D1075087

THE CAMBRIDGE HISTORY OF

EARLY CHRISTIAN LITERATURE

The writings of the Church Fathers form a distinct body of literature which shaped the early Church and built upon the doctrinal foundations of Christianity recently established within the New Testament and by oral and ecclesiastical tradition. Christian literature in the period *c.* 100–*c.* 400 constitutes one of the most influential textual oeuvres of any religion. Written mainly in Greek, Latin and Syriac, patristic literature emanated from all parts of the early Christian world and helped to extend its boundaries. The works of Irenaeus, Origen, Hippolytus, Eusebius, Athanasius, Gregory of Nyssa, Augustine, John Chrysostom, Ephrem, the gnostics, the Montanists and the Cappadocians are among the best-known examples of an extensive set of texts grappling with the theological issues at the heart of early Christianity – many of which still lie at its heart today. This *History* is the first systematic account of that literature and its setting for many years. The work of individual writers in shaping the various genres and forms of Christian literature is considered, and the volume also offers three general essays covering distinct periods in the development of Christian literature. These pieces survey the social, cultural and doctrinal context within which Christian literature arose and within which it was used by Christians. The book is intended for use by theologians and historians, providing a landmark reference work for scholars, teachers and students.

Frances Young is Edward Cadbury Professor of Theology at the University of Birmingham.

Lewis Ayres is Assistant Professor of Historical Theology at the Candler School of Theology and Graduate Division of Religion, Emory University.

Andrew Louth is Professor of Patristic and Byzantine Studies at the University of Durham.

THE CAMBRIDGE HISTORY OF EARLY CHRISTIAN LITERATURE

*

Edited by
FRANCES YOUNG
LEWIS AYRES
ANDREW LOUTH

Assistant editor: Augustine Casiday

CAMBRIDGE
UNIVERSITY PRESS

PUBLISHED BY THE PRESS SYNDICATE OF THE UNIVERSITY OF CAMBRIDGE
The Pitt Building, Trumpington Street, Cambridge, United Kingdom

CAMBRIDGE UNIVERSITY PRESS
The Edinburgh Building, Cambridge, CB2 2RU, UK
40 West 20th Street, New York, NY 10011–4211, USA
477 Williamstown Road, Port Melbourne, VIC 3207, Australia
Ruiz de Alarcón 13, 28014 Madrid, Spain
Dock House, The Waterfront, Cape Town 8001, South Africa

http://www.cambridge.org

First published 2004

Printed in the United Kingdom at the University Press, Cambridge

Typeface DanteMT 10.5/13 pt. *System* LaTeX 2ε [TB]

A catalogue record for this book is available from the British Library

Library of Congress Cataloguing in Publication data
The Cambridge history of early Christian literature / edited by Frances Young, Lewis Ayres, Andrew Louth.
p. cm.
Includes bibliographical references and index.
ISBN 0-521-46083-2
1. Christian literature, Early–History and criticism. I. Young, Frances M. (Frances Margaret) II. Ayres, Lewis. III. Louth, Andrew.
BR67.C25 2004
270.1–dc22 2003055726

ISBN 0 521 46083 2 hardback

Contents

B · CONTEXT AND INTERPRETATION

PART TWO
THE THIRD CENTURY
A · LITERARY GUIDE

B · CONTEXT AND INTERPRETATION

Contributors

LEWIS AYRES, Emory University
JOHN BEHR, St Vladimir's Orthodox Theological Seminary
SEBASTIAN P. BROCK, University of Oxford
HENRY CHADWICK, University of Cambridge (Emeritus)
JOHN DAVID DAWSON, Haverford College
SUSAN ASHBROOK HARVEY, Brown University
RONALD E. HEINE, Puget Sound Christian College
DAVID G. HUNTER, Iowa State University
ANDREW LOUTH, University of Durham
R. A. MARKUS, University of Nottingham (Emeritus)
OLIVER NICHOLSON, University of Minnesota
RICHARD A. NORRIS, JR., The Union Theological Seminary (Emeritus)
KAREN JO TORJESEN, Claremont Graduate University
MARK VESSEY, University of British Columbia
FRANCES YOUNG, University of Birmingham

Editors' preface

The excellent Cambridge Histories have not so far included a scholarly compendium on the literature of early Christianity. This volume seeks to fill that gap, while taking note of new developments in the field, which make it particularly appropriate to undertake the production of such a volume at this time.

This literature has traditionally been studied by students of Christian theology and Christian scholars with an interest in the doctrinal and organizational development of the Church. It has commonly been described using the adjective 'patristic', since these authors were considered the 'Fathers' of the Church, and introductory handbooks have been known as 'Patrologies'. It is not intended to ignore the concerns of this clientele, though it is hoped that a wider readership may also turn to this volume as a standard work of reference. Increasing historical interest in the late Roman and early Byzantine worlds has made the subject much more interdisciplinary. Indeed, it could be argued that this material is simply a subclass of the literature of late antiquity, and a reference work should include the whole range of material. However, this would consign the material in this volume to a small section, and since it is a substantial and historically significant subclass, there is a case to be made for examining it in its own right, as long as the wider historical context, and the sharing of perspectives and concerns with non-Christian contemporaries, are made clear.

This greater interdisciplinary focus has been particularly important, however, since it has meant that the material is now studied with a broader range of issues in mind. Feminists have challenged the designation 'patristic', and questions of social identity and social level have become important, together with issues such as the parting of the ways with Judaism, and the process of Christianization. 'Heretics' have been re-habilitated, and their motivations and ideas studied with greater sympathy, especially as they were history's losers. New material, such as the Nag Hammadi find and the Tura papyri, have occasioned more intensive research. This material can no longer be presented simply as sources for the history of the development of Christian doctrine, important though that project remains.

At the same time the hermeneutical questions raised in relation to New Testament interpretation have hardly begun to touch the field, so that questions of appropriation are ripe for consideration. Conversely, there has been an awakening interest in early Christian interpretation of Scripture, as perspectives other than the historical have opened up in biblical studies. These questions are of particular interest to the editors, and attention to them should have a considerable place in a volume of this kind. The adoption of the canon and the formative place it held in Christian thinking, as interpreted by the exponents in the Church, also have their background in the ancient veneration for literature and the place of rhetoric and literary study in the educational system.

It is hoped that, given this overall context, this work will provide a major volume of reference, distilling the present lively developments in the subject area and essaying some pioneering directions. The policy adopted has not been to provide a comprehensive encyclopedia or dictionary, of which there are already recent worthy representatives, such as *Dizionario Patristico e di Antichità Cristiane* (1983–8), edited by Angelo di Berardino, translated into English as *Encyclopedia of the Early Church* and published in 1992, or *Encyclopedia of Early Christianity*, edited by Ferguson and others, and published in 1990. Instead of brief introductory articles in alphabetical order by an enormous variety of scholars, an attempt is made to provide a coherent focus, and to concentrate on the literature, its interpretation and significance, and its context, historical, social, philosophical. The work takes account of heterodox as well orthodox, heretic as well as bishop. It provides essays on the major figures and authors, and assesses the major schools of Alexandria, Antioch, Edessa and Nisibis. It discusses the major controversies, not abstracting the important Christological struggle from a context in which other issues were at stake, such as Origenism and asceticism. It embraces feminist and sociological approaches to the material.

In some respects this work may replace the Patrologies, now thirty to forty years old, though without adopting the same style or pretending to offer comprehensive bibliographies. Some overlap in material and approach with Frances Young's volume, *From Nicaea to Chalcedon*, may justly be suspected, but this should be complementary to that work: the A sections cover the literature of a much broader period and geographical location in relatively briefer compass, with the additional advantage of engaging a team of contributors with varied expertise, while the B sections of each Part enable the generation of a greater sense of perspective than was possible in a series of essays on individual authors, as well as giving an opportunity to explore new hermeneutical questions.

This is meant to be a reference work, not necessarily a book to be read consecutively from cover to cover. Sections A and B are deliberately set up as different approaches to approximately the same material and some degree of overlap is to be expected, though in each period the A sections deal simply with extant material, surveying the literary deposit which has come down to us, while the B sections explore the contexts into which that material needs to be placed if it is to be understood in an informed way, including reference to significant works which are no longer extant and such fragmentary sources as contribute to reconstruction of those contexts.

This is not simply a general history, but a literary history, seeking to take questions concerning the genre and rhetoric of the texts seriously. It is also meant to be not just a contribution to the study of the past and its 'objective' reconstruction – the long-standing project of modernist historiography – but also a contribution to the interpretation and present appropriation of texts from the past; in other words, a resource for theological thinking that goes beyond the simple repetition of formulae or the use of past labels for present controversies.

This volume has been long in gestation. Its 'onlie begetter' was Frances Young, who designed the shape of the volume and commissioned the contributors. Soon, however, she was overwhelmed by the burdens of university administration, and the other two editors were invited to see the project through to completion. (In the final stages, the assistant editor, Dr Augustine Casiday, one-time research student at the University of Durham, proved invaluable in helping draw up the bibliography, preparing the chronological table, and compiling the index.) The final state of the volume is the responsibility of all three of us.

Abbreviations of patristic and other texts

AcPT = *Acta Pauli et Theclae*
AcJ = *Acta Justini*
Ad Nov. = *Ad Novatianum*
Adol. = *Ad Adolescentes de legendis libris gentilium*
Ad Phil. = *Ad Philippense*
Ad Serap. = *Ad Serapionem*
Afric. = *Epistula ad Africanum*
AH = *Adversus Haereses*
An. = *De Anima*
APet. = *Acta Petri*
Apol. = *Apologeticum* or *Apologia*
Apol. c. Hier. = *Apologia contra Hieronymum*
Apol. c. Ruf. = *Apologia contra Rufinum*
Ar. = *Contra Arianos*
Autol. = *Ad Autolycum*
Bapt. = *De Baptismo*
Barn. = *Epistula Barnabae*
Bibl. Cod. = Photius, *Bibliotheca*, cited by codex
Bon. = *De bono mortis*
BPud. = *De Bono Pudicitiae*
Carn. = *De Carne Christi*
Cast. = *De Exhortatione Castitatis*
Cat. = *Catechesis*
Cels. = *Contra Celsum*
CG = *Contra Gentes*
Chron. = *Chronicon*
I Clem. = *Prima Epistula Clementis*
II Clem. = *Epistula Secunda Clementis*
Coet. = *Oratio ad sanctorum coetum*

Comm. in Mt. = *Commentarius in Matthaeum*
CommPs. = *Commentarius in Psalmos*
Conf. = *Confessions*
Cor. = *De Corona*
CTheod. = *Codex Theodosianum*
Dan. = *in Danielem*
Dec. = *De Decretis*
Dem. = *Demonstratio Praedicationis Apostolicae*
Demetr. = *Ad Demetrianum*
Dial. = *Dialogus*
Did. = *Didache*
Diog. = *Epistula ad Diognetum*
EcProph. = *Eclogae Propheticae*
Enn. = *Enneades*
Ep(p). = *Epistulae*
Ephes. = *Ep. ad Ephesios*
ETh. = *Ecclesiastica Theologia*
Eun. = *Contra Eunomium*
Fug. = *De Fuga*
Graec. = *Oratio ad Graecos*
Greg. = *Ep. ad Gregorium*
Haer. = *Refutatio omnium haeresium* or *Haereticarum fabularum compendium*
HE = *Historia Ecclesiastica*
Herac. = *Disputatio cum Heracleida*
Herm. = *Adversus Hermogenem*
HExod. = *Homilia in Exodum*
Hom. in Jud. = *Homilia in Judices*
HR = *Historia Romana*
Idol. = *De Idololatria*
Idola = *Quod idola dii non sint*
Ieiun. = *De Ieiunio*
Il. = *Ilias*
In Eph. = *In Ephesios*
In Rep. = *In Rempublicam*
Inst. = *Institutiones* or *Institutiones Divinae*
Inv. = *De Inventione*
Io. = *Commentarius in Ioannem*
Ira = *De Ira Dei*
Laps. = *De Lapsis*

Laus. = *Historia Lausiaca*
Leg. = *Legatio*
Magn. = *Ad Magnesios*
Mand. = *Mandata*
Marc. = *Adversus Marcionem* or *Contra Marcellum*
Mart. = *Exhortatio ad Martyrium* or *De Martyribus Palestinae*
Med. = *Meditationes*
Mon. = *De Monogamia*
Mort. = *De Mortibus Persecutorum*
MPol. = *Martyrium Polycarpi*
Nat. = *Adversus Nationes*
NHC = *Nag Hammadi Codices*
Noet. = *Contra Noetum*
Od. = *Odysseas*
Opif. = *De Opificio Dei*
Or. = *De Oratione* or *Oratio*
Paed. = *Paedagogus*
Paen. = *De Paenitentia*
Pan. = *Panarion*
Pan. Or. = *Panegyrica in Origenem*
Pass. Perp. = *Passio Perpetuae*
Pass. Scil. = *Passio Sanctorum Scillitanorum*
Philad. = *Ad Philadelphenos*
Polyc. = *Epistula ad Polycarpum*
Praescr. = *De Praescriptione*
Prax. = *Adversus Praxean*
PrEv. = *Praeparatio Evangelica*
Princ. = *De Principiis*
Procat. = *Procatechesis*
Pud. = *De Pudicitia*
Q. = *Quaestio*
Ref. = *Refutatio Confessionis Eunomii*
Rep. = *Respublica*
Res. = *De Resurrectione Carnis*
Rom. = *Ad Romanos*
Ruf. = *Adversus Rufinum*
Scap. = *Ad Scapulam*
Scorp. = *Scorpiace*
Sim. = *Similitudines*

Smyrn. = *Ad Smyrnaeos*
Spect. = *De Spectaculis*
SpS = *De Spiritu Sancto*
Strom. = *Stromateis*
Syn. = *De synodo* or *De synodis*
TestDom. = *Testimonium Domini*
Tom. ad Ant. = *Tomus ad Antiochenos*
Trall. = *Ad Trallianos*
Trin. = *De Trinitate*
Ux. = *Ad Uxorem*
Val. = *Contra Valentinianos*
Virg. = *De Virginitate*
Vir. Ill. = *De Viris Illustribus*
Vis. = *Visio*

Other abbreviations

These abbreviations are used in the notes, and in the bibliographies, where publication details can be found.

ACO: *Acta Conciliorum Oecumenicorum*
ACW: Ancient Christian Writers
AGLS: Alcuin / Grove Liturgical Studies
ANF: The Ante-Nicene Fathers
ANRW: *Aufstieg und Niedergang der römischen Welt*
BGL: Bibliothek der Griechischen Literatur
BLE: *Bulletin de littérature ecclésiastique*
BMus: *Bibliothèque du Muséon*
CAH: *Cambridge Ancient History*
CCSG: Corpus Christianorum. Series Graeca
CCSL: Corpus Christianorum. Series Latina
CHLG: *Cambridge History of Later Greek and Early Medieval Philosophy*
CSCO: Corpus Scriptorum Christianorum Orientalium
CSEL: Corpus Scriptorum Ecclesiasticorum Latinorum
CPG: *Clavis Patrum Graecorum*
CPL: *Clavis Patrum Latinorum*
CSS: Cistercian Studies Series
CWS: Classics of Western Spirituality
DCB: Dictionary of Christian Biography, Literature, Sects and Doctrines
DEC: *Decrees of the Œcumenical Councils*
DLT: Darton Longman and Todd
DSp: *Dictionnaire de spiritualité ascétique et mystique, histoire et doctrine*
ECF: Early Church Fathers
EEC: *Encyclopedia of the Early Church*
ET: English translation
FC: Fathers of the Church

GCS: Griechischen Christlichen Schriftsteller
Greg.: *Gregorianum*
GTS: Grazer Theologische Studien
HeyJ: *Heythrop Journal*
HeyM: Heythrop Monographs
HTR: *Harvard Theological Review*
HUT: Hermeneutische Untersuchungen zur Theologie
JAC: *Jahrbuch für Antike und Christentum*
JECS: *Journal of Early Christian Studies*
JSNT: *Journal for the Study of New Testament*
JSOT: *Journal for the Study of the Old Testament*
JTS: *Journal of Theological Studies*
LCC: Library of Christian Classics
MGH: Monumenta Germaniae Historica
OCA: Orientalia Christiana Analecta
OCP: *Orientalia Christiana Periodica*
ODCC: *Oxford Dictionary of the Christian Church*
OECS: Oxford Early Christian Studies
OECT: Oxford Early Christian Texts
PG: *Patrologia Graeca*
PIOS: Pontificium Institutum Orientalium Studiorum (now, Pontificio Istituto Orientale)
PL: *Patrologia Latina*
PO: *Patrologia Orientalis*
PPS: Popular Patristics Series
PTS: Patristische Texte und Studien
RBen: *Revue Bénédictine*
RechSR: *Recherches de science religieuse*
REL: *Revue des Études Latines*
SA: *Studia Anselmiana*
SBAW: Sitzungsberichte der bayerischen Akademie des Wissenschaften
SBL: Studies in Biblical Literature
SC: Sources chrétiennes
SCH: *Studies in Church History*
SEA: *Studia Ephemeridis ≪Augustinianum≫*
SecCent: *Second Century*
SP: *Studia Patristica*
ST: Studi e Testi
SWGS: Schriften der wissenschaftliche Gesellschaft in Strassburg

TCH: Transformation of the Classical Heritage
ThH: Théologie Historique
TRE: *Theologische Realenzyklopädie*
TS: Texts and Studies
TTH: Translated Texts for Historians
TU: Texte und Untersuchungen
VigChr: *Vigiliae Christianae*
ZAC: *Zeitschrift für antikes Christentum/Journal of ancient Christianity*
ZKG: *Zeitschrift für Kirchengeschichte*
ZNW: *Zeitschrift für die neutestamentliche Wissenschaft*

Chronological table of early Christian literature

Featuring key writers, works and events

Writers	Works	Events
Philo of Alexandria (*fl. c.* 30–45)		
Clement of Rome (*fl. c.* 95)	*The Shepherd of Hermas* (90–150)	Domitian's persecution? (95–96)
Ignatius of Antioch (*fl. c.* 100–115)	*Didache* (100–150)	Trajan's proscription of Christianity? (112)
	Apocalypse of Peter (*c.* 125–150)	
	Aristides of Athens, *Apology* (*c.* 120–138)	
	Papias, *Explanation of the Sayings of the Lord* (*c.* 130)	
	Epistle of Barnabas (130–131)	
Valentinus at Rome (*c.* 136–165)	Justin Martyr, *Dialogue with Trypho* (*c.* 138)	Bar Kochba's revolt (138)
Marcion at Rome (*fl.* 144–?)	Justin Martyr, *First and Second Apologies* (148–161)	
Clement of Alexandria (*c.* 150–215)	*Acts of John* (150–180)	
Bardaisan (154–*c.* 222)		
Tertullian (155–*c.* 220)		
Polycarp (d. 156)		Polycarp's martyrdom (156)
Justin Martyr (d. 165)	*The Acts* (= Martyrdom) *of St Justin and his companions* (165)	
	Melito, *Peri Pascha* (*c.* 167–168)	

(*cont.*)

Writers	Works	Events
	Tatian, *Discourse to the Greeks* (*c.* 165–180)	
Irenaeus (*fl. c.* 175–180)	Athenagoras, *Supplication for the Christians* (*c.* 177)	
	Theophilus of Antioch, *To Autolycus* (180)	
	The Acts of the Martyrs of Scilli in Africa (180)	The Martyrs of Scilli in Africa (17 July 180)
Origen (185–253)	*Gospel of Peter* (before 190)	
	Acts of Paul and Thecla (before 190)	
	Acts of Peter (before 190)	
	Acts of Thomas (*c.* 200–250)	Septimius Severus' persecution? (*c.* 202–212)
Cyprian (200/210–258)		The martyrdom of Perpetua and Felicity (7 March 202)
Hippolytus (*fl.* 212–235)		
Callistus, pope of Rome (*regn.* 217–222)	Origen, *On first principles* (*c.* 220–230)	
	Origen, *On prayer* (233–234)	
	Origen, *Exhortation to martyrdom* (235)	
	Apocalypse of Paul (*c.* 240–250)	
	Origen, *Against Celsus* (246)	
Novatian (*fl.* 250–253)		The Decian persecution (250–253)
Antony the Great (250–356)		
Arius (256–336)		The Edict of Valerian (257–260)
Paul of Samosata (*fl. c.* 260–268)		Cyprian of Carthage's martyrdom (14 September 258)
Eusebius of Caesarea (263–339/340)		
Athanasius (295–373)		
Lactantius (*fl.* 303–317)		Diocletian's persecution (303–305)

(*cont.*)

(*cont.*)

Writers	Works	Events
Ephrem the Syrian (*c.* 306–373)		
	Arnobius of Sicca, *Against the pagans* (*c.* 311)	Donatism (311–411)
Didymus the Blind (313–398)	Eusebius of Caesarea, *Church History* (*c.* 312–325)	The 'Edict' of Milan (313)
Pachomius (*fl.* 320–346)	Eusebius of Caesarea, *Preparation for the Gospel* and *Proof of the Gospel* (*c.* 314–315)	
Constantine (regn. 325–337)	Athanasius, *On the Incarnation* (*c.* 320)	Council of Nicaea I (325)
Basil the Great (330–379)		
Gregory of Nazianzus (330–389/390)		Dedication of Constantinople (330)
Gregory of Nyssa (335–394)		
Ambrose (*c.* 340–397)	Aphraat, *Demonstrations* (*c.* 337–345)	
Jerome (340/342–420)		
Evagrius Ponticus (*c.* 345–399)		
Rufinus (*c.* 345–410)		
Cyril of Jerusalem (*fl.* 348–386)		
John Chrysostom (344/354–407)		
Hilary of Poitiers (*fl.* 350–368)		
Victorinus Afer (*fl.* 353–362)		
Augustine of Hippo (354–430)	Athanasius, *Life of St Antony* (*c.* 356)	
John Cassian (*c.* 360–435)		
Julian the Apostate (regn. 361–363)		
Diodore of Tarsus (*fl.* 362–394)	Basil, *Hexaemeron* (before 370)	
	Basil, *On the Holy Spirit* (375)	
	Epiphanius of Salamis, *Panarion* (377)	Death of Valens at Adrianople (378)

(*cont.*)

Writers	Works	Events
	Gregory of Nyssa, *Life of St Macrina* (379)	
	Gregory of Nazianzus, *Five theological orations* (380)	
	Didymus (?), *On the Trinity* (*c.* 381–392)	Council of Constantinople I (381)
	Theodore of Mopsuestia, *Catechetical Homilies* (*c.* 388–392)	
Theodore of Mopsuestia (*fl.* 388–428)	Gregory of Nyssa, *On the life of Moses* (*c.* 390–392)	
	Nemesius of Emesa, *On the nature of man* (*c.* 392–400)	
	Augustine, *On Christian doctrine* (397–426)	
	Augustine, *Confessions* (*c.* 400)	
Theodoret (*c.* 393–458)	*Doctrine of Addai* (*c.* 400)	
	Palladius, *Dialogue on the life of St John Chrysostom* (*c.* 408)	
	Augustine, *City of God* (413, Bks 20–22: 426)	Alaric enters Rome (the 'Fall of Rome') (410)
	Palladius, *Lausiac History* (419–420)	
	Philostorgius, *Ecclesiastical History* (425–433)	Council of Ephesus (431)
Cyril of Alexandria (*fl.* 428–444)	Cassian, *Conferences* (426–429)	
Nestorius (*fl.* 428–450)	Socrates, *Ecclesiastical History* (*c.* 440)	
	Sozomen, *Ecclesiastical History* (*c.* 439–450)	
	Theodoret, *Religious History* (*c.* 440)	
John of Apamea (*fl. c.* 450)	Theodoret, *Ecclesiastical History* (448–449)	
Jacob of Sarug (451–521)		Council of Chalcedon (451)

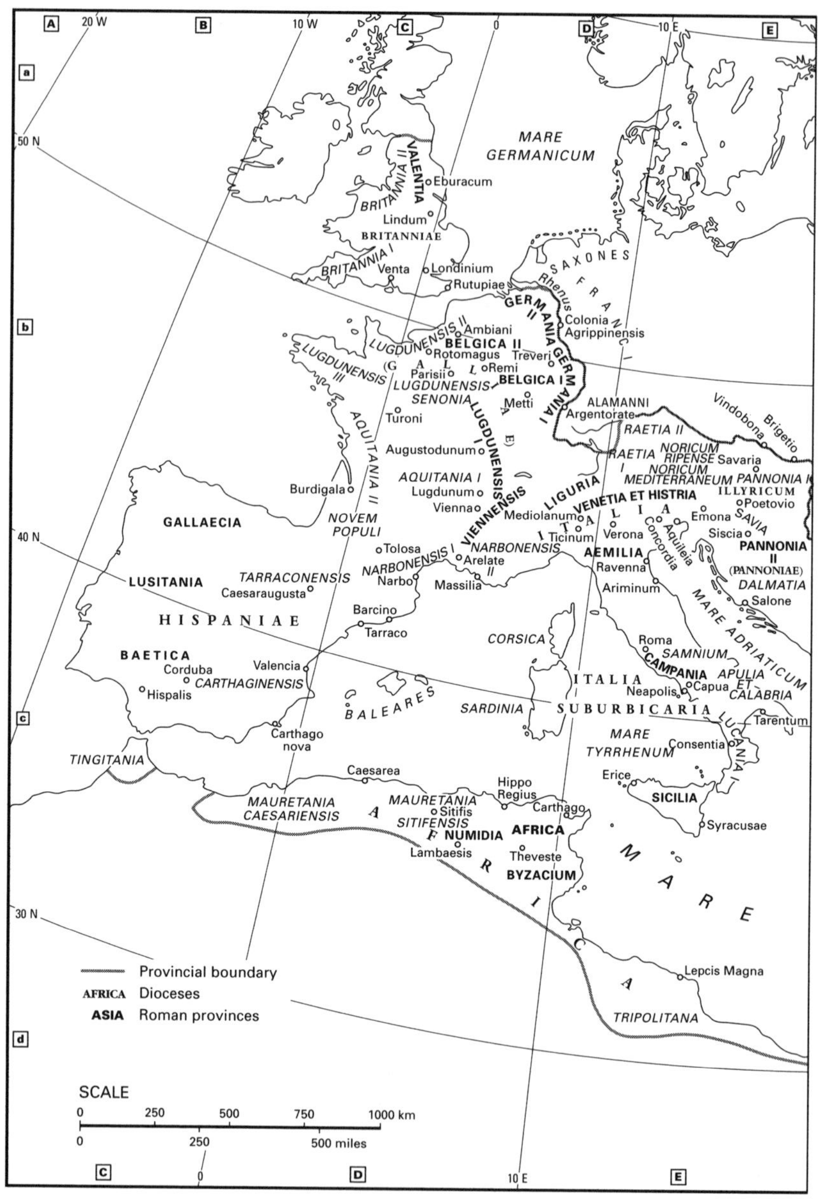

Map: The Roman Empire in the late fourth century AD

PONTUS EUXINUS
INTERNUM
Sirmium
Singidunum
Ratiaria
Danuvius
SCYTHIA
MOESIA I
DACIA RIPENSIS
MOESIA II
Marcianopolis
Naissus
DACIA
Serdica
THRACIA
HAEMIMONTUS
Hadrianopolis
Constantinopolis
Nicomedia
EUROPA
RHODOPA
MACEDONIA
Thessalonica
EPIRUS NOVA
EPIRUS VETUS
THESSALIA
Heraclea
Cyzicus
Nicaea
BITHYNIA
HONORIAS
PAPHLAGONIA
HELENOPONTUS
Chersonesus
Trapezus
PONTUS POLEMONIACUS
Ancyra
GALATIA I
GALATIA S
HELLESPONTUS
PHRYGIA
ASIA
LYDIA
Sardis
Smyrna
Ephesus
Athenae
ACHAIA
CARIA
PISIDIA
PAMPHYLIA
LYCIA
INSULAE
CRETA
CYPRUS
Salamis
LYCAONIA
Iconium
ISAURIA
CILICIA I
CILICIA II
Tarsus
Antiochia
SYRIA
SYRIA S
CAPPADOCIA I
CAPPADOCIA II
Caesarea
ARMENIA I
ARMENIA II
Melitene
Amida
MESOPOTAMIA
Nisibis
Samosata
Edessa
OSRHOENA
EUPHRATENSIS
Euphrates
Tigris
Ctesiphon
Emesa
PHOENICE
PHOENICE I
Berytus
Damascus
PALAESTINA II
Caesarea
ARABIA
PALAESTINA I
Hierosolyma
PALAESTINA SALUTARIS
ORIENS
PONTICA
MACEDONIA
DACIA
ASIANA
Cyrene
LIBYA SUPERIOR
Alexandria
Scetis
LIBYA INFERIOR
AEGYPTUS
ARCADIA
THEBAIS
Phbow
Nag Hammadi
Thebae
20 E
30 E
40 E
50 E
60 E
50 N
40 N
30 N

PART ONE

*

THE BEGINNINGS: THE NEW TESTAMENT TO IRENAEUS

A.

*

LITERARY GUIDE

I

Introduction: the literary culture of the earliest Christianity

FRANCES YOUNG

The last 200 years have seen considerable swings in the literary assessment of the earliest Christian literature, including as it does the texts which became the canonized Scriptures of the Church, but not just those. The pendulum has been affected partly by new discoveries, but changing perspectives have also played their part. A series of interrelated questions has emerged from the principal debates:

(1) In what sense are Christian texts 'literary'? How do they relate to other literature that has survived from antiquity?
(2) Which texts should be included in the category 'Christian'?
(3) From what social level and cultural milieu did these texts issue? To what extent are they to be assessed as the deposit of an oral and non-literary environment? How is the transition to written texts to be evaluated?
(4) Do peculiarities of language, rhetoric or genre set these texts apart? Or are they typical of the time and circumstances from which they emerged?
(5) How are these texts to be read? Is it enough to evaluate them as historical documents, relating them to the historical circumstances in which they were generated and the literary culture to which they originally belonged?

Some of these questions will be considered in Part I B, but it is an illusion to think that a description of the literature can be offered without essaying some answers.

Investigators of the nineteenth century had inherited and challenged certain distinctions. The first was the distinction between texts deemed to be canonical and the rest, that is, those that had been included in the New Testament and associated with the Old Testament to form the Bible, and those that were not so privileged yet still held authoritative as 'patristic', being the work of the Fathers of the Church. Whereas in the Orthodox East such works are believed to contain all of theology and to be the authoritative texts for interpreting the Scriptures (a position analogous to the role of the Talmud in Judaism), the effect of the Protestant Reformation in the West had been to reinforce the distinction. This was now challenged, however, on historical grounds: certain texts eventually excluded were earlier in date than some that were included in the biblical canon. The tracing of a historical sequence reflecting historical development required the abandonment of canonicity as a criterion in assessing the literature.

Against that background there emerged the notion of distinguishing between the 'primitive literature' of the Christian movement and that produced after the adoption of the forms of Greco-Roman literary culture. It was, of course, evident all along that judged by the standards of classical literature the earliest Christian texts fell short. The ancient charge[1] that the apostles were illiterate and ignorant and that Christianity flourished among women and slaves carried some weight because scholars trained in the classics could immediately see how these texts were wanting in sophistication of style and composition. In the earlier half of the twentieth century, the low-class, 'popular' nature of the movement and its literature seemed to be confirmed by comparing the language, style and genres with the many everyday papyri – accounts, business letters, legal and personal documents, etc. – discovered in Egypt.[2] So the letters of Paul were treated as occasional, personal letters, not to be compared with literary epistles, and the Gospels as the assemblage of sayings and stories that had circulated for at least a generation in oral form. Indeed, 'gospel' was treated as a new and unique literary genre, invented by Mark and then to be aped by other writers, both orthodox and heretical.

The second distinction inherited and challenged in the nineteenth century was that between orthodox and heretical literature. The transmission of the texts from antiquity had been in the hands of the Church. The Church was interested in what was dogmatically sound. Anti-heretical literature was preserved, but not the texts of those condemned. Orthodoxy was regarded as the pure and pristine truth revealed, later distorted by heretics. The notion that doctrine developed through history, however, stimulated an interest in the contribution made by heresy to that development. Furthermore, concern to discover the historical Jesus or the historical Socrates was paralleled by a fascination with reconstructing the life and teaching, not only of approved characters, but also of notorious heretics. This interest was reinforced by remarkable new discoveries, ever increasing as the twentieth century proceeded, and these discoveries became part of the literature now to be studied.[3] The long-familiar extant literature had to be placed in a much larger literary context, indeed an ever-expanding environment as theories of the non-Christian – indeed pre-Christian – origins of gnosticism subordinated the orthodox texts within a larger interpretative framework. This larger literary world was not the world of the classics, of high culture, but a kind of literary underworld, lying at the confluence of oriental religions and Hellenistic mysteries.

These two challenges to the way the texts had been received arose from modern historical consciousness, and the literary guide in Part I A reflects both: canonical and non-canonical, orthodox and heretical writings are introduced side by side. But postmodern literary and hermeneutical questions may reopen issues concerning canonicity and authority, and sociological approaches mean that the world from which these texts emerged can now be viewed rather differently, at least partly because questions about their literary character have been raised in new ways.[4] Perspectives are refined (1) if questions are asked not so much in terms of reconstructing a religio-cultural milieu by exploiting parallels between texts (the History of Religions approach) but in terms of intertextuality; (2) if rhetorical intent and social function assume greater importance than questions of authenticity, authorship and date; (3) if anxiety about the historicity of events behind the text is submerged by focus on interpreting the text itself; (4) if the character of the discourse is analysed, in terms of the effect it could or should produce, the world it creates and into which it invites the reader; and (5) if the identification of genre is taken as a crucial clue to how a text is to be read.

Early Christianity had its matrix among Jews. This obvious fact has to assume importance in considering the character and environment of early Christian literature, if only because an examination of its 'intertextuality' shows a deep acquaintance with the literature of the Jewish community, at least in its Greek form. The Law and the Prophets, the Psalms and some wisdom-books are not only quoted but frequently alluded to or in various ways aped in the whole range of material under consideration. The particular genre of 'apocalyptic' was produced by Jewish and Christian authors over a period of some 500 years spanning the genesis of Christianity. It is likely, given their traces in early Christian literature, that 'testimony-books' were produced, collections of 'oracles' culled from the Law and the Prophets, sometimes with adaptations or commentary to demonstrate fulfilment, and that likelihood is enhanced by the discovery among the Dead Sea Scrolls at Qumran of fragmentary texts of that form, 4Q Testimonia and 4Q Florilegia. It is in Jewish texts that precedent can be found for the ways in which biblical material is shaped and interpreted in works such as the Epistle of Barnabas, not to mention the writings within the New Testament.

'Judaism' (Ἰουδαϊσμος) was a word parallel to 'Hellenism'. It referred to the culture of the Jewish race (ἔθνος). Just as the Greeks had lawgivers, and the prophetic oracles of the Sibyls, and a literature of great antiquity on the basis of which all education was conducted, including the moral formation of the citizen, so the Jews had their own great lawgiver, Moses, and their own books of prophecies, and a literature which the young were trained to read and live by. The earliest Christians were Jews nurtured in the Jewish tradition. Crucial to the understanding of early Christian literature was the question raised increasingly in the latter part of the twentieth century: how are we to conceive 'the parting of the ways' between Jews and Christians? What are the implications of the fact that gradually it was not people of Jewish but of other ethnic origins who took over the literature of the Jews, claiming it as their own, and who, while rejecting the literary culture of their own upbringing, actually read their adopted books, and wrote their own, with the assumptions of 'Hellenism'? There lies the significant transition, rather than a supposed shift from oral to written culture, or indeed a change from 'primitive', unselfconscious, writing to the norms of the literary elite. Early Christianity was always rooted in a 'book' culture, but from the standpoint of the Greco-Roman world it was alien – 'barbarian', in fact.

There is, however, another remarkable aspect of this early Christian book culture which has been revealed by accumulating archaeological evidence. Literature was normally inscribed on rolls. Christian texts from the earliest known date appear in codex form, the forerunner of the book. Wax-tablets had long been joined by leather thongs to form 'notebooks', but no one before the Romans thought of arranging parchment or papyrus in this way. Even then such 'notebooks' were only used in schools and businesses; they were not 'proper books'. For literary texts the transition from roll to codex did not take place until the fourth century, and for the copies of Torah ceremonially read in the synagogue Jews have retained the scroll form to this day. How is it then that the Christians adopted the codex form for their texts – not just their compositions, but even the Scriptures they had taken over from the Jews? The oddity is reinforced by the fact that Christian scholars of the third century went back to having their works written on rolls!

Explanations have been sought, sometimes practical, such as greater convenience for quick reference or for travelling missionaries to carry, sometimes more ideological, such as precedents set by the original form of Mark's Gospel or the Pauline Epistles,[5] or the use of notebooks to assemble 'testimonies'. Probably a complex range of factors contributed, including maybe the 'blasphemous' reduction of the sacred Jewish texts to the status of mere witnesses to Jesus Christ – Ignatius insists on the superiority of Christ to 'ancient books' (*Philad.* 8). But most significant here is the point that the book culture of early Christianity was physically that of day-to-day business, suggesting that, at any rate at first, those who belonged to the communities that valued this literature, though not aspiring to any kind of literary or educated elite, were nevertheless accustomed to dealing with documents. This coheres with other research which has modified the idea that the earliest Christians were low-class or belonged to some kind of underworld.

Ancient society was not stratified by class, so much as made up of competing households which were themselves hierarchies, consisting not only of the kinship group but also of employees, dependents, servants and slaves. The Christian communities were based in such urban households,[6] and their patrons and leaders must have had some social status and considerable economic power. Levels of literacy would have been extremely varied across the household community; doubtless for the most part it would have been a pragmatic skill required for business. On the other hand, most city dwellers would have some awareness of literary norms, since all reading was aloud, often in social settings, and all public communication reflected rhetorical conventions. Indeed, the majority of illiterate people would have been familiar with writing and its uses, employing scribes to write letters or other necessary documents. The 'notebook' would be the everyday vehicle for records rather than the literary roll; so here is the context in which handy collections of teachings or testimonies would begin to be compiled. Here, too, is the context in which the letter would become the primary genre.

The very earliest Christian texts are the letters of Paul, a Jew and Pharisee formerly known as Saul. The old attempt to distinguish letters and epistles can hardly be sustained, though in origin the authentic letters were certainly occasional documents issuing from the practical need to maintain communication and sort out problems. These 'everyday' letters in fact follow the generic conventions of letters from the wider Greco-Roman world, yet radically adapt them to specific Christian needs (see below chapter 2). The Pauline letters are after all rooted in the wider world of the literatures of antiquity yet at the same time distinctive. A similar case can be made for the Gospels: they have significant analogies with the biographical literature of the period, though also distinctive features.

The Pauline letters also set a precedent: letters are the actual or assumed genre of a great deal of the earliest Christian literature. Furthermore a letter from an 'apostle' became the authoritative form in which to address the difficulties of a subsequent generation. Indeed, pseudonymity is a feature of a good deal of the material purporting to come from the first two hundred years of Christian literary activity – how much remains a contentious issue. Modern critical scholarship has been exercised with determining which texts are authentic, whether traditional attributions have any basis, and what might be the provenance of anonymous texts such as Hebrews. Postmodern critical theory, with its emphasis on the 'death of the author', might enable a greater focus on the nature of these texts as rooted in communities. The significant thing about attribution has to do with what Foucault would call the 'author-function':[7] it is not without significance that the process of canon-formation involved the attempt to distinguish writings that were 'apostolic'. The reception of the texts may be as significant in terms of literary history as their provenance.

So the nineteenth-century challenges to the way this literature has for the most part been received may need to be reviewed. In biblical studies, canon criticism has reopened the question whether the formation of a canon and the effective turning of many books into one does not change the way the texts are read. Are we to read these works simply as documents which provide windows on to the past? Or should our reception of them take into account, not only what they implicitly claim to be through their genre and discourse, but also the effect of their transmission, as scripture, as 'patristic', as heretical? To such questions we will return in chapter 10.

Notes

1 Origen repeatedly faces such criticisms from Celsus: e.g. *Cels.* 1.62.

2 E.g., the classic study by Adolf Deissmann, *Light from the Ancient East*.

3 E.g., the discovery of the Mandaean literature dramatically affected the researches of the History of Religions School in the early twentieth century; the Nag Hammadi library, found in Egypt in the 1940s, fuelled continued research into gnosticism in the second half of the century.

4 Frances Young, 'From Suspicion and Sociology to Spirituality: on Method. Hermeneutics and Appropriation with Respect to Patristic Material', 421–35.

5 See C. H. Roberts, 'Books in the Greco-Roman World and in the New Testament', and Harry Y. Gamble, *Books and Readers in the Early Church: A History of Early Christian Texts*.

6 The importance of the household for understanding the ancient social context of Christian groups has been repeatedly emphasized in New Testament studies since around 1980; e.g. David C. Verner, *The Household of God. The Social World of the Pastoral Epistles*.

7 M. Foucault, 'What is an author?', in P. Rabinow, ed., *The Foucault Reader* (New York: Pantheon Books, 1984), 101–20.

2

The apostolic and sub-apostolic writings: the New Testament and the Apostolic Fathers

RICHARD A. NORRIS, JR.

The expression 'Apostolic Fathers' corresponds to an idea of seventeenth-century origin. It originated as the label for a set of writings, then in the process of being recovered and edited, whose authors, though mere 'fathers' and not apostles, were taken to have been close to figures of the apostolic age and thus to possess a certain tincture of apostolic authority. Their writings were therefore both associated and contrasted with those contained in the New Testament, since the latter were assumed to have been written either by apostles proper or by first-generation contemporaries and disciples of theirs.

Historical-critical study of the New Testament has since eliminated the chronological gap that this scheme postulates between the New Testament and the Apostolic Fathers. It is now recognized that apart from the genuine letters of Paul, the books of the New Testament were all written in the period between (roughly) AD 70 and 140, and are thus largely contemporary with those contained in the collection of Apostolic Fathers (– and also, of course, with certain 'apocrypha' and gnostic writings). What distinguishes the latter collection, then, is simply the fact that its writings are relatively primitive, that they belong to traditions counted orthodox, and that they did not become part of the New Testament (though at least three of them – *I Clement*, *The Shepherd of Hermas* and *Didache* – appeared on certain lists of New Testament books).

This primitive Christian literature takes a variety of forms, but by far the most frequent form is that of the letter. Of the twenty-seven separate writings contained in our New Testament, only six do not present themselves as letters. Letters are also central in the traditional collection of the Apostolic Fathers, which contains missives written in the names of Ignatius of Antioch, Polycarp of Smyrna, and of the Church of Rome (*I Clement*), not to mention the so-called *Epistle of Barnabas*, which is alleged by its title to be a letter but is not.

In the Roman-Hellenistic world letters were a common, if not frequent, means of communication among ordinary folk, for personal or business purposes. They were often written by professional scribes, who of course employed conventional forms. At the same time, letters of a more studied (but not less conventional) style, which were sometimes 'published' and handed down as literature, served members of the educated classes for maintenance of the bonds of personal and political friendship and could sometimes, as in the case of the so-called 'Moral Epistles' of Seneca, be given over to paraenesis: that is to say, exhortation and advice. This was often accompanied by exposition of relevant philosophical doctrine, whether moral, psychological or cosmological. A letter could, then, function as a short treatise.

Of the letters in the New Testament, fourteen were traditionally attributed to Paul. Of these, the unquestionably genuine ones are 1 Thessalonians, 1 Corinthians, 2 Corinthians, Philippians, Philemon, Galatians and Romans. They were written, most probably in that order, between AD 50 and 60. Of these seven, one – the Letter to the Romans – now combines two letters (Romans 16 appears to be an addition), and two of them, 2 Corinthians and Philippians, amount to little anthologies of the apostle's correspondence with the Christians in Corinth and Philippi. These modify the conventions of the Hellenistic letter in ways that reflect both Paul's Jewish background and his Christian belief. Thus his salutations name sender and recipients but alter the normal greeting by using the formula 'grace and peace' (the latter term representing standard Jewish usage, and the former, a Christian theme). Normally this would be followed by a prayer for the recipients; Paul observes this custom by introducing a thanksgiving to God for his correspondents, which in turn contains or is co-ordinated with an assurance of his prayers. It is also in accord with accepted practice that Paul closes by conveying greetings to individuals. He uses a blessing in place of the customary 'Farewell'.

The body of a Pauline letter is structured more by its subject-matter than by any set of conventions. Nevertheless it can contain conventional materials (lists of virtues or vices, for example, or commentary on biblical materials).

Paul's letters were occasional. They dealt with issues, practical and doctrinal, that arose within the churches he founded, sometimes, as in 2 Corinthians and Galatians, because of the teaching of persons Paul treated as intruders and competitors. Most of the letters, as far as we can tell, were fairly brisk. Of the two that are more elaborate, 1 Corinthians concerns itself first with party conflicts reported to Paul by visitors to Corinth, and then with a series of questions submitted to Paul by his correspondents. Only Romans, in which Paul introduces himself to a church where his person and message were unknown (save no doubt by report), approaches the character of an essay-letter.

Paul had many detractors, but he also had disciples, people who in effect came to constitute a Pauline 'school'. Like most schools, it included folk who developed their master's ideas in quite different ways. It is from such circles that we have the so-called 'deutero-Pauline' letters: 2 Thessalonians, Ephesians, and the Pastoral Epistles (1 & 2 Timothy and Titus). The authorship of Colossians, whose language and ideas were appropriated by the writer of Ephesians for his own purposes, is still a matter of some debate; but the letter should probably be included in this list. These works imitate the form of the Pauline letters; and like most pseudepigraphical literature of the time, they seek not only to claim the apostle's name and authority for what they say but, even more perhaps, to perpetuate and defend that authority by developing the master's teaching in new circumstances.

It is difficult to date the deutero-Pauline writings. The Pastoral Epistles, reflecting as they do a scene in which certain differences among Christians are hardening into serious disagreement and even alienation, doubtless belong in the first quarter or so of the second century. Ephesians, on the other hand, belongs to an earlier period, very likely the eighties of the first century. Even earlier dates may be sought for Colossians and 2 Thessalonians.

The influence of Paul both as a letter-writer and as a teacher was not confined to his 'school', however, with its tendency to publish under his name. Included in the traditional list of Pauline letters is one – the so-called Epistle to the Hebrews – that is certainly not, despite its closing verses, a letter, and does not claim to be Paul's. This anonymous work does, however, rework themes that are present in Paul's letters, and this may explain why it was early accepted in the East as Pauline. The Roman Church was apparently sceptical of Hebrews' apostolic credentials but nevertheless valued the work (it was cited around AD 96 in *I Clement*). This lends plausibility to the hypothesis that Hebrews, whoever its author was, was a treatise (or sermon?) addressed to the Roman Church in the eighties of the first century.

On this view of Hebrews, one must set alongside it the New Testament letter styled 1 Peter. According to Papias, this letter was written from Rome, but it is, to say the very least, doubtful whether the Apostle Peter was its author. More likely, it belongs to the same period as Hebrews and therefore outside the life-span of Peter; but it attests the possible existence of a 'school' of Peter at Rome, which had some of the interests and attitudes one finds in Hebrews – which, that is to say, belonged in general to the world of a Hellenistic

Jewish Christianity. The letter contains reminiscences of Pauline teaching, and therefore represents a point of view that does not oppose Peter and Paul.

Apparently in AD 96, the Roman Church addressed an admonitory letter to the Church at Corinth. There, for reasons the letter does not reveal, the established elders had been deprived of office by younger members of the church. The letter is styled *I Clement* because, according to Eusebius of Caesarea, a man named Clement, who perhaps presided over the Roman board of elders or acted as its corresponding secretary, actually composed the letter. It is in any case a formal, carefully constructed, letter written in excellent Greek – the work of a competent rhetorician. *I Clement* does not defend the Corinthian elders so much as it does the very idea or principle of order in the Church. It argues not only on moral grounds, but also from the order in nature, from the order given to the Aaronic and Levitical priesthood by Moses, and from the authority of the apostles, that it is illegitimate and dangerous to overturn the constituted leadership of the Church.

By contrast with *I Clement*, which reads like a formally constructed didactic essay, the seven authentic letters of Ignatius of Antioch are hasty, personal, and, even allowing for their occasional imitation of the 'Asian' style in rhetoric, thoroughly breathless and inelegant. They were written, probably around AD 113, by a man who describes himself as the former 'shepherd' of 'the church in Syria' (*Romans* 9.1), now under arrest and being transported to Rome, where he believes and hopes that he will undergo the final test and privilege of martyrdom. Ignatius plainly knows some at least of Paul's letters, but he does not consciously imitate them. He turns his journey into spectacle, and at two stops receives delegates from churches to whom he then writes his letters in return. Thus from Smyrna, whose church, with Polycarp its bishop, received him cordially, he writes letters to the Christians at Ephesus, Magnesia and Tralles, and another to the Roman Church by way of self-introduction, anticipating his arrival there. Then later, from Troas, he addresses the churches at Philadelphia and Smyrna, composing a separate letter to Polycarp. The burden of these letters reveals a man concerned with unity within the churches, who for this reason commends in strong terms communion with, and obedience to, the local chief pastor, the bishop, and condemns certain sets of views – docetic or 'Judaizing' – which threaten to divide the churches.

Ignatius' letters were collected, it seems, by Polycarp himself. Shortly after Ignatius continued his journey to Rome, Polycarp wrote a letter – or possibly two letters – to the church at Philippi, the fundamental aim of which was paraenetic. It is here he indicates that he is sending along a set of Ignatius' communications (*Philippians* 13).

In this same period – i.e., the two decades on either side of the year 100 – the three letters attributed to John were probably composed. The 'John' in question was of course traditionally identified at once as John the Son of Zebedee, as 'the beloved disciple' (cf. John 21:20, 24), and as the author of the Fourth Gospel. Contemporary criticism, however, tends to sees not an individual but a Johannine 'school' and its tradition behind this literature: a school based in a Jewish-Christian community set in some Hellenistic metropolis. On this basis it is possible to understand the affinities and the differences – of style, vocabulary and thought – among the four works. The First Letter of John is not a letter in form, but an anonymous sermon or tract, one of whose concerns – the problem of docetism – links it to the Ignatian correspondence. Like Ignatius, the author is troubled by the denial 'that Jesus Christ has come in the flesh' (4:2), which he associates (apparently) with a further denial that Jesus is the same (person) as 'the Son' or 'the Christ' (2:22f.). 2 and 3 John are very brief letters written by one who calls himself 'the Elder', and who shares the anti-docetic interests of 1 John. The first of these is addressed to a church, the second, a letter of recommendation, to an individual (Gaius).

Clearly, then, by the opening years of the second century, questions about correct belief were agitating many churches and occasioning serious divisions. It is customary nowadays to see these debates as occasioned by 'gnosticism', whether in a full-blown or a partial and preliminary form. The arguments were passionately and not always rationally pursued; and this is nowhere plainer than in the two writings titled, in the New Testament, Jude and 2 Peter. The former takes its stand on 'the faith which was once for all delivered to the saints', and denounces in no uncertain terms persons who, the unknown author says, have denied Christ and perverted 'the grace of our God into licentiousness'. This invective is in its substance reproduced in the second chapter of 2 Peter, a piece of Christian pseudepigraphy that rebukes 'false teachers' who 'follow cleverly devised myths' and misinterpret not only the prophets but the letters of Paul, which the author counts as 'scriptures'. This letter is reckoned to be one of the latest, if not the latest, of the works included in the New Testament.

Perhaps a decade earlier than 2 Peter, around AD 130, and in Alexandria, a Christian writer addressed a letter-treatise styled *The Epistle of Barnabas* to a general audience ('sons and daughters') at a time, as he saw it, of crisis (perhaps that of the Bar Kochba revolt in Palestine). His aim is to dissociate Christianity from Judaism, which he does by trying to show how Torah, when its deep – i.e., allegorical – meaning is evoked, bears a Christian sense. To this treatise on biblical exegesis there has been joined another form of the ethical catechesis that opens the *Didache* (see below).

The term 'gospel' eventually came, in early Christianity, to identify works of widely differing sorts. The Valentinian *Gospel of Truth* appears to be a sermon or treatise. The *Gospel of Thomas* is an anthology of sayings of Jesus. The *Gospel of Philip* is also an anthology, but of gnostic reflections on the Christian life. Originally, however, 'gospel' as used of a literary work denoted a narrative account of Jesus' ministry and destiny, and the four such works that open the New Testament define in and of themselves a distinctive genre.

The characterization of these works as 'gospels' may be attributable to the title given the earliest of them: 'The Gospel of Jesus Christ the Son of God' (Mark 1:1). In the second century, this Gospel was attributed to Mark, whom we meet as a companion of Paul (cf. Acts 12:12, 25; 15:36ff.; Col. 4:10). The attribution was made, however, on the ground that the work conveyed the reminiscences of Peter. Whether or not this attribution is correct, the writing itself was anonymous, as were the other three Gospels. They came to be described as Gospels 'according to' Mark, Matthew, John and Luke only in the second century (see Irenaeus, *AH* 3.1.1).

Mark's Gospel was likely written around the year 70, in the atmosphere of crisis engendered by the Roman siege (and ultimate destruction) of Jerusalem after the Jewish revolt of 66. This date also marks the approximate point at which the Christian communities lost their primary first-generation leaders: James, Peter, Paul, and no doubt others as well. In this situation Mark drew together traditions about Jesus, whether in oral or in written form: stories of Jesus' baptism and miracles, particular gnomic sayings, and perhaps a collection of his parables (cf. Mark 4). Mark combines these with the story of Jesus' passion and resurrection, which he may have known in written form. This account becomes the culmination of his narrative in the sense that it exhibits the meaning of Jesus' ministry and at the same time the logic of Christian discipleship, both of which Mark envisages as opening out upon the imminent, and final, coming of the Son of Man.

Together with those attributed to Jesus' disciple Matthew (cf. Matt. 9:9) and to Paul's companion Luke (Col. 4:14), Mark's is counted as one of the 'Synoptic' Gospels, so called because there is a literary relationship among them. Mark, in fact, seems to have been known and used by the other two, though often with significant omissions and changes of detail. Mark, however, is not the only source they have in common. Each of them also reproduces the contents of a tradition of the sayings of Jesus. This tradition is usually taken nowadays to have been set down in writing, and is referred to as 'Q' (from the German term *Quelle*, 'source'). In addition to this sayings-source, however, Matthew and Luke employ other materials to supplement Mark. Luke knows a set of sayings and parables that are not paralleled in any sources now available; and both Matthew and Luke preface their Gospels with (differing) accounts of the birth and early life of Jesus.

The changes made in Mark (or for that matter in Q), however, while revealed in alterations of language, detail and relative order, are not so much the outgrowth of issues about 'facts', as they are of somewhat different understandings of the significance of Jesus. Like present-day constructions of 'the historical Jesus', Matthew and Luke *see* Jesus in perspectives different from that of Mark.

Matthew, the earlier of the two (this Gospel seems to stem from West Syria in the eighties of the first century), is concerned with the relevance of its story to the continuing, day-to-day life of the Church. The sense of imminent crisis that Mark had evinced is missing. This is replaced by a perception that Jesus' words, deeds and sufferings display a pattern for the Christian conduct of personal and communal life under the increasing pressures of misunderstanding and hostility. Matthew presents this pattern in such a way as to render his work almost a handbook of Christian faith and practice – an expression that defines fairly exactly the way in which it has been read and appropriated over the centuries.

Luke's Gospel, which cannot be understood properly apart from its sequel and complement, the Acts of the Apostles, is governed by a reflective theological thematic that can be read equally well as apology and as programme. The author's world is that of Hellenistic Jewish Christianity and its mission to the Gentiles. He sees that mission, of which Paul becomes his symbol in the Acts, as an outgrowth of Jesus' ministry, death and triumph. Thus the imminent judgment and transformation of the cosmos, which seem to lie just on the other side of the close of Mark's Gospel (Mark 16:8), are in Luke displaced into an unspecified future time. Attention is focused instead on the time 'in between'. The significance of this – the Church's – time is intimated in Acts by the journey of Paul from Jerusalem to Rome, and is grounded in the time of Jesus, who moves, deliberately and portentously, from Galilee to Jerusalem (see Luke 9:51) for the sake of the 'exodus which he was to accomplish' there (Luke 9:31).

Like Matthew and Luke, the Fourth Gospel belongs to the last quarter of the first century. A very early appendix to the Gospel appears to attribute it to 'the disciple whom Jesus loved' (John 20:21; cf. 13:23, 19:26f.), whom a second-century tradition then identified as John the son of Zebedee; but this is more than doubtful. In any case, this Gospel, whether or not its final redactor knew any of the Synoptics, differs from them regarding many details of the chronology of Jesus' ministry, and introduces incidents of which they know nothing (e.g., the wedding at Cana, the raising of Lazarus). Furthermore, it portrays Jesus and his teaching very differently. The discrete and relatively brief and pointed 'sayings' of the Synoptic tradition, as well as the parables that typify Jesus' teaching in that tradition, disappear. They are replaced by meditative and dramatic dialogues and monologues on themes related to seven 'signs' that Jesus performs (2:1–12:50), and by his lengthy farewell discourse with its concluding prayer (13:1–17:26). These signs are intended to evoke faith and discernment of the identity of Jesus as the unique Son and revealer of God (1:18), who as Word or *Logos* of God is the divine Wisdom dwelling with human beings, and in whom all the finalities for which the Synoptics looked to the future are present realities: resurrection, eternal life, and judgment.

This Fourth Gospel, then, retains the general form of the Synoptics, and may very well have known one or more of those works themselves; but it has sources of its own (e.g., a 'Book of Signs'), traditions which it prefers to those which the Synoptics convey (e.g., about the length of Jesus' ministry, and the day of his execution), and above all a manner of reflection that mirrors on the one hand the particular experience of a continuing community, and on the other the ideas and habits of mind of a developing 'school', one that perpetuated the insights of a founder it remembered as 'the disciple whom Jesus loved'.

Alongside letters and gospels of the canonical form, three other types of writing are prominent in Christian literature of this primitive period. The first is the apocalypse ('unveiling'), a record of visions and revelations accorded a seer, usually with the assistance and mediation of a heavenly guide or guides. The typical subject-matter of such works is ultimate mysteries: the character and inhabitants of the divine or heavenly realm, the predetermined course of cosmic history, and the ultimate fate of the world. Apocalypses tended to appear in situations of crisis in which events had created acute doubts about the justice of God and the destiny of God's righteous servants.

The Revelation to John is the principal – though uncharacteristic – representative of this genre in the New Testament, for while in content it has all the marks of apocalypse, in its technical form it is a letter 'to the seven churches that are in Asia' (1:4; cf. 22:21). Further, it is not written, as was customary, under the pseudonym of some past worthy; for the author names himself. Who this John was it is impossible to say. From the language and style of his book, not to mention its contents, one can be sure that he was not the author of the Fourth Gospel or of the letters attributed to John; but this tells nothing about his identity. He regards himself as a prophet (1:10), and no doubt this, together with the letter-form that the work assumes, explains why he can name himself. He writes at a time when, as he sees it, the churches in Asia are facing the prospect of serious persecution, and the common opinion of scholars identifies this time as the reign of the Emperor Domitian.

Among the Apostolic Fathers, some at least of the characteristics of the apocalyptic literature are shared by *The Shepherd of Hermas*, which stems from the Roman Church of the early second century; but this fascinating text, which offers materials for a portrait of the Church of Rome in the first half of the second century, is less concerned with strictly eschatological issues than the here-and-now question of whether God will allow another repentance for the recidivist Christian community at Rome. The answer revealed to Hermas by his 'shepherd' is 'Yes, but only one'.

Finally, in a work titled *The Teaching of the Twelve Apostles to the Nations*, more commonly referred to as the *Didache*, we have what its posterity has treated as the first Christian church-order. In its present form, the work is a composite of earlier materials and dates from the first half of the second century. It opens with an ethical catechesis that delineates 'two ways, one of life and one of death'. This is followed by instructions for performing baptism and eucharist as well as advice regarding the leadership of a Christian community. The New Testament does not by any means lack interest in such problems (see, e.g., most of 1 Cor.; Matt. 20:20ff., 18:15–18), but it contains no work whose form parallels that of the *Didache*.

3

Gnostic literature

RICHARD A. NORRIS, JR.

'Gnosticism' and 'gnostic' are not easy terms to define. Traditionally, they were used to describe certain second- and third-century Christian groups or teachers that claimed to possess a special saving knowledge (γνῶσις), which had been revealed to their predecessors and passed on to them. Such persons, we learn, described themselves, using Pauline language, as 'spiritual' or 'perfect', and sometimes perhaps as 'gnostics' (possessors of a life-giving awareness).[1] This knowledge could not be received by everyone: it was an esoteric knowledge destined only for the elect. Christians who received and accepted it seem to have thought of it as the real or 'deep' meaning of ordinary Christian teaching, which, therefore, they appeared to affirm on one level and to deny on another. It was this circumstance, with the differences of belief and behaviour that accompanied it, that made these gnostics seem at once puzzling, threatening, and alien – and not least because for Christian communities, already hard pressed to survive in an increasingly hostile world, cohesiveness was not only a virtue but a necessity.

This traditional understanding of gnosticism as a deviant form of Christianity – a heresy or assemblage of heresies – is consistent with the character of the literary sources from which knowledge of it was drawn. These sources were the reports of gnosticism's dedicated Christian opponents. In some cases, they quoted passages from the writings of gnostic thinkers. Clement of Alexandria, perhaps the mildest of gnosticism's detractors, preserves in his *Stromateis* (*Miscellanies*) bits of the writings of Valentinus and Basilides. In his *Excerpts from Theodotus*, he muses critically over the ideas of a later Valentinian author. Origen in his *Commentary on John* cites important fragments of the earlier commentary of the Valentinian Heracleon. Epiphanius of Salamis, a fourth-century heresiologist, transmits the important *Letter to Flora* of the Valentinian thinker Ptolemy (essentially a protreptic work, though in the form of a discussion of the sources – i.e., the authors – of the Mosaic Law). These texts are valuable, but scanty; and scholarship had for the rest to rely on writers who summarized gnostic documents and teachings – notably, Irenaeus of Lyon in Book 1 of his treatise *Against Heresies* (*c.* 180), where Valentinian and pre-Valentinian myths of creation and redemption are accurately but unsympathetically retailed; and Hippolytus of Rome (*c.* 220) in his *Refutation of All Heresies* (or *Philosophoumena*).

In the polemic of these often angry opponents of Christian gnosticism, one strain of criticism asserted, though in a fashion somewhat confused and indiscriminate, that the source or sources of gnostic teaching were foreign to Christian tradition: that it drew for its basic ideas on Stoic or Platonist philosophy, or on magical theories and practices, or on the cults of the traditional Mediterranean gods. Such accusations had more truth to them, and less, than their authors could have known. For this to become apparent, however, it was necessary to have a wider selection of authentic gnostic literature; and that became available only through discoveries made in more recent times.

Thus in 1785, the British Museum came into possession of a Coptic manuscript of the fourth century that was part of the estate of a London physician and antiquary named Askew. This *Askew Codex* contains a series of dialogues between the risen Jesus on the one hand, and Mary Magdalene and other disciples on the other. It was first published, with Latin translation, in 1851 under the title *Pistis Sophia*, and has since been translated frequently into modern languages.

Then in 1848 the Bodleian Library at Oxford acquired a manuscript that had been purchased in Egypt by James Bruce, a persistent Scottish searcher for sources of the Nile. This *Bruce Codex*, rebound to its detriment in 1886, was only usefully published in 1892,[2] and in English translation only in 1978. It contains two tractates, of which the first is titled *The Book of the Great Initiatory Discourse*, and the second is without title (though only by reason of the state of the manuscript). Both are in the form of dialogues between Jesus and his disciples: the first is concerned essentially with formulae that grant access to the transcendent world, and the second with a hymnic characterization of its depths, which are interior to as well as independent of the beings to which it gives rise.

In addition to these two eighteenth-century finds, the Berlin Museum in 1896 acquired a papyrus manuscript (*Berlin 8502*) which contained three hitherto unknown works: a *Gospel of Mary*, a work titled *The Apocryphon of John*, and another called *The Sophia of Jesus Christ*. These were writings that were potentially of great moment for the study of gnosticism, but by reason of two successive world wars they were not published until 1955.

By that time, however, further discoveries had been made. Between 1947 and 1949, the scholarly world was made aware of the discovery of a series of mid-fourth-century Coptic codices, on papyrus, in the vicinity of the town of Nag Hammadi in Upper Egypt. One of these – the so-called *Codex Jung* – left Egypt and became the property of the C. G. Jung Institute;[3] the others were acquired, after some delay, by the Cairo Museum, and in 1956 the process by which they were to be prepared for publication was begun. By that time, the academic world had been informed of the contents of the *Codex Jung*. It included five works, of which two – the *Gospel of Truth* and a *Treatise on the Resurrection* (also known as the *Epistle to Rheginus*) – excited instant attention. Publication of the contents of the *Codex Jung* began in 1955; but the publication of the whole of the Nag Hammadi find required more than two decades.

In the thirteen codices of the Nag Hammadi corpus (of which the twelfth and the thirteenth are in exceedingly fragmentary condition) there are a total of fifty-one distinct writings. Some of these are duplicated within the collection (there are, for example, three versions of the *Apocryphon of John* to add to the version given in *Berlin 8502*), and a few are also known from other sources. Even a superficial survey of their content reveals several significant points. Above all, however, the collection is remarkably variegated. It was of course assembled by Christians, and the great majority of the writings it contains are gnostic in their tone and content. Nevertheless, (a) not all of the writings it contains exhibit a gnostic sensibility; (b) not all of the plainly gnostic writings belong to the same 'school' or tendency within the gnostic 'movement'; and above all (c) not all of the gnostic writings are Christian. The people who collected and read it, therefore, were probably not deeply interested in the differences of point of view between, say, a Valentinian anthology (*The Gospel of Philip, NHC* II, *3*), a document in the Hermetic tradition (VI, *6*), a brief section of Plato's *Republic* (VI, *5*), and slightly varying accounts, in varying forms, of the origins of the cosmos. They would no doubt have used these documents more as vehicles for meditation and insight than as textbooks of dogmatic truth; and this of course marks an important difference between them and someone like Irenaeus, who had construed the gnostic writings he knew in precisely the opposite way.

More important still, this odd collection, providing as it does a window on both Christian and non-Christian gnosticism, enables students to assess gnostic teaching on the basis of its own testimony, and above all to assess it as a movement that cannot be understood simply in terms of its relation to Christianity, that is, as a product, whether natural or perverse, of Christian faith. To this extent, the suspicion evinced by gnosticism's early opponents, to the effect that it was an 'import' into Christianity, has a certain amount of justification. On the other hand, investigation of the affinities of gnostic writings and teachings have tended to suggest that its early cohabitation with Christianity was at least partly occasioned by the fact that it shared a cultural and social 'location' with the Christian movement – a location defined by a significant overlapping of speculative tendencies in early Judaism (not without a basis in scriptural exegesis) with other currents of religious practice and philosophical thought.

This point can even be illustrated from the literary forms assumed by the writings in the Nag Hammadi Corpus. One of the most common of these forms was the so-called 'revelation dialogue'. This genre – as the English term 'revelation' indicates – is a type of apocalypse. The writer reports an experience or experiences in which a heavenly figure of some sort explains and conveys transcendent truth in converse with a human being. One example of such a dialogue is of course the New Testament book of the Revelation to John; others, such as the writings attributed to Enoch or Ezra (Esdras), can be sought among the apocrypha and pseudepigrapha of the Old Testament. Within the Nag Hammadi collection, an illuminating example is *The Apocalypse of Adam* (*NHC* V, *5*). In this work, which affords no obvious evidence of being affected by Christian ideas or symbols, there is contained 'the revelation which Adam taught his son Seth in the seven hundredth year'.[4] Adam first relates how he and Eve lost 'the eternal knowledge of the God of truth', and then how three powers from the transcendent world conveyed to him knowledge of three descents of a saviour-figure ('Illuminator') to rescue Seth's descendants, 'the generation without a king over it,' by wakening them to knowledge of their own heavenly derivation and identity. Like many other apocalypses, then, this work is primarily intended to convey hope – in this case, no doubt, to a community of 'Sethian' gnostics – by giving assurance of the divine destiny of the seed of Seth and their ultimate rescue from the clutches of the death-dealing Creator God of this cosmos. *The Apocalypse of Adam* is thus reminiscent not only of earlier apocalypses, but also of the sort of writing one finds in the *Testaments of the Twelve Patriarchs* (for this revelation is Adam's legacy to his son); yet the reader does not actually hear the conversation between Adam and his heavenly interlocutors. Rather, what is heard is a summing-up of its content for Seth, so that the body of the apocalypse reads almost like a treatise (with a lengthy hymnic insertion).

The same is not true of the writing called *Zostrianos* (*NHC* VIII, *1*), however, in which the speaker directly relates his question-and-answer dialogues with 'the angel of the knowledge of eternal light' (and others). This too – another Sethian work, though one that betrays the influence of late Platonism – is an apocalypse. Like the apocryphal *Ascension of Isaiah*, it relates a journey through the divine world, in the course of which the speaker is baptized into higher and higher levels of *gnosis*, so that on his return to earth he can record his knowledge for the benefit of those who are drawn to a nobler level of life, i.e., for the seed of Seth. Another example of this genre is the second part of the tractate called *The Hypostasis of the Archons* ('Reality of the Rulers,' *NHC* II, 4), which, apart from an opening allusion to St Paul, contains no Christian materials. This opens with a tendentious paraphrase of Genesis 1–6, but follows that with a revelation delivered to the speaker (Norea, a female equivalent of Seth) by Eleleth, 'the great angel', concerning the origin and character of the 'rulers' – the wicked Creator God and his powers.

But it is not only in these Sethian and non-Christian writings that the revelation dialogue appears in gnostic literature. *The Apocryphon of John*, for example, which stands squarely in the Sethian tradition, has been at least superficially Christianized through the identification of the Saviour or Revealer with Jesus. As a result of this, however, the character of the dialogue itself has been changed. It has become a dialogue between the risen Jesus and one of his disciples, John the son of Zebedee. Jesus, then, becomes the heavenly revealer, who appears in glorious light in threefold form, to dispel John's puzzlement and doubt by conveying roughly the same truth that is conveyed in *The Hypostasis of the Archons* or *The Apocalypse of Adam*. In this way, gnostic teachings – about the spiritual overworld, the origins of the cosmos, and the salvation of the elect – are given the authority of the Saviour himself, not to mention that of the Apostle John. The device used to accomplish this is conflation of the classical apocalyptic dialogue between a seer and a heavenly revealer with conventional Christian accounts of post-resurrection communications delivered by Christ to his earthly disciples. The plausibility and attractiveness of this procedure was no doubt strengthened by the established convention, which went back to Plato and Xenophon, of using dialogue as a means of conveying philosophical ideas, and by the fact that question-and-answer was a well-known teaching method.

The form of *The Apocryphon of John* reappears in a number of other works in the Nag Hammadi corpus. *The Book of Thomas the Contender* (*NHC* II, 7), for example, which is entirely innocent of Sethian exegeses of Genesis or Sethian accounts of world origins, presents a revelation dialogue between Jesus and his 'twin', the Apostle Judas Thomas, in which the superiority of a life attuned to spirit as opposed to flesh is commended in the face of Thomas' (no doubt disabling) complaint, and fear, that Jesus' teachings will be despised by the world. This work obviously belongs to the Syrian 'Thomas'-literature also represented by *The Gospel of Thomas* (*NHC* II, 2) and *The Acts of Thomas*.

To take another example, *The Sophia of Jesus Christ* (*NHC* III, *4*; with a longer version in *Berlin 8052*) is particularly interesting as a work of this genre in that it represents a Christianized version of a gnostic original – *Eugnostos the Blessed* (*NHC* III, *3* & V, *1*) – which immediately precedes it in one of the Nag Hammadi folios. *Eugnostos* is in form a letter and presents a fundamentally Sethian account of the structure of the divine overworld of which, it avers, 'philosophers' have been uniformly ignorant. *The Sophia of Jesus Christ*, which transforms its original into a revelation dialogue, makes this interest explicit by explaining that the 'disciples and seven women' to whom Jesus appeared like 'a great angel of light' were troubled about 'the underlying reality of the universe and the plan and the holy providence and the power of the authorities[5] and about everything that the Saviour is doing'. Its subject-matter, then, is quite different from that of *The Book of Thomas the Contender*, and indeed it appears to have roughly the same agenda as *The Apocryphon of John*. What all of these have in common, however, is the fact that they portray themselves as dealing with the puzzlement and doubt that trouble believers, whether Christian or gnostic or both. They are not, then, addressed to the world at large and are, in that sense at least, esoteric. This seems moreover to be the case with other gnostic writings in the form of the revelation dialogue. Thus the *Apocalypse of Peter* (*NHC* VII, *3*),[6] in which Jesus interprets for Peter the meaning of three visions which the latter has had, is clearly addressed to Christian gnostics who find themselves under attack by the leaders and other members of the Church. It explains this phenomenon as due to the congenital spiritual blindness of those whose natural home is this world; and it assures Peter that he, to whom 'mysteries' have been revealed, will convey them 'to those of another race who are not of this age'.

The revelation in dialogue form is by no means the sole form taken by gnostic writing, though it is certainly a frequent and characteristic one. One of the most remarkable and interesting remains of gnostic literature is *The Gospel of Truth* (I, *3*; XII, *2*), which is a treatise or sermon whose aim, like that of Ptolemy's *Letter to Flora*, seems to be protreptic: i.e., it aims to attract people to the Christian message as Valentinian gnostics understand it. A work of great rhetorical skill, it carries neither a title (the title given it is taken from its opening words) nor the name of its author (though many have attributed it, not implausibly, to Valentinus himself). Its subject-matter is the salvation to be attained through knowledge of 'the Father of truth' revealed by the Word from God or the Saviour, who is identified with Jesus. It is probably this *Gospel of Truth* that Irenaeus of Lyon mentions in his work *Against Heresies* (3.11.9) as 'recently written down' by the Valentinians and as proof that they reckon 'more gospels than there actually are'. Perhaps if he had read it, he would not have written so, since it is in an entirely different form from his Four Gospels, and there is no evidence that his adversaries, however seriously they took its teaching, thought of it as a fifth item on that particular list.

A similar protreptic aim informs another treatise, this time cast in letter-form (though the writer is never named): the so-called *Treatise on the Resurrection* or *Epistle to Rheginus*. Here the writer is dealing with a much-debated subject from the point of view of a thoughtful, philosophically instructed Christian gnostic. He writes as to a pupil or disciple who has come to him with honest questions about 'resurrection'. Much that he says might have been acceptable to an orthodox writer like Origen (though surely not to an Irenaeus or a Tertullian). What marks him out as a Valentinian is his identification of resurrection with a putting off of the visible cosmos and a (mental) return of the spiritual self to the supernal home whence it came.

By contrast with such protreptic works, the Nag Hammadi corpus also contains writings that almost certainly reflect the cultic practices of committed gnostic believers. Thus *The Gospel of the Egyptians*,[7] also titled *The Holy Book of the Great Invisible Spirit* (*NHC* III, *2* & IV, *2*) recounts the Sethian myth at length, but as a story of salvation that comes to its end in what looks like a baptismal ritual. Similarly, the *Trimorphic Protennoia* (*NHC* XIII, *1*), which takes the form of a self-declaration, in alternating poetic and prose sections, on the part of the three-formed Wisdom, recounts the elements of the Sethian myth and ends with a description of baptism and of the descent of the Saviour. Valentinian practice is reflected in the work titled *A Valentinian Exposition*, which expounds the story of creation and redemption, the *gnosis* which believers understand, and provides instruction on the meaning of baptism and what look like elements of a eucharistic prayer. These writings, more than the protreptic works, provide useful hints of the way gnostics – Christian but also non-Christian – talked in their own circles.

Notes

1 It is as a result of a usage of Irenaeus of Lyon (which his orthodox successors in the early Church did not imitate) that 'gnostics' has become a designation for all such groups indiscriminately.

2 C. Schmidt, ed., *Gnostische Schriften in koptischer Sprache aus dem Codex Brucianus*.

3 After the death of Jung himself, the codex was returned to the Cairo museum to be kept there with its fellows. It is commonly counted as the first codex of the series of thirteen.

4 This and other quotations from writings in the Nag Hammadi corpus are taken from J. M. Robinson, ed., *The Nag Hammadi Library in English*.

5 I.e., the 'archons' or rulers of the visible cosmos.

6 This writing must not be confused with the apocryphal apocalypse that bears the same title.

7 Not to be confused with the apocryphal Gospel of the same title.

4

Apocryphal writings and Acts of the martyrs

RICHARD A. NORRIS, JR.

'Apocrypha' and 'apocryphal' originally signified something hidden or secret, and they were applied in this sense to esoteric writings, that is, writings which circulated only within a narrow group of persons 'in the know'. Thus one second-century Christian writer speaks of '*apocryphal* and spurious writings' produced by Marcosian gnostics.[1] However, the term soon enough came, in Christian circles, simply to mean 'false' or 'spurious'.[2] Taken in this sense, the label might convey one or more of the following judgments: that the work contained falsehood or doubtful teaching; that it made an illegitimate claim as to authorship; or, finally, that it was no part of a church's received list of authoritative books. The expression 'apocryphal literature' is thus a vague one. In practice it refers to what might be called the popular literature of early Christianity or some sector thereof. Not many such writings were actually candidates – in whatever circle or locale – for official or canonical status; but all were taken seriously by their audiences, many had a wide audience, and some had an abiding influence on Christian belief and practice. In this category it is reasonable to include the literature of the so-called 'Acts of the Martyrs'; for while these never claimed official status in any locale, they were no doubt widely circulated and read (perhaps even, on occasion, at assemblies of the church), and constituted a literature that at once inspired, entertained, edified and persuaded.

First in this general category must come gospels, which here means writings that concern themselves with some aspect of the story of Jesus, whether or not they take the same form as the canonical four. Certain of these served minority or sectarian communities. Christian writers of the second through the fifth centuries refer to *Jewish-Christian* gospels, for example. Concerning the character and titles of these they are somewhat confused (perhaps because the titles they use are most often descriptions assigned by themselves and other outsiders). Thus there circulated in Egypt in the second century a *Gospel according to the Hebrews*, known to Clement of Alexandria and Origen. The few fragments of this writing suggest dependence on Matthew, but it elaborates on the canonical Gospel in a manner that seems gnostic in mood and inflection if not in substance.

The same title is assigned by Eusebius, in Palestine, to what is certainly a different writing, 'in which those of the Hebrews who have accepted Christ take great pleasure' (*HE* 3.25.5); and this work Eusebius classifies, along with the Revelation to John, as 'disputed' or marginal, but not among the 'spurious' (such as *The Shepherd of Hermas*). It must, then, be a work that Eusebius knows, or knows of, as written in Greek. Eusebius also reports, however, that Hegesippus had quoted from a 'Syriac' gospel as well as from the *Gospel according to the Hebrews*. Later still, Epiphanius of Salamis mentions a 'Gospel of the Nazoreans', whom he identifies as Jewish Christians living in Berœa. This he says is a version of Matthew in 'Hebrew' (= Aramaic). It seems likely that this is the same work that Eusebius describes as 'Syriac'; and the question is whether it is also identical with what he calls the *Gospel according to the Hebrews*, and if so, whether the Greek or the Aramaic form is earlier. In any case, it cannot have been regarded as heretical and certainly belongs to the first part of the second century.

The same cannot be said for the *Gospel of the Ebionites*, which was an abbreviated and much revised form of Matthew. The narrative in this work was put in the mouth of the apostles themselves, and it omitted the Matthaean birth-narrative (preferring a gnostic-style Christology focused on the baptism of Jesus). It was probably, as Goodspeed suggested, written to impugn the authority of the dominant four-Gospel canon, which it therefore presupposes.

Mention is often made of *the Gospel of the Egyptians*,[3] quoted six times by Clement of Alexandria in the third book of his *Miscellanies* and alluded to by Origen and Hippolytus. Clement associated it with Encratites who forbade marriage, and the citations he gives, two of which are paralleled in *II Clement* and *the Gospel of Thomas* (see below), are all concerned with that issue. Nothing is known of the shape or content of the rest of this writing, which therefore remains something of a cipher.

Several apocryphal gospels are attributed to apostles, thus tacitly claiming apostolic authority for their content. The so-called *Protevangelium of James* or *Book of James* is a narrative attributed to 'the brother of the Lord', and probably comes in its earliest form from the last quarter of the second century. Much altered and elaborated as it was copied over the centuries, this writing, which draws on the canonical Gospels, the Old Testament stories of Samuel, and legendary materials orally transmitted, is concerned basically with the story of Mary – her miraculous birth, her perpetual virginity, and the birth of Jesus.

A similar work of piety referred to as the *Infancy Gospel of Thomas* (to avoid confusion with the *Gospel of Thomas*) probably comes, like other writings that bear Thomas' name, from Syria and may date to the late second century. It conveys various stories about the child Jesus, calculated to portray him as endowed with unusual, indeed miraculous, powers, knowledge and insight. Like the *Book of James*, it enjoyed wide popularity, was translated into many tongues, and was read well into the medieval period.

Of more interest to historians are the *Gospel of Thomas* and the *Gospel of Peter*. The first of these is known only from the Nag Hammadi corpus, and therefore in a Coptic translation of the original Greek. It almost certainly originated in eastern Syria and belongs to the history of gnostic Christianity, even though it exhibits little if any sign of affinity with Valentinianism. The *Gospel of Thomas* is in form not a Marcan-style gospel at all, but a collection of sayings of Jesus, many of them closely related to those in the so-called 'sayings-source' ('Q') shared by the Matthaean and Lucan Gospels. It presents Jesus as the revealer of saving insight (wisdom). The question whether the *Gospel of Thomas* is dependent on the Gospels of Matthew or Luke tends now to be answered in the negative, and some scholars think it is an alternative version of the source Q drew on. In any case it is relatively early and belongs to the end of the first, or the beginning of the second, century.

The same may be true of the *Gospel of Peter*, which Bishop Serapion of Antioch (*fl. c.* 200), on a visit to Rhossus where the book was a subject of debate, eventually stigmatized as non-Petrine and as docetic in its view of Christ (Eusebius, *HE* 6.12.3–5). Of this writing we now have a single papyrus fragment dating from well after the Arab occupation of Egypt. The text takes up just after the scene in the trial of Jesus in which Pilate washes his hands (cf. Matt. 27:24) and ends with an account of Jesus' resurrection. The narrative can at certain points be construed in a docetic manner, but need not be so taken. The most striking elements in this fragment are perhaps its claim to give an eyewitness account of the actual resurrection of Jesus, with attendant wonders, and its strengthening of the anti-Jewish sentiment in the canonical Gospels. The *Gospel of Peter* seems to depend on the canonical four and possibly derives from western Syria early on in the second century.

The claim to apostolic authorship made by some of these later gospels is also made for a document of an entirely different form. The *Letter of the Apostles* (*Epistula apostolorum*) was unknown even by title until the last decade of the nineteenth century, when a partial Coptic text was discovered, slightly later supplemented by a complete text in Ethiopic and some Latin fragments. The work claims to be written by the eleven apostles and is addressed to all

Christians everywhere. It relates, like many of the gnostic documents in the Nag Hammadi corpus, a dialogue between the risen Christ and its authors; but its aim is clearly anti-docetic and anti-gnostic. Thus it insists not only on the reality of Christ's body, but on the bodily resurrection of believers, and at the same time exhibits the ethical and moral rigorism of much of the Christianity of its time, orthodox and not-so-orthodox. It probably belongs to the first half of the second century and comes from Asia or Syria.

Alongside these 'gospel' materials must be set another group of works of a quite different sort, the literature that relates the deeds or 'acts' (πράξεις) of various apostles. These writings are similar in form if not always in style, and clearly were immensely popular in the churches of the first four centuries, at all levels of their membership. Each narrates the journeys, speeches and miracles of a single apostle, drawing on mostly legendary materials that circulated in early oral tradition. Their titles, containing as they invariably do the word 'acts', invite comparison with the Lucan Acts of the Apostles, and the comparison is not wholly without point. Like the canonical Acts, these apocrypha are narratives which interest themselves in the visions, wonders and conversions that occurred as their subjects fulfilled an apostolic mission. On the other hand, while they convey and commend the beliefs and commitments of popular Christianity and so perform a teaching function, they do not evince the theological concerns that preoccupy the canonical Acts, nor are they parts of larger works. They are meant to entertain and edify even more than to instruct, and therefore can with equal profit be compared to the romantic fiction of the late Hellenistic Age, i.e., to works such as Longus' *Daphnis and Chloe*, or even Apuleius' *Metamorphoses*. In this instance too, however, the differences seem, in the end, as great as the similarities. The form of the travel narrative is common to both, but the Christian 'acts' literature lacks any real element of plot even as Hellenistic romances, for all their love of appalling perils and narrow escapes, lack the acts' focus on works of saving power and interest in martyrdom. The early Christian literature of apostolic acts, then, has affinities with various literary genres in the Roman world (not excluding the sort of thing one finds in biographies of philosophers like Pythagoras or even Plotinus); but it does not conform precisely to any of them.

Like the *Gospel of Thomas*, the *Acts of Thomas*, an early third-century composition, identifies its subject as 'Judas Thomas, also called Didymus'. Since *thomas* in Aramaic and *didymos* in Greek both mean 'twin', this Judas is meant to be identified as the twin brother of Jesus. There is little doubt that the work, again like the *Gospel of Thomas*, stems from an east Syrian setting, since Syrian tradition made Thomas the founder of the church at Edessa. It was very likely composed in Syriac, but quickly translated into Greek. Later translations into, for example, Latin and Armenian indicate its wide-ranging popularity and its influence – as does the fact that it was admired not only by gnostics and Manichaeans, but also by the orthodox (who in translating it would often polish up its doctrine). The story-line is based on the Lord's assignment of India to Thomas as his sphere of mission, and concentrates on the latter's miracles and conversions there. The individual 'acts' (thirteen in number) provide the writer with opportunities to insert various prayers and hymns – which doubtless reflect liturgical practices – into the text; and one of these, 'The Song of the Pearl', is a well-known allegory of the fall and redemption of the soul. It is plain – from this hymn as well as from many other elements in the story – that the *Acts of Thomas* derives from a milieu where a form of Christian gnosticism was practised; it is full of themes that also appear, often in more developed and explicit forms, in other gnostic sources. It also commends a rigorist lifestyle, making of Thomas a practitioner of sexual continence who lives upon bread and water (with salt) alone, and whose notion of what to do with money is to give it to the poor.

Perhaps several decades earlier than the *Acts of Thomas* is the *Acts of Peter*, which, however, is now known only in incomplete form and for the most part in Latin translation. Here is found the famous *Quo vadis?* incident (*APet.* 35) and the tradition that Peter was crucified with his head downwards (*APet.* 37). The centrepiece of this work appears to have been Peter's conflict with Simon Magus at Rome. This culminates in a scene in the Forum, where it is established that whilst Simon has the power to kill, only Christ through Peter can restore the dead to life. There is no trace of gnostic sensibility in the *Acts of Peter*, but the same stern style of life is evinced here as in the *Acts of Thomas*. Riches are for sharing, the values of this world are to be deprecated, virginity is praised, and indeed Peter is attacked for persuading a wife to leave her husband's bed.

The same tone is maintained in the *Acts of Paul*, which apparently knows and uses the *Acts of Peter* and appears to belong to the closing decades of the second century: it was known to such authors as Origen and Tertullian. Only after 1904, however, when a fragmentary Heidelberg Coptic manuscript was first edited and published, did scholars realize that significant sections of the *Acts of Paul* had circulated separately as the *Acts of Paul and Thecla*, the *Martyrdom of Paul*, and possibly *3 Corinthians* (a pseudo-Pauline letter that for a time was in the canon of the Armenian and probably the Syrian Churches). With the help of another manuscript discovered in 1936, a substantive portion of the Greek text became available, though significant parts of the text are still unknown.

This writing follows the normal pattern of the 'acts' literature, and is further typical of it in its contempt for worldly goods, its advocacy of continence, and its low view of marriage. The latter theme is especially prominent in the *Acts of Paul and Thecla*, a work whose popularity can be measured by the spread of a cult of Thecla, who, though she seems to have been a legendary figure, was venerated as martyr and virgin in West and East alike and came to have a shrine at Seleucia. In the *Acts*, Thecla is encouraged by Paul to teach, contrary to the express prohibition of 1 Timothy, and she administers baptism.

Also from the second century, we have works titled the *Acts of John* and the *Acts of Andrew*. The latter is the most difficult of these works to reconstruct, since, while scholars have a clear notion of its extent, the original text is not available in anything like a complete form. It too was a travel narrative replete with wonders, inculcating an encratitic manner of life, and culminating in a story of the hero's martyrdom. The *Acts of John* differs from this pattern only in that its hero is not martyred, but simply steps, after a prayer of thanksgiving, into a grave his disciples had just dug, lies down, and cheerfully surrenders his spirit. The sections 94–105 seem to have been inserted in the text as an independent whole: their form, language and atmosphere, and in particular the splendid hymn to which Jesus and his disciples dance, are gnostic and must stem from an earlier period than the rest of the text.

The early Christians further wrote and consulted works of the sort that are styled 'apocalypse'. An apocalypse is a written record of a revelation given through a mediating figure (often an angel) in the form of visions or auditions or both. Its immediate subject-matter is the transcendent divine world, which is seen to be temporally and spatially separated from the human world as presently experienced. The apocalyptist's central concern is the ultimate (re-)integration of these two worlds and the consequent cure, destruction or punishment of evil: in a word, eschatology, though not without an intimation of the implications of this future for the conduct of life in the present. Its normal occasion is a set of events, just past or plainly impending, that create a crisis in the lives of the community to which the seer's revelation is addressed and so raise the question of evil in an acute form.

One such work, the *Apocalypse of Peter*, was included, though in the category of disputed works, in the so-called Muratorian canon, a third-century Roman list of authoritative books. Composed in the first half of the second century, it is now known only in an Ethiopic version (with a substantive Greek fragment). Widely read and admired in the early Church, the book consists largely of descriptions of the different states of the righteous and the wicked after the ultimate divine judgment. It nicely adjusts punishments in hell to fit sins on earth and from a functional rather than a formal point of view ought probably to be classified as paraenesis. It draws on Greek and Hellenistic pictures of the underworld and is a principal source of classical Christian portrayals of heaven and hell. Similar pictures of the fates of righteous and wicked can be found in later works: the *Apocalypse of Paul* (fourth century), for example, which draws on the *Apocalypse of Peter*; or the *Apocalypse of S. John the Theologian* (ninth century).

Another type of apocalypse is represented by the *Ascension of Isaiah*, which combines an old Jewish legend of the martyrdom of Isaiah, originally perhaps in Hebrew (1–5), with a Christian interpolation (3:13–4:22) and supplement (6–11, which relate the 'ascension' proper), originally in Greek. The whole text is now known only in an Ethiopic translation, though there are fragments of versions in Latin, Coptic and Slavonic. The different sections were no doubt composed at different times and by different hands, but the whole probably belongs to the second century. Chapters 6–11 relate an experience accorded Isaiah, in which he is guided by an angel through the successive heavens to the seventh. There he has a vision of the descent of the Christ ('the Beloved') through the heavens and down to the unhappy earth, as well as of his birth, death and resurrection, and his return through the heavens. Formally a typical apocalypse, the *Ascension of Isaiah* is nevertheless not focused on eschatology but on the (past) work of the Christ and on Isaiah's vision of the series of heavens. The *Book of Elchasai*, a sectarian piece dating from the reign of Trajan, is quoted briefly in the writings of Hippolytus and Epiphanius. It may well have belonged to the genre of apocalypse, though because of the paucity of evidence certainty on this score is impossible.

Finally, account must be taken of early (i.e., primarily second-century) martyrs' *acta*: which is to say, accounts of the trials, sufferings and deaths of Christians at the hands of Roman authorities. The earliest of these is the *Martyrdom of Polycarp*, a writing commonly reckoned among the Apostolic Fathers. It is in the form of a letter from the Church of Smyrna to all 'dwellings of the holy Catholic Church everywhere' and to the Church of Philomelium in particular. It speaks only in general terms of those who died before the bishop, but goes into detail in suggesting how Polycarp tried to evade capture, how he was taken, how he conducted himself at his trial, and how he was finally killed (with a knife because 'his body could not be consumed by the fire'). The letter of course intends to glorify Polycarp and the other martyrs for their nobility and patience under suffering, not to mention their devotion to Christ, and suggests that Polycarp died 'in order that we might become imitators of his'. The *Letter of the Churches of Lyon and Vienne* (Eusebius, *HE* 5.1.3–5.2.8), directed from Gaul to the churches of Asia *c.* 177, is similar in form to the *Martyrdom of Polycarp* and evinces some of the same aims – namely, to encourage Christians who might suffer persecution themselves with the example of sisters and brothers who through the power of the Spirit had triumphed in the contest with Satan (to whom the persecution is attributed: the mob and the Roman authorities appear to be no more than the devil's pawns). There are of course similarities between these accounts and the stories of the Maccabaean martyrs, with which second-century Christians were certainly acquainted.

A different form of narrative is found in the *Acts of Carpus, Papylas, and Agathoniké*; the *Acts of Ptolemaeus and Lucius*; the *Acts of Justin and Companions*; and the *Acts of the Scillitan Martyrs*. Each of these employs, or partially takes the form of, a court record of the exchange between the accused and the Roman magistrate who presided over the proceedings; and their rhetorical power depends to a certain extent upon the bare-bones simplicity and realism of their style. All refer to events in the latter half of the second century, and for the most part in the reign of Marcus Aurelius. The next great spate of martyrs' *acta* come from the third century, for the most part from the persecution under the Emperors Decius and Valerian.

Notes

1 Irenaeus, *AH* 1.20.1; cf. Clement of Alexandria, *Strom.* 1.15.69.

2 Tertullian, *Pud.* 10.12, classifies *The Shepherd of Hermas* among 'apocryphal and false' writings, though Irenaeus had cited it as scripture.

3 Not to be confused with the work of the same name in the Nag Hammadi corpus.

5
The Apologists

RICHARD A. NORRIS, JR.

The term 'Apologists', as applied to Christian writers of the early period, denotes a series of authors who in the course of the second century composed and circulated addresses and pleas (cf. Justin, *I Apol.* 1.1: προσφώνησιν καὶ ἔντευξιν) to emperors and others in public authority on behalf of their fellow Christians. The aim of such writings was in general to persuade the authorities that the frequent local persecutions of Christians were unjust, unnecessary, and unworthy of enlightened rulers. This aim entailed some explication of Christian beliefs, practices and morals, and of course the explication tended to grow imperceptibly into defence, the content of which might range from reassurance (e.g., that Christians did not practice cannibalism, or that they had not joined forces, whether in principle or in practice, with rebels against the Roman order) to argument (e.g., that Christianity was, despite impressions to the contrary, neither novel nor irrational by the standards of current philosophical religion). Apology in this narrow sense might of course pass over into direct refutation of critics of Christianity or attempts to establish the superiority of Christian faith to the polytheism and idolatry that characterized popular religious practice in the Roman Empire.

These Apologists were not without precedents for their work. Hellenistic Judaism had produced writings that served the purposes and aims of apology; and earlier Christian literature contained instances of discourse that pursues apologetic aims and methods: the speech attributed to Paul in Acts 17:22ff., for example, or 1 Peter 2:13–15, which advises obedience to the authorities as a way of silencing 'the ignorance of foolish men'. The apologetic writings of the second century could and did draw on such resources as these as well as on the commonplaces of Hellenistic rhetoric and on the language of Middle Platonist (and Stoic) religious cosmology and theology. They were, then, the products of authors who enjoyed a fuller education in the Greek manner than the majority of Christians, and who could therefore envisage and present their faith in a way that might make it appear comprehensible and tolerable, if not attractive, to initially hostile readers. It is perhaps typical of this mentality that an apologist like Justin Martyr could envisage – and present – Christianity as siding with the cause of reason and philosophy against the immoral and implausible 'myths' of the (classical) poets: i.e., the stories of the gods whose cults were practised throughout the Mediterranean world. Thus he intimates that Jesus was a latter-day Socrates, and more, the incarnate divine original of every Socrates. As a defence against the charge of 'atheism' (i.e., refusal to honour the accepted gods, the charge brought against Socrates) this was a useful tactic even if some might have thought it a bit too clever, and even if to ordinary Christians it might have sounded dangerously compromising.

The first apologist mentioned in our sources was one Quadratus, of whom the church historian Eusebius (*HE* 4.3.1–2) reports that he 'composed a defence' (ἀπολογίαν) addressed to the Emperor Hadrian (AD 117–38). Eusebius elsewhere describes this Quadratus as a 'disciple of the Apostles', and indicates that the address was presented to the emperor in Athens, where the emperor visited in 124 and 129. Eusebius does not identify the 'wicked men' whose efforts to trouble Christians, he says, evoked this apology; and he gives only a brief excerpt from Quadratus' work, which concerns the reality and enduring character of the (miraculous) 'works' of Jesus.

In his very next breath (*HE* 4.3.3), Eusebius mentions another apologist – one Aristides – who, he reports, addressed a 'defence' to Hadrian at about the same time as Quadratus. He seems not to have seen a text of this apology, but assures readers that it has been preserved by 'many'; and indeed a Syriac text of it was found on Mount Sinai in 1889 by J. Rendel Harris. On the basis of this discovery, a Greek text of *The Apology of Aristides* was shortly thereafter identified as figuring in a novel, *Barlaam and Josaphat*, that had been written in Palestine in the tenth century. The Syriac text disagrees with Eusebius' statement that the work was addressed to Hadrian and sets it instead in the reign of Antoninus Pius (AD 138–61), but three Armenian manuscripts that contain the opening lines of the *Apology* concur with Eusebius. The Greek version is shorter and may have been revised and enlarged at some point. Aristides' *Apology* is of interest not only for its attack on polytheism and its account of the God whom Christians worship, but also for its defence of Christian morality and its characterization of Christians as a third γένος, race, alongside Jews and Gentiles (whom Aristides divides into three races: viz., 'Chaldaeans and Greeks and Egyptians').

Aristides' *Apology* has much in common with another, probably still earlier, writing from which fragments are quoted by Clement of Alexandria and which Clement titles *Κήρυγμα Πέτρου* ('Peter's Message')[1]. It was also known to Heracleon, the second-century Valentinian commentator on the Gospel of John, and to Eusebius, who may not have read it but certainly rejects it as an apostolic and canonical writing (*HE* 3.3.2). Examination of the fragments suggests that the work contained discourses that claimed Peter's authority (if not necessarily his authorship) and sounded many of the same themes touched on by Aristides: the picture of Christians as a 'third race'; insistence on the uniqueness of the God who though invisible 'sees all things' and though uncontained contains all things; assertion that it is Christians alone who worship God rightly, 'through Christ in a new way'; stress upon the prophets' prediction and anticipation of the death and triumph of Jesus. Indeed it may well have served Aristides and others as a source or a model. The title of the work – *Κήρυγμα* – is significant in that it indicates the character of this sort of 'apology': it is less a defence, perhaps, than a form of missionary proclamation that involves at the same time a critique of rival, but older and more established, religious traditions.

During the reign of Antoninus Pius, but after the emperor had elevated his adoptive son Marcus Aurelius to share his rule in 146, Justin Martyr, a Christian teacher of Middle Platonist leanings and a native of Flavia Neapolis (the ancient Shechem and the modern Nablus) in Palestine, addressed an apology to him and his 'sons' Verissimus (i.e., Marcus) and Lucius. It was possibly the martyrdom of the aged Polycarp of Smyrna (*c.* 156) that stimulated this appeal, which was written in Rome, perhaps in 156 or 157. The complete Greek text of the apology is known only through one fourteenth-century manuscript (now in the National Library at Paris) and a later copy of it. Eusebius of Caesarea, who lists eight works of Justin's (*HE* 4.18.1–6; cf. 4.16.1), counts among them two apologies, one addressed to Antoninus Pius, his sons, and the Roman Senate, and another, to his successor Antoninus Verus (i.e., Marcus Aurelius). If this report is correct, then we do not possess the text of the second; for the text which the manuscripts place first (allegedly addressed to the Roman Senate) is clearly the conclusion of, or more likely an appendix or supplement to, the one they place second. (It is nevertheless customary to cite the *Apologia* proper as the 'First Apology' and the supplemental piece as the 'Second Apology'.)

Justin, who in a somewhat stylized manner recounts, in another work, his philosophical education and his conversion to Christianity (*Dial.* 2.1–8.2), does not call his writing an *apologia* but, as noted above, an 'address and petition'. By comparison with the *Apology* of Aristides, it is quite long. It appeals to the emperors as 'pious and philosophers and guardians of justice and lovers of culture [παιδεία]' (*Dial.* 2.2). It seems to be a piece of what the ancients called deliberative rhetoric,[2] i.e., its purpose was to present arguments to commend and justify a course of action. Justin's narrow aim appears to have been a simple one: to induce the authorities to restore in Asia the policy of Hadrian, who had discouraged mob action against Christians, required their accusers to be present in court and liable for false accusation, and made the ground of accusation 'the Name' (i.e., of Christian). Justin clearly disapproves of this last principle, but what he immediately seeks is not to see it voided, but something a bit more likely of accomplishment: action to assure that if Christians are brought to court on the basis of other charges (e.g., 'atheism' or infanticide), they be examined and tried on those charges and not be put to death for the Name, as though being a Christian were *ipso facto* an admission of the truth of such accusations. He is confident that investigation would show these other charges to be false (cf. *II Apol.* 14.2).

Behind this narrow and immediate purpose, there lies of course a larger interest. Justin wants not only to assert the innocence of Christians in the face of certain false accusations; he also wants on the one hand to indicate how and why he can believe and assert that Christianity is intrinsically superior to other cults, and on the other to understand and explain why, if this be so, Christians are nevertheless persecuted. In both connections Justin's arguments assume that he and the imperial philosophers and rulers whom he addresses share a common culture. His claim is that the highest elements in that culture, which he tends to identify with the philosophical tradition that stems from Plato, are akin to Christian belief because the 'reason' (λόγος) it appeals to is a participation in that divine Wisdom and 'Word' (Λόγος) which became incarnate in or as Jesus. Thus in Justin's mind Jesus' teachings represent both the original and the culmination of philosophical wisdom, and Justin's rhetoric effects, or seeks to effect, a marriage between two divergent religious and cultural traditions. An essential element in this argument is, of course, his contention that the Hebrew prophets, under the guidance of God and the Word, anticipated the Christian dispensation. As to the question why Christians are persecuted if all this be true – and if the real, ingenerate and unnameable God is indeed the sponsor of Christianity – Justin's response is not to blame the emperors whom he makes bold to address as fellow philosophers. Rather, he blames the demons who, even as they have enslaved the human race to themselves by deceit, now dress Christian teachings up in a costume (περίβλημα) deliberately calculated to repel people (*II Apol.* 13.1; cf. 5.4f.).

It is in his *Dialogue with Trypho the Jew* that Justin develops his Christian understanding of the Law and the Prophets. This work, which assumes a literary form that goes back to Plato and Xenophon, is of no inconsiderable length. In it Justin depicts a conversation between himself, a Christian, and a Hellenistic Jew (probably fictional), and he prefaces it with an account of his conversion at the hands of a Jewish Christian. In the broadest sense of the term, the *Dialogue* is no doubt a piece of apologetic: its business is to render credible not merely the content of Christian exegesis of the Jewish Scriptures (for the most part as translated in the Septuagint), but also, no doubt, to turn the tables on Marcion by providing a vivid justification of Christian use of them, while at the same time showing (in the wake of the Bar Kochba rebellion) that Christians were not – or were no longer – to be confused with Jews and so tarred with the brush of disloyalty to the Roman order. The *Dialogue* supplies, then, evidence of Justin's views on a variety of subjects of theological or ecclesial interest; but above all it provides more than just a taste of the sort of exegesis of Law and Prophets that was predominant in second-century Christianity but was, even as Justin wrote, being questioned not only in Marcionite circles but also by Christian gnostics. Justin reads the books of Moses and the Prophets wholly in the light of his understanding and experience of the New Covenant in Christ: i.e., he sees them as foreshadowing or as explicitly predicting the universal redemptive work of Christ.

If Justin's *Apology* fell in the reign of Antoninus Pius, his death by martyrdom (*c.* 167) fell in that of Marcus Aurelius (161–80). Marcus had a distaste for Christians, whom he tended to regard as stubbornly seditious. His reign, moreover, had more than its share of problems and disorders, which created insecurities in some sections of the Empire and encouraged popular hostility to Christians: e.g., the revolt of L. Avidius Cassius (175), who controlled Egypt, Syria and Asia for six months; unremitting wars along the northern Danube frontier to stem waves of invasion occasioned by migrations in central Europe; and the spread of a new bout of plague. Growing distrust of Christians in intellectual and imperial circles was perhaps reflected in an uncompromising attack on Christianity, *The True Word*, penned by one Celsus; and it may have been fanned in sections of the East by the spread after 171 in Asia of the Montanist movement, named after the Phrygian prophet Montanus who led it. This movement revived the spirit of apocalyptic and fomented a lust for martyrdom as well as contempt for the established order of things – all of which constituted bad publicity for churches whose leaders were attempting to give the appearance of been staid, normal and loyal.

Not surprisingly, then, the reign of Marcus Aurelius witnessed the composition of a number of pleas for and defences of Christianity. Thus Eusebius mentions an anti-Montanist writer named Miltiades who wrote an apology addressed to the 'worldly rulers' (κοσμικοὺς ἄρχοντας) in addition to treatises 'against the Gentiles and against the Jews' (*HE* 5.17.1, 5); but none of his writings has been preserved. Eusebius further tells of one Apollinaris, the bishop of Hierapolis, who in addition to writing against Montanism and composing the statutory treatises against Greeks on the one hand and Jews on the other, directed an 'apologetic discourse' to Marcus Aurelius (*HE* 4.26.1, 4.27) in 176. In the course of this he attributed the rain- and thunder-storm which saved a Roman army on the Danube frontier to the prayers of the Christian soldiers of the Twelfth Legion (*HE* 5.5.4). The bishop had his facts quite wrong, to be sure; but his claim illustrates the seriousness with which he and other apologists sought to reassure the authorities of the firm adhesion of Christians to the Roman order – which of course Celsus in his *True Word* had questioned,[3] and the Montanists, whom Apollinaris sought to refute, challenged.

More important than Apollinaris, however, are four contemporaries of his, of whom the first was his fellow Asian Melito of Sardis, who may have been bishop of the Christian community there. On the account of Eusebius, Melito – described a decade or two later as 'the eunuch whose whole career was in the Holy Spirit' (*HE* 5.24.5) – was an extensive writer (*HE* 4.26.2), among whose many compositions was a 'book [addressed] to the Emperor' (βασιλεῖ). Eusebius preserves three interesting extracts from this work (*HE* 4.26.5–11). Melito notes that Christians ('the race of the godly') are persecuted because of 'new decrees' that obtain throughout the proconsular province of Asia and render them potential victims of informers and blackmailers; and like his predecessors he asks, in properly flattering tones, that the emperor ascertain for himself whether the accusations are just. He also suggests that the waxing of Roman power and prosperity under Augustus and his successors is linked to the birth and spread of Christianity, and argues that it is only two wicked emperors, Nero and Domitian, who were inept enough to persecute Christians, but that their folly was corrected by Hadrian and Antoninus Pius. The implication of this historical argument was clear enough.

Eusebius also preserved a fragment of one of Melito's letters, addressed to one Onesimus, which not only contains the first use of the expression 'Old Covenant (*or* Testament)' to denote a set of books, but also the earliest Christian list of the contents of that set (*HE* 4.26.13f.). Like Justin and Irenaeus, Melito was one of those who used 'the ancient books' as the explicit sources of his proclamation and teaching, but tended to refer to the Christian Gospels and other authoritative writings more allusively, even though it was they that determined for him the sense of the Law and Prophets. This is apparent from the text of Melito's homily *On Pascha*, which between 1932 and 1960 was discovered and identified in a series of manuscript sources. This remarkable document – written in Greek in the elaborate, rhythmical 'Asiatic' style of the Second Sophistic – attests the writer's studied ingenuity as a rhetor. It is a sermon, preached after a reading of Exodus 12, on 'the mystery of the Pascha' (i.e., Passover). For Christians, this meant the death and resurrection of Christ, for which the Exodus was taken to be as it were the Artist's preliminary model. The sermon thus provides insight into the themes associated with celebration of the Christian Passover, though it does not indicate whether or not Melito and his fellow Christians at Sardis were Quartodecimans, observing the Christian celebration on the same day as the Jewish. What is clear, however, is that the homily belongs not only to the Greek culture that produced Melito's Asiatic style, but also to the Jewish culture that produced the Passover *haggadah*, with the traditions of which Melito is clearly acquainted. For all this, his sermon is an excellent example of Christian anti-Jewish polemic, which in his case is more than merely ritual or traditional. Sardis was a significant centre of diaspora Judaism, and Melito's stance towards Judaism – that of one who was at once an ungrateful tributary and an indebted foe – illustrates the general position of Christianity in relation to Judaism in his time, a position that people like Marcion and the Christian gnostics would have rendered somewhat more rational and self-consistent.

Roughly the same ambiguity characterized the stance of Christians towards the Hellenistic culture that was native to them as (for the most part) Gentiles. One of Melito's contemporaries was a Christian writer named Athenagoras, of whom almost nothing is known save what can be gathered from the text of his *Embassy* [or *Plea*: πρεσβεία] *on Behalf of the Christians*. This work, unknown to Eusebius but rescued from obscurity in the tenth century, is addressed to Marcus Aurelius and his son and co-emperor Commodus and dates from the period 176–80. Athenagoras – who is described as an Athenian, a philosopher and a Christian in the title of his work – penned an address in the accepted manner of forensic oratory. He is obviously learned and capable of apt quotation of classical poetry and philosophy, and his materials are selected, organized and handled skilfully. The defence of Christians and Christianity he offers does not appear to have any particular occasions or events in mind. Rather is it a thoughtful and careful reiteration of the normal themes of Christian 'defences'. Like Melito, Athenagoras is flattering to the emperors in the manner dictated by rhetorical practice, protesting Christian loyalty to the throne; and like Justin, he defends Christians against the charge of atheism by arguing that their monotheism is sounder than popular polytheism and more in accord with the philosophical tradition, though of course this could not explain in any adequate way the refusal of Christians to participate in normal civic rites: i.e., the 'anti-social' disposition associated with the exclusivity of their monotheism. Athenagoras' appeal to the philosophical tradition – like Justin's – fails not because it is insincere or even wrong-headed, but because there was more to the political and religious culture of the Mediterranean world than it could embrace; and this becomes obvious enough when he turns to the requisite criticism and refutation of prevailing religious practice, which, again like Justin, he associates with the deceptions of evil demons. Athenagoras is, then, a tributary, but in the end a disloyal one, of the high culture which his Atticizing *Plea on Behalf of the Christians* illustrates.

Such ambiguity appears in an alternative form in the so-called *Address Against the Greeks* (*Πρὸς Ἕλληνας*) of Tatian, a disciple of Justin Martyr at Rome who was born in 'Assyria' (the region across the Euphrates) and eventually, at some point after Justin's martyrdom, returned there to teach. The most plausible date for this work is slightly after the popular rising against Christians at Lyon and Vienne in Gaul (*c.* 177),[4] in the course of which Marcus Aurelius approved the execution of Christians who were Roman citizens. Not long after this time, Tatian had acquired the reputation (which has stayed with him) of being not merely a leader of the 'Encratites', who disapproved of marriage and practised vegetarianism, but a gnostic of sorts. His most influential work, however, the *Diatessaron*, which wove the narratives of the four Gospels into one, was the foundation of the Syrian churches' New Testament until the fifth century; and his *Address Against the Greeks* too was read and valued in orthodox circles. It is the work of one who has enjoyed and takes pride in a Greek-style education in rhetoric and philosophy, but who nevertheless repudiates and ridicules this cultural, intellectual and religious heritage and announces that he has found 'barbarian writings' (i.e., the Old Testament) to be 'older . . . and more divine'. Tatian's work is not really an 'apology' at all, but a broadside aimed at Greek culture; yet it is written in a consciously mannered style that reflects the rhetorical taste of his era and the sorts of learning it valued. His repudiation of Greek culture is at the same time a product of that culture.

The *Epistle to Diognetus*, traditionally reckoned among the Apostolic Fathers, is actually the product of a later period, and very likely belongs to the same general era as the writings of Melito, Athenagoras and Tatian. The identities of its author and of its addressee have long been subjects of learned speculation; but no hypothesis has been or, given the state of the evidence, can be, established. The work is in the style of an address, not a letter, and as we have it is incomplete: there is a gap after chapter 10, and 11–12 most likely come from a sermon extolling knowledge of the divine *Logos*. The first ten chapters appeal to 'Diognetus' to put aside prejudice and acknowledge the superiority of Christians' understanding and service of God to that of Greeks and Jews. The author goes on to dwell on the love of God evinced in God's self-revelation in the *Logos*-Son, and on the possibility of human imitation of and likeness to God.

The final author traditionally mentioned among the Apologists of the second century is Theophilus, bishop of Antioch, whose work *To Autolycus* (in three books) appears to span the borderline between the reigns of Marcus Aurelius and his son Commodus. The three books seem to have been written separately, and each can certainly be read independently. The first book is intended to persuade Autolycus, who is neither an emperor nor a provincial governor, to 'obey' God 'by believing him' (*Autol.* 1.14), to which end Theophilus provides the normal critiques of Gentile and of Jewish religion but concentrates on the Christian understanding of God and the resurrection. Book 2 he calls a 'treatise' (σύγγραμμα) which he hopes will demonstrate 'the vain labour and the empty religious observance in which you are confined' (2.1); and over against the confusions of poets and philosophers alike he sets the wisdom of the prophets, primarily as represented by the opening chapters of Genesis, of which Theophilus gives a lengthy exegesis. Book 3 is a collection of materials whose tendency is to show 'the antiquity of our writings', and to this end Theophilus, who by now can be recognized as a man of not inconsiderable learning, enters into complicated questions of historical chronology. Taken together, the three books *To Autolycus* do not constitute an apology in the ordinary sense but are more a work of controversy combined with elementary instruction.

Notes

1 See W. Schneemelcher, ed., *New Testament Apocrypha*, II, 99–102 for the fragments.
2 See P. Keresztes, 'The Literary Genre of Justin's First Apology', *VigChr* 19 (1965), 99–110.
3 Origen, *Cels.* 8.67–8.
4 See the arguments of R. M. Grant, *Greek Apologists of the Second Century*, 113f.

6
Irenaeus of Lyon

RICHARD A. NORRIS, JR.

Irenaeus, head of the Christian community at Lyon (Lugdunum) in Gaul after *c.* 177, was a central figure in the second-century debate stimulated in the Christian churches by gnosticism and by the teachings of Marcion. His principal writing on these subjects – the treatise now known as *Against Heresies* – was significant not only for its criticisms and denunciations of his opponents, but also for its contribution to (a) the churches' development of authoritative norms of teaching and (b) their 'theology', i.e., their interpretation of these norms for catechetical purposes.

Irenaeus was not a native of Gaul or a citizen of Lugdunum (a Roman colony founded in 43 BC, shortly after Caesar's victories in Gaul). Like most Christians there, he was an immigrant. He himself tells us (*AH* 3.3.4; cf. Eusebius, *HE* 5.20.5ff.) that in his 'youth' he saw Polycarp, the bishop of Smyrna who was martyred *c.* 156. The likelihood is, therefore, that Irenaeus was born in Smyrna during the thirties or perhaps the forties of the second century. As to when and how he came to Lyon – which was the principal centre for trade, transport and government in central and northern Gaul – it is impossible to say with any certainty, though it seems probable that he sojourned for a time in Rome on his way. Somewhere, and almost certainly in Smyrna, he acquired a basic rhetorical education which in the end he put to good use. If the doxographic information he deploys in *Against Heresies* 2.14 is a proper clue to the extent of his acquaintance with the philosophical tradition, he did not graduate to any serious study of that subject; but he seems to have been a systematic reader of earlier Christian writers (not excluding some of his opponents), and through them he seems to have absorbed and mastered concepts that were current in his day in cultured discussions of God, the human constitution, and the like.

It was around 177, in the summer, that the populace of Lyon turned on the Christians there and by their onslaught instigated the sequence of events that led to the violent deaths of a number of martyrs. Irenaeus – or so Eusebius relates (*HE* 5.4.1) – was a presbyter at the time, and was dispatched to Rome with a message for Bishop Eleutheros. It was on his return that he was chosen to succeed the martyred Pothinus as bishop.

One may assume that Irenaeus' hostility to Christian gnosticism as well as to the teachings of Marcion was brought with him from Asia, and that his stays at Rome not only confirmed his views but perhaps clarified them. It may have been at Rome that he came upon the gnostic writings, and held the conversations, that he alludes to in *Against Heresies* 1.*pr*.2 and, by implication, in 4.*pr*.2. But there were, as he tells us, followers of Marcus the Magician living and teaching in the Rhone valley (*AH* 1.13.7), and clearly the gnostic movement in the shape of certain disciples of Ptolemy was infecting the congregation at Lyon. Irenaeus' attack on gnostic teachings, therefore, was not undertaken out of general interest in the issues they raised, but because of a real threat to his own church, whose members were no doubt rendered the more susceptible to gnostic suasions by the doubts about divine providence that would have been stimulated by the persecution they had endured.

In any case, little is known about the career of Irenaeus after he became bishop in Lyon. The last action reported of him is that he wrote a letter to Victor, bishop of Rome, asking Victor to be tolerant of Quartodeciman practice in Asia (*HE* 5.24.11ff.). This would have occurred around AD 190, and most authorities reckon that Irenaeus would have died at some point in the course of the next decade. Essentially, then, nothing is known of Irenaeus' later life save that he was, or continued to be, active as a writer, though Gregory of Tours (d. 594) knew a tradition that held Irenaeus to have been a martyr.

In his *Ecclesiastical History*, Eusebius of Caesarea mentions a number of writings of Irenaeus. First he speaks of a work titled *Exposure and Refutation of the Pseudo-Knowledge*[1] (*HE* 5.7.1), to which he elsewhere assigns the title *Against Heresies* (*HE* 3.18.2), no doubt because it was simpler. This, he tells us, was written in five books. In yet another place, he explains that Irenaeus was the author of various letters, presumably of the sort that amounted to brief treatises or essays:

> . . . one addressed *To Blastus* on the subject of schism; another *To Florinus* on the subject of the sole rule [of God], to the effect that God is not the author of evil, for Florinus seemed to be defending this opinion. For his sake too, when he was attracted by the Valentinian error, a work was composed by Irenaeus *On the Ogdoad* . . . (*HE* 5.20.1)

Finally Eusebius notes that in addition to his 'treatises' (συγγράμμασιν: i.e., the five books *Against Heresies*) and letters, Irenaeus also wrote a 'brisk and extremely cogent' discourse *On Scientific Knowledge* against the Greeks, and another discourse 'for the proof of the apostolic preaching'.

All save two of the works in this list have, as far as anyone now knows, perished. Of the two survivors, the later to be written was the so-called *Proof of the Apostolic Preaching*, which indeed at one point refers to *Against Heresies* by title (*Dem.* 99). It became available only in the last century, when the text of an Armenian version of it was published by its discoverer, Dr Karapet Ter-Mekerttschian, in 1907, together with a German translation by Adolf von Harnack, who is responsible for the division of the text into one hundred numbered sections (*Texte und Untersuchungen* 31.1). The second is of course the lengthy work *Against Heresies*. This latter at any rate was widely read in the early centuries of the Christian movement, for even though we lack the complete text in its original Greek, we possess the full ancient Latin version, probably of the third century, as well as thirty-three fragments of a Syriac version and a complete Armenian version of books 4 and 5. The severely literal Latin translation has been preserved in four principal manuscripts, ranging in date from the ninth to the fifteenth century. It was first printed in the 1526 edition of Desiderius Erasmus; but the standard edition until recently has been that of R. Massuet (1712), who introduced the current chapter- and paragraph-divisions into books 1–4 (those in book 5 had been provided by François Feu-Ardent in his edition of 1575). It is Massuet's edition that is reprinted in volume 7 of J.-P. Migne's *Patrologia Graeca*.

The question of the structure of the five books *Against Heresies* has occasioned much exercise of scholarly imagination, perhaps because Irenaeus did not plan or execute the work with exacting care. The whole of it is, of course, an attack on Christian gnostic teaching and practice: a series of λόγοι which, as the original title suggests, embody not so much a defence as an enacted prosecution. The elements that make up this indictment and refutation, however, are of different sorts and have different aims; and more than that, Irenaeus often pursues aims of different orders simultaneously.

This circumstance can be illustrated by the argument(s) of book 1. Scholars are agreed that this book contains what Irenaeus refers to in his own title for the work as the ἔλεγχος or 'scrutiny' of the γνῶσις his adversaries claim to possess. For him, this is a focal element in his whole argument: first, because he believes that he has, as his predecessors had not, discovered the essential content of that γνῶσις; and secondly, because he thinks that by reason of this discovery he can identify the fundamental themes that characterize *all* heretical teaching. In addition to all this, however, Irenaeus also believes that he can provide a genealogy of heresy.

His scrutiny begins, therefore, with the presentation of a grand myth of world-generation and world-reintegration that he attributes to the Ptolemaean teachers he knew at Lyon or Rome; and into this account he inserts reports of the scriptural exegeses by which his adversaries defend their story (*AH* 1.1–8). This takes up almost a quarter of the first book: and understandably, for it represents the keystone of his argument. Having set this myth out and indicated why he takes exception to it (*AH* 1.9–10), he then traces its connections: to the doctrine of Valentinus, whom he takes to be its immediate parent, and to its siblings, more particularly the teaching of Marcus the Magician. He has already indicated (*AH* 1.11.1) that he thinks Valentinus, in his turn, derived much of his inspiration from a 'sect called "gnostic"'; but for the moment he does not develop this intimation. Instead he offers an indication of the teachings that he thinks all heretical sects share in spite of their variety (*AH* 1.22.1); and then, adapting materials he has taken over from Justin Martyr, he traces a 'succession' of heretical 'schools' back to their origin in Simon Magus (cf. Acts 8:9–13), whom he, following Justin, takes to be the single historical root of all heresy (*AH* 1.23–8). Only after this does he return to his 'gnostics', the predecessors of Valentinus; for since (as it happens) their writings are anonymous, he cannot fit them into Justin's succession of heretical 'schools of thought' with nameable founders or leaders. There is, then, a unity about book 1; for it aims to present a picture of the people Irenaeus is accusing. As it turns out, however, these 'people' are not simply contemporaries of Irenaeus who espouse a particular type of false or dangerous teaching: they are 'all the heretics', which means at once (a) the heirs of Simon Magus, and (b) any who denigrate the Creator God and deny the salvation of the flesh. It does not occur to Irenaeus that these two categories may not coincide, or that there may be heretics who fit neither of them, or that Justin's obsession with Simon Magus may have been misplaced.

Book 1 is the ἔλεγχος, the scrutiny and exposure of the sort of teaching Irenaeus proposes to refute. Obviously, then, book 2 begins the ἀνατροπή, the 'overthrow' or refutation that is the second element promised by the original title of *Against Heresies*. Book 2, however, is odd in that it seems intended not as a first step, but as a complete refutation in its own right. It deconstructs, in the manner prescribed by the then-current canons of literary and philosophical criticism, the whole of the grand myth set out in *Against Heresies* 1.1–8 (and also addresses certain heretical teachings from other sources) in order to show the absurdity of the whole affair. The question has been raised, therefore, whether Irenaeus did not originally intend this critique to bring his work to an end, so that books 3–5 would represent an afterthought. This question, however, fails to understand Irenaeus' assessment of his opponents' 'hypothesis'. He believes that almost everything said in the grand Ptolemaean myth *falls outside the scope of the Scriptures*. One cannot therefore, in his view, refute this 'fiction' from the Scriptures; one can only point to difficulties, improbabilities, or inconsistencies in it. When, in the later books, he takes up the particular challenges of Valentinian or Marcionite exegesis, it is not so much to deconstruct the Valentinian myth as it is to show, and insist, that the 'plot' or story the Scriptures tell is a different one. That story, he thinks, revolves around the one and only God, the one who creates and redeems the world and humanity; around the incarnation of God's Word and the outpouring of the Spirit; and around the salvation of the very 'earthy' humanity spoken of in Genesis 2:7.

It is with these matters, then, that books 3–5 of *Against Heresies* are concerned. The Valentinian myth is always in the immediate background, to be sure; but the foreground is occupied with 'proofs drawn from the Scriptures' (*AH* 3.*pr*.). What is to be established by such proofs is 'the sole true and life-giving belief', which, Irenaeus insists, is identical at once with 'the teaching of the Son of God' and with the teaching of the apostles transmitted to the churches (ibid.). Irenaeus' opponents allege, to be sure, that the apostles 'preached before they had perfect knowledge' (*AH* 3.1.1) and that the Scriptures, including the apostolic writings, are ambiguous until they are understood in the light of the gnostics' secret tradition. But Irenaeus denies the first proposition, and counters the second with the assertion that the public teaching tradition of the Church (the 'kerygma of the truth': *AH* 3.3.3) is guaranteed as apostolic by the fact that it has been handed down from the apostles through a clear succession of teachers, the churches' bishops. This tradition, moreover, is not secret but is conveyed in the Church's ordinary catechesis, the content of which Irenaeus calls 'the Rule of Truth' or 'the hypothesis of the Truth', i.e., the 'plot' which actually informs the Scriptures. The catechetical tradition, then, and the Scriptures (the writings of the prophets and apostles) announce the same divine scheme. Hence Irenaeus' definition of his task in book 3: to show, by reference to their writings and to the authoritative reports of their message, that all the apostles 'have handed down to us one God, announced in the Law and the Prophets to be the Maker of heaven and earth, and one Christ who is the Son of God' (*AH* 3.1.2).

To this task he proceeds, first addressing the question of the identity of the ultimate God with the cosmic Creator. He makes allusion to the prophets and St Paul, replying to two Valentinian objections (*AH* 3.5–8). He then turns to the testimony of the authors of the Gospels and defends the fourfold Gospel canon he uses (*AH* 3.9.1–3.11.7). Finally he adduces the Book of Acts, from which he draws evidence to show what Peter, Philip and Stephen taught; and, still appealing to Acts, defends Paul against both Marcion's excessive adulation and the hostility of the 'Ebionites' (*AH* 3.12–15). In the last section of book 3, Irenaeus turns to his second agenda item, the unity of Christ. Here there is no discernible order in his citations of the Scriptures, though his argument is still based primarily on *apostolic* testimony, and in particular that of John and Paul.

From this account, one can see why Irenaeus' treatises may seem confused. He defines the content of book 3 in two ways: by reference to the *issues* (God and Christ) it will address, and by reference to the *materials* (apostolic writings) it will employ; and he organizes the book along both lines simultaneously. Furthermore, he turns aside at certain points to justify his use of the particular writings he employs or to deal with particular and prominent objections to his line of argument, and this creates lengthy parentheses in his exposition. Nevertheless, by the end of book 3, two things are clear. Irenaeus' 'New Testament' is basically a collection of works conceived to be written by, or to report the teaching of, *apostles*; and while he differs radically from Valentinians about how such books should be read, he does not, save in the case of the Acts, seem to differ with them about the books that constitute the core list. It is Marcion, not the gnostics, whom he openly accuses of truncating the list of essential Christian Scriptures.

The issue upon which Marcion and the Valentinians concur is their belief that the God who reveals himself in the Law and Prophets is not the supreme Father whom the Christ made known; and it is this issue – in effect another form or phrasing of the question whether the Creator God is the ultimate God – that Irenaeus takes up in *Against Heresies* 4. He takes it up, however, on the basis of *words of the Lord* (as reported in the Gospels), rather than on that of the teachings of the apostles. In a series of parallel arguments, he looks at sayings of Jesus to meet arguments of his opponents, insisting that the same God is God of both the Mosaic and the Christian covenants. This requires him not only to develop an account of God's history with the human race, but also to deal with the questions of how the Invisible and Incomprehensible can be thought of as having been 'seen' and 'known' in and through prophetic vision, action and utterance, and of how and why human freedom participates in the making of this history of salvation. Book 4, then, like book 3, operates at several levels simultaneously: it develops at once a discussion of hermeneutics, a vision of salvation history, and a many-sided reiteration of Irenaeus' thesis about the identity of the God whom Christ reveals.

The third item on Irenaeus' fundamental agenda, i.e., the issue of the redemption of 'flesh', is the centrepiece of *Against Heresies* 5, which after an introductory section turns first to the exegesis of crucial Pauline texts, obviously because it was Paul to whom the Valentinians appealed for their denial that the material body is a proper subject of redemption. Central to this argument is the question of Pauline – and, in general, Christian – anthropology, but also that of eschatology, especially as Paul treats of it in 1 Corinthians 15. Accordingly, book 5 concludes with a lengthy consideration of human destiny, in the course of which Irenaeus' millenarianism emerges, as does also his affection for the Revelation to John.

The second of Irenaeus' extant works, the *Proof*[2] *of the Apostolic Preaching*, professes to be a letter of sorts but is not, and looks to the casual reader like a piece of catechesis. Certainly it is clear, from the opening sections of the work, that its aim is to deal with the basic content of catechesis ('to set forth in brief the preaching of the truth . . . in the form of notes on the main points': *Dem.* 1), i.e., with what Irenaeus also calls 'the body of the truth' (ibid.) and 'the rule of faith' (*Dem.* 3). This is summarized under the three heads of the baptismal confession ('God the Father . . . , Jesus Christ the Son of God, who became incarnate and died and was raised, and . . . the Holy Spirit of God', *Dem.* 3), which Irenaeus then, in the remainder of his introductory section, expands and comments on. He then proceeds (8–42*a*) to the same point whence he had set out (i.e., the baptismal faith) by way of a summary of the history of salvation, which he obviously takes to be another way of expounding the rule of faith. At *Dem.* 42*b*, however, Irenaeus brings exposition to an end and passes on to what he, like Justin Martyr, regards as the real proof of the content of the apostolic preaching, namely, the fact that the whole οἰκονομία of salvation 'was foretold by the Spirit of God through the prophets'. Here plainly he, like Justin in the *Dialogue*, employs a collection of *testimonia* (passages from the Law, the Prophets, and the Psalms arranged under headings that indicated their relevance to elements of the Christian dispensation), from which he makes selections. In the course of this, he stresses not only the events of the story of Christ, but also the supersession of the Law and the superiority of Christianity to Judaism. He concludes with a warning against heresy, which reminds the reader that this work is inspired by more than just catechetical motives: that for Irenaeus this 'preaching of the truth' is 'the manner of our salvation' and 'the way of life' (*Dem.* 98), from which it is dangerous to depart. The *Proof* too has a polemical sub-text and is reiterating the basic message of *Against Heresies*.

Notes

1 Ἔλεγχος καὶ ἀνατροπή τῆς ψευδωνύμου γνῶσεως: for the last phrase see 1 Tim. 6:20.

2 The Greek title had Ἐπίδειξις, which means 'showing' in both of its senses: i.e., demonstration and indication or exposition. The translation of the *Proof* quoted here is that of J. P. Smith in *St. Irenaeus: Proof of the Apostolic Preaching*.

B.

*

CONTEXT AND INTERPRETATION

7

Social and historical setting

JOHN BEHR

The first two centuries of the history of Christianity were crucial. It was a period of struggle for survival and the crucible in which the basic elements of Christian identity and church organization were forged. During this time, Christians had to find ways of explaining their relationship to the Jews and the broader pagan world, while suffering sporadic persecution from both, and also learn to resolve internal differences in matters of teaching, liturgy and calendar, and church organization and order. By the end of the second century, there were Christian communities scattered throughout the Empire, from Edessa in the East to Lyon in the West, displaying a remarkable diversity but also a concern to hold a common faith and pattern of life.

The early Church in Jerusalem must have initially appeared as yet another group within the remarkably variegated Judaism of the time. It was a given for Christians that what God had done in Christ must be continuous and consistent with the revelation of God in Scripture, yet it was no less clear that they were reading Scripture in a different manner. Thus while they continued to attend the Temple, the apostles also proclaimed their message from Solomon's Portico and met in their own homes to break bread (Acts 2–3). The apostles' preaching gathered adherents from most sections of Jewish society apart from the Sadducees. Of particular importance were the Hellenized Jews (cf. Acts 6), those Jews who preserved their religion but were otherwise culturally assimilated to their Gentile environment, and their counterparts, the God-fearers, those Gentiles attracted by the moral teaching and monotheism of the Jews but reluctant to embrace the Law fully (cf. Acts 10). It was through the Hellenistic synagogues of the Jewish diaspora, located in cities throughout the Empire, that Christianity would spread. It is probable that there were Christian Jews in the countryside surrounding Judaea and perhaps north into Galilee, but they soon disappeared from history. More important was the spread of Christianity further north into Damascus and Antioch, the capital of Syria and the third city of the Empire, the place where they were first called 'Christians'

(Acts 11:26). In Acts this spread of Christianity beyond Jerusalem is described as a result of a persecution of the Christians there, occasioned by Stephen's speech against the Temple and his subsequent stoning (Acts 6–8, 11:19). Saul, a Pharisee from Tarsus and a student of Rabbi Gamaliel at Jerusalem, was present at this stoning, and continued and intensified the persecution, until his encounter with the risen Christ on the road to Damascus persuaded him to use his zeal for proclaiming the gospel to the Gentiles. Whatever intentions there had been to spread Christianity to the Gentiles throughout the Empire, Saul became the dominant figure in this mission and, as Paul (Acts 13:9), was thereafter thought of as the apostle to the Gentiles. His letters to the newly founded communities are the oldest Christian writings we have, and appear to have been collected together early; already at the beginning of the second century, Ignatius refers to the 'letters' of Paul.[1] After his first missionary journey with Barnabas, around AD 46, from Antioch to Cyprus, Pamphylia, Pisidia and Galatia, the issue of the inclusion of the Gentiles, and the demands to be placed upon them, implicit already in the account of the Hellenists and Stephen, became critical. There are two differing accounts of the resulting 'Council of Jerusalem' (*c.* AD 48/9; Acts 15:1–29 and Gal. 2:1–10). Though both agree that circumcision should not be expected of Gentile converts, Acts further adds that such converts should abstain from food with idolatrous associations and unchastity, while the only further stipulation Paul mentions is to 'remember the poor'. After breaking with Barnabas and Peter, who had refrained from eating with Gentile Christians at Antioch when men from James of Jerusalem arrived representing the 'circumcision party' (cf. Acts 15:36–40; Gal. 2:11–14), Paul set out with Silas on further missionary journeys, visiting the communities he had previously established and moving out further into Asia, Macedonia and Achaia. It is probably from Corinth, in the late 50s, that Paul wrote his letter to the Romans, preparing the way for his coming visit to Jerusalem so that the community there would accept the collections he had gathered on their behalf (Rom. 15:30–2). When he arrived in Jerusalem, he was greeted with hostility and imprisoned by the Romans for his own safety. After further commotions and plots on his life, he was moved to Caesarea for a couple of years, and finally, as a Roman citizen, to Rome itself for trial in the early 60s. According to the writers of the second century, Paul, along with Peter, was martyred under Nero (cf. Eusebius, *HE* 2.25.5). By the second half of the second century, monuments had already been built for Peter on the Vatican hill, and for Paul on the road to Ostia (*HE* 2.25.7).

As most of the surviving literature is concerned with the development of the Gentile communities, we know relatively little about the Christian community in Jerusalem after the middle of the first century. James, 'the brother of the Lord', was the leader of the church in Jerusalem after Peter's departure (Acts 12) until his martyrdom in AD 62 (*HE* 2.23, citing the second-century church historian Hegesippus). It is possible that the Jewish War of AD 66–70 prompted Christians to leave the area for Asia. According to second-century writers, John, the son of Zebedee, resided in Ephesus, while Philip the apostle, together with his four prophetess daughters, lived in Hierapolis in Phrygia (Irenaeus, *AH* 3.3.4; *HE* 3.31.2–5). Also from Asia in the early second century, Papias recorded what he claimed were the oral reports of those who had known the apostles, describing the origin of the Gospels: Mark is said to have been the interpreter of Peter in Rome, setting down accurately, but not in order, everything he remembered concerning the words and actions of the Lord, while Matthew composed his oracles in Hebrew (*HE* 3.39.15–16). It is possible that Papias also knew the Gospels of Luke and John, and that what are later regarded as the four canonical Gospels were already beginning to circulate together in codex form in Asia at the turn of the second century.[2] It is only from the middle of the third century onwards that legends start appearing that identify other apostles as the founders of other Christian communities, such as Mark in connection with Alexandria.[3] According to Hegesippus, James, the 'brother of the Lord', was succeeded by Symeon, the 'cousin of the Saviour', as the head of the Jerusalem community (*HE* 3.11). This need for a familial relationship to the Lord as a qualification for leadership seems to have continued at Jerusalem (cf. *HE* 3.20.6), until, as a result of the Bar Kochba rebellion (AD 132–5), Hadrian forbade Jews from entering Jerusalem, which he renamed Aelia Capitolina, and so the succession of the 'bishops of the circumcision' ceased (*HE* 4.5.2–3). No substantial information survives concerning the existence of these Jewish Christians thereafter. They had been excluded from the synagogue and subjected to a curse from about AD 85, and were later required by Bar Cochba to recognize his messianic status and to deny Jesus under the pain of execution.[4] Accepted neither by their own kinsfolk nor by the increasing body of Gentile Christians, by the end of the second century they were known as a deviant Christian sect, the Ebionites, 'the poor ones'. However, it would be wrong to assume that contact between Jews and Christians ceased completely in the middle of the second century. Interaction between the two groups continued for several centuries, as John Chrysostom's polemic against those Christians infatuated with Judaism indicates.[5]

As Christianity spread beyond the bounds of Judaea, most often through towns and cities that already contained Hellenistic Jewish communities, it was unavoidable that Christians should come to the attention of the state. The

Roman Government was usually tolerant of foreign cults and religions, provided that they did not encourage sedition or weaken traditional values.[6] The various local deities of the provinces encompassed by the Roman Empire were easily absorbed into the pantheon and the diverse spectrum of religious life. The God of the Jews, however, demanded exclusive adherence, that sacrifices be performed only at Jerusalem, and prohibited all images. On account of the antiquity of their religion, and their loyalty to the ways of their ancestors, both highly valued by the Romans, the Jews were treated with toleration and were even granted privileges by Augustus and later by Claudius. Christians, however, despite their claims to the ancient Scriptures of the Jews, appeared as newcomers.[7] During the first and second centuries, Christians were not subject to any wholesale attempt at repression, but they were subjected to occasional persecution. When Nero was suspected of causing the fire which destroyed much of Rome in AD 64, he directed the blame upon the Christians. According to Tacitus, Nero executed an 'immense multitude' of Christians,[8] some in the Arena, some by crucifixion and others by fire, using the latter 'to illuminate the night when daylight had failed' (*Annals* 15.44). By the time that Tacitus recorded the event, some fifty years later, while he is non-committal about the allegation, he accepts that Christians deserved to be punished on account of their 'hatred of the human race'. Christians were thought of as 'a class of men given to a new and wicked superstition' (Suetonius, *Nero* 16.2), which, in the popular imagination, included nocturnal meetings at which cannibalism and incest were practised. Nero's actions, though not instigated for ideological reasons, nevertheless set a precedent for condemning Christians to death for no other reason than being Christian. It is probable that pressure on Christians in Rome continued during the following decades. The Letter to the Hebrews, written around this time and connected with Rome, urges Christians not to become disheartened, apostasize from faith in Christ and revert back to their former ways. The situation worsened when Domitian promoted veneration of himself as the divine Augustus and insisted on being addressed as 'lord and god'. After putting a number of senators to death on the suspicion of treason in AD 95, Domitian had the consul Flavius Clemens executed and his wife Domitilla, the granddaughter of Emperor Vespasian, banished. According to Dio Cassius the charge was 'atheism', the abandoning of the Roman gods and the adoption of Jewish practices (*Epitome* 67.14). However, as the Jewish religion was a recognized religion, it is possible that the charge of 'atheism' actually indicates adherence to the Christian faith. Eusebius, describing the events under Domitian, also refers to a Domitilla, this time the niece of Flavius Clemens, who was banished for being a Christian (*HE* 3.18.4). Even if Domitilla herself was not a Christian, it seems that she patronized the practice of Christianity in her household and that her estate was adopted as a Christian cemetery at the beginning of the third century.[9]

Early in the second century (*c.* AD 112), Pliny, the governor of Bithynia in Asia Minor, wrote to Trajan requesting guidance about the correct way to treat Christians (*Ep.* 10.96). According to his reports, Christianity had penetrated not only the cities but also the villages and the surrounding countryside. Pliny knew that there was a precedent for the execution of Christians, but was unsure about the exact nature of their crime, whether they should be punished for their profession of Christianity or for the secret crimes associated with the name. Either way, Pliny had no hesitation in executing those who kept to their profession, as their 'obstinacy and unbending perversity deserve to be punished': a worse crime than being Christian. This had only resulted, however, in an increased number of accusations. When Pliny examined some lapsed Christians, including two deaconesses, he found no evidence of crime: they described how they were accustomed to assemble before daylight on certain days, to sing hymns to Christ as a god, to take an oath that they would abstain from crime, and that they met again later to eat ordinary food (not murdered infants). They had, furthermore, even refrained from meeting in this way when the emperor had forbidden secret societies. In his reply, Trajan assured Pliny that he had acted properly, and that he should pay no heed to anonymous accusations nor initiate any inquisition. If a proper charge was brought against someone (so that the accuser could be accused of slander, and incur a similar penalty), and if the accused was convicted, he or she should be allowed to recant and be pardoned, but otherwise punished (Pliny, *Ep.* 10.97). The same position was taken by Hadrian, around AD 125, in a rescript sent to Caius Minucius Fundanus, the proconsul of Asia. During the second century a number of individuals suffered martyrdom, including Ignatius, bishop of Antioch, in Rome (under Trajan), Polycarp of Smyrna (*c.* AD 155), and Justin in Rome (*c.* AD 162–7). The letters of Ignatius exemplify a conviction which, while not necessarily seeking out martyrdom, welcomes it, fearing only that he might be persuaded to turn aside from his triumphal following in the passion of his God (*Rom.* 6). The martyrs became celebrated figures, not only after their death, as with Polycarp, whose bones were valued as 'more precious than precious stones and finer than gold' and around which the Christians gathered 'to celebrate the birthday of his martyrdom' (*MPol.* 18), but also before their death, as they awaited their final trial. For Ignatius, martyrdom was also a test for correctness of faith against those who claimed that Christ only 'appeared' to suffer, with the implication that His followers do not need to undergo such tribulations themselves (*Trall.* 9–11). Only under Marcus Aurelius, in AD 177, did a large, violent persecution break out, stirred by popular suspicion and hatred, against the Christians of Lyon and Vienne in Gaul. It is possible that stronger measures began to be adopted because of an increase in voluntary martyrdom, which Marcus Aurelius found distasteful (*Med.* 11.3), combined perhaps with the provocative behaviour associated with the Montanists.[10] However, there is no suggestion of any misplaced enthusiastic zeal in the *Acts of the Scillitan Martyrs*, seven men and five women executed three years later in North Africa; rather, the martyrs request a calm hearing as they make their serious confession. Popular sentiment had not been contained by the rulings of Trajan and Hadrian, and the suspicions about the obscenities practised by Christians lingered, as did the conviction that the Christians' refusal to worship any god but their own alienated the goodwill of the gods and precipitated various disasters. Their devotion to their God, neither ancient nor ancestral, but recently condemned as a common criminal, made ready scapegoats of Christians. As Tertullian later commented wryly, 'If there is an earthquake, a famine or pestilence, the cry is raised "the Christians to the lions"' (*Apol.* 40).

However, it must be remembered that during the second century these persecutions were only sporadic, isolated and local events; they were not a deliberate attempt to eradicate Christianity. In this period, although Christians were formally in official disrepute and were socially stigmatized, informally they were usually left to do as they pleased, and were even able to protest against their treatment. For instance, Chadwick describes how, when a certain governor in Asia Minor began to persecute Christians, 'the entire Christian population of the region paraded before his house as a manifesto of their faith and as a protest against the injustice'.[11] By most accounts, the second century was a remarkable period of peace, stability and well-being in the history of the Roman Empire, enabling freedom of travel around an extended realm in a quite unprecedented fashion. Trajan's comment to Pliny that anonymous accusations are 'not in keeping with the spirit of the age' is typical of the self-confidence that could extend generous tolerance to others (Pliny, *Ep.* 10.97). Nor did this escape the Christians. Justin, in his *First Apology*, addressed to Antoninus Pius and his sons, was at pains to point out that Christians, far from being subversive adherents of an illegal sect, were in fact exemplary citizens and that, although they prayed to God alone, they prayed for the emperor (*I Apol.* 17). Justin was even prepared to see the sign of the cross in the legionary ensigns and trophy poles used by the Roman Army (*I Apol.* 55). For Justin, it was not the state itself that was wrong, but rather its failure to recognize the truth of Christianity. A couple of decades later, Athenagoras, in an treatise addressed to

Marcus Aurelius and Commodus, noted the profound peace which the Empire enjoyed by virtue of their wise rule, though he regretted that the equality which all had before the law was not extended to the Christians (*Leg.* 1.2–3). At about the same time, Melito of Sardis pointed out the providential beginning of Christianity under the *Pax Romana* established by Augustus and the fact that it flourished together with the Empire (*HE* 4.26.7). The relative toleration of the second century provided a time during which Christian communities could consolidate and address internal problems of community, identity and organization.

If the persecutions themselves were neither sustained nor widespread, the effects of the martyrdoms on the developing churches were profound and universal. By the 60s, a whole generation of Christians had passed away without seeing the expected return of Jesus. The readiness of James, Paul and Peter to die for their faith, undaunted by the delay of the Second Coming or the small number of their followers, was an effective testimony against any crisis of confidence. The faith demanded total commitment, and this dedication, which Pliny perceived as 'obstinacy', served to strengthen the community immeasurably.[12] The pagan philosopher Celsus, around AD 180, commented that 'the love which Christians have for one another exists because of the common danger and is more powerful than any oath' (Origen, *Cels.* 1.1). It was not, however, as Celsus assumed, simply as a result of social stigmatism that Christians had a common bond. The injunction to love one another, as a way of loving God and as a reflection of His love for the human race, was a novelty in the pagan world where, as gods were held to be incapable of feeling love in response to that offered, religion tended to be approached in a self-interested, contractual spirit.[13] That this love should be manifest in care for strangers was even more striking. For Ignatius, martyrdom was not the only test of faith, just as important was active love: he claimed that those who hold incorrect beliefs about Christ 'have no care for love, none for the widow, none for the orphan, none for the distressed, none for the afflicted, none for the prisoner, or for him released from prison, none for the hungry or thirsty' (*Smyrn.* 6). Demanding a great deal from the Christians, both in terms of commitment and charity, the churches were also able to offer much to both the spirit and the flesh. That in later centuries the various churches cared for numerous widows, virgins and orphans, and looked after strangers and the destitute, is well known. Julian the Apostate complained that 'the impious Galileans support not only their poor, but ours as well; everyone can see that our people lack aid from us' (*Ep.* 22), and tried to initiate comparable charities, but failed, lacking any religious basis for such activity. Such activity took on an even more heroic quality when disasters struck. In the early centuries, the Christian communities were located primarily in the urban centres of the Empire. But far from being the ordered, civilized places that their ruins suggest, the Greco-Roman cities were overcrowded nightmares.[14] As Stark describes it, people would have 'lived in filth beyond our imagining . . . The smell of sweat, urine, faeces and decay permeated everything.'[15] They were rife with infectious diseases, such that most people would have suffered from chronic health conditions, and those who survived had a life expectancy of less than thirty years. Cities were subject to frequent fires, collapsing buildings and other disasters. To maintain their populations, the cities needed to be repopulated by newcomers more or less continually, leading to high rates of crime and frequent riots. In such conditions, the Christian church could provide a new basis for attachments and an extended sense of family. When an epidemic struck, such as the first appearance of smallpox from AD 165–80, the fatalities were enormous, probably about a quarter to a third of the total population.[16] The typical response of the pagans, even doctors like Galen, was to leave the cities for the countryside until the danger passed. When another epidemic struck in AD 251, Cyprian of Carthage and Dionysius of Alexandria reported how the Christians, having learnt how not to fear death, remained in the cities nursing the sick, and thereby gaining an immunity so that they could pass among the afflicted, apparently invulnerable. Galen also noted that the Christians' 'contempt of death and of its sequel is patent to us every day'.[17] The newly forming Christian communities offered, in Stark's words, 'a *new culture* capable of making life in Greco-Roman cities more tolerable'.[18]

This new culture had a particularly dramatic effect for women in the Christian communities. In a culture where female infanticide was normal, where girls were often married at the age of twelve, and if they did not die as a result of childbirth or abortions, were often widowed at a young age and encouraged to remarry, sometimes under the pressure of penalty, so that they could again be productive members of society, while their inheritance would pass to the new husband, Christianity offered a radically different alternative. The respect in which virgins and widows were held, and the willingness of the churches to support those virgins and widows who were less fortunate, gave women a real choice to remain single, and if they inherited an estate, to keep it and dispose of it as they chose. If they decided to (re-)marry, the prohibition on abortion and infanticide (cf. *Did.* 2.2) prolonged their life-expectancy and also increased their fertility rates, while the rejection of male double-standards concerning fidelity opened up further dimensions in the marital relationship. During the first and second century, the population of the Empire was in decline. Augustus had promoted legislation encouraging people to have more children, but to little effect.[19] Dio Cassius attributed this barrenness, especially among the upper classes, to a shortage of females (*Roman History* 54.16). In the new culture of Christianity, however, the ratios were reversed. That the predominant number of Christians were female was a fact recognized by Christians and pagans alike. It brought mockery from pagans such as Celsus (cf. Origen, *Cels.* 3.55), and necessitated practical considerations, such as Callistus' decision, at the beginning of the third century, to tolerate 'just concubinage', so that Christian women need not lose their status and legal privileges by having to marry beneath their rank.

The preponderance of women, especially among the upper classes, had significant implications not only for their role with respect to family life, but also within the Christian communities, at least until the fourth and fifth centuries when, as Christianity became the dominant religion, the ratios levelled out. It has already been noted how Pliny examined two deaconesses. Half a century earlier, Paul's letters indicate that women were fulfilling significant roles in the churches. Though in 1 Corinthians 14:34–6 he enjoins the women to keep silent in the churches, learning from their husbands at home, he also makes it clear that they have his consent to pray and prophesy in public (cf. 11:5, with the head veiled). In the same letter Paul also mentions Aquila and Prisca and the church gathering in their house (1 Cor. 16:19); that Prisca is even named suggests that she was an important person. This is confirmed by Romans 16:3, where she appears first: 'Greet Prisca and Aquila, my fellow workers in Christ Jesus, who risked their necks for my life, to whom not only I but also all the churches of the Gentiles give thanks; greet also the church in their house.' Prisca is clearly a missionary, alongside Paul, and a patron of the community that meets at her house. In the preceding verses, Paul commended 'our sister Phoebe, a deaconess of the church at Cenchreae', who has been a leader or patron (προστάτις) for Paul and many others (Rom. 16:1–2). Whether or not the term διάκονος here should be taken as representing an office (as it perhaps does in Phil. 1:1), Phoebe was evidently a woman of means and importance within the community. In the remainder of Romans 16 no less than eight other women are singled out for personal greetings. Colossians 4:15 also refers to a church meeting in the house of Nympha, and the same is probably indicated by Paul's reference to 'Chloe's people' (1 Cor. 1:11).

Something of the impact and controversy created by the new roles which women were assuming within the Christian communities is reflected in the popular apocryphal acts, especially those claiming the authority of Paul. In the *Acts of Paul and Thecla*, a betrothed virgin called Thecla chances to overhear

Paul speaking publicly about virginity. She is converted to this new lifestyle, miraculously escapes the male authorities, who are furious with Paul, 'a sorcerer who has misled our wives' (*AcPT* 15), but is supported by the women of the city. After baptizing herself (*AcPT* 34), she cuts her hair short and dresses as a man, and then sets off to follow Paul. Paul directs her to 'teach the word of God' (*AcPT* 41), which she does, 'enlightening many by the word of God' before falling asleep (*AcPT* 43).[20] The radical freedom from societal constraints advocated by such Christianity was expressed concretely in self-control (ἐγκράτεια) and represented by a pure, virgin or celibate body.[21] By the end of the second century, such ascetic tendencies were described as 'Encratite', and its advocates were accused of rejecting the use of wine and meat, and insisting on total sexual abstinence for all Christians; these tendencies are often associated with Tatian, who taught at Rome in the middle of the second century, before returning home to Syria, taking with him his *Diatessaron* and perhaps his ascetic leanings.[22] The later Pastoral Epistles, on the other hand, again laying claim to the authority of Paul, tended to emphasize the subordination of women within the general household order expected of the Christian communities, and rejected any desire for disruptive asceticism. Nevertheless, women still played an important role, not only as widows and deaconesses, but also as prophetesses. Papias held the daughters of Philip, and their prophetic words, in high regard (*HE* 3.39.9). And Miltiades, an anti-Montanist writer in the late second century, spoke of a prophetess Ammia with respect, arguing that the 'Montanist women' did not inherit her prophetic gift (*HE* 5.17). He was referring to Maximilla and Prisca (or Priscilla), the associates of Montanus who, probably in the early AD 170s, had proclaimed a new dispensation and outpouring of the Spirit expressing itself in the form of a new and authoritative prophecy. Montanism, or 'the (New) Prophecy', soon spread beyond Phrygia, advocating greater enthusiasm and more rigorous disciplinary practices. The movement brought to a climax various unresolved tensions which had been simmering during the second century, and gave further occasion to consolidate the developing forms of church organization.

The basic locus for these church communities was the private house. Chapter 16 of Romans, written in the late AD 50s, suggests that alongside the 'house church' of Prisca and Aquila (vv. 3–5), there were at least four other distinct groups (vv. 10, 11, 14, 15) in Rome, each associated with particular names. There is no indication that the Church of Rome had corporate ownership of any property during the first two centuries; the later designation of the older churches in Rome as *tituli* churches, of which twenty have no record of their foundation and so may well date from the earliest days, implies, under Roman law, private ownership.[23] When great teachers, such as Justin, Valentinus and Marcion, arrived in Rome in the second century, their disciples gathered in private property. In the *Acts of Justin and Companions*, Justin claims that he and his disciples meet 'above the baths of Martin', while Valentinians seem to have met at a villa on the via Latina.[24] Various models have been suggested for the formation of these communities, such as burial societies, voluntary associations, philosophical schools and cultic associations.[25] It is important to note that these Christian house communities embraced all the dimensions of church life. Justin's community was not simply a school or a place of catechesis alongside, and independent from, an otherwise constituted church. To those who assembled around him, Justin did indeed 'impart the words of truth' (*AcJ*), yet none had been converted by Justin. Justin's precious description of the liturgical life of his community is also set within the same context (*I Apol.* 61, 65–7). Here he describes how the newly baptized are brought in to join the brethren, and how the president (the προεστώς) of the brethren celebrates the eucharist, which the deacons distribute to those present, and later to those who were absent. He also comments that the community gathers together weekly, on Sundays,[26] for the reading of Scripture, instruction and exhortation by the president, and the offering of prayer and the eucharist. Though Justin does not use the language of bishops (ἐπίσκοποι – lit. 'overseers') or presbyters, his community does clearly reflect the two offices, *episcopos*-presbyter and deacons, described in the Pastorals as the model of church organization (1 Tim. 3, 5:17; Titus 1:5–7; in 1 Tim., both are described, in various contexts, as 'presiding', cf. 3:4, 5, 12, 5:17).

Although there were a number of different communities in Rome, there was also a sense of communal identity. When Paul, and later Ignatius, wrote to the Christians of Rome, they sent a single letter, clearly intending that it be circulated amongst the various congregations, though Ignatius' awkward phrasing in his opening greeting ('to the church . . . in the place of the country of the Romans') betrays a certain hesitation about the location of the church to which he is writing.[27] A glimpse of the relations between these various communities in the first half of the second century is offered in *The Shepherd of Hermas*. In one of his visions, Hermas is instructed to write two books, and to give one to Clement and the other to Grapte: 'Clement will then send one to the cities abroad, for this has been committed to him, and Grapte shall exhort the widows and the orphans. But you shall read them to this city accompanied by the presbyters who preside over the church' (*Vis.* 2.4.3). The terminology of presbyter, president and bishop (ἐπίσκοπος) was still fluid; Clement himself used the terms presbyter and *episcopos* interchangeably (cf *I Clem.* 44.4–5), and even at the end of the second century Irenaeus could still use these terms as equivalents (cf. *AH* 3.2.2, 3.1; cf. *HE* 5.24.14). Hermas also suggests that there was only one such presbyter-president in each community and that he held 'the chief seat' (πρωτοκαθεδρία; *Mand.* 11.12, cf. *Vis.* 3.9.7). It seems, therefore, that in Rome there was a general assembly of the presbyters or presidents of the various communities, with someone charged with the specific duty of communicating with other churches on behalf of the Roman assembly, and another with the oversight (ἐπισκοπή) of charity. Thus, a letter could be written anonymously on behalf of the Church of Rome to Corinth, though it was generally known to have been written by Clement (cf. *HE* 4.22.2, 23.11). And, while each presbyter-president was responsible for the distribution of charity within his own community (cf. Justin, *I Apol.* 67), as the church in Rome increased in size and wealth, the responsibility for administering charity at large and abroad also became more important: Dionysius of Corinth praised Soter of Rome for increasing Rome's ancestral custom of sending contributions to the many churches in every city (*HE* 4.23.10). In addition to these offices held on the part of the Roman Church at large, the various congregations used to express their communal identity by the exchange of the eucharistic gifts, later known as the *fermentum* (cf. *HE* 5.24.15). In this arrangement, especially as there was no common, corporately owned, property, excommunication was a self-chosen affair. In the case of Cerdo, for instance, Irenaeus describes how he sometimes taught secretly and at other times confessed openly, but when refuted for his false teaching 'he separated himself from the assembly of the brethren' (*AH* 3.4.3). Rather than share in the common teaching, Cerdo preferred to break with the brethren, probably symbolized by the refusal to exchange the *fermentum*. Even though such communities were outwardly similar to the others, by the time of Irenaeus such a decision would be described, pejoratively, as the founding, of a school with its own succession of teaching (Ptolemy from Valentinus, *AH pr.*2; Marcion from Cerdo, *AH* 1.27.2), all ultimately deriving from Simon Magus (*AH* 1.22.2ff.) and so not part of the succession of teaching which was traced back to the apostles (*AH* 3.3).

Elsewhere, in the early part of the second century, there are two other important witnesses to church organization. The *Didache* (c. AD 100) seems to indicate a community in transition. Several chapters describe how to receive itinerant apostles and prophets, with a special concern for detecting false prophets (*Did.* 11–13), and the direction to 'let the prophets celebrate a Eucharist as they will' (*Did.* 10.7). But, in addition, the congregation is enjoined to appoint bishops and deacons as permanent local ministers, and it further specifies that 'they also minister to you the ministry of the prophets and the teachers' (*Did.* 15.1). With Ignatius of Antioch the ministry of itinerant charismatics has completely disappeared. He emphasizes that as a bishop he does not have the authority to give orders as did the apostles (*Trall.* 3.3; *Rom.* 4.3), though he seems to claim for himself the right to speak with prophetic authority (*Philad.* 7.1). Most important, however, is Ignatius' insistence on three distinct clerical orders, bishop, presbyters and deacons, and the central role of the bishop in the church. Ignatius exhorts the Smyrnaeans, for example, to be sure to follow the bishop as Christ follows the Father, doing nothing pertaining to the church without the bishop, and always to be present wherever the bishop appears, just as wherever Christ is 'there is the catholic church' (*Smyrn.* 8). But Ignatius' emphasis on the centrality of the bishop for the community within any given geographical area, his 'monepiscopacy', must not be construed in terms of the later 'monarchian' position of the bishop.[28] The obedience that the Smyrnaeans owe their bishop is also due to the presbyters (*Smyrn.* 8.1). Similarly, the Magnesians and the Ephesians are exhorted to do nothing without the bishop and the presbyters and are to obey them both, as well as be subject to one another (*Magn.* 7.1, 13.2; *Ephes.* 2.2, 20.2). Ignatius also speaks of the bishop and the presbyters as both 'presiding', the one in the place of God and the others in the place of the council of apostles (*Magn.* 6.1). And, again, the heretics are the ones who have separated themselves from the body of the church, choosing not to join the common assembly (*Ephes.* 5.3), rather than having been excluded by an episcopal decision.

The date at which monepiscopacy became established at Rome is a matter of debate.[29] But another practice from the East certainly contributed to its establishment there. A number of churches in Asia Minor were accustomed to celebrate Easter, the Christian Passover, on the same day as the Jewish Passover, the fourteenth day of the month Nisan, whatever day of the week it might be, and so are described as Quartodeciman. Other Christians, however, perhaps desiring to distinguish themselves from the Jews after AD 135, kept their celebration of Easter on the Sunday following Passover. It is difficult to determine how early either practice is: Eusebius records a letter from Polycrates of Ephesus, which defends the Quartodeciman practice as being the ancient tradition, upheld by luminaries like Philip and John (*HE* 5.24.1–7), but provides no comparable evidence for the celebration of Easter on Sunday. According to Eusebius, after receiving this letter from Polycrates, Victor, who 'presided at Rome' (AD 189–98), tried 'to cut off from the common unity all the dioceses (*paroikias*) of Asia along with the adjacent churches, on the grounds of heterodoxy, and he placarded this by means of letters, proclaiming that the brethren there were absolutely excommunicated. But all the bishops were not pleased by these events' (*HE* 5.24.9–10). These events, which Eusebius reconstructs, in fourth-century terms, as an action of the pope of Rome against churches in a different country, should probably be understood as the unilateral action of the *episcopos*-presbyter of one community in Rome against the other communities *there*, an action which not surprisingly caused consternation. This presumptuous action was criticized by Irenaeus of Lyon, who wrote to Victor, pointing out that not only was a plurality of practices possible, but that 'the presbyters before Soter, who presided over the church of which you are now leader, did not themselves observe it, . . . though they were at peace with those from the dioceses where it was kept when they came to them,' and that 'no one was ever rejected for this, but the presbyters before you [Victor] who did not observe it sent the Eucharist to those from other dioceses who did' (*HE* 5.24.14–15). Irenaeus continued by reminding Victor that when Polycarp of Smyrna had visited Rome, in the middle of the second century, 'Anicetus was not able to persuade Polycarp not to observe it . . . nor did Polycarp persuade Anicetus to observe it,' but both kept respect for each other and peace was preserved in the church (*HE* 5.24.16–18). It is probable that prior to Soter (i.e., before AD 165) there was no fixed celebration of Easter at Rome, at least there is no evidence for it, so that the divergence of practice was more than simply a matter of dates.[30] Nor is there any evidence, despite Eusebius' fourth-century convictions, that there were any councils of bishops meeting over this controversy and coming to a unanimous agreement for celebrating Easter on Sunday (*AH* 5.23); in fact, the only two letters which Eusebius goes on to cite, Polycrates and Irenaeus, argue for recognition of diversity.[31] Rather, just as Polycarp's discussion with Anicetus concerned the practices of Christians in Rome, so also the point of Irenaeus' letter was to restore peace between the communities, and their leaders, in Rome.[32] Although the date for Easter was one of the primary topics treated at the Council of Nicaea, the Quartodeciman practice continued, especially in Asia Minor, into the fifth century.[33] Nevertheless, the flurry of letter writing the affair occasioned, like the Montanist controversy (cf. *HE* 5.19), certainly contributed towards a greater awareness of the Church as a universal body. This unity was one perceived both by Christians themselves, such as Avircius Marcellus, the bishop of Hieropolis in Phrygia at the end of the second century, who on his own epitaph describes how he has travelled from Nisibis to Rome and found the same faith, serving the same nourishment, everywhere,[34] and by pagans such as Celsus, who differentiated between various sects and 'the Great Church'.[35]

Notes

1 *Ephes.* 12.2. Cf. Gamble, *Books and Readers*, 58–65.

2 Cf. C. E. Hill, 'What Papias Said About John (and Luke): A "New" Papian Fragment', *JTS* n.s. 49/2 (1998), 582–629. Needless to say, the location and occasion of the New Testament writings has been endlessly debated; for a summary, see R. E. Brown, *An Introduction to the New Testament*, The Anchor Bible Reference Library (New York: Doubleday, 1997).

3 Cf *HE* 2.16.1, which is phrased in deliberately vague terms. There is very little information on Christianity in Alexandria and Egypt during the second century. This silence, together with the fact that prior to the episcopate of Demetrius (*c.* 189–230) we hear only of figures such as Basilides and Valentinus, seems to support Bauer's claims about the priority of 'heresy'. Cf. W. Bauer, *Orthodoxy and Heresy in Earliest Christianity*, 44–60. However, the numerous papyri suggest the substantial presence of those who would later be called 'orthodox'. C. H. Roberts, *Manuscript, Society and Belief in Early Christian Egypt*; C. Wilfred Griggs, *Early Egyptian Christianity*.

4 Cf. Justin Martyr, *I Apol.* 31; S. G. Wilson, *Related Strangers: Jews and Christians 70–170CE*.

5 Cf. W. A. Meeks and R. L. Wilken, *Jews and Christians in Antioch in the First Four Centuries of the Common Era*; R. Stark, *The Rise of Christianity*, 63–9.

6 Cf. R. MacMullen, *Paganism in the Roman Empire*.

7 On the appropriation of Scripture, and the claim that classical culture was derivative from it, see F. Young, *Biblical Exegesis and the Formation of Christian Culture*, 49–75.

8 M. Sordi suggests that, in the horror caused by the events, 'a few hundred victims' would merit this description, *The Christians and the Roman Empire*, 31.

9 On the two accounts about 'Domitilla' and the catacomb bearing that name, see J. S. Jeffers, *Conflict at Rome: Social Order and Hierarchy in Early Christianity*, 48–62; and P. Lampe, *Die stadtrömischen Christen in den ersten beiden Jahrhunderten*, 166–72 (ET: 198–205).

10 Cf. Sordi, *Christians*, 72–3; for qualification see C. Trevett, *Montanism: Gender, Authority and the New Prophecy*, 123–9.

11 H. Chadwick, *The Early Church*, 55.

12 Cf. Stark, *Rise*, 163–89.

13 Cf. MacMullen, *Paganism*, 52–3; Stark, *Rise*, 86.

14 Estimates for the population density of Rome range from 200 to 300 inhabitants per acre; modern-day Manhattan has 100, yet in Rome it was illegal to build private buildings higher than 20 metres. For Greco-Roman cities, see Stark, *Rise*, 147–62; J. Carcopino, *Daily Life in Ancient Rome*.

15 Stark *Rise*, 153–4.

16 On epidemics, see ibid., 73–94; W. H. McNeill, *Plagues and People* (New York: Doubleday, 1976).

17 Cited in R. Walzer, *Galen on Jews and Christians*, 65.

18 *Rise*, 162.
19 For a collection of sources, see Jo-Ann Shelton, *As the Romans Did: A Source Book in Roman Social History* (New York and Oxford: Oxford University Press, 1988), 28–9.
20 J. K. Elliott, *The Apocryphal New Testament* (Oxford: Clarendon Press, 1993), 364–72. Cf. V. Burrus, *Chastity as Autonomy: Women in the Stories of the Apocryphal Acts*.
21 Cf. P. Brown, *The Body and Society*; A. Rousselle, *Porneia: On Desire and the Body in Antiquity*.
22 Cf. H. J. Drijvers, 'East of Antioch: Forces and Structures in the Development of Early Syriac Theology', in *East of Antioch: Studies in Early Syriac Christianity*, ch. 1.
23 Cf. A. Brent, *Hippolytus and the Roman Church in the Third Century: Communities in Tension before the Emergence of a Monarch-Bishop*, 399–400; Lampe, *Die stadtrömischen Christen*, 304 (ET: 362).
24 Cf. Lampe, *Die stadtrömischen Christen*, 257–64, 306 (ET: 298–313, 364–5).
25 Cf. R. L. Wilken, 'Collegia, Philosophical Schools, and Theology', in S. Benko and J. J. O'Rourke, eds, *The Catacombs and the Colosseum: The Roman Empire as the Setting of Primitive Christianity*, 268–91; W. A. Meeks, *The First Urban Christians: The Social World of the Apostle Paul*, 75–84.
26 On the emergence of Sunday as the regular weekly day of worship, see S. Bacchiocchi, *From Sabbath to Sunday*; W. Rordorf, *Sunday*; Wilson, *Related Strangers*, 230–5.
27 Cf. Brent, *Hippolytus*, 410.
28 Cf. A. Brent, 'The Relations between Ignatius and the *Didascalia*'.
29 Lampe, *Die stadtrömischen Christen*, argues for the time of Victor (189–98); Brent, *Hippolytus*, places the crucial period slightly later with Callistus (217–22).
30 Cf. Wilson, *Related Strangers*, 235–41.
31 Cf. W. L. Petersen, 'Eusebius and the Paschal Controversy', in H. Attridge and G. Hata, eds, *Eusebius, Christianity, and Judaism*, 311–25.
32 Cf. Lampe, *Die stadtrömischen Christen*, 322–3 (ET: 381–7); Brent, *Hippolytus*, 412–15.
33 Cf. A. Strobel, *Ursprung und Geschichte des frühchristlichen Osterkalenders*.
34 Text in J. Stevenson, *A New Eusebius*, 143.
35 Cf. Origen, *Cels.* 5.59–61.

8
Articulating identity

RICHARD A. NORRIS, JR.

By the last decades of the first century, the Christian communities around the Mediterranean basin had entered upon a process that would, over a period of two or more centuries, produce a relatively stable, widely shared, and socially embodied sense of who they were and what they stood for. This identity-forging process was impelled by at least two related circumstances, and it was strongly encouraged, to say the least, by others. One of its essential conditions lay in the tendency of these communities, however different from one another in their versions of Christian faith and life, to see themselves as constituting a single people, scattered though their outposts were. The literature of the New Testament and the Apostolic Fathers, and of later periods as well, indicates how natural, not to say habitual, it was for these communities and their representatives to expect one another's recognition and to interfere in one another's business. From the beginning, then, the history of Christianity was a history of controversy. It exhibits not only a high incidence of disagreement or misunderstanding within and among churches, but also a prevailing sense of mutual involvement and even mutual dependence; and these two factors conspired together to stimulate attempts to arrive at a common public mind and a shared practice.

Correlative with this quarrelsome cohesiveness was a second circumstance: Christian awareness of alienation from the world-order in which the churches were set. If that world tended at first to see Christians as errant, narrow fanatics, socially and religiously rootless, and potentially dangerous, they for their part tended to envisage their world as being under the domination of powers inimical to God and to Christ. The process of articulating Christian 'identity', therefore, was not simply a product of Christians' sense of belonging to a single 'people', but also of their sense – elicited as much by pressures from without as by internal needs – of being out of place in a world to which they did indeed belong, but only, in the last resort, as 'strangers and exiles on the earth' (Heb. 11:13); for by hypothesis a set of strangers and exiles cannot derive their common identity from that world as it is.

This 'world', however – which to early Christians meant neither the κόσμος of ancient philosophy nor the 'society' of modern theorists, but 'the present age' (ὁ νῦν αἰῶν: cf. 1 Tim. 6:17) – was a complex affair, to which churches were related in a correspondingly complex way. The sphere of the Roman Empire, i.e., the territories bordering the Mediterranean with their hinterlands, constituted for its peoples the οἰκουμένη, the place of human habitation. This world had a shared high culture: the 'Hellenism' disseminated in the East in the wake of Alexander the Great's conquests, and then Latinized by the Roman conquerors of Alexander's successors. There were of course corners of the Mediterranean world where this high culture scarcely penetrated and the Greek and Latin languages were infrequently heard. Where it did penetrate, moreover, it was influenced by local institutions, beliefs and usages, with the result that 'Hellenism' could take variant forms, the most common factors in which were the Greek language itself and, of course, the Greek institution of the πόλις.

The original Christians, however, had no place in this world *as Christians*. They were Jews with an odd set of convictions: a messianic sect within the larger body of Second Temple Judaism, whose members believed, in the light of Christ's resurrection, that they were living on the very brink of the 'last times', the 'restoration of all things'. It is wrong therefore to think of primitive Christianity as a distinct 'religion' that grew up alongside Judaism. Rather did it appear *within* Judaism, only to be separated out by a gradual process. Like the Essene movement portrayed in the literature of the Qumran community, it was a purely Jewish group that was nevertheless alienated in significant ways from the tradition that produced it.

If it is wrong to conceive of primitive Christianity as an independent 'religion', it is equally wrong to picture Second Temple Judaism – i.e., Judaism before the revolts that brought about the destruction of the Temple (AD 70) and the exile of Jews from Judaea under Hadrian (*c.* AD 135) – as simply an incipient form of the rabbinic Judaism that established itself step by step in the second and following centuries of the Common Era. Judaism in the days of Jesus and Paul, in Judaea and in the diaspora as well, was a more differentiated phenomenon. It found unity in study and observance of the Torah given by God to Moses, in attachment to the Jerusalem Temple, and in the patterns of personal and communal prayer that grew up in the diaspora as substitutes and equivalents for Temple worship.

Furthermore, Judaism in the Roman-Hellenistic age produced a variegated literature, not only in Aramaic or Hebrew, but also in Greek. *The Wisdom of Solomon*, for example, or 2 *Maccabees*, was basic reading for early Christians, as, needless to say, was the entire Greek translation of the Jewish Scriptures, the Septuagint, which was begun in the third century BC in Alexandria for the use of Greek-speaking Jewish communities, and became the first Christian Old Testament. Not less important was the literature of apocalypse, beginning with the Book of Daniel, which Christians not only pondered, but also contributed to and, in the end, preserved when it had ceased to be popular with Jews. Second Temple Judaism, then, if one takes account of its several forms, framed the thought-world of primitive and early Christianity.

This is particularly true with regard to Christian perceptions of the churches' environment – religious, political and cultural – and is most apparent in Christian attitudes towards the religious practices of 'the nations'. Jewish perception of the nations' gods as mere idols (cf. Ps. 115), and the conviction, native to apocalypse, that the present age was dominated by fallen spirits, determined Christian estimates of the traditional deities of the Mediterranean peoples. By the same token, early Christians were largely at one with Jews in perceiving the Roman order as hostile to the governance of the true God, and in believing that it would in the end be overthrown; but like Jeremiah (cf. Jer. 29:4–9, 24–32), the Pharisees, and the later rabbis, they came to believe, on the whole, that the present state of things was of God's permission, and professed an interim loyalty to their rulers (cf. Rom. 13:1–7; 1 Pet. 2:13–17).

A similar ambiguity informed Jewish attitudes towards the high culture of the Hellenistic world and the teachings of the philosophical schools. Such traditions, not unlike Judaism, inculcated ways of life and based these 'ethics' on beliefs about the structure of reality and of human nature: beliefs that could furnish both criticisms of popular religion and alternative interpretations of it. Philosophical sects were thus natural competitors of Judaism (and Christianity) for the allegiance of educated persons. Nevertheless diaspora Jews who were brought into close contact with such teachings – and the inevitable example of this is Philo the Alexandrian – often discerned in them an affinity not only for monotheism but also for the way of life enjoined by Torah. Thus they found, in Middle Platonism and Stoicism, tools for their apologetic and for the understanding of their own tradition; and some maintained that Plato and his successors had found inspiration in the more ancient teaching of Moses. Here too Christians followed a road that diaspora Judaism had already travelled. On the one hand they distrusted philosophy and saw it as a demonically inspired rival, while on the other they could envisage it, in Justin's manner, as a tradition, however corrupted, whose origins lay in God's revelation, and whose fulfilment was Christ.

These evidences point not so much to Christian 'indebtedness' to Judaism, as merely to the fact that Christianity was originally a form of Judaism. As in the case of Christian reliance on Moses and the prophets, they call attention not to borrowings but to unremarkable continuities. It is only against the background of such continuities that the question how there occurred a final social, institutional and doctrinal separation between Judaism and Christianity can be properly raised.

It is not possible to assign a date to this separation. Some have attributed it, largely or in part, to the introduction, a decade or more after the destruction of Jerusalem, of a 'benediction against heretics' (*birkat ha-minim*) into the synagogue liturgy; but the evidence supporting this explanation is uncertain, and in any case it wrongly presupposes that Judaism at that time possessed a functioning central authority. One can only say that the seeds of this separation were planted even before the Jewish revolt of AD 66–70, that reactions to the destruction of the Temple in 70 encouraged it, and that it appears to have become more or less complete in the wake of the revolt led by Bar Kochba (AD 135).

The original seed of the process must no doubt be sought in the admission of uncircumcised Gentiles to Christian 'assemblies' (ἐκκλησίαι), which, on the evidence of the Book of Acts, seems to have begun with a persecution in Jerusalem that 'scattered' a group of Greek-speaking Jewish Christians who, like their leader Stephen, entertained deviant views about the Temple cult (see Acts 6:8–8:4). This practice created severe problems. Some Christians (whom Acts in one place describes (15:5) as belonging 'to the party of the Pharisees') objected to the practice of preaching the gospel 'to uncircumcised men' as well as to eating with them (Acts 11:3; cf. 15:1). At Antioch in Syria, a controversy arose over table-fellowship between Gentile and Jewish Christians (Gal. 2:11ff.); and behind this practical problem there no doubt lurked the larger issue of whether Gentile converts to Christianity ought not to become observant Jews.

This was not a quarrel between Jew and Christian, but between two groups of Christian Jews whose differences followed out points of view already known in the Judaism of the Second Temple era. The course of the debate is difficult to reconstruct because the narratives in Acts 15 and Galatians conflict. For present purposes, however, the sequence of events is of less interest than the reason given in Acts for a 'liberal' decision on this matter. James 'the Lord's brother', we are told, adduced a Jewish tradition to the effect that with the dawning of the messianic age the Gentiles would be incorporated into God's people. Since, however, the end-time foreseen by the prophets had indeed dawned, as demonstrated by the Gentiles' reception of the Holy Spirit (Acts 15:8; cf. 10:45–7), the door into the eschatological people of God was opened to 'all the Gentiles who are called by my name' (Acts 15:17*b*). Hence the 'apostles and elders' limited themselves to defining minimal conditions of table-fellowship between Jewish and Gentile Christians.

Two assumptions governed this decision. The first held that the Christian sect represented the renewed Israel, the Israel of the messianic age. The second held that Gentiles could belong to this renewed Israel: that God had willed their incorporation into the people. These assumptions Acts presents as common ground among the disputants. They did not however entail that the Law was suspended for such Gentiles; and of course the great majority of Jews in the diaspora communities touched by Christian preachers accepted neither of the assumptions. Thus the presence of Gentiles within the churches created tensions both within the Christian movement and between its members and non-Christian Jews. Thence it came about that in cities where the Pauline mission, or others like it, operated, Christians were from the beginning compelled to meet apart from the synagogue community and thus to assume some sort of tentative identity of their own – often in the form of societies grouped around a particular household or group of households. At the same time, the question whether Gentile Christians must accept the yoke of the Law continued to be debated in the churches.

The earliest contributor to this debate who can be consulted directly is the Apostle Paul. In Galatians and Romans, Paul wrestles with the issue of the status of the Mosaic Law, both in Israel and in the renewed Israel that incorporates Gentiles. A Pharisee at heart, he revered the books of Moses; but on the other hand, as against 'the circumcision party', he insisted that the only basis of anyone's status as a child of God in the age that had dawned with the gift of the Spirit was faith in Christ; and therefore he argued that no one 'is . . . justified by works of the law' (Gal. 2:16). Thus he argues, from the text of the Law, that Gentiles, by sharing the faith of Abraham in God's promise, can be justified 'apart from law, though the law and the prophets bear witness to' this gift (Rom. 3:21; cf. 4:13–17). Here he allows the Law the prophetic function of attesting the Christ's fulfilment of God's promise to the patriarch, and, to that end, of intimating the priority of 'faith' to 'works'; but since 'works of the law' have never been salvific in themselves, the only function he can assign to the Law in the economy of salvation is that of revealing sin, or of bringing it to a head (or, in Galatians, of serving a preliminary disciplinary function as a 'pedagogue'). The problem he then has to struggle with (in Rom. 9–11) is not whether or how Gentiles can be incorporated into the end-time Israel, but why Jews, who surely are its natural citizens, are not rushing to join it.

Another phase in the relation of Christianity to Judaism was introduced by the destruction of Jerusalem and its Temple in AD 70. One result of that event was the disappearance of the Jerusalem Church (whose leader, James, had been executed even before the great revolt) and with it the marginalization of Christian groups whose members, whether Jewish or Gentile, observed the Mosaic Law.[1] Such groups did not disappear, not even when harassed by the adherents of Bar Kochba in the Judaean revolt under Hadrian. We hear of them well into the fourth century, and they seem to have maintained an ongoing polemic against Paul; but as early as the middle of the second century, other Christians perceived them as eccentric and deviant, partly no doubt because in most places where churches had been established their point of view had become unfamiliar.

Another result of the disappearance of the Jerusalem Temple, given the insecurities it doubtless occasioned in some quarters of diaspora Judaism, seems to have been the expulsion of Jewish-Christian cells that had existed within certain synagogue communities. The Gospel of Matthew – with its insistence on the one hand that neither jot nor tittle of the Law shall pass away, and on the other its acid polemic against the Pharisees – probably reflects the experience of such a community. Even more clearly is this the case with the Gospel of John. Modern readers who note the latter's hostility to 'the Jews' tend to equate it with modern European and American anti-Semitism (of which its language has indeed been a source). In reality, however, the members of the early Johannine community seem to have been Jews themselves. What the Gospel's language reflects is the sort of 'division among the Jews' (19:19; cf. 7:43, 11:45f.) to which its text regularly alludes; and of course 'the Jews' who are its opponents are fairly obviously identified as members of a particular 'school', that of the 'Pharisees' (e.g., 9:13, 18; cf. 3:1!). Here no question arises about the status of Gentiles or whether they ought to observe the Law, as in the Pauline communities. Nor is there any question (as there is at Gal. 3:19; cf. Acts 7:53) of the Law's being given by anyone save God. The Law is subordinated to the 'grace and truth' that have come through Christ (1:17); but then it is also true, as Jesus says (5:46), that Moses in the Law 'wrote of me' and that 'Abraham rejoiced that he was to see my day' (8:56). These Johannine believers did not maintain, then, that the Law should not be observed; but they seem to have held that Jesus, as the Wisdom or Word of God dwelling amongst human beings, was the true content of the Law, just as they held that the true 'Temple' was Jesus' 'body' (2:21). Here, one suspects, division was encouraged not so much by repudiation of the Law as by the claim that the Law must be read Christologically.

By the end of the first century, then, three assumptions governed the churches' perception of themselves. One was that observance of the Mosaic Law was not necessary for Gentile believers, and increasingly, therefore, not for Jewish Christians either. This was the practical upshot of the Pauline polemic against 'Judaizers', and it is interpreted by the writer of Ephesians, himself a Jew, as signifying the breaking down of 'the dividing wall of hostility' and the creation in Christ of 'one new humanity' (2:14f.) out of Jew and Gentile. A second assumption, implicit in this eschatological (and universalist) claim, is that through their faith in Christ, Gentile believers become heirs of the promises of God made to Israel and thus 'members of the household of God' and indeed parts of the new temple of God (2:19, 21f.): in other words, that the ἐκκλησία, inclusive of both former Jews and former Gentiles, is indeed the renewed, end-time people of God, Israel. A final assumption is that, even though the Law is formally outmoded by life in the Spirit (Gal. 5:16–23; cf. Eph. 4:30), the Law and the Prophets are a revelation of the same God who has published his eternal purpose 'in Christ' (Eph. 1:9), and are therefore themselves witnesses to Christ.

These assumptions indicate wide differences of perception and belief as between Christians and Jews. As time went on, moreover, new factors operated to distance Jews and Christians even further from each other. During the period of the disastrous Jewish rebellions of AD 115 (in Cyrenaica and Egypt) and 135 (in Judaea), Christians were beginning to be noticed (and intermittently persecuted) by the Roman authorities as an independent cult, partly no doubt because they could no longer find concealment in the penumbra of the synagogue. Yet even after the events of AD 135 – when with the defeat of Bar Kochba Judaea was renamed Syria Palaestina and the former Jerusalem, now forbidden to Jews, was given the name Colonia Aelia Capitolina – Rome continued to tolerate Judaism as a *religio licita*. It was rebellion, not the ancient and respectable religion of the Jews, that Rome abhorred. Christian churches on the other hand were subject to persecution precisely because theirs was not the traditional religion of a recognizable people, but an upstart cult, fanatic and hostile to the gods, a cult at whose origin there lay, in the crucifixion and resurrection of Jesus, a double symbol of alienation from the present order of things.

Under these circumstances, Christian leaders seem to have reacted in two ways. On the one hand, they now developed an apologetic directed specifically *against* Judaism – an apologetic that can be studied in second-century writings as various as the so-called *Epistle of Barnabas*; Justin's *Dialogue with Trypho*; Melito of Sardis' homily *On the Passover*; and Tertullian's tract *Against the Jews*. This apologetic has traditionally been thought to have arisen out of Christian anger at the hostility of Jews to the claims of Christ (and of the churches), out of envy of the relatively secure status of Jews in the Roman world, and out of a need to counter the attractions of Judaism to many Gentiles. However real such reactions may have been, examination of rabbinic and patristic literature of the period after *c.* 135 does not suggest that the two groups continued to have much real knowledge of, or dialogue with, each other. The claims of Christianity do not seem greatly to have exercised the rabbis, and it can be argued that the 'Jews' portrayed in Christian polemic are stereotypical figures constructed to serve the purposes, not of authentic debate with living opponents, but of in-house Christian reflection on the course of salvation history. Certainly Christian writers of this era give the – unexpected – impression that they tended to construe Judaism fundamentally as a phenomenon of the past.[2]

In this connection it is instructive to read chapters 9–30 of Justin's *Dialogue with Trypho*. There Jews are portrayed – on the basis of their past – as a uniformly stiff-necked and rebellious people who not only slew the prophets but now 'have slain the Righteous One . . . and . . . reject those who set their hope on him' (*Dial.* 16.4). This complicity in the death of Christ and repudiation of Christians explains why Judaea is 'a wilderness' and no Jews are any longer allowed in Jerusalem (*Dial.* 16.3). The Mosaic Law too, with its sabbaths, its feast-days, its food-laws and its sacrifices, was given precisely because of the Jews' habit of disobedience: i.e., in effect, as a punishment (a view that would have astonished even the Paul of Galatians). Here one sees almost for the first time a Christian criticism of Judaism that not only represents the perspective of people who see themselves as standing outside the boundaries of the historical Israel, but also responds not to the Jewish position in any contemporary debate or situation, but to Israel's past historical record. Not only is the Church – 'us', as Justin puts it – 'the true, spiritual Israel' (*Dial.* 11.2, cf. 11.4), but Judaism itself is tacitly treated as belonging to the past.

This negative apologetic, however, did not mean that Christians like Justin simply rejected their Jewish heritage or ceased to define themselves in relation to Israel: i.e., to see themselves and Judaism as successive moments in the same story. Justin himself insisted that the God who raised Jesus Christ from the dead was the very God who by the hand of Moses led the Israelites out of

Egypt, who gave the Law to Moses, and who called and inspired the prophets. Christians naturally looked to the Mosaic Law to suggest, e.g., how their own priesthood should be ordered (*I Clement*); and if Justin rejected the 'ceremonial' laws of the Pentateuch, he was confident that its 'moral' legislation was of universal validity – was, indeed, little more than a publication of natural law. Further, it was to the Law and the Prophets that they looked, as Christians had looked from the beginning, for the predictions, previsions, portents and intimations which assured them that the Christian dispensation was implicit in God's purposes from the beginning. This, indeed, was the function, for them, of Moses' 'ceremonial' legislation.

Another motive also operated in Christian appeal to the books of the Law and the Prophets. One of the strongest charges brought by 'Greeks' against Christians was that Christianity was unworthy of respect because it was an upstart religion, a novelty that bore none of the wisdom of the past and belonged to no historic people (like the Jews). In the face of this critique, it was natural enough for Christians to claim that, on the contrary, one had only to consult Moses and the prophets to realize that Christian faith had a pedigree more respectable than most. The 'deep' or 'spiritual' meaning of the Jewish Scriptures was a Christian meaning; and that fact explains why the churches represented, as Justin says, the new spiritual Israel.

That is why these early Christians tended in fact to think of themselves, at least in the first instance, as a nation (or a citizenry): an attitude that corresponded not only to their claim to be Israel's 'successor', but also to the perception, current in their day, that religious practice was correlative on the whole with membership in some group that possessed a given cultural or political unity, or both. They thought of themselves as a scattered people, living in the territories of other nations or citizenries (not unlike Jews of the diaspora, with whom they thus tacitly compared themselves), but observing their own laws and customs.

The truth is, however, that in the case of the churches this belief did not quite correspond to reality. They were composed of folk of a wide variety of local cultures and citizenries, and their membership in the Christian movement was, to begin with, more a matter of attraction and choice than of birth and upbringing. Hence the 'nation' or 'people' constituted by Celtic, Egyptian, Semitic, Greek and Latin Christians (to mention no others) was to find that its common identity depended to an unusual degree upon more or less explicit commitments and agreements with regard to certain fundamental practices, structures of authority, and beliefs. Christians, said Tertullian, are made not born; and the same seems to have been true of the Church as a whole.

It is a commonplace of contemporary scholarship that there never was an undifferentiated 'faith once delivered to the saints' (Jude 3): i.e., a way, or a body, of teaching about faith and practice that all Christians were originally agreed upon. Even the New Testament canon, as it gradually took shape during and after the second century, brought together in a single collection writings that represented a wide variety of teaching and emphasis. On the other hand, this variety was not unlimited. Christianity was an identifiable phenomenon even before the drawn-out, and relatively self-conscious, process of acknowledging and constructing a shared 'identity'. It was identifiable because, by the end of the first century, Christian communities around the Mediterranean basin tended to share certain focal themes of thought and discourse: as, for example, Jesus the Christ of God, the Spirit of God discovered or conferred as the source of a new life, and 'resurrection' as the destiny of the saints. Such themes did not constitute anything even vaguely like a coherent 'theology' (a word which, like 'orthodoxy', was not in use at that time among Christians). What they represented was at most an agenda for catechesis, i.e., for an elementary account of the relationship to the Divine that originated from, and had its primary instantiation in, Jesus; was actualized as life in and of the Spirit; and issued in, or entailed, 'resurrection'.

Nevertheless, as the churches left the opening decades of the second century behind them, it became clear not only that there were differing, and indeed inconsistent, interpretations of the common themes of Christian catechesis (whence the doctrinal conflicts of the later second century), but also, and in the first instance more significantly, that there were equally serious differences about what counted as authoritative sources of Christian teaching and what voices in the Church counted as authoritative interpreters of these sources. The making of what is now called 'orthodoxy' was the process by which an initial settlement of these closely intertwined issues was achieved and a public 'identity' established for the churches. The process was, needless to say, informal, desultory and confused. Early Christianity was not an 'organization', even in the most elementary sense, but a collection of hard-pressed local communities whose interchanges with one another were necessarily occasional (and in any case some of these communities lay outside the growing network of communication). Hence the Christian movement in the second century lacked the procedural rationality and decisiveness associated with established committee structures and clear chains of command. It is much easier to say what, on the whole and in the end, seems to have come about than to trace precisely the process by which it happened.

One thing at any rate is clear: there were two ultimate sources of authority for Christian believers. One was Jesus himself, the living Christ, and the other, the Spirit that he had conferred upon his disciples. The significant questions, then, were on the one hand how to obtain access to these two authorities, and on the other hand how they were related.

The beginnings of answers to these questions are best sought in the churches' characteristic institutions; for these in fact represent the starting-point of later developments. From the New Testament, and from later writings like the letters of Ignatius, *I Clement* and *Didache*, it is apparent that, at any rate from the middle of the first century, there were at least two basic institutions that focused and shaped the life of most, if perhaps not all, Christian communities: baptism and the Lord's Supper or eucharist. Little can be known about the precise shape taken by these communal practices in any particular place or at any particular time; but it can be said with fair certainty both that they were liturgical observances (i.e., regular ritual practices that involved a whole community), and that their aim was, in the largest sense, the establishment and maintenance of communication between the Church and the sources of its life and hope, i.e., Christ and the Spirit of Christ, both understood as gifts and manifestations of God. Without doubt these liturgical practices functioned as inchoate articulations of the churches' identity: or better, perhaps, as matrices for the development of such articulations.

Take the case of baptism. From the earliest times, a ritual of water-baptism was employed to mark conversion to the new faith, endowment with the Spirit, and entrance into the fellowship of both the local and the extended community. Variously described as 'putting on Christ' (Gal. 3:27), 'enlightenment' (Heb. 10:32), and 'rebirth' (John 3:3, 5; Titus 3:5), this ritual of washing soon became the liturgical centrepiece of a long initiatory process. The process culminated in participation in the eucharist, but – more important for present purposes – it was also, formally or informally, prefaced by certain preparatory activities: acts of repentance, exorcisms, and above all catechesis, teaching that in one form or another dealt both with the conduct required of Christians, and with the truths that converts acknowledged and assented to in the explicit confession of faith which, at least in the second century, came to accompany the very act of baptism. This meant that local churches were regularly, perhaps even rhythmically, preoccupied with the processes of formation and instruction by which prospective members of the church were brought to their second birth as children of God (Gal. 4:6f.). Moreover, the eucharist itself, whose observance marked the weekly, and annual, celebration of the Christian Passover, the death and resurrection of Christ, included extended readings and expositions of the Scriptures, which candidates for baptism, not to mention established members of the community, were expected or required to attend.

Thus the local branches of the Christian 'nation' or 'people' in its diaspora could take on more the aspect of schools than of proper ethnic groups. To outsiders, no doubt, churches looked like neither of these, but more like what the Romans called a *collegium*. This was a voluntary association or club or society that met regularly for purposes of fellowship, had its own customs and rituals, elected officers (some of whom were sometimes called ἐπίσκοποι, 'overseers' or perhaps 'guardians'), maintained a common purse, and often provided services to its members (e.g., a decent burial). Pliny the Younger in his well-known letter to the Emperor Trajan seems to perceive the local congregation of which he speaks as such a body; and a century later Tertullian recognizes the similarity between such *collegia* and churches when, in his *Apology*, he describes the Church in such terms for the benefit of outsiders. Nevertheless, perception of churches as schools – that is, as communities devoted to the teaching and learning of a way of life – was, together with the quite different image of it as a 'people', more common among insiders, since it was rooted in commonplace and even ritual activities that went on within congregations.

This is the picture of the Church that Justin Martyr entertains when he describes Christianity as a 'philosophy'; for that word refers in the first instance not to a body of speculative theory but to a sect or 'school' like that of the Pythagoreans or Stoics, who inculcated and practised a certain way of life on the basis of their characteristic teachings (δόγματα) about the nature of the world within which human life is conducted. Justin thought, then, that Christianity was the true philosophy, and he appears to have set up a Christian 'school' in Rome, which would no doubt have trained people in Christian belief and practice. Clement of Alexandria too thought of life within the Church as a discipleship in which progress is made from the faith that accepts baptism to the life of the mature Christian 'gnostic': a life in which the Word of God is the ultimate teacher, but in which human teachers too have their place. Indeed, a close description of the structure of the church at Alexandria in Clement's day – if such a thing were possible for us – might well have to make reference to the presence of more than one such Christian 'school', some of which masters like Clement himself, or Origen later, would have repudiated as heretical.

Where such a structure existed, the teachers, each presiding over a relatively tightly knit group of disciples, would have been principal, and perhaps dissonant, voices of authority in a local church. Superimposed on this structure, however – and indeed on the primitive structure of household-churches with their heads – there came to be another in which the central figure was the individual styled 'overseer' (ἐπίσκοπος, 'bishop'). That term, whose first known Christian use appears in Paul's correspondence with the Christians at Philippi (Phil. 1:1), clearly refers to some sort of leader in the church who was closely associated with deacons ('assistants'?). The word is initially – as in *I Clement* and the *Didache* – employed in the plural, perhaps as a rough synonym for 'presbyter' ('elder': cf. 1 Pet. 5:1; Acts 20:17) or as denoting the members of a particular class of presbyters. In the letters of Ignatius (*c.* 113), however, there is revealed what appears to be a relatively novel structure in which each local church has as its head a single bishop, who presided over the elders; and it is this structure which, as the second century progressed, came to prevail in church after church until it represented the norm.

Ignatius clearly envisages this figure as a centre of unity within the local church, and that role itself is focused in the bishop's presidency at the eucharist. As far as Ignatius is concerned, this presidency guarantees that the assembled people is indeed 'church', and the liturgy itself an act of the church in Christ; so that apart from the bishop there is no 'real' eucharist. The bishop, then, is in charge of the church's characteristic doings at its regular meetings: i.e., of its liturgy. This understanding implied, moreover, that the bishop was also in charge of the processes of initiation into the church, including the catechesis that preceded baptism (and eventually of the processes later associated with the 'second baptism', that is, the reconciliation of excommunicate but penitent sinners). The bishop thus came to control the door to membership of the community and, at the same time, to be the church's principal teacher and 'supervisor' of teaching: a rival – potentially if not always actually – of figures like Justin and Origen. It was through the bishop, then, in his presidency within the liturgy, that the members of the assembly had access to the unity, holiness and truth that resided in Christ and the Spirit.

This structure developed and came to prevail fairly early on in the second century. It was everywhere in place, even in Alexandria, by *c.* 200. Its advance, however, was not without significant obstacles and serious challenges. One possible obstacle was, as we have suggested, the authority of the heads of Christian 'schools'. Another inevitable challenge was represented by those who had suffered and confessed their faith under persecution, and especially those who had borne the ultimate 'witness' (μαρτυρία) – death – to their allegiance to Christ; for these were assumed not merely to be endowed with the Spirit (cf. Matt. 10:20; John 15:26), and to image the paradigmatic martyr,

Christ himself (cf. 1 Tim. 6:13), but to share with him even now in the new life of the resurrection. Even in death, the martyr was a figure of authority; and the cult of the martyrs provided a focus of devotion distinct from that of the bishop's liturgy (a fact intimated, in the days after persecution had ceased, by the architectural distinction between martyrs' shrines and ordinary places of assembly). In the second century, bishops and the cause of the martyrs were allied as over against gnostics, who were thought to deprecate martyrdom and to have compromised with the 'powers': the 'orthodox' churches stood for the moral significance of martyrdom and the obligation of Christians under persecution to 'confess' and 'bear witness'. At a later date, there was conflict between 'confessors' (persons imprisoned for their faith and thus endowed with special gifts of the Spirit) and bishops when the former interfered in the administration of penance in the case of persons who had dishonestly evaded confession of their faith, or when the bishops themselves gave the appearance of deserting their responsibilities by hiding from the authorities in a time of persecution. In the end, however, these two foci of spiritual authority achieved reconciliation as episcopal authority clothed itself in that of the martyrs: there is well-known evidence of one form of this in the traditional association of the bishops of Rome with the martyred Peter, and eventually with his shrine-church on the Vatican Hill.

A more serious challenge to episcopal authority came in the last third of the second century with the rise of the so-called 'New Prophecy' in Asia Minor. This movement represented a revival, originating in Asia Minor around 170, both of prophecy and of millennialism. Montanus, the founder of the movement, with his companions Priscilla and Maximilla, spoke as under the control of the Paraclete whom Jesus had promised, that is, the Spirit who would 'guide' his disciples 'into all the truth' (John 16:13); and he predicted that the New Jerusalem would descend at a site near the village of Pepusa in Phrygia. The disappointment of this expectation did not give pause to his movement: it spread widely and was known in Rome (where, it seems, Bishop Victor first applauded and then opposed it), in Gaul, and in North Africa, where the apologist and moralist Tertullian was converted to it, more, apparently, because of the moral rigorism and enthusiasm for martyrdom it commended than because of any propensity for religious frenzy it represented. There is no indication that Montanists deviated from the ordinary pattern of Christian teaching and belief; but the role they gave to prophecy made of the Spirit-endowed prophet a figure of authority to rival that of the bishop.

More serious in the end, at least as measured by the character of the reaction it evoked, was the challenge to the authority of the emerging episcopal system represented on the one hand by Marcion and his separatist churches, and, on the other, by Christian gnosticism. The latter had deep roots in the churches: roots that reached back into the first century and into the Jewish soil of Christianity; but it achieved notoriety in the course of the second century, especially through traditions associated with the names of Basilides and Valentinus, both Alexandrian Christians by origin. Marcionites and gnostics handled the question of authority in the Church in quite different ways; but they both drew on the sources to which the emerging consensus about the content of catechesis itself appealed. At the same time they severely criticized that consensus in the light of their own prepossessions.

The episcopal system, founded as it was on the bishop's presiding role in the local church's primary liturgies, made of him a mediating figure. In the liturgy of baptism, he was the church's primary catechist, and the minister through whom the Holy Spirit was conferred on believers. In the eucharist, his blessing of the bread and wine and his exposition of the Scriptures (no doubt shared with other presbyters) were essential to the church's communion with Christ and to its dwelling in the mind of Christ. The head of the community thus had a central role in the church's maintenance of communication with the sources of its life and identity; and insofar as the media of such communication were written texts or other verbal formulae he exercised the authority of the interpreter *par excellence*.

The primary texts used in the churches' liturgies were of course those contained in the Septuagint. To these Scriptures Christian teachers appealed both to validate their accounts of Christ and of the revelation or redemption he brought, and also to elicit the meaning of his life, death and resurrection. More direct accounts of Christ appeared in the form of orally shaped traditions concerning Jesus: traditions that gradually, as the first century drew to its close, came to be written down, primarily though not exclusively in the literary form originally represented by the Gospel attributed to Mark. This appeal to Jesus, however, was also – and inevitably, since he left no written account of himself or his views – an appeal to the original transmitters of his teaching and bearers of his message. It was thus generally assumed that authentic Christianity was the Christianity of the first generation of teachers: i.e., that communication of their Spirit-inspired doctrine brought people into agreement with the mind of Christ. Accordingly the four Gospels that eventually formed one of the core elements of the New Testament were in the course of the second century attributed to 'apostolic' figures as their authors, whether these were members of the Twelve or other first-generation leaders. Similarly, there had been churches that treasured collections of Pauline letters, and of course other writings taken to embody apostolic teaching or to have apostolic authors.

Such a library – i.e., the 'prophetic'[3] and 'apostolic' books – was thus inevitably a focus of the second-century debates that marked the churches' 'crisis of identity'. These focused upon questions having to do primarily, as indicated above, with *the criteria of authentic Christianity.* They involved questions of doctrine (or, to be more precise, of the content of catechesis), to be sure; but even more basically, they involved questions about the reliable sources of such teaching and about the manner in which, and of course the persons by whom, the sources were to be authoritatively interpreted.

In no case is this clearer than in that of the crucial debate occasioned by Marcion, a native of Pontus who taught in Rome around 140. History has remembered him as the one who denied that the Jewish Scriptures could have any authority for Christians, a position he took on the ground that the Mosaic creator and lawgiver was a God different from, and morally inferior to, the one made known in Jesus Christ. Marcion counted the Apostle Paul the only trustworthy witness to the true gospel of Christ and denigrated traditions that were attached to the names of other first-generation teachers. He saw the 'Father' of Christ as a forgiving and loving God who sent his Son to rescue souls from the tyranny of the oppressive deity of Sinai. In his teaching, then, there was no place for any notion of continuity between the 'prophetic' and the 'apostolic' writings; and indeed the only apostolic writings he recognized as authoritative were the Pauline corpus as he knew it and an abbreviated form of the Gospel of Luke. These works he established as an official κανών ('normative list') for his churches, thus creating the first stable version of a 'New Testament'. No doubt the form of this brisk list – i.e., its construction out of the two basic elements of gospel and apostolic letter – reflected common practice in churches he had known; but the idea of an official definition of works to be reckoned as authoritative was novel and may have been inspired by a need to find a substitute for the Jewish Scriptures.

There is much that is of interest in the content of Marcion's teaching; but the attention of his adversaries was focused on his refusal of books whose interpretation and exposition were central to the churches' catechesis. Hitherto the authority of the Jewish Scriptures had simply been presupposed. To be sure, traditional Christian use of the Septuagint required that it be treated as inspired prophecy or as 'type', an extreme form of which approach can be found in the so-called *Epistle of Barnabas*; and Marcion's way with the Jewish Scriptures depended, by contrast, on his habit of confining interpretation to their plain or 'literal' sense. Nevertheless it was not his exegetical method, or even his exclusivist Paulinism, but rather his refusal of the Jewish Scriptures that captured the attention of his adversaries; and the decision against Marcion rests less on later, elaborate refutations of him from the pens of Irenaeus and Tertullian, than simply upon the churches' inability to take his attack on the books of the Mosaic Covenant quite seriously. They continued to read the books of Moses and the Prophets (not to mention the Writings), as authoritative Scripture, and set Marcion aside, almost automatically, as a deviationist.

This entrenched habit of seeking authoritative truth in the Jewish Scriptures was not repudiated by the Christian gnostics, the heirs of Valentinus and Basilides, whose teaching and practice constituted a yet more fruitful stimulus to early Christian self-definition. These teachers did not set the Jewish Scriptures aside but, as Ptolemy's *Letter to Flora* indicates, offered a thoroughly critical assessment of them, one which tended to show that while on the level of obvious meaning the books of Moses reveal the teaching of an inferior Creator God (the 'Demiurge', i.e. 'Artisan', as the Valentinians would have it), they, like the other scriptural books, contained intimations of a higher truth and a higher reality than those explicitly conveyed by the Demiurge to the prophets. This higher reality was the spiritual world of which spiritual individuals knew themselves to be members and for which they were ultimately destined; and acquaintance with this truth, revealed in and by the Christ, was the 'knowledge' that transformed the life of the person 'in the know', the gnostic. Gnostics, then, could accept the Scriptures rendered in the Septuagint, on the condition that they be interpreted on the basis of their own experience of enlightenment: and the same was true of the distinctively Christian Gospels and the letters of Paul, on which much of their self-understanding was based.

For this reason, the followers of Valentinus and Basilides could not like Marcion be summarily dismissed. Nor for that matter were they in the position of erecting a 'canon' of their own to rival the Gospels and other Christian writings which, by the middle of the second century, were widely, if only by custom, read in the Church's liturgy. To be sure, they had a literature of their own and took it seriously, accepting, for example, accounts which taught that truths merely hinted at in the Church's books were explicitly revealed by Christ to certain chosen disciples after his resurrection. They did not, however, seek to substitute this literature for what would become the canonical New Testament. On the contrary, the Valentinians were sedulous interpreters of the very Christian writings to which 'the great Church' made its appeal. It was a Valentinian author – Heracleon – who composed the first commentary on the

Fourth Gospel; and even Irenaeus makes it plain how much of his opponents' teaching depended on exegesis both of the Synoptic Gospels and of the Pauline corpus.

These Christian 'gnostics', then were differently related to the churches than the followers of Marcion. They seem frequently to have formed cells or 'schools' within churches rather than to have organized themselves separately; and this circumstance is reflected in their attitudes to the writings, Jewish and Christian, that churches tended to treat as weighty or authoritative, and even to the catechesis in which Christian beliefs were inculcated. In both cases they allowed these customary authorities to stand, but insisted, on one ground or another, that they had two levels of meaning, the inferior one of which was the one disseminated in the churches. Their own teaching, by contrast, conveyed a deeper truth, which was for the most part merely intimated by the obvious sense of the churches' writings and teachings.

In the case of the Christian gnostics, then, it was not enough, as it was in that of Marcion, for opponents to insist upon the authority of a set of writings: or even, as Irenaeus did, to insist additionally upon the apostolic authority of the ordinary content of the churches' catechesis (which, in his several summaries of it, he called 'tradition', or 'the message' or 'the rule of truth'). The Valentinians, with whom Irenaeus was immediately concerned, claimed apostolic validation for their own way of taking these authorities. They laid claim to an esoteric tradition embodying that 'secret and hidden wisdom' which Paul had conveyed only 'among the perfect' (1 Cor. 2:6f.). An Irenaeus might question the credentials of this alleged tradition; and he might further insist upon the superiority of the ordinary catechesis, handed down (as he believed) in apostolically founded churches from teacher to teacher in the succession of elders or bishops, whom he plainly regarded as its authoritative bearers and legitimate interpreters (thus tacitly likening bishops to the successive heads of a philosophical school, accredited interpreters of the founder's principles). Nevertheless it was necessary to deal directly with the content of the Valentinians' secret wisdom and to raise the question whether it really did represent the 'deep' sense of the prophetic and apostolic teaching.

As early as Justin Martyr (*c.* 150), we find a general characterization of the teaching of the Valentinians and others: they all 'teach people to blaspheme the maker of the universe, and the Christ he prophesies as coming, and the God of Abraham and Isaac and Jacob' (*Dial.* 35.5). These *gravamina* Irenaeus – not to mention Origen (in his own distinctive way), Tertullian, and Hippolytus in the next generation – later took up and supplemented. The central doctrinal issue stemmed from gnostic erection of another, ultimate God, and a whole spiritual universe, above and beyond the Creator God of Genesis 1 and the visible cosmos that he brought into being. These writers further agreed in opposing denial of the identity of the God of Abraham and the prophets with the Father of Jesus Christ, and, further, denial that the true Saviour, as distinct from the Creator God's Messiah, possessed a fleshly (i.e., bodily) dimension. They went on to insist against Marcion and the gnostics that bodiliness is an essential dimension of the human self, and that salvation – i.e., resurrection – pertained to body as well as soul.

In defining these principles as representing the true sense of the established Scriptures and the emerging 'New Testament', Irenaeus had focused attention on his alternative to the Valentinian 'secret tradition'. This was, roughly speaking, the scheme or story of salvation implicit in the baptismal confession of faith and the catechesis that accompanied and interpreted it. These authorities, he thought, had invariably spoken, in a way clearly contrary to Marcionite and gnostic teaching, of one God, the Creator, and therefore of one Christ, one cosmos, and one humanity. This 'canon of the truth' he believed, as we have seen, to be apostolic as to its source, and he saw two ways of establishing this proposition. One, which we have already noted, was by appeal to apostolically founded churches (and the Roman Church in particular), in which this kerygma had been handed down in the succession of those who had inherited the apostolic teaching office, i.e., the heads of the communities. The second was by appeal to the writings of the apostles themselves; for he believed that the books currently accepted as apostolic, while often obscure, propounded, in their more frequent lucid bits, the very scheme he insisted upon, and, further, that his opponents' scheme was foreign to the Scriptures generally, i.e., that neither the prophets nor the apostles knew anything of it and in fact did not even address the questions it tried to answer.

Out of this debate, then, two authorities emerged, which were seen to interpret and support each other: the Scriptures on the one hand, and, on the other, the baptismal confession with its accompanying catechesis, which in turn was summarized in various forms and wordings of the 'rule of faith' or 'ecclesiastical canon'. A secondary, but not less crucial, authority was vested in the head of the community, the bishop, who was charged with the responsibility of preserving and conveying this truth. The 'orthodox' definition of the criteria of authentic Christianity, then, drew on informally established, but still evolving, practices and institutions that functioned within the liturgies of baptism and eucharist; and in the process no doubt assigned them a new prominence and assisted in the definition of their contours and content as vehicles of the churches' sense of their identity.

To be sure, the repudiation of central gnostic theses on the basis of these criteria of authentic Christian teaching did not by any means entail the disappearance – or even the rejection – of the gnostic sensibility as such or of a wide range of gnostic attitudes and beliefs: the identity crisis of the second century, considered from the point of view of doctrine, was focused on a very narrow, if fairly basic, range of issues, and 'orthodoxy' itself, as it came to be defined, could embrace a wide range of 'theologies'. The heart of the argument lay, as has been said, in questions about the *criteria* of catechesis; and these were discerned in two mutually interpreting sources: the accepted outline of the standard catechesis itself, and the prophetic and apostolic Scriptures. Even these norms, however, were established more by practice and by spreading custom than by any *fiat* of ecclesiastical authority. Indeed it would have been difficult in the second century to discover an ecclesiastical authority capable of uttering a *fiat*, though of a certainty folk like Irenaeus would have been glad if there had been.

Notes

1 It is for such groups that most scholars reserve the label 'Jewish-Christian'.
2 But see most recently, James Carleton Paget, 'Anti-Judaism and Early Christian Identity'.
3 Early Christians classed the whole of 'the Law and the Prophets' as *prophetic* books and also included in this category the psalms attributed to David (though not the writings taken to be Solomon's).

9

Christian teaching

FRANCES YOUNG

The literary deposit of early Christianity is most often used as source material for tracing the development of doctrine. But religion in the ancient world was not dogmatic. The Latin words *religio* and *pietas* referred to the obligations a person owed not merely to the gods but also to society, to parents and family; the Greek word εὐσέβεια meant offering respect to divinities through customary rituals. Traditional practice was far more important than belief or unbelief. This was true for Jews as well as Gentiles. In the second century Christians were accused of being atheists because they withdrew from conventional religious practices.

Dogmata or *doctrina* (both words meaning 'teaching(s)') belonged not to religion but to schools, and it was the philosophical schools which principally generated doctrine, whether about metaphysics or morals. Philosophers might debate the existence and nature of the gods, but on the whole endorsed convention.[1] Thus, apart from the Epicureans, they avoided the accusations faced by the Christians. The Christian retort was to attack false gods and claim that they worshipped and obeyed, in a rational and moral way, the one true God,[2] the divinity philosophers acknowledged but in their case with no practical consequences. Only through the Christian claim to teach the truth were religious practice, ethics and doctrine integrated and dogma made central to religion. Within the social context of the ancient world, the placing of literature at the heart of the community's activities also suggests something more like a school than a religious gathering.

Scripture and its reading

For the reading of Scripture at Christian assemblies there was, of course, Jewish precedent, and it was the Jewish Scriptures that were read throughout the second century. Justin notes the reading of the memoirs of the apostles (*I Apol.* 67), presumably meaning the Gospels, and it is likely that such reading practice paved the way for the development of a distinctively Christian canon, but this took time and was completed beyond the period with which we are presently concerned. Meanwhile the earliest Christians, who were Jews, had passed on the practice of meeting weekly or daily to read and interpret the Law and the Prophets, and of worshipping through the singing of psalms and the offering of prayers and spiritual thanksgivings. This is what Jews had long done whenever they were distanced from Jerusalem, the location of their only Temple and place of sacrifice, sacrifice being for them, as for everyone else in antiquity, the normal religious activity. Their gatherings to study Scripture, however, together with their exclusive devotion to one God and their high ethical standards, had long since earned them the admiration of Aristotle and the reputation for being philosophers. Jewish religious activity had already appeared school-like, as Christian practice would also.

For the reading of literature lay at the heart of ancient educational activities. Through study of the classics youngsters were not only given practice in construal of the text and reading aloud, not only given stylistic models to emulate in their own composition and a more profound understanding of rhetoric and communication, but were initiated into a literary culture and given moral guidance. Literature provided ethical maxims and heroes to imitate, and criticism enabled the differentiation of good and bad behaviour. The educational use of the poets by sophists had once been challenged by philosophers, notably Plato, as had popular conceptions of the gods and unbecoming tales of their dubious exploits. But Plutarch's works show how these challenges had been met.[3] The rhetorical schools focused on moral criticism, while philosophers developed allegory, and the classical literature remained the revered canon of wisdom passed down from ancient times for each generation to benefit from.

The Jews had their own distinct body of literature: even Hellenized Jews like Philo who were given to reading their Scriptures with Platonist spectacles. This literature gave them their national history, as Greek literature did for the Greeks. As the Athenians had their lawgiver, Solon, the Jews had Moses. Superficially at least Jewish books played a role in the Jewish community similar to that played by Greek books in the Hellenistic schools. Yet the veneration of the scrolls was enhanced by their ritualized reading in religious contexts, and the belief that the words were the very words of God. Increasingly religion had centred on texts which validated the exclusive behaviour of Jews in the Greco-Roman world.

Obedience to the word of God and the use of books in gatherings for worship became characteristic of Christians also. But there were subtle shifts. Paul, the Apostle to the Gentiles, had fought for the acceptance of non-Jews into the

Church without the requirement that they took on all the ethnic marks and traditional practices of the Jewish community, notably circumcision and the dietary laws. Thus the increasingly Gentile Church accepted the Scriptures without accepting the commandments taken to be specific to the Jews. Yet they did receive the Law of Moses as writings about morality within which divine instructions about ethics and lifestyle were to be discovered.

Thus the predominant use of Scripture found in early Christian texts is to provide *paraenesis*. The earliest non-canonical texts, the Apostolic Fathers, are full of collages of maxims and proverbs drawn from the Jewish Scriptures, their choice guided, it would seem, by the slant provided by traditions about the teaching of Jesus.[4] The Valentinian *Letter to Flora* makes distinctions between laws given by God, which have universal validity, notably the Ten Commandments, laws given by Moses for the Jews only, and laws intended to be symbolic of deeper and more spiritual truths. Such distinctions were far from uncommon in early Christianity, though usually without the gnostic twist of this text. Increasingly, however, Gentile Christians would read the Scriptures with the critical tools of the Hellenistic schools: they would exercise moral judgment about the literal meaning, while finding the texts full of exemplars and ethical teaching.

The finding of exemplars, or 'types', is particularly important. When the Epistle to the Hebrews catalogues lists of biblical heroes who exemplify 'faith', or *I Clement* similarly warns against jealousy or recommends obedience by presenting outstanding cases of these qualities found in the scriptural narratives (Heb. 11; *I Clem.* 4–5, 9–12), they are using the Jewish classics as Greek and Latin literature was used in the schools of the Empire. Intertextuality of this kind is already found in Hellenistic Jewish material, such as the works known as Ecclesiasticus and the Wisdom of Solomon, both of which would become part of the Septuagintal canon, that is, the Greek books received as Scripture by the Church. But in early Christianity we find another kind of 'typology' in use, namely the discerning by hindsight of prophetic *mimesis* of the Christian story in biblical narratives and even the deliberate shaping of one narrative in terms of another so as suggest prefiguration or prophecy.

Such typology, to which we will return, reflects the other shift in early Christian reading of the Scriptures, namely the increasing extent to which the Jewish Scriptures were treated as belonging to the genre of prophecy, as collections of oracles. This was hardly without Jewish precedent. Commentaries found among the Dead Sea Scrolls are good examples of the tendency to treat prophetic texts piecemeal as oracles and through exegesis to report contemporary fulfilments. The Hellenistic period was that in which apocalyptic literature flourished, and these revelatory texts frequently reworked prophetic texts to provide new prophecies of the approaching denouement in which God's plan for the cosmos would be finally achieved. Early Christian texts, canonical and non-canonical, betray the influence of apocalyptic literature and of oracular exegesis of the prophets. The argument between Jews and Christians, as Justin's *Dialogue with Trypho* shows, was not about the principle of prediction through inspired seers, but about the reference of these prophecies.[5] Establishing that reference proved the truth of the prophecies, and so provided an important apologetic argument in the wider Greco-Roman world.

For Christians it was obvious that both the traditional messianic prophecies and many other texts pointed to Christ: fulfilment was 'now' in the life of Jesus or the Church. Sometimes they could argue this by using allegory, again a technique used by others before them, sometimes from the 'literal' sense of the text. For example, in *I Apology* 32, Justin discusses Genesis 49:10:

> The sceptre shall not depart from Judah, nor a lawgiver from between his feet, until he come for whom it is reserved; and he shall be the expectation of the nations, binding the foal to the vine, washing his robe in the blood of the grape.

Justin first enquires up to whose time the Jews had a lawgiver and king of their own, and concludes that the descendents of Judah ruled their own land up to the time of Jesus Christ. He then considers the phrase 'the expectation of the nations' and points out that there were by then among all races believers who expected the return of the one crucified in Judaea, after whom the land of the Jews was taken in war. So far the argument seeks to discern the prophetic reference through taking phrases at their face value. Now, however, we find symbols of what was to happen in Christ:

> The foal of an ass stood at an entrance to a village tied to a vine, and he sent his followers to get it. When brought, he mounted and sat on it to enter Jerusalem, where was the great Temple of the Jews, later destroyed by you (= the Romans).

'Washing his robe in the blood of the grape' is taken to be a reference to the passion, his robe being believers who are washed by his blood, which is the power of God.

This example is a good one for showing how little the distinction between literal and allegorical interpretation meant to those who sought to find prophetic reference. Being an interpretation of Genesis, it is also a reminder of the fact that all the books of the Law and the Prophets were likewise treated as predictive.

But predictions were not simply found by seeking the reference which the verbal forms of the text implied. Prophecy was found in the shapes etched into the narratives: Moses holding up his arms to enable victory was a 'type', according to the *Epistle of Barnabas* (*Barn.* 12), and the consequent rout of the Amalekites became a standard precursor to the destruction of the powers of evil by Christ's arms outstretched on the cross. Luke's birth-narrative implies that Hannah prefigures Elizabeth, and Hannah's Song the Magnificat. In the hands of Melito, the Passover *haggadah* becomes the celebration of the passion, the escape from Egypt being the 'type' of human escape from the power of evil which had dominated since the sin of Adam and Eve, an escape effected through the sacrifice of Christ. Recent work has shown that there are 'inner-biblical typologies'[6] which provided precedents for this, the prophetic 'typology' alluded to earlier. The confluence of biblical and Hellenistic cultures generated Christian typology.

It is an over-simplification to say that whereas Jews treated all Scripture as belonging to the genre of 'law', Christian interpretation took the genre to be 'prophecy'. In the context of apologetic, to which much of the extant material may be said to belong, readings of the texts as prophetic were bound to be argued as 'proof' of Christian claims. No doubt this also happened in the homiletic context, as Christian identity was confirmed and consolidated. But to go back to the point with which we began, in the second century, Scripture was predominantly the source of teaching about how to live as Christians under the eye of God, the Creator of the universe. Warnings to the Jews of old became warnings to contemporary Christians (e.g. Hebrews and *II Clement*); biblical commandments and moral maxims became instructions in the Christian lifestyle.

And that is one reason why the Church may be said to demonstrate the characteristics of a school rather than a cult.

Doctrine, philosophy and apologetic

Yet it was a peculiar school. The *Epistle to Diognetus* presents its oddity:

> The difference between Christians and the rest of humanity is not a matter of nationality, or language, or customs . . . The doctrine they profess is not the invention of busy human minds and brains, nor are they like some, adherents of this or that school of human thought. They pass their lives in whatever

township – Greek or foreign – each man's lot has determined; and conform to ordinary local usage in their clothing, diet, and other habits. Nevertheless, the organization of their community does exhibit some features that are remarkable, and even surprising . . . (*Diog.* 5–7)[7]

There follow comments on the way they behave as 'resident aliens' whose citizenship is really elsewhere, on their refusal to expose infants or share wives.

They obey the prescribed laws, but in their own private lives they transcend the laws. They show love to all; and all persecute them . . .

Summing up, the claim is made that the relation of Christians to the world is that of a soul to a body. Diffused throughout, the soul holds together the body; so it is Christians who hold the world together. They have the truth imparted by a messenger from the God of all.

And that truth is the very essence of rationality, as Justin informs us:

What we possess appears greater than every human teaching because of the fact that rationality *in toto* has become the Christ who appeared for our sake, body, mind and soul. Whatever philosophers or lawgivers enunciated was wrought by partial insight into the Logos. Since they did not have knowledge of the whole of the Logos, which is Christ, they often contradicted themselves. (*II Apol.* 10)

The more one considers this statement, particularly in association with the way Justin uses words about teaching and learning elsewhere in his *Apologies*, the more it teases the normal assumptions about what doctrine is. Justin is not talking about the dogmatic propositions of Christology. He is talking about Christ being both the entire content of rational understanding and the whole vehicle of sound teaching. Christ communicates and embodies the true, which includes a corresponding way of life.

As far as Justin is concerned, Christian teaching begins with the fact that God, the Maker of all, has an eye on everything, and there will be judgment (*I Apol.* 10, 12). What 'we have received by tradition', 'have been taught, are convinced of and believe', is that God is present and sees everything, and that God accepts those who imitate the excellent qualities that are God's own. Justin names these as temperance, justice, love of humanity and whatever is characteristic of a God who is nameless, thus weaving together philosophical and biblical virtues (*I Apol.* 10). It is impossible to escape God's eye (*I Apol.* 12).

That means that how to please God is the most crucial teaching of all. Reason, the λόγος embodied in Jesus, has persuaded the Christians to abandon idolatry and worship of the daimons, and to worship the Maker of all, who needs no sacrifices, libations or incense. They have been taught to praise this God with the word of prayer and thanksgiving for all things provided, offering this as the only worthy tribute, not consuming by fire what has been supplied for sustenance, but using it as intended for themselves and for the needy. As far as God is concerned, it is adequate to offer thanksgivings for creation, health and all sorts of things, together with petitions for immortality through faith. But this shows that no sober-minded person could imagine that Christians were atheists, pleads Justin (*I Apol.* 13).

Indeed, the God Christians seek to please is the one who brought everything into being from formless matter (*I Apol.* 10), and they have been taught that God did not create the world aimlessly (*II Apol.* 4). Rather, this was done for the sake of humankind out of God's goodness, and those who show themselves worthy of God's intentions by their deeds will be delivered from corruption and suffering, to reign and have fellowship with their Creator (*I Apol.* 10). Those who are persuaded and 'believe what we teach is true and undertake to live accordingly' are regenerated by water. At birth we had no knowledge and choice, says Justin, but the new birth through baptism means that the children of necessity and ignorance become children of choice and knowledge, illuminated in their understanding (*I Apol.* 61). Justin's expressions betray the fact that he is reading the Christian tradition with the spectacles of Hellenistic philosophy and its predominant interests and questions. Early Christian apologetic opposed the fatalism of certain philosophies and of widespread practices such as astrology. Choice and free will undergirded their ethical stance, and it was not perceived to be at variance with their view of providence or prophecy. God could allow freewill while still working to effect the divine plan for the universe.

The lifestyle Christians chose was taught by Christ and followed Gospel precepts: praying for enemies, giving to the needy, living in chastity. Justin describes a woman who 'came to knowledge of the teachings of Christ' (*II Apol.* 2), and the story makes it clear that the principal effect was to turn her from sexual licence to chastity, so incurring the wrath of her unconverted husband. Adultery and second marriages may have been prime sins, but Christ called sinners to repentance. Patience, freedom from anger, turning the other cheek, refusal to swear, and rendering to Caesar the things that are Caesar's: these were what Christ taught (*I Apol.* 15, 16–17).

Now Justin's use of the language of teaching and learning shows how much he teaches the teachings received from Christ as a philosophy. Like contemporary Stoics and Cynics, he places manner of life at the heart of everything, and what metaphysical interest there is provides warrants for the way of life taught. His understanding of creation (out of formless matter rather than nothing) is closer to Platonism than the Christian doctrine would become. It is, of course, possible to pick out passages from which may be deduced Justin's 'doctrines' in the later sense of Christian dogmatics: Justin has a Christology, partly implicit, occasionally explicit, and also views about God which from time to time slip out for one reason or another. But the teachings that matter to him are those spelt out above.

Is this simply the result of Justin's apologetic aim? In other words, does he present Christianity as teaching a distinctive and honourable lifestyle to make a point against those who accuse Christians of atheism and immorality? One might be tempted to think so if it were not for the fact that this lack of what we have come to regard as 'dogmatic interest' and this focus on precepts for life is even more true of the earlier material found in the Apostolic Fathers, not to speak of the writings of the New Testament. From the Pastoral Letters through the writings of Clement of Rome, Ignatius and Polycarp, the all-seeing God looms as the warrant for ethical teaching revealed by Christ, the true teacher and lawgiver. Furthermore, Justin correctly represents the concern with chastity and sexual ethics in second-century Christianity. It was only as the assumptions that gave warrant to the ethics came to be contested that explicit doctrines concerning God, creation, Christology, Trinity, and so on, began to be spelt out. The struggle with the gnostics was the first such defining process.

Doctrine and hermeneutics

Doctrine in our sense, then, has to be distilled from this literature by the benefit of hindsight. The approach of most 'patristic' studies has an anachronistic flavour, at least as far as the second century is concerned. New Testament scholars have long since recognized this: the doctrine of God as Trinity is a classic case of Christian truth being deduced from texts of Scripture through a process of debate and then becoming the hermeneutical key to interpretation; the doctrine is not obviously there in the New Testament, let alone in the writings which became the Christian Old Testament, but all these texts were later taken to bear witness to it. What is being suggested here is that second-century Christian material is in the same case.

It is all too easy to read second-century texts in the light of later concerns, to see them as part of the process of doctrinal development, finding later doctrines embryonically present. Doubtless such an approach has a certain validity, especially in a context where different readings are legitimated (see below chapter 10). But such reading by hindsight has not yet been adequately challenged by historico-critical analysis. Helped by sociological approaches we have already set the whole idea of 'doctrine' in a different context. Should we not begin by attempting to read the texts in terms of their world rather than as immature steps on the way to something more perfect?

Even if we do attempt this, some 'doctrine' in our sense will emerge. For, as we have seen, a particular understanding of the world and humanity as God's creatures validates and undergirds the explicit, predominantly ethical, teaching. What we find articulated will be, on the one hand, features that are distinctive compared with rival accounts and, on the other, points which become contested within the set of common assumptions made by most of the early Christians. So it turns out that by far the most important doctrinal issue in second-century texts is the issue of creation.

It is often assumed that the doctrine of creation out of nothing was simply inherited from Jewish tradition. But it would seem that that assumption rests on a combination of unexamined presuppositions and superficial reading of the textual evidence.[8] It has already been noted above, but without comment, that Justin wrote of the one who brought everything into being 'from formless matter'; clearly he read the 'chaos' of Genesis in terms of that Platonic notion, as he could not have done if the doctrine of creation out of nothing had been clearly established prior to Justin's time. Philo seems to have accepted the same Platonic notion, while speaking of the creation of all that exists out of the non-existent. For without form nothing specific did exist; the language of 'non-being' was distinctly ambiguous in Greek, and would continue to be so. The gnostic Basilides spoke of the non-existent God creating a non-existent world out of the non-existent (Hippolytus, *Haer.* 7.20–1), but he hardly meant there was nothing but absolute nothingness. Rather, God's 'non-existence' was a way of speaking about infinity, formlessness and incomprehensibility. It was only in the face of challenges from Hellenistic philosophy and gnosticism that the doctrine of creation out of nothing, meaning out of absolute nothingness, was forged.

It would be Tertullian (see Part II) who would rehearse the arguments for adopting *ex nihilo*: God cannot have created out of the divine self, or everything would be God; God cannot have created out of pre-existent matter because that would mean two eternal beings, or two gods; so the only possible conclusion is that God created out of nothing (*Adversus Hermogenem*). This is a retrospective summary of the options available in the second century to those who wished to claim belief, as Christians did, in One God Creator of All.

For what Christians did believe they had inherited from the Jews and found attested in Scripture was the truth that there is One God, and that that sovereign God is Lord over the universe he created. This was, as we have seen, the lens through which the world, the Scriptures and ethical obligations were focused; in other words, it was the hermeneutical key for second-century Christians. As in the case of Jews, they were distinguished from others by this view of the way things are and the lifestyle it validated. But it was this that had been challenged among second-century believers by Marcion and the gnostics. Its defence had to clarify what was meant. If the second alternative entertained by Tertullian was the view of Platonist Christians like Justin and Hermogenes, the first was typified by gnostic emanations. Yet the gnostics, along with Marcion, had challenged the unity of God; so Tertullian's argument implies their inconsistency. Tertullian therefore reflects the Christian response to challenges on more than one front. His position had been anticipated by other second-century apologists, such as Tatian and Theophilus, who argued that God was greater than any human craftsman precisely in not needing wood or stone or any other material from which to make things; divine power and sovereignty are evident in creation out of nothing (*Graec.* 4–5; *Autol.* 1.4; 2.4, 10, 13).

'One God, the Creator of everything out of nothing' could be said to be the first Christian doctrine to be firmly established. As long as that was contested, other things which would later give cause for concern and so require more precise definition would remain as unquestioned traditions and assumptions. There was no Christological problem until the incompatibility of that first doctrine with traditions about Christ caused a sufficiently uncomfortable cognitive dissonance for puzzled believers, whether spontaneously or through hostile inquiries such as those of Celsus. It is a good question why the earliest Christians did not find their increasing veneration of Christ inconsistent with the monotheism by which they set such store, as had Jews before them.

Indeed, the earliest Christians were Jews. The proclamation of one God and one Lord was the work of Paul, once Saul, the Jewish Pharisee. Why did Paul not perceive a problem? As far as the New Testament documents are concerned there has been great energy expended in tracing the precedents for the names, titles and roles attributed to Jesus Christ. Some, such as prophet or Messiah, even Son of God, implied no more and no less than God's predestined servant. Others suggested angelic origin. For despite, or in some cases because of, its exclusive monotheism and its adherence to a nameless and transcendent God, the spectrum of contemporary Jewish belief in angels, mediators and forms of divine appearances was wide. It has been plausibly suggested that what Paul saw on the Damascus road was analogous to the visions of Jewish mystics,[9] and he identified the manifest human form of God revealed to seers with the risen Christ. A number of New Testament passages pick up previous speculations about God's Wisdom or Word being immanent in the universe, in the Torah, in prophets and wise men, and suggest this was supremely embodied in Jesus Christ. Nowhere do we find speculations that suggest Jesus was or had anything to do with a God other than the God of Abraham, Isaac and Jacob. Rather, it is the one God of all creation who is at work in Jesus Christ, whose coming is the culmination of the Creator's plan for the human race. There was no need to provide rationalization or explanation.

One crucial second-century challenge was the differentiation between the Father of Jesus Christ and the Creator God offered by Marcion and the gnostics; the other was the tendency to protect the divine Christ from contamination with the realities of human flesh. Perhaps it was preoccupation with these issues that obscured the problem for monotheism of claiming divinity for Christ. The apologists developed the notion of Jesus being the embodiment of God's Word, utilizing Stoic notions of the immanent, cosmic *logos* to provide an intellectual framework, as Philo had done before. Unlike the Stoics but like the Jew Philo they affirmed a God transcendent and unknowable, but since this God was the source of all, and God's wisdom pervades all creation, and since all human wisdom, rationality and knowledge depend upon this immanent divine *logos* within the human mind, no great problem was perceived in conceiving of this *logos* as being God's own Mind at work in creation and incarnation, fulfilling God's purposes. We have seen such teaching expounded by Justin. It is found in others such as Tatian and Theophilus. It explains things to their audiences in recognizable terms, and shows no sign of perceiving any threat to the monotheism proclaimed elsewhere in the same texts.

The distinction between the human and the divine was in any case blurred in Greek thinking, whether philosophical or mythological. Myths of deified heroes encouraged the Euhemeran view of religion, that is, the theory that the gods were simply great men of the past who had come to be venerated as gods, an idea borrowed from the philosophers and exploited to the full by the apologists in their attacks upon traditional religion. The conventional apotheosis of the emperor confirmed the idea and reinforced its openness to ridicule. More difficult to resist, however, were assumptions about the eternity of the soul and its kinship to the divine. A clear distinction between Creator and creatures would not emerge before the Arian controversy of the fourth century. Christ as the embodiment of God's wisdom immanent in creation, and especially in the souls of the righteous, could be easily accepted in Christian circles without the threat to monotheism being perceived, while an opponent like Celsus could quickly discern the similarity between Euhemeran apotheosis and the divinization of Jesus. Christology becomes explicit as Christian claims about Christ are contested, and therefore specifically in the following century.

It is sometimes said that second-century theology was binitarian, and that there was no clear distinction between the pre-existent *Logos* and the Spirit; indeed, *Logos*-theology really leaves no room for the Spirit. What has been said already may put a slightly different complexion on this. My contention would be that the term binitarian is no more appropriate than trinitarian. Second-century Christianity was fundamentally monotheist but, like contemporary Judaism, took seriously the immanent activity of God in the world through a variety of agencies. Christian apologists were most anxious to give some kind of account of this activity in and through the person of Jesus Christ, and they used the concepts of *Logos* and Wisdom to accomplish this. But second-century Christian authors also spoke of the Holy Spirit, particularly as inspiring the prophecies which bore witness to Christ, but also as the agent of sanctification in baptism and of continuing prophetic activity in the Church. The fact that there was no very clear distinction between such immanent divine activities and the functions of angels should hardly surprise us. Nor should the variety of derivative divine beings in the gnostic forms of Christianity. All are of a piece. And yet, in those texts which later orthodoxy transmitted, there is a kind of hierarchy which sets apart the *Logos* and the Spirit. It is not altogether surprising to see Irenaeus refer to these as the two hands of God (*AH* 6.1.3; vi.1).

Irenaeus is usually treated as the first great Christian theologian. Modern interest in tracing what constitutes the original contribution of key figures to the process of doctrinal development obscures the fact that his prime concern, as of all the Fathers, was not to be innovative, but to discern and reinforce the tradition truly received from the apostles. But one thing reiterated in studies of Irenaeus is important, namely the key significance of his rehearsal of the Rule of Faith, or Canon of Truth.

Facing what he saw as distortions of the tradition in the teaching of the gnostics and Marcion, Irenaeus provided summaries of the faith which offered the hermeneutical key to the contested Scriptures (*AH* 1.10.1, 22.1; 3.4.1; *Dem.* 6). There are a number of features to be noted. The first is that these summaries never appear in precisely the same wording or form: in other words, we cannot yet speak of a creed to be memorized despite the creed-like flavour of the material. The second is that they all select much the same key elements from the Scriptures so as to indicate the beginning, middle and end of the overarching single narrative of the universe which unifies them. The third is that they describe three characters and their roles in that narrative: the one God and Creator of all; the Son of God, Jesus Christ, who was incarnate, crucified, dead, buried and resurrected, and will come again as Judge; and the Holy Spirit who inspired the prophecies of Christ. For Irenaeus, such summaries provide the yardstick against which all doctrines and readings of Scripture must be tested. The criteria for Christian doctrine, and for a Christian hermeneutic of the biblical canon, are hereby established.

To some extent, then, the matters usually treated under the heading 'dogma' do figure in second-century texts. Furthermore, the second century is important for establishing that 'doctrine' is what Christianity is about. It is not a 'new superstition', whatever observers like Tacitus may have thought. It is not 'atheism', however much it might seem so to critics. Rather, it is a way of life, taught by one who spoke with the authority of the one true God, Creator of heaven and earth. This being so it fulfils all that has gone before in Greek philosophy, as well as the inspired predictions of the Hebrew prophets, and involves a 'school-like' teaching and learning process more than religious activity as then understood. This is the context in which words for teaching (*dogma* and *doctrina*) come to represent what Christianity is.

To summarize, then, at this stage, ethics and lifestyle were as important as metaphysical or theological dogmas. The call to 'virginity'[10] figured as controversially in that society as the refusal to offer sacrifice or incense to the gods. The challenge to contemporary norms, such as the exposure of infants, was grounded in commitment to the life given by the Creator, as was the refusal of military service. Purity of heart and of body was demanded by the expectation that this God would call all to account at the final Judgment. It was therefore important to know what was the revelation of the divine will for human life. And the precondition of being able to learn what that might be and practise it was freedom of the will and the possibility of choice. Second-century texts have far more to say about these subjects than those which normally fill histories of doctrine. It is later orthodox hermeneutics that searches for the precursors of classic doctrinal definitions. What we find here are exhortations to living according to the precepts of Scripture and Jesus the Teacher, alongside narratives typologically shaped to provide prophecy and precedent, and material which intends to explain and justify the ways in which Christians differentiated themselves from both Jews and Greeks. The truth about the one God, Father of Jesus Christ, who created and oversees all, and against whose demands all will be judged, is the core of second-century Christian teaching.

Notes

1 Cicero, *De Natura Deorum*, is a classic expression of this.

2 Demonstrated in the work of the Apologists, e.g. Justin, *I Apology*; Athenagoras, *Legatio*; the *Epistle to Diognetus*; Theophilus, *Ad Autolycum*.

3 Plutarch, *Moralia*, especially *De liberis educandis* and *Quomodo adolescens poetas audire debeat*.

4 Good examples are provided by the Two Ways tradition found in *Did*. 1–6 and *Barn*. 18–20. Cf. also passages such as *I Clem*. 21–3.

5 See O. Skarsaune, *Proof from Prophecy. A Study in Justin Martyr's Proof-Text Tradition: Text-Type, Provenance, Theological Profile* and discussion in Young, *Biblical Exegesis*, 122 ff.

6 M. Fishbane, *Biblical Interpretation in Ancient Israel*.

7 ET: Maxwell Staniforth and Andrew Louth, Early Christian Writings, Penguin Classics (Harmondsworth: Penguin, 1987).

8 See G. May, *Creatio ex nihilo. The Doctrine of 'Creation out of Nothing' in Early Christian Thought*; and further discussion in F. Young, '"*Creatio ex nihilo*": a Context for the Emergence of the Christian Doctrine of Creation'.

9 A. F. Segal, *Paul the Convert*.

10 See Brown, *Body and Society*.

10

Conclusion: towards a hermeneutic of second-century texts

FRANCES YOUNG

Many of the earliest Christian texts are letters. They were addressed to specific recipients in the first or second century. Evidently twenty-first-century readers are not the addressees. We cannot read them as their first readers would. The original 'reading genre' is therefore not open to us.[1] How then are they to be read? For other reasons the same question must be asked not just of letters but of all the different types of extant material, including that which has been newly discovered.[2]

The development of historical consciousness has meant that for most of the modern period it has simply been assumed that the appropriate way to read these texts is as historical documents. Scholarship has even taken this view with respect to the canonical material. Thus all these texts have been treated as windows through which we can see into a different world, reconstruct past events, discern the evolution of ideas, give a plausible account of early Christianity which is objective. This is not, however, to approach them as 'works' in their own right, but as data, material evidence for a historical project which is other than reading the texts.

For those texts which became Scripture the postmodern period has seen some re-evaluation. Structuralism, critical theory, literary approaches and hermeneutics have all grappled with the question about present meaning and reacted against the supposedly objective attempt to determine past meaning. But this is driven by the fact that there are present readers for whom these texts matter, for whom they remain part of the Holy Bible. Are the same issues important when it comes to those texts which would appear to have no other relevance than as historical documents? Certainly it would seem that some textual deposits have no value except as 'traces' of the past. Bills and contracts have no abiding significance: the flotsam and jetsam of a past world has a fascination, whether coins, hairpins or everyday correspondence, but their interest is solely as clues to entering a dead world about which we may now feel boredom as much as passionate curiosity. The archaeologist is of course highly motivated, and that same motivation may inspire the reader of such second-century texts as we have that throw light on Christianity and its borderlands. The attempt to reconstruct has its own validity, but it is as well to be self-conscious about the consequences. The material is being exploited for ends other than those inherent in the texts themselves, or implied at the point of production. Those bills were meant to be paid, those contracts fulfilled.

Most of the texts discussed in the literary guide were meant to persuade. True, they were produced in a particular context for a particular audience, so that the question how to place them historically has a bearing on their interpretation: hence the succeeding chapters. To 'hear' these texts demands a certain imaginative placing within the world from which they came. Understanding them is enhanced by the acquisition of the skills of the 'implied reader': ability to read Greek, for example, or awareness of the then current social and intellectual assumptions about the way things are. Yet is this enough?

Texts, especially authoritative texts, create worlds as well as reflect them: for readers and institutions are formed by them. Great literature speaks across cultures and centuries: for audiences and readers respond. Maybe these texts are not great literature, and most of them did not acquire the authority of Scripture. Yet some have contributed to the formation and transmission of an authoritative reading of Scripture, and in every case their preservation implies that someone somewhere valued them. Most of them claim to offer the reader something worth having. Should we be prepared to open ourselves to the possibility of entering their world, of being persuaded or offended, appropriating or rejecting their claims? Postmodern criticism would suggest that we should at least raise the question.

Feminist readings have already challenged the influence of patriarchal texts and rehabilitated texts dismissed as apocryphal, such as the *Acts of Paul and Thecla*,[3] or rejected as heretical, such as the newly discovered gnostic literature.[4] There is a proper place for the hermeneutic of suspicion. Readers sit in judgment on texts received as authorized, while using others to create an alternative history. Heretics are given their due and their story is reclaimed from the obscurity imposed by their labelling, while women's contribution is discerned, whether in the story behind the texts or in their transmission. But this remains largely a process wedded to historical method and the use of texts as data, despite the fact that the motive of unearthing the suppressed history of women is clearly relevant to the interests of some in our contemporary world, and indeed can be used to validate the emergence of women's groups in tension with the institutionalized Church, like the gnostic or celibate groups from which these texts are thought to have emerged.

That may be one clue to the manner in which some of this material may be appropriated. It is analogous to the 'typology' so characteristic of the way early Christians read texts themselves.[5] 'Types' or models are found in the literature of the past because they provide precedents, validate current behaviour, encourage current struggles, or instance the universal human story into which we each and all fit. This approach can indeed enable a reading of these texts which is questioning but also respectful. The arguments of apologists must perforce be earthed in the context which they were addressing, yet it is worth asking whether the old apologetic traditions can still provide models, whether their dialogue and confrontation with their world can teach contemporary believers how to deal with an increasingly non-Christian environment, whether the implicit universalism of their *Logos*-theology might not provide a 'type' for dealing with a world of many faiths. Such a programme would necessitate the articulation of difference, but in the interests of tracing fundamentals and mapping parallels.

That coheres with the key 'mimetic' approach which the ancients took to literature, and therefore comes near to doing justice to their claim upon the reader. Texts were meant to 'mirror' life and to be a 'possession for ever',[6] able to teach by exemplar. But attention to ancient rhetoric may take us even further. In seeking to instil the techniques of persuasion, teachers both analysed texts and offered theories. Things can be said in a variety of different ways; the subject-matter was clothed in diction, and the choice of style, of vocabulary, of figures of speech, had to be appropriate to what was to be said if it was to carry conviction. This was not just a matter of making lies plausible, because the *logos* (that is, the discourse and its subject-matter) had to ring true. But *pistis* (belief, conviction) depended also on the *ethos* (character and lifestyle) of the speaker, as well as the audience's *pathos*, its response, its being moved by the speaker and the message to the point of acceptance. Communication theory arrives at a similar position. Author, text and reader constitute a triangle, and no hermeneutic is adequate which does not pay attention to each. The authors of these texts would in many cases have recognized that dynamic, and for us to do so would be to honour their expectations. This allows us both to articulate the differences between ourselves and authors of the second century, known or anonymous, but also to enter into a critical and dialogical reading of their texts.

This 'reading strategy' would also attend to issues raised about 'ethical reading'.[7] Such a reading requires that readers do not simply exploit texts for their own interests, refusing to examine their own presuppositions, but attempt to be open to the 'other' and to listen, acknowledging difference, recognizing that the author has something to say and endeavouring to hear that, while reserving the right of challenge and differentiation, of refusal to be taken over. Second-century texts bear the marks of the new marginalized Christian *ekklesia* forming its sense of identity by differentiating itself from others. Its claim to supersede Hellenism and be the true philosophy may seem remote from the concerns of readers now, but its claim to supersede Judaism has echoes that have reverberated down the centuries with devastating effects in this century. Texts such as the *Epistle of Barnabas* and Melito's *Homily on the Pasch* cannot be read now without some sense of offence. Yet to be true to those texts and the contexts from which they came we must also recognize the closeness of their thinking and exegesis to that of their Jewish contemporaries. These texts belong not to the culture of anti-Semitism, but to passionate quarrels between relatives. Ethical reading involves awareness of that past as well as of its dire legacy.

That example has taken us into the hermeneutical problems of specific texts, but some more focused discussion of select texts is needed to earth these hermeneutical questions, brief though it must perforce be. We will contrast a newly discovered document with texts that were passed down in the tradition and eventually canonized.

The so-called Pastoral Letters are among those which were canonized. Since the Reformation they have provided scriptural justification for the ministerial offices characteristic of differing denominations, and correspondingly different historical reconstructions of the development of ordained personnel. Thus they have been transmitted to us with authoritative status for any who claim to belong to one of the Christian churches, though with differing 'readings'. For many believers there are further major difficulties. Modern scholarship has demonstrated that it is extremely unlikely that St Paul was their author, so there appears to be a lie inherent in texts claiming to communicate truth. Furthermore, the world they recommend is hierarchical through and through, monarchical symbolism creating difficulties for a society which values democracy, and patriarchal assumptions offending readers committed to equal opportunities. Take them at face value and you are not only deceived but you perpetuate a hidebound institution, fundamentalist, Catholic or Orthodox, increasingly marginalized and rejected in the current social context. Yet these writings belong to Holy Writ.

Some readers will, of course, find this combination of circumstances intolerable and will reject the authority of these texts. Others will treat them simply as historical documents, revealing for what they show about how Paul and his teaching were transmitted to the next generation. Others, however, may wish to respect and accommodate them because of their commitment to the Christian tradition, and so will seek a hermeneutic of appropriation. To do this necessitates a recognition of difference, together with a willingness to try and discern how these texts worked in relation to the world of the past from which they emerged, and so how their stance might be played out in a very different world.

What is noticeable about the stance of these texts is the tension between assimilation to the environment within which their readers lived and differentiation from it. The texts create an alternative world which both mirrors and challenges that of the Roman Empire and of a typical household within it, but is actually the Kingdom or household of God. Their hermeneutic requires a sympathetic reading of their injunctions in terms of that world prior to a translation of the results into an equivalent stance in the different world we now inhabit. Such a programme need not be unfruitful.[8]

But before we pursue that further let us turn to the *Gospel of Truth*. Newly discovered documents naturally stimulate excitement, but the discovery of the Nag Hammadi library did more than that. It placed in a more sympathetic light forms of early Christianity that the traditional narrative, stemming from Irenaeus, dismissed as false and absurd. Historical scholarship discovered two things, first how close to 'orthodoxy' some forms of gnosticism were, secondly why gnostic ideas were attractive to early Christian believers. Historians, then, have sought to do justice to those who had been suppressed, while those struggling with the vestiges of an old authoritarianism found comfort in early Christian groups which they could identify as freethinking and feminist, and others in this postmodern pluralist world have even gathered groups of gnostic believers who have welcomed these texts into new canons and developed gnostic rituals of worship. Thus these texts have been appropriated in ideological and practical ways, though 'orthodox' scholars of early Christianity have tended to treat them with a certain suspicion while finding them historically interesting. Reading these texts has provoked different responses from readers in the current climate, and much depends on the reader's starting-point and presuppositions.

The hermeneutic of canonical texts cannot but be affected by familiarity, by the long history of accommodating and domesticating exegesis. The hermeneutic of newly discovered texts begins in a different place. Specialists are indispensable, for only they have access to the language: Coptic in the case of the *Gospel of Truth*. The implied reader is not a postmodern English-speaking internationalist. The specialist's translation, however, may make the text accessible to such a reader, despite the *aporiai*, evident where there are gaps in a text with bits missing or unclear, implicit because inbuilt decisions have had to be made by the translator about how to construe obscure passages. There are ways, then, in which it is now a different text; indeed, given that the Coptic version is not the original, the text is at third remove. The actual reader has a long journey of exploration to undertake to have any hope of approximating to the implied reader, even if we speak of the implied reader of the codex written in Coptic and concealed in the jar by Pachomian monks in the mid-fourth century, rather than the original, presumably Greek-speaking, gnostic reader of perhaps the second century. The assessment of a newly discovered text from the past can take years of scholarship, and even then it is inevitably impoverished by the absence of the liturgical context and the oral tradition that accompanied the reading of the text. The process is a reminder that the hermeneutic of canonical texts can be enhanced by a parallel process, by the discovery of their unfamiliarity, by attempting to set them in the strange world of the past from which they came, and finding the evidence wanting.

The world of the *Gospel of Truth* is indeed strange. It has been described as an 'Apocalypse of the Mind'.[9] The reader is drawn into a curious world of imaginative speculation, a world which negates the reality of everyday experience, ignores the concreteness of historical existence and offers the restoration of a fulness of mystical life which is monist, individualist and disembodied, expressible only in metaphor and allegory. This may indeed have an appeal to 'New Age' spirituality, for both handle social and political alienation by offering transcendence. It would seem surprising that a liberating hermeneutic could be based on a text such as this if that liberation is supposed to have corporate or social effect. The 'freethinking and feminist' hermeneutic depends, not upon reading the text, but on setting the text in a reconstructed social and historical world which is taken to be patriarchal, hierarchical and authoritarian: indeed, the supposed world of the Pastoral Letters.

So it might be that entering the contrasting worlds of these texts is not unlike living in the contemporary pluralist world of the early twenty-first century. Perhaps one might indulge in a certain 'typological' or exemplary reading, which makes allowances for the difference between our own social world and that from which these texts emerged while appropriating the contrasts of principle. The Pastorals seek to affirm life in the concrete world of politics and everyday existence, for the world belongs to its Creator, and has responsibility for living according to the Creator's intentions. The fact that surrounding society cannot see this and does not do it means living in tension with it, affirming its order and its role in restraining evil and criminality, even mirroring its structures in the 'household of God', while also challenging it even to the point of suffering martyrdom for refusing to deny the truth. The *Gospel of Truth* requires no such stance. It might be read as offering self-indulgent withdrawal from moral engagement, while rehearsing a nice ethic of love.

The Pastorals recognize the importance of corporateness and community, of the need for leadership and respect, for the acceptance of duties and responsibilities if a group is to function effectively, as well as the importance of not thinking too highly of oneself, of recognizing one's role and place in a larger whole and offering obedience and honour to God and those who represent God on earth. The social norms were not adequately challenged by the elements of service and of resistance to 'success'-values which seem embodied in the teaching and example of Christ; hierarchy was too easily reinforced. But one could argue that freethinking, individualism, assertion of 'rights' and 'doing one's own thing' is as much a betrayal of Christian identity as ever authoritarian hierarchies were. 'Have this mind in you, which was in Christ Jesus'. An ethical reading respects and challenges both text and reader. It may also confirm the old decision to canonize the Pastorals and not the *Gospel of Truth*.

Notes

1 See further Werner Jeanrond, *Text and Interpretation as Categories of Theological Thinking*, ET T. J. Wilson (Dublin: Gill and Macmillan, 1988).
2 For fuller discussion of the issues and methods, see Young, 'From Suspicion and Sociology'.
3 Dennis R. MacDonald, *The Legend and the Apostle: the battle for Paul in story and canon* (Philadelphia: Fortress, 1983).
4 Elaine Pagels, *The Gnostic Gospels*.
5 Young, *Biblical Exegesis*, especially chapters 7 and 10.
6 Thucydides' famous dictum, κτῆμα ἐς αἰεί.
7 Wayne Booth, *The Company We Keep* (Berkeley: University of California Press, 1988); Frances Young, 'The Pastorals and the Ethics of Reading', *JSNT* 45 (1992), 105–20.
8 See further the final chapter of Frances Young, *The Pastoral Letters*.
9 David Dawson, *Allegorical Readers and Cultural Revision in Ancient Alexandria*.

PART TWO

*

THE THIRD CENTURY

A.

*

LITERARY GUIDE

11

The Alexandrians

RONALD E. HEINE

The Alexandrian Christian literature known to us begins at the end of the second century with the works of Clement (*c.* 150–215), and his later contemporary, Origen (*c.* 185–254). What we surmise about what preceded them is based on scraps and hints. Eusebius, relating what was probably only a legend, says that Mark, the associate of Peter, took Christianity to Alexandria (*HE* 2.16.1). Apollos is the first Christian associated with the city whose name we know. He is described as learned in the Scriptures, but having a somewhat imperfect understanding of the faith (Acts 18:24–6).[1] Scholars are generally agreed that Christianity had been established in Alexandria by the middle of the first century, and that there was a strong strain of heterodoxy, or at least of diversity, there until the early third century.[2] The two famous gnostic teachers, Basilides and Valentinus, had been associated with the city in the first half of the second century.

Clement, who was probably born in Athens of pagan parents, came to Alexandria *c.* 180 on his educational pilgrimage (*Strom.* 1.1.11.1–2). There he attended the lectures of the Christian Pantaenus, and succeeded him as leader of the school.[3] In 202–3, during the persecution of Septimius Severus, he fled Alexandria, and joined his friend Alexander in either Cappadocia or Jerusalem.[4] Clement died in exile, some time before 215 (Eusebius, *HE* 6.11; 6.14.8).

Eusebius is our main source for the list of Clement's works. He knew the *Stromateis* in eight books, the *Hypotyposeis* also in eight books, the *Protrepticus* in one book, the *Paedagogus* in three, a book entitled *Who is the Rich Man Who is Saved?*, a treatise *On the Pascha*, the discourses *On Fasting*, *On Slander*, and *Exhortation to Endurance*, or *To the Recently Baptized*, and a book entitled the *Ecclesiastical Canon*, or *Against the Judaizers* (*HE* 6.13.1–3). The primary manuscript containing the *Stromateis* includes two additional works entitled *Excerpta ex Theodoto* and *Eclogae Propheticae*, which scholars also assign to Clement.[5] In 1973 M. Smith published portions of a letter attributed to Clement that he had discovered in the Mar Saba monastery in Palestine. The letter fragment, two and a half pages long, was copied on the end pages of a seventeenth-century printed volume of Ignatius' letters. It has the title, 'From the letters of the most holy Clement, the author of the *Stromateis*, to Theodore'.[6] Of the works in Eusebius' list, the *Protrepticus*, *Paedagogus*, *Stromateis*, and *Who is the Rich Man Who is Saved?* are extant, and there are enough fragments of the *Hypotyposeis* to gain an idea of its contents and manner of approach.

The only certain date connected with Clement's life and work concerns the composition of the first book of the *Stromateis*, which was written some time in the reign of Septimius Severus (AD 193–211: *Strom.* 1.21.144.1–5). A. Méhat has suggested the following possible dates for the major works: *Protrepticus c.* 195, *Paedagogus c.* 197, *Stromateis*, book 1 *c.* 198, books 2–5 *c.* 199–201, and after his departure from Alexandria, *Stromateis* books 6–7 and *Who is the Rich Man Who is Saved? c.* 203, *Eclogae Propheticae c.* 204, and *Hypotyposeis c.* 204–10.[7]

The *Stromateis* is Clement's longest and most important surviving work. Because Clement refers in the opening of the *Paedagogus* to his intention to write a trilogy consisting of *Protrepticus*, *Paedagogus* and *Didascalus*, and no work by the latter title is known, some earlier scholars considered the *Stromateis* to be the conclusion of this trilogy. This view is now rejected. No one considers the *Stromateis* to follow the two earlier works in any kind of logical sequence. Whether the present book 8 in the manuscript was the actual concluding book of the *Stromateis* is also questioned. Book 8 is much shorter than the other books of the *Stromateis*, and is a discussion of philosophical method. It treats Stoic demonstration, Aristotelian syllogisms, genera, species, categories and causes, and Platonic definitions. It is a strange and anticlimatic conclusion if it were intended to follow the discussion of the spiritual perfection of the Christian gnostic in book 7. R. P. Casey considered everything after book 7 of the *Stromateis* in the manuscript tradition, i. e., book 8, *Excerpta ex Theodoto*, and *Eclogae Propheticae*, to be notebooks of Clement which someone later attached to books 1–7 of the *Stromateis*.[8]

The *Stromateis* gives the impression of a rambling series of jottings, as the meaning of its title (*Miscellanies* or *Patchwork*) suggests.[9] Clement himself calls attention to this, and suggests that the impression of aimless rambling is intentional, and that there is a plan to his work, even a Greek literary genre that he is consciously following.[10] He speaks of it, indeed, as 'systematic' (*Strom.* 1.1.14.2). He has adopted this form, he says, to hide the truth from all but those who truly seek it, and who are worthy of it (*Strom.* 1.1.13.3; 8.1.1.3–2.2). His method, he claims, puts responsibility on the reader as well as the writer. The latter must be qualified to speak, and the former to hear (*Strom.* 1.1.5.1). The reader must exercise 'care and inventiveness' to understand the text (*Strom.* 7.18.111.3).[11]

Clement is especially concerned in the *Stromateis* with the broad subjects of the nature of God, creation, and faith. He explores these subjects, and their implications, from such perspectives as how God can be known, how Greek philosophy relates to Christian faith, how faith relates to knowledge, how a Christian should view martyrdom, whether a Christian should marry, and how one's concept of God affects such practical aspects of piety as prayer. He makes extensive use in this work, as also in *Protrepticus* and *Paedagogus*, of Greek literature, dotting his pages with quotations. On the whole, his evaluation of Greek culture is more positive than most Christians of his time, though he maintains a running critique of what he considers objectionable. He is especially fond of using Greek sources to criticize Greek views. The literature of Hellenistic Judaism, particularly that of Philo, is very important in his argumentation.[12] Clement is aware that he is addressing four different groups of people. He is making a defence of the Christian faith to the intelligent pagan (*Strom.* 7.1.1.1),[13] he wants to refute certain views of the heterodox gnostics, he wants to avoid alienating the simple believers, and he wants, above all, to appeal to educated Christians to become what he calls 'true gnostics'.[14]

The *Hypotyposeis* appears to have been Clement's most extensive exegetical work. Eusebius describes it as containing brief explanations of all the canonical Scriptures, including even those Eusebius classed as disputed, namely Jude and the other catholic epistles, the *Epistle of Barnabas*, and the *Apocalypse of Peter* (*HE* 6.14.1). Photius asserts that it covered both the old and new Scriptures, but this hardly seems possible in light of the fragments that remain (*Bibl. Cod.* 109). First, all the fragments are concerned with the New Testament, and secondly, the fragments that are assigned to a specific book in the sources begin with book 4, and in these fragments of book 4 Clement is already discussing 1 and 2 Corinthians. We know, from some of the fragments in Eusebius which are not ascribed to any particular book, that he discussed the Gospels. These must have preceded book 4. If, therefore, the work included the Old Testament as well, it must have treated only a few selected books of it as well as only selected verses from the books. Cassiodorus has preserved a Latin translation of brief comments on 1 Peter, Jude, and 1 and 2 John with the title, 'Adumbrations of Clement of Alexandria on the Canonical Epistles'. These appear to have come from the *Hypotyposeis*, and demonstrate that the work had the form of what we know as scholia.

Photius claimed that the work contained heterodox as well as correct doctrine. He asserted that, among other things, Clement taught that matter is eternal, that the Son is a creature, that there is metempsychosis, that there were many worlds before Adam, that Eve was derived from Adam in a shameful way, and that the Word became flesh only in appearance. Nothing of this nature has survived in the fragments.

The *Protrepticus* and *Paedagogus* may be considered together as the second was composed as the complement to the former. The *Protrepticus*, or *Hortatory Address*, was a common literary genre which encouraged one to the study of philosophy. Both Aristotle and Cicero had composed such addresses. Clement defines the role of his *Protrepticus* in the opening of the *Paedagogus*. It is to persuade cultivated unbelievers to salvation. It begins with a critique of Greek mythology as expressed in literature, religion, and the visual arts, and culminates with a presentation of the divine Word revealed in the prophetic Scriptures.[15] The *Paedagogus* is, then, intended to take charge of the new convert and to train his soul to the virtuous life (*Paed.* 1.1.4). It is especially for the role of the ancient *paedagogus* in forming the moral character of the child that Clement chooses this title. He carefully distinguishes the *paedagogus* from the teacher, or *didascalus*. The latter provided intellectual instruction for the child. The first book of the *Paedagogus* is concerned to identify the 'children' of whom the *paedagogus* has charge, the *paedagogus* who leads them, and the means he uses to form Christian character. The other two books treat a variety of themes related to morality and etiquette,[16] with the discussion sometimes degenerating to such trivial topics as the style and firmness appropriate in one's bed.

The treatise *Who is the Rich Man Who is Saved?* is an exegetical discourse which discusses the problem of Mark 10:17–31. The renunciation demanded in the text should not be understood, Clement asserts, of material possessions, but of the human passions. The wealth that should be sought, on the other hand, is the wealth of virtue. Clement doubts that the passions can be eradicated all at once, but thinks they must be corrected over a period of time with the help of God, the brethren, and genuine repentance. This leads him to affirm the efficacy of post-baptismal repentance, which he makes quite explicit in his closing story of the Apostle John and the repentant convert who had become a thief.

The *Excerpta ex Theodoto* and *Eclogae Propheticae* appear to be notebooks, probably not intended for publication, at least in their present form. The former contains excerpts from a Valentinian gnostic named Theodotus with some critical comments from Clement, and the latter are excerpts from the Scriptures with occasional comments. Neither contribute much to our understanding of Clement.

The authenticity of the Mar Saba letter is still debated.[17] The letter begins by complementing Theodore on silencing the teachings of the Carpocratians. It then relates that Mark came to Alexandria from Rome and there wrote a more spiritual gospel, which he entrusted to the church in Alexandria on his death. The Carpocratians had obtained access to this gospel and corrupted it. The letter then proceeds to cite a few lines from this gospel to refute the corruptions of the Carpocratians. The focus of attention in studies of the letter has been on the alleged 'secret gospel' of Mark. If genuine, however, the letter also pushes back the tradition related by Eusebius connecting Mark with Alexandria by a century.

The relationship between Clement and Origen is difficult to ascertain. Eusebius, who provides most of our information concerning Origen's life (*HE* 6),[18] asserts that he had been a student in Clement's school at Alexandria, and implies, at least, that he succeeded Clement as head of the school. Origen, however, never refers to Clement in any of his surviving works, and Bardy has argued, against Eusebius, that there was no continuity between the school later headed by Origen in Alexandria and that presided over by Pantaenus and Clement.[19] In contrast to Clement, Origen appears to have been an Alexandrian by birth, and a child of Christian parents. He was thoroughly educated in the Scriptures from his childhood, but he also received the standard classical education of a young man of that time, for after the martyrdom of his father he was able to support himself by teaching as a grammaticus. And when he decided to turn exclusively to the teaching of sacred literature, he was able again to support himself modestly from the proceeds of selling his classical library (*HE* 6.2.15; 6.3.8–9).[20]

Origen's literary career falls into three periods, separated by two major interruptions. He began his writing in Alexandria at the request of Ambrose whom he had converted from Valentinianism. The latter became Origen's patron and furnished him with a corps of stenographers who recorded his words, first, probably, as he lectured, and later, in Caesarea, also as he preached.[21] He composed a commentary on the first twenty-five psalms in Alexandria, a commentary on Lamentations in five books, the first eight books of his *Commentary on Genesis*, a treatise *On the Resurrection* in two books, another entitled *Stromateis* in ten books, the *On First Principles* in four books, the first five books of his *Commentary on John*, and began, at least, work on his textual study of the Septuagint called the Hexapla (*HE* 6.23–4).[22] We can only surmise the date that Origen began writing. It must have been in the early years of the reign of

Alexander Severus (AD 222–35), for Eusebius places it immediately after Origen's visit to Antioch at the invitation of the emperor's mother (*HE* 6.21.3–4; 23.1). Eusebius is precise, however, about the end of Origen's Alexandrian period. He left in the tenth year of Alexander Severus, i.e. 232 (*HE* 6.26),[23] and went to Caesarea in Palestine where his friend Theoctistus was bishop. His departure came as the culmination of a long and bitter conflict with Demetrius, bishop of Alexandria (*Io.* 6.1–12).

Approximately three years after his arrival in Caesarea Origen's life as a scholar was again interrupted by the persecution of Maximinus (AD 235–8). He took refuge in Caesarea in Cappadocia where he was kept by the virgin Juliana.[24] In the short period before the persecution he resumed work on the *Commentary on John*, composing at least books 6–10, wrote the treatise *On Prayer* and, some time in the first half of the year 235, composed his *Exhortation to Martyrdom.*[25]

Origen resumed his life in Caesarea of Palestine after the death of Maximinus. He founded a school where Gregory Thaumaturgus, later bishop of Pontus, was one of the students. He preached the majority of his homilies in the Church of Caesarea in this period,[26] and wrote the bulk of his treatises. He completed the *Commentary on John* in thirty-two books probably in 241–2,[27] and wrote his *Commentary on Isaiah*, of which Eusebius knew thirty books. He began a commentary on Ezekiel in Caesarea, and finished its twenty-five books on a visit to Athens, where he also wrote the first five books of his *Commentary on the Song of Songs*. He finished the latter in five additional books composed after his return to Caesarea (*HE* 6.32.1–2). He composed another, larger commentary on the Psalter, reaching at least to Psalm 78, and a briefer *Scholia on the whole Psalter*. He carried on an extensive correspondence. Eusebius knew of a collection of more than a hundred letters, among which were letters to Fabian, bishop of Rome, the Emperor Philip, and the emperor's wife (*HE* 6.36.3–4). Letters to his student Gregory and to Africanus survive, and portions of a letter to some friends at Alexandria. Some time in this period Origen composed a commentary on Romans in fifteen books, a treatise *On the Pascha* in at least two books, and a *Dialogue with Heraclides*. The *Commentary on Matthew* in twenty-five books, the *Commentary on the Twelve Prophets* also in twenty-five books, and the treatise *Against Celsus* in eight books were works of Origen's final years (*HE* 6.36.1–2).

Origen was arrested and tortured in the persecution of Decius. Decius was killed in battle in June 251. Origen was released and died, probably, in 254.[28]

What survives of Origen's works exists in three forms. First, a few of the works survive either complete or in large portion in Greek manuscripts.

Second, a number of his works have been preserved in Latin translations done by Rufinus, Jerome, and an unknown translator. Finally, a large number of fragmentary excerpts are quoted in the works of others, both friends and enemies of Origen, and especially in the later commentary genre known as catenae. The following discussion treats only the works in the first two categories. These works will be treated in the three traditional groups of commentaries, homilies, and works not primarily exegetical. This is an artificial division, for biblical exegesis lies at the heart of all of Origen's works, and they are also all equally concerned with theology. Just as one did philosophy in this period either by writing commentaries on the works of the classical philosophers, or by treating particular themes exegetically,[29] so Origen did theology in relation to the Bible.

Of Origen's commentaries, three on New Testament books survive in large measure, and one on a book of the Old Testament. I treat them in their chronological order. Nine of the thirty-two books of the *Commentary on John* have been preserved in Greek.[30] Book 19 lacks several pages at both the beginning and end, book 10 lacks, perhaps, the first page, and books 2 and 6 may also lack something at the end. The thirty-two books reached only John 13:33, but there is no evidence that Origen wrote more than this on the Gospel. The commentary begins with a long general introduction (*Io.* 1.1–89) which has certain similarities to introductions in philosophical commentaries.[31] He then devotes a lengthy discussion to the first two verses of John (*Io.* 1.90–2.69) to refute the monarchian understanding of God.[32] In discussing John 1:3, Origen introduces the views of the Valentinian Heracleon (*Io.* 2.100–4), who may have written a commentary on the Gospel. Although Origen cites and attempts to refute Heracleon's views at several points in the commentary, it is too much to say that his reason for writing the commentary was to refute Heracleon's exegesis of John.[33] His purpose in writing was, as he himself says at the conclusion of the introduction, 'to explain the mystical meaning stored up like a treasure in the words' of the Gospel (*Io.* 1.89).[34]

The *Commentary on the Song of Songs*, consisting originally of ten books, has been partially preserved in a Latin translation of Rufinus. The introduction, books 1–3, and the beginning of the fourth book are extant, covering Song of Songs 1:1–2:15. Besides not including the later books of the commentary, Rufinus also omitted all of Origen's more technical discussions of the text. Jerome, in the prologue to his translations of Origen's homilies on the Song of Songs, noted that in the commentary, in addition to commenting on the text of the Septuagint, Origen had also commented on the versions of Aquila, Symmachus, Theodotion, and another version he had found near Actium. No reference to any of these versions can be found in the translation of Rufinus. The introduction, like that to the *Commentary on John*, has similarities with those of philosophical commentaries.[35] Origen treats the Song as a drama which he interprets schematically in relation to its literal meaning, its meaning in relation to the Church, and finally its meaning concerning the individual soul. Some have seen elements of a Christian-Jewish polemic reflected in the exposition of the early verses.[36]

The *Commentary on Romans* consisted of fifteen books. When Rufinus translated the commentary in the early fifth century he noted in his preface that some of the books were lost, and doubted his ability to 'supply' what was missing and to 'restore' the work's continuity. He also noted his intention to 'abbreviate' the work. Rufinus' abbreviated Latin version in ten books is extant.[37] The papyri found at Tura in 1941 contain Greek excerpts from books 5–6 of the commentary treating Romans 3:5–5:7, corresponding to books 3–4 of Rufinus' translation.[38] The comparison of these fragments with Rufinus' translation led to a generally positive evaluation of Rufinus' work.[39] Chadwick suggested that book 11 (corresponding to Rufinus' book 7) on Romans 9:1ff. was not available to Rufinus, and that he drew the discussion of the hardening of Pharaoh's heart from that in book 3 of *On First Principles* and supplied the remainder of the exegesis himself.[40] Hammond Bammel has argued that book 14, treating Romans 12–14, also was not available to Rufinus, and that he drew his exegesis for this section from the now lost *Stromateis* of Origen.[41]

Books 10–17 of the *Commentary on Matthew* are extant in Greek. They treat Matthew 13:36–22:33. In addition, there is a Latin translation of the commentary by an unknown translator which covers Matthew 16:13–27:66.[42] P. Gorday has noted that the works of Origen's Caesarean period are less speculative than those of his Alexandrian period, and that they are more concerned with practical aspects of Christian piety and the relationship between Christianity and Judaism.[43] R. Girod thinks that controversy between Christians and Jews was a primary reason for the composition of the *Commentary on Matthew*.[44] H. J. Vogt considers the commentary to contain Origen's final word on many questions, either confirming or correcting his earlier opinions.[45]

There are 205, and possibly 279, homilies of Origen that are extant either in Greek or in Latin translations.[46] Of these, there are twenty on Jeremiah and one on 1 Samuel extant in Greek, sixteen on Genesis, thirteen on Exodus, sixteen on Leviticus, twenty-eight on Numbers, twenty-six on Joshua, nine on Judges, nine on Psalms 36–8, and one on 1 Samuel[47] in Rufinus' Latin translation, and in the Latin translation of Jerome, two homilies on the Song of Songs, nine on Isaiah, fourteen on Jeremiah (of which twelve correspond to homilies preserved in Greek), fourteen on Ezekiel, thirty-nine on Luke, and possibly seventy-four on the Psalms.[48]

These homilies were preached in the church at Caesarea, with the exception of the two on 1 Samuel which were delivered in Jerusalem. Nautin has argued convincingly that they were all preached in a three-year liturgical cycle some time between 238 and 244,[49] preceding the *Commentary on the Song of Songs*, where Origen refers to homilies on Judges, Exodus, Numbers, and a work on Leviticus. The homilies are concerned with scriptural exposition intended 'to edify the Church'.[50] They discuss the scriptural reading for the particular day.[51] This reading sometimes replaces the traditional prologue of the homily. The exposition itself follows the progression of the biblical text. The epilogue is usually short, and concludes with a doxology drawn from 1 Peter 4:11 or Revelation 1:6.[52]

The *On First Principles*, written at Alexandria, is the earliest of the works of Origen that are not primarily exegetical. It exists in its entirety in Rufinus' Latin translation of 397. Rufinus was convinced, as he states in his preface, that the work had been interpolated by heretics. He, therefore, either omitted objectionable passages concerning the Trinity, or corrected them on the basis of what he found in Origen's other writings. Besides Rufinus' translation there is a Greek text for books 3.1 and 4.1–3 preserved in the book of Origen's excerpts called the *Philocalia* compiled by the Cappadocian Fathers in the fourth century.

The study of the *On First Principles*, which has occupied centre stage of Origen studies since the fourth century, has been advanced significantly in the last two decades. M. Harl and her students, following some seminal observations of B. Steidle,[53] have established the literary genre and structure of the treatise. The treatise belongs to the genre represented by the *On the Gods and the World* of Sallustius, and treats the subject that was called physics, i.e., the relation of God to the created world. Such works contained two parts. The first summarized the author's teaching on these subjects, and the second investigated details related to the larger issues in the first part. Origen expanded this basic format by adding a preface in which he set forth the rule of faith, and a concluding summary. Applied to the *On First Principles*, this schema yields the following structure: Preface, Part One (*Princ.* 1.1–2.3), Part Two (*Prin.* 2.4–4.3), and Summary (*Prin.* 4.4).[54]

The treatise *On Prayer*, preserved entire in Greek, and written after Origen's move to Caesarea but before the persecution of Maximinus, was occasioned by a letter from his friends Ambrose and Tatiana (*Or.* 2.1) setting forth certain objections that had been raised against prayer (*Or.* 5.6). Origen begins by answering these objections, and then discusses prayer in general, before providing a lengthy commentary on the Lord's Prayer (*Or.* 18–30). The work concludes with a discussion of subjects connected with the practice of prayer such as the place of prayer, the direction to face when praying, and what subjects are appropriate for prayer.[55]

The *Exhortation to Martyrdom*, also preserved entire in Greek, was written some time after the beginning of the persecution of Maximinus in the first half of 235.[56] Origen's friend Ambrose and a presbyter at Caesarea named Protoctetus had been imprisoned. Origen wrote his treatise in praise of martyrdom to encourage his friends to faithfulness and courage in their imprisonment. The treatise is significant because it not only provides information concerning the Church's teaching on martyrdom, but also reveals some of the disagreement on the subject which the persecution elicited. It is also significant historically as a major document deriving from the time of the persecution.

The papyri discovered at Tura in 1941 contained the Greek texts of two previously unknown works of Origen. Neither work can be dated precisely, though both were probably written after the persecution of Maximinus. The one, a treatise *On the Pascha* in two books,[57] might also be listed among the commentaries, or even, perhaps, the homilies. It is a spiritual exegesis of Exodus 12, concerned specifically with the topic of the Passover. Origen begins by showing that, contrary to popular understanding among Christians, the term Pascha has no connection with the suffering of the Saviour, but is derived from a Hebrew word meaning 'passage'. Exodus 12 then becomes the story of the celebration of the true 'passage out of Egypt' in the Christian rebirth (4.16–35).

The other previously unknown text discovered at Tura has the title, *Dialogue of Origen with Heraclides and the Bishops with him concerning the Father and the Son and the Soul.*[58] It purports to be the record of a synod examining the orthodoxy of a certain Bishop Heraclides. The synod cannot be dated, though it seems more likely to have occurred in Origen's later period at Caesarea. Heraclides appears to have held some form of monarchian theology, for Origen is at pains to elicit a confession from him that the Church confesses two Gods who are a unity. After accomplishing this, and expounding this doctrine, Origen then responds to questions addressed to himself on the resurrection, the soul, and the soul's immortality. The latter issue, put forward as an assertion of what Origen taught by a bishop named Demetrius, put Origen on the defensive, and seems to have flustered him a bit. His response is little more than pettifoggery.

The three preserved letters all stem from the Caesarean period of Origen's life. One, partly preserved in the Latin translation of Rufinus, is addressed to friends in Alexandria.[59] In this letter Origen asserts that he never taught that the devil would be saved, and cites two cases in which either his text or his teaching had been altered by someone, and then circulated as his work. The letter to Gregory, preserved in Greek in the fourth-century *Philocalia*, urges Gregory, a former student in Caesarea, to 'spoil the Egyptians', i.e., to appropriate everything in Greek philosophy that can be applied profitably to the study of the Scriptures. The letter of Africanus to Origen and Origen's reply are both extant in Greek.[60] N. de Lange, the most recent editor of the letters, places the correspondence in the same time period as the composition of the *Commentary on Matthew*.[61] Origen's letter was written from Nicomedia, where he was staying with the family of his friend Ambrose. Ambrose composed the letter as Origen dictated (*Afric.* 21, 24). Africanus had pointed out to Origen that the latter had erred in treating the story of Susanna as genuine, and that it was a later Greek addition to the Hebrew story of Daniel. Origen's letter is a lengthy rebuttal of Africanus' argument, and is a good example of erudition supporting an error.

Against Celsus, preserved complete in Greek, was Origen's last treatise.[62] Ambrose had requested that Origen provide an answer to a book entitled *The True Doctrine* which attacked Christianity, and which had been written some time in the second century by an unknown Middle Platonic philosopher named Celsus. Celsus was relatively well informed about Christianity and had read parts of the Bible and some Christian literature. He attacked the Church's basic doctrines concerning Christ, God, and man, ridiculed the low status of the people the Church attracted, and complained of the detrimental effect of Christianity on the state because Christians would neither participate in the common political affairs, nor serve in the military. In his reply Origen drew freely on the Greek philosophers and poets as well as the Bible to provide a rational basis for holding the Christian faith. The work is a magisterial defence of the faith against 'its cultured despisers'.

Notes

1 Codex D adds that he had been instructed in the word of the Lord in his homeland.

2 See C. W. Griggs, *Early Egyptian Christianity*, 13–78; Bauer, *Orthodoxy and Heresy*, 44–60; and somewhat differently understood, Roberts, *Manuscript, Society and Belief*.

3 Eusebius, *HE* 6.13.2; 6.6.1. On the school of Alexandria see G. Bardy, 'Aux origines de l'école d'Alexandrie'; M. Hornschuh, 'Das Leben des Origenes und die Entstehung der alexandrinischen Schule'; Dawson, *Allegorical Readers*, who follows Bardy against Eusebius; and A. van den Hoek, 'How Alexandrian was Clement of Alexandria? Reflections on Clement and his Alexandrian Background', who

gives more credence to Eusebius; and C. Scholten, 'Die alexandrinische Katechetenschule', *JAC* 38 (1995), 16–37.

4 P. Nautin, *Lettres et écrivains chrétiens des IIe et IIIe siècles*, 138–41, has argued that Clement's exile was in Jerusalem, and not Cappadocia as is usually assumed.

5 For other works known only from the appearance of their titles in Clement or elsewhere, see J. Ferguson, *Clement of Alexandria*, 179. The fragments of lost works which can be ascribed with reasonable certainty to Clement are collected in O. Stählin, GCS 17 (1909), 195–230.

6 M. Smith, *The Secret Gospel*; M. Smith, *Clement of Alexandria and a Secret Gospel of Mark*.

7 A. Méhat, *Étude sur les 'Stromates' de Clément d'Alexandrie*, 54.

8 R. P. Casey, *The Excerpta ex Theodoto of Clement of Alexandria*, 3–4.

9 H. Chadwick, *Early Christian Thought and the Classical Tradition*, 31; Dawson, *Allegorical Readers*, 183.

10 E.g. *Strom.* 1.1.13.1–14.3; 4.2.4.1–7.8; 7.18.111.1–3. See the studies of Méhat, *Étude*, and L. Roberts, 'The Literary Form of the *Stromateis*', 211–22.

11 Roberts, 'Literary Form', 213.

12 See A. van den Hoek, *Clement of Alexandria and His Use of Philo in the Stromateis*.

13 See J. Bernard, *Die apologetische Methode bei Klemens von Alexandria*.

14 See Chadwick, *Early Christian Thought*, 52–4.

15 See T. Halton, 'Clement's Lyre: A Broken String, a New Song'.

16 On the relation of the two see B. Leyerle, 'Clement of Alexandria on the Importance of Table Etiquette'.

17 See M. Smith, 'Clement of Alexandria and Secret Mark: The Score at the End of the First Decade'; Ferguson, *Clement of Alexandria*, 188–9; E. Osborn, 'Clement of Alexandria: A Review of Research, 1958–82'; A. H. Criddle, 'On the Mar Saba Letter Attributed to Clement of Alexandria'.

18 But see the criticisms of Eusebius in P. Nautin, *Origène: sa vie et son oeuvre*, R. Grant, *Eusebius as Church Historian*, and the summary of these and other criticisms in R. Heine, *Origen: Homilies on Genesis and Exodus*, 2–7.

19 See the works cited in note 3 above. Alexander, bishop of Jerusalem, in a letter to Origen appears to indicate that Clement was one of those through whom he had come to know Origen (Eusebius, *HE* 6.14.8–9).

20 See B. Neuschäfer, *Origenes als Philologe*.

21 See R. Heine, 'Three Allusions to Book 20 of Origen's *Commentary on John* in Gregory Thaumaturgus's *Panegyric to Origen*'.

22 Origen's works are far too numerous to list in their entirety in this discussion. I list only the works of which major portions are extant, with a few of the more important lost works mentioned by Eusebius. Eusebius refers to a complete catalogue of Origen's works which he included in his (now lost) life of Pamphilus (*HE* 6.32.3). Jerome, on the basis of this catalogue, says there were about 2,000 works (*Ruf.* 2.22), and in his *Ep.* 33 lists 786 titles. Jerome's list omits some of Origen's works which we possess.

23 See R. Heine, *Origen: Commentary on the Gospel according to John, Books 13–32*, 4, note 12.
24 See ibid., 5–13, and, for a different view, H. Crouzel, 'Origène s'est-il en Cappadoce pendant la persécution de Maximin le Thrace?'
25 Heine, *Origen: Comm. Jn. 13–32*, 11–12, 14–15.
26 Nautin, *Origène*, 389–409.
27 Heine, *Origen: Comm. Jn. 13–32*, 15–18.
28 There is another tradition that puts Origen's death in 250–1, and makes him a martyr. See R. Grant, 'Eusebius and His Lives of Origen'.
29 Cf., for example, the works of Alexander of Aphrodisias.
30 Books 1, 2, 6, 10, 13, 19, 20, 28 and 32, with brief fragments of books 4 and 5.
31 See R. Heine, 'The Introduction to Origen's Commentary on John Compared with the Introductions to the Ancient Philosophical Commentaries on Aristotle'.
32 R. Heine, 'Stoic Logic as Handmaid to Exegesis and Theology in Origen's Commentary on the Gospel of John'; A. Orbe, 'Origenes y los Monarquianos'.
33 Heracleon is not mentioned in books 1, 28 or 32.
34 Trans. R. Heine, *Origen: Commentary on the Gospel according to John Books 1–10*, 51.
35 I. Hadot, 'Les introductions aux commentaires exégétiques chez les auteurs néoplatoniciens et les auteurs chrétiens'.
36 R. Kimelman, 'Rabbi Yohanan and Origen on the Song of Songs: A Third-Century Jewish-Christian Disputation'; E. E. Urbach, 'The Homiletical Interpretations of the Sages and the Expositions of Origen on Canticles, and the Jewish-Christian Disputation'; Y. Baer, 'Israel, the Christian Church, and the Roman Empire', esp. 98–118.
37 See C. P. Hammond (Bammel), 'Notes on the Manuscripts and Editions of Origen's Commentary on the Epistle to the Romans in the Latin Translation by Rufinus'. She has also published a new critical edition of the text, *Der Römerbriefkommentar des Origenes. Kritische Ausgabe der Übersetzung Rufins*, in three volumes.
38 J. Schèrer, ed. *Le commentaire d'Origène sur Rom. III.5–V.7 d'après les extraits du papyrus No 88748 du Musée du Caire et les fragments de la Philocalie et du Vaticanus Gr. 762*.
39 H. Chadwick, 'Rufinus and the Tura Papyrus of Origen's Commentary on Romans'.
40 Ibid., 40–1.
41 C. P. Hammond (Bammel) 'Die fehlenden Bände des Römerbriefkommentars des Origenes'.
42 See R. Girod, 'La traduction latine anonyme du commentaire sur Matthieu'.
43 P. Gorday, *Principles of Patristic Exegesis*, 47–8. See also Trigg, *Origen*, 166–200. H. Crouzel, *Origen*, 43, calls the *Commentary on Matthew* 'less mystical and more pastoral' than that on John.

44 R. Girod, *Origène, Commentaire sur l'Évangile selon Matthieu*, I, SC 162 (1970), 10–13. On Origen and the Jews in Caesarea see N. R. M. de Lange, *Origen and the Jews*, esp. 75–102; H. Bietenhard, *Caesarea, Origenes und die Juden*; and L. I. Levine, *Caesarea Under Roman Rule*.

45 H. J. Vogt, *Der Kommentar zum Evangelium nach Mattäus*, I, 49–50.

46 The discrepancy concerns the 74 homilies on the Psalms attributed to Jerome, but which V. Peri (*Omelie origeniane sui Salmi*) has argued Jerome translated from Origen with only minor changes. See M.-J. Rondeau, *Les commentaires patristiques du Psautier*, I, 54–5.

47 On the question of the translator of this homily see P. and M.-T. Nautin, *Origène: Homélies sur Samuel*, 35–43.

48 See note 46 above.

49 Nautin, *Origène*, 389–409. Cf. R. P. C. Hanson, *Origen's Doctrine of Tradition*, 15–24, who dates the homilies differently.

50 É. Junod, 'Wodurch unterscheiden sich die Homilien des Origenes von seinen Kommentaren?', 62–81.

51 E.g. *HExod.* 1.1; 4.1.

52 Junod, 'Die Homilien', 60–2. On Origen's preaching see also P. Nautin, *Origène: Homélies sur Jérémie*, I, 100–91.

53 B. Steidl, 'Neue Untersuchungen zu Origenes' Peri Archon', 236–43.

54 See esp. M. Harl, 'Structure et cohérence du Peri Archôn', and G. Dorival, 'Remarques sur la forme du Peri Archôn'. H. Crouzel and M. Simonetti have adopted this format in their new edition of the treatise in *SC*. Cf. C. Kannengiesser, 'Divine Trinity and the Structure of *Peri Archon*'.

55 See the translation and notes by J. E. L. Oulton in J. E. L. Oulton and H. Chadwick, eds, *Alexandrian Christianity*, 171–387.

56 See Heine, *Comm. Jn. 13–32*, 5–13.

57 O. Guéraud and P. Nautin, *Origène, Sur la Pâque*.

58 J. Scherer, *Entretien d'Origène avec Héraclide et les évêques, ses collègues sur le Père, le Fils, et l'âme*. ET by H. Chadwick in Oulton and Chadwick, eds, *Alexandrian Christianity*, 430–55.

59 *PG* 17, 624–6.

60 Ed. N. de Lange in *Origène: Philocalie, 1–20 et La lettre à Africanus*, 471–578.

61 Ibid, 498–501.

62 See the annotated translation of H. Chadwick: Origen, *Contra Celsum*.

12

The beginnings of Latin Christian literature

RONALD E. HEINE

The precise date and exact provenance of the emergence of Latin Christian literature are obscure. It seems to have appeared first in North Africa. Roman Christian literature is in Greek up to the time of Hippolytus in the mid-third century. Tertullian dominates the discussion because of the number of his extant treatises. He did not, however, like Athene, spring forth fully grown from the head of Zeus, armed and shouting his battle cry. There was a Latin Christian literature before him. Unfortunately, we cannot say how extensive this literature was, because its remains are so meagre.

The first Latin Christian literature appears to have been translations of portions of the Bible. These translations have not been preserved, but are posited from traces left in the biblical citations of Tertullian and Cyprian in North Africa, and Novatian in Rome. A distinction is made between 'North African' and 'European' translations on the basis of differences which appear in the authors from the respective locales.[1] The earliest reference to such translations is in the Latin *Acts* of the martyrs of Scilli in North Africa (AD 180) where it is stated that the martyrs had copies of 'books, and letters of Paul'. The former were probably copies of the Gospels. It is assumed that these books and letters would have been in Latin.

J. Daniélou has argued that there was an extensive Latin Christian literature before Tertullian stemming from Judaeo-Christianity of the second century.[2] He appeals to the evidence of *V Esra*, and the three treatises of Pseudo-Cyprian, *Adversus Judaeos*, *De Centesima Sexagesima Tricesima*, and *De Montibus Sina et Sion*. His evidence for a date prior to Tertullian for the Pseudo-Cyprianic treatises, however, has been subjected to a rigorous critique, and shown to be invalid.[3] *V Esra*, on the other hand, may have been composed around 200. Daniélou is on somewhat firmer ground when he argues for a second-century date for the Pseudo-Cyprianic treatise, *De Aleatoribus*. Harnack suggested Victor, bishop of Rome (AD 189–99) as the author. Jerome refers to Victor as writing short treatises, and implies at least that he wrote in Latin (*Vir. Ill.* 34, 53).

If Victor were the author of this treatise, it would be the earliest surviving Christian document written in Latin at Rome.[4] Daniélou's dating of the Latin translations of *I Clement* and *The Shepherd of Hermas* in the second century is in accord with the scholarly consensus on these translations. He also assumes that the Muratorian canon was a second-century Latin text. That the canon stems from the end of the second century is possible, but it appears to have been composed in Greek, and translated into Latin in the fourth century.[5]

The small *Passio Sanctorum Scilitanorum* is the earliest preserved Latin Christian document. It is the transcript of a portion of a trial of five Christians in Carthage in 180. The instant reply of their spokesman, when asked if they would like time to deliberate before the sentence was pronounced, reveals the uncompromising tone of early North African Christianity, 'In a case so just, there can be no deliberation.'

Passio Sanctorum Felicitatis et Perpetuae, which stems from the beginning of the third century (*c.* 203), relates the imprisonment and martyrdom of a group of Christians, again in Carthage. The document contains first-hand accounts of dreams of the imprisoned Perpetua and Saturus in a narrative structure supplied by a later unknown editor. It shows several Montanist traits, not all of which are limited to the editorial comments, but which suggest that Perpetua and Saturus may have held Montanist views. Some have suggested that Tertullian was the editor of the treatise. The evidence is inconclusive at best, and some of it clearly suggests otherwise.[6]

Minucius Felix was the author of an apology entitled *Octavius*. Whether his location was Rome or Africa is uncertain. Some think he was the first Christian author in Rome.[7] Others understand his theology to be that of early African Christianity.[8] The setting of the treatise, at least, is Rome. Similarities between this work and Tertullian's *Apologeticum* have inspired a debate concerning which was prior. Current opinion favours the priority of Tertullian.[9] The work has the form of a dialogue between a pagan and a Christian, with Minucius as arbiter. The author is well-read in classical literature and cites it frequently. The apology is unusual in that it cites no Scripture, and never mentions Jesus Christ by name.

Commodian is a mystery. Placed by some in the early third century, and by others in the fifth, he has been located in such disparate places as North Africa, Gaza, Arles, Illyria, Gallia Narbonensis, and Rome. The current consensus favours a date in the mid-third century, and a North African provenance.[10] His writings consist of a collection of eighty acrostic poems in two books entitled *Instructiones*, and a poem in hexameters entitled *Carmen de Duobus Populis*, or *Carmen Apologeticum*. As poetry, his work is undistinguished.[11] Book 1 of *Instructiones* is addressed to pagans, and book 2 to the Church. *Carmen* addresses Jews and Christians. The poems reflect a modalistic monarchian view of God, and a millenarian eschatology. These, and other factors, suggest a third-century date.

Tertullian of Carthage is the first Latin Christian author who can be located and identified with relative precision. His life can be placed in the approximate period of 160–220.[12] Virtually no information about him exists outside that supplied by his own writings. Jerome, it appears, had no source of information beyond Tertullian's works, except for a conversation with a certain Paul of Concordia who related a story about Cyprian's respect for Tertullian (*Vir. Ill.* 53).[13] Eusebius' information was probably based on a Greek translation of *Apologeticum* from which he quotes (*HE* 2.2.4).

A few earlier assumptions concerning Tertullian have been either discarded or seriously questioned by modern studies. He is not to be identified with the jurist of the same name mentioned by Justinian. His usage of legal concepts, once appealed to as evidence for his juristic training and used to explain some of his central theological views, has been shown to be imprecise.[14] His father was not a soldier, and Tertullian himself was probably not a priest.[15]

The chronology of Tertullian's works, beyond certain general limits, is not precise. Barnes worked out a minute chronology in 1971, placing all of Tertullian's works between 196 and 212, but noted several points that needed revision in the reissue of his book in 1985.[16] F.-C. Fredouille follows R. Braun and places the works in the time frame of 197–217. His arrangement of the order of some of the works also differs from that of Barnes.[17]

Tertullian's conversion to Christianity occurred, perhaps, in 193, and his earliest writings, *Ad Martyras*, *Ad Nationes* and *Apologeticum*, can be dated in 196–7 on the basis of historical allusions to the immediate aftermath of the battle of Lugdunum. *Ad Scapulam* refers to an eclipse of the sun which can be dated in 212.[18] In *De Pudicitia* 1, Tertullian refers to an 'edict' offering forgiveness for the sins of adultery and fornication which had been issued by the *Pontifex Maximus*. If this 'edict' is connected with Callistus' policy of forgiveness attacked by Hippolytus (*Haer.* 9.12.20ff.), then this treatise must have been written in 218 or later. Although the latter is a strongly debated point, it seems probable to me.[19]

Within the time frame of 196–218 a further distinction can be made between those works which show no influence of Montanism and those which show such influence. The first datable reference to Montanism in Tertullian is in the first book of *Adversus Marcionem*, which, on the basis of a reference to the Emperor Severus, can be assigned to 207–8 (1.29.4; 15.1).[20] Even this, however, is not unambiguous, and itself underscores one of the difficulties in dating Tertullian's works precisely. He sometimes revised and reissued the same work. He says at the beginning of *Adversus Marcionem* that the present edition is the third. Some think the Montanist reference belongs to the last revision. If this is so, then its connection with the date of 207–8 is called into question, with the consequence that all of Tertullian's Montanist works may be later.

The thirty-one surviving treatises of Tertullian can be grouped into the categories of apologetic writings, anti-heretical writings, and parenetic writings. *De Pallio* does not fit well in any of these categories, but is considered among the last.

The two books of *Ad Nationes* were Tertullian's first apology. The main themes are the same as those of his *Apologeticum*, and the work reads like a preliminary draft of its much more polished successor. *Apologeticum*, with its careful organization,[21] breadth of treatment, forceful arguments, and oratorical flair, is the masterpiece of second-century apologies. In it Tertullian answers the common accusations against Christians, launches an attack on the illegality of their trials, and condemns the corruption and superstitions of pagan society. These first two apologies follow the tradition of the Greek apologists of the second century. Tertullian knew the apology of Justin, and perhaps that of others as well.

De Testimonio Animae, composed within a year of *Apologeticum*, is in a completely different style. It develops what would have probably been a footnote at *Apologeticum* 17.4–6, had ancient authors had the use of footnotes. Tertullian appeals to certain common sayings and attitudes of humanity concerning God and related subjects, and treats these as the view of the soul itself, and hence the natural testimony of the human soul to God. With *Adversus Judaeos*, he enters the different arena of Christian-Jewish polemic.[22] Again he enters a stream of tradition. Justin's *Dialogue with Trypho* is our most extensive extant earlier apology against a Jewish antagonist, and Tertullian's approach resembles Justin's, although the work is not a dialogue. The overarching argument, which frames the major section of the treatise (chs 7 and 14), concerns the conversion of the Gentiles as a proof that the Christ who has come is the Christ who was to come.

In 212, prompted by the outbreak of a new persecution in Carthage, Tertullian returned to the standard apologetic genre with his *Ad Scapulam*, addressed to the proconsul of Africa (211–13). It treats in abbreviated form many of the themes addressed in *Apologeticum*. The approach, however, is different. He writes, he says, not on behalf of the persecuted Christians, who rejoice in being condemned for their faith, but out of concern for the persecutors. He would spare both the individuals and the state the consequences of fighting against God.

Tertullian's ten anti-heretical treatises were composed between *c.* 198–213 in, perhaps, the following order:[23] *De Praescriptione Haereticorum*, *De Baptismo*, *Scorpiace*,[24] *Adversus Hermogenem*, *Adversus Valentinianos*, *De Anima*, *De Carne Christi*, *De Resurrectione Mortuorum*, *Adversus Marcionem*, and *Adversus Praxean*.

De Praescriptione Haereticorum is directed at heresy in general. Tertullian blames heresy on philosophy and the insatiable curiosity it fosters. In opposition to the heretics' cleverness in manipulating the Scriptures, he proposes faith in the fixed contents of the 'rule of faith'. He argues that heretics have no right to the Scriptures on the basis of the legal concept of the *praescriptio*.[25] At the end of the treatise he promises to treat specific heresies in separate works.

In *De Baptismo* Tertullian defends the necessity of baptism against an attack by a woman of the Cainite heresy[26] who had been successful in making converts in Carthage. The treatise provides important information about the understanding and practice of baptism in the third century. In *Adversus Hermogenem* Tertullian draws on philosophy to refute Hermogenes' assertion that God created everything from pre-existing matter. J. H. Waszink has argued that both Hermogenes' arguments and Tertullian's refutation reflect the influence of Middle Platonism.[27] The treatise *Adversus Praxean* refutes the monarchian view of God, and argues for an economic trinitarian view. *De Anima* rejects Plato's doctrine of the soul, which Tertullian saw to be the basis of the views of various (gnostic) heresies. He appeals to the Stoics, the physician Soranus of Ephesus, the Gospel story of Dives and Lazarus, and the vision of a (Montanist) sister to establish the corporeal nature of the soul against Plato, and argues that it has a beginning simultaneous with the body.

Tertullian addressed four treatises either in their entirety or in part against the Valentinians.[28] He 'desacralizes' their myth in *Adversus Valentinianos*,[29] and defends martyrdom against their views in *Scorpiace*. In the closely related *De Carne Christi* and *De Resurrectione Mortuorum* he attacks the views of Marcion, Apelles and Valentinus in the first, and adds Basilides, in name at least, in the latter. In the former each heresy gets separate treatment, with the emphasis falling on Marcion and his denial of Christ's nativity,[30] while in the latter the heresies are rarely distinguished or identified. The heretics derive their views from Scripture, he asserts, either by mutilation (Marcion) or misinterpretation (Valentinus).

Marcion posed the greatest danger to the faith in Tertullian's view. I have already noted two treatises in which Marcion's error is attacked. *Adversus Marcionem* was Tertullian's most extensive treatise. Begun as a single book, it was expanded into five in two successive revisions.[31] The first book denies the god proposed by Marcion,[32] the second shows that God is both Creator of the world, and good, and the third shows, by the argument of prophecy and fulfilment, that the Christ promised in the Old Testament is the same as the Christ revealed in the Gospels. The latter book draws on Justin and Irenaeus for much of its argument.[33] In the fourth book Tertullian examines Marcion's gospel, a truncated version of Luke, and in the fifth he considers the epistles of Paul recognized by Marcion. He argues in the last two books that Marcion's own scriptures refute his position.

There is an additional anti-heretical treatise, probably not by Tertullian, entitled *Adversus Omnes Haereses*, which is appended to the end of *De Praescriptione Haereticorum* in most manuscripts. It contains a list of thirty-two heresies, beginning with Simon Magus, and extending to that of the modalistic monarchians in the early third century. It appears to be a summary of Hippolytus' lost *Syntagma*.[34] The author knew Tertullian's *Adversus Praxean*, for he substitutes Praxeas for Noetus as the author of the modalistic monarchian heresy. Praxeas is mentioned otherwise only by Tertullian.

The sixteen preserved paraenetic writings of Tertullian span his entire writing career, from his earliest *Ad Martyras* composed in 196 to his strongest attacks on the Catholics as a Montanist at the end of his life. Two of the treatises deal with the important third-century subjects of persecution and martyrdom. In the short treatise *Ad Martyras* Tertullian praises the martyrs like a spectator, he says, cheering on athletes. He returned to the subject, but from a different perspective, in *De Fuga in Persecutione*, one of his last treatises, written after he had taken the viewpoint of the Montanists in opposition to the Catholics. Here he argues forcefully against those who would justify the attempt to escape from persecution.

Three treatises treat the proper dress for Christians, if indeed the strange *De Pallio* may be so considered. *De Pallio* argues for the ancient, simple Punic pallium to be the dress of men in place of the more fashionable and modern Roman toga. Book 2 of *De Cultu Feminarum*, which may have been composed before book 1,[35] argues for modesty in female apparel, and book 1 attacks the 'pomp' of women. In *De Virginibus Velandis* Tertullian argues that virgins, as well as wives, should be veiled. He appeals to the authority of the Paraclete to support his view, but the view was not particularly Montanist. He had argued for the same position in his earlier *De Oratione* (21–2), which shows no Montanist tendencies.

Tertullian also addressed various virtues and disciplines of the Christian faith. In his early, pre-Montanist *De Patientia*, in which he says he is qualified to write on his subject only as an invalid praising health, he makes impatience, which he locates first in Eve, the fountain of all sin, and patience, conversely, the central virtue of the Christian life from which all the other virtues and disciplines flow. *De Oratione*, also an early, pre-Montanist treatise, first gives an exposition of the Lord's Prayer, and then treats various subjects connected with the practice of prayer. In the late *De Ieiunio Adversus Psychicos* Tertullian defends the Montanist practices of frequent fasts, dry diets and prolonged stations.

The apostolic decree of Acts 15:29, charging Gentile Christians to abstain from idolatry, blood and fornication was an important text for Tertullian.[36] He often took the reference to blood to mean murder, identified fornication with adultery, and the latter with second marriages, and associated the decree with the commands in the Decalogue found in Exodus 20:4, 13–14. He considered these three commands to have been bound over on Christians by the apostles. He doesn't give much attention to murder, except to note that it was considered unforgivable by the Church (*Pud.* 22), but the other two subjects are discussed repeatedly in his parenetic writings. *De Idololatria* is devoted exclusively to the subject of idolatry, and the subject plays a major role in the treatises *De Spectaculis* and *De Corona Militis*. He attacked second marriages in the three treatises, *Ad Uxorem* 1,[37] *De Exhortatione Castitatis*, and *De Monogamia*. The argument increases in intensity from one treatise to the next, as they represent his pre-Montanist phase, his early acceptance of the Montanist position, and finally his vituperative attack on the Catholic view near the end of his life.

Acts 15:29 also played an important part in Tertullian's later view on the forgiveness of post-baptismal sins. He treated the subject first in the early *De Paenitentia*, which predated his adoption of Montanism. He shared the view of the second-century Church, that no sin should be committed after baptism, but grudgingly allowed for a second and 'last' repentance. He described this repentance as a humiliating public confession, which many, he said, avoided because of the humiliation. He excluded no sin from this second repentance. In the late *De Pudicitia*, in contrast, Tertullian exploded against an 'edict' which offered forgiveness for the sins of adultery and fornication on the basis of repentance. Drawing on the Johannine distinction between sins 'not unto death', and sins 'unto death', he divided sins into those forgivable by the Church and those not. The latter involve the commands of Acts 15:29, and can be forgiven only by God.

The significant advances made in understanding the influence of the classical rhetorical tradition on Tertullian deserve attention,[38] especially as they modify the view that he was radically antithetical to classical culture. Not only do his writings reflect the structural patterns of the various styles of speeches, but the way he approaches and develops a subject shows the influence of his rhetorical training.

Adversus Praxean illustrates well Tertullian's knowledge and use of classical rhetoric. Structurally, the treatise is a textbook model of the construction of a speech. The introduction, chapters 1–2, contains all of the four possible parts of an introduction, *exordium*, *narratio*, *partitio* and *propositio*.[39] This is followed by a *praemunitio*, chapters 3–10, in preparation for the main argument.[40] The main body, chapters 11–26, consists of a mixture of *reprehensio* and *confirmatio*. This is followed by an *amplificatio*, chapters 27–30,[41] and an emotionally charged conclusion, chapter 31.

The material of the main body of the *Adversus Praxean* is provided by the Bible, and shows how Tertullian's exegesis is indebted to the rhetorical tradition. The rhetoricians had rules and techniques for treating cases that 'turned upon written documents'.[42] One of the problems in such cases involved ambiguity. Cicero suggested several ways to resolve ambiguities, among which were appealing to (1) the immediate context, (2) the larger context of an author's writings, acts and whole life in order to show his intent, and (3) what would need to have been written for the opponent's interpretation to be correct.[43] Quintilian added that one should make a grammatical analysis of the words in question.[44] Tertullian uses the third technique in chapters 13 and 15.[45] He applies Quintilian's grammatical analysis to John 10:30 in chapter 22. He appeals to the immediate context to interpret Isaiah 45:5, a favourite text of the monarchians (*Prax.* 18, cf. 20). He follows this immediately with the rhetorical practice of *occupatio*, and anticipates how the monarchians will attempt to nullify his interpretation (*Prax.* 19).[46] In chapters 21–5 he treats both the immediate context and the larger context of the whole Gospel of John to show the inadequacy of the monarchian use of John 10:30 and 14:9–10. He urges the opponents to go through the 'whole Gospel', and closes by noting that he has done that, and has thereby shown the intent of the Gospel (*Prax.* 25).[47] Finally, he says that his examination of John has shown many passages of clear meaning which should be used to interpret the few ambiguous passages the monarchians appeal to rather than vice versa (*Prax.* 26).[48] This latter reflects yet another rhetorical rule, that one should always 'proceed from the certain to the uncertain and not the other way around'.[49]

The treatise *Adversus Valentinianos* demonstrates Tertullian's ability to adapt the rules of rhetoric to serve his own purposes. This treatise departs from the usual rhetorical structure in that it consists of only the first two parts of a speech, the *exordium* (1–6) and the *narratio* (7–39).[50] A *narratio* could be historical in nature, legendary, imaginary (using comic themes), or psychological.[51] Tertullian states at the end of the *exordium* that he is disposing with the discussion, i.e. refutation and confirmation, and resting content with exposition, i.e. *narratio*. He then indicates the kind of *narratio* he will use. Some topics deserve to be laughed at. The rhetorical tradition was very reserved, however, with regard to the methods of comedy. Tertullian observes this reserve. He adds at the end of his *exordium* that the laughter must not be 'unseemly'. Fredouille has noted the difference between Tertullian's parody of the Valentinians and those common to the comedy and satire of that period. One need recall only the ribald caricatures in the *Golden Ass* of Tertullian's fellow North African Apuleius in the mid-second century to perceive the difference.

Fredouille has called attention also to Tertullian's use of the rhetorical subgenre of the portrait, in which, with a few deft phrases, the physical features or psychological character of a person are depicted.[52] Tertullian employs it negatively in his refutations of Hermogenes, Marcion, Praxeas, the Valentinians, and feminine vanity,[53] and positively to illustrate a moral ideal in a miniature of hypostasized Patience.[54] Despite his famous disclaimer,[55] Tertullian knew how to use Athens' arguments to defend Jerusalem's truth.

Notes

1 T. P. O'Malley, *Tertullian and the Bible*, 1–63. But see Philip Burton, *The Old Latin Gospels* (Oxford: Oxford University Press, 2000).

2 J. Daniélou, 'La littérature latine avant Tertullien'. This argument is repeated and expanded in J. Daniélou, *The Origins of Latin Christianity*, 5–98.

3 A. P. Orbán, 'Die Frage der ersten Zeugnisse des Christenlateins'. Orbán does not treat *V Esra* in this study. G. Quispel, 'African Christianity before Minucius Felix and Tertullian', questions the reliability of the type of Orbán's arguments, but without good grounds, it seems to me.

4 S. T. Carroll, 'An Early Church Sermon Against Gambling'. Carroll's article includes an ET of the text.

5 See A. C. Sundberg, Jr, 'Canon Muratori: A Fourth-Century List', 2. Sundberg argues for a fourth-century Greek origin, a position recently supported by G. M. Hahneman, *The Muratorian Fragment and the Development of the Canon*. For the traditional date, see E. Ferguson, 'Canon Muratori: Date and Provenance'.

6 T. D. Barnes, *Tertullian. A Historical and Literary Study*, 79–80.

7 E. Heck, 'Minucius Felix und der Römische Staat', *VigChr* 38 (1984), 154; cf. J. Quasten, *Patrology*, II, 155.

8 C. J. De Vogel, 'Platonism and Christianity: A Mere Antagonism or a Profound Common Ground?' *VigChr* 39 (1985), 23, following G. Quispel.

9 See Heck, 'Minucius Felix', 154, especially note 1. Quispel, 'African Christianity', 309–21, however, argues for the priority of Minucius.
10 See A. Di Berardino, 'Commodian', in Quasten, *Patrology*, IV, 259–65.
11 See K. M. Abbott, 'Commodian and His Verse'.
12 Barnes, *Tertullian*, 57–9, proposed that he was born *c.* 170 and died in middle life shortly after 212.
13 Ibid., 3–10.
14 R. D. Sider, 'Approaches to Tertullian: A Study of Recent Scholarship', 238; Barnes, *Tertullian*, 22–9.
15 Barnes, *Tertullian*, 11–21.
16 Ibid, 30–56; 326–9.
17 F. C. Fredouille, *Tertullien et la conversion de la culture antique*, 487–8.
18 Barnes, *Tertullian*, 32–4, 38, 328.
19 The most recent survey of the debate is by C. Micaelli, in C. Micaelli and C. Munier, eds, Tertullien, *La Pudicité*, 9–38, who thinks the edict referred to by Tertullian should not be connected with Callistus. Barnes, *Tertullian*, 30–1, also rejected the identification.
20 Barnes, *Tertullian*, 37, 46.
21 See R. D. Sider, 'On Symmetrical Composition in Tertullian', 408–18, 423.
22 Some have questioned the authenticity of this work. See Fredouille, *Tertullien et la conversion*, 254–5, note 92 for a listing of the literature in the debate. Fredouille, 254–71, argues for its authenticity, and I think he is correct in this.
23 Barnes, *Tertullian*, 55, who has *Bapt.* first, would place them all between 198 and 210/11; Fredouille, *Tertullien et la conversion*, 487–8, differs most significantly on the following treatises: 208–12 *Val.*, *An.*, *Carn.*, *Res.*, *Marc.* V; 211–12 *Scorp.*; 213 or later *Prax.*
24 Barnes' date for this treatise, 203/4, is considerably earlier than most date it. I find his arguments for a pre-Montanist date in 'Tertullian's Scorpiace' convincing.
25 See R. D. Sider, *Ancient Rhetoric and the Art of Tertullian*, 25–6, on the rhetorical structure of the treatise.
26 Barnes, *Tertullian*, 279–80; cf. *Praescr.* 33.10; Ps.-Tertullian, *Haer.* 2; and Epiphanius, *Pan.* 38.
27 J. C. Waszink, 'Observations on Tertullian's Treatise against Hermogenes'.
28 Five, if the *An.* should also be included.
29 J-C. Fredouille, ed., Tertullien, *Contre les Valentiniens*, I:14.
30 See Sider, *Ancient Rhetoric*, 27–8; 55–60.
31 *Marc.* 1.1.1; cf. Barnes' summary of Quispel's conclusions (*Tertullian*, 326–7).
32 See Sider, *Ancient Rhetoric*, 49–54 for its approach.
33 Tertullian may have also used Irenaeus for book 1, and the lost *Adversus Marcionem* of Theophilus (Eusebius, *HE* 4.24) for book 2. So Quispel, cited in Barnes, *Tertullian*, 327.
34 P. Nautin, *Hippolyte, Contre les heresies,* 15–70.
35 Barnes, *Tertullian*, 53, 55.

36 See *Idol.* 24; *Pud.* 12; and cf. his choice of the corresponding laws from the Decalogue to quote in *Spect.* 3. He takes the command concerning blood in its literal sense also, in *Apol.* 9.13 and *Mon.* 5.4. In *Mon.* 7 he alludes to the decree as removing the burdens of the Law. See Quispel, 'African Christianity', 286–7.

37 *Ux.* 2 forbids widowed Christians to marry unbelievers.

38 Sider, *Ancient Rhetoric*; Fredouille, *Tertullien et la conversion*, 29–178; H. Steiner, *Das Verhältnis Tertullians zur antiken Paideia*.

39 Sider, *Ancient Rhetoric*, 23–4.

40 Ibid., 35–7.

41 Ibid., 38.

42 Ibid., 74, 85–100.

43 *Inv.* 2.40.116–41.121.

44 *Inst.* 7.9.10, cited in Sider, *Ancient Rhetoric*, 86.

45 Sider, *Ancient Rhetoric*, 98–9.

46 See J. H. Waszink, 'Tertullian's Principles and Methods of Exegesis', 23.

47 Cf. Sider, *Ancient Rhetoric*, 98.

48 Cf. *Prax.* 20 which is the programmatic introduction to Tertullian's investigation of John.

49 Quintilian, 5.10.8; cited in Sider, *Ancient Rhetoric*, 50. See also Waszink, 'Tertullian's Principles', 27.

50 Sider, *Ancient Rhetoric*, 30.

51 Fredouille, *Contre les Valentiniens*, 1.12–20.

52 *Tertullien et la conversion*, 38–47.

53 Ibid., 49–58.

54 Fredouille, ibid., 59–63, calls this an allegorical portrait.

55 *Praescr.* 7.9.

13

Hippolytus, Ps.-Hippolytus and the early canons

RONALD E. HEINE

Hippolytus is one of the most enigmatic figures in the history of the early Church. He appears to have been a man of great importance, but both his identity and his writings are surrounded with problems. The traditional depiction of his life, since the discovery and publication in 1851 of the *Refutation of All Heresies*, places his activities in Rome in the first third of the third century. He was a priest there perhaps as early as the bishopric of Victor (189–99). He strongly opposed the endorsement of modalistic monarchianism by the bishops Zephyrinus (199–217) and Callistus (218–22), and what he considered to be the lax penitential policy of the latter, and consequently he became bishop of a schismatic church in Rome in opposition to Callistus. He was the author of a large number of exegetical works, two works against heresies, a work concerning the universe, a chronicle, a computation of the dates of Easter, and a work on church order. In 235 he was exiled to Sardinia, along with Pontianus, bishop of Rome, by the Emperor Maximinus Thrax. Both men died there as martyrs. Before suffering martyrdom, however, it is assumed that Hippolytus was reconciled with Pontianus, for Fabian, bishop of Rome (236–50), brought both back to Rome for burial, and Hippolytus was later recognized as a martyr by Damasus (bishop 366–84). Some, however, relying on a reference in the *Chronicon Paschale* to Hippolytus, bishop of Porto near Rome, take the latter to have been the author and martyr, and not the priest who became head of a schismatic church in Rome.

This depiction was challenged by P. Nautin in 1947,[1] who argued that the *Refutation of All Heresies* and all the works inscribed on the so-called statue of Hippolytus should be attributed to an obscure Christian named Josephus. Nautin took his argument further in a subsequent study, arguing that the treatise *Against Noetus*, which he took to be the concluding section of the *Syntagma* referred to by Photius, could not be the work of the person who wrote the *Refutation of All Heresies*. He would attribute only the *Syntagma* and the exegetical works to Hippolytus.[2] Nautin's hypothesis has not won general acceptance, especially his attribution of works to a Christian Josephus. It has, however, brought into sharp focus the many ambiguities and problems connected with the body of works loosely labelled Hippolytan. Some reject Nautin's solution, but attribute the exegetical works and *Against Noetus* to an otherwise unknown Hippolytus of Asia, and the remainder of the corpus to Hippolytus of Rome. Others argue that there was only Hippolytus of Rome, and that he was the the author of all or most of the works noted above. Most recently, A. Brent has proposed a solution along the lines followed by New Testament scholars in their approach to the problem of the Johannine corpus. He argues that the works are those of a school with two or more authors, one of whom was Hippolytus of Rome, who also edited some of the earlier works of the school.[3] In what follows, I use the name Hippolytus without qualification of all the works, but take notice of the disputes over authorship in the discussions.

Prior to the mid-nineteenth century, only a few of Hippolytus' works were available, and these mostly in brief fragments. In 1841 a single manuscript containing a *Refutation of All Heresies* was discovered and eventually attributed to Hippolytus. In the late nineteenth and early twentieth century the complete texts of some of his commentaries and homilies were discovered in Slavonic, Armenian and Georgian translations, and a few portions of his works in Greek. The following sources constitute the main materials available for sorting out what is genuine and what is spurious.

Eusebius, who provides our earliest information about Hippolytus, names him, along with Beryllus of Bostra and Gaius of Rome, as one of the learned churchmen of that time. He says Hippolytus presided over a church, but, in contrast to Beryllus and Gaius, he does not name the place (*HE* 6.20).[4] He provides a list of seven works of Hippolytus which he knows: *On the Hexaëmeron*, *On what followed the Hexaëmeron*, *Against Marcion*, *On the Song*, *On Parts of Ezekiel*, *On the Pascha*, *Against All the Heresies* (*HE* 6.22). He dates the *On the Pascha* in the first year of the Emperor Alexander (AD 222), saying that this formed the terminus for the sixteen-year cycle of the Pascha.

Jerome, in dependence on Eusebius, says Hippolytus was a bishop, but doesn't know where. He twice refers to him as a martyr,[5] and, like Eusebius, attributes a work *On the Pascha* to him whose calculations extend to the first year of Alexander. He lists eighteen titles, five of which correspond with Eusebius' list (*Vir. Ill.* 61). Theodoret of Cyrus cites excerpts from nine works which he attributes to Hippolytus, none of whose titles appear in other lists. The accuracy of his titles, however, is questioned. Photius refers to an otherwise unknown *Syntagma Against Thirty-Two Heresies* by Hippolytus, and the fourteenth-century Ebed-Jesus refers to four works of Hippolytus, two of which have parallels in Jerome's list.

In 1551 a statue was found in the vicinity of the catacomb of Hippolytus the martyr in Rome. It was the torso, without head, of an unidentified figure seated on a throne. Engraved on the base of the throne is a computation of dates for Passover and Easter beginning from the first year of Alexander Severus, and on the right rear post a list of thirteen works, of which the first two are unreadable. The remaining eleven works in the list are: *On the Psalms*, *On the Pythonissa*, *On behalf of the Gospel of John and the Apocalypse*, *Apostolic Tradition concerning Charisms*,[6] *Chronicles*, *Against the Greeks and against Plato* or *Concerning the Universe*, *Exhortation to Severina*, *Demonstration of the Times of the Pascha according to the Table*, *Odes on all the Scriptures*, *On God and the Resurrection of the Flesh*, *On the Good and the Source of Evil* (PG10, 875–84). This statue, restored as a figure of Hippolytus in the sixteenth century and now standing at the entrance of the Vatican library, was identified with Hippolytus on the basis of the similarity of some of the titles of the works inscribed on its base with those in the lists of Eusebius and Jerome,[7] and because of the area in which it was discovered. It has since been shown that the statue dates from the second century, and originally depicted a female figure. The inscriptions on the base, however, must be dated after AD 222, the first year of the reign of Alexander Severus.

Many of the works in these lists exist only fragmentarily, and others not at all. The extant works attributed to Hippolytus will be discussed in the four groupings of exegetical works, anti-heretical works, historical and philosophical works, and works concerned with church discipline.

There are six exegetical works ascribed to Hippolytus which are extant more or less entire. The *Commentary on the Song of Songs*, cited by both Eusebius and Jerome, is the oldest of Hippolytus' surviving works. It covers chapters 1:1–3:8 of the Song, and is extant in its entirety in a Georgian translation made from an Armenian version in the ninth century or later. There are also fragments of the work in Syriac, Armenian and Slavonic, and a paraphrastic summary in Greek.[8] This was the first Christian commentary on the Song, and it initiated the practice of interpreting the book as speaking of Christ and the Church.[9]

The treatise *On Christ and the Antichrist*, known by Jerome, survives entire in Greek as well as in Slavonic, Ethiopian and Georgian translations.[10] It is dated around AD 200, preceding the *Commentary on Daniel*, where it is mentioned. It is an exegetical study treating themes and texts which appear, from their recurrence in several of his works, to have been dear to Hippolytus. Texts from

Daniel, the Apocalypse, the blessings of Jacob (Gen. 49), and the blessings of Moses (Deut. 33) are especially important in the treatise.

Jerome, Photius and Ebed-Jesus refer to a *Commentary on Daniel* by Hippolytus. The work survives in large part in Greek and entire in a Slavonic translation.[11] It consists of four books, and includes the story of Susanna, who is taken to represent the Church. It was written in 204, during the persecution by Septimius Severus. It treats the Antichrist again, and provides historical identifications of the various kingdoms alluded to enigmatically in Daniel. Another of Hippolytus' central concerns in this work, as also in others, is to warn his readers against expecting an imminent end of the world, an idea encouraged, no doubt, by the persecution. He argued that the world must endure 6,000 years from the time of creation, and that the Christ was born in the year 5,500. There would be, therefore, approximately two and a half centuries before the end.

The commentary *On the Blessings of Isaac, Jacob, and Moses* is not referred to explicitly by any of the ancient witnesses to Hippolytus' works, but is attributed to him in the Georgian and Armenian manuscripts. It consists of two books, the first covering the blessings of Isaac and Jacob (Gen. 27 and 49), and the second those of Moses (Deut. 33). The first book is extant in Greek, though attributed to Irenaeus, and also in Armenian and Georgian versions.[12] The second is extant entire only in Armenian and Georgian versions, with four fragments in Greek. The two books clearly constitute one work, as the second begins with a brief summary of what was discussed in the first book. Hippolytus' references in the work to the Messiah's descent from Levi as well as Judah, his association of the Antichrist with Dan, his typological treatment of Benjamin and Joseph, and the attempt to justify Simeon and Levi's treatment of the Shechemites cause Daniélou to posit that he was indebted to the type of Jewish exegesis represented in the *Testaments of the Twelve Patriarchs*.[13]

Two exegetical homilies are extant. One is entitled 'An Exposition of David and Goliath', and is attributed to Hippolytus in the manuscript. There is a complete Georgian version, plus some Armenian fragments.[14] The sermon begins by noting that deeds as well as words can be prophetic, which, as Daniélou notes, is directly related to the view of Justin and Irenaeus that the Old Testament consists of type as well as prophecy.[15] Hippolytus then develops a David-Christ typology, and takes the battle between David and Goliath to represent that between Christ and the devil. Some of Hippolytus' favourite themes are again treated, such as that of the Antichrist and a reckoning of the age of the world.[16]

The other exegetical homily is on the first two psalms. It is extant almost entire in Greek,[17] and there are some Syriac fragments. The Greek text is anonymous, but the homily is attributed to Hippolytus in the Syriac fragments.[18] A large section is devoted to the whole of the Book of Psalms, and treats the questions of authorship and the authenticity of the titles. It argues that David was the author of the whole, though not of each individual psalm, and that the titles were inspired just as the psalms themselves. The final two chapters give a Christological interpretation to the first two psalms, and use this interpretation to explain why they were placed first, and why they have no titles. The question of whether this homily should be identified with the work *On the Psalms* in the lists given by Jerome and the statue, and whether it should be assigned to the same author as the other exegetical works, has been the subject of an extensive debate.[19] Beyond these six works, Hippolytus' other exegetical works are represented only in brief fragments, some in Greek, and some in other languages.

Both Eusebius and Jerome ascribe a treatise *Against All Heresies* to Hippolytus, and Photius refers to a *Syntagma* of Hippolytus against thirty-two heresies, beginning with the Dositheans and ending with Noetus and the Noetians. Among the extant works ascribed to Hippolytus is a 'Homily of Hippolytus, Archbishop of Rome and Martyr against the Heresy of a certain Noetus'. These works against heresies have been the centre of the storm in studies of Hippolytus.

The first point of dispute was the relationship between the *Syntagma*, known only from its mention by Photius, and the preserved treatise *Against Noetus*. The latter begins with an exposition and refutation of the heresy of Noetus, and concludes with a 'demonstration of the truth'. In the seventeenth century it was proposed that the *Against Noetus* was a fragment from the end of the *Syntagma*. Since then the debate has been over whether the *Against Noetus* was an independent work, perhaps a homily as its title claims, or represents the end of the lost *Syntagma*.[20] In 1865 R. A. Lipsius added some new information to the question of the *Syntagma* when he argued that Epiphanius, Philastrius, and Ps.-Tertullian had all drawn on the *Syntagma*, and that the little treatise of Ps.-Tertullian, *Against All Heresies*, preserves the list and order of the thirty-two heresies of the *Syntagma*, and is, in effect, a brief summary of the latter. He also considered *Against Noetus* to be a fragment from the end of the *Syntagma*. Lipsius' arguments concerning Ps.-Tertullian and the *Syntagma* have generally prevailed to the present. No agreement has been reached, however, on the question of the relationship between the *Syntagma* and *Against Noetus*.

The treatise that goes under the title of *Refutation of All Heresies*, or *Elenchus*, has had a very chequered history. Because the first book is a doxography of Greek philosophy, it appears to have been separated from the remainder of the work very early and to have had its own independent existence under the title of *Philosophumena* as a source for the study of philosophy. It has been preserved in five Greek manuscripts.[21] The book is ascribed to Origen in the manuscripts, but the fact that the author indicates in the preface that he is a bishop led scholars to dismiss the ascription to Origen. The author says that his purpose in beginning with a synopsis of Greek philosophy is to show that the teachings of the heretics derive not from Scripture, but from philosophy, the mysteries and the astrologers. At the end of the first book he says he will next present the mysteries and the doctrines concerning the stars.

Books 2 and 3 of the treatise have been lost, but in 1841 a manuscript containing books 4–10 was discovered. The beginning of book 4 is missing. It begins in the midst of a discussion of astrology. Books 5–9 attack the heresies, beginning with the Naasenes and culminating with Noetus and his disciple, Callistus. The Elkesaites are then discussed, followed by a brief account of the Jews. Book 10 summarizes what has preceded, and ends with a brief presentation of the 'doctrine of the truth'.[22] No author is indicated in the titles of the books, but at 10.32.1, where the demonstration of the truth begins, a title is inserted ascribing the views to Origen.

The text of this manuscript was first published in 1851 and was attributed to Origen. In the same year others argued that it was the work of Hippolytus. The attribution to Hippolytus prevailed, with a few hesitations, until Nautin's attack in 1947.[23] Nautin noted that the author refers to a treatise *On the Universe* which he had written (10.32.4), and that Photius had read a work by this title written by Josephus. Nautin also found references to a work of similar title attributed to Josephus in John Philoponus and in the *Sacra Parallela*. Using this as his starting-point, he concluded that the *Refutation of All Heresies* was written by a Christian named Josephus who had been confused with the well-known Jewish historian of that name. Further, since the list on the statue contained a work *On the Universe*, Nautin argued that the entire list there should be attributed to the same Josephus, especially since he had also found a reference in a Byzantine *Memorandum* which ascribed a *Chronicle* to Josephus, another work alluded to by the author of the *Refutation* (10.30.1) and included in the list on the statue.

A group of scholars, represented especially in the work of V. Loi and M. Simonetti, have attempted to solve the problem of Hippolytus by positing an Asian and a Roman Hippolytus. The exegetical works, along with the *Against Noetus*, which is *not* to be identified with the *Syntagma*, are assigned to an Asiatic bishop of unknown see named Hippolytus. The *Refutation of All Heresies*, the *Syntagma*, and the works engraved on the statue make up the other block of works. These are assigned to Hippolytus of Rome who opposed Callistus, and who died as a martyr.[24]

Marcovich, the most recent editor of the *Refutation*, argues for Hippolytus of Rome as its author, along with the remainder of the Hippolytan corpus.[25] Frickel also concludes that there was only one Hippolytus, that he was honoured with the statue, and wrote both the *Against Noetus* and the *Refutation of All Heresies*, plus the other works that have been attributed to him.[26]

Brent, who proposes a school of Hippolytus in Rome, must radically reinterpret the statue for his solution to work. This reinterpretation is a twofold process. First, the figure itself is taken never to have been intended to represent Hippolytus, or any other specific person, but to have been symbolic of the ethos of the school. Consequently, if the figure did not represent a specific person, there is no reason to assume that the works in the list were written by one person and not several who were part of the school. The founder of the school was radically opposed to the monarchian Christology of Callistus, and wrote the *Refutation* plus the other works on the statue which can be associated with it. Hippolytus succeeded him as leader of the school, and attempted a rapprochement with Callistus' Christology, as seen in the *Against Noetus*. In addition to the latter, he wrote the *Commentary on Daniel* and related works, and also made editorial revisions in some of the works of his predecessor. The *On the Psalms* was written by a third member of the school.[27] No general consensus has been achieved on these basic questions concerning Hippolytus' person and works, nor does it appear that one is likely.

Two works cited on the statue alone appear to have been philosophical works. We know nothing of the one entitled *On the Good and the Source of Evil*. The other, entitled *On the Universe*, is referred to in the *Refutation of All Heresies* (*Haer.* 10.32.4). Photius read it under the name of Josephus, but questioned his authorship because of its Christian contents. He thought it more likely the work of Gaius. He says it consisted of two small books, and gives a brief description of the contents.[28] A few Greek fragments have been preserved.[29]

Two works concerned with chronology have also been attributed to Hippolytus. Eusebius refers to a work entitled *On the Pascha*, which reckoned the dates of Easter up to the first year of Alexander Severus,[30] and a work with a similar title is listed on the statue. Most of the engravings on the statue, as noted above, consist of two computations, the one reckoning the sixteen-year cycle for Passover from AD 222–333, and the other the corresponding dates for Easter Sunday.[31] A work entitled *Chronicles* is also listed on the statue, and the author of the *Refutation* refers to an earlier work of his treating Jewish history (*Haer.* 10.30.1). There is an anonymous *Chronicle*, preserved partly in Greek, and completely in Latin, Armenian and Georgian translations. This work is attributed to Hippolytus on the basis of internal evidence and the reference on the statue. It claims in the title to cover the time from the creation to the present day, and its contents extend from Adam to Alexander Severus. If by Hippolytus, it must have been published shortly before his deportation in 235. Among the many common features with other works of Hippolytus is the warning against expecting an imminent end of the world.[32]

The two works that go under the titles of the *Canons of Hippolytus* and the *Apostolic Tradition* represent a specialized field of study in themselves. Their contents have great intrinsic interest for the early history of church order and worship, treating such subjects as ordination, baptism, worship and prayer in the manner of manuals explaining how and when they are to be performed.[33] The two texts are clearly related to one another, and have a complicated and intertwined history. The *Canons* are extant only in an Arabic version which is thought to be derived from a Coptic translation of an original Greek text. The work known as the *Apostolic Tradition*[34] appears in several collections of Church Orders dating from the fourth century, and is sometimes in longer and sometimes in shorter form. It exists in Sahidic, Bohairic, Arabic, Ethiopic and Latin versions. The Oriental versions are interdependent, the Bohairic and Arabic versions deriving from the Sahidic, and the Ethiopic from the Arabic.

The *Canons* were attributed to Hippolytus by H. Achelis in 1891, who argued that the *Apostolic Tradition* and the other Church Orders were derived from it.[35] This attribution was later rejected by E. Schwartz and R. H. Connolly, who argued that the *Apostolic Tradition* was the source of all the Church Orders, and that the *Canons* were a later adaptation made between the fourth and the sixth centuries.[36] Some have argued since for a date in the middle of the fourth century for its composition, and an Egyptian provenance, but no one has been willing to see more than the shadow of Hippolytus in the *Canons* since the work of Schwartz and Connolly.[37] The *Apostolic Tradition* was attributed to Hippolytus at the beginning of the twentieth century on the basis of the work by the same title listed on the statue of Hippolytus. This attribution has been widely, but not universally, accepted. There is general agreement, however, that the work derives from Rome in the first half of the third century.[38]

Notes

1 See J. A. Cerrato, 'The Hippolytan Biblical Commentaries and the Identity and Provenance of their Author,' Theology Faculty, University of Oxford, DPhil Thesis, 1996, 44–54, for a discussion of earlier authors who supported an Eastern rather than a Roman provenance for Hippolytus.

2 P. Nautin, *Hippolyte et Josipe*; Nautin, *Hippolyte, Contre les hérésies*; P. Nautin, 'Hippolytus', *EEC* I, 383–5.

3 These positions are treated more fully in the discussion of the anti-heretical works below.

4 J. Frickel, *Das Dunkel um Hippolyt von Rom*, 3–9, argues that Eusebius' silence on the place of Hippolytus' see does not mean that he did not know its location.

5 *PL* 26.20B; *Ep*. 36.16. For other references to Hippolytus by Jerome, see Frickel, *Das Dunkel*, 9–13. The fourth-century Latin poet Prudentius devotes a lengthy hymn to the martyr Hippolytus (*Liber Peristephanon* 11).

6 It is not certain if this should be read as one title or two.

7 Only the work on the Pascha matches any of the titles in Eusebius' list. This and four others have similarities with titles in Jerome's list.

8 G. Garitte, *Traités d'Hippolyte sur David et Goliath, sur le Cantique des cantiques et sur l'Antéchrist*, CSCO 264. Garitte provides a Latin translation of the three works in this volume, and the Georgian text in ibid. 263.

9 See J. Daniélou, *Gospel Message and Hellenistic Culture*, 258–60.

10 Note 8 above. Unless otherwise noted, critical editions of the extant Greek texts of Hippolytus can be found in GCS.

11 M. Lefèvre, Hippolyte, *Commentaire sur Daniel*, goes beyond the edition in GCS by taking into account more recent discoveries. GCS has announced that a new edition of the commentary is in preparation.

12 Greek text with the two versions and a French trans.: *PO* 27.1–2 (1957); Greek text alone: *TU* 38.1 (1911), 1–43. German trans. of a Russian trans. of the Georgian: *TU* 26.1a (1904), 1–78.

13 *Gospel Message*, 260.

14 Note 8 above. German trans.: *TU* 26.1a, 79–93.

15 *Gospel Message*, 262.

16 The latter differs from that in *Dan*. in that there the Saviour comes in the year 5,500, but here, because Goliath's armour weighs 5,000 shekels, he comes in, or after, the year 5,000.

17 See Rondeau, *Commentaires*, I, 33.

18 P. Nautin, *Le dossier d'Hippolyte et de Méliton dans les florilèges dogmatiques et chez les historiens modernes*, 161, 103.

19 Rondeau, *Commentaires*, I, 27–32, 37. On the three fragments on the psalms in Theodoret see ibid., 37–43.

20 For a summary of the debate and the literature, see Nautin, *Hippolyte, Contre les hérésies*, 1–70, who argues that it is the end of the *Syntagma*, and R. Butterworth,

Hippolytus of Rome: Contra Noetum, 1–33, who argues that it is an independent homily.

21 M. Marcovich, *Hippolytus Refutatio Omnium Haeresium*, 1–8.

22 On the contents of the treatise and its aim and methods see I. Mueller, 'Heterodoxy and Doxography in Hippolytus' "Refutation of All Heresies"'; G. Vallée, *A Study in Anti-Gnostic Polemics*, 41–62; C. Osborne, *Rethinking Early Greek Philosophy*; and J. Mansfeld, *Heresiography in Context: Hippolytus' Elenchos as a source for Greek philosophy*.

23 Note 2 above.

24 See the essays in *Ricerche su Ippolito*, *Nuove Ricerche su Ippolito*, and the summaries in E. Norelli, *Ippolito, L'Anticristo*, 9–32, and Rondeau, *Commentaires*, I, 30–2.

25 *Hippolytus*, 8–17.

26 Frickel, *Das Dunkel*.

27 A. Brent, *Hippolytus and the Roman Church in the Third Century*.

28 Photius, *Bibliotheca*, 48.

29 M. Richard, 'Hippolyte de Rome', col. 542; W. J. Malley, 'Four Unedited Fragments of the *De Universo* of the Pseudo-Josephus found in the *Chronicon* of George Hamartolus (Coislin 305)'.

30 Jerome repeats Eusebius' notice.

31 On the problems of identifying the computations on the statue with the references in Eusebius and Jerome, and the suggested solutions, see Frickel, *Das Dunkel*, 70–5, and the literature cited there.

32 Richard, 'Hippolyte', col. 541; R. Helm, *Der Chronik des Hieronymus*, GCS 46 (1955), ix.

33 See J. A. Jungmann, *The Early Liturgy*, 52–86, 97–108.

34 It lacks both title and author's name in the MSS.

35 H. Achelis, *Die Canones Hippolyti*.

36 E. Schwartz, *Über die pseudoapostolische Kirchenordnung*; R. H. Connolly, *The So-called Egyptian Church Order and Derived Documents*.

37 H. Brakmann, 'Alexandreia und die Kanones des Hippolyt'; P. Bradshaw, ed., and G. Bebawi, trans., *The Canons of Hippolytus*, 6–7.

38 Bradshaw and Bebawi, *Canons*, 4–5; cf. Richard, 'Hippolyte', col. 545.

14

Cyprian and Novatian

RONALD E. HEINE

Much of the mid-third century is scantily documented for both secular and Church history. We are fortunate, however, to have an abundance of material concerning Cyprian and the church in Carthage for the ten-year period from May 248 to September 258. All of Cyprian's twelve, or thirteen, treatises have survived, plus eighty-two letters from his extensive correspondence. There are, in addition, a *Vita Cypriani* written shortly after Cyprian's death by his deacon, Pontius, and the *Acta Proconsularia Cypriani*.

Our sources, however, are almost exclusively concerned with Cyprian's career as bishop. We know nothing certain about his birth or family. From references to his property, gifts, and the social status of some of his friends, it is assumed that he came from a Carthaginian family of wealth and rank. C. A. Bobertz has argued that he belonged to the social strata of municipal *decuriones*.[1] Jerome says that he had taught rhetoric before his conversion by the presbyter Caecilius (*Vir. Ill.* 67). The date of his conversion (245–6) is also a matter of conjecture. Cyprian describes his conversion in the *Ad Donatum*, but in a general and 'rhetorically stylized' way.[2]

He was chosen to be bishop of Carthage in 248–9,[3] while still a neophyte in the faith. His biographer says he was the unanimous choice of the people, but notes some opposition. The opposition consisted of five influential presbyters in Carthage, who, despite Pontius' suggestions to the contrary, continued to be a barb in Cyprian's bishopric.

Most of Cyprian's literary activity was generated by crises. Shortly after his election as bishop, the Church was thrown into disorder and confusion by the ravaging persecution of Decius which lasted from January 250 to the spring of 251. Cyprian took refuge in this persecution, but maintained contact with the church in Carthage by correspondence. Some Christians were arrested, and thereby attained the honoured position of 'confessors'. Far greater numbers, however, complied with the demands of the emperor, and were termed the 'lapsed'. This situation created the problems which dominated the remainder of Cyprian's episcopate.

In the relative peace between the Empire and the Church from the summer of 251 until 256, the church in Carthage was disturbed by a devastating plague, and by fears of a persecution under Gallus (253). The persecution appears not to have affected Carthage, nor to have developed beyond the arrest of Cornelius, bishop of Rome, and his successor, Lucius.[4]

In 257 the Emperor Valerian initiated a new persecution. Cyprian was brought before the proconsul of Carthage on 30 August 257. When he confessed to being a Christian and a bishop he was exiled to nearby Corubis. On 13 September 258 he was again brought in for trial, and on 14 September, he was executed.

Cyprian's writings fall into the two general categories of letters and treatises. Of the eighty-two letters, sixty are his, and six others are synodal letters of the African Church written by him. The remaining sixteen are letters addressed to him, or are letters to which he responded.[5] The letters have been transmitted in the manuscripts in confused order and with a great diversity in their total number. No manuscript has all eighty-two, and only one has eighty-one. The one additional letter was first published in 1944.[6]

The treatises, by contrast, seem to have been collected and arranged in their order soon after Cyprian's death, and to have survived intact.[7] The *Quod Idola Dii Non Sint* is the only treatise in the collection whose Cyprianic authorship has been seriously questioned.[8] Its arguments, which attack the disbelief of the Jews as well as pagan idolatry, show the influence of Tertullian's apologies, and that of Minucius Felix.

Most of Cyprian's writings are addressed to specific occasions, and can, therefore, be dated rather precisely. The *Ad Donatum*, written in 246, was his first treatise. It speaks of his conversion, and deplores the degenerate nature of Roman society. M. Szarmach has shown, from both its form and content, that it belongs to the genre of the protreptic address.[9]

Cyprian's first writings as bishop were composed between his election (May 248/9) and the beginning of the Decian persecution (January 250). The *Ad Quirinum*, or *Testimonia*, was written no later than 249.[10] He appears to have written it first in two books, and later to have added the third. It is a compendium of Scriptures arranged according to topics. The first book treats the disobedience of the Jewish people and their demise as the people of God, and the second treats the nature of Christ and his fulfilment of Old Testament prophecies. The third book treats a miscellany of topics related to the Christian life, some doctrinal, but most concerning discipline. The *De Habitu Virginum* was also composed in this period. It is addressed primarily to a group of wealthy virgins who insisted on their right to dress lavishly, attend immodest parties, and frequent the public baths. It shows the influence of Tertullian's *De Cultu Feminarum*. *Letters* 1–4 may also belong here, as they contain no reference to persecution. This, of course, does not necessarily mean that they preceded it. Some also place *Letter* 63 in this period on stylistic grounds, but the date is disputed.[11] It argues for mixing wine with water in the eucharistic cup, against some who used water alone.

Letters 5–43, written during his first exile (January 250–Easter 251),[12] make up the next group of Cyprian's writings. About half of this correspondence is addressed to his clergy in Carthage. Two letters are addressed to the laity, and three more include them in the address. The remaining correspondence is between Cyprian and the clergy in Rome, and the confessors in Rome and Carthage. The correspondence reveals the chaos into which the Church was thrown by the persecution, and the host of internal problems which arose.

The writings composed between March and the summer of 251 treat the immediate aftermath of the Decian persecution. Cyprian faced two immediate problems when he returned to Carthage. First, Felicissimus, one of the presbyters who opposed his election to the bishopric, had formed a laxist church, and was readmitting the lapsed without penance (*Epp.* 41–3). Cyprian issued his *De Lapsis* in March shortly after his return to counteract Felicissimus' influence. After praising the confessors and the faithful, and identifying himself with those mourning for the lapsed, he attacks those offering reconciliation without penance as purveyors of false hope. He then makes his own proposal for the lapsed. They are to confess their sin, mourn, pray, and apply themselves to good works, especially to almsgiving. He had noted earlier that many who lapsed had done so to protect their property. He now argues that this wealth which caused their fall should be used to heal their wound. The restoration promised, however, is complete. Those who make such satisfaction 'will earn not merely God's forgiveness, but His crown' (*Laps.* 36).[13]

The other problem arose from the execution of Fabian, bishop of Rome, at the beginning of the Decian persecution. The Roman Church had waited until the persecution was over before choosing a new bishop. During this period, Novatian had taken a leading role among the presbyters at Rome. He was passed over, however, in the election in favour of Cornelius. Novatian contested the appointment of Cornelius, and when this failed, assumed the title of bishop for himself, and, with the support of some prominent Roman confessors, set up a rival church in Rome.[14] Cyprian had to decide which man to recognize as bishop. After an investigation into the election of Cornelius by envoys he sent to Rome, he recognized Cornelius. Not only was Novatian outraged by this rejection, but Cornelius was angered by the delay. *Letters* 44–54 all concern this episcopal dispute in Rome.

The laxist church which Felicissimus led in Carthage, and Novatian's rigorist church in Rome, splintered the unity of the Catholic Church. Cyprian addresses this issue in his most famous treatise, *De Ecclesiae Catholicae Unitate*. The treatise, written in March or April 251, argues for the unity of the Church based on the unity of its episcopacy. Scholars are divided, however, over whether the treatise was written to combat the local problem which Felicissimus had created, that in Rome stemming from Novatian, or both. They are also divided over whether it was intended for the council of African bishops which began meeting in Carthage in late April 251, or for the laity in Carthage.[15] However one may decide on these questions, Cyprian certainly thought its contents relevant to the Roman situation when he wrote to the Roman confessors who had returned to the Catholic Church from that of Novatian (*Ep*. 54.3.4). The transmission of the text of chapter four of this treatise in two versions has also generated a lengthy debate. One version, called the Primacy Text (PT), stresses the primacy of the chair of Peter. The other, called the *Textus Receptus* (TR) lacks this reference, and insists, instead, on the equality of all the apostles. TR was long considered the original version, and PT was thought to be a later interpolation to support the papacy. It is now thought that Cyprian first issued the text as it stands in PT, but later, perhaps during the controversy with Stephen, revised and reissued it as it stands in TR.[16]

The fourth group of Cyprian's writings can be dated between late summer 251 and late spring 254. The *De Dominica Oratione* must have been written early in this period. There are no references to contemporary problems that allow us to date it precisely. Cyprian finds the whole of Christian doctrine summarized in the petitions of the prayer. *Letters* 55–66 fall into this period, and treat a variety of topics.[17] *Letters* 57–8, written perhaps in 253, are especially important in that they express Cyprian's fear that another persecution is imminent. Two of the treatises, written probably in 252–3, treat situations caused by the plague. The *De Mortalitate* describes the suffering it was causing, and addresses the fears and questions it was raising in the Church. The *Ad Demetrianum* is an apology. Demetrianus had raised the old accusation that Christian 'atheism' was the cause of plagues and famines. Cyprian argued that both the plague and the impending persecution (*Ep*. 58) were signs that the end of the world was approaching. The *De Opere et Eleemosynis* may also have been written in 252–3.

It presents works of mercy as a means for the forgiveness of sins committed after baptism.

The return to the Catholic Church of converts baptized in Novatian's church raised the question of the legitimacy of baptism performed in a schismatic church. *Letters* 67–75, and the treatises *De Bono Patientiae*, written early in 256, and *De Zelo et Livore*, written in the summer of the same year, are all related to the dispute over schismatic baptism between Cyprian and Stephen of Rome (May 254–August 257). Cyprian insisted that persons baptized outside the Catholic Church must be rebaptized, and Stephen argued that they need not be.[18] Not all of Cyprian's fellow African bishops agreed with him on this issue. In *Letter* 73 he refers to his efforts to maintain harmony among his colleagues on such questions, and says he has recently composed a treatise to this effect entitled *De Bono Patientiae* which he encloses with the letter. Praising patience, however, proved inadequate, and the treatise was followed by one condemning jealousy and envy.

Cyprian's final writings were produced during his year of exile in the persecution of Valerian (August 257–September 258). The *Ad Fortunatum*, another compendium of Scriptures, was compiled in exile to prepare Christians for the persecution already afflicting them. *Letter* 80, which predates Cyprian's arrest by perhaps a month, warns fellow bishops of the imminent persecution on the basis of inside information he has received of Valerian's rescript against the Christian clergy and other Christians of rank in society. *Letters* 76–9 are correspondence between Cyprian and fellow bishops suffering in the persecution, and *Letter* 81 is addressed to his congregation in Carthage.[19]

There is no speculative theology in Cyprian's works. His theology is intensely practical. He is concerned with the Church in its constitution and its daily life. These concerns were called forth partly by the turbulence in the Church in the mid-third century which we have noted, and partly by the social world of late antiquity. Several recent sociological studies of Cyprian's works have shed light on his situation. Bobertz, concentrating on the letters written during Cyprian's first exile, and the two treatises issued immediately on his return, argues that Cyprian's relationship with the church in Carthage was a patron–client relationship. He thinks Cyprian was chosen as bishop by the laity against the wishes of the majority of the clergy. The laity saw the bishop as their patron who provided them with both material benefits (alms) and spiritual benefits (forgiveness). The opposition clergy led by Felicissimus attempted to undermine Cyprian's authority during his absence by moving to seize control of these two bases of power, and thereby to establish their own patronage relationship with the Church. Cyprian's chief concern in both the correspondence from exile and the two treatises, then, was to maintain his control of the distributions to the poor and of the process of administering forgiveness to the fallen.[20] This understanding will undoubtedly be modified as other elements of the complex situation are brought to bear on it. It does, nevertheless, illuminate several aspects of the writings in question, of Cyprian's career, and of the situation in Carthage. Bobertz does not address how Cyprian's understanding of the patronage of a Christian bishop differed from that aristocratic Roman patronage which he critiques in the *Ad Donatum*. C. E. Straw, who also applies the patronage model to Cyprian's bishopric, is sensitive to this latter problem. Focusing on the *Ad Donatum* and the *De Opere et Eleemosynis*, she argues that Cyprian refashioned the patronage system as a Christian by making it a system that had a genuine concern for the poor.[21] H. Montgomery uses the same model of patronage to explain why Cyprian avoided martyrdom in the Decian persecution, but accepted it in that of Valerian.[22]

Novatian was probably a better stylist than Cyprian, and certainly a better theologian, but because he was excommunicated as a heretic most of his literary work has perished. Jerome refers to nine treatises of Novatian, and says there were many more (*Vir. Ill.* 70). He also knew of a collection of Novatian's letters (*Ep.* 10.3).[23] Only four treatises and three letters, however, have survived, and these not under Novatian's name. The letters were preserved among the correspondence of Cyprian, and the treatises *De Spectaculis* and *De Bono Pudicitiae* were transmitted under Cyprian's name. The *De Cibis Iudaicis* and *De Trinitate* survived among the works of Tertullian.[24]

We have very little trustworthy information about Novatian's life. The style of his writings and his knowledge of Stoic philosophy[25] suggest that he was educated, and probably came from Rome, and not Phrygia, as Philostorgius asserts (*HE* 8.15).[26] He may have received clinical baptism by affusion when he was very ill, as Cornelius reports in his defamatory letter about Novatian to Fabius (Eusebius, *HE* 6.43). The further assertions of Cornelius, however, that Novatian never received confirmation, that he was ordained a presbyter by the bishop contrary to the wishes of the whole clergy and many of the laity, and that he hid and refused to perform his ministry during a persecution, are highly suspect. The introductions to his three shorter treatises that have survived reveal that he was separated from his congregation when he wrote them, but neither the date nor the circumstances of the separations are known. As noted earlier, Novatian took a leading role among the Roman presbyters during the persecution of Decius and, when Cornelius was chosen to be bishop of Rome, formed a rigoristic schismatic church in Rome with himself as its bishop.[27] Socrates, writing in the fifth century, says Novatian was martyred in the persecution of Valerian (*HE* 4.28). There is, moreover, a tomb on the Via Tiburtina in Rome discovered in 1932, with the inscription, 'To the most blessed martyr Novatian . . .' The identity of the latter, however, cannot be confirmed, nor can the information given by Socrates.

The *De Trinitate* is the earliest of Novatian's treatises that have survived. It seems to have been written some time in the decade preceding the Decian persecution, when Novatian was a loyal presbyter of the church in Rome. It is the first theological treatise written in Latin at Rome. It is, moreover, a theological work of distinction, capable of standing alongside those of Irenaeus, Hippolytus and Tertullian. A. Harnack even compared it with Origen's *De Principiis*, though he thought it inferior to the latter in speculative philosophical theology.[28] The title of the treatise is improper, for the term *trinitas* never appears in the work. It is a commentary on 'the rule of truth', which A. d'Alès takes to be the baptismal creed.[29] As such, it is divided into four parts, treating the Father (1–8), the Son (9–28), the Holy Spirit (29), and how both the Father and Christ can be God, and God still be one (30–1). The standard problems of late second- and early third-century theology are treated. In discussing the Father, Novatian is concerned to refute both gnostic and simple, literalistic views of God. In the large section on the Son, he argues briefly against the docetists, and extensively against the dynamic and modalistic monarchians whose theology had disturbed Rome in the first quarter of the third century.[30] His treatment of the Holy Spirit may have Montanist teachings in view, when he argues that it is the same Spirit who was at work in the Old Testament, who was poured out on the apostles, and who is at work in the Church today. His understanding of the work of the Spirit in the Church shows the influence of Tertullian's modified Montanism when he indicates that the Spirit's work is to direct discipline, explain the rule of truth, and guard the gospel (29.17–19).[31]

Letter 30 in Cyprian's correspondence was, by Cyprian's own testimony, written by Novatian on behalf of the presbyters and deacons in Rome (*Ep.* 55.5). *Letters* 31, from the Roman confessors, and 36, from the presbyters and deacons in Rome, are ascribed to Novatian on the basis of stylistic similarities to *Letter* 30.[32] All three letters treat the problem caused by the presbyters in Carthage who were granting readmission to the lapsed on the recommendation of a few confessors. The Roman clergy and confessors agree with Cyprian's policy to postpone a final decision on the lapsed until due consultations after the persecution, and otherwise to grant forgiveness only in cases of extreme illness. Novatian was only the secretary composing these letters, so they cannot be pressed too far in search of his own views. Nevertheless, signs of his rigorism are evident in various expressions and emphases in the letters.[33]

The circumstances and dates of the composition of the three pastoral treatises, *De Cibis Iudaicis*, *De Spectaculis* and *De Bono Pudicitiae*, are a puzzle. All three refer to the author's absence from his congregation, and in the last he refers to himself as a bishop. The general view is that all three were composed after Novatian became bishop. It is assumed by most that the separation to which the *De Cibis Iudaicis* refers was caused by a persecution, and the work is, therefore, dated during the persecution of Gallus (253), when Cornelius was exiled from Rome. The other two are then dated in the period 253–60. This dating, however, is rejected by Vogt, who argues that the *De Cibis Iudaicis* was written before the Decian persecution, and, therefore, before Novatian was bishop of a schismatic church. Vogt then puts the *De Spectaculis* in the same period, arguing that it must have been written when no Christians either were being, or had recently been, martyred. He further argues that the *De Bono Pudicitiae* was written after the schism, but before the beginning of the Valerian persecution in 257.[34]

The *De Cibis Iudaicis* argues that the Jews were blind to the true meaning of the food laws of Leviticus, and interprets them in the tradition represented in the second-century *Epistle of Barnabas*. The other two treatises are moralistic works, the one attacking Christians who attended the public shows, and the other praising sexual purity in the descending order of virginity, continence, and marriage.

Notes

1 'Cyprian of Carthage as Patron: A Social Historical Study of the Role of Bishop in the Ancient Christian Community of North Africa', 51, 75ff.

2 Ibid., 86–7.

3 See *Ep*. 59.6.1, which can be dated in the summer of 252, and the note on the somewhat ambiguous term, *quadriennium*, in G. W. Clarke, trans., *The Letters of St. Cyprian of Carthage*, III, 244.

4 See ibid., III, 4–17.

5 The letters can best be read in English today in G. W. Clarke's annotated translation.

6 Ibid., I, 8. Clarke includes it as Letter 82. For details concerning the text of this letter see ibid., IV, 319ff.

7 Ibid., I, 7–8.

8 See M. M. Sage, *Cyprian*, 373.

9 Szarmach, ' "Ad Donatum" des heiligen Cyprian als rhetorischer Protreptik'.

10 H. J. Vogt, 'Cyprian – Hindernis für die Ökumene?', 13–14.

11 See Clarke, trans., *Letters*, III, 287–91.
12 The individual letters are not in chronological order in this or the following groupings. For a suggested chronological order within each time period see the appropriate sections in the introductions of the 4 volumes of Clarke's *Letters*.
13 Bévenot, *Cyprian: De Lapsis and De Ecclesiae Catholicae Unitate*, 55.
14 See ch. 18 below.
15 See the summary by C. A. Bobertz, 'The Historical Context of Cyprian's *De Unitate*'. Bobertz argues that the schism of Felicissimus is addressed, and that the treatise was written for the church in Carthage, and not for the council of African bishops. See also Clarke, trans., *Letters*, II, 301–2.
16 See Bévenot, *Cyprian*, xi–xv.
17 On *Ep*. 63, which may belong here, or at the beginning of Cyprian's career, see note 12 above.
18 See Vogt, 'Cyprian – Hindernis', 7–8.
19 *Ep*. 82 appears to belong to the earlier Decian persecution.
20 Bobertz, 'Cyprian of Carthage'.
21 C. E. Straw, 'Cyprian and Mt 5:45: The Evolution of Christian Patronage'.
22 H. Montgomery, 'The Bishop Who Fled: Responsibility and Honour in Saint Cyprian'.
23 See also Socrates, *HE* 4.28, and Cyprian, *Epp*. 44.1; 45.2; and 55.1, 5.
24 Nineteenth-century scholarship also attributed the treatises *Quod Idola Dii non Sint*, *De Laude Martyrii* and *Adversus Judaeos* to Novatian (A. Harnack, 'Novatian. Novatianisches Schisma. Kirche der Katharer', *Realenzyklopädie für protestantische Theologie und Kirche*, 3rd edn (Leipzig, 1896–1913), XIV, col. 226). The work of A. d'Alès, *Novatien. Étude sur la théologie Romaine au milieu du IIIe siécle*, 2–25, and others has rejected these latter treatises.
25 Cyprian, *Ep*. 55.16.1; J. Daniélou, *Origins of Latin Christianity*, 233–50.
26 See H. J. Vogt, *Coetus Sanctorum. Der Kirchenbegriff des Novatian und die Geschichte seiner Sonderkirche*, 17, and *Novatiani Opera*, ed. G. F. Diercks, *CCSL* 4 (1972), viii.
27 See above at p. 154, and Cyprian, *Ep*. 55.
28 A. von Harnack, *Lehrbuch der Dogmengeschichte*, I, 632.
29 D'Alès, *Novatien*, 84.
30 See ch. 18 below.
31 Cf. Tertullian, *Virg*. 1.6–8.
32 See Clarke, trans., *Letters*, II, 133–4, 165, and the literature cited there.
33 See R. J. DeSimone, trans., *Novatian*, 180–1.
34 Vogt, *Coetus Sanctorum*, 27–37.

15

The earliest Syriac literature

SEBASTIAN P. BROCK

Although Jesus and his apostles undoubtedly used Aramaic as their main language of communication, nevertheless we know singularly little about the early spread of Christianity among the Aramaic-speaking population of the eastern provinces of the Roman Empire (covering approximately modern SE Turkey, Syria, Lebanon, Jordan and Israel) and of the Parthian Empire further east. In view of this lack of information particular interest is attached to the earliest surviving Syriac literature, most of it belonging to the third and fourth centuries, since this offers the best evidence for the distinctive character of Aramaic-speaking Christianity in a milieu that was for the most part still comparatively unHellenized.

It is likely that some time before the end of the second century AD a large proportion of Aramaic-speaking Christians came to adopt as their literary language the local Aramaic dialect of Edessa, known today as Syriac. Inscriptions in this dialect, which has its own distinctive script, are already known from the first century AD, and from the mid-third century there survive three legal documents from Edessa (modern Urfa in SE Turkey) and its vicinity. As will be seen, it is likely that Syriac had already been adopted as a literary language by local Jews as well as by pagans before it was taken up by Aramaic-speaking Christians.

The origins of Christianity in Edessa are unfortunately shrouded in obscurity, and with one exception (Bardaisan), it is not until the fourth century (by which time Christianity was well established in the area) that we begin to have any clear evidence. According to a local tradition already in circulation *c.* 300, and recorded by Eusebius (*HE* 1.13.6–22), Abgar the Black, the king of Edessa and its surrounding territory, having heard of Jesus' miracles, had sent a letter to him, asking him to come and heal him of an illness. In his reply, Jesus promised to send one of his disciples after his ascension. Once this had taken place Judas 'who is also Thomas' sent Thaddaeus, one of the Seventy, who duly healed him and preached the gospel in Edessa. Eusebius claims to have translated the text from Syriac, and indeed the legend also comes down to us in a much expanded form in Syriac, in a work known as the Teaching (or Doctrine) of Addai (Addai being the Syriac equivalent of Thaddaeus).[1] This work, which belongs to the early decades of the fifth century, is more interesting for the light it sheds on Edessene Christianity of that time than for any reliable information it can give of the origins of Christianity in Edessa.

Modern scholars have taken basically two very different approaches to this legend (which obviously reflects the general search for apostolic origins, characteristic of the fourth century). Some would dismiss it totally,[2] while others prefer to see it as a retrojection into the first century of the conversion of the local king at the end of the second century:[3] in other words, Abgar (V) the Black of the legend in fact represents Abgar (VIII) the Great (*c.* 177–212), contemporary of Bardaisan. Attractive though this second approach might seem, there are serious objections to it, and the various small supportive pieces of evidence that Abgar VIII became Christian disappear on closer examination.[4] Accordingly, the wiser course is to acknowledge that the Thaddaeus/Addai legend can tell us nothing about the origins of Christianity in Edessa, and to turn to the single early Christian writer of Edessa whose name we know and who is definitely a historical figure, namely Bardaisan.

Bardaisan (154–222) frequented the court of Abgar VIII (where Julius Africanus met him) and had evidently received a good education in Greek culture, even though he wrote only in Syriac. Known as 'the Aramaean philosopher', he had a speculative mind and was well versed in current trends in Greek philosophy. Since his views on certain topics, such as creation, did not conform to what subsequently emerged as orthodox Christian teaching, later writers regarded him as a heretic, some associating him with Valentinian doctrine, while others (among them, Ephrem) saw him as providing the basis for Mani's teaching. Since one result of this later condemnation of his views was the loss of his writings, his teaching has to be reconstructed on the unsatisfactory basis of the biased reports of the heresiographical tradition.[5] We know from Ephrem, however, that one of the vehicles for his teaching was poetry, thus making him the earliest representative of one of the most distinctive features of Syriac literature of the patristic period, namely the use of verse as a medium for theology. The particular genre he used was the stanzaic *madrasha*, conventionally (but not very satisfactorily) translated 'hymn', which was also the one which Ephrem himself used to such great effect.

One extant work, of a very different nature, is often ascribed to Bardaisan: *The Laws of the Countries*.[6] This short book, a discussion on free will known to (and quoted by) Eusebius in a Greek translation under the title of *Dialogue on*

Fate (*PrEv.* 6.10.1–48),[7] is in fact the product of one of his disciples. Significantly, it takes the form of a philosophical dialogue, whose opening words – 'A few days ago we went up to visit our brother Shemeshgram. Bardaisan came and found us there . . . and he asked us, "What were you talking about . . . ?"' – deliberately reflect the beginning of a Platonic dialogue. This work thus introduces into Syriac literature a genre which was specifically Greek in character. Bardaisan and his followers provide an excellent example of the way in which a local Aramaic culture came to be Hellenized: philosophical and theological ideas that were current in the contemporary Greek-speaking world were introduced into Syriac on two different levels, the first using what will certainly have been a native Syriac genre, the verse *madrasha*, no doubt aimed at a wider audience, and the second introducing a Greek literary genre, probably intended for a smaller and highly educated group of readers.

A passage in *The Laws of the Countries* implies that Christianity had spread fairly widely in the East by the first half of the third century, and it is virtually certain that by that time much of both the Old and the New Testament would have been available in Syriac translation. Although there is nothing that specifically links the earliest Syriac biblical translations to Edessa, the fact that the dialect of Aramaic used was known in antiquity as 'Edessene' strongly suggests that they must belong to this general area. The Syriac Old Testament, known as the Peshitta, is definitely a translation directly from Hebrew, and the earliest books to be translated (no doubt the Pentateuch among them) probably go back to the second century AD, thus almost certainly constituting the earliest surviving monument of Syriac literature. The question of whether the Peshitta Old Testament was the work of Jews or of Christians has been long disputed. One thing, however, is certain: as in the case of the Septuagint, different books were translated by different people and at different times. It is in fact very likely that the earliest translations were the work, not of Christians, but of Jews from the Edessa region;[8] this is suggested by, among other things, the presence both of a number of exegetical translation traditions that are closely paralleled in rabbinic literature, and of certain phraseology such as 'he spoke before God' or 'God was revealed over him', characteristic of the Targum tradition. If some other later books of the Syriac Old Testament were translated by Christians, then these Christians will have had a knowledge of Hebrew quite exceptional in the early Church, and this suggests that they may well have been converts from Judaism, or that they came from a Christian community that still maintained close ties with its Jewish roots.

Such a scenario may shed light on the controversy among scholars over the character of earliest Syriac Christianity: was the background of the earliest

Christian mission to this area still deeply rooted in Judaism (as the Addai legend implies)? Or was it of predominantly Gentile background, as the Greek orientation of Bardaisan's teaching seems to suggest?[9] Those who reject the idea of any historicity lurking behind the Addai legend have normally opted for the second position, but this leaves the indirect evidence provided by the case of the Peshitta Old Testament without any satisfactory explanation. Probably it is better to suppose the existence of two different strands present in earliest Syriac Christianity, one with a pagan background and a Hellenizing orientation, and the other with background and orientation both Jewish. It would be tempting to go on and suppose that these two streams represent two different strata within Edessene society: since the former is inevitably linked with Bardaisan, it is likely to have been associated with the Hellenized upper classes, while the latter would then have been characteristic of the less Hellenized strata of society.[10]

Some further light on this matter is thrown by the earliest Syriac translations of books of the New Testament. It is now generally accepted that the earliest form of the Gospels in Syriac was the *Diatessaron*, or Harmony of the Four Gospels associated with the name of Tatian, and this remained in current use into the first half of the fifth century, when a successful policy of suppressing it was carried out. But was the Syriac *Diatessaron* (lost now apart from quotations) identical with Tatian's *Diatessaron*, and if so, did he compose it in Syriac, or was it translated from Greek? And if it was written in Syriac, how is this to be related to the western *Diatessaron* tradition in Latin and medieval vernacular languages? Also, to what extent did Tatian introduce encratite features, or make use of other sources besides the four Gospels?[11] All these questions remain matters of uncertainty and dispute; what is certain, however, is that the Syriac *Diatessaron* exercised a considerable influence on early Syriac writers and a commentary on it, attributed to Ephrem, survives, providing us with the best direct evidence for its readings. It is also likely that the Syriac *Diatessaron* was responsible for many of the harmonizing readings to be found in the earliest Syriac translation of the separate four Gospels, known as the Old Syriac and preserved (in slightly different forms) in two early manuscripts (the *Sinaiticus* and *Curetonianus*). Though various dates have been suggested for the Old Syriac translation of the Gospels,[12] ranging from the second to the early fourth century, it is perhaps most likely that it belongs to the early third. Two features deserve special mention here. In the first place, it is significant that, perhaps already in the *Diatessaron* but definitely in the Old Syriac, Old Testament quotations in the Greek Gospels have often been adapted to the wording they have in the Peshitta Old Testament;[13] this not only provides a useful *terminus ante quem* for the translation of particular Old Testament books into Syriac, but it also indicates that, for the community for whom the translation was made, the Peshitta Old Testament had greater authority in this matter than the wording of the Greek New Testament. Secondly, certain features in the terminology and phraseology used in the Old Syriac Gospels strongly point to a milieu that has its roots in Judaism; thus, for example, for 'the Law', Greek νόμος is not simply transliterated *nāmōsā*, as later became the standard practice, but is frequently rendered by *'urāytā*, the normal term in Jewish Aramaic. Similarly, we here and there encounter in the Old Syriac Gospels phraseology which is characteristic of the Targum tradition: thus at Luke 1:13 where in the Greek the angel tells Zacharias 'Your prayer has been heard', the Old Syriac provides 'Behold, God has heard the voice of your prayer', using a phrase which occurs a number of times in the Palestinian Targum of the Pentateuch (e.g., Neofiti at Gen. 30:17), but never in the Peshitta Old Testament. Features such as these cannot have arisen in a Christian community whose sole origin lay in a mission that was wholly or predominantly Gentile in orientation.[14]

Like many early translations from Greek into Syriac, the Old Syriac Gospels are in places a fairly free rendering; furthermore, it had been made from an early form of the Greek text that subsequently fell out of use, to be replaced, in the Syrian area, by a precursor of the standard Byzantine *textus receptus*. Accordingly it is hardly surprising that in due course it was felt necessary to bring the Old Syriac closer into line with the Greek. This process was at first a gradual one, and traces of it can already be seen in the two surviving Old Syriac manuscripts; some time around the beginning of the fifth century, however, a particular (rather inconsistently) revised text[15] was so successfully promoted that it rapidly became the standard Syriac New Testament text, known today as the Peshitta. Besides the Gospels the Peshitta covers Acts, the Pauline Epistles, and part of the Catholic Epistles (James, 1 Peter, 1 John; the remaining books, which did not form part of the Syriac canon, were not translated into Syriac until the sixth century). Although no Old Syriac manuscript of these books survives, quotations in early writers suggest that there must have been an Old Syriac version, though it may not have differed as noticeably as is the case in the Gospels from the Peshitta revision. Among the Pauline Epistles read in this lost Old Syriac version was 3 Corinthians.

Two very important monuments of early Syriac literature almost certainly belong to the second and third centuries, and both have often been associated with Edessa, though again it is only the fact that they are written in Edessene Aramaic (i.e. Syriac) which can offer any real evidence in support of this, and here it must be recalled that, once Syriac had been adopted as the literary language of Aramaic-speaking Christianity, its use will have rapidly spread to other areas as well.

The forty-two *Odes of Solomon* constitute a unique document of early Christian literature.[16] These short lyric poems vividly express the joy of an intimate relationship between the Odist and Christ:

> As the sun brings joy to those who await the day,
> so is the Lord my joy,
> for He is my Sun,
> His beams have raised me up;
> His light has dispelled all the darkness from my face.
> (Ode 15:1–2)

Though some odes are straightforward and offer no particular problems of interpretation, many are highly allusive and employ striking imagery, while a small number remain extremely obscure (e.g. 38) and have defied any satisfactory explanation. Direct biblical references are absent, but numerous possible allusions can be identified. Even the association with Solomon remains unclear: is it simply due to the fact that the odes were evidently often transmitted together with the Psalms of Solomon (of very different character), or does the name reflect a deliberate choice on the part of the unknown author? In the light of this it is perhaps not surprising that date, background and original language all remain uncertain and matters of dispute.

For some, the *Odes* go back to the late first century, emanate from Johannine circles, and have some links with Qumran literature (*Ode* 5 opens, as do some of the *Hodayot*, with the words 'I give thanks to You, Lord'); others see them as originating in the kind of Valentinian milieu that produced the *Gospel of Truth*; others again have seen in them polemic aimed against Marcionite and even Manichaean teaching (this last would mean that their date is to be lowered at least to the late third century); yet others have read them as early baptismal hymns. None of these positions carries full conviction, but there is something to be said for seeing the *Odes* as expressing the joy felt at the experience of the realization of what baptism signifies; furthermore, if the phrase 'without envy', used no less than seven times of God, is indeed aimed against Marcionite teaching (known to have been present in Syria), then this places the *Odes* at least in the second half of the second century. A late second-century date would also suit the notable parallels to be found in Clement of Alexandria for the striking feminine imagery used of God in *Ode* 19, where 'the Son is the cup (of milk), and the Father is He who was milked, and the Holy Spirit is She who milked Him'.[17]

The *Odes* survive almost complete in Syriac, but one ode (11) is known in Greek, and five in Coptic (incorporated into the gnostic *Pistis Sophia*); there is also a quotation in Latin by Lactantius. All of this indicates that the *Odes* must once have circulated quite widely, but in what language were they originally written? Inconclusive arguments have been adduced both for Greek and for Syriac; another, though perhaps remote, possibility is that they were originally written in some other Aramaic dialect (or even Hebrew). While most scholars at present favour Syriac, it remains puzzling that they are not written in any recognizable Syriac poetic form, yet they are clearly intended as poetry. Although the more complete of the two surviving Syriac manuscripts dates from as late as the fifteenth century, only a few possible allusions to them can be found in the works of Ephrem, while no traces at all in the rich Syriac liturgical tradition have ever been located.

By far the most extensive piece of early Syriac literature is the narrative concerning the Apostle Thomas's journey to, and time in, India, known as the *Acts of Thomas*[18] (the apostle is in fact always referred to as Judas Thomas, or Judas the Twin, *sc.* of Jesus). Unlike most of the other apocryphal Acts of the Apostles, the *Acts of Thomas* were composed in Syriac, and not in Greek; an early Greek translation, however, survives and this happens to preserve some archaic features which have been removed in the surviving form of the Syriac text. The work is usually dated to the early third century and has often been associated with Edessa, though there are no strong reasons to support this and Edessa never receives a single mention. The work, which is divided into 14 Πράξεις, or 'Acts' (the last of which concerns the martyrdom of Judas Thomas), belongs to the Hellenistic Greek literary genre of the 'Romance'. This genre had already been taken over in Judaism and adapted as a vehicle for religious teaching in the *Romance of Joseph and Aseneth*, and the *Acts of Thomas* likewise will have been aimed at imparting a religious message. It would seem that the prime aim of the book was to promote the ideal of an encratite lifestyle: thus both Judas Thomas and the women and men whom he converts are presented as models of chastity, for whom profane marriage (but not necessarily the institution of marriage itself) is something to be abhorred and rejected. It was no doubt this encratite aspect of the *Acts of Thomas* that made them also popular in Manichaean circles.

It seems likely that the intended readership of the *Acts* was expected to pick up various latent typological hints, in particular the parallel between Judas Thomas, sold by Jesus, his 'twin', to a merchant in order to go to preach in India, and Joseph (another model of chastity), sold by his brothers to end up in Egypt where in due course he rose to a position of authority. The *Acts of Thomas* in fact serves as a major source for our knowledge of early Syriac theology; furthermore, the various descriptions of baptisms (chs 27, 121, 132, 157), often with accompanying prayers, are of great importance for an understanding of the early Syriac baptismal tradition.

Incorporated into the *Acts of Thomas* are two earlier allegorical hymns in (it seems) a six-syllable metre, on the Bride of Light (chs 6–7), and the famous Hymn of the Pearl (or Soul; chs 108–13), whose origins and significance have been the subject of much debate:[19] the main characters in the narrative poem – the king and queen of the East, the prince their son who is sent to Egypt to rescue a pearl that is guarded by a dragon, and the prince's double who meets him on his return – can all be interpreted in several different ways. Some have claimed the hymn as a pre-Christian witness to an otherwise unknown Iranian form of gnosticism, but on the whole a Christian origin seems more likely. In any case, it is clear that the East represents the heavenly realms, and Egypt the world: a correlation which must depend ultimately on the biblical narrative of Genesis and Exodus. The triad, king, queen and prince, reminiscent of the divine triad 'our lord, our lady, and the son of our lord and lady', found in inscriptions at Hatra, may well represent the Christian Trinity (and was certainly understood as such by later Christian readers); if this is correct, then the prince, who is both saviour and in need of being saved (before he can rescue the pearl, which probably represents the soul), is best understood as representing both First Adam and Second Adam: such a close identification of the two Adams can in fact be paralleled elsewhere, above all in the Ps.-Clementine literature. Many of the other details, however, remain problematic, and no modern interpretation provides a satisfactory explanation of everything.

The appellation 'Judas Thomas' also occurs in a few of the Coptic texts from Nag Hammadi, notably the *Gospel of Thomas*. This has (no doubt correctly) been taken as an indication of Syrian provenance, though whether any of these works had originally been written in Syriac or some related Aramaic dialect remains a matter of conjecture.

A few further early Syriac texts survive, notably a letter of a certain Mara to his son Serapion, and some Apologies. In the *Letter of Mara*,[20] Mara is portrayed as being from Samosata by origin, but at the time of writing he appears to be a captive in Seleucia; in the course of his Letter he gives various counsels of advice, of a generally Stoic nature, to his son, warning him of the vanity of the world. At one point mention is made of the Jews, who killed 'their wise king', as a result of which their city Jerusalem was sacked. It is known that captives were taken from Samosata by the Parthians in 72 and 161/2, and by the Sasanians in 256, and the Letter has been associated with each of these by modern scholars.

The question of date is an important one, since the Letter quotes a snatch of poetry, which may thus represent the earliest example of isosyllabic poetry in Syriac. The early date and the pagan authorship of the Letter have, however, been convincingly challenged, on the grounds that the linking of the death of Jesus with the destruction of Jerusalem is an essentially Christian motif, and one that only came into currency in the post-Constantinian period. Accordingly the Letter should be seen as the work of a Christian posing as a pagan; this in itself is interesting, for it points to the existence of a phenomenon not hitherto known from early Syriac writings, but familiar from Greek Christian ones.

Three early texts in Syriac belong to the genre of the Apology: since two of these are definitely translations from Greek, they are of only marginal interest here. The *Apology of Aristides* happens to survive independently only in Syriac translation, for the Greek original is known only from the form incorporated into the Christianized Buddhist tale, *Barlaam and Ioasaph*, whose Greek text is attributed to John of Damascus. Though no Greek work with the title '*Hypomnemata* which Ambros<ios>, a chief man of Greece, wrote' (as an *apologia* to his fellow senators) is known, this early Syriac work is in fact just a translation of the *Apology of Pseudo-Justin*. Of more interest is an unduly neglected *Discourse of the philosopher Meliton which took place* (or: *who was*) *in the presence of Antoninus Caesar*.[21] This Antoninus has been variously identified as Marcus Aurelius or Caracalla. If it was indeed delivered in the emperor's presence, then this apology too will certainly have been written originally in Greek, but it is also possible that the claim is just a literary fiction, in which case there is a serious possibility that the work was written in Syriac; if so, we would then have another example, alongside the book of *The Laws of the Countries*, of what one might call biculturalism, where a Syriac author takes over a purely Greek literary genre.

A further text which may belong to the earliest period of Syriac literature is a collection of a hundred or so wisdom sayings attributed to Menander the Sage.[22] These have no direct connection with the Greek Menander Sentences. Their origin is uncertain, but they are probably a translation from a lost Greek collection of sayings, and they may originate from Egypt in the early Roman period, where possibly they were the work of a 'God-fearer'.

One final point is worth making. Although surviving Syriac literature is almost entirely of Christian provenance, it is important to remember that Syriac (or a closely related Aramaic dialect) also served as an important literary vehicle for Manichaean literature. Today only some diminutive fragments of Manichaean writings in Syriac survive, but it is very possible that several texts extant in other languages, such as the Greek *Life of Mani*, are translations from

Syriac. It is also quite possible that there was a pagan literature in Syriac, produced largely at Harran, not far from Edessa; of this, however, only a few alleged fragments, attributed to a prophet Baba, survive.[23]

Notes

1 English translations in G. Phillips, *The Doctrine of Addai the Apostle*, and G. Howard, *The Teaching of Addai*. For the background to the work, see S. P. Brock, 'Eusebius and Syriac Christianity', in Attridge and Hata, eds, *Eusebius, Christianity, and Judaism*, 212–34 (repr. in S. P. Brock, *From Ephrem to Romanos. Interactions between Syriac and Greek in Late Antiquity*, ch. II).

2 Notably Bauer, *Orthodoxy and Heresy*, 1971, and H. J. W. Drijvers, 'Facts and Problems in Early Syriac-speaking Christianity', *SecCent* 2 (1982), 157–75 (repr. in his *East of Antioch*, ch. 6).

3 Notably F. C. Burkitt, *Early Eastern Christianity*, ch. 1, and H. E. W. Turner, *The Pattern of Christian Truth*, 39–46, 85–94.

4 See Brock, 'Eusebius and Syriac Christianity'.

5 A reconstruction is provided by H. J. W. Drijvers, *Bardaisan of Edessa*.

6 Text and ET in H. J. W. Drijvers, *The Book of the Laws of Countries*.

7 The work is also quoted in the *Clementine Recognitions* 9.19–29, and in Ps.-Caesarius, *Erotapokriseis* 108–9.

8 See especially M. P. Weitzman, *From Judaism to Christianity: Studies in the Hebrew and Syriac Bibles*, ch. 1; and in general, S. P. Brock, 'Ancient Versions (Syriac)' in *The Anchor Dictionary of the Bible*, VI (New York and London: Doubleday, 1992), 794–9.

9 Thus especially H. J. W. Drijvers.

10 See S. P. Brock, 'The Peshitta Old Testament: between Judaism and Christianity', *Cristianesimo nella Storia* 19 (1998), 483–502.

11 An excellent guide is provided by Petersen, *Tatian's Diatessaron*.

12 See especially B. M. Metzger, *Early Versions of the New Testament*, ch. 1.

13 See J. Joosten, 'Tatian's Diatessaron and the Old Testament Peshitta', *Journal of Biblical Literature* 120 (2001), 501–23.

14 For Jewish features in early Syriac literature as well as in the Syriac Bible, see S. P. Brock, 'Jewish Traditions in Syriac Sources', *Journal of Jewish Studies* 30 (1979), 212–32 (repr. in *Studies in Syriac Christianity*, ch. IV), and 'Palestinian Targum Feature in Syriac', *Journal of Jewish Studies* 46 (1995), 271–82.

15 In the past this has often been associated with Rabbula, bishop of Edessa from 411–36, but the evidence for this is inadequate.

16 The best ET is that by J. A. Emerton, in H. F. D. Sparks, *The Apocryphal Old Testament* (Oxford: Clarendon Press, 1984), 683–731. A detailed commentary, by M. Lattke, is in the course of publication (1999–).

17 On this ode see H. J. W. Drijvers, 'The 19th Ode of Solomon: its interpretation and place in Syrian Christianity', JTS n.s. 31 (1980), 337–55.

18 ET by A. F. J. Klijn, *The Acts of Thomas*. A good introduction is given by H. J. W. Drijvers, 'Thomasakten', in W. Schneemelcher, ed., *Neutestamentliche Apokryphen* (1997b), 289–303.

19 A survey is given by P.-H. Poirier, *L'Hymne de la Perle des Actes de Thomas* (Louvain: Peeters, 1981).

20 ET in W. Cureton, *Spicilegium Syriacum* (London: Rivingtons, 1855), 70–6. On this Letter see especially K. E. McVey, 'A Fresh Look at the Letter of Mara bar Sarapion to His Son', V Symposium Syriacum (Orientalia Christiana Analecta 236) (Rome: Pontificio Istituto Orientale, 1990), 257–72.

21 ET in Cureton, *Spicilegium Syriacum*, 41–51. For the possible dates, see F. Millar, *The Roman Near East, 31 BC–AD 337*, 478, with note 21; also I. Ramelli, 'L'apologia siriaca di Melitone ad Antonio Cesare', *Vetera Christianorum* 36 (1999), 259–86.

22 ET, with good introduction and notes, by T. Baarda in J. H. Charlesworth, ed., *The Old Testament Pseudepigrapha*, II, 583–606.

23 ET in Brock, *Studies in Syriac Christianity*, ch. VII, 233.

16

Concluding review: the literary culture of the third century

FRANCES YOUNG

The reader of this literary guide to the third century[1] will have been struck by the continuities and discontinuities with the material discussed in the earlier section. The continuities are enough to alert one to the artificiality of any chronological division, and it is the case that those divisions are far from absolute: the apocryphal New Testament material, for example, is by no means confined to the earliest period though we have treated it in Part I. Yet with the Alexandrians a new note is struck, and the birth of a Christian literature in Latin and Syriac marks a shift of which account must be taken. Christian texts are altogether becoming more embedded in the cultural and linguistic worlds around them, and their genres reflect that reality.

The epistolary form remains important, though those extant demonstrate subsequent interest in preserving those epistles which, having emanated from significant figures or councils, could be used to settle questions of belief or church order. Thus, apart from the collected correspondence of Cyprian, most letters from the period have survived because appeal was made to them in later controversial situations: for example, the correspondence of the two Dionysii, bishop of Rome and bishop of Alexandria, preserved by Athanasius. Others were preserved by Eusebius because they testified to the issues he was reporting. It is clear, however, that correspondence remained a significant way of keeping the scattered Christian communities in touch, and of communicating decisions which were taken to have wider import. There is both continuity and development here, paving the way for the 'official' communications of councils in the coming centuries, and in the case of Cyprian, for the collected correspondence of persons with standing which will become a feature of the fourth century. The latter is a clear case of higher-class Christians conforming to the literary culture around them; the former of the adoption of current styles of imperial governance.

That observation coheres with the impression that the literary guide must have created: more and more Christian authors were adopting the genres of the educated culture around them, and operating in a more sophisticated literary world. As already observed in chapter 1, the literary culture of the earliest Christianity is no longer regarded as 'low-class' in the same sense as it was at the beginning of the twentieth century. Yet the adoption of the codex is a clue to the fact that the earliest Christians had no literary ambitions; and the fact that debates are still continuing about the background of, and parallels to, so much of the earliest Christian literature bespeaks a continuing level of scholarly hesitancy about placing it in the mainstream of Greco-Roman literary culture. With the third century such hesitancy disappears. Clement and Origen adopted well-known philosophical genres: *Protreptikos* indicates by its title an exhortation to adopt the philosophical way of life; *De Principiis* is a Christian treatise following a standard format for discussing 'physics' (see chapter 11). Even the culture critic, Tertullian, exploits the norms of rhetoric (chapter 12) and, as the first substantial Christian author writing in Latin, demonstrates, like the great pagan orator Cicero before him, the extent to which literature written in Latin had conformed to Greek norms. Even the earliest Syriac literature was subject to the same Hellenizing pressures (chapter 15).

An unexpectedly striking example of the increasing debt to mainstream culture lies in the adoption of the methods of Hellenistic textual and literary criticism in commenting upon the books of Scripture. This constitutes the emergence of formal biblical scholarship within the Christian tradition. There is exegesis to be found in earlier texts, both letters and homilies, but it is not systematic. The commentaries and sequences of exegetical homilies which emerge in the third century, particularly with Origen but also Hippolytus, indicate a level of professional attention to the texts that owes something to Jewish precedent but much more to the way in which Hellenistic scholars and philosophers approached the classical texts.

It is worth pausing for a moment, however, to note that even here Christians did not simply conform to existing norms, and as a result the origin and nature of commentaries and homilies, so characteristic of the literary remains of Christianity, is not by any means transparent. The *Hypotyposeis* of Clement of Alexandria would appear to have been scholia, that is, annotations. These, usually marginal, notes on difficulties in classical texts had long been the main vehicle for recording scholarly comment in the Greco-Roman world, and it would appear that Clement collected similar jottings on the New Testament. But what lies behind the very definition of a scholion is the fact that most commentary was oral not written. In the schools of *grammatikos*, *rhetor* and *philosophos* education was based on classical texts, read and discussed in class. In the Hellenistic age school manuals and compendia were to some extent provided, and sometimes philosophers wrote commentaries on Plato or Aristotle. But most of the exegetical activity that went on in antiquity was never written down. The same must be true of the early Church, with its 'school-like' character (see chapter 9). It is only with the Alexandrians that the recording and dissemination of comment on Scripture is undertaken. Origen's patron, Ambrose, would seem to have initiated and facilitated that process.

The recording and dissemination seem to have taken two forms which have become distinguishable genres of exegetical activity. The ascription 'commentary' is usually taken to mean a self-consciously literary form, whereas 'homily' is taken to be a 'talk', given in a liturgical context and either transcribed by stenographers or prepared subsequently for publication. This distinction is useful and does characterize differences in Origen's works. The *Commentary on John* introduces itself as a kind of philosophical commentary and is addressed to the patron who financed the secretariat that produced it as a literary publication, while the *Commentary on Matthew* provides good examples of his discussion of issues that might be regarded as technical, such as text-critical points. The homilies, on the other hand, provide moral and spiritual exhortations which seem directed at a congregation Origen perceives to have reached different levels on the Christian way. But such distinctions cannot be overpressed.

There is a more fundamental reason for challenging the distinction than the fact that Origen is always, in Commentaries as well as Homilies, looking for the moral or spiritual meaning to be discerned in the texts he is treating. In a sense all literature in the ancient world was oral. We should never forget that publication and copyright are terms which have taken on specific meanings in the era of the printing press. In the ancient world there is a sense in which all writing was taken to be recorded speech, publication was more like a public reading, and many authors, Origen included, worried about their lack of control over the subsequent process of copying and dissemination, protesting at interpolation or distortion in pirated editions. In the case of later commentators there are sometimes grounds for debate as to whether a commentary was actually produced by editing homilies. Yet the distinction is important, and Origen's activities are one reason for pressing it.

The distinction between commentary and homily may be loose and hard to apply, but it does say something important about the context in which the exegetical activity was taking place. We have noted in Part I the school-like character of the early Church. Yet it was not in its gatherings precisely like a school. It had characteristics more like the Jewish synagogue insofar as a prime purpose was not just to read and interpret the received authoritative literature but to do so in the context of prayers and thanksgivings: indeed, in the case of the early Church, in the same assembly as the commemoration of the death of Jesus Christ in the 'bloodless sacrifice' of the eucharist. The bishop sitting on his *cathedra* expounding the sacred books with the congregation standing around him may have looked a bit like a schoolteacher giving a *homilia*, or informal talk; but this was the word of the Lord and by the third century the liturgical and religious character of what followed was increasingly clear as sacrificial and mystical characteristics attached themselves to the liturgical actions. The homily belongs to the liturgical context and is delivered to the whole gathered Christian community.

By comparison the commentary belongs to the world of learning. Alongside the Church, and to some extent in tension with it, a tradition had grown up, it would seem, of semi-independent Christian teachers, people like Justin or Origen who found in Christianity the framework for the true philosophical understanding of the world and undertook professional activities on that basis. Origen's school in Alexandria is supposed to have been inherited from Pantaenus and Clement, and tradition spoke of it as a catechetical school to which Origen was appointed by his bishop. But a number of hints suggest that the situation was not so straightforward: (i) under Ambrose's patronage, Origen was clearly trying to produce a Christian philosophical scholarship which could rival that of mainstream culture as well as the pretensions of the gnostics; (ii) his relations with the bishop of Alexandria became increasingly difficult, and he eventually set up in Caesarea where he was more welcome, a fact that suggests a certain potential rivalry between his school and the wider Christian community; (iii) the curriculum outlined by his pupil, Gregory Thaumaturgus, is hardly that of a catechetical school; rather, Origen was developing a complete cursus of studies such as was common in the educational system of antiquity, but with Christian philosophy as its goal. The difference between the commentary and the homily is, roughly speaking, that between the lecture and the sermon.

But the Christian scholars of the third century not only adopted more of the norms of the surrounding literary culture; they also further developed different types of controversial literature already characteristic of the second-century Church, notably, apologetic and anti-heretical works.

Origen's work *Contra Celsum* is usually described as an 'apology'. It takes a rather different form from the 'addresses and pleas' of earlier apologists, for it takes as its starting-point the anti-Christian work of Celsus, *The True Doctrine*, and answers it point by point. Indeed, in terms of 'form' the question might well be asked whether it is appropriate to speak of a 'genre' of apologetic.[2] Yet whether in the surface form of letters, petitions to authorities, dialogues or whatever, there is a recognizable literary interest and developing tradition of writing in defence of Christianity, which, beginning in the second century, is carried through the third century and into the fourth. Precise precedents are somewhat elusive, but apologists certainly owed something to both the standard defence-speech and to previous attempts to explain 'Jewishness' to the Greco-Roman world. Christian apologists increasingly rehearsed a number of standard motifs. Tertullian's *Apologeticum* is a valuable example of the genre, if we are to designate it such, from which the similarities and differences of other apologetic works can be plotted.

Christian literature, however, was not simply concerned to establish Christian identity over against the wider culture and to distinguish it from Judaism. There was also the issue of where the true tradition lay, and Irenaeus' attempt to expose the falsehood of some claims to *gnosis* was taken up in further compendia which critically detailed the teachings of heretics, such as those of Hippolytus. Again this type of controversial literature would be passed on into the fourth century, each compendium usually being dependent on previous work, to which additions and editorial modifications were made. A great deal of early Christian literature is polemical, and polemical elements enter other 'genres', such as the commentaries, homilies and letters on which comment has already been made.

This polemical aspect of Christianity accounts for another striking feature of the third-century material surveyed in this section: so much of what was produced has been lost or destroyed, not least because its transmission was affected by the fact that the orthodoxy of the principal literary figures did not survive the scrutiny of later heresy-hunts. Attention to detail will soon uncover the fact that different circumstances affect different authors: much of Tertullian survives despite his espousal of the Montanist teachings; Origen's massive literary output must have suffered not merely from deliberate destruction after his condemnation, but from simply not being copied; the work of Hippolytus is doubtless elusive because of his historically dubious status; because theologically sound, some of Novatian's work is extant despite his having caused schism. But all of this reinforces the point that the transmission of early Christian literature has been profoundly related to perceived authority.

In other words, authors are authors because they are authorized. The chance discovery of the text from Tura that purports to be the minutes of a synod examining the orthodoxy of Heraclides perhaps indicates that the authority of Origen's name once ensured the transcription of significant events at which he spoke; but, despite his profound influence on the development of Greek Christian literature and the vital necessity for the historian to unearth every trace possible, his authority became contested and with that went increasing literary oblivion. Many factors contribute to the fact that, in spite of this eclipse, it is not impossible to reconstruct much of Origen's life and work. As chapter 13 demonstrates, it is that much more difficult with Hippolytus. Historico-critical questions are unavoidable if we are to get any kind of handle on the literary culture of the third century. The authenticity and dating of so much of the literature has to be established before questions concerning its literary heritage and ambience can be properly addressed. It is perhaps not surprising that hermeneutical issues with respect to this literature have hardly been raised when a full account of the material requires the rehabilitation of authors who became, in one way or another, unauthorized.

But the issue of transmission can alert us to other features of this literary culture. We can see two pressures at work in the development of Christian literature: on the one hand, it is the literature of a community, older documents being taken up into later, larger compendia, the original authors often being unimportant; on the other hand, the authority of certain authors is such that their deposit is progressively enlarged, many works of later provenance being attributed to them. Examples of the latter feature include the libraries attributed to Ignatius and Justin Martyr (perhaps it is not surprising that second-century authors were subject to this treatment, but it occurred also in relation to the great orthodox authorities of the fourth century). Examples of the former are to be found (i) in the anti-heretical literature, Epiphanius' great work of the fourth century taking up and apparently superseding earlier works, with Hippolytus' work being a stage between Irenaeus and later encyclopedias; (ii) in the collections of canons, where works such as the *Didache* and the *Apostolic Tradition* become 'books' within larger volumes; and (iii) in the way catenae will abstract from commentaries and homilies of various different authors, sometimes preserving extracts from lost works in the process.

These features of early Christian literature are another reason why historico-critical questions have so dominated the study of this material. The question of sources has been as vital as the question of authenticity and dating. Furthermore, the literature of the fourth century demonstrates by its quotations and allusions that major controversies in the third century provide the background to the production and transmission of the material, and without painstaking reconstruction of those debates, we cannot grasp the picture into which this literary culture fits.

One final aspect of this developing Christian literary culture cannot be ignored: the primary activity of the community which produced it was worship. Texts which belong directly to this context are very limited, though, as we have seen, homilies originally did belong there, and there are substantial collections of these, especially from Origen. There could be an argument about whether poetic texts, such as the *Odes of Solomon*, originated in the context of communal worship: certainly the many references to singing imply, not merely the use of the biblical Psalter, but the emergence of singable Christian texts. Some would claim to find traces of these in some of the earliest Christian material; but for the most part such material is lost. What we do have in the third century are some texts which describe liturgical procedures, like the *Apostolic Tradition* associated with the name of Hipploytus; some relevant treatises, such as the works of Origen and Tertullian on prayer; and many references to worship in other texts, such as the letters of Cyprian. Once again, serious attention to this aspect of the literary culture of early Christianity requires painstaking historical reconstruction.

So the principal conclusion of this literary review must be that historical and contextual questions cannot but remain paramount in assessing and interpreting this material. That is one reason why importance is attached to the following studies of the third-century social setting, of third-century controversies, and of the Christian teaching that emerged within the third-century cultural context (chapters 17–19). Nevertheless many of the features of third-century Christian literature to which attention has been drawn here will clearly be of significance when questions of hermeneutics and appropriation are then addressed (chapter 20).

Notes

1 The material in this chapter is principally a comment on what precedes and readers are referred back to earlier chapters for footnotes and references.

2 See further the volume edited by Mark J. Edwards, ed., *Apologetics in the Roman Empire: Pagans, Jews and Christians*.

B.

*

CONTEXT AND INTERPRETATION

17

Social and historical setting: Christianity as culture critique

KAREN JO TORJESEN

The third century is often cast as a period of increasing conformity to Roman institutions and values, one that carried Christianity further and further from its true and original identity. This story of conformity implies an interaction between two disparate cultures in which the weaker culture is modified and somehow diminished through its adaptation. Such a model imagines Christianity as a missionary enterprise seeking to take root in an alien culture. What this narrative obscures is the fact that Christianity was a movement originating within Roman society, invented as it were by 'Romans'.[1] It is precisely the fact that Christians lacked a unique cultural identity that made the emergence of Christianity such a dilemma for the Empire. Christians did not have a common ethnic identity – that distinctive dye of language, custom, ritual and local history that located other individuals and groups on the cultural map of the Roman Empire. Since the Roman elites were fastidious about their 'Romanness', expressed in the values of *auctoritas*, *dignitas*, *romanitas* and *mos maiorum*, these ethnic identities remained a powerful force in imperial society. When the imperial military and political map bestowed sometimes unwanted regional identities on areas organized into provincial administrative units, the custodians of this regional culture created a hybrid culture by crossing the values and traditions of this 'Romanness' with those of the proud, albeit local, elites.[2] Christianity was shaped by the powerful cultural forces at work within the imperial and regional societies where it germinated.

However, the notion that Christians constituted a distinct culture, an ἔθνος, was central to the early self-portrait of Christianity. As Christian intellectuals and preachers were seeking to create an identity of otherness and difference, Christianity was, in fact, fashioning itself as a πολιτεία. By the strategic use of the term ἔθνοι or *nationes* for outsiders, they placed themselves at the centre of civilization and culture, in effect reducing all outsiders to foreigners or barbarians. In their claims to be a people, they were following the example of the Greeks, Jews and Romans who used the caricature of the uncivilized outsiders to set off the superiority of their own ethnic cultures.[3] A more adequate way of understanding Christianity is as a process of culture critique within Roman society. Christianity originated within the matrix of Roman society and, as Roman society spawned Christianity, it was also changed by it. Christianity, in turn, was continuously shaped and constrained by the values, world-view and institutions of Roman society.

If we interpret the evolution and growth of Christianity in the third century as the sum of the processes taking place in Christian communities from Gaul to Africa and from Asia Minor to Egypt, we see that third-century Christianity was the creation of Christians who were city officials, members of the imperial household, local *patres familiarum*, upper-class matrons, independent widows, despised handworkers such as potters, tanners, entrepreneurial freed persons, and slaves, all of whom were deeply entrenched in their regional cultures. Furthermore, we will see that third-century Christianity was shaped by very Roman notions of family solidarity, class aspirations and ethnic loyalty. The imperial bureaucracy, civic institutions, public values, patronage, and Roman notions of *honor*, *mos maiorum*, *pietas*, *disciplina* and *Romanitas* moulded Christianity as much as its ecclesiastical crises and doctrinal disputes.

Influence of patronage on religious customs

Patterns for human relations within society influenced the way relations between humans and gods were imagined. Protocols and rituals formed the language of honour by which a client acknowledged the dignity and worth of a patron, a worth they possessed by virtue of their superior social rank. Family rituals secured the benevolence and protection of the ancestors. Private prayers and gifts at temples sought a similar patronage from gods and goddesses such as Asclepius, Venus and Juno. Romans saw in their deities powerful patrons whose protection, favour and benevolence they sought to retain through affirmations of loyalty and rituals of honour. The state likewise sought the patronage of Roman and foreign gods and goddesses. The calendar of festivals honouring these deities was set by a government official, the priests who performed these rituals were supported by the state, and the temples themselves were civic building projects.[4] Maintaining the patronage of these powerful deities was not left to the spontaneous devotion of Roman citizens but was rather a significant state enterprise. The foundation of Roman greatness rested on the piety of the Roman state and the scrupulous care with which Roman priests performed the rituals of honour both to the patron gods of Rome and the foreign gods who generously acquiesced in Rome's conquest of their peoples.

Although slanderous rumours of incest and cannibalism among the populace dragged Christians into Roman courts, it was their repudiation of state religion that subjected Christians to investigative torture and execution as criminals.[5] Christians were not faulted for their neglect of participation in private religion, but for their open attack on public or civic religion. It was common for ethnic groups to boast of the superiority of their patron deities. This could be read as exaggeration or simple arrogance, but the Christians went further and demoted these powerful patrons to the rank of daimons: shadowy, intermediary divinities who lacked the honour and power of the glorious patron deities. Homage to the state deities, Tertullian claimed, was nothing more than homage to powerless daimons (*Idol.* 15). Far from being honourable gifts dedicated to respected deities, the burning of incense and the blood of sacrificial animals counted as nothing more than food for mangy daimons that hover around temple altars. Such flagrant and flamboyant insults to the honour of Roman patron deities left Christians open to the charge that periodic outbreaks of war, famine, drought and pestilence were the angry outbursts of public patron deities whose honour had been offended.

This contempt for the religion of the state could easily be interpreted as high treason (*intentatio laesae divinitatis*). In response to this danger, Christian apologists mounted both a defence and a counter-attack. They defended recalcitrant Christians by insisting on their loyalty to the emperor, to whom they were bound in love and for whom they offered prayers, since they deemed him to be appointed by their own God. Cyprian argued that because these deities were in fact former kings, honoured after their deaths through statues, festival days and sacrificial animals, there was, in fact, no clear connection between the festivals honouring these patrons and the glory of Rome (*Idola* 1). Conversely, Christians ought to be considered the most valuable of all citizens because they secured for the emperor the patronage of the eternal, true and living God.

Their counter-attack moved within the same logic of patronage. The wars, pestilence, famine and droughts were outbursts of the Christian God who had been grievously offended by the persecution of the Christians. Tertullian pointed to the recent eclipse of the sun as a sign of God's anger, Lactantius to the grisly deaths of persecuting emperors and proconsuls (*De Mortibus Persecutorum*). To drive home his argument against the Stoic notion of the impassibility of God and to defend the possibility of an angry God, Cyprian claimed that the Christian God was a creator and had the right to punish his own slaves for the crimes of idolatry and persecution; the anger of a Creator God could only be assuaged by making 'satisfaction to God and emerging from the darkling superstition into the bright light of true religion' (*Demetr.* 25).

State persecution, social class and the episcopacy

For two hundred years the persecutions of Christians had been regional and sporadic, generally in response to mobs inflamed by rumours of incest, of cannibalism, or by anonymous accusations provoked by envy, animosity or greed.[6] As traumatic as the ordeal of arrest, trial and execution was, the numbers remained few. When governors demanded that Christians sacrifice, it was part of the judicial procedure which would establish whether, in fact, the accused was a Christian. The guilty were executed for failing to comply with an imperial order.

In the trials, Christians encountered Roman political power concretized in the form of judicial authority. It was this judicial authority that they contested; Christ was the true judge and the Roman governors would have their day in his court. To defuse the suspicion of rebellion or insurrection, Christians protested that neither they nor their Christ had political aspirations. Nevertheless, the question 'Caesar or Christ?' – whether posed by the Roman magistrate or the Christian defendant – created an equivalence between these two loyalties. Christians in their rhetoric claimed that they were renouncing the religious authority of the Roman gods, but the drama of the martyrdom itself established Christ as a divine authority who could and must lay claim to political allegiance. Through the drama of martyrdom, the nature of Christ's authority shifted subtly. Earlier preaching proclaimed Christ as teacher, prophet and healer, but in the martyrologies and apologies he was proclaimed as judge and ruler.

The Emperor Decius (a general proclaimed emperor by his victorious army) was an Illyrian by ethnicity who gained entry to the Roman aristocracy through marriage. To legitimate his accession, he took extraordinary measures to align himself with the aristocratic tradition of ancient republican Rome. He restored the republican office of Census and in a great display performed the annual sacrifice to Jupiter on the Capitol. It was, however, a radical break with tradition in the year 250 when Decius ordered that a similar sacrifice be performed in all the provincial capitals. What made Decius' edict remarkable and even radical was the use he made of public religion. Before Decius, a publicly appointed magistrate or priest serving under the jurisdiction of a city council was the person responsible for holding a sacrifice (letting out the contract for the animal, presiding over the sacrifice, leading the victim, and supervising the temple staff). Even the wine for libations and incense for offerings were provided by the city government. The sacrifice itself was clearly an act of the city government performed by public officials with public monies to secure the well-being of the city under the twofold patronage of the imperial family and the Roman gods.

Decius' edict that the entire populace was required to sacrifice shifted radically the meaning of the city sacrifices. The implication was clear: every person living under the jurisdiction of Roman administrative authority bore some modicum of responsibility for honouring the gods. Decius turned what had been a public civic function celebrating a city's loyalty to Rome into a personal test of loyalty to the Roman emperor and to the Roman gods.[7] City officials drew up individual certificates for each person who sacrificed, certifying their participation. In this way, each individual was made to feel the obligations and the burden of 'Romanness', loyalty to the Roman emperor and devotion to the Roman gods. In Decius' vision of the new Roman order, the religious and civic duties carried out by the civic elites should now also be borne by the populace. 'In effect, Decius tried to treat the empire as though it were a city.'[8]

Decius' demand for universal participation in the Roman cult was a totally new experience for the Christian laity. If the obligations to sustain the patronage of the state gods now fell on individuals, then all Christians were locked in mortal combat with the Empire. Christians who were members of the municipal elites understood immediately the dire implications of this policy change. As members of the decurial class, they were the instruments through which the conquered populace was woven into the fabric of Empire. They secured the welfare of their city (and their own positions) through the melding of imperial and local interests. Dionysius of Alexandria wrote that 'of the more eminent persons some came forward immediately through fear, others in public positions were compelled to do so by their business' (Eusebius, *HE* 6.41.10–12). The Roman proconsul of Africa, Aspasius Paternus, informed the Christian bishop of Carthage that those who did not practise Roman religion still ought to acknowledge Roman rites. Cyprian refused to accept the distinction between the religious and civic dimensions of the festival. The bishop's refusal to participate was the more egregious because he was a member of the Carthaginian elite. As such he bore a greater burden of Romanness – of loyalty to the Roman emperor and the Roman gods – than did his social inferiors.[9] Cyprian was executed in 258 under Galerius Maximus, Paternus' successor, for refusing to participate in what were by then called the *ceremoniae romanae*.

The question why so many Christians lapsed during the Decian persecution obscures the fact that martyrdom was not considered a universal calling and an entire Christian community had never before been forced to choose martyrdom as a testimony of their faith, although both martyrs and ascetics were highly respected. The edict itself was without precedent and it was more a demand for civic allegiance than religious allegiance. Valerian spelled this out six years later in the distinction between adherence to Roman religion and participation in Roman ceremonies. The Jews were not required to sacrifice and their political allegiance was accepted without this ritual. Even the ensuing divisions and schisms between churches on the basis of a strict or lenient discipline were not new. Yet in the aftermath of the Decian persecution, Christianity underwent a convulsive evolution.

Those who succumbed to the threat of confiscation, fear of judicial torture, the humiliation of public trial, and the terror of execution became the lapsed, bearers of the stigma of unbelief: for their act of denial had cancelled their act of faith. Those who had undergone arrest, trial, confiscation, fines, torture or punishment and had survived became the confessors. Their courage in the face of fear, fortitude in the face of suffering, and faithfulness in the face of death confirmed the power and presence of the spirit in them. Confessors did not need to undergo a ritual of ordination; they were deemed to hold the rank of priest.

Once the fear of state retribution had passed, the fear of divine retribution supplanted it. Many of the lapsed sought spiritual safety once again in the arms of the Church and turned to the confessors and sought their patronage in the form of letters of recommendation. The clergy were quick to honour the sponsorship of the confessors and received the penitents into communion.[10]

Cyprian had gone into hiding during the Decian persecution and was judged by many of his clergy to have abdicated his role as bishop. Nevertheless, from hiding he relentlessly pursued his episcopal prerogatives. He was strongly opposed to the traditional procedures for dealing with the excluded. He felt new measures were required because of the scale of the problem of the lapsed – *totius orbis*. According to the old procedure, individual members of the clergy and confessors could restore penitent individuals. The innovation that Cyprian urged on the clergy was a centralized process of readmission, entrusted to a panel or commission to review each case individually on its own merit: a kind of judicial review. Cyprian provided a set of categories into which individuals might fall and created a ritual of readmission through the laying on of hands by the bishop and the clergy. According to his guidelines, those with recommendations whose lives were endangered should be reconciled to the Church after penance. For the rest, a deathbed reconciliation could be offered only after a lifetime of penance. This the Carthaginian clergy felt was far too severe.[11]

The pastoral concerns were not the only ones. Equally compelling for Cyprian and for many of his colleagues was this question: who should constitute the visible Church? Cyprian was convinced that the Church must be a society of those who were worthy. He grieved the laxity that thirty years of peace had brought the Church. There were bishops who were too involved in agriculture, trade and banking to govern their flock. There were deacons living with *subintroductae*, virgin female companions. The wealthy women of the congregation were worldly. Cyprian's procedure of a quasi-judicial investigation was designed to make sure that only those deserving be readmitted. He had no sympathy for the fashionable lapsed who did not care to do penance or the influential lapsed who used their status to gain readmission (*Ep.* 52). Novatian, one of the leaders in the Roman Church, held views even stronger than those of Cyprian. The visible Church was the company of those purified by baptism who kept their purity, if necessary at the price of martyrdom. These were the only ones who should share the eucharistic table. No penance could restore that baptismal purity.

Roman social order and Christian polity

The Decian persecution struck the Church at a time of burgeoning growth and upward mobility. The penetration of Christianity into the public classes made Christianity appear more threatening to the *romanitas* of those classes so essential for Roman hegemony. It was not until Christian converts appeared in the decurial class that Christianity posed a threat to imperial authority and Roman culture, for by the middle of the third century a significant number of bishops belonged to his class.[12] The changing character of Christianity in the third century can be traced through the transformations of liturgical space, shifts in the locus of authority, and the adoption of new organizational paradigms.

By the third century, local Christian communities were able to buy houses and remodel them for use by the worshipping community. The first stages of remodelling involved removing a wall to create a larger rectangular room, thus transforming a dining room to an assembly hall. In the house churches the social space of the *triclinium* (dining room) created and affirmed social bonds between those who participated in the common meal and emphasized the full membership of each individual in the community, mediated by access to the table. The new social space created by the assembly hall shifted the nature of the social bonds. A dais was placed at one end of the hall and the bishop's chair was placed on the dais. In this new orientation of communal space towards the bishop's chair, social bonds within the community came to be mediated through the bishop.

Along with the creation of a hall, the doors to the assembly rooms were widened and sometimes arched, making the space more public through providing a larger and more ceremonial entrance. The addition of a forecourt or portico, often colonnaded, created a vestibule which lent a greater sense of formality. The commissioning of wall paintings, the laying of a mosaic floor, and the addition of columns to the courtyard signified an increase in the wealth and status of members.[13] These architectural changes reflect and were concurrent with a rise in the social status of members of the Christian community. Renovations such as mosaic floors, wall paintings and marble revetments were often gifts from affluent members whose function as patrons for the church reflected their social status in the city.

As the architectural space of early Christian meetings came more and more to resemble the assembly hall of the city, the leadership of the Christian churches came increasingly from members of the local elites, the curial class. Just as in the cities holding any of the various priesthoods was a means of upward social mobility, so it was also in the Christian churches.[14] Rank and status within the church paralleled rank and status outside.[15] As municipal office holders, these church leaders were members of the curial class, rather than private persons such as seamen, tile workers, potters and tanners. As members of the curial classes their vocation was simply public service. Through their influence, the proceedings of the Christian community came to have more in common with the procedures and concerns of city councils than they did with the rituals performed at the municipal temples.[16]

During this process, the Christian communities began to replicate the socio-political order of Roman society. The essence of Roman political philosophy can be summed up in a single principle: rule by the propertied classes. An official ceremony marked the entry of an individual into these classes, once the property qualification was met (there was also a fee). Entry into the *ordo* brought both privileges and responsibilities, above all the obligation to be involved in public life. Theologians of the third century began to describe the Church as a *corpus* or *societas*, terms used for the body politic.[17] The congregation was organized into orders that corresponded to the classes of Roman society. The distinction between the *ordo clericus* (clergy) and the *ordo laicus* (laity) paralleled the distinction between the *honestiores*, the public classes (senatorial, equestrian and decurial *ordines*) and the *humiliores*, private persons (the plebeian *ordo*). The *ordo clericus* of the Christian Church, made up of bishops, priests, widows, virgins, sub-deacons and lectors, was modelled on these Roman *ordines*. Ordination was the ceremony for entry into the *ordo*, membership was for life and both privileges and responsibilities accrued to members. Tertullian speaks of the *ius dandi baptismi*, *ius docendi*, *ius delicta dandi* and *ius offerendi* as belonging to the ordo (the legal rights to baptize, teach, discipline and offer the eucharist).[18] Like their counterparts of the senatorial, equestrian and curial classes, the clergy as the *ordo ecclesiasticus* represented and manifested the honour and authority of the Church; therefore it was imperative that they exemplify the moral discipline of the Church.[19] The *ordo clericus* was likewise the deliberative and decision-making body of the Church.

While the presidency of the municipal councils rotated yearly (magistrates like the *duoviri* were elected for a one-year term), the presidency of the clergy, the office of bishop, was a lifetime calling. Consequently, the authority of the Christian bishop over the clergy was anomalous and the full monarchical authority of the bishop developed only gradually. During the Decian persecution, the Roman clergy dealt directly with the Carthaginian clergy, ignoring Cyprian who, though in hiding, remained an active administrator. Likewise, when Novatian challenged the election of Cornelius as bishop of Rome, the Council of Carthage communicated directly with the Roman clergy and not with Cornelius. During the persecution, while Cyprian was in hiding, the clergy in Carthage continued to act independently and resisted Cyprian's attempts to control them by accepting into communion the lapsed who had *libelli*.

Cyprian's rapid ascent to the episcopacy was not propelled by the clergy. Five presbyters remained bitterly opposed to his ordination throughout his tenure. Rather, a popular acclamation elected him: 'the *plebs* would listen to no refusal' (*Epp.* 43 and 66). It is this experience that shapes Cyprian's theory of episcopal office: each bishop is elected by his own *plebs*.[20] The authority of the bishop derives from the laity and the laity should withdraw their grant of authority if the bishop is a sinner. Indeed, Cyprian worked actively to circumvent the authority of the Carthaginian clergy. As the persecution began to wane, he set up a commission of three bishops and two presbyters to distribute aid to those whom the persecution had stripped of their resources through confiscation.[21] The deacon Felicissimus fought Cyprian's attempt to circumvent the clergy, insisting that whoever sought aid from the commission would receive neither aid nor communion. Carthaginian Christians were forced to choose to be either clients of Cyprian or clients of the clergy. In its embryonic state during the middle of the third century, the monarchical episcopate was a fragile institution. Witness Cyprian's unending struggle to impose it on the Carthaginian clergy.

Roman rhetoric and Christian persuasion

Rhetoric was among the principal tools of power for the elite.[22] One cannot overestimate the value of training in rhetoric for establishing authority. Cyprian's beautifully crafted letters to the schismatic Roman confessors persuaded them to abandon Novatian and return to Cornelius (*Ep.* 50). Cyprian was able to rally African, Roman and Italian bishops, clergy and laity alike to his plan for dealing with the lapsed. His training in the arts of persuasion – argument, style, invective and praise – served as his principal tools of power while in hiding. In preserving and publishing his correspondence, he was following Roman provincial administrators like Pliny who showcased simultaneously their policies and their literary prowess. Cyprian, a master stylist, edited Cicero's dictionary of phraseology for Christian use. When Cyprian secured one of the letters from the Roman clergy which had ignored his authority, he returned it to its author with stinging remarks on stylistic infelicities. Cyprian's training in forensic rhetoric made him effective in controlling the deliberations of a council through careful sequencing in the presentation of the evidence and the setting out of the terms of the argument.

Councils and the consolidation of regional Christianities

Shifts in power were also taking place at the regional level. The second-century synods dealing with the date of Easter and controversy over Montanism were not dominated by the bishops of the provincial capitals. These second-century synods were gatherings of no more than twelve to eighteen bishops. By the third century, synods were convened in the provincial capitals and drew as many as sixty bishops. The pattern of the second-century synods shows a loose confraternity of bishops within a geographical region, but by the third century, the provincial capitals hosted the synodal meetings and their bishops dominated them. The lines of power between the churches of a region began to flow along the same well-worn channels as Roman administrative power.

The politics of the African churches were dominated by Carthage, the city at the heart of Romanized Africa with direct lines to imperial power.

Carthage assumed a natural dominance over against Numidian Africa whose relationship to Rome was that of a client state now elevated to the status of ally for their support of the Romans in their battle to subdue the Carthaginians a century earlier. In Egypt, the Alexandrian bishops dominated the politics of the Egyptian churches, gaining a natural authority from the fact that all of Egypt was under the administrative control of Alexandria. The bishops of Rome were particularly concerned with the primacy of their city and the goals of its Empire, authority, conformity and uniformity.

Regional differences surface when one examines ecclesiastical and doctrinal concerns. A comparison of what caused an ecclesiastical crisis in Alexandria with what precipitated an ecclesiastical crisis in Carthage is instructive about the regional differences. The third-century Alexandrian bishops (Dionysius and Peter) engaged in contemporary debates on the Godhead, on natural philosophy, on the coming of the Saviour, on the resurrection. The famous Alexandrian teachers Clement and Origen produced the first great systems of Christian philosophy. In contrast, Western intellectuals like Hippolytus and Irenaeus compiled long catalogues against speculative theology (*philosophumena*, *syntagma*). For African intellectuals, the triumph of Christianity was a moral one rather than a philosophical one and their writers produced moral treatises on women's dress, the wearing of the victor's crown, and on second marriages. Intellectuals of the Latin West were especially concerned about Judaism's relation to Christianity. Hippolytus wrote *On the date of Easter*, Novatian *On Circumcision*, *On the Sabbath*, *On Jewish Food*. Tertullian wrote against the Jews as did an anonymous Latin writer, Ps.-Cyprian.

Bishops of the major cities in the third century were actively consolidating episcopal power. In Hellenistic Alexandria it was the authority of the philosopher teacher that was perceived as a threat to the consolidation of episcopal power; in Carthage it was the moral and spiritual authority of the confessors. The Alexandrian Bishop Demetrius struggled to impress upon the famous Christian philosopher, Origen, the prerogatives of episcopal power and assert episcopal authority over the freedom of the teacher. He was not entirely successful; for one of his successors, Alexander of Alexandria, was faced with a similar problem a century later with the teacher Arius. The Carthaginian Bishop Cyprian sought to make the bishop the mediator of the spiritual merit of the confessor. Nor was he altogether successful, for a century later African bishops would still be struggling to assert their authority over against Donatist bishops who saw their churches as heirs to the spirituality of the confessors.

Gender and religious authority

In Roman religion, women presided over both public and private festivals in the roles of *sacerdos*, *magistra*, *ministra* and *flaminica*. Often these were public offices and thus woman officiated at state functions, performed sacrifices, and were responsible for the administration of temple sites.[23] Interestingly, women's gender was never seen as a handicap or a liability in their holding these public offices. Neither public office nor presence in public space nor officiating at a public event was perceived by Roman society as transgression of the boundaries that set off the public political jural domain from the female domestic domain. Those points at which Romans perceived a clear transgression of the boundary between the public and private domains was in the exercise of *curia*, a form of power that was gendered masculine. The Roman historian Dio Cassius comments on the vast political power exercised by Livia (wife of the Emperor Augustus and mother of the Emperor Tiberius), that 'she undertook to manage everything as if she were sole ruler' except 'that she never ventured to enter the senate chamber or the camps or the public assemblies' (*HR* 57.12). What these three arenas have in common is the exercise of public speech as a form of public authority. Christian women were also heads of congregations and leaders of house churches. They were appointed deacons, ordained priests and presided as bishops, though not always without opposition. A female bishop from Caesarea successfully resisted the attempts of two male colleagues to discredit her through exorcism (Firmilian of Caesarea, *Ep.* 75.10). Epitaphs from Egypt (Artemidorus), Phrygia (Amnio), Greece (Epiktas) and Sicily (Kale) honour Christian women who were priests.[24] A letter of Pope Gelasius forbidding the ordination of women as priests confirms the fact that women were ordained, as do epitaphs from southern Italy.[25] Many of the churches of the new prophecy elected female clergy (Epiphanius, *Panarion* 49.236). Likewise the churches that embraced a wisdom soteriology readily acknowledged the authority of women clergy.[26] Epitaphs attest the activities of women deacons in Cappadocia (Maria), Achaia (Aggipiane), Melos (Agliasis), Macedonia (Matrona), Delphi (Athanasia), Bithynia (Krazalia), and Jerusalem (Sophia).[27] However, the institutions that possessed status were those of the political jural realm, not those of the domestic.[28] The presence of women and the prominence of their leadership could represent neither status nor power in the Roman understandings of gender. Only a fully masculinized leadership could do that. Third-century writers, such as Tertullian, challenged the legitimacy of women teaching, preaching and prophesying because in doing so they were 'usurping' a male prerogative, the power inherent in public speech.

Tertullian chastises 'the impudence of that woman who assumed the right to teach' (*Bapt.* 17). The transition from domestic to public space, from private to public classes, from a community organized along the model of a household to one modelled on the Roman body politic, undermined the legitimacy of women's leadership and brought about a masculinization of leadership during the third and fourth centuries.[29]

Roman roots of Christian asceticism

Early Christians evolved a distinctive lifestyle and set of values expressed in Christian asceticism. Roman society provided two distinct paradigms for renunciation as a vocation and Christian asceticism borrowed from both. Elite men marked for public life (which meant managing their family's assets, contributing to the prestige of the city, and building their own careers through the *cursus honorum*) could renounce their public life for a life of philosophical retirement. Simplicity of dress (signified by the philosopher's *pallium*), renunciation of an active sexual life, the discipline of the passions, a simple life and a hard bed were the markers of philosophical asceticism. A prototype for a female version of asceticism can be found among elite women. Traditional Roman mores expected widows of elite men to demonstrate their loyalty to their deceased husbands by choosing a vocation of chastity rather than remarrying. Chastity figured as a distinctly female virtue and formed the very core of female honour. When Christian teachers urged Christian women to pursue a vocation of chastity either as widows or as unmarried virgins, they were demonstrating that Christian women excelled at this most Roman of female virtues.

Women were the first professional ascetics within the Christian churches and the earliest institutionalization of asceticism was in the orders of widows and virgins. Through the orders of widows and virgins, the churches practised a vicarious asceticism and, in exchange, conferred on the widow and virgin the honours of both rank and office. Up until the fourth century, these were the only professional ascetics among the clergy. From the fourth century forward, ascetic authority is gradually assimilated to ecclesiastical authority as the ascetic values of renunciation of wealth and withdrawal from the world become important signifiers of clerical authority.[30]

The success of the orders of widows and virgins lay in the fact that they were anchored in women's social roles.[31] The order of virgins sacralized the identity of the chaste, protected, dependent daughter; the order of widows enshrined the image of the powerful *mater familias*. The ideal of the Roman mother was a formidable figure, a forceful personality, a strong disciplinarian, a custodian of Roman culture, and the guardian of traditional morality.[32] As a widow she became the guardian of her family.[33] When the leadership roles of the second-century Church were organized into the clerical orders of the third-century Church, the widows became one of the orders within the clergy. They were seated in the front of the church with the rest of the clergy who officiated during the liturgy. In Africa, the penitents seeking readmittance into the church prostrated themselves in front of the widows (Tertullian, *Pud.* 13). In Syria, the widows were entrusted with all the ministries to women (*TestDom.* 17.83). The third-century Church took the letter to Timothy as the charter for the office of widow. Their office was 'to continue in prayer and supplication night and day' (1 Tim. 5:5). The potency of the prayers of the widows was greater than that of other Christians because their ascetic practices – renunciation of sexuality, fasting, prayer and good works – endowed them with a superior piety (Ignatius, *Polyc.* 3).

Men and women of the laity were also attracted to ascetic practices, especially prayer, fasting and sexual renunciation.[34] In the churches where prophecy reigned, Christians experienced themselves as living along the border of the divine realm. Their services of worship were regularly graced with signs of the divine presence: dreams, visions, prophecies and revelations. For those who lived so close to the divine, ascetic practices were necessary disciplines for preparing the soul for this commerce with the divine. In these churches, every member was expected to give herself to the regular disciplines of fasting and prayer. An inscription in Phrygia remembers Nonas, a prophetess, as a woman of long powerful prayer, noted for visitation of angels, mighty in the gift of tongues.[35] Men and women were expected to take up the vocation of chastity once released from marriage by the death of a spouse. Even marriage itself became a school for continence and spouses who could agree together to renounce intercourse entered on a vocation of chastity while still embedded in the institution of marriage.

Another version of household chastity was practised by men and women linked neither by marriage nor by family who shared a domicile while each pursued a vocation of chastity. Women in these arrangements were called *subintroductae*. Tertullian was so bold as to enjoin chastity on the Roman male:

> Let us look at our own inner world, think how a man feels in himself when he abstains from a woman. He thinks spiritual thoughts; if he prays to the Lord he is next door to heaven; if he turns to the scripture, he is all of him

> present to them; if he sings a psalm, it fills his whole being with enjoyment; if he exorcises a demon he does it in confidence in his own strength.
>
> (*Cast.* 10.1)

Chastity as a Christian vocation was gaining ground in the third century.

Christian forms of piety: prayer and hagiography

The Psalms functioned as the earliest prayer book in the house churches. Early Christians believed that the Psalms were written by David the prophet, who foresaw Christ and composed them to reveal the state of Christ's soul. Early Christians praying the Psalter could use them as meditations on Christ. Not surprisingly, the first line-by-line commentaries on biblical books were interpretations of the Psalms. Both Origen of Alexandria and Hippolytus of Rome wrote commentaries on the Psalms. During the third century, liturgical arts flourished in every region. Prayers were composed to consecrate the eucharistic bread and wine, to ordain bishops, priests, deacons, widows, and to bless the cheese, olives, oil, milk and honey brought to the altar. Prayers sanctified the baptismal waters and the oils used for anointing; prayers effected exorcisms. The language of prayers and hymns was borrowed from the vocabulary of honour with which the excellence, dignity, worth and value of patrons, divine and human, was celebrated. Praise and petition marked the circle of patronage between Christians and their God, just as it did for the devotees of Zeus, Asclepius and Hera.

Family religion in Christian homes honoured God with rituals of prayer recited three times a day (*Did.* 4). Tertullian gives a Christian interpretation to the traditional Roman posture of prayer: Christians pray, 'gazing up heavenward . . . with hands extended because they are innocent . . . head uncovered because we are not ashamed . . . without a guide because we pray from the heart' (*Cor.* 3). Christians were exhorted by sermon and treatise to be diligent in their private prayers and to pray at set intervals of the day: the third, the sixth and the ninth hours, and even to rise at midnight to wash their hands and pray. Tradition makes of these hours a memorial of the crucifixion. In private, they could pray kneeling, sitting, or even lying and facing the east. Following Roman burial customs, Christians prayed for their dead, especially on the anniversary of their death. Especially the Christian widow offered prayers as a sacrifice for her husband's soul and for his refreshment in the interim and for fellowship with him in the resurrection (Tertullian, *Mon.* 2).

The first impulses toward Christian panegyric, or what the Church would later call hagiography, can be traced through an African composition, *The Life of Cyprian*. Written by his deacon Pontius, *The Life of Cyprian* unites the themes of asceticism and martyrdom in a Christian version of panegyric. Pontius' familiarity with the genre of epideictic rhetoric makes his omissions all the more striking. He is silent on Cyprian's family, the illustriousness of his ancestors, the extent of his wealth, his role as a civic servant, his education and the honours conveyed to him by the city; although these were all clearly known to him, he will not 'speak of his earthly lineage, but of his heavenly birth'. It is not for civic virtues that Cyprian is praised, but rather for ascetic virtues. He was continent, 'that the heart might become what it ought to be and the mind attain to the full capacity of truth'. He had renounced the world, wealth, and ambition. Only in his description of the trial and execution does Pontius call attention to his 'illustrious fame in the city'.[36] All of his achievements as a bishop are framed by Pontius as stages along the way to martyrdom. He restrained virgins to the fitting discipline of modesty, brought penitence to the lapsed, truth to the heretics, unity to the schismatics. He consoled the martyrs and animated the confessors. 'His was the first to decorate the insignia of his heavenly priesthood with the glorious gore of martyrdom.' Cyprian, the illustrious bishop, is praised for his ascetic virtues and for his martyrdom, for it is the stories of the martyrs and the renunciation of the ascetics that sets the terms for Christian hagiography – the glorification of the suffering self.[37]

Notes

1 The Empire created by Rome was actually a colourful mosaic of distinct cultural groups with their own laws, languages and customs, united under Roman military and administrative authority. When speaking of this Empire as a composite society, I use the term Roman, but the term can be misleading for most often a 'Roman' was also a Jew, a Phrygian, or an Alexandrian.

2 J. B. Rives, *Religion and Authority in Ancient Carthage*, gives an excellent account of the role of the municipal elites in creating this hybrid culture. Christian elites would undertake a similar process to institutionalize Christian values and practices by adapting Roman paradigms.

3 Christian apologists created the category of 'pagan' as a way to give a definitive content and systematic character to the culture they wished to critique. For a complete portrait of this duality of Pagan and Christian see Robin Lane Fox, *Pagans and Christians*.

4 See *On Roman Time. The Codex-Calendar of 354 and the Rhythms of Urban Life in Late Antiquity*, M. R. Salzman's study of the Roman calendar as a repository for Roman cultural traditions.

5 The Christian apologist Minucius Felix gives a literary reprise of the rumours and suspicions directed against Christians in popular culture in his book *Octavius*. See FC 10, 321–402.

6 W. H. C. Frend, *Martyrdom and Persecution in the Early Church*.

7 There was no universal priesthood because there was no direct control of religion in the provinces by the emperor. What the imperial cult reinforced was a version of *romanitas* with the deified emperor as its primary symbol.

8 Rives, *Religion and Authority*, 260.

9 Bishops Fabian at Rome and Byblas at Antioch were executed. Alexander of Jerusalem died in prison, Dionysius of Alexandria escaped arrest, and Cyprian of Carthage went into hiding.

10 There were other ways as well to fall out of communion with the Church. Bishops, priests, deacons and widows all carried some responsibility for correction and discipline. The severest form of discipline was exclusion from communion; however, through penance and the recommendation of a sponsor, a penitent could be reconciled. This sponsorship was a form of patronage. Catechumens also had sponsors who accompanied them through the process and stood surety for them at baptism.

11 When Cyprian came out of hiding in the spring of 251 and convened the first Council of Carthage, they accepted the basic outlines of Cyprian's proposal. When a popular uprising against the Christians threatened to unleash another persecution, a second council in 252 reversed the earlier decision and admitted all those penitents who were still seeking admission. The pastoral concern of the bishops was that especially these penitents needed the strength that flowed from the eucharist to fortify themselves in the face of another persecution.

12 Theodore Klauser, 'Bischöfe als staatliche Prokuratoren im dritten Jahrhundert?'

13 Michael White, *Building God's House in the Roman World. Architectural Adaptation among Pagans, Jews and Christians*, 120ff.

14 Ibid., 147ff.

15 Ibid., 57.

16 Ibid., 85. Upward mobility also meant that the community – pagan, Christian, or Jewish – had become influential enough to count as valuable clients and therefore attract the patronage of leading citizens who were not necessarily members of the community.

17 Elisabeth Herrmann, *Ecclesia in Re Publica*, 42; Alexander Beck, *Römisches Recht bei Tertullian und Cyprian*, 51–8.

18 *Cast.* 17 (baptizing); *Bapt.* 1 (teaching); *Pud.* 21 (disciplining); *Cast.* 7 (offering).

19 Beck, *Römisches Recht*, 54.

20 Cyprian sees himself not only as the patron of the poor, the *plebs* in the Church, but also seeks to make patronage the model for the relationship between the bishop and the clergy. Here is where conflict is sparked. His ongoing problem with the Carthaginian clergy is their refusal to behave as clients. His strategy is to recruit client clergy in order to establish the patron-client relationship as the foundation for episcopal power.

21 It is interesting to note that in establishing a five-member commission he is imitating imperial practice. Decius set up five-member commissions in each town to supervise the universal sacrifice. Cyprian appointed them, their authority derived from him, and they were in effect tutors or executors of his finances, operating under his instructions.

22 Averil Cameron, *Christianity and the Rhetoric of Empire. The Development of Christian Discourse*; Peter Brown, *Power and Persuasion in Late Antiquity.*

23 Amy Richlin, 'Carrying Water in a Sieve: Class and Body in Roman Women's Religion'.

24 Egypte: *Cahiers de recherches de l'Institut de Papyrologie et d'Egyptologie de Lille* 5 (1974), 264, no. 1115; Phrygia: *Greek, Roman and Byzantine Studies* 16 (1975), 437–8; Greece: *Bulletin de correspondance hellénique* 101 (1977), 210, 212; Sicily: *L'Année epigraphique* (1975), 454; see also Ute E. Eisen, *Arntsträgerinnen im frühen Christentum.*

25 Giorgio Otranto, 'Note sul sacerdozio femminile nell'antichità in margine a una testimonianze di Gelasio', see ET in Mary Ann Rossi, 'Priesthood, Precedent and Prejudice'.

26 Pagels, *Gnostic Gospels*, 60ff.

27 Since the Latin cultures of the western Mediterranean did not insist on gender segregation during worship, a specialized female order of deacons does not appear in the Latin sources. Greece: *Supplementum Epigraphicum* 29 (1978), 425; Melos: M. Guarducci, *Epigrafica greca*, IV (Rome: Il Poligrafico, 1978), 368–70; Macedonia: G. H. R. Horsley, ed., *New Documents Illustrating Early Christianity* (Sydney: Macquarie University Press, 1977), 109; Delphi: Guarducci, *Epigrafia greca*, IV, 345–7; Bithynia: *Zeitschrift für Papyrologie und Epigraphik* 18 (1995), 46; Cappadocia: *Supplementum Epigraphicum Graecum* 27 (1978), 947a; Jerusalem: Guarducci, *Epigrafia greca*, IV, 445.

28 The Christian churches were constituting themselves as a political/jural realm through the development of the bishops' courts in the third century. Christians were instructed to settle disputes and claims within the Christian community. By the third century the bishop functioned as a judge and the bishop's court was a full-fledged legal institution which, by the fourth century, was placed on an equal footing with the imperial courts by the Christian emperor, Constantine. Church offices were listed alongside civic offices in contracts and bills of sale and on inscriptions and epitaphs, as recognized forms of public honour.

29 Karen Jo Torjesen, *When Women Were Priests*. Virginia Burrus in *The Making of a Heretic: Gender Authority and the Priscillianist Controversy* traces these cultural

forces at work in the Priscillianist controversy, and then in the Arian controversy in *Begotten, Not Made: Conceiving Manhood in Late Antiquity*.

30 Philip Rousseau, *Ascetics, Authority and the Church in the Age of Jerome and Cassian*.

31 Kate Cooper, in *The Virgin and the Bride*, shows the continuity between the idealized womanhood of antique culture and female asceticism among Christians.

32 Suzanne Dixon, *The Roman Mother*.

33 Judith Hallett, *Fathers and Daughters in Roman Society*, 76ff.; Dixon, *Roman Mother*, 31–5.

34 Brown, *Body and Society*.

35 C. H. Emilie Haspels, *The Highlands of Phrygia: Sites and Monuments* (Princeton: Princeton University Press, 1971), I, 338–9, no. 107, plate 630.

36 *Life of Cyprian*. It is likely that Pontius forgoes the opportunity to praise Cyprian for the excellence of his social standing and civic achievements because Cyprian's easy transit to the episcopacy via patronage made his assets of wealth and status controversial.

37 Judith Perkins, *The Suffering Self*.

18

Articulating identity

RONALD E. HEINE

The attempt to articulate the boundaries of Christian identity in the third century involved inner-Church debates between groups which held different views on what constituted Christianity. Some of the concerns overlapped with those of the second century. The problem of what to appropriate and what to reject in contemporary culture, for example, was a perennial concern.

The major inner-Church conflicts of the third century, however, concerned the definition and understanding of faith and discipline. These were the two primary boundary markers of Christian identity. What must a Christian believe, and how must he or she live? The main tenets of Christian faith had, by this time, been summarized in what was known as the rule of faith. This was not yet a normalized and fixed document, but there was a body of generally recognized doctrine that could be referred to by this term. Not everyone agreed, however, on how the contents of the rule should be understood. Scripture, of course, was important to all the groups concerned with Christian identity in the third century, but there were different ways of reading Scripture, and these different ways of reading produced different results. Each group in conflict, as we will see, called upon Scripture to support its views.

The debates concerning Christian identity in the third century were anything but clear-cut cases. One cannot conclude that the group on one side was Christian and that on the other was not. Groups such as the gnostics, who deviated significantly from the rule of faith, had already been excluded. While treatises continued to be written against them in the early third century, they were no longer major participants in the debates about identity. The Montanists, on the other hand, who deviated from the Catholics more in discipline than in doctrine, continued to be major participants in the person of Tertullian. Tertullian adopted their viewpoint and radically criticized Catholic policy in regard to discipline. At the same time he continued to hold and defend the rule of faith with the Catholics, and may never have left the Catholic Church in Carthage. Novatian and his Catholic opponents were, likewise, in agreement on the rule of faith, but differed on questions of discipline and hierarchy. The lines of Christian identity were ambiguous even in those cases that concerned the interpretation of the rule of faith. In the monarchian debates, for example, Callistus, bishop of Rome, held a view of the relation between the Father and the Son that Hippolytus rejected as heretical. He put Callistus at the apex of his discussion of heretics. On the other hand, Hippolytus himself appears to have been bishop of a schismatic church in Rome. Origen wanted to remain faithful to the rule, but develop a system of speculative thought using philosophy and the Bible to address questions not treated in the rule. When one thinks of the towering figures in the third century who made major contributions to the shaping of subsequent Christian thought, Tertullian, Hippolytus and Origen were all considered at one time or another to stand, at best, on the margins of the tradition that prevailed.

The following subdivisions move back and forth between these two major markers of Christian identity. The monarchian issue concerned faith. What must the Christian believe about Jesus and his relation to God? With Tertullian the focus turns to discipline. What should the Church demand in the lifestyle of its members? The discussion of Origen shifts back to faith, and especially to its relationship with the surrounding culture. The Novatian schism raises the question of discipline again, but in a new context, and also highlights the issue of the Church's hierarchy in the question of Christian identity.

From monarchianism to Paul of Samosata

The beginning of the third century was a period of ferment in the Church's thinking about Christ. Two propositions had become axiomatic. The first, inherited from the Church's Jewish roots, was that God is one. The second, distinctively Christian, was that Jesus is God. Both propositions were central to the issue of Christian identity. The problem was how to maintain the second without contradicting the first.

The Church had been engaged in a long struggle against the gnostic view of God, and that of Marcion. The former separated the highest God from the Creator God of the Old Testament, and the latter separated the Creator God of the Old Testament from the redeeming God of Jesus. This polemic had heightened the Church's sensitivity to the importance of the doctrine of God's oneness.

The Apologists of the second century were the first to address systematically the question of what it means to call Jesus God. They stood in the philosophical tradition of Middle Platonism which had assimilated the Stoic *Logos* doctrine to Plato's creative Demiurge. Middle Platonists, therefore, had a first God, the intellectual One of Plato, and a second creator God, the *Logos*. The Apologists used this concept to explain how God could be transcendent and impassible and yet create and redeem the material world, and further, how Jesus could be called God without contradicting the doctrine of monotheism. The *Logos*-theology of the Apologists was refined into the doctrine of the economic Trinity by Irenaeus. The latter doctrine was accepted, with minor alterations, by Hippolytus and Tertullian in the early third century. It was by no means, however, universally acknowledged as the explanation for the relationship between Jesus and God.

Two reactions to this Middle-Platonic-based doctrine arose in the late second and early third centuries.[1] Both are referred to as monarchianism, since they were ways of preserving the monarchy of God. The two approaches were considered together as ways to avoid proclaiming two Gods as early as the mid-third century (Origen, *Io.* 2.16). The approaches themselves, however, were quite different, and are distinguished by modern scholars by the adjectives modalistic, and dynamic.

Tertullian, in the early third century, first labelled monarchian those whom we call modalistic monarchians. Their doctrine made no substantial distinction between the persons of the Trinity, but asserted that the various names referred to the particular manner of manifestation of the one God. Tertullian asserted that this was the viewpoint of the majority of believers, whom he called 'the simple' (*Prax.* 3). Hippolytus claimed that the heresy had arisen in his own time, and was led by 'ignorant' persons (*Haer.* 9.6). It seems to have been a widely held view, but, as I will show in what follows, its leaders were anything but simple or ignorant. The argument between the modalistic monarchians and those holding some form of the *Logos*-theology had roots in philosophical schools that affected their respective interpretations of Scripture.

Hippolytus claims that this teaching originated with Noetus of Smyrna (*Haer.* 9.7; *Noet.* 1).[2] Noetus began to teach either in the last decade of the second century or the first decade of the third. His teaching was taken to Rome by a disciple named Epigonus, where it found a spokesman in Cleomenes. The doctrine was accepted in Rome by the two bishops, Zephyrinus and Callistus, according to Hippolytus, who was not an unbiased witness regarding either. Callistus excommunicated Sabellius as a political move, according to Hippolytus, to mask his own similar theological position (*Haer.* 9.12.15). Tertullian addressed a treatise against Praxeas, another modalist who came from Asia Minor to Rome.[3]

The core of Noetus' teaching was 'that Christ himself is the Father, and that the Father himself was born, suffered, and died' (*Noet.* 1). Those who stood in the tradition of the Middle Platonic *Logos*-theology rejected this teaching because it involved God the Father directly in the material world, and especially in suffering.[4]

Noetus' central doctrine was based on an argument which combined Scripture and Stoic logic.[5] First, using Old Testament Scriptures, he established the proposition that there is only one God,[6] namely the Father. He then assumed that Christ should be considered to be God, which most Christians would not have questioned.[7] The Noetians then structured these two propositions into a Stoic argument known as the first undemonstrated argument.[8] The argument has the form: If A, then B; A is true, therefore B is true. They argued: (A) if Christ is God (based on the common faith of the Church), then (B) he is the Father himself (based on the Old Testament passages about the oneness of God), and concluded: (A), Christ is God, is true, therefore (B), he is the Father himself. This conclusion was then used as the first proposition in a subsequent argument of the same kind to prove that it was the Father who suffered.[9]

This logic yielded a God who, though not immanent in the material world, was much more directly involved in it than the Platonists' God. God the Father created the material world without the intervention of an intermediate *Logos*, and God the Father redeemed the material world without the intervention of an intermediate *Logos*.[10]

Callistus, as also Praxeas, if they were, indeed, two different people,[11] modified this doctrine slightly to avoid saying that the Father suffered. He identified the Son who suffered with the flesh born of the virgin, and the Father with the Spirit who was in the Son, and said that the Father did not suffer himself, but suffered 'along with the Son' (Hippolytus, *Haer.* 9.12.18–19; Tertullian, *Prax.* 29).[12]

Sabellius, the most famous proponent of the modalistic doctrine, added further refinements. First, he made the Holy Spirit an explicit part of the teaching, saying that 'the same one is Father, Son, and Holy Spirit' (Epiphanius, *Pan.* 62.1.4). The three, he said, are one subsistence (*hypostasis*), and one person (*prosopon*) with three names (Theodoret, *Haer.* 2.9, cf. Epiphanius, *Pan.* 62.1.4–6, Eusebius, *ETh.* 3.6.4). Second, he added the argument of temporal sequence to the various manifestations. In the Old Testament, God gave the Law as Father; in the New Testament, he became incarnate as Son; finally, he visited the apostles as Holy Spirit (Theodoret, *Haer.* 2.9; Epiphanius, *Pan.* 62.1.7–9).

An alternative explanation for the relationship between Jesus and God also made its way from Asia Minor to Rome at approximately the same time as Noetus' doctrine. Theodotus, referred to as a cobbler from Constantinople, went to Rome about 190. He taught that Jesus was a human being, in common with all other human beings, except that he had been born of a virgin, who, he said, in dependence on Luke 1:35, had been overshadowed by the Holy Spirit. Because of his superior religious nature, Jesus received the Christ in the form of a dove at his baptism. This descent of the Spirit on Jesus made him Christ, but not God. The followers of Theodotus were divided over whether Jesus ever became God. Some thought he did after his resurrection (Hippolytus, *Haer.* 7.35; cf. 10.23). Theodotus' explanation of the relationship between Jesus and God is called dynamic monarchianism, because of the 'power' (δύναμις) which Jesus received at his baptism.

Theodotus was excommunicated by Victor, bishop of Rome (189–99), for teaching that Christ was a 'mere man'. He appears then to have formed his own congregation in Rome, for Eusebius relates a story about a confessor named Natalus who was persuaded by followers of Theodotus to become a bishop 'of this heresy' in the time when Zephyrinus was bishop (Eusebius, *HE* 5.28.6–10).

Theodotus' followers appear to have accepted the philosophy of Aristotle,[13] been especially interested in logic, rejected the allegorical exegesis of the Bible for a more grammatical and literal exegesis, and applied the Greek philologists' methods of textual criticism to the text of the Greek Bible. Eusebius cites an early source which refers to their admiration of Euclid, the geometrician, Aristotle and his disciple Theophrastus, and the philosophical physician Galen (Eusebius, *HE* 5.28.13–19). R. Walzer argued that it was especially Galen, who was a contemporary in Rome, whose influence should be seen in all of these areas, and suggested that Theodotus' followers may have attempted to restate the teaching of the Church in a way that would appeal to an audience such as that represented by Galen.[14]

Eusebius connects Artemon, also called Artemas, with the teaching of Theodotus, and links him, in turn, with Paul of Samosata (*HE* 5.28.1; 7.30.16–17). We know little about Artemon. He may have still been alive in 268.[15] He appears to have added the argument of antiquity to Theodotus' teachings, claiming that this view of Christ went back to the apostles, and that it had been corrupted only in the time of Zephyrinus (Eusebius, *HE* 5.28.3; cf. Theodoret, *Haer.* 2.4). He thereby claimed, implicitly at least, that Victor had himself shared this view, something which the author of Eusebius' source was quick to contradict by pointing out that Victor had excommunicated Theodotus. The latter loses some of its argumentative power, however, if we remember the somewhat later Callistus-Sabellius affair reported by Hippolytus. Some have attempted to corroborate Artemon's claim by pointing to the adoptionist Christology in Hermas (*Sim.* 5.6). The claim to antiquity, however, must have been mainly an exegetical argument, based, if we may assume that Artemon appealed to the same texts to which Epiphanius says Theodotus appealed, on texts primarily from Luke-Acts, such as Luke 1:35 and Acts 2:22.[16]

In the second quarter of the third century Origen was called upon to interrogate Beryllus, bishop of Bostra in Arabia, at a synod convened to deal with the latter's view of Christ. Beryllus had denied pre-existence to Christ, as well as any divinity except for that conferred on him by the indwelling of the Father (Eusebius, *HE* 6.33.1–3). Eusebius, curiously, does not mention Theodotus, Artemon, or Paul of Samosata in relation to Beryllus, who obviously held views in common with them. The reason, probably, was that Beryllus was not considered a heretic, since he succumbed to Origen's arguments and was restored 'to his former sound opinion'.

In 268 Paul of Samosata was deposed as bishop of Antioch, for teaching a similar doctrine.[17] The synod that deposed him consisted of bishops who held Origen's views. Paul had enough local political power, however, as well as popular support in his church, to resist the decision and retain control of the church property. The emperor had to be called upon to settle the matter concerning the property. He settled it against Paul (Eusebius, *HE* 7.30.18–19).

Eusebius is our most reliable witness to the teachings of Paul of Samosata, for he had read the synodal letter composed by the bishops who deposed him (*HE* 7.30.1–17). Unfortunately, the passages he has excerpted from that letter do not say much about Paul's view of Christ. The bishops asserted that he forbade psalms to be addressed to Christ in worship, that he would not acknowledge with them that the Son came 'down from heaven', that he said that 'Jesus Christ is from below'; and they concluded by associating Paul's teaching with that of Artemas. In his *De Ecclesiastica Theologia*, Eusebius says that Paul of Samosata taught that Jesus is the Christ of God, and that there is one God over all things. He did not confess, however, that Christ is the Son of God, and that he was God before he became flesh (*ETh.* 1.14.2). Eusebius' statements place Paul of Samosata in the dynamic monarchian tradition.[18]

Neither modalistic nor dynamic monarchianism died with its most notorious advocate. They were both pushed to the periphery, however, as the Platonic theology represented pre-eminently by Origen in the third century took over the centre of the Church's understanding of its doctrine. Platonism triumphed theologically in the Church at about the same time that it triumphed philosophically in the Empire. Alexander of Aphrodisias, who received an imperial appointment as teacher of Aristotelian philosophy at the beginning of the third century, was the last significant Aristotelian philosopher in antiquity. After him, even those who wrote commentaries on Aristotle did so as Platonists.[19]

The dynamic monarchian doctrine was condemned for denying the deity of Christ (Eusebius, *HE* 5.28.6; Origen, *Herac.* 128). The latter was thought to be inseparably connected with the eternal pre-existence of the *Logos*-Christ with God. The modalistic doctrine was condemned for involving the Father too intimately in this physical world. The views influenced by Aristotle and the Stoics, both of which emphasized the phenomena of this physical world, were marginalized by the higher vision of Plato. Both doctrines, nevertheless, cast long shadows which fell across the Christological debates between the monophysites and dyophysites in the fifth and sixth centuries.

Tertullian and Christian radicalism

Christian identity, as previously noted, concerned discipline as well as doctrine. Tertullian had a deep concern for both. The focus in this section is on discipline, but we begin with a brief look at his faith, for he considered discipline to follow faith (*Mon.* 2).

Tertullian's faith is often remembered for its radical expression in the question, 'What has Athens to do with Jerusalem?', together with the assertion that the death of the Son of God 'is credible because it is foolish', and his resurrection 'is certain because it is impossible'. As we have already noted, however, Tertullian was not as hostile to the learning of classical culture as these paradoxes suggest.[20] Nevertheless, he grounded faith on, and demanded that it be tested by, the two touchstones that by now were the common intellectual property of the Church, namely Scripture and the 'rule of faith'.[21] Both, he insisted, proceeded from the earliest days of the Church. This antiquity was significant, for what is earliest, he asserted, is true and authoritative. What comes later is derivative, diluted, and (usually) deviant.[22]

The rule of faith, which Tertullian thought went back to Christ himself (*Praescr.* 13), was the more basic of the two touchstones. It is 'faith', Tertullian notes, that saves one, not skill in exegeting the Scriptures, and 'faith', he says, 'has been placed in the rule' (*Praescr.* 14). The heretics could find their teachings in the Scriptures because their exegesis was not controlled by the 'rule' (*Pud.* 8).

The rule of faith, which Tertullian sets forth in three different treatises, never in exactly the same wording, but always with the same basic structure and content (*Praescr.* 13, cf. 36; *Virg.* 1; *Prax.* 2),[23] summed up the basic doctrines of the Church. It begins with a short statement about the one God who created all things from nothing by his Word. Then follows a much longer section identifying this Word as the Son of God, and setting forth the basic beliefs related to his birth, life, death, resurrection, ascension, sending of the Spirit, and return to reward and judge mankind. This was the *sine qua non* of the Church. To alter this rule, or to depart from it, was to cease to be Christian (*Apol.* 46.17). Even after he had accepted the new prophecy of the Montanists, Tertullian continued to insist that the rule of faith was unalterable. The new revelations of the Montanist prophets, he asserted, could affect only 'discipline and life' (*Virg.* 1.4–5).

Tertullian's views on discipline are focused in his teachings concerning post-baptismal sins, asceticism, and martyrdom. His views on these subjects were strict from the beginning, but they became even stricter after his acceptance of the new prophecy. We cannot here discuss the tangled question of whether Tertullian withdrew from the Catholics and became a part of a Montanist Church in Carthage, or whether he remained in the Catholic Church but adhered to Montanist views.[24] Whichever side one takes, it is abundantly clear that Tertullian shared the Montanist viewpoint in his later writings and severely criticized Catholic teachings from this perspective.

Tertullian's concern for purity of doctrine was matched by his concern for purity of life in the Church. Prior to his adoption of the Montanist viewpoint, he had already applied the imagery of the Lord purging the threshing floor to the Church. Those who were subverted from Christian perseverance were dismissed as 'the chaff of a fickle faith' blown away by the 'blast of temptation', and leaving the heap of corn to be stored in the Lord's granary purer (*Praescr.* 3).[25]

The gulf that baptism cut in life between one's past in the world and one's present in the Church was so deep that it should be delayed, he thought, until one was fully cognizant of the responsibilities it imposed, and was in a reasonable position to fulfil those responsibilities (*Bapt.* 18).[26] It is repentance, however, which effects forgiveness, and not baptism. Baptism seals the forgiveness, and can be valid only if one has actually stopped sinning (*Paen.* 6).

Tertullian compared Christians to people delivered from shipwreck. Just as the latter feared further sea travel so as not to tempt fate, so should Christians fear sinning after baptism. He recognized, however, that the devil is determined to regain those whom he has lost. Consequently, although baptism shuts the gate of forgiveness, God leaves it open a crack for one last repentance. Tertullian was hesitant to speak of this, for he feared it might relax Christian discipline.

Nevertheless, he asserted that one who has need of this remedy should use it without shame (*Paen.* 7). He indicated no sins which could not be included in this second repentance. Tertullian's views in this regard seem to reflect those of the early Church in general.[27]

Tertullian's doctrine of post-baptismal repentance narrowed, however, after he embraced the rigorist discipline of the Montanists. He states that he has changed his opinion concerning the forgiveness of those Christians guilty of adultery and fornication, among whom he included widowed people who remarried (*Pud.* 1). He subsequently divided sins into the categories of 'remissible' and 'irremissible', with idolatry, murder, adultery and fornication forming the latter category (*Pud.* 2). He did not exclude the possibility that God could forgive such sins in the eschaton, if the guilty did penance throughout their lifetime, but he refused them any reconciliation with the Church. He argued that the presence of such a sinner spoils the purity of the whole Church (*Pud.* 13). Tertullian grounded this view on both the Scriptures and Montanist prophecy. The latter rested on an oracle which he attributed to 'the Paraclete himself': 'The Church can pardon sin, but I will not do it, lest they also commit other offences.'[28] Tertullian's concern for purity had become an instrument of division under the influence of Montanist rigorism.

Tertullian also considered asceticism an important part of Christian discipline. In contrast to ascetics in the East, however, he did not renounce marriage.[29] His attitude towards virginity was ambivalent. He never wrote a treatise in praise of virginity, nor did he praise it frequently in his other treatises. The one treatise devoted to the subject is a criticism of the practice of allowing virgins to appear unveiled in Church. Even in this treatise, as in several others, he ranked continence above virginity as the more difficult attainment (*Virg.* 10; *Mon.* 1; *Cast.* 1, 10; *Ux.* 1.8). As a Montanist he saw the divine instruction concerning marriage progressing in three stages. First, the Law of Moses allowed divorce and second marriage. The new law then denied divorce, and, finally, the new prophecy denied second marriage (*Mon.* 14). He saw the Montanist rejection of second marriages to be a mean between the prohibition of marriage by heretics and what he considered to be the multiplication of marriages allowed by Catholics (*Mon.* 1).

The Montanist practices of fasting frequently, eating only dry foods, and avoiding wine had come under Catholic attack and were vigorously defended by Tertullian. He considered these practices to be another form of continence parallel to that which he had already defended in regard to marriage (*Ieiun.* 1). The biblical prophetess Anna was his heroine, for she united in herself the continence of long widowhood and of frequent fasts. He used her example to show that those who practise continence in regard to sex and food have a superior ability to recognize Christ (*Ieiun.* 8; cf. *Mon.* 8). The Montanists, as Christians and non-Christians before them, appear to have used fasting and dry diets to encourage visionary experiences (*Ieiun.* 12; *An.* 48).[30]

Martyrdom always had high honour in the Church, except among the gnostics, and it appears to have been especially honoured at Carthage.[31] It is, in fact, difficult to see appreciable differences between the views of the Catholics and the Montanists on this subject. It has been argued, however, based on his interpretation of the oracle of the Spirit which urged Christians to desire martyrdom over any other form of death (*Fug.* 9.4; *An.* 55.1–5), that Tertullian may have advocated voluntary martyrdom.[32] The oracle in question is cited in Tertullian's argument against current use of Matthew 10:23. Voluntary martyrdom is not at issue. Tertullian is arguing against those who want to justify flight in persecution. He argues on the basis of the rhetorical rule of considering both the immediate and the larger context of a statement to determine its meaning.[33] He begins with the immediate context of Matthew 10 (*Fug.* 6), then takes in the larger context of Jesus' life (*Fug.* 7–8), moves next to the context of the teaching of the apostles (*Fug.* 9.1–3), and, since he believes that the Spirit who spoke in the Bible speaks also in the new prophets, he appeals finally to the words of an oracle of the Spirit in this even larger context (*Fug.* 9.4). And what Tertullian understood the Spirit to say was that one should choose death as a martyr instead of flight. The question concerned standing firm in persecution, not pursuing or provoking martyrdom. Tertullian was so adamantly opposed to fleeing persecution because he saw the crux of persecution to concern the confession of Christ, which related it directly both to the rule of faith and to the irremissible sin of idolatry.

There are two passages in the *Ad Scapulam*, written during Tertullian's Montanist period, which refer to Christians coming forward of their own accord in time of persecutions. Both are intended as statements to show the governor how much Christians despise the dangers of persecutions (*Scap.* 1, 5).[34] The latter reference is accompanied by a reference to a persecution in Asia in which all the Christians in a particular city offered themselves for martyrdom to the governor.[35] Tertullian uses this illustration as a warning to Scapula. Such a thing *could* happen in Carthage too. Then what would Scapula do, with such a mass of people, comprising every age and rank of society? How could Carthage endure such an outrage? It seems unlikely that Tertullian is thinking only of Montanists reacting in this way, and not of the entire Christian body in Carthage coming forward. Tertullian expresses neither approval nor disapproval in these references to Christians giving themselves up to the authorities voluntarily. It should be noted, however, that these, plus the other arguments of this apology, are intended to convince Scapula to desist from persecuting Christians, which is rather incongruent if he were seeking an opportunity for himself and others to become martyrs.

The major point of difference between the Catholics and the Montanists on martyrdom in the third century was their differing views on avoiding it. While the Catholics considered martyrdom to be the highest possible attainment of the Christian faith, they insisted that it should not be pursued intentionally, and should be avoided if one could do so without compromise.[36] Both Cyprian and Origen were arrested for the faith in the mid-third century. The former was martyred, and the latter would have been had not the persecution ended, but both men had fled to avoid martyrdom in earlier persecutions. The Montanists, however, appear not to have sanctioned flight in persecution under any circumstances.

Tertullian's own view on this subject appears to have been modified only minimally by his acceptance of Montanism. He may have grudgingly allowed flight from persecution as an alternative to denying the faith before he became a Montanist. It is obvious, however, that he did not recommend it. It was, at best, a concession granted to weakness (*Ux.* 1.3).[37] It stood among things permitted, not among things recommended, and, he adds, 'What is *permitted* is not *good*' (*Ux.* 1.3). In a Montanist work he castigated pastors who fled as 'lions in peace', but 'deer in the fight' (*Cor.* 1). In his Montanist treatise devoted specifically to the subject, he argued, first, using Job as his paradigm, that because persecutions come from God they ought not, and ultimately cannot, be avoided (*Fug.* 1–4), secondly, that fleeing out of fear of denying is already a denial (*Fug.* 5), thirdly, that both proper exegesis of Scripture and the testimony of the Paraclete show that Matthew 10:23 is not applicable to the persecutions suffered by the Church (*Fug.* 6–11), and finally, that bribery to avoid persecution is wrong (*Fug.* 12–13). He concludes the treatise by relating his position directly to his Montanist stance, when he says that those who have received the Paraclete 'practise neither flight in persecution nor bribery to avoid it' (*Fug.* 14.3).

Tertullian's concern for the purity of the Church reappears explicitly in this treatise. At its beginning, he cites the imagery of the threshing floor, and says that persecution is the winnowing fan which separates 'the grain of the martyrs from the chaff of the deniers' (*Fug.* 1). At the end of the treatise, he asserts that standing firm in persecution keeps Christ's 'betrothed virgin pure' (*Fug.* 14).

Christianity was a stern affair for Tertullian even before he adopted the new prophecy of the Montanists. W. H. C. Frend and C. B. Daly have each labelled him a 'puritan'.[38] The latter thinks his attitude and views were the source of Novatianism,[39] and the former calls him 'the father of Donatism'.[40] R. L. Fox has noted that the discipline of the Montanists 'appealed to over-achievers'.[41] It certainly attracted one in Tertullian.

The new *paideia*: Origen

Origen's Christian discipline was as strict as that of Tertullian, at least prior to the latter's adoption of Montanism. He too spoke out against 'certain persons' who presumed to forgive the sins of idolatry, adultery and fornication, and thereby exceeded the power of their priestly office (*Or.* 28.10). He was a rigorist ascetic by any standard, even disallowing the stories of his self-mutilation, and he considered faithfulness to death in persecution the highest confession of Christ, suffering in prison himself as a confessor.

Origen also had a high regard for Scripture and the rule of faith, which, though he considered it to be a somewhat looser body of teaching than Tertullian, he nevertheless believed to derive from the apostles. It is in his understanding and use of the rule, especially, that the great distance between Origen's understanding of the faith and that of Tertullian is obvious. Tertullian used the rule as a means of excluding Greek philosophical speculation from the faith. For him Athens and Jerusalem represented opposing camps. Heresy was the child of the union of Greek philosophy and Christian faith. Origen, on the other hand, recognized that the rule of faith left several issues of importance to Christian thought untouched, and felt that a coherent body of doctrine needed to be constructed from the rule by using Scripture and logical arguments (*Princ.*, Pref. 10). To this end he urged his students to 'spoil the Egyptians', and make philosophy the handmaid of theology (*Greg.* 1–2).[42]

It is by this combination of such a positive evaluation of the contribution of Greek *paideia*, and particularly of its philosophy, with a Christian faith, deeply rooted in the Christian Scriptures, that Origen, better than any other Christian in the first half of the third century, achieved the Christian synthesis that W. Jaeger termed 'the new paideia'.[43] Porphyry, a younger pagan contemporary of Origen, thought the two elements which Origen brought together in his life incompatible. He derided him for living like a Christian, but thinking like a Greek (Eusebius, *HE* 6.19.7). Origen's achievement, while never unproblematical, was to have a powerful and permanent effect on the Church. It is to him, as J. Trigg has said, that we owe, more than to any other individual, the fact that 'Athens and Jerusalem belong equally to our Western heritage'.[44] Many Christians, nevertheless, shared Porphyry's view.

The combination of Greek *paideia* and the Judaic-Christian tradition had a long history in Alexandria.[45] Its beginnings go back at least as far as the work of the translators of the Hebrew Bible who produced the Greek version known as the Septuagint. It was continued, on the Jewish side, through the works of Aristobulus and Philo. Pantaenus, the Christian teacher of Clement, must have united the two, as Clement certainly did.[46]

Origen grew up as a child of the Church and was thoroughly educated in the Scriptures by his father, whose martyrdom impressed him deeply (Eusebius, *HE* 6.2.2–10). He later studied philosophy with the Alexandrian Platonist Ammonius,[47] read the works of Philo and Aristobulus (*Comm. in Mt.* 15.3; *Cels.* 4.51), and probably heard the lectures of Clement (Eusebius, *HE* 6.6.1). The Middle Platonic philosophy of the late second century, which borrowed freely from the teachings of Aristotle and the Stoics and blended the borrowings into a Platonic framework, was, along with the Bible and its world of thought and imagery, assimilated into the depths and structure of Origen's thought.[48]

Having taught as a grammaticus for a time, Origen could cite classical authors by name as readily as anyone, though he rarely did so outside the *Contra Celsum*. The influence of Greek *paideia* on Origen is revealed, not in his citations, but in the way he thinks and works. The question is not whether Origen was a Christian or a Platonist.[49] Nor should it be assumed that Origen chose to use Platonic philosophy because he wanted to respond to gnosticism. That he did respond to gnosticism with Platonic philosophy, among other things, cannot be questioned. Platonic philosophy, however, provided the intellectual framework within which Origen understood the world and his own Christian faith. It provided, especially, a world-view of an ordered cosmos controlled by God in which God's *Logos* was an active participant.

From Origen's conscious perspective and intention at least, Greek *paideia* was always subordinate to Christian faith. In teaching his students, his syllabus began with the disciplines of Greek education, namely dialectic, physics, geometry, astronomy and ethics, and concluded with the study of theology, for which the earlier studies were preparatory (Gregory Thaumaturgus, *Pan. Or.* 7–15; Origen, *Cels.* 3.58).

Origen did his theological work as an exegete of the Bible. This was so whether he was writing commentaries, preaching, or treating subjects thematically, as in the *On First Principles*, *On Prayer*, and *Exhortation to Martyrdom*. The latter category of works is largely exegetical, treating passages from the Bible where the appropriate themes appear.

In both this general exegetical approach to his work, and in the particular way he went about it, he reveals his indebtedness to the philosophical culture of his day. The usual way of doing philosophy at this time was either to write commentaries on the classical philosophers of antiquity, or to take a theme and treat it by an exegetical study of what the earlier philosophers had said on the theme.[50] The writings of the earlier classical philosophers represented philosophical authority. This authority was represented to the Christian Origen in the ancient books of the Jews and Christians which the Church called its sacred Scriptures. The fact that Origen's life work was focused on these Scriptures sets him and his work apart from Greek *paideia* at the same time that the methodology which he applied to the interpretation of the Scriptures identifies him with it.

Origen went about his exegetical work in the manner of a Greek grammaticus, applying the techniques long used by Alexandrian classical scholars to establish the authenticity of an ancient text and to illumine its meaning.[51] These techniques were applicable primarily to what Origen called the literal meaning of the text. His chief concern in interpreting the Bible, however, was with the spiritual meaning, which he considered to be hidden in the text. For this purpose Origen took over the allegorical interpretative method of the philosophers.[52] He was aware of Plato's critique of the epic tradition. Plato had banned the Homeric poems from the educational curriculum of his ideal state because their teachings about the gods were unworthy of the gods. Marcion, in the second century, had rejected the Church's use of the Old Testament with a similar critique. As later philosophers, including Platonists, reclaimed the Homeric poems by allegorical interpretation, so Origen reclaimed the Old Testament for the Church.[53] The God of the Old Testament was stripped of anthropomorphisms by allegory in the same way that Homer's gods were stripped of their immoralities.

In seeking the hidden spiritual meaning of the biblical text Origen often used an intertextual principle that the grammarians referred to as 'Homer interpreting Homer', and the philosophers called 'Aristotle interpreting Aristotle', etc.[54] Origen used the terminology of Paul, and called the principle 'comparing spiritual things with spiritual'. He considered it to be the way in which the Holy Spirit illuminated the biblical text in the mind of the interpreter.[55] This very principle, however, so clearly established in the Greek grammatical and philosophical exegetical traditions, points up the complexity of Origen's mind. He says that he learned the principle from a Jewish teacher, and in the way he relates the story it sounds as though he had heard it directly from the teacher himself (*PG* 12, 1080B). While one might think immediately of the Alexandrian Jewish allegorical tradition represented in the work of Philo, N. de Lange has pointed out that the rabbis also used such a procedure in interpreting Scripture.[56] Origen had certainly learned his Hebrew from Jewish teachers in Alexandria, and perhaps he had learned some of his exegetical procedures from them as well. This does not, however, alter the fact that Origen's thought moves in a Greek framework.

It is not just his work as an exegete and his methodology in that work, however, that point to the influence of Greek *paideia* on Origen. The agenda of his exegesis was largely set by the questions that troubled the intellectuals of his day. Is God corporeal or incorporeal? How could an incorporeal, transcendent God create the material world? Is there a divine providence? Are the choices and actions of mankind free or determined? What is the source of evil? Origen was not, of course, the first Christian to think on such themes. The gnostics, especially, had been troubled by such questions and had proposed answers. It was their answers, in many cases at least, which caused Origen to address the questions anew.[57] He seeks the answers within the Christian Scriptures, but he reads these Scriptures in the framework of the Platonic world-view. This world-view, however, was also modified in Origen's mind by Christian teaching. This modification is most apparent and important in the particularization of the abstract philosophical *Logos* in the historical Jesus of Nazareth. While Origen's *Logos* doctrine had many facets that went beyond the picture of Jesus in the Church's Gospels, he never denied the importance of this historical appearance, nor did his thought ever become docetic.[58] It is this combination of agenda, world-view, Scriptures, Christian tradition, and working method which constitutes the synthesis that Origen achieved.

The journey to Egypt which Origen urged on his students, and which he himself had taken before them, was a perilous journey. He knew, or at least thought that he knew, its hazards, but considered it worthwhile and necessary (*Greg.* 2). History has largely judged him correct in this, though a century after his death Epiphanius closed his lengthy attack on Origen's teachings by charging him with being 'blinded by Greek *paideia*' (*Pan.* 64.72.9).

The Novatian schism

With Novatianism we return to the spirit of Tertullian, and the issue of Christian discipline. The Novatian schism began from a very specific occasion. In the episcopal election at Rome in March 251, Cornelius, rather than Novatian, was chosen as the successor of Fabian who had been martyred at the beginning of the Decian persecution. Novatian responded by establishing a rigorist Church of the 'Pure' (Eusebius, *HE* 6.43.1), which granted no reconciliation to those who had lapsed during the persecution, and had himself ordained as its bishop. Cyprian's *Letters* 44–54, written in the weeks immediately following the election, document Novatian's angry reaction. The author of the anonymous *Ad Novatianum*, written only a few years later, hints that it was this rejection that prompted Novatian to set up a rival church, when he compares Novatian to Saul who was 'once a good man', but who turned against David out of 'envy' (14.4).

Cornelius and Novatian were both presbyters in Rome (Cyprian, *Ep*. 45.2.5). Cornelius had risen to his position through all the lower clerical offices (ibid. 55.8.2). Novatian's ordination to the presbyterate, so Cyprian implies, at least, and Cornelius asserts, had followed a different, and perhaps questionable, course (ibid.; Eusebius, *HE* 6.43.17). The two men had radically different views on the reconciliation of those who had lapsed during the Decian persecution. Cornelius' attitude was conciliatory, and Novatian's was strict and rigid. This latter must have been a factor in the selection of Cornelius over Novatian.[59]

Evidence of Novatian's rigorist understanding of the Church before the schism can be found in *Letter* 30 of Cyprian's correspondence, which Novatian composed on behalf of the clergy in Rome during the persecution.[60] He speaks there of the 'just severity of the gospel discipline' which keeps one on course and ensures 'the safety of the Church'. This 'strictness' is ancient, stemming from the earliest days of the Roman Church, and must not be relaxed (*Epp*. 30.2.1–2; 3.3). He juxtaposes God's mercy and 'strict justice' in a series of sentences, which are so constructed that justice counteracts mercy in each instance. What is, perhaps, more important, he juxtaposes Matthew 10:33, where Christ says he will deny those who deny him, with Matthew 18:32, which speaks of the forgiveness of all debts, in such a way that the former counteracts the latter (*Epp*. 30.7.1–2). Matthew 10:33, as we shall see, provided the leitmotif of Novatian's position.

It appears that in the beginning, at least, Novatian's rigorism denied forgiveness only to the lapsed. Cyprian attacks the inconsistency of this position. He denies penance and pardon to the lapsed, but has adulterers, so Cyprian says, in his fellowship (*Epp*. 55.26.1–27.2). Both, of course, were mortal sins. Adultery, however, had been forgivable in Rome at least since the bishopric of Callistus, and perhaps for as long also in Carthage.[61] There is an apparent inconsistency in Cyprian's attack, however, for he insinuated earlier that, like the Stoics, Novatian considered all sins equal (*Ep*. 55.16.1). What Cyprian must have meant by this is that Novatian made no distinctions among the various circumstances under which different people had lapsed during the persecution.

If Novatian's rigorism applied only to the lapsed in the beginning, however, there is evidence that it was later extended by his church, if not by himself, to include all mortal sins, and perhaps even all post-baptismal sins. Discussing adultery in the *De Bono Pudicitiae*, written some time after he had become bishop, he says that adulterers will not possess the Kingdom of Heaven (*BPud.* 6, citing 1 Cor. 6:9). He says nothing about pardon for adultery. Everything is aimed at prevention rather than cure. The adulterer, he says, has no excuse, for he either has, or could have had, a wife. He returns to the subject at the end of the treatise where he asserts that adultery 'kills the soul' (*BPud.* 14). This latter assertion is very similar to his statement in the earlier *De Trinitate*, where he says that to deny Christ results in the 'destruction of the soul' (*Trin.* 14.10).[62] This suggests that by the time he wrote the *De Bono Pudicitiae* Novatian included adultery with idolatry as unforgivable. Penance, moreover, is described in the same treatise as the 'shameful attestation of sins which have been committed' (*BPud.* 13.4). D'Alès has called attention to the statement which the Novatianist Sympronianus presented to Pacian of Barcelona a century later, which denies repentance after baptism, and says that the Church cannot remit mortal sins on the grounds that the Church itself perishes if it receives sinners.[63] This latter point reflects Novatian's own view that the admission of an idolater pollutes the whole Christian community, and his concern to protect 'the safety of the Church' (Cyprian, *Epp.* 55.27.2–3; 30.2.1).

Novatian's rigoristic religion found a following that lasted several centuries. Cyprian's prediction of its rapid demise after the initial enthusiasm cooled down proved wrong (*Ep.* 55.24.3). The Novatianist churches spread widely and rapidly, and could still be found in the fifth century in the West, and till the eighth century in the East.[64]

The Novatian schism raised anew the question of the nature of the Church. Cyprian looked at the Church from the top, so to speak, and defined it in terms of the ordination of its episcopate (*Ep.* 69.3). Those people associated with and obedient to a properly ordained bishop constituted the Church. Novatian looked at the Church from the standpoint of its membership and the success of the latter in being 'purity's ornament' (*BPud.* 2.3). Those who kept the laws of the gospel constituted the Church. These were not, as we have noted, the only alternatives for defining the nature of the Church, nor were they the only elements in the ecclesiology of either Cyprian or Novatian.[65] They were, however, the primary points in conflict between Cornelius and Cyprian on the one side, and Novatian on the other. Cyprian conceived of the Church as a mixture of saints and sinners. He was not unconcerned about its purity, but he did not think the presence of sinners destroyed the Church, nor that even serious sins committed after baptism were unforgivable. When he wrote to the Roman confessors who had returned to the Catholics from Novatian's church, he granted that there might be tares among the wheat. Rather than leave the Church, he said, our duty 'is to strive to become wheat ourselves' (*Ep*. 54.3.1). Novatian, on the other hand, thought he could 'divide the tares from the wheat', and that he had been commissioned 'to wield the winnowing fan and to cleanse the threshing floor' (*Ep*. 55.25.1).

Many factors must have contributed to the origin of Novatian's schism, including, of course, the episcopal election and his own personality. Two factors of special significance, however, were noted by his ancient opponents. Cyprian pointed to the role of Stoic philosophy in forming the severity of Novatian's character and his view of sin (*Ep*. 55.16.1). Modern studies have confirmed that Novatian's thought in many respects is strongly indebted to the Stoic tradition.[66] Vogt would hold Stoicism responsible for the schism.[67]

The anonymous author of the *Ad Novatianum* pointed to another factor. He accused Novatian of using a faulty hermeneutic to interpret the Bible (*Ad Nov.* 9.1). There were two errors in Novatian's hermeneutic. First, he used the single verse of Matthew 10:33 to interpret the whole. 'Stop frightening the unwary', the author says to Novatian, 'with the sophism of one little text' (*Ad Nov*. 12.1). He alludes to Matthew 10:33, Novatian's favourite text, and then cites Scriptures from Exodus to Revelation in which the Lord exhorts the sinful, without qualification, to repent. Tertullian had accused the modalistic monarchians of a similar hermeneutical fallacy. They selected a few verses of Scripture which supported their view, and then made the rest of the Bible yield to these verses (*Prax*. 20). Both the anonymous author of the *Ad Novatianum* and Tertullian are applying the rhetorical rule for interpreting written texts of reading the part in the context of the whole rather than interpreting the whole by a part.[68]

The other hermeneutical error with which the anonymous author charges Novatian is failure to ask what Matthew 10:33 means (*Ad Nov*. 7.1–8.6; 12.2). Novatian read Matthew 10:33 as a transparent text, and applied it without question to the situation of the lapsed in relation to the Church in his own time. The anonymous author again uses the rule of the larger context to interpret Matthew 10:33. He first raises the question of the time to which the text refers, and argues that it does not refer to the present time, but to the future, final judgment depicted in Matthew 7:22–3. He supports his point by asking the Novatians, 'Whom of those who left or denied the Lord while he was still here did the Lord deny?', and then cites the telling case of Peter (*Ad Nov*. 7.1–8.6). Finally, the author asks to whom Jesus' statement is applicable.

Does he have the penitent in mind? Again, the context of the whole Bible is brought to bear to show that the compassion of God never turns the penitent away (*Ad Nov.* 12.2–15.4).

It would be overly simplistic, as we have already noted, to suggest that the Novatian schism was due to a single factor. On the other hand, the significance of the hermeneutical error should not be underestimated, especially in the perpetuation of the schism. This schism, like many others, depended on a particular way of reading a few biblical texts to the exclusion of the teaching of the entire Bible.[69]

Notes

1 J. Moingt, *Théologie trinitaire de Tertullien*, I, 87–134, interprets the situation differently, and argues that the trinitarian theology developed in reaction to the modalistic monarchian view.

2 For some possible distinctions between Noetus' doctrine and that of his successors, see S. N. Mouraviev, 'Hippolyte, Héraclite et Noët (Commentaire d'Hippolyte, Refut. omn. haer. IX 8–10)'. On Noetus' doctrine see R. E. Heine, 'The Christology of Callistus'.

3 Moingt, *Théologie trinitaire*, I, 90–1, suggests that *epigonus* be taken as the common noun meaning 'descendant' or 'successor' and treated as a pseudonym in Hippolytus, and that Praxeas was the name of the person involved.

4 See Epiphanius, *Pan.* 57.1.2, who reduced Noetus' error to the assertion that the Father suffered.

5 On the modalists' dependence on Stoic philosophy in general, see H. Hagemann, *Die Römische Kirche*, 346–71.

6 Hippolytus, *Noet.* 2, lists Exod. 3:6, 20:3, and Isa. 44:6. On the rabbis' use of these Scriptures against the Christians, see E. F. Osborn, *The Emergence of Christian Theology*, 29. Nautin, *Hippolyte, Contre les hérésies*, 134–5, questions the historical reliability of Hippolytus' assertion that the Noetians used these Scriptures on the basis of the rhetorical ploy of anticipating the arguments of the opponent and answering them in advance. They obviously used Scripture, however, and it seems to me that Hippolytus would not have made such a good case for them had there not have been a basis in fact.

7 See, for example, *II Clem.* 1.1; Ignatius, *Ephes.* pref; Pliny, *Epp.* 10.96.7.

8 See J. B. Gould, *The Philosophy of Chrysippus* (Leiden: Brill, 1971), 82ff.

9 Hippolytus, *Noet.* 2. Novatian, *Trin.* 25, 26 and 30 gives similar examples of the logic of the modalists.

10 Not even in his most vigorous ascription of the creation to God himself did Irenaeus associate the material world with the Father without the intervention of his agents, or 'hands' (*AH* 2.30.9). Osborn, *Emergence*, 183.

11 For the attempt to identify them see Hagemann, *Römische Kirche*, 234–57, and A. Harnack's rejection of this, and other identifications of Praxeas, *Lehrbuch der Dogmengeschichte*, I, 741–3.

12 On Callistus' doctrine see Heine, 'The Christology of Callistus,' 56–8, esp. 74–8.

13 See Hagemann, *Römische Kirche*, 345–7.

14 Walzer, *Galen on Jews and Christians*, 75–86. Cf. R. M. Grant, *Heresy and Criticism*, 67–72.

15 See R. H. Connolly, 'Eusebius, H.E. v.28', *JTS* 49 (1948), 76, who argues that Artemon was living in the vicinity of Antioch.

16 See Epiphanius, *Pan.* 54.3.5, 9. They also used Deut. 18:15, which is cited in Acts 3:22 and 7:37 (Epiphanius, *Pan.* 54.3.1).

17 It is important to note that there were also non-theological charges brought against Paul of Samosata. See F. W. Norris, 'Paul of Samosata: Procurator Ducenarius', 50, 67–70.

18 For the modern debate over the teachings of Paul of Samosata and the other later sources which refer to his teachings see the works listed in the Bibliography. The most significant variant interpretation is that of F. Loofs, *Paulus von Samosata*, who, on the basis of later sources, attempted to interpret Paul's teaching in the tradition of Tertullian and the doctrine of the economic Trinity. Loofs' view has not been generally accepted.

19 See R. W. Sharples, 'Alexander of Aphrodisias: Scholasticism and Innovation', *ANRW* II.36.2, ed. W. Haase (Berlin and New York: Walter de Gruyter, 1987), 1179.

20 See ch. 12.

21 On the 'rule of faith', see A. Outler, 'Origen and the *Regulae Fidei*', esp. 134–5, and L. Countryman, 'Tertullian and the *Regula Fidei*'.

22 For Tertullian's appeal to the argument of antiquity see *Praescr.* 29–31; *Herm.* 1; *Apol.* 19.1ff.; 47.10–11; *Prax.* 2; and *passim*. This same argument was later somewhat of an embarrassment to Tertullian when some of his Montanist views were attacked by the Catholics as being novel (see *Virg.* 1; *Mon.* 3–4; *Ieiun.* 1, 14).

23 On the differences and similarities see Countryman, 'Tertullian and the *Regula Fidei*', 208–11, and Moignt, *Théologie trinitaire*, I, 66–75.

24 On this question see especially, D. Powell, 'Tertullianists and Cataphrygians', *VigChr* 39 (1975), 33–54; W. Tabbernee, 'Remnants of the New Prophecy: Literary and Epigraphical Sources of the Montanist Movement', *SP* 21 (1989), 193–7; G. L. Bray, *Holiness and the Will of God: Perspectives on the Theology of Tertullian*, 10–11, 54–63; C. B. Daly, *Tertullian the Puritan and His Influence*, 10–15; Sider, 'Approaches to Tertullian', 236–8; D. Rankin, *Tertullian and the Church*, 41–51; Trevett, *Montanism*, 66–76.

25 I follow generally the translations in ANF 3 and 4, with occasional modifications.

26 Cf. Daly, *Tertullian the Puritan*, 4.

27 See ibid., 81–96, esp. 95, note 114.

28 R. E. Heine, *The Montanist Oracles and Testimonia*, 7.

29 See Brown, *Body and Society*, 79–102.

30 Cf. Fox, *Pagans and Christians*, 395–6.

31 See *Pass. Scil.* and *Pass. Perp.* Perpetua and her companions may have been Montanists, but they were, nevertheless, honoured as martyrs by the Carthaginian Church (Barnes, *Tertullian*, 77–9). For the gnostics' views of martyrdom, see Tertullian's *Scorp.*; Pagels, *Gnostic Gospels*, 70–101; and Frend, *Martyrdom and Persecution*, 243–7.

32 W. Tabbernee, 'Early Montanism and Voluntary Martyrdom', *Colloquium* 17 (1985), 36–8; cf. A. Jensen, *Gottes selbstbewüßte Töchter* (Freiburg, 1992), 293–6.

33 See ch. 12 above, p. 138. note 48.

34 The reference in *Scap.* 1 might even be an allusion to the illustration cited in 5.

35 It is sometimes assumed that these were Montanists, but, as Tabbernee points out, there is no evidence for this other than the assumption that Montanists were voluntary martyrs ('Early Montanism', 41).

36 See, for example, Origen, *Io.* 28.192–201, 209, 244; *Comm. in Mt.* 10.23; 16.1; *Cels.* 1.65; *Hom. in Jud.*, 9.1; Clement, *Strom.* 4.9.71–73.1; 4.10.76–7; Cyprian, *Ep.* 81; and the views related and opposed by Tertullian, *Cor.* 1.

37 Barnes, *Tertullian*, 54–5, puts this treatise between 198 and 203, and thus at least two years before Tertullian's earliest dated Montanist work, *Cor.*, in 205.

38 Frend, *Martyrdom and Persecution*, 366; Daly, *Tertullian the Puritan*.

39 *Tertullian the Puritan*, 190–202.

40 *Martyrdom and Persecution*, 366.

41 *Pagans and Christians*, 409.

42 Cf. Gregory Thaumaturgus, *Pan. Or.* 6, 11, 13, 14. This does not mean, of course, that Origen was uncritical of Greek philosophy (see H. Crouzel, *Origène et la philosophie*, 9–101; idem, *Origen*, 156–63; and Chadwick, *Early Christian Thought and the Classical Tradition*, 101–23).

43 Jaeger, *Early Christianity and Greek Paideia*, 63.

44 Trigg, *Origen*, 9.

45 See C. Bigg, *The Christian Platonists of Alexandria*, and Dawson, *Allegorical Readers*.

46 This passes over the work of the gnostics Basilides and Valentinus, whom the Church, at least, considered to have gone seriously wrong in their appropriation of Greek culture.

47 So Porphyry (Eusebius, *HE* 6.19.6). See ibid. 6.19.8 for a list of some of the Middle Platonic philosophers Porphyry asserts that Origen studied.

48 See Berchman, *From Philo to Origen*; Lyman, *Christology and Cosmology*, 39–81.

49 Chadwick, *Early Christian Thought*, 122.

50 See, for example, R. Sorabji, 'The Ancient Commentators on Aristotle', in R. Sorabji, ed., *Aristotle Transformed: The Ancient Commentators and their Influence* (London: Duckworth, 1990), 24; De Faye, *Origène: sa vie, son oeuvre, sa pensée*, I, 87–8. Cf. the comments above in ch. 11 on the introductions to Origen's commentaries on John and the Song of Songs, and Dawson, *Allegorical Readers*,

on the differing, but nevertheless exegetical, procedures of the Alexandrians Philo, Valentinus and Clement.

51 De Faye, *Origène*, I, 75, 89–90, who notes that the general procedure of commenting on a text was the same, whether the commentator was a grammarian or a philosopher. See also Neuschäfer, *Origenes als Philologe*; R. M. Grant, *The Earliest Lives of Jesus* (New York: Harper and Brothers, 1961); Heine, 'Stoic Logic as Handmaid'.

52 De Faye, *Origène*, I, 91–4.

53 Plato himself, as Marcion too, rejected the use of allegory.

54 See R. Lamberton, *Homer the Theologian: Neoplatonist Allegorical Reading and the Growth of the Epic Tradition*, 109; L. G. Westerink, 'The Alexandrian commentators and the introductions to their commentaries', in Sorabji, ed., *Aristotle Transformed*, 343; P. Sellew, 'Achilles or Christ? Porphyry and Didymus in Debate over Allegorical Interpretation', *HTR* 82 (1989), 83.

55 C. Jenkins, ed., 'Origen on 1 Corinthians', *JTS* 9 (1908), 240. See also PG 12, 1080BC; 1000B; *Cels.* 7.11.

56 De Lange, *Origen and the Jews*, 110–11. De Lange notes that the principles of exegesis used by the rabbis were 'broadly the same as' those of the Greek exegetes.

57 See H. Koch, *Pronoia und Paideusis*, 13–15.

58 See *Io.* 2.61; 10.26; cf. Heine, *Origen: Comm. Jn. 13–32*, 35–8.

59 See Clarke, *Letters of St. Cyprian*, III, 184.

60 See ch. 14 above.

61 See Hippolytus, *Haer.* 9.12.20ff.; Cyprian, *Epp.* 55.20.2; 21.1; 73.19.1.

62 This assertion is based on Matt. 10:33.

63 D'Alès, *Novatien*, 167, citing PL 13, 1063D.

64 See Vogt, *Coetus Sanctorum*, 183–290.

65 See Daniélou, *Origins of Latin Christianity*, 429–64; Vogt, *Coetus Sanctorum*, 57–138.

66 Vogt, *Coetus Sanctorum*, 136–8; Daniélou, *Origins*, 233–50; d'Alès, *Novatien*, 164–5.

67 Vogt, *Coetus Sanctorum*, 138.

68 See the discussion above in ch. 12, p. 138.

69 Cf. Vogt's perceptive comments on Cyprian's failure to listen to the entire Bible in the rebaptism controversy ('Cyprian – Hindernis', 14–15).

19
Christian teaching

JOHN DAVID DAWSON

With unprecedented breadth and depth in the work of Origen of Alexandria, Christian teaching in the third century displayed a complex integration of spiritual sensibility, textual interpretation, and philosophical reflection. Such multifaceted Christian teaching unfolded amidst a developing Neoplatonist philosophical and pedagogical tradition which, from Plotinus to Proclus, sought a comparable spiritual, textual and metaphysical synthesis. Although the tradition of moral and intellectual transformation to which both Christian and polytheist Platonists were indebted was firmly rooted in the dialogues of Plato, by the end of the third century AD, Plato's heirs had diverged from the master's teaching in a variety of ways. Their chief departure was a thoroughgoing effort to recover the pedagogical significance of authoritative texts – for the Christian Platonists, the books of the Old and New Testaments; for the polytheist Platonists, a variety of Greek poetic texts, pre-eminently the Homeric epics.

The distinctiveness of Christian teaching in the third century is not to be found in formal interpretative techniques such as allegorical reading, which leading intellectuals like Origen shared with fellow Platonists concerned to demonstrate the coherence of spiritual and metaphysical teaching with traditional texts. Nor can Christian distinctiveness be located simply in the extent to which Christian theologians tried to show the biblical character of their conceptual reflections, for both Christian and non-Christian Platonists were increasingly concerned to display just such integration of textual explication and philosophical reflection. Instead, Christian teaching diverged from polytheist Platonist teaching in distinctive ways according to the degree and manner in which authoritative texts were allowed to shape thought and behaviour in ways deemed consonant with the character of the stories they told.

Wandering stories vs. things in themselves: Plato on the poets

To understand the cultural significance of the decision of Christian teachers to make the text of the Bible the privileged context for conceptual reflection on their faith, one must understand the shifting fortunes of Greek poetry in the formation of Greek *paideia*. Greek moral education before Plato (and after him, despite his criticisms of it) was rooted in the memorization and recitation of poetry.[1] Strong identification with poetic narrative was intended to inculcate patterns of evaluation and action under the governance of a paradigmatic description (where 'governance' implies no independent contribution on the part of the listener). Surrender to, and memorization of, the poetry was for the sake of identification with its heroes, and this was best accomplished through dramatic recitation, in which rhapsode and audience sought to reproduce in themselves the emotions and dispositions of the narrative's leading characters. Over time, reciter and listeners built up within themselves a whole set of emotionally rooted reflexive responses that conditioned them to respond as poetic heroes had once done in analogous life-situations. To learn the poets by heart was to prepare oneself for life.

Pedagogical aspirations within the Platonist tradition began with Socrates' sharp denunciation of the role of traditional poetic texts in shaping human character. In the *Republic*, Plato has Socrates vehemently oppose the poetic narratives that had long been the centrepiece of Greek moral education. When the members of the rhapsode's audience identify with the characters and events of a well-sung tale, or when theatre-goers become emotionally involved with the dramas they witness on stage, they allow their souls to be dragged away from things as they really are, toward the shifting, illusory realm of human action and passion, generation and decay. To bury oneself in narrative texts is to ensure that one will never be able to know things as they really are in themselves, but only as they are represented by, and related to, other things. Someone immersed in the drama of the *Iliad* will never know, for example, what anger really is by itself, but only what Achilles is like when he is angry with Agamemnon. Those entranced by remembered poetic narrative may well be able to recall instances and examples, but will never be able to offer a definition. If asked, then, to explain why justice is praiseworthy, such an unfortunate may be able to cite examples of persons and acts that the poets praise as just, but will be unable to explain what justice itself is apart from the examples that elicit praise. To find oneself in such a state is, Plato insists, never to find one's self at all. A person seduced by poetic texts will fail to become an independent, autonomous, self-identical self. Such a person will not be able to act solely on the basis of reasons that he or she has discovered, but only by imitating others. Like the Achilles he imitates, such a person will be angry today, calm tomorrow, angry the next day – but will never come to achieve a stable and abiding identity.

Plato's philosophy provides the necessary antidote for this textually induced disease, a way out of the labyrinth of narrative desire. One cannot, simply by an act of will, make a clean break from one's poetically deformed past; instead, a difficult process of disengagement will be required, a therapy of withdrawal. One must return, as Freud later recommended, to the narratives that had deformed one's identity and do something other than recite and memorize them. Instead, by means of interrogation, one must call a halt to recitation. The Socratic interrupting question is designed to break the spell of the poetic narrative, to make listeners stop, step back, and turn the narrative text itself into an object of knowledge. And by making the text an object of knowledge rather than a context for immersion and self-formation, one makes oneself into an independently knowing subject for the first time. The soul is born in the process of abstracting from the text that had made its birth possible. One no longer re-enacts Achilles' wrath or Priam's grief – one interrogates them. What is the nature of anger or grief? What are its effects on the self? How desirable are those effects? Learning to pose and answer such questions will finally release one from the grip of the 'wandering stories' that had formerly obscured the definitions of things as they are 'in themselves'.

Despite his unfavourable contrast of writing with speech in the *Phaedrus*, writing aided Plato in his programme of unrelenting abstraction. For writing enabled one to locate and 'stabilize' a text that had hither been 'in motion' orally between speaker and listener; it allowed one to turn the slippery oral text into a different kind of text, one that stood still long enough to put questions to it. Writing helped transform the text as a mutually enacted performance of speaker and listener into an object of a single reader's measurement, analysis and dialectic. What Plato sought for in this double procedure of abstractive reading was an entity that was finally one rather than many, timeless rather than temporal. The syntax of narrative was destined to give way to the syntax of mathematics.

Polytheist Neoplatonist recovery of text as symbol

When polytheist Neoplatonic philosophers returned to Greek poetry and read it allegorically as a source of philosophical insight, they did so – surprisingly, to those familiar with the *Republic* – in the name of Plato himself. This Neoplatonic return to poetic narrative was aided by a new emanationist ontology and a theory of poetry as symbolic rather than mimetic. The emanationist scheme eased the earlier Middle Platonic dichotomies of matter and mind, building a potential bridge between the sensible poetic images of poetry and abstract philosophical meaning.[2] And a new conception of the poetic text as symbolic avoided Plato's criticism of poetry as a harmfully misleading imitation of reality. Although Neoplatonic hermeneutical innovations are evident as early as the *Enneads* of Plotinus, they receive a much fuller elaboration in the later writings of Porphyry and Proclus. Plotinus refers both explicitly and obliquely to Greek poetry from time to time but makes no extended effort to show how a proper reading of it would be congruent with his philosophical ideas (it seems clear that he assumes this to be the case, but he has no stake in showing it to be so). But Porphyry makes Plotinus' assumptions about the philosophical value of poetry explicit, and, somewhat later, Proclus offers the most extensive and systematical display we have of the Neoplatonic allegorical reading of the Homeric epics. In his wide-sweeping integration of Neoplatonic ontology with allegorical reading of the large portions of the Homeric epics, Proclus provides an especially useful comparison with Origen, who produced an even more massive integration of metaphysical reflection with biblical interpretation. Hence, if we want to probe the convergences and divergences between polytheists and Christians working in the Neoplatonic tradition, we should not be forced by mere chronological juxtaposition into comparing Origen only with Plotinus. Instead, at least with respect to the exegetical dimensions of philosophical reflection, it is the fifth-century Proclus rather than the earlier Plotinus who can illuminate the distinctiveness of Origen's third-century biblical Platonism.

Plotinus had laid the essential groundwork for later Neoplatonic theory of language by describing language as a mediation between the material world and spiritual reality. Language was a metaphor for the devolution of the *hypostases* (the One, the Mind, the Soul) that structured reality:

> For as the language [λόγος] spoken by the voice is an imitation [μίμημα] of that in the soul, in the same way as the one in the soul is an imitation of the one in the other [*hypostasis*, mind], likewise, just as the language pronounced by the lips is fragmented [into words and sentences] in contrast to that in the soul, so is the one in the soul (which is the interpreter of that previous language) fragmented by comparison with the one that precedes it.
>
> (Plotinus, *Enn.* 1.2.3.27–30)[3]

Despite this oblique hint of the possibility of linguistic mimesis, the thrust of Plotinus' thought is finally rigorously apophatic – away from what the discursive language of poetry could communicate about spiritual reality, for 'in that which is totally simple, what discursive description can there be?' (*Enn.* 5.3.17.24–5). If there is to be a relationship with the One beyond discursive language and thought, it will come not through language but through mystical vision: 'One must trust that one has seen it when the soul is suddenly illuminated' (*Enn.* 5.3.17.28). Hence, poetry and myth can finally have no mimetic value for Plotinus; they may hint at a higher realm, but they can bear no essential or intrinsic relation to it. As the classicist Robert Lamberton concludes, 'Myth may be used to enliven Plotinus's exposition of his world-system, but the elements of myth remain subservient to that exposition and constitute a poetic language whose referents can be shifted as needed.'[4]

Proclus looked for a more essential relation between poetic myth and Neoplatonic philosophy. He agreed with Plato that if Homer's poetry was mimetic, then its depictions of the gods were certainly inappropriate. But upon close examination, one could see that Homer's poetry was not mimetic but symbolic. The Homeric symbol does not straightforwardly depict reality but indirectly 'hints' at it, and the relation between the symbol and what it reveals is far more subtle than are relations between perceptible things. The reader of poetry as symbol must seek out these obscure correspondences; to recognize that water is a symbol of the phenomenal world, one would need to discern the hidden correspondence between the formlessness of water and the shifting, mutable character of the natural world. Only a hopelessly literalist reader would think that Homer only intended to represent an actual body of water. But only a reader sufficiently attentive to the symbolic character of Homer's poetry could come to recognize that water was no arbitrary sign but an image intrinsically related to what it signified. No less than Proclus, Origen also wanted to display both the deeper meaning of biblical narrative and the intrinsic relation between the literary character of that narrative and its meanings.[5] What follows is a brief display of how these two Platonist exegetes sought to articulate the correspondences between text and meaning that made the reading of authoritative texts important for the process of philosophical teaching. The character of that correspondence – and of the ways in which its importance was conceived – will help identify Origen's distinctively Christian permutations of his inherited Platonic tradition.

Plato had soundly rejected Homer's story of Hephaestus hurrying again to the aid of his mother Hera, who was at risk of another beating at the hands of her husband Zeus:

> Patience, mother!
> Grieved as you are, bear up, or dear as you are,
> I have to see you beaten right before my eyes.
> I would be shattered – what could I do to save you?
> It's hard to fight the Olympian strength for strength.
> You remember the last time I rushed to your defence?
> He grabbed my foot, he hurled me off the tremendous threshold
> and all day long I dropped, I was dead weight and then,
> when the sun went down, down I plunged on Lemnos,
> little breath left in me. But the mortals there
> soon nursed a fallen immortal back to life. (*Il.* 1.586–94)[6]

Although Proclus agrees with Socrates that such stories are unsuitable for children, he insists that philosophers should recognize that they are actually symbols of deep truths about the cosmos (*In Rep.* 181.28–82.9). It is true that words in this story ('hurling forth,' 'bondage') appear to attribute characteristics to the divine that the divine cannot possess. But one must understand that such terms describe not the divine but only human perceptions of the divine by persons mired in the realm of ordinary sensibility. In order to get at the aspect of the perception that truly corresponds with divine reality, one must strip away the distortions produced by human misperception. So for each term, Proclus first identifies its purely human connotation: 'bondage' suggests coercive restraint, 'hurling' a violent act at the hands of another. One must then abstract from the words meanings relevant to the divine and set aside misleading connotations: from 'bondage' one abstracts union, setting aside constraint; from 'hurling' one abstracts single progression, setting aside violent coercion (*In Rep.* 1.82.23–9). In each instance, Proclus seeks out an underlying affinity between the meaning the term has in the ordinary world and its meaning as applied to the divine. Plato had argued that abstract Forms or Ideas were implied by our ordinary use of categories: particulars denoted by the same term implied that they were all instantiations of a single form or εἶδος (*Rep.* 596a). But the search for εἴδη became complicated when one encountered the multiplicity of mythical narratives and intensified further when key terms in the narrative seemed to denote violent coercion and fragmentation in the realm of the divine. Proclus seeks to move from the surface of the text to the world of forms in a way that connects with the meanings of the words in ordinary usage. The key task is to display the conceptual structure that such a meaning shares with the world of forms. On the issue of oneness and diversity, then, Proclus – in contrast to Plato – wants to have it both ways at once: the plurality of narrative and the unity of the divine realm are merged through the category of emanation. Unlike Plotinus, for whom there can be no relation between discursive descriptions and the 'totally simple', Proclus gives poetry a productive role, but only as long as one understands it to be a collection of non-mimetic symbols.

A similar reading strategy helps build a bridge between the temporality of poetic narrative and the timelessness of the gods. Plotinus had faced the same dilemma, evident in his effort to suppress the temporality and passion of the sufferings of the dead in Homer's treatment of Heracles in the first *nekyia* of the *Odyssey* (*Od.* 11.601–2). He argues that the image of Heracles that Odysseus sees in Hades will finally dissolve as Heracles' higher soul, already among the gods, gradually loses all memory of the material world.[7] But once again, as, for example, in the case of the Homeric theomachies, Proclus seeks in poetry more evidence of the integration of spiritual and material reality than Plotinus had sought. Like Socrates, Proclus believes that the theomachies, if taken mimetically, utterly mischaracterize the divine nature (*In Rep.* 1.89.10–24). He observes that Homer sometimes offers descriptions of the gods that are literally true: for example, that the gods are eternally at rest and beyond all strife (*Od.* 6.42–6). When Homer depicts the gods with imagery of strife and battle, though, he is not offering a straightforward description of divine activity; instead, he is depicting through the use of symbols a paradoxical quality of the divine – its unity in itself apart from the flux of the material world, and its entry into that world for the exercise of providence. Consider, for example, how Homer hints at this paradoxical activity of the divine at the opening of book 20 of the *Iliad*. After Zeus orders Themis to call the gods to the summit of Olympus, Poseidon asks why the gods have gathered in Zeus' house. Is it because the Trojans and Achaeans are poised for war once more? Zeus replies: 'These mortals do concern me, dying as they are. / Still, here I stay on Olympus throned aloft, / here in my steep mountain cleft, to feast my eyes / and delight my heart. The rest of you: down you go, / go to Trojans, go to Achaeans. Help either side / as the fixed desire drives each god to act' (*Il.* 20.21–5).

According to Proclus, this scene hints at the property of the divine that the subsequent battles of the gods represent: they are simultaneously within the godhead (the gods are within Zeus' house) and yet flow outward into the world of human action and passion. Proclus observes first that Zeus himself remains above the battles, containing within himself all the other gods, who distinguish themselves from him while simultaneously remaining in him, insofar as they are the means of Zeus' extension of providence to the lower realms. Proclus has symbolically interpreted Zeus' call to the gods to gather within his palace as a call to gather within himself, and his subsequent dismissal of them and their direct intervention in the human battlefield as an account of Zeus' own exercise of providence in human affairs. Proclus bolsters his interpretation by observing that Homer does not describe battles among those gods who remain within Zeus, who exercises his providence transcendently (*In Rep.* 1.90.22–8). Homer's theomachies concern only those lower deities who implement providential activity directly in the world of human affairs (*In Rep.* 1.90.28–91.4). But even this implementation entails no human passion on the part of the divine. The depiction of gods fighting with one another as they take sides in the human conflict serves only to represent the human reception of divine 'powers'. Such depictions should not be taken to suggest that the gods *themselves* are subject to passions such as anger. What is said about these lower deities is merely a symbolic reflection of the power of their interventions to shape human life.[8]

Although Proclus distinguishes the lower gods from Zeus (much as Plotinus had contrasted Heracles' 'image' with his higher, divine soul) and also distinguishes the gods from their lower 'powers' (or other administrative emissaries), Homer clearly names the gods by name in his theomachies. Proclus counters by insisting that the gods simply share the same name with their powers and administrators. Yet even though the suffering of the lower administrative beings may properly be referred to the higher gods who share their names, those higher gods do not themselves suffer: their implementation of Zeus' providential regard entails no fundamental change in the divine nature. Proclus' allegorical reading of Homer does not, then, simply dissolve the temporal dimensions of poetic narrative into timeless truths, as Plotinus was more inclined to do. Instead, his reading construes a temporal sequence in Homer (Zeus calls the gods to his house and then sends them forth) as symbolic of two simultaneous realities: the gods remain within Zeus, yet also proceed outward to administer (through lower managers) Zeus' providential will. The high god is thereby able to intervene in the human world on behalf of human beings without putting his divine atemporality and changelessness at risk. But this high god's act of providence is fundamentally alien to the most crucial attributes of the divine nature, and the reason why this god might wish to engage in providential activity at all remains mysterious.

Christian Platonist subordination of philosophy to Scripture

In his effort to subordinate Greek philosophy to Scripture through allegorical interpretation, Origen stands in the tradition of Philo rather than Clement.

Rarely referring to polytheist poetic or philosophical texts by name and quoting from them infrequently, Philo used allegorical reading to subordinate textually liberated Greek ethical and philosophical concepts to the particular textual features of the authoritative Pentateuch. In contrast, Clement displayed a much more favourable attitude toward the religious significance of Greek polytheist literature, discovering in Greek poetic classics no less than in Jewish and Christian Scripture the medium through which the divine *logos* spoke. For Philo, critique and revision of classical culture were accomplished through textual usurpation; through allegorical reading, one could come to see that Moses had delivered the wisdom of the Greeks in the very textual details of the Pentateuch. But for Clement, Christian critique and revision of classical culture was grounded not in the textual details of Scripture (or any other text) but in the pre-textual, authoritative voice of the *logos* that had finally become incarnate as Jesus of Nazareth.[9] As philologist, textual critic and biblical exegete, Origen shared Philo's commitment to the religious significance of textual detail, and like Philo (but quite unlike Clement) rarely quoted polytheist literature as though it were as capable as Scripture of manifesting the voice of the *logos*.

Before probing some of Origen's Christian divergences within the Platonic cultural current in which he found himself, it is worth noting just how far the preceding account of Proclus' Homeric interpretation already departs from the dualistic metaphysical assumptions of the second-century Middle Platonist Celsus, who declared in his *True Word* that

> God is good and beautiful and happy, and exists in a most beautiful state. If then He comes down to men, He must undergo change, a change from good to bad, from beautiful to shameful, from happiness to misfortune, and from what is best to what is most wicked. Who would choose a change like this? It is the nature only of a mortal being to undergo change and remoulding, whereas it is the nature of an immortal being to remain the same without alteration. Accordingly, God could not be capable of undergoing this change.
> (*Cels.* 4.14)[10]

Like Celsus, Proclus assumes that God – in the highest sense – could not undergo this change. But unlike Celsus, Proclus wants to explain how a god who cannot change could nonetheless intervene providentially in human affairs. Hence, as we have seen, Proclus links an emanationist scheme (in which deity can assume multiple levels of being or instantiations) to the Homeric texts that describe divine interventions. Origen is as devoted as Proclus or Celsus to the notion of God's immutability (though with some qualifications to be introduced shortly). But he is also committed to the notion of divine providence, especially as enacted by God's self-emptying in the person of Jesus on behalf of humanity (Phil. 2). Hence Origen responds to Celsus initially with the concise affirmation: 'While remaining unchanged in essence, He comes down in His providence and care over human affairs' (*Cels.* 4.14). This, in a nutshell, is perhaps the single most fundamental Christian teaching in the third century, and we are now in a position to ask: What about its articulation by Origen serves to identify it as distinctively Christian teaching? In what ways does Origen's resistance to Celsus' formulation differ from Proclus'?

The heart of Origen's resistance lies in his exposition of the phrase 'came down'. What can it mean for a God who is 'entirely uncorruptible, simple, uncompounded, and indivisible', a God who Scripture insists is 'the same' and 'change[s] not', to 'come down'? At first, Origen exploits the easy opening that Celsus' aesthetic and moral language affords: God's descent is not a change 'from good to bad' because Scripture insists that the incarnate God did not sin. The descent was not a change from 'beautiful to shameful' because the incarnate God 'knew no sin'. It was not a change 'from happiness to misfortune' because the Word was happy even in his self-humiliation. And the descent was not a change from 'what is best to what is wicked' because goodness and love for humanity are not wicked things.

But these various reversals of moral and aesthetic evaluation do not address the heart of Celsus' critique because they do not yet confront its metaphysical premise – that divine nature cannot undergo an essential change. Origen recognizes that he shares with Celsus too many metaphysical views about the divine essence to tackle this insistence on divine impassibility head on. He also recognizes that the biblical witness, despite its reference to divine incarnation, also insists that God does not somehow lose divinity or alter the divine character by virtue of becoming incarnate. Hence biblical testimony oddly enough reinforces at least some of the implications of essential unchangeability. Nonetheless, the Bible insists that God providentially 'came down' to humanity. Proclus' way out of the dilemma posed by Celsus' radical dualism was to invoke the Neoplatonist emanationist scheme already articulated by Plotinus, creating a spectrum of the divine nature, ranging from a high divine nature that was unchangeable to lower, quasi-divine natures that could intervene without themselves changing. But the 'quasi' hides the ontological difficulty, and one can readily see why Origen's direct contemporary Plotinus dropped the poetic accounts of multiple gods in favour of the singular One beyond all being. Origen wrestles with the same conceptual problem:

> If the immortal divine Word assumes both a human body and a human soul, and by so doing *appears* to Celsus to be subject to change and remoulding, let him learn that the Word remains Word in essence. He suffers nothing of the experience of the body or the soul. But sometimes he comes down to the level of him who is unable to look upon the radiance and brilliance of the Deity, and becomes *as it were* flesh, and *is spoken of* in physical terms, until he who has accepted him in this form is gradually lifted up by the Word and can look even upon, *so to speak*, his absolute form. (*Cels.* 4.15)

How can the Word remain 'Word in essence' yet really (and not just 'as it were') enter human life? This passage shows that Origen's approach to this problem does not lie in either the flat declaration of essential unchangeability, or in the various rhetorical qualifications ('as it were', 'so to speak'). Instead, what is fundamental is the divine intent to save by bringing the human being into a direct encounter with the divine reality. In other words, Origen avoids the impasse created by the juxtaposition of essential impassivity and apparent transformation into the human in order to insist on a more fundamental theological point: whatever 'coming down' means, it must at a minimum mean that the God who 'comes down' is fully God throughout that descent, that the descent brought about no religiously significant change in the *character* of God – because only by encountering God as God really is can the human being achieve salvation. Origen's way of sidestepping Celsus' either/or is to relocate the starting-point for reflection on the topic: that starting-point is not a definition of the divine nature (the heresy of the later Neo-Arians), but testimony to the divine intent to save (the orthodoxy of the later Arius himself). If Celsus 'had understood what is appropriate for a soul which will have everlasting life, and what is the right view of its essence and origin, he would not have ridiculed in this way the idea of an immortal person entering a mortal body; (our view here does not accept the Platonic doctrine of the transmigration of souls, but a different and more sublime view)' (*Cels.* 4.17).

But what is this more sublime view, and how does it differ from transmigration? Above all, the divine *nature* must be understood according to the divine *character*, as manifested in the biblical account of the already-enacted divine intention to save, and not on independent philosophical grounds. Platonic philosophy insists that the divine nature cannot change, but Origen counters that while this is, in a profound respect, true (God's nature does indeed not change, in the sense that God remains forever 'in character'), the truth of the claim of unchangeability lies not in its philosophical consistency but in its compatibility with the biblical affirmation that God assumed a human being to heal humanity. Origen expounds this compatibility on two levels: that of the nature of God, and that of the soul of Jesus. With respect to the nature of God, Origen makes food rather than abstract Platonic form the key to 'essence'.

> Concerning the nature of the Word, just as the quality of food changes in a mother into milk suitable for the nature of her infant, or is prepared by a physician with the intention of restoring a sick man to health, while it is prepared in a different way for a stronger man, who is more able to digest it in this form; so also God changes for men the power of the Word, whose nature it is to nourish the human soul, in accordance with the merits of each individual. (*Cels.* 4.18)

The nature of the human predicament calls forth a certain solution from God, and God's nature is capable of providing that solution. While Origen's earlier qualifications ('so to speak', 'as it were') testify to his belief that God undergoes no essential change in providing this solution, his food analogy is designed to show that those qualifications cannot be taken in a docetic sense – 'as it were' does not point to unreality, to a deception or lie: 'Surely the Word is not false to his own nature when he becomes nourishment for each man according to his capacity to receive him; in so doing he does not mislead or tell lies' (*Cels.* 4.18). In Origen's estimation, Celsus' problem is not his insistence that God does not change, but rather his failure to grasp God's resolution of the human predicament. That resolution is the full expression of the divine nature, and that divine resolution is every bit as unchanging as one could wish, or need.

Origen's second strategy is to probe the nature of God's transformative act at the level of Jesus' soul. He begins again by endorsing Celsus' valuation of changelessness: 'Concerning Jesus' soul, if anyone supposes that there was a change when it entered a body, we will ask what he means by a "change". If he means a change of essence, we do not grant this, either of his soul, or of any other rational soul.' But, Origen continues, 'if he means that it undergoes something because it has been mixed with the body and because of the place into which it has come, then what difficulty is there if the Word out of great love to mankind brings down a Saviour to the human race?' (*Cels.* 4.15). Origen allows for what he calls Jesus' 'undergoing something' – how can this be compatible with essential changelessness? It can be compatible only if one once again subordinates an *a priori*, philosophically generated concept of essential changelessness to the biblical depiction of Jesus' willing service on behalf of humanity. Doing so allows one to conclude that the Saviour descended 'of his own free will to accept the limitations of humanity on behalf of our race'.

To Origen, the will's acceptance of limitation is no limitation of the will, for such a will is like the food that does not betray its essential nature when it nourishes (no matter what alteration of form might be required for it to nourish effectively). Indeed, the will's act is not 'like' the food that remains essentially nourishing – it is the *same* event: the Saviour's willing acceptance of limitation in order to save ('he did not count equality with God a thing to be grasped') *just is* God's characteristic (unchanging) will to assume salvifically efficacious form. So paramount for Origen is the divine will to save, that God will accept whatever self-limitation might be required to bring it about:

> There is nothing wrong if the person who 'heals sick friends' healed the human race which was dear to him with such means as one would not use for choice, but to which he was confined by force of circumstances. Since the human race was mad, it had to be cured by methods which the Word saw to be beneficial to lunatics that they might recover their right mind.

'Jesus', Origen concludes, 'is clearly said to have accepted everything for the sake of sinners, that he might deliver them from sin and make them righteous' (*Cels.* 4.19). And as for the metaphysical concern about essential divine changelessness: the respect in which it can be used to affirm a Christian truth must be subordinated to the biblical account of what God has 'in fact' already done. What God has done must be regarded as fully congruent with and revelatory of how God 'essentially' is, or, conversely, 'it is not in accord with God's character not to stop the spread of evil and bring moral renewal' (*Cels.* 4.20). To think otherwise is to fail to grasp the meaning of the Christian Scriptures, and 'Celsus', Origen acidly remarks, 'does not understand the meaning of our scriptures at all.' Origen's closing rebuke indirectly highlights the exegetical character of his departures from Platonist precedent: '[Celsus'] criticism touches his own interpretation and not that of the Bible' (*Cels.* 4.17).

Despite the enormous influence of Origen's allegorical hermeneutic, it would be misleading to suggest that Christian teaching in the third century consisted solely in conveying the results of biblical interpretation and theological reflection. For these activities were only components of a much richer and multifaceted exposition of an entire way of life. Origen envisaged Christian existence as a life of continual ἄσκησις or 'discipline', in which the individual goal of personal spiritual purification through prayer and fasting was matched by the equally important injunction to public demonstration of one's faith, even to the point of martyrdom. For Origen, biblical interpretation, conceptual reflection, personal prayer, fasting and martyrdom were not unrelated acts, and even characterizing them as 'interrelated' fails to do justice to the way he understood them as multiple expressions of the Christian believer's transformative relationship with the Creator God. Indeed, nothing stands outside the scope of the Creator's wisdom, which embraces all the particularities of the natural, material world no less than the world of Scripture:

> the wisdom of God has permeated the whole of Scripture even to the individual letter. This is indeed why the Saviour said: 'Not one iota or one stroke will pass away from the law, until everything comes to be' (Matt. 5:18). For just as the divine skill in the fabrication of the world appears not only in sky, sun, moon, and stars – all of these being bodies through which it courses – but it has acted on earth in the same way even in the meanest material object, since even the bodies of the tiniest creatures are not despised by the Artisan, and even less the souls present in them, each of which receives in itself a particular property, a saving principle in an irrational being. Nor does the Artisan despise the earth's plants, since he is present in each of them with respect to their roots, leaves, possible fruits, and different qualities. So with regard to everything recorded by the inspiration of the Holy Spirit we accept that, since divine providence has endowed the human race with a superhuman wisdom by means of the Scriptures, he has, so to speak, sowed traces of wisdom as saving oracles, in so far as possible, in each letter. (*CommPs. 1–25*, pref. 4)[11]

In light of this expansive vision, reading Scripture becomes a primary vehicle of prayer, which in turn purifies one's soul. The one who prays 'becomes more ready to be mingled with the Spirit of the Lord, who has filled the whole world and has filled the whole earth and heaven'. Through the resulting 'purification', the one who prays 'partake[s] of the Word of God' . . . 'who is never absent from prayer, and who prays to the Father with the person whose Mediator he is. For the Son of God is a High Priest who makes offerings for us . . . and with the Father. He prays for those who pray and appeals along with those who appeal' (*Or.* 10.2).[12] As High Priest, the Son has also 'offered Himself as a sacrifice', bringing 'cleansing to the world'. Those who are 'the priests of whom He is High Priest offer themselves as a sacrifice', and such a person thereby 'holds fast to his confession and fulfils every requirement the account of martyrdom demands' (*Mart.* 30).[13] The purificatory practice of private prayer thereby finds its culminating expression in the public act of martyrdom. The expression of spiritual purity in the ideology of martyrdom has long been associated with the name of Tertullian in the Latin West, but Origen's articulation and enactment of the martyr's stance is no less striking. His hermeneutical resistance to pressures for cultural accommodation was complemented by a series of bodily disciplines and public practices ranging from asceticism to prayer and martyrdom. Christian teaching in third-century Alexandria, no less than in third-century North Africa, was always on public display.

Christianity and Greek culture: towards a Christian paideia

Some fifty years ago, the classicist Werner Jaeger argued that the character of ancient Christian teaching is best understood in light of the synthesis it achieved with Greek cultural ideals. Literary and philosophical strands in Greek culture had long been at odds with one another, and early Christian teachers exploited that internal cultural debate by endorsing Greek philosophy's demythologization of poetic, mythical traditions and by identifying parallels between pagan philosophical and Christian theological ideas.[14] In Jaeger's still widely shared view, the resulting 'mixing' of Greek and Christian conceptions was achieved at the deep level of a philosophically articulated set of humanistic ideals.[15] The problem with this view is not the claim that 'Christian faith' and 'Greek cultural ideals' intermixed, but rather the suggestion that ancient Greek Christians could espouse a 'Christian faith' that was, in its essential origin or character, somehow sufficiently independent of Greek culture to make its subsequent 'mixing' with that culture possible. On the contrary, there was no Christian faith for a Greek Christian that was not, from the very outset, an ingredient in that individual Christian's existing cultural formation. To suppose otherwise (i.e., that faith is inherently separate from culture) – if only to argue for a subsequent intermixing between them – is to posit an intrinsic opposition between religion and culture that could only be credible on the basis of a theological claim about the a-cultural (or even anti-cultural) nature of divine revelation.[16]

Yet to reject such unnuanced contrasts between religion and culture is not the same as giving up the task of discerning the distinctive features of Christian identity. In the third century, and pre-eminently in Alexandria, Christians fashioned their distinctively Christian identities within the context of a prior and ongoing cultural formation they could not escape even had they wanted to. The fashioning of Christian identity in the third century did not turn principally on the alliance between Christian theology and Greek philosophy against the mythological texts of Greek religion. Instead, it turned on the displacement of culturally authoritative Greek texts by the Christian Bible, a displacement that entailed a radical criticism of some of Platonism's most central affirmations. This contest – of Christian Bible and theology against Greek poetry and philosophy – was not a struggle between 'Christian faith' and 'Greek culture'. It was instead a contest fought out by members of Greek culture over competing constructions of their identity, as authorized by alternative authoritative texts. No less than their non-Christian opponents, Christians wished to privilege certain texts and make a place for conceptual reflection. But at a surprisingly early date, culturally elite thinkers such as Origen helped changed the rules of subsequent cultural debate. By elevating to cultural pre-eminence texts whose most philosophically problematic particularities he refused to evade, Origen and those who followed him were able to make even Platonic philosophy the site of a distinctively Christian *paideia* grounded not only in theoretical reflection and hermeneutical ingenuity, but in the practices of bodily ἄσκησις, personal and corporate prayer, and freely accepted martyrdom.

Notes

1 The following account of Greek moral education through poetic narrative, as well as Plato's rejection of it, is outlined in Eric A. Havelock, *Preface to Plato*. The implications of Havelock's work for understanding early Christianity's engagement with Greek poetry and philosophy through the construction of its own, counter-polytheist, *paideia* remain largely unexamined.

2 Cf. R. Lamberton, *Homer the Theologian: Neoplatonist Allegorical Reading and the Growth of the Epic Tradition*, 163.

3 The following analysis is derived from ibid., 88–90.

4 Ibid., 106.

5 For further exposition of this point, see David Dawson, 'Allegorical Reading and the Embodiment of the Soul in Origen', 26–43.

6 Translation taken from: *Homer: The Iliad*, translated by Robert Fagels; Introduction and Notes by Bernard Knox (New York: Viking, 1990). Plato, *Rep.* 378D, argued that whether or not they contained hidden meanings, such stories could not be saved by allegorical interpretation because their surface meanings unavoidably misshaped the souls of young listeners.

7 Lamberton, *Homer the Theologian*, 102.

8 Cf. Proclus, *In Rep.* 1.91.4–11.

9 For further discussion of the differences between the allegorical hermeneutics of Philo and Clement, see Dawson, *Allegorical Readers*, chs 1 and 3.

10 Translation taken from: Chadwick, trans., *Origen: Contra Celsum*.

11 Translation from: Trigg, *Origen*, 71. This passage displays the characteristically Philonic aspect of Origen's commitment to the revelatory character of the Bible's textuality.

12 Translation from: Greer, *Origen*, 100–1.

13 Translation: ibid., 62.

14 For an excellent account of the philosophy of Clement and Origen in relation to the non-Christian (especially Platonic) philosophical views of their age, see H. Chadwick, 'Philo and the Beginning of Christian Thought' in *CHLG*, chs 8–11.

15 Jaeger, *Early Christianity and Greek Paideia*, 39–40: 'In reality the Greek cultural ideals and Christian faith did mix, however anxious we may be to keep each

of them immaculate. There was on both sides a powerful desire for mutual penetration, regardless of how reluctant to assimilate these two languages were, each with its different ways of feeling and metaphorical self-expression. Both sides must finally have come to recognize that, beneath all that, an ultimate unity existed between them, and a common core of ideas, which so sensitive a thinker as Santayana did not hesitate to call "humanistic," though he perhaps did not mean this to be taken as unqualified praise.'

16 Jaeger is himself aware of the extent to which his project may appear to trade precisely on the very opposition between religion and culture that he wishes to undermine. His lectures open with the straightforward declaration that 'I shall not undertake to contrast religion and culture as two heterogeneous forms of the human mind, as might appear from the title, especially in our day, when theologians such as Karl Barth and Brunner insist on the fact that religion is not a subordinate part of civilization, as the old school of liberal theologians often took for granted when they talked of art, science, and religion in one breath' (p. 3). But if Jaeger is not going to make a religion/culture contrast, someone will need to make it, or else his overall argument about the synthesis of Christian faith and Greek cultural ideals will remain unintelligible. As it turns out, it is the ancient Christians themselves who make the necessary, invidious contrast:

> Origen had given the Christian religion its own theology in the style of the Greek philosophical tradition, but what the Cappadocians had in mind was a whole Christian civilization. They brought to that task a broad culture that is manifest everywhere in their writings. Notwithstanding their religious convictions, which are opposed to the revival of the classical Greek religion attempted by powerful forces in the state at their time, they do not conceal their high esteem for the cultural heritage of ancient Greece. This is the sharp line of demarcation that they draw between Greek religion and Greek culture. Thus they came to revive the positive and productive relation of Christianity and Hellenism that we found in Origen, but in a new form and on a different level.
>
> (Jaeger, *Early Christianity and Greek Paideia*, 74)

Jaeger's claim for a synthesis between Christian religion and Greek culture first requires an opposition between Christian religion and Greek religion. Since the only opposition is between competing religions, once the Greek religious elements are removed from Greek culture, there is no opposition between that culture and the Christian religions because they are essentially (at their 'common core of ideas') the same. But without any real contrast at the outset, any subsequent synthesis seems predetermined, if not altogether illusory.

20

The significance of third-century Christian literature

FRANCES YOUNG

From a historical point of view the significance of third-century Christian texts is incontestable. This is a fundamentally important era in the formation of Christianity. This material reveals the extent to which the Church conformed to social norms in the Greco-Roman world while remaining counter-cultural. It testifies to the pressures that increasingly focused the mind of the community on credal definitions. It provides insight into the problems of discipline and the difficulties of maintaining unity. Yet only the attempt to delve behind the principal literary deposits can reveal this, for they largely emanate from towering but problematical figures most of whom would later be judged at best on the margins of orthodoxy.

Characteristic of modern scholarship has been a suspicion of the tradition through which the deposits of the third century were transmitted. The major outcome of the historical approach has been the rehabilitation of Origen. He has rejoined the 'Fathers' of the Church, and his profound influence on the development of Christian theology has been fully recognized. Estimates of his achievement have oscillated from lightly Christianized philosopher to Hellenized biblical scholar. Both characterizations presuppose the same outlook, comprising the following elements: (1) the assumption that an author's work is to be understood in terms of its historical and intellectual environment; (2) the focus on the author as one whose originality and influence is to be assessed; (3) the tendency to produce what purports to be a 'God's eye' or objective view of the past, the truth about which tradition had suppressed or distorted.

This historical approach implies detective work, all the more evident in relation to a figure such as Hippolytus. The literary guide describes as 'traditional' an account of his life which dates merely from 1851, introduces the complex modern debates about who he was and what he wrote, and provides us with a contrast between the sketchy information which can be gleaned from ancient sources, such as Eusebius and Jerome, and the expanding list of works attributed to him as a result of modern discoveries in a range of languages such as Slavonic, Armenian and Georgian. Works by this Hippolytus were apparently valued and transmitted, though his person was obscure. Even apart from the problems of Hippolytus, the state of the extant deposit requires historical detective work before any assessment of significance is possible. Reconstruction of the social situation and indeed of the major controversies of the third century depends upon evidence being gleaned from elsewhere, such as material preserved by Eusebius in writing his history in the next century.

But the suggestion that the Christian literature of the third century is only of historical importance is contestable. Precisely because of the historico-critical programme and its apparently secure results, some of this literature has had a remarkable influence on modern developments. The prime example is the *Apostolic Tradition* attributed to Hippolytus. Seized upon as the earliest witness to Christian liturgy, it has deeply influenced twentieth-century liturgical revision in the mainstream churches. Behind that fact there doubtless lurks a continuing sense that to strip away later accretion and get back to the original is to find what one seeks in its pristine, and therefore true, form. Thus the motivation which fired the development of the historico-critical movement is both exposed and justified. It never was simply and solely a matter of reconstructing the past for the sake of it. It was an extension of the spirit of the Reformation, reinforced by the apologetic need to prove the truth of Christianity by divesting its origins of myth and tracing the facts in the face of modern polemics against its historical claims. For such reasons, the treatment of early Christian literature as documentary evidence for reconstructing history has been dominant. Such scholarship has had impressive results, results which are not confined to revising that history.

Now, however, the intellectual context of scholarship has changed.[1] In literary theory the importance of the 'author' has been challenged; in hermeneutics a classic text's ability to transcend its own time has been re-emphasized. The subjectivity and contingency of the interpreter has been recognized, and this challenges the possibility of establishing once and for all the truth about the past; indeed, ongoing debates about Hippolytus provide a good example of the fact that in many cases the truth cannot be convincingly established even when historical critics share the same approach and presuppositions. Now, with the constellation of things referred to as postmodernism, the fact that there must always have been a plurality of meanings is exposed, and it is no good asking precisely what was meant any more. What are the implications for the study of third-century Christian literature of this major shift in the way literary critics and interpreters approach texts?

Clearly our own situation as readers will have a determinative effect on the outcome of any study we undertake: 'reading genres' is a term that has been used for the different reading modes involved when, first, a letter of Paul is read by its original addressees, then later it is read as the Word of God in a liturgical setting.[2] So what are the potential 'reading genres' of third-century Christian literature? What interests are involved in its interpretation? The lack of a continuous tradition of reading this material as authoritative must mean the question has to be treated differently from when it is asked of Scripture, or indeed of the major figures of the fourth century. Clement and Cyprian alone have been canonized and continuously recognized as Fathers of the Church. Interest in the rest has been resurgent with the historico-critical programme. The question is, then, whether 'historical document' is the only possible 'reading genre' for this material, or whether there are ways of appropriating it: that is, discerning its abiding significance for at least some present readers. Maybe that question can only be answered work by work. Two general approaches, however, may be briefly considered:

I. In the case of the third-century material, a major issue is how the total deposit of the Christian community in that period is to be handled, including the traces and evidence not covered by the literary guide, not to mention the surd of all that missing material. If we were to shift attention from authors whose status as teachers of the Church is problematic and recognize that the truly significant thing about this literature is that it testifies to the life of a community which was at a crucial stage in the formation of its identity and which has a continuing, if fragmented, existence, then the question of 'reading genre' and appropriation might take on a different complexion. For members of this community might then be engaged in reading critically the past which created the world it continues to inhabit.

Such an approach would have to take up and affirm the struggle to trace lost material, to discuss sources and dates, to do justice to the losers who are represented to us only through the words of those who triumphed: in other words the historico-critical programme which postmodernism has deconstructed. For the communities which claim to be in continuity with that which produced this literature need to re-engage with the issues of identity that were so hard fought in the third century, to grapple again with the arguments that led to definitions and exclusions, whether in matters of faith or practice. To do that they need to understand something of the factors that created a climate in which certain arguments would seem plausible and others not; for they cannot simply take over the same discourse in a totally different social and cultural world. They need to read the texts with a mixture of suspicion and empathy, to enter into a critical dialogue with the third-century community to which this literature alone gives access, however inadequate that access may be.

Three examples, one ecclesiological, one ethical, one doctrinal, may help to illustrate this, brief and merely suggestive though the treatment here must be:

(i) *Extra ecclesiam nulla salus*: outside the Church there is no salvation. This well-known tag has had a life of its own. Originating in the struggle with Novatian, it has become detached from the context in which Cyprian wrote his treatise on Church unity. In the post-Reformation era the question was which body was the true Church outside which there was no salvation: there were rival claimants. But this exclusivist claim now has to be faced in a post-Christian civilization, where mainstream Christian bodies embrace the ecumenical movement as they face a world of many faiths and none.

Suppose we put Cyprian's tag back into context. Faced with a massive pastoral crisis, Cyprian realized that the health of the Church was threatened by its perfectionist stance. The demand for post-baptismal purity from sin, as if the existential Church were straightforwardly the eschatological community, ran counter to compassion for human weakness under unprecedented pressure. Some thought that to compromise was to betray the Church; others that they could trade in forgiveness. Cyprian saw that it was necessary to marry discipline with mercy. Only a certain quality of Christian community which achieved this could bring health and salvation. It is perhaps that perception which could enable a reappraisal of boundaries and identity-markers.

(ii) Abortion is a subject on which present Christian bodies profoundly disagree. Tradition bans it on the grounds that all life is sacred – surprisingly, since that is a general philosophical principle with apparently no distinctively Christian warrant. The early Christians had other warrants for adopting an uncompromising stance on this issue.

Our own 'horizon'[3] and that of the third century barely coincide. The ethos of antiquity meant that there was no taboo, in literature if not in fact, on 'exposing' at birth unwanted infants, let alone disposing of them earlier through abortion. Conceptually, then, there was a single spectrum and birth did not provide a determinative boundary, whereas now the taboo on doing anything after birth puts pressure on the ante-natal period. Jews and Christians stood out against all of this because of their respect for what God had created, and the biblical commandment against taking life.

Thinking through again these theological warrants for early Christian attitudes might create different approaches in the context of the twenty-first century, where the population explosion has replaced infanticide as the social context, and a woman's right to choose has to be balanced against the rights of the unborn child, especially when the known outcome is inevitable dependence through serious disability. A theological warrant of a different kind might be found in the compassionate love of God revealed in Jesus Christ.

(iii) Recent theology has seen a revival of interest in the Trinity. The notion of God as being in some sense community in relationship has been attractive to those who wish to challenge modern individualism. The pluralism within postmodern theology has produced feminist and liberationist interpretations of the doctrine. Furthermore, monarchianism is not dead. Groups which have basically taken the 'adoptionist' line, such as the Unitarians and the Christadelphians, may have effectively been excluded from the ecumenical movement, but more serious is the emergence of the so-called Oneness-Pentecostal Churches, which, on the basis of many of the same scriptural texts as Tertullian's opponent 'Praxeas', argue powerfully against a Trinitarianism which appears tritheistic and defend a concept of God as One Spirit, transcending and pervading all things, incarnate once in Jesus and now at work in the Spirit-filled churches: in other words a form of modalism. For traditional churches the mystery of the Trinity is a fundamental identity-marker; but a widening ecumenism which embraces Pentecostalism cannot avoid the challenge this presents, since the Pentecostal churches are themselves divided over the Trinity.

The third-century material demonstrates that the notion of Trinity was fiercely contested and only the fourth-century controversies refined a doctrine which has never been entirely unproblematic. It is instructive to re-examine the arguments of one such as Tertullian and see how bound they are to the presuppositions of his time. Does Scripture have to be read his way? The issues are both theological and hermeneutical. The notion that doctrines developed once but now must stand as truth for evermore is becoming increasingly hard to sustain. We need an 'ethical reading' of the arguments and debates which is prepared to respect third-century arguments and our own very different rationality. We need a readiness to grapple with analysis of the material so as to determine how far multiple interpretations may or may not be legitimate. For Christian identity over time requires some attention to the ability of truth claims to transcend a plurality of cultural embodiments.

Of course it has long been true that groups in mainstream churches have used the names of ancient heresies as sticks with which to beat theologians with whom they do not agree. But what is suggested here is not quite so simple. The suggestion is that the broad spectrum of third-century debate be revisited without the prejudice implied in the labels that have stuck since the fourth century determined what was to be received as the authentic tradition. The hermeneutical stance being recommended here is similar to that proposed earlier (chapter 10). It is fundamentally 'typological', though a typology that is dependent upon the, admittedly provisional, results of historical reconstruction rather than simply the reading of extant texts. It is a plea to Christian communities not to be tied to the conclusions of third-century debates but to 'replay' them with the same seriousness, but perhaps in a less polemical style. The Church in a pre-Christian age may inform the Church in a post-Christian world.

II. There remains, however, the literary question as to how the extant texts are to be read, and whether this can go beyond a merely historical reading. It is here that the identification of genres becomes paramount. Different genres expect different reading stances. Homilies written down imply readers who wish to enter imaginatively into the world of the liturgy and to make a committed response to what was said by the preacher. Commentaries imply readers who wish to enter the world of biblical scholarship. Letters seek to communicate with the recipients and imply a certain relationship between the sender and those who receive them. All ancient texts imply the rhetorical intention to persuade, and this is particularly true of controversial literature, treatises composed to expose and contest the arguments of opponents. To take the genres seriously may lead to a reading that is more than merely historical.

Yet we are not the implied readers (see also chapter 10); this is explicit in the case of letters, implicit in the case of all this literature since we do not belong to the socio-linguistic world from which it stemmed. The transmission of Origen's homilies, often in translations from the Greek by later apologists like Rufinus who wished to gloss what seemed by then less than orthodox, denies us not only the original form of the text but also a sense of that liturgical context which the original implied reader would doubtless have had. This distance between ourselves and the texts is an unavoidable gap, and an ethical reading has to recognize the 'otherness' of the text. Perforce any reading today must have an element of critical distance, of suspicion. We cannot just take over texts from the past as if that distance were not there.

Nevertheless, the postmodern situation in which we find ourselves has already created renewed interest in the biblical exegesis of early Christian scholars like Origen, and has generated the question whether there is not more in it than used to be thought in the heyday of the historico-critical approach. A greater degree of empathy and more readiness to appropriate is emerging as people are liberated to allow that multiple meanings of Scripture are possible, as Origen did.

And for the Christian intellectual a figure like Origen may be a significant 'type': for he is a paradigm of what it means to undertake serious engagement with the questions for Christian belief raised by the rationality of one's own time, and in the process to stimulate both respect and hostility. His story is replayed again and again in Christian history. For Christianity has always been, on the one hand, 'school-like', an important intellectual and scholarly tradition based on books and their interpretation; but also on the other hand, as ancient critics perceived, a kind of superstition, liable to uncritical acceptance of irrational ecstasies like those of Montanism, to obscurantist appeals to Scripture which fail to take account of the metaphorical nature of language, to unquestioning fundamentalisms couched in slogans inherited from previous controversies, to an appeal to faith which has no place for reason. Perhaps modern scholars subject to similar pressures have instinctively warmed to Origen, and that is why his name has been rehabilitated. Tertullian has faired less well at the hands of modern readers who place him in the obscurantist camp. This contrast should surely reinforce the point that the situation and presuppositions of the reader are as important in interpretation as those of the author.

The text, its readers implied and actual, its author, and rhetorical intent: attention to all of these is essential to responsible reading of third-century Christian literature; and inevitably the result will be a plurality of readings, not least because these texts will be used for different ends as they are interpreted. There cannot be one answer to the question of significance. Yet it remains true that the literature and debates of the third century contributed to the creation of a world into which we are invited, to the genesis of 'the faith' or the overarching credal narrative which is the *logos* that constitutes Christianity. If that subject-matter is to carry conviction and so be appropriated as truth, it is through the channel of fourth-century transmission; so further exploration must await the discussion of hermeneutics in chapter 40.

Notes

1 I refer to the many elements now attributed to a shift from modernity to post-modernism. The principal features affecting interpretation of patristic texts were sketched in Young, 'From Suspicion and Sociology'.

2 Werner Jeanrond, *Text and Interpretation as Categories of Theological Thinking*, ET, T. J. Wilson (Dublin: Gill and Macmillan, 1988).

3 The notion of 'horizon' in hermeneutics entered the discussion with Gadamer whose work is classically discussed by Anthony Thiselton, *The Two Horizons* (Exeter: Paternoster, 1980).

PART THREE

*

FOUNDATION OF A NEW CULTURE: FROM DIOCLETIAN TO CYRIL

A.

*

LITERARY GUIDE

21

Classical genres in Christian guise; Christian genres in classical guise

FRANCES YOUNG

Often designated the 'Golden Age of Patristic Literature', the fourth and fifth centuries provide us with a mass of material which carries weighty literary and theological significance. For this was the period which later ages looked back to as that in which the authoritative 'Fathers of the Church' set out the faith handed down to them, and there is an important sense in which this determined the transmission of earlier texts as well as those originating in this period. It was also a time in which classical genres appeared in Christian guise, and Christian genres achieved their classic form.

There are, of course, discernible continuities and discontinuities with what has gone before. These can best be focused by noting two determinative moments for the character of Christian literature. The first marks the beginning of the period: the final attempt to eradicate Christianity followed by Constantine's patronage of the Church. The second is the reaction to Julian's attempt to reverse what had happened and construct a revived paganism sufficiently robust to challenge the power of this new kind of religion with credal foundation and institutional scaffolding. The latter will throw retrospective light on the former.

In a sense Christians had in the past engaged in a battle of literatures.[1] The Bible was to replace the classics as the literature of a Christian culture that stood over against the culture of the Greco-Roman world. In particular the gods and idols omnipresent in the classics were to be rejected; and the theatre was taboo. Julian took this anti-culture tradition seriously. If Christians refused to believe the literature on which all education was based, they should cease to be schoolteachers: and Christians were banned from the schools. There were two reactions to this.

In the first place, Christian rhetoricians began to produce a new literature which had classical styles and genres but Christian content. As the historian Sozomen put it:

> Apollinaris employed his great learning and ingenuity in the production of a heroic epic on the antiquities of the Hebrews to the reign of Saul, as a substitute for the poem of Homer . . . He also wrote comedies in imitation of Menander, tragedies resembling those of Euripides, and odes on the model of Pindar. In short, taking themes of the entire circle of knowledge from the scriptures, he produced within a very brief space of time, a set of works which in manner, expression, character and arrangement are well approved as similar to the Greek literature. (*HE* 5.18)

In the second place, indeed well after the crisis was over, classically educated Christian leaders, like Basil of Caesarea and Gregory of Nazianzus, produced justifications for Christian participation in traditional schools. It was generally recognized that, as noted by Sozomen introducing the account already quoted, Julian's sole motive for excluding the children of Christian parents from instruction in the learning of the Greeks was that he considered such studies conducive to the acquisition of argumentative and persuasive power.

In other words: rhetorical training empowered Christian leaders. Indeed, Gregory of Nazianzus would later use his rhetorical power to produce a couple of anti-Julian orations[2] which show how much he regarded this attack as tantamount to persecution, as a real bid to undermine the Church. He refused to accept that λόγοι (words) and ἑλληνίζειν (being Greek in language, thought and culture) belonged, as Julian claimed, only to those who would worship the Greek gods. Less directly inspired by reaction to Julian, but in the same period, Basil wrote a treatise for his nephews explaining the usefulness of Greek classical literature in their education.

Clearly the Constantinian revolution had reinforced the tendencies, already noted in the third century, for Christians to come from the educated literary elites and to adapt classical modes of writing to Christian ends. But whereas at that earlier stage conversion had often carried with it an explicit exchange of one culture for another with implicit transference of fundamental presuppositions, now, in a society where Christianity was increasingly dominant, the surviving pedagogy was 'secularized', and the interpenetration of the two cultures enhanced. This would diversify very considerably the range of literary genres produced by leading Christian authors. At the same time, however, there would be those who reacted against the cultural sell-out, maintaining the tradition of Christianity as critique of culture and celebrating orally the simplicity of those who withdrew into the desert to challenge the world, the flesh and the devil in stories of their illiteracy that would eventually be collected and, somewhat paradoxically, recorded in writing. A figure like Jerome (chapter 28) would construct for himself a literary *persona* that somehow straddles the contradictory traditions of radical rejection of the classical tradition and profound assimilation to it.

For, indeed, the fourth century produced self-conscious Christian *literati*, in both East and West, and much of the literature to be surveyed in this section consists of *corpora* of works produced by persons who aspired not only to the life of the resurrection, but to the kind of immortality that comes from leaving a literary legacy to posterity.[3] Collections of letters are an indication of such ambitions, mirroring as they do the collections of rhetorical compositions left by classical authors: obvious examples include the letters of Basil of Caesarea, Theodoret of Cyrrhus, and Jerome. But other indicators are to be easily found. Gregory of Nazianzus retires to write poetry; Gregory of Nyssa composes a counterpart to Plato's *Phaedo*; Proba constructs a *cento*; Ambrose produces a *De Officiis* like Cicero; Eusebius is the first, but not the last, to write history. Jerome's very attempt to catalogue Christian authors with their works betrays the construction of a self-conscious Christian literary heritage to match that which transmitted the classics of ancient Greece and Rome.

In constructing this literary guide Jerome owed much to Eusebius. Eusebius lived through the first of our two determinative moments, and marks a significant transition. He inherited Origen's library in Caesarea, and when Constantine came east he was already an old man who had lived through the last great persecution. Long before that he had begun to piece together the first history of the Church,[4] as if he sensed that the right moment had come to gather the story together from the beginning, select the significant figures, whether bishops or scholars, and record their achievements so as to transmit their legacy to future generations. The various editions show how he was prepared to struggle with the question of God's providence as the Church's fortunes turned. If persecution was a divinely intended lesson for a Church that had become lax, patronage by a professedly Christian emperor was the goal of God's plan.

History in the ancient rhetorical tradition had likewise sought to use narrative of the past as a way of conveying moral lessons and exploring the outworkings of fate.[5] But Eusebius' historical writing did not straightforwardly conform to the classical conventions. As in his other great works, usually described as apologetic, he adopted a documentary mode of presentation, supporting his argument with long quotations;[6] it is extraordinary how often we are reliant upon Eusebius' work for extant fragments of the writings of antiquity, whether from Hellenized Jews, Greek philosophers or Christian authors. History, for Eusebius, had become a kind of apologetic, an alternative method of proof that Christianity was true.

And that in itself is a pointer to the problems of generic analysis. Little of the Christian literature of the fourth and fifth centuries escapes influence from the classical traditions of antiquity, yet little of it can be analysed neatly according to the classical genres. There are *encomia* and *consolationes*, but generally speaking the classical genres, where slavishly copied, produced works that failed to survive: nothing remains of the great literary labours of Apollinaris that we hear of from Socrates. What makes generic analysis difficult is the fact that many different forms are used as vehicles for a single given tradition of Christian argument. As a result patrologies classify 'patristic literature' in terms of content rather than form; the standard categories are 'dogmatic', 'apologetic', 'moral', 'ascetical', 'exegetical', rather than 'history', 'epic', 'dialogue', 'essay', 'novel'. The time has come for the issue of genre to be faced more explicitly as we pause at the moment of convergence between the heritage of the Church and of the classical world.

Let us begin by considering the so-called 'genre' of apologetic.[7] Eusebius, whether self-consciously or not, may seem to offer a fairly precise definition, for in his *Ecclesiastical History* he uses the word *apologia* to describe the works of Quadratus and Aristides (*HE* 4.3), Justin (*HE* 2.13, 4.11–12, 16), Melito (*HE* 4.13) and Tertullian (*HE* 3.33, 5.5). He seems to treat Quadratus and Aristides as the first Christian authors to address a discourse to the emperor in defence of the faith, and the others as following in this tradition. He does not use the word to describe works of Theophilus (*HE* 4.24) and Tatian (*HE* 4.29) which are now usually embraced within the genre 'apologetic'. They were not speeches addressed to the emperor: Tatian addresses 'the Greeks', Theophilus the individual Autolycus.

Strictly speaking, *apologia* belongs to the world of forensic rhetoric: it was the speech for the defence in a law-court. By writing his *Apology* for Socrates, Plato had perhaps set a precedent for literary apologies, and Demetrius' catalogue of letter-types includes the apologetic letter, defined as one that 'adduces with proof arguments that contradict charges that are being made'. But the general defence of a particular community undertaken by the Christian 'apologists' has no direct precedent. The best surviving exemplar of what Eusebius seems to regard as an 'apology' is in fact a work he apparently did not know, that of Athenagoras. The title of that work is *presbeia*, an embassy or deputation. In fact, the 'deputations to the emperor' which Eusebius calls 'apologies' bear comparison with the situation described by Philo in his *Embassy to Caius*. It would be interesting to know how far back the use of *apologia* as a title for the works of Justin and the others actually goes.

Whatever the answer to that question, it would appear that Eusebius intends a fairly particular form of writing to carry the title *apologia*, whereas 'apologetic' now generally embraces many different forms of writing, designating simply the intention to defend or prove the truth of Christianity against detractors. Origen's 'apologetic' work *Against Celsus* is no address to the emperor, but rather a refutation of Celsus' *True Doctrine*, a work written against Christians. It has successors in works *Against Porphyry* and *Against Julian*; Eusebius' own treatises entitled *Praeparatio Evangelica* and *Demonstratio Evangelica* are treated as apologetic. All these develop a literary form in which the opposition's words are quoted to be refuted, or the testimony of friend or foe is cited as confirmation of a point. That Eusebius could write a 'history' that adopted the same tactic of documentation demonstrates the argument that clear generic analysis is often problematical.

The same kind of argument could be developed with respect to other writings conventionally grouped together more on the basis of content than form. 'Dogmatic' writings are of many kinds. The contentious character of early Christianity is often remarked, and it has surely left its marks on the extant literature. Thus 'dogmatic' works may take the same form as some of the apologetic material just considered; for they were directed against particular opponents, this time heretics, and polemically examine their position point by point, the only difference being that the conflict is internal rather than external. But contention might also be dressed up as a dogmatic 'dialogue', as in the case of Theodoret's *Eranistes*; one or both sides may appear in extant polemical correspondence about dogma like that between Cyril and Nestorius; or the issues may be addressed in quite other forms of writing. In fact the term 'dogmatic' is impossibly vague as a way of designating a 'genre'; for there are orations, homilies, letters, treatises, even expositions of Scripture which may be described as 'dogmatic' because they expound particular teachings of the Church and provide patristic testimony to what became the agreed 'dogma'. They are 'dogmatic', at least to some extent, by hindsight. They carry authority because certain authors have been authorized by posterity as the purveyors of sound teaching.

The descriptions 'apologetic' and 'dogmatic' both appear then as subsequent classifications, and raise questions about what is meant by 'genre', and what is the point of generic analysis. 'Genre' is one of the ways in which meaning is encoded in a literary text. The proper identification of a genre enables the reader to make judgments about sense. Not to identify the fictional character of a novel and to confuse it with biography is to misread the text, and to attribute false intentions to the narrator. Generic analysis will only assist the reading of texts if it serves that kind of function. And it can only do this if it takes seriously the history of literature and its intertextuality, thus enabling the reader's apprehension of what kind of 'implied reader' is embedded in the text by the very fact that the author chose to adopt and adapt a certain set of literary conventions.

That kind of analysis can probably only be done work by work. But we may provide a hint of what is possible by taking an example. Among the *Orations* of Gregory of Nazianzus are several *encomia*,[8] speeches commemorating the life of friend or family member. An intertextual analysis soon demonstrates that their generic model is provided by the traditions of classical rhetoric, and the standard *topoi* are clearly followed. *Amplificatio* and *comparatio* serve to enhance the character-sketch; the climax is a *consolatio* encouraging a philosophical attitude towards bereavement. But whereas classical *encomia* would have been full of allusions to and quotations from classical literature, Gregory's speeches are full of Scripture. His sister Gorgonia's character is described in terms of the ideal wife of Proverbs 31 and a number of biblical heroes who embody key virtues; comfort for the premature death of Caesarius is drawn from the Psalms and the promise of resurrection. The 'implied audience' is one that can spot the biblical allusions while recognizing the traditional conventions of epideictic rhetoric. The familiar patterns of English understatement do nothing to prepare the present reader for all this. Texts of this kind can only be appreciated by learning how to approximate to the 'implied reader', that is, by generic and intertextual analysis.

Such analysis is required text by text. Yet a start can be made by recognizing the fact that all literature in the ancient world was meant to persuade, and though written down was rhetorically never far from oral presentation. The Christianity of the ancient world comes over as very earnest, prepared to exploit all known techniques to carry conviction, and ready to adapt and experiment for the end envisaged rather than simply follow the textbooks slavishly. The *Life* became a significant Christian literary form, but it was transformed into martyrology and hagiography as the subject was presented as 'type' or model to be emulated as well as hero(ine) to be celebrated. The object was to affect the audience, the intention to convince and change lives.

So the form or surface-genre, often problematic as we have seen, is perhaps in many cases less significant for providing literary clues than the audience or context to which the work is directed. If much of the literature reflects a world of debate and contention, much else takes its character from the context of worship, from the desire to form a Christian people inspired by the Scriptures to live in a certain manner and for the sake of certain goals.

Authoritative exposition of Scripture recorded for posterity is therefore one of the characteristic features of Christian literature of this period. Such exposition often gathers up elements of contemporary controversy, deducing 'orthodox' teachings, warning against 'heretical' interpretations; but it also underlines moral maxims and garners 'types' of the spiritual or moral life. Thus it is rooted in a continuous tradition, but at the same time malleable to contemporary needs; it has precedents in school exposition of the classics, but achieves its own character and purpose. What is recorded of this activity, however, is extant because it has been regarded as authoritative. That is why it has been transmitted. Figures of great reputation lent authorial weight to the texts. The interplay of authoritative authors and community transmission is to be seen in the fact that catenae would be produced, commentaries composed of extracts from the great expositors of this period.

Similar, but now focused on authoritative exposition of 'the faith' or the right teaching, would be the development of *florilegia*, collections of extracts from different authorities claimed as documentation that a particular doctrine is approved and traditional. Such collections began in this period, one example being Theodoret's collections of testimonies at the end of each of the dialogues that make up his *Eranistes*: he is claiming support for his own position from Athanasius and others to whose authority his opponents also appeal. The attribution of spurious texts to such authority figures is hardly surprising. But perceived authority is also fundamental to the collections of 'community' documents that begin in this period: the record of councils, creeds and canons, which provided the authorized fulcrum through which the tradition was handed down and, for our purposes most significant, through which the literature was transmitted.

Which brings us full circle to where we began. This period is crucial for the transmission of all the literature covered in this volume. It is this period which is responsible for challenging the authority of Origen and others, thus creating the problematic situation addressed in Part II. Characteristic of the Christian literary tradition is a concern with authority, an authority bound up with the status of the author, but also with the nature of the content – for valued works would be preserved by attribution to known authority figures. That Eusebius documents history is typical of the need for 'proof', in the sense of bringing the reader or audience to conviction (*pistis*). The old rhetoric, together with the old genres, was both borrowed and transformed.

Notes

1 See further, Young, *Biblical Exegesis*, ch. 3.
2 Gregory of Nazianzus, *Or.* 4 and 5.
3 For details concerning the following examples, see relevant chapters in the literary guide.
4 See, however, ch. 23, below.
5 Glenn F. Chesnut, *The First Christian Histories Eusebius, Socrates, Sozomen, Theodoret, and Evagrius*, shows how Eusebius shifts this into a focus on free will and providence.
6 A. Momigliano showed how this distinguished Eusebius' work from that of pagan historiographers in 'Pagan and Christian Historiography', in A. Momigliano, ed., *The Conflict between Paganism and Christianity in the Fourth Century*, 79–99.
7 See further the volume edited by Mark J. Edwards, *Apologetics in the Roman Empire*.
8 See further Frances Young, 'Panegyric and the Bible', *SP* 25 (1993), 194–208; reproduced as ch. 5 in *Biblical Exegesis*.

22

Arnobius and Lactantius

OLIVER NICHOLSON

Rhetoric was the core of ancient education. The production of 'good men skilled in speaking' was not a literary affectation; it was a practical necessity in a world where public business was carried on orally. Rhetorical correctness became, therefore, the mark of the educated man; a writer who could not express himself properly was one who would not be taken seriously, like a modern scientist ignorant of mathematics. Lactantius and Arnobius were both professors of rhetoric; indeed, though neither mentions the other in his surviving works, Arnobius taught Lactantius. Both men knew that their intelligent contemporaries despised Christianity because it was crudely expressed: 'The language is trivial and sordid,' Arnobius' opponents complained (*Nat.* 1.58.2); 'They think nothing true except what is sweet to listen to,' wrote Lactantius; 'they do not therefore believe in the divine utterances because they lack adornment, and they do not trust those who interpret them because such people are generally ignorant' (*Inst.* 5.1.17–18). The objection was not frivolous; it expressed a sense that Christianity was fundamentally incompatible with what was known about the way the world worked. The Christians were frankly stupid; *stultitia*, said their persecutors, had laid hold of them (so Galerius: *Mort.* 34.2; cf. *Inst.* 5.18.12). Lactantius and Arnobius confronted this judgment on their convictions in contrasting ways.

The seven books *Against the Pagans*, the only known work of Arnobius, is less a defence of Christianity than a vigorous counter-attack on a broad range of pagan religious thought and practice, deploying a detailed knowledge of Latin literature and Roman myth. Arnobius, a professor of rhetoric at Sicca, a city in the hinterland of Roman North Africa, had been an opponent of Christianity, but was converted by dreams (Jerome, *Vir. Ill.* 79; *Chron.* p. 231g, Helm). When the local bishop did not believe him, Arnobius wrote an assault on his former religion and so was accepted. It is reasonable to suppose that the surviving seven books, written soon after his conversion (*Nat.* 1.39), and at some date later than the First Edict of the Great Persecution in 303 (4.36), are those the bishop read. This then, perhaps uniquely, is the work of a Christian convert convinced but not yet instructed in the faith.

Much of *Against the Pagans* is made up of acrimonious altercation with an unnamed pagan, whose assertions are repudiated with arguments rooted in a common culture rather than with appeals to what is characteristically Christian. Scripture is quoted possibly twice (*Nat.* 1.6; 2.6); the only expositions of distinctively Christian notions come in the second book, where Arnobius answers the charge of Christian stupidity with an attack on philosophical wisdom, and in the latter part of the first book. Here he asserts that all men know by nature that God is Lord of all (1.33) and that it is no use to claim (as the Stoic did in Cicero's dialogue *On the Nature of the Gods*) that this supreme God is the same as Jupiter (1.35: cf. 3.7). Christ had come to reveal the character of the Most High (1.60); he was not, as critics complained a condemned criminal (*Nat.* 1.36), a mere mortal (1.42) or a magician (1.43). Only his human form perished on the cross (1.62); he brought healing for all ills to those who believe and yet he and his followers are savagely persecuted (1.65).

What furnished the rationale for persecution was the public religion of cities, particularly that of Rome, the paradigm city for the Romans of North Africa, *domina Roma* (*Nat.* 2.12). Roman religion protected cities from natural disasters, pagans thought: ' "it is on account of the Christians", they say, "that the gods send all evils, and that destruction comes upon the crops from above" ' (1.13; cf. 1.1). The answer of Arnobius' first book is that the communities of the Roman world had endured natural disasters long before there had been Christianity, and that anyway it demeans the whole notion of the divine to think that famine, plague and pestilence are caused by pique on the part of the gods at Christian neglect of the rites of Roman religion (1.23). In any case, the Most High was greater and more ancient that the pagan gods. 'Does Apollo rain for you, does Mercury rain for you?' (1.30); there was a time before they were born, yet even in those ages there was rain and weather.

In later books Arnobius carries his attack into the pagan camp. The second book takes to pieces the claim to superior wisdom of the educated, among them certain *viri novi*, who may be Neoplatonist philosophers (*Nat.* 2.15); Christ is a wiser and more powerful master than any philosopher (2.11). There is, though, more than philosophy at issue; Arnobius argues that the entire apparatus of ancient learning, literature and law, which makes the learned so proud, is stupidity in the eyes of the First God (2.6).

The three central books concentrate on the pagan gods. It was in mythology that the characters of the immortals were defined, but the myths make them seem both human and immorally involved in mortal matters such as love and war. Besides, the complexities of myth could not possibly be an accurate representation of divine reality: ' "How do we know," says someone, "if writers on the Gods have recorded what they have investigated and discovered, or, as it has seemed and indeed is the case, have they published wanton fiction?" ' (4.18). Allegory, which understands myths as accounts of natural forces, so that the limbs of Father Liber scattered across the land are the stems of the vines and Proserpina carried off into the underworld is the seed buried in the ground, is inadequate as a way of explaining the stories and fails to eradicate their filthiness.

The two final books criticize the festivals and sacrifices celebrated by cities to appease and honour their gods. True gods would not be impressed by such physical activities (*Nat.* 6.2). They are not like people and are not given to passions such as anger (7.15), still less are they pleased by the proper performance of festivals (7.33) and annoyed to the point of vengeance when the celebration is inadequate or inaccurate (7.38–44). Arnobius compares the gods who regulated the practicalities of life in a Roman city to an elevated conception of divinity which owes as much to classical philosophy as it does to Christianity. *Against the Pagans* would have lost much of its force when the apparatus of public paganism disintegrated. Its only known ancient readers were St Jerome and (presumably) the bishop of Sicca, and it survives in only two manuscripts. Often rambling but always caustic, it gives a sharp idea of religious dissension in the cities of Africa in the generation of the Great Persecution.

Lactantius, taught by Arnobius at Sicca, had acquired wider horizons than his master by the time he wrote his surviving works in later life. He was called to be professor of Latin rhetoric at the imperial city of Nicomedia in Asia Minor (Jerome, *Vir. Ill.* 80), in extreme old age he was tutor to the son of the Emperor Constantine (Jerome, *Chron.* p. 230*e* Helm), and there may even be political overtones to his elegant elegiacs *On the Phoenix*. His enthusiasm for court gossip is most evident in his vitriolic pamphlet *On the Deaths of the Persecutors*, an important source for the political history of the years which saw the Great Persecution (303–13) and the rise to supreme power of Constantine the Great (306–37). It was written in 313/15, soon after Constantine and his ally Licinius had brought the persecutions to an end, and recounts recent history in detail to show by 'great and wonderful examples' how God's judgment has destroyed emperors who dared to harm the Christians; 'it has come late, but heavily and in the way it ought' (*Mort.* 1.6). The message may have influenced Constantine directly: the peroration of a sermon preached by the emperor to the Christians at his court enumerated the unsavoury circumstances in which his persecuting predecessors had perished (*Coet.* 24–5). *On the Deaths of* *the Persecutors* is notable for its argument as well as for the historical details it records; it is the first application by a political insider of Christian notions about God's involvement in human history to the realities of practical politics.

Lactantius' other surviving works were the product of the same eventful decades as *On the Deaths of the Persecutors*. The seven books of the *Divine Institutes* were composed during the Great Persecution, *On the Workmanship of God* earlier, probably at the start of the persecution, and *On the Anger of God* after 313, when the persecutions had ended. In his old age Lactantius made an *Epitome of the Divine Institutes* and was at work on a revised edition of them, complete with laudatory dedications to Constantine, when he died, probably around 325. Lactantius wrote in prose that earned him in the Renaissance the soubriquet 'the Christian Cicero'. His Christianity was uncompromising but it was presented in a manner palatable to people like his own pupils, men with a decent middlebrow education, more rhetoric than philosophy, who were intending to take their places in public life (cf. *Inst.* 3.16.2). Such people considered Cicero both the perfect orator and the highest philosopher (1.15.16; 3.14.7). It was pointless to impress upon them arguments based on Scripture (5.4.4–8); better to sweeten the rim of the medicine-cup with the honey of knowledge shared in common (5.1.14) – the image is of course borrowed from the poet Lucretius (*De Rerum Natura* 1.936–42). Even the horror of the crucifixion is made to seem more horrible by a comparison with the tortures denounced in Cicero's orations *Against Verres* (*Inst.* 4.18.10).

Lactantius wrote in troubled times. The *Divine Institutes* replied to the writings of two contemporary publicists, one a philosopher, the other a provincial governor, who attempted to show the Christians the error of their ways (*Inst.* 5.2–3): the discussion of righteousness (*iustitia*) is much taken up with the injustice of the persecutions (5.8–23). But Lactantius' polemic against 'those who accuse justice' was intended to have a perennial relevance: 'I have thought I ought to conduct this case so that I may overturn earlier writers and what they have written and take away from future opponents any opportunity of writing or replying' (5.4.1–2). Not that Lactantius was one to win the argument but lose the sympathy of his readers. His definitive apologetic was a work of controversy, but it also aimed to 'open to the contemplation of the truth the eyes of the heart' (4.26.4), to enable people to see the world in a Christian perspective, to bring them 'to the full and overflowing fountain of knowledge' (1.1.22). For Lactantius' Christian classic was intended also as a text which could give thorough basic instruction in the faith, in the same way that the Institutes of the civil law constituted a permanent handbook for those engaged in legal study (1.1.12). Lactantius felt that such Christian education was 'to be thought a profession much better, more useful and more glorious than that of oratory, in which we have long been engaged and used to bring up the young not to virtue but simply to cunning wickedness' (1.1.8).

Romans distinguished between *religio*, what was done to sustain the relationship between Gods and men, and *sapientia*, the knowledge of matters human and divine. Lactantius opined that pagan *religio* lacked any connection with ethics; it subordinated the spiritual to the physical and was concerned merely with matters of ritual. Philosophy was not true *sapientia*, not least because it lacked any way of worship. It is only where there is worship of one God that *sapientia* and *religio* come together, where all life and activity relate to one head and to one supreme whole, where indeed the teachers of wisdom are the same as the priests of God (4.3.1–7).

Lactantius lays out the united *religio* and *sapientia* of Christianity in seven books: the first three demonstrate the falseness of pagan cult and philosophy, the latter four true wisdom and the religion of the One God, its duties and rewards. From an assertion of the unity of God, backed by a wide range of non-Christian witnesses (1.2–8), the reader is led to an exposition of the myths as a garbled account of the deeds of ancient rulers mistakenly honoured as gods. Lactantius can even put a date to them: Saturn, ancestor of the gods, ruled on earth 322 years before the Trojan War, so about 1500 BC (1.23.2–5). Book 2 describes the demonic forces which engineered the invention of idolatry and in doing so outlines Christian belief about the way the world was created out of nothing, a topic important in the instruction of those preparing for baptism. Lactantius then shifts attention to a 'greater and more difficult struggle' (2.19.2). Philosophy, as Cicero and the Academics had argued, furnishes no certain knowledge; it is useless because it is inconclusive (3.7.9): 'those who teach philosophy are already old and dead before they have decided how they ought to live' (3.14.11). Lactantius' alternative is simple: 'the whole wisdom of man is in this one thing, that he should get to know God and worship him' (3.30.3).

Having thus cleared the ground, Lactantius describes the Christian conception of universal history foreshadowed in books 1 and 2. God made man to know and worship him (7.6.1; cf. 4.4.3); originally, then, wisdom and the religion of the Most High were universal, but were worn away by the rise of idolatry and the increasing infidelity of the Jews (4.1–2; 4.10.5–8). 'As the end of the age approached', God sent his Son to reclaim the human race, to teach righteousness (*iustitia*) and to found a temple for him, for the temple of the true God is made up of people (4.10.1; cf. 6.25.15). Book 4 expounds the centrality of Christ to God's plan, again following the lines of pre-baptismal instruction.

Book 5 illustrates what *iustitia* means in practice, particularly in relation to suffering and persecution. The first duty of *iustitia* is the worship of God, the second is mercy or *humanitas*, which alone can furnish the rationale of a common life (6.10.2). Book 6 gives details of the whole duty of man, in the manner of Cicero's *De Officiis*; it incorporates Lactantius' notions, novel in the Roman world, about the right management of the passions and the way they may be directed towards the augmentation of moral strength (*virtus*). The reward of *virtus* is immortality; the final book of the *Institutes* justifies the hope of the individual Christian (7.2–13), and then, in an extensive eschatological prophecy, shows how, at the end of six thousand years of world history, God will inaugurate a final millennium of bliss for the righteous before he winds up the entire world process (7.14–26).

The *Divine Institutes* were designed as a comprehensive introduction to Christianity, and their *Epitome* as an abbreviated version of the great work, which gave disproportionately large space to the demythologizing of the pagan gods. Lactantius' two shorter treatises, *On the Workmanship of God* and *On the Anger of God*, were rather different in purpose. The former was written not to interest the public at large but 'to make more wise the philosophers of our sect' (*Opif.* 1.2). It is a detailed account of human anatomy, drawing heavily on contemporary learning, which demonstrates how a person's body and soul are all God's work and so may be employed for the purposes for which he designed them; it has been called 'a manufacturer's handbook for all body-owners'. *On the Anger of God* is directed specifically at those who affirm the unity of the Most High God but cannot think that so lofty a being could be affected by passions, particularly not those which cause harm (*Ira* 2.5; 2.7–8). Lactantius argues that to deny God's capacity for feeling is to destroy the relationship between God and man created by religion; in particular, if God is capable of showing his kindness and mercy he must also have the capacity to show a righteous anger with that which is evil. The treatise engages a wide range of philosophical opinion on this most discussed of ancient emotions. It may also be seen as a theological exposition of the message put forward through historical examples in *On the Deaths of the Persecutors*. One can only speculate whether or not the Donatus to whom it is dedicated is the same as the confessor Donatus for whom *On the Deaths of the Persecutors* was written.

Lactantius was not concerned with speculative theology. He alludes only once to a Greek theologian (*Inst.* 1.23.2), and that was a catechetical writer already over a century dead. His secular Latin learning, though, was substantial and was deployed to show that contrary to appearances Christianity was not 'unworthy of a sane individual's credence'. In time his Mere Christianity came to seem conservative; the *Divine Institutes* is ostentatiously ignored in Augustine's *City of God* (18.23.70), though the intentions of the two works are remarkably similar. Lactantius wrote in a time of the breaking of nations. If Arnobius shows us the tensions behind the Constantinian Revolution in a provincial city, Lactantius gives us an idea of the issues which separated Christians from pagans at court. If we are to understand the sort of Christianity to which Constantine the Great was converted, it is to Lactantius that we must turn.

23
Eusebius and the birth of church history

ANDREW LOUTH

Eusebius was born in the early 260s, probably in Caesarea, which was to be the centre of his activities for most of his life. He became bishop of Caesarea in about 313 (probably in succession to Agapius, who had ordained him priest and seems to have survived the Great Persecution), and died on 30 May 339. We know comparatively little about his life: a *Life* was written by his successor at Caesarea, Acacius, but this has been lost. This is doubtless because, though posterity valued some of his works, it had little veneration for the man and bishop, for during the controversy over the doctrines of the Alexandrian priest, Arius, Eusebius found himself on the losing side. Consequently, though a good deal has survived of Eusebius' literary activity, it is probably only a small part of the total, which makes it very difficult to form a rounded view of him.

Three events profoundly shaped Eusebius' life and activity. The first was his encounter with Pamphilus. Pamphilus was a great admirer of the work of Origen, though he had never known the man himself. He had studied in Alexandria under Pierius, whose devotion to Origen was such that he was known as 'Origen Junior' (Jerome, *Vir. Ill.* 76), and towards the end of the third century settled in Caesarea, where Origen had taught after his expulsion from Alexandria.[1] There he set about restoring Origen's heritage by making copies of all his voluminous works and continuing his labours on the text of the Scriptures. Eusebius must have become Pamphilus' disciple almost as soon as he arrived in Caesarea, and he evidently caught his enthusiasm for Origen. He shared in Pamphilus' scholarly labours, and collaborated with him on his *Defence of Origen*, which he completed, writing book 6 after Pamphilus' martyrdom in 309. He preserved the memory of his mentor both in a *Life* (which is lost) and in the prominent place he gives to Pamphilus in his *Martyrs of Palestine*: more personally, he took Pamphilus' name, calling himself *Eusebius Pamphili*, Pamphilus' Eusebius.

The second great event that affected Eusebius' life was the toleration of Christianity, and indeed the growing imperial patronage of the Church, in the years following Constantine's victory at the Milvian Bridge in 312. Eusebius became bishop of Caesarea soon after; his was an episcopate that experienced the dramatic change in the relationship between the Christian Church and imperial authority. One consequence of that change was the emperor's interest in Church matters, including matters of belief. At the council held in Nicaea in 325, which was to come to be thought of as the first 'Œcumenical' council, Eusebius found himself in the opposition, although he finally accepted, as did virtually all the bishops, the decision of that council. Imperial favour also nurtured his interest in discovering and celebrating the sites associated with Christ's birth, death and resurrection: sites which lay in the territory, over which, as bishop of Caesarea, Eusebius was metropolitan.

The third event, though it perhaps loomed larger in Eusebius' imagination than in reality, was his encounter with the Emperor Constantine himself, and his finding himself commissioned to compose a panegyric for his *tricennalia*, the celebration of thirty years' rule from Constantine's acclamation as *Augustus* by the army in York in 306, and the *Life of Constantine*, which he began after Constantine's death in 337 and on which he was still engaged when he died himself.

The apprenticeship with Pamphilus marked everything that Eusebius wrote; Eusebius emerged as a man of wide reading and great scholarly erudition. It is as such that posterity valued him, with the consequence that any other virtues Eusebius may have had – pastoral or spiritual qualities, theological insight into the interpretation of Scripture – have been obscured. Nevertheless, it is proper to begin with some appreciation of what was clearly of great importance to him, though comparatively little of it has survived: his biblical scholarship.

In the catenae, the 'chains' whose links consist of usually brief explanatory passages drawn from the writings of the Fathers arranged as a commentary on biblical books, there are passages from Eusebius commenting on nearly all the books of both the Old and New Testaments. Although what has survived in the catenae does not amount to much, its range suggests that a great deal has been lost. It is not improbable that biblical commentary loomed large among Eusebius' concerns. In the case of Isaiah, our knowledge of Eusebius' biblical scholarship has been greatly deepened by the discovery of a nearly complete commentary on the prophet in the margin of a Florentine biblical manuscript (discovered in 1934, eventually published in 1975).[2] From this it emerges that Eusebius' exegesis is much more concerned with the historical meaning of the text than might have been expected from such a devoted Origenist; it also adumbrates a theology of the Church almost entirely free of the imperial ideology that is so conspicuous an aspect of the ecclesiology of the imperial *encomia*. Eusebius' biblical scholarship is also manifest in his *Gospel Canons*, a way of locating parallel *pericopae* in the four Gospels,[3] and, in a rather different way, in his *Onomasticon*, a gazetteer of the Holy Land, presumably compiled for the Empress Helena's visit in 326.[4] He also wrote a work called *Gospel Questions*, of which only an epitome and fragments survive.

Apart from commentaries and sermons on the Scriptures, early Christian theology was either of an introductory catechetical nature, or apologetic, that is, defence of Christianity against Jews, who disputed Christian use of the Scriptures they held in common, or against traditional classical culture. Eusebius represents the culmination of this tradition of apologetic theology, at least in terms of the scholarly resources he brought to this task. His main apologetic works are prefaced, both in substance and chronologically, by the *General Theological Introduction*, also called *Prophetic Selections* (*Eclogae Propheticae*), since the books that survive (books 6–9) consist of discussion of messianic passages from the prophets. This is perhaps more catechetical than apologetic, and references to the persecution during which it was written (*EcProph*. 1.8), make attractive Barnes' suggestion that 'it replaced the formal, organized instruction of catechumens which was now forbidden by law'.[5] Eusebius' great works of apologetic are the fifteen books of his *Preparation for the Gospel* and the twenty books of his *Proof of the Gospel* (of which only books 1–10 and a lengthy fragment of book 15 survive). In the first of these he makes a revealing claim to originality – 'the purpose that we have in hand is to be worked out in our own way' (*PrEv*. 1.3.5) – which is perhaps explained when he says later: 'I shall set down not my own words, but rather those of them who have been most diligent in their piety to those whom they call gods' (ibid. 1.6.14). This indicates what is most remarkable about Eusebius' apologetic method: its extensive and careful documentation. With Origen's *Against Celsus*, Eusebius' *Preparation for the Gospel* is one of the main sources for our knowledge of the views of many ancient philosophers cited by them, whose works have otherwise been lost. It is certainly not the content that is original: Eusebius follows the earlier apologists in attacking Greek myths, oracles, belief in fate, and then goes on to show that anything of value in Greek philosophy, especially in Plato, is derived from Moses and the prophets who lived long before the Greek philosophers. The *Proof of the Gospel* forms a sequel directed against Jewish objections to Christianity. It begins by claiming that Christianity is the re-emergence of the ancient and universal religion of the patriarchs: the Mosaic dispensation was an interlude the real purpose of which was to prepare for the coming of Christ. Book 2 shows how the downfall of the Jewish state, the coming of Christ and the calling of the Gentiles were all predicted by the prophets. Books 3–10 show how the prophets predicted the humanity and divinity of the coming Messiah, and the events of his earthly life, culminating in his passion and death. The rest of the *Proof of the Gospel* presumably dealt with the resurrection, ascension, the coming of the Spirit and the foundation of the Church. The *Preparation* and the *Proof* seem to envisage the peace of the Church, and thus presumably belong to the early years of Eusebius' episcopate. Another of Eusebius' apologetic works, which seems to be a kind of condensation of these, is his *Theophany*, or *Divine Manifestation*, in five books (the fifth book is expressly based on *Proof*, book 3). Only fragments survive of the original Greek, but the whole text survives in a early Syriac translation. It seems to belong to the period of Constantine's sole rule (after 324), and has some similarities both in structure and detail with Athanasius' early work, *Against the Pagans – On the Incarnation*.

All this does not exhaust Eusebius' apologetic work. In addition, he wrote works directed specifically against the pagan attack on Christianity, which it is argued prepared for and accompanied the Great Persecution. There is a brief *Against Hierocles*. Hierocles had been governor of Bithynia at the beginning of the Great Persecution and became prefect of Egypt in 307, in both places enthusiastic in his persecution of Christianity. In his *Truth-loving Discourses* he attacked Christianity by comparing Jesus with the pagan sage and wonder-worker, Apollonius of Tyana. His work is lost, but Eusebius' reply survives. A similar, but presumably much more substantial, work was his reply to the famous *Against the Christians*, written by Plotinus' disciple and editor, Porphyry. Porphyry's attack survives in fragments, but Eusebius' reply is lost. In addition to this apologetic work, Eusebius wrote two pieces of polemical theology, against Marcellus of Ancyra, who was the preferred target for those who were unhappy with Nicaea and its use of the term ὁμοούσιος. These are his *Ecclesiastical Theology* and his *Against Marcellus*.

It is out of his apologetic concern that Eusebius' greatest achievement – his *Church History* and other historical works – grew. In writing a history of the Church, Eusebius was conscious that he was a pioneer:

> I am the first to venture on such a project and to set out on what is indeed a lonely and untrodden path; but I pray that I may have God to guide me . . . As for men, I have failed to find any clear footprints of those who have gone this way before me; only faint traces, by which in different fashions they have left us partial accounts of their own lifetimes. (*HE* 1.1.3)[6]

One recalls his claim to originality at the beginning of the *Preparation for the Gospel* (which may be very nearly contemporaneous). Here he is original in conception, as well as execution, but it is the method he claimed as original in the *Preparation* that he applies in his *Church History*: viz., that of letting the original documents speak for themselves. For what is striking about the *Church History* is that, though Eusebius had plenty of models in earlier historical writing (with which he is familiar, and which he sometimes uses: Josephus' *Jewish War*, for instance, in the early books), he does not attempt to produce a conventional historical narrative; rather, he sees his role more as that of a compiler.[7] There is hardly any narrative structure – the sense of historical progression is provided by the first of the purposes Eusebius set himself in writing his history of the Church: viz., to record 'the lines of succession of the sacred apostles, stretching from the time of our Saviour to our own'.

These lines of succession Eusebius took from an earlier historical work of his, the *Chronicle*. The nature of this work further confirms both the apologetic roots of Eusebius' conception of Church history and the originality of his scholarship. The *Chronicle*, which survives complete only in an Armenian translation, consists of two parts, the first brief epitomes of the history of the Chaldaeans, Assyrians, Hebrews, Egyptians, Greeks and Romans, the second a table of dates arranged in columns so that contemporary events in the histories of the different nations would be on the same line – a synchronic world chronicle (the second part survives in a Latin translation, augmented and brought up to date, by Jerome). The apologetic purpose of this is plain: to demonstrate the superior antiquity of those Jewish traditions that Christians had made their own. And although in the compilation of this work Eusebius made use of the labours of predecessors, notably Julius Africanus, it seems that the notion of a synchronic world chronicle is his own (and he knew it):[8] it was to be the basis for all later world chronicles in the medieval West, and in the Byzantine Empire, as well as in Oriental, Slav and Celtic languages.[9]

Into the documentary framework provided by the succession lists of the bishops of Rome and Alexandria, and also (though less reliably) Jerusalem and Antioch, Eusebius fitted information illustrative of a number of themes he lists at the beginning: (a) important events in the life of the Church and outstanding leaders and heroes; (b) the names and dates of heretics; (c) the calamities that overwhelmed the Jewish race after their conspiracy against the Saviour; (d) the persecutions of the Church; and (e) the 'martyrdoms of later days down to my own time, and at the end of it all the kind and gracious deliverance accorded by our Saviour' (*HE* 1.1).[10] The documentary material Eusebius used in his *Church History* was diverse: it included already published work, Josephus' *Jewish War* for instance (in books 2 and 3); earlier Christian compilers of historical material, notably Hegesippus and Julius Africanus; dossiers on Montanism and Quartodecimanism, which were probably already to hand, and a work on heresy in Rome called *The Little Labyrinth*. He uses early Christian theologians, and makes a point of listing their writings, often revealing the existence of works that have now been lost (or only recently discovered: e.g., the *Didache*). He draws on collections of episcopal letters, especially those of Dionysius of Alexandria; and the account of the life of Origen, in book 6, is probably based on the *Defence of Origen* he wrote with Pamphilus. Particularly important is the collection of *Acts of the Martyrs* that Eusebius says he had made (*HE* 4.15.47). In most cases, Eusebius is our sole source for these documents; where they have survived independently, they confirm his accuracy (as is the case with the imperial documents preserved in his *Life of Constantine*). His historical material is, however, limited to what one might expect to find in the libraries of Caesarea and Alexandria: Eusebius is poorly informed about the Latin West.

Book 1 acts as a kind of preface to the *Church History* and makes unmistakable the apologetic concern of the whole work, as it presents belief in the creator Word who was to become incarnate as a religion as old as creation, with the Jewish dispensation having no other function than to prepare for Christ, with whose coming it was to be dissolved. The rest of the *Church History* falls into two distinct parts: books 2–7, which pursue themes (a)–(d), set out above, and books 8–10, which pursue (e). Books 2–7 present the history of an institutional Church, defined in terms of communities led by bishops, whose role is to defend the integrity and purity of the Church and its teaching against heretics and persecutors. Books 8–10 relate the Great Persecution, from the perspective of Palestine for the most part, and the inauguration of the period of imperial favour. How these fit together poses several problems. First, and more fundamentally, while the sunny introduction leads one to see the period of persecution as nothing more than an interlude before inevitable victory, the beginning of book 8, however, presents the Great Persecution as a divine judgment for the way in which the Christian Church had responded to its increasing acceptance in Roman society with 'arrogance and sloth', rancorous disunity and 'unspeakable hypocrisy and dissimulation carried to the limit of wickedness'. But secondly, and much discussed, there is the problem of the evolution of the *Church History*.

Book 10 is conceived of as an addition or appendix: it is separately dedicated to Paulinus, bishop of Tyre from at least 313 until 326, and consists of Eusebius' sermon of dedication for the new basilica in Tyre and a dossier of letters illustrating the imperial favour now shown to the Church (the way in which it presents Constantine and Licinius as comrades-in-arms makes it clear that it belongs to the period between 313 and 316/17, when war between the two emperors broke out). In its present form two further chapters have been added (9–10), celebrating Constantine's final victory and assumption of sole power in 324 (the Syriac version gives evidence of still later modifications). The evolution of books 8 and 9, which cover the Great Persecution (book 8 dealing with the period up to May 311, when Galerius halted the persecution; and book 9 with the renewal of persecution under his junior partner Maximin in November 311), is bound up with another of Eusebius' works, his *Martyrs of Palestine*. This exists in two forms: a longer version, preserved in Syriac, and a shorter version, which survives in some manuscripts of the *Church History*. The long recension covers the persecution in Palestine (mainly at Caesarea) month by month from 303 to 311, and gives the impression that it came to an end in May 311, with Galerius' edict of recantation. The short recension, though it covers no more ground, seems, from the way it refers to Maximin, to envisage the renewal of persecution in November 311. As it stands, the short recension has neither beginning nor end, but there seems to be a reference back to book 8 of the *Church History* (cf. *Mart*. 12 with *HE* 8.2.2ff.), which suggests that it is a continuation of, or an appendix to, book 8; further, the short recension ends on the point of quoting Galerius' edict of recantation, quoted at the end of book 8. As for books 8 and 9 of the *Church History* itself, they seem to belong together in that book 8 seems to look forward to events recorded in book 9; further, the 'appendix' to book 8 (found in some manuscripts only) is presented as a conclusion, since it records the fate of the four Emperors who began the persecution in 303. Various solutions to all this have been suggested. It seems clear that the long recension of the *Martyrs of Palestine* was finished between May and November 311. The short version is either an appendix to book 8 recording in more detail the persecution in Palestine,[11] or more radically (and more credibly) the short recension, preceded by the present beginning of book 8 (up to 8.2.3) and followed by the edict of recantation and the 'appendix' to book 8, is in fact the original form of book 8. This was presumably abandoned and replaced by the present books 8 and 9, because the account of the Great Persecution in the *Martyrs of Palestine*, confined as it is to events in Palestine, seemed parochial and out of place in the *Church History*.[12]

The big question, though, is: what was the *first* edition of the *Church History*? Put another way, in discussing the evolution of book 8–10, are we discussing how the conclusion of the *Church History* took shape, or the making of a later appendix? Traditionally it has been thought that the original version of the *Church History* ended with some part of books 8–10 – either book 8 (in some form), or books 8–9 or 10 – so that it belongs either to 311 or some time before 316/17. More recently the view has gained favour (though the traditional view still has its supporters) that the first edition of the *Church History* consisted of books 1–7 (which in their present form have been touched up) and was composed in the latter years of the third century, during the false peace of the Church that Eusebius seems to envisage at the beginning of book 8: a peace so rudely shattered by the Great Persecution.[13] This question raises large issues about the nature of the *Church History* – is it, as Westcott put it, a work which 'gathers up and expresses . . . the experience, the feelings, the hopes of a body which had just accomplished its sovereign success, and was conscious of its inward strength',[14] or, as Barnes has it, 'contemporary evidence for the standing of the Christian Church in Roman society in the late third century'?[15] And that in turn raises questions as to how deeply Roman society had been Christianized prior to Constantine's conversion.

Eusebius' other works of history are his *encomia* of the emperor. The *Praises of Constantine* consist of two distinct works: the panegyric delivered by Eusebius in the palace at Constantinople on 25 July 335, at the beginning of Constantine's celebration of his *tricennalia* (chapters 1–10), and the treatise presented to the emperor by Eusebius at the dedication of the Church of the *Anastasis* (or the Holy Sepulchre) in Jerusalem on 13 September 335 (chapters 11–18). The *Life of Constantine*, left unfinished on Eusebius' death, survives in four books and is notable both for its (to many nauseous) eulogy of the emperor (which is no more than what was required of an *encomium*) as well as for the (typically Eusebian) inclusion of letters and edicts. There is considerable dispute as to how much of the text we have is genuinely Eusebian, and no scholarly consensus.

The vast influence of Eusebius is unquestionable. His view of the emperor as friend and imitator of the Word of God formed the basis of the Byzantine (and Carolingian) imperial ideology. But as world chronicler and church historian, he created the forms in which later Christians expressed their historical consciousness. No one attempted to repeat the historical work of Eusebius: Gelasius, Jerome and Rufinus, Socrates and Sozomen take up where Eusebius left off (Rufinus having provided a Latin translation of books 1–9 before continuing), and extend his notion of Church history into their own times.

Notes

1 For Pamphilus' life, see Jerome, *Vir. Ill.* 75, and Photius, *Bibl. Cod.* 118.

2 Discovered by A. Möhle, 'Der Jesaiakommentar des Eusebius von Kaisareia fast vollständig aufgefunden', *ZNW* 33 (1934), 87–9. The text has been edited by J. Ziegler: *Eusebius' Werke*, IX, *Der Jesajakommentar* (GCS, 1975). See M. J. Hollerich, *Eusebius of Caesarea's* Commentary on Isaiah.

3 See E. Nestle and K. Aland, eds, *Novum Testamentum Graece* (Stuttgart: Würtembergische Bibelanstalt, 1963[25]), 32*–37*.

4 For another view, that the *Onomasticon* should be dated *c.* 295, see T. D. Barnes, 'The Composition of Eusebius' *Onomasticon*'.

5 T. D. Barnes, *Constantine and Eusebius*, 169.

6 Translation by G. A. Williamson: Eusebius, *The History of the Church*, 2.

7 Something emphasized by A. Momigliano in his 'Pagan and Christian Historiography in the Fourth Century A.D.', *in Conflict between Paganism and Christianity*, 79–99, esp. 90f.

8 See *Praep. Ev.* 10.9.2, and his preface to the *Chronicle: Die Chronik des Hieronymus*, ed. R. Helm, *Eusebius' Werke*, VII (GCS 47, 1956), 8.

9 See B. Croke, 'The Originality of Eusebius' *Chronicle*', *American Journal of Philology* 103 (1982), 195–200 (repr. as item I, of *Christian Chronicles and Byzantine History, 5th–6th Centuries*).

10 Eusebius, *HE* 1.1.

11 So Lawlor, *Eusebiana*, 243–91, esp. 285ff., and Lawlor and Oulton, *Eusebius of Caesarea: The Ecclesiastical History and Martyrs of Palestine*, II, 9ff.

12 So Barnes, *Constantine and Eusebius*, 149ff., based on his article, 'The Editions of Eusebius' *Ecclesiastical History*', *Greek, Roman and Byzantine Studies* 21 (1980), 191–201.

13 See Barnes, 'Editions', and from rather a different perspective R. Grant, *Eusebius as Church Historian*. For a critique of Barnes' position, see A. Louth, 'The Date of Eusebius' *Historia Ecclesiastica*', *JTS* n.s. 41 (1990), 111–23.

14 Quoted by J. B. Lightfoot, 'Eusebius (23) of Caesarea', DCB II, p. 323.

15 T. D. Barnes, 'Some Inconsistencies in Eusebius', *JTS* n.s. 35 (1984), 470–5, at 471.

24

The fourth-century Alexandrians: Athanasius and Didymus

ANDREW LOUTH

Fourth-century Alexandrian theology is more or less summed up in the writings of two theological giants, Athanasius, pope of Alexandria from 328 until his death in 373 (not counting various periods of deposition and exile), and Didymus the Blind, a scholar of enormous renown in his own day, who was appointed head of the Catechetical School in Alexandria by Athanasius, a position he held until his death. The contrast that will be revealed between their theological methods and teaching suggests that, although Didymus taught with the approval and support of Athanasius, it is hazardous to speak too confidently of an 'Alexandrian school of theology'.

Athanasius

Since Athanasius' election as bishop of Alexandria in 328 was challenged on canonical grounds, it is likely that he had then barely attained the canonical age of thirty, which would mean that he was born at the very end of the third century. We know nothing about his upbringing and education, though from his writings it would seem a fair deduction that he acquired a good knowledge of Greek, without having had a formal education. His knowledge of classical philosophy and rhetoric is far from non-existent: he has a genuine admiration for Plato, whom he calls 'great among the Greeks', and shows skill in rhetorical methods of argument, but his style (of writing, as well as thinking) has a simple home-spun quality. He must soon have attracted the attention of the pope of Alexandria, or his circle, for already in his twenties he became one of his deacons, and attended the Council of Nicaea with Alexander (325). It is unlikely that he played any significant role there, though the suggestion has often been made (his hand has also been detected in either or both of the letters Alexander issued before the council, but there is no consensus about this). Alexander died soon after his return to Alexandria; Athanasius was elected his successor. During his long episcopate of nearly forty-five years,

Athanasius came to be seen as a stalwart defender of the faith of Nicaea, for which he suffered deposition and several periods of exile. During his early exiles in the West (in Gaul: 336–7; in Rome: 339–46), he established important links with Western churchmen. During his later exiles he fled to the Egyptian desert where he found support within the growing monastic movement. It is not therefore surprising that all Athanasius' writings are occasional in form, though this does not mean that in them he had no grand design, especially with regard to posterity.

Because the occasional form predominates, letters form the largest single category of Athanasius' genuine works. However, Athanasius' fame in his own time and later as a champion of orthodoxy has meant that the largest category of works ascribed to Athanasius are those now judged to be dubious or spurious (139 items compared with 80 genuine items in Geerard's *Clavis*). This needs to be borne in mind, as some traditional judgments about Athanasius (e.g., his wide classical learning) are derived from works now thought to be spurious. Other categories, which sometimes overlap with the epistolary, are the apologetic, the polemical and the ascetical; a little exegetical material survives, mainly in the catenae, but, surprisingly, no sermons. Some important genuine writings of Athanasius are no longer preserved in their original Greek: notable examples are the *Festal Letters*, written each year (often from exile) to announce the date of Easter and prepare his clergy and people for the celebration of that feast, and many of his ascetical writings. There is no evidence that Athanasius wrote in any other language than Greek, though it is very likely that he could speak Coptic, the vernacular of his diocese, in which language many of his works are preserved.

Against the Pagans – On the Incarnation

Athanasius' earliest work, his two-part *Against the Pagans* and *On the Incarnation*, stands in the apologetic tradition. It is generally regarded as early, as it bears no obvious trace of the Arian controversy which dominated Athanasius' consciousness as a bishop, although it has been argued forcefully (by Charles Kannengiesser) that it belongs to the mid-330s and envisages the Arians in its attack on schism, and it has even been placed in the context of the revival of paganism under Julian the Apostate. It is not original – there are striking parallels, even in some of its wording, with Eusebius' late apology, the *Theophaneia* – but it is compelling, and the second half is one of the most attractive doctrinal works of patristic literature. It begins by presenting a fundamentally contemplative understanding of human existence – human beings were made to contemplate God – and sees the Fall of humanity as a turning of attention away from God to a self-centred concern with created things. Paganism in all its forms is a consequence of the Fall. Athanasius goes on to outline two ways in which the fallen soul can return to God, through contemplation of the cosmos and through the soul itself. The second part, *On the Incarnation*, argues that, though the soul can see the way back to God, this can only be accomplished by the Word of God's making himself personally present in the created order, and overcoming the metaphysical or ontological consequences of the Fall – corruption and death – by absorbing them through his own encounter with, and embracing of, death. As a result of the Word of God's becoming human, human beings are enabled to become God: to incarnation there corresponds deification. This pattern, fundamental to most later Greek and Byzantine theology, is nowhere laid out so concisely and clearly as here.

This work exists in two recensions: a long one and a short one, which seems to be a revision of the long one. Both recensions survive in Greek, but the short recension survives also in a very early Syriac version (the extant MS is sixth-century, so the version may be as early as the fourth century). It has been argued that the short recension persistently plays down the significance of the human element assumed by the Word in the incarnation, though it is not clear that even in the long recension Athanasius attributes much more significance to the human than the fact of its assumption by the Word. It has even been argued that Athanasius is responsible for both recensions, though why or when he made the revision is not clear.

Anti-Arian writings

To this (non-literary) category belongs the bulk of Athanasius' writings. He composed three *Orations against the Arians* (probably *c.* 340: the 'fourth' oration is spurious), a *Defence* (or *Apology*) *against the Arians* (349), *On the Nicene Decrees* (352), *Letter to the Bishops of Egypt and Libya* (spring 356), *History of the Arians* (357), and *On the Councils of Ariminum and Seleucia* (autumn 359). To this category should probably be added his *Defence before Constantius* (353 in the original version) and his *Defence of his Flight* (357), for, though they have more limited ends, they form part of Athanasius' literary construction of Arianism and his struggle against it. The influence of this body of texts has been enormous. They present a picture of Athanasius, the unsullied champion of orthodoxy, who at times stood virtually alone against heresy: *Athanasius contra mundum*. This picture was largely taken up by those (including the Church historians, Socrates, Sozomen and Theodoret, not to mention the Latins, Rufinus and Jerome) who told the story of the Arian controversy at the end of the fourth century and in the fifth, when Nicene orthodoxy had become settled imperial policy. Much recent scholarship has been devoted to deconstructing the Athanasian account. Significant elements in this deconstruction include: awareness of genuine resistance to Athanasius in his own diocese by those, principally the Meletians, who had suffered from Athanasius' high-handed methods; a defence of the Emperor Constantius' treatment of Athanasius as actually following the canonical procedures that Athanasius demanded; but perhaps most significant, an increasing resistance to seeing the doctrinal struggle of the mid-fourth century as essentially an 'Arian' controversy, rather than a much more broadly based and complex dispute in Eastern theology over the doctrine of the Trinity (a 'disposing of the effects of Origenism', though even that may be too narrow).

To turn to more specifically literary points. Although Athanasius is at pains to present the controversy as simply between Arians (and fellow-travellers) and the orthodox, in most of his anti-Arian writings the nature of this orthodoxy is not usually identified with the doctrine of the *homoousion*, enshrined in the Nicene creed, that became the hallmark of the later 'Nicene' orthodoxy of the Council of Constantinople of 381 and later œcumenical councils. In fact, the term 'consubstantial' (ὁμοούσιος) does not seem to be a natural part of Athanasius' theological vocabulary, not at least until after 362. Athanasius' own doctrine seems to embrace a number of points – that the Son is not created out of nothing, that he derives from the Father, and is distinct from the Father but not separate from him – but he has no settled vocabulary for expressing this. It is also striking that Athanasius' opponents remain Arius, disowned by everyone after his death, and Asterius ('the sophist'), who again ceases to be a significant figure after 341. This is perhaps less surprising than it appears at first sight, as it is by no means unusual for late antique polemic to deal with traditional enemies rather than actual ones (cf. Augustine's concern with classical Arianism, rather than the contemporary Arianism of the barbarian tribes). Another feature of Athanasius' anti-Arian polemic, especially of his *On the Nicene Decrees*, *Defence against the Arians*, and *On the Councils of Ariminum and Seleucia*, is his concern to preserve documentation. Despite the possibility of bias, this has proved a fruitful quarry both for ancient Church historians and for modern scholars.

Later doctrinal treatises

These, all in epistolary form, include the *Letters to Serapion on the Holy Spirit* (*c.* 360), the *Tome to the Antiochenes* (*Tomus ad Antiochenos*) and the *Letter to the Emperor Jovian*, which report on the anti-Arian doctrinal consensus, achieved at the Council of Alexandria, held under Athanasius' presidency on his return to his see after the Emperor Julian's general amnesty for exiled bishops, and the *Letter to Epictetus* (*c*. 370). The first, concerned with a group who accepted the divinity of the Son, but denied that of the Holy Spirit, extend Athanasius' arguments concerning the *homoousion* to the Spirit, though Basil seems to have been following Athanasius' example in requiring for admission to communion nothing more than a denial that the Spirit is a creature (see Basil, *Epp*. 113, 114, 125, 128, etc.; cf. Athanasius, *Ad Serap*. 1.33 and *Tom. ad Ant*. 5). The *Tomus ad Antiochenos*, as well as recording agreement over the essential faith in the Trinity between those who used *hypostasis*, and those who used *ousia*, to express the divine unity, also attempts to clarify the nature of the union between the Word and humanity in the incarnation. This is discussed further in the *Letter to Epictetus*, which later assumed huge significance in the Christological controversy between Cyril and Nestorius. These Christological assertions have been taken as being aimed at Apollinarianism, and though they could be taken in this way it is by no means clear that they were intended thus. The anti-Apollinarian argument is much clearer in the two books of *On the Incarnation against Apollinaris*, ascribed to Athanasius but certainly spurious. Another later doctrinal work ascribed to Athanasius is the so-called 'Athanasian Creed' (*Quicunque vult*), which is a Latin summary of 'Athanasian' orthodoxy.

Ascetic works

These, again, are almost all in the form of letters. Among them should be included the *Festal Letters*, concerned, as they are, with an 'asceticism of everyday life', in contrast with the others which mainly envisage the monastic life. The letters preserved in Greek – to Ammoun, Dracontius, and Marcellinus (an important discussion of the Christian use of the Psalms), two to Horsesius, and two to monks in general – have long been regarded as authentic. Most of the rest survive in versions (mainly Coptic and Syriac), and there has been long dispute as to their authenticity. It now seems likely that the two letters to virgins, a treatise on virginity, fragments from *On Sickness and Health*, a letter *On Charity and Continence*, and various other fragments are authentic.[1] The *Festal Letters*, which, apart from fragments (and *Ep*. 39 which contains Athanasius' ruling on the biblical canon), survive complete only in Syriac, raise a particular problem. These letters, announcing the date of Easter for each year, are assigned to particular years in Athanasius' episcopate: it has long been suspected that, in assigning the letters to years, the compiler had no certain information and several times assigned a letter to another year when Easter fell on the same date. Recent research has only strengthened this suspicion.[2]

The most important ascetic work ascribed to Athanasius is the *Life of Antony*. Although Athanasius' contemporaries thought he had written a *Life* of St Antony of Egypt (see Gregory Nazianzen, *Or.* 21.5, written 379/80), and a Latin translation of such a *Life* had reached the other end of the Empire some time before 386 (see Augustine, *Confessions* 8.6.15), there have been persistent doubts as to whether the Greek *Life* we have is a genuine work of Athanasius. It has been argued that there was a lost Coptic original (on which the undoubtedly later Syriac version was based), and that the Greek *Life* is too Hellenistic a work to be Athanasian.[3] However, it seems unlikely that the versions provide access to anything more original than the Greek *Life*,[4] leaving little reason to doubt that Athanasius was its author. The importance of the *Life of Antony* lies not only in the early witness it furnishes of desert monasticism, but also in the fact that it became the archetype of the saint's life, perhaps the most popular Christian literary genre for the next thousand years (although it should be noted that neither it, nor any other fourth-century source, presents Antony as the 'first monk', as has often been stated or presumed in modern times).

Didymus the Blind

During his lifetime, Didymus was a figure of immense renown. Among his disciples he counted Rufinus and Jerome; Socrates, the Church historian, rated him as a bulwark against Arianism in Alexandria alongside Basil and Gregory Nazianzen in their cities (*HE* 4.25–6), and Theodoret ranked him with 'Ephrem the wonderful' in Edessa (*HE* 4.29). He died in 398 at the age of eighty-five, having lost his sight when a child of four. According to Rufinus, he was appointed by Athanasius as head of the Catechetical School in Alexandria (*HE* 2.7). What is meant by this is less clear. In the literary warfare between Rufinus and Jerome over Origenism, he is referred to as a defender and interpreter of Origenism,[5] but that is no warrant for supposing that the 'catechetical school' over which he presided was organized along the lines of Origen's academy in Caesarea, as depicted in Gregory Thaumaturgus' *Panegyric to Origen*. Later ages, however, remembered him as an Origenist (he was condemned along with Origen and Evagrius at the fifth Œcumenical Council in 553), and few of his works were preserved. Jerome tells us that 'among many other works', he wrote commentaries on all the Psalms, Isaiah, Hosea, Job, and the Gospels of Matthew and John, as well as two books *On Doctrines and against the Arians*, and *On the Holy Spirit*. We also know that he wrote a commentary on (and in defence of) Origen's *On First Principles*.[6] Of all this only fragments survived – in the catenae, and preserved by John Damascene in his *Sacra Parallela*. Ironically, given Jerome's later antipathy to everything Origenist, his translation of *On the Holy Spirit* preserved it for the West. In the eighteenth century, Mingarelli published what he believed to be the Greek text of (most of) the three books *On the Trinity*, mentioned by Socrates (*HE* 4.25). More recently books 4 and 5 of Basil's *Against Eunomius* (which are certainly not by Basil) have been identified with *On Doctrines and against the Arians*, as the 'first treatise', frequently referred to in *On the Trinity*.

Our knowledge of Didymus, however, has been transformed by the discovery in a munitions dump at Tura, in Egypt, of papyri which include, as well as works of Origen's, several of Didymus' biblical commentaries: on Zechariah, on Genesis 1–17, and on parts of Job, Psalms and Ecclesiastes. These enable us to form some idea of the biblical scholarship for which Didymus was renowned. They confirm him as an 'Origenist', following Origen's own practice of seeking a deeper ('allegorical') meaning beyond the literal meaning (which he is keen, however, to establish), rather than Origen's prescription (in *On First Principles* 4.2.4) of a threefold meaning in Scripture. He uses varied terminology to refer to this deeper meaning; a good deal of attention has been paid to his use of the terms ἀλληγορία and ἀναγωγή, and attempts have been made to detect both a theological, as well as a more strictly hermeneutical, methodology in Didymus' exegesis.

The authenticity of Didymus' dogmatic writings is still contested. *On the Holy Spirit* is certainly authentic, as is a brief, and acephalous, treatise *Against the Manichees*. His defence of the deity of the Holy Spirit develops the argument of his bishop, Athanasius (to whom he does not, however, refer), but with much greater serenity: it is mainly concerned with expounding relevant biblical passages. The same is true of *On the Trinity*, and the work preserved as books 4 and 5 of Basil's *Against Eunomius*. The authenticity of these works has, however, been contested: largely on grounds of lack of 'provenance' and alleged inconsistencies with authentic commentaries discovered in Tura. The argument that both *On the Trinity* and *Against Eunomius* 4–5 are by the same person is perhaps stronger than the argument that that person is Didymus.

Notes

1 D. Brakke, 'The Authenticity of the Ascetic Athanasiana', *Orientalia* 63 (1994), 17–56. The most important of these are translated by Brakke in *Athanasius and the Politics of Asceticism*, 274–319.

2 T. D. Barnes, *Athanasius and Constantius*, 183–91.
3 T. D. Barnes, 'Angel of Light or Mystic Initiate? The Problem of the *Life of Antony*', *JTS* n.s. 37 (1986), 353–68.
4 D. Brakke, 'The Greek and Syriac Versions of the *Life of Antony*', Muséon 107 (1994), 29–53.
5 Rufinus, *Apol. c. Hier.* 2.12,25; Jerome, *Apologia contra libros Rufini* 1.8, 2.16, 18, 3.27.
6 Socrates, *HE* 4.25; cf. Jerome, *Apol.* 2.16.

25

Palestine: Cyril of Jerusalem and Epiphanius

ANDREW LOUTH

At the Council of Nicaea in 325, the Fathers decreed in their seventh canon that the honour paid to the bishop of Aelia by 'custom and ancient tradition' was to be preserved, without prejudice to the rights of the metropolitan city (of Caesarea). 'Aelia' (in full: Aelia Capitolina) was the name given to the city established on the site of ancient Jerusalem in 135 after that city had been razed to the ground by the Romans. The canon witnesses to the tensions focused on the city of Jerusalem, with its Gentile name erasing its Jewish associations, while 'custom and ancient tradition' honour it as the site of the central events of the Christian faith: the death and resurrection of the Lord. 'Custom and ancient tradition' accomplished a good deal in the years following the Œcumenical Council, enabling the Emperor's mother Helena, on her pilgrimage to the Holy Land in 326 or 327, to identify many of the sacred sites, as well as discovering the relics of the True Cross. Within a decade of the council, these sites had been adorned by splendid new buildings, raised at imperial expense, not least the complex of buildings on the site embracing Golgotha and the tomb whence Christ had risen, including the Church of the Resurrection (the *Anastasis*), or the Holy Sepulchre, dedicated on 13 September 335. In this way the tension between secular 'Aelia' and religious 'Jerusalem' was resolved in the Christian city of Jerusalem, set to become the Holy City of Christendom, the goal of pilgrimage and guardian of the places where God had lived his incarnate life. Whether or not Jerusalem had earlier been a place of Christian pilgrimage, the Christian city established by imperial bounty witnessed pilgrimage on a hitherto unthinkable scale, and, as the pilgrims returned with their memories, became a potent influence throughout the whole Christian world. Jerusalem, then, saw itself transformed in the fourth century, but the consolidation of its position only began in the fifth century. Jerusalem was raised to patriarchal status, in return for Juvenal's compliance with imperial orthodoxy, at the Council of Chalcedon (451), and the real development of Palestinian monasticism belongs to the fifth century, with the foundations of St Euthymius and St Sabas (the 'Great Lavra'), the heroes of Cyril of Scythopolis' *Lives of the Monks of Palestine*. Later still, after the fall of Palestine and the Eastern provinces to Islam, these monasteries became a beacon of orthodoxy, exercising a powerful influence, both theological and liturgical, throughout the world of Byzantine Christendom.

Of such a future there is little trace in the literature to be surveyed in this chapter: Jerusalem was marginal to the theological currents of the fourth and fifth centuries, and though it became a geographical focus for the controversy over Origenism, this was largely because of the presence in the Holy Land of Jerome and other Latins, who can hardly be classed as Palestinian, even though Jerome spent almost half his long life there.

Cyril of Jerusalem

We know nothing about Cyril until, in 348, already a priest of the Church of Jerusalem, he was consecrated bishop by Acacius of Caesarea and Patrophilus of Scythopolis in succession to Maximus. In 357 he was deposed by a council held in Jerusalem, either because he had failed to toe the doctrinal line laid down by his metropolitan Acacius, or perhaps because he had sought to establish the independence of his see from the metropolitan see of Caesarea (developing the spirit, though not the letter, of canon 7 of Nicaea). He was briefly reinstated in 359 by the Council of Seleucia, but with the triumph the next year of Acacius and the homoeans again deposed. He returned to his see on the death of the Emperor Constantius (362), but this time fell foul of the Arianizing policy of the Emperor Valens and in 367, or shortly after, was yet again deposed. He took charge of his see again in 378, attended the Second Œcumenical Council at Constantinople in 381, and died later that decade, probably on 18 March 387. Such a disjointed episcopal career was by no means unusual in the mid-fourth century, but unlike some others affected similarly, Cyril can hardly be claimed as a martyr for orthodoxy: he seems to be a representative of those Eastern bishops (perhaps a majority), initially mistrustful of Nicaea, who came finally to accept the creed of that council, and the doctrine of the *homoousion*.

Cyril's main literary work is a collection of *Catechetical Homilies*. Prefaced by a 'procatechesis', there are twenty-three sermons, eighteen of which were given during Lent, and five, expounding the rites of initiation themselves (baptism, anointing and the eucharist), the so-called 'mystagogical catecheses', given during Easter week itself (and thus after those who heard them had been initiated). Because of a casual reference to the heresy of Mani as being seventy years old (*Cat.* 6.20), it is generally held that these sermons were delivered early in Cyril's episcopate, perhaps in 350, though it is possible they were delivered in 348, Cyril, then still a priest, deputizing for his bishop, Maximus. In some manuscripts the five 'mystagogical catecheses' are ascribed, not to Cyril, but to his successor John: there is no scholarly agreement as to which of them they belong to.

These form the earliest collection of catechetical homilies to survive: from later in the century there survive such homilies by John Chrysostom (twelve in all, but not all from the same series; none of them 'mystagogical'), by Theodore of Mopsuestia (sixteen in all, six 'mystagogical'), and, in the West, Ambrose (all 'mystagogical'). The first eighteen of Cyril's sermons, together with the introductory procatechesis, were given in the course of Lent to those who were to be baptized on Easter Eve – to 'those about to be enlightened' (φωτιζόμενοι). The catechumenate normally lasted several years, though it seems that children of Christian parents were generally admitted as catechumens shortly after birth, and their names enrolled, along with those who had completed their catechumenate, at the beginning of the Lent before their baptism. The procatechesis welcomes the candidates, and emphasizes the seriousness of the step they are about to take in baptism, in which sins are forgiven once-for-all: there is no second chance. The note of mystery, which is to resound throughout the mystagogical catecheses, is already sounded: 'already you stand on the frontier of mystery. I adjure you to smuggle no word out' (*Procat.* 12). The catechetical sermons that follow deal with the importance of forgiveness and Bible reading, penitence and the danger of the devil and temptation; the third deals in general with the meaning of baptism; the fourth contains a summary of Christian doctrine; the fifth discusses faith; and the rest expound, article by article, the baptismal creed which the candidates will profess when baptized. In the course of the last sermon the φωτιζόμενοι recited, one by one, the baptismal creed they had committed to memory. These sermons were given in the *Martyrion*, the basilica erected by Constantine over the crypt where the True Cross had been discovered, the largest building on the Golgotha site that included the Church of the *Anastasis*. In the fourth sermon, Cyril, for confirmation of the historicity of the crucifixion, appeals to 'this sacred Golgotha where we have now come together because of him who was crucified here' (*Cat.* 4.10). The 'mystagogical catecheses' were given, whether by Cyril or John, to the newly baptized in the Church of the *Anastasis* (so the Spanish pilgrim Egeria informs us) in the course of Easter Week. These remarkable sermons convey a powerful sense of the awesome mystery of the eucharistic celebration, that 'most dread hour' (φρικωδεστάτη ὥρα), in which Christ himself is present through the invocation (ἐπίκλησις) of the Holy Spirit, and given to the faithful in the elements of bread and wine.

Apart from another sermon (on the healing of the paralytic), there also survive one (or possibly two) letters from Cyril. One of these letters has long been known: the letter, written in 351 to the Emperor Constantius, informing him of the miraculous cross of light that appeared over Jerusalem on 7 May 351,[1] during the Paschal season. In this letter he recalls the discovery of the True Cross, 'fraught with salvation', though he does not name the Empress Helena, and more surprisingly makes no mention of Constantine's vision of the Cross which, according to Eusebius, occasioned his conversion, even though he takes the miracle as a good omen for Constantius, as he set out 'under the trophy of the cross' against the usurper Magnentius, whom he ultimately defeated. The other is a letter preserved in Syriac, attributed to Cyril, about the attempted rebuilding of the Temple in Jerusalem under Julian the Apostate.[2] Although the modern editor of his letter is not inclined to accept its authenticity, it seems to belong to Cyril's circle, and fits closely with his conviction that Jerusalem has now become a Christian city, the city of the Cross.

Epiphanius of Salamis

Epiphanius' place in the literary history of Palestine is rather different from Cyril's, not least because he spent the latter half of his life as bishop of Constantia, ancient Salamis, in Cyprus (365–403). He was, however, born in about 315 in Palestine, in Eleutheropolis not far from Gaza, where around 335, after making a tour of the monks of Egypt, he founded a monastery, over which he ruled for about thirty years. Even though he spent the latter part of his life in Cyprus, he maintained contact with Palestine, and was instrumental in stirring up the Origenist controversy there in the last decade of the fourth century. He seems to have studied in Alexandria, and acquired knowledge of Greek, Syriac, Hebrew, Coptic and some Latin: Jerome referred to him as *vir Epiphanius πεντάγλωττος* (*Ruf.* 3.6). He had no time for the classical ideals of his contemporaries, the Cappadocian Fathers, and his Greek is what Karl Holl called an 'elevated Koine', apparently readily understood by his contemporaries, learned or not (so Jerome, *Vir. Ill.* 114), but as it has reached us, tortuous and sometimes barely comprehensible.

His main works, which belong to the mid-370s, are the *Ancoratus* ('One firmly anchored') and his compendium of heresy, the *Panarion* ('Medicine Chest', so-called because it provided remedies for those bitten by the serpent of heresy). The *Ancoratus* is a lengthy defence of the orthodoxy that was to be triumphant at the Second Œcumenical Council in 381, at which Epiphanius himself was not present. It is a long and rambling defence, which often seems to move by association of ideas rather than any logic of argument, and ends with a lengthy creed of Epiphanius' own composition, preceded by a creed practically identical with that endorsed at the Second Œcumenical Council (the 'Niceno-Constantinopolitan creed'), to which the anathemas that formed part of the original creed of the Council of Nicaea are appended. There is, however, general scholarly agreement that Epiphanius originally included the genuine creed of Nicaea, for which the liturgically more familiar creed was substituted at a later date.

The *Panarion* is a list of, and refutation of, eighty heresies. It is the most important collection of heresiological material to survive, and formed the basis for later such collections, notably John Damascene's account of 100 heresies, which formed part of his *Fountain Head of Knowledge*. One is tempted to characterize it as a compendium of largely inaccurate information, but its earlier sections provide access to lost works, notably Justin Martyr's work on heresies, the Greek of Irenaeus' *Adversus Haereses*, and Hippolytus' *Syntagma*. But it is perhaps even more important for what it professes to be: an analysis, or better diagnosis, of heresy. The Greek word αἵρεσις was originally quite neutral in its connotation: it indicated a choice, a way of life or way of thought. It was used of the schools of philosophy, and by extension (by Josephus, for instance) of the different groups within Judaism. In Christian use it came quickly to mean a *wilful* choice, a chosen departure from the one orthodox tradition. It is perhaps first used in this sense by Hegesippus, who, according to Eusebius, named seven 'heresies' among the Jews, 'all hostile to the tribe of Judah and the Christ', which introduced into the 'virgin Church' spawned the heresies of various groups that we would call 'gnostic' (*HE* 4.22): many of the names of these heresies, as recorded by Eusebius, are preserved in the early parts of Epiphanius' *Panarion*. It is a picture of an original unitary purity – that of orthodoxy – splitting up into a multiplicity of heresies. Drawing on earlier attempts, Epiphanius seeks to provide a genealogy of this process, but the significance of Epiphanius' effort lies, in part, in its date, and the way in which it provided valuable support to the emerging neo-Nicene orthodoxy that was to receive imperial endorsement from Theodosius I and the Second Œcumenical Council, called by him in 381.

Epiphanius begins with the 'four mothers' of pre-Christian heresy (derived, it seems, from Col. 3:11), and the sixteen heresies that have flowed from them. The first is 'barbarism', the antediluvian heresy that prevailed from the Fall, proceeding from Adam's disobedience, the second, 'Scythism', which prevailed from the Flood until the Tower of Babel (or Terah, the first potter, who made possible idolatry – Epiphanius' account is not at all clear), marked by 'error proceeding from the nature of the individual will, not from what was taught or written' (*Pan.* 2.3). The third mother of heresy is Hellenism, which is identified with idolatry, and the fourth, Judaism, marked by circumcision. None of these was properly a heresy, but rather opposition, in various forms, to 'the faith, so to speak, which now holds sway in the holy Catholic church of God, so recently founded, a faith which was in the beginning and which later was revealed again' (ibid.). From these flow the sixteen pre-Christian heresies: four philosophical schools (Stoics, Platonists, Pythagoreans and Epicureans) and twelve Jewish sects (Hegesippus' seven, augmented). There follows an interlude, telling of the incarnation of the Word, after which Epiphanius embarks on his account of the sixty Christian heresies: from assorted gnostics to the various trinitarian heresies of the fourth century, closing with Mariolatrous Collyridians and the Messalians. Epiphanius' structure is an elaboration of the apologists' claim to the pristine nature of the Catholic faith: it is a kind of sociology of knowledge establishing the authenticity of orthodoxy.

One of Epiphanius' heresies, already a concern in the *Ancoratus*, is Origenism. In the 390s Epiphanius was instrumental in fomenting the Origenist controversy in Palestine, and securing the support of Jerome, once an admirer of the great Alexandrian. One of his letters from this period is preserved, in Jerome's translation, as *Letter* 51 in the collection of Jerome's letters. That letter contains a dramatic example of Epiphanius' iconoclasm, further examples of which are to be found in a pamphlet, a letter to the Emperor Theodosius I, and the Testament to the community of which he was bishop, fragments of which were salvaged by Karl Holl from the refutation of Epiphanius composed by the great iconodule patriarch of the ninth century, Nicephorus. Several other works of Epiphanius survive, but most of what came to be attributed to him is spurious.

Notes

1 This is the date normally given, with Cyril referring to Constantius' preparations for the battle of Mursa (28 September 351). It has however been argued that the date should be 350 (by H. Grégoire and P. Orgels, *Byzantion* 24 (1954), 596–9) or 353 (J. Vogt, 'Berichte über Kreuzeserscheinungen aus dem 4. Jahrhunderts n. Chr.', *Annuaire de l'institut de philologie et d'histoire orientales* 9 (1949), 602–3).

2 Sebastian Brock, 'A Letter Attributed to Cyril of Jerusalem on the Rebuilding of the Temple under Julian', *Bulletin of the School of Oriental and African Studies* 40 (1977), 267–86 (reprinted as item X of *Syriac Perspectives on Late Antiquity*).

26

The Cappadocians

ANDREW LOUTH

The grouping together of Basil of Caesarea, with his friend, Gregory of Nazianzus, and his brother, Gregory of Nyssa, as the 'Cappadocian Fathers' (originally the 'great Cappadocians') is a product of modern scholars,[1] who have regarded as significant the family links, geographical locality and common theological commitment they perceived in them. It is not a traditional designation: the three Fathers of the fourth century singled out by the Church as 'universal teachers' (οἰκουμενικοὶ διδάσκαλοι) are Basil 'the Great', Gregory 'the Theologian' (i.e., Nazianzen), and John 'of the Golden Mouth' (or Chrysostom), celebrated together on 30 January. We should perhaps pause before linking the 'Cappadocians' too closely together: they had individual minds, although the courses of their lives were undoubtedly interwoven.

Basil and his friend, Gregory of Nazianzen, were probably of like age, both born in 329 or 330, the sons of well-off, land-owning families. Their friendship went back to their studies together in Athens in the early 350s. They were both highly accomplished rhetors, skilled in the literary Greek of the classical period. Gregory of Nyssa, Basil's younger brother, born perhaps in the late 330s, was no less accomplished, though he seems not to have followed him to Athens, but owed his rhetorical training directly to his elder brother. Basil and his friend Gregory were soon drawn to the ascetic life, and in 356, after completing his studies at Athens, Basil went on a tour of monastic settlements in Coele-Syria, Mesopotamia, Palestine and Egypt. On his return he was baptized and retired to his family estate at Annisa in Pontus (near the confluence of the rivers Iris and Lycos) where he joined his mother, Emmelia, and his sister, Macrina, in their life of asceticism. From here he wrote to Gregory Nazianzen, inviting him to join him. To begin with Gregory resisted, pleading family commitments, but later joined him (for probably quite a short period). During their first period together at Annisa, the two friends compiled an anthology from the great Alexandrian theologian, Origen, of texts concerned largely with the interpretation of Scripture and the freedom of the rational will, which they called the *Philokalia* (or 'anthology', literally: love of the beautiful). The common inspiration they found in Origen, to which this work is a monument, is significant both for their theology and for their desire for an ascetic life of withdrawal and contemplation.

In 360, Basil was ordained reader in Caesarea, the metropolis of Cappadocia, by its bishop, Dianius, and then returned to Pontus. The following year, Julian became emperor. Julian, brought up a Christian, had also pursued philosophical studies, and was briefly (in 355) Gregory's contemporary at Athens (though it is doubtful whether they encountered each other). During his short reign (361–3), Julian declared himself a worshipper of the old gods (thus: the 'Apostate') and, because of the intimate link between Greek literature and Greek paganism, forbade Christians to teach the classics: an action which, though welcome to some Christians, struck at the root of the Christian culture of such as the Cappadocians. In 362 Gregory was ordained priest, against his will, by his father, Gregory, bishop of Nazianzus, and fled to Annisa. Later that year Basil returned to Caesarea, probably to attend the deathbed of Bishop Dianius, and was ordained priest by his successor Eusebius. A year after, as a result of a misunderstanding with Eusebius, Basil left Caesarea for Pontus, where he spent the rest of the decade. In 370, after the death of Eusebius, Basil became bishop of Caesarea.

Basil sought, as bishop, to win the church of the East for Nicene orthodoxy, and saw the division of the province of Cappadocia in 371 by the Arian Emperor Valens as an attempt to undermine his authority. To bolster his authority, Basil sought to place those he could trust in newly created sees, and consecrated Gregory his friend bishop of Sasima, and his brother Gregory bishop of Nyssa. Gregory of Nazianzus refused to go to Sasima ('a thoroughly deplorable and cramped little village'), and remained in Nazianzus until his father's death in 374 and probably later: the friendship between the two men did not survive this episode. Gregory the brother, a married man who perhaps continued to live with his wife as a bishop, went to Nyssa. The rest of the decade saw Basil's continued struggle against what he regarded as a continuation of Arianism in the teaching of Aetius and Eunomius. He died on 1 January 379 on the threshold of victory, for Valens had died the previous year in the disastrous battle of Adrianople, and on 19 January the Western Emperor Gratian raised Theodosius to the purple in his stead.

Theodosius was committed to Nicene orthodoxy and soon invited Gregory of Nazianzus to Constantinople, a largely Arian city, to be orthodox pastor in the Church of the Resurrection. He preached eloquently in defence of Nicene orthodoxy, his sermons there including the five 'theological' orations, to which he owes his title 'the Theologian'. In 380, on the death of the Arian Demophilus, he succeeded him as bishop of Constantinople, and was involved in the preparations for the œcumenical council held in Constantinople in 381 to define the Christian orthodoxy that Theodosius was to enforce. After the death of Meletius, bishop of Antioch, who was president of the council, Gregory succeeded him, but was soon deposed from both see and presidency, the ostensible grounds being the ban on episcopal translation by the First Œcumenical Council of Nicaea (for Gregory was nominally bishop of Sasima). He retired to his family estates at Nazianzus, where he remained until his death in about 391.

Gregory of Nyssa also took part in the Second Œcumenical Council, shortly after defending his brother's doctrinal position in the first two books of his *Against Eunomius*. Such was his standing that he was chosen to preach the funeral oration for the deceased Meletius of Antioch, and appointed by Theodosius one of the inspectors of orthodoxy for the civil diocese of Pontus. For a few years he became something like court preacher, delivering the funeral orations for the emperor's wife, Aelia Flacilla, in 383 and his daughter, Pulcheria, in 385. He was still alive in 393, and it is assumed that he died shortly afterwards.

From this brief account of the interlocking lives of the 'great Cappadocians' it is evident that the acmae of the three men – Basil's in the 370s, Gregory Nazianzen's 379–80, and Gregory Nyssen's 380–5 – represent successive stages in the establishment of the orthodoxy sealed at the Second Œcumenical Council, which became the ideology of Theodosius' Christian Empire.

Basil of Caesarea

The writings of Basil the Great (so-called in his lifetime) can be divided into several categories: ascetic works, dogmatic works, homiletic works, letters, and a liturgy.

During his time at Pontus, and later at Caesarea, Basil founded several monastic communities, and provided them with guidance on how to live the monastic life. Originally this guidance was given in various forms: letters, *erotapokriseis* ('questions and answers'), and sermons, on both details and the principles of the monastic life. Despite the example of Pachomius, with which he was acquainted from his visit to Egypt, Basil hardly provides anything in the form of rules. The form in which Basil's monastic directions came to be most widely known, however, was in the form of a collection of 'Longer and Shorter Rules' – not 'rules', properly speaking, but a series of questions and answers (fifty-five treated at length, and 313 more briefly, sometimes very briefly) – prefaced by a series of prologues, mostly ascetic sermons by Basil, and in many manuscripts accompanied by letters (or conflations of letters) from Basil's correspondence, as well as other material. This collection, called the 'Great Asceticon', represents the end of a long period of evolution. The main lines of this development were worked out by the late Dom Jean Gribomont, mainly on the basis of the scholia, the editorial comments, added by the editor of the sixth-century 'Vulgate' text on which subsequent tradition and printed editions are based, and also on the Latin translation of the Rule made by Rufinus.[2] The earliest form was called by the editor the 'Small Asceticon' and seems to be identical with the Greek text on which Rufinus' Latin translation is based: it is in question and answer form, much shorter than the Longer and Shorter Rules, including elements from both series, but presenting them in a single series. It was drawn up by Basil, before he became a bishop, for ascetics with whom he had personal contact. But the editor knew of other collections: one that Basil 'sent' somewhere, dating from before 370, and collections of material from Pontus, Caesarea and somewhere else. The division into long and short rules was present in the Pontus material, but not in the material from Caesarea. The Pontus collection was known by the editor as the 'Ascetic Outline', ended at *Shorter Rules* 286, and was considered by him to be early. What all this suggests is that Basil's 'monastic rule' originated in his own practice of the ascetic life, before he became a bishop, and that it developed independently at Pontus and Caesarea, drawing on material Basil prepared for his own communities, as well as on reflections on the monastic life prepared for a much wider audience.

But within this development there are pressures at work only dimly discernible to us. Basil's early involvement in the ascetic movement was bound up with his relationship to Eustathius, in pursuit of whom he made his monastic tour, and who later became bishop of Sebaste. As bishops they fell out, Basil regarding Eustathius as little more than an Arian. However, the church historian, Sozomen, at one point asserts that some regarded Eustathius as the author of the 'ascetic treatises commonly attributed to Basil of Cappadocia' (*HE* 3.14). This at least suggests, what we would anyway expect, close affinity between the ascetic ideals of the early Basil and Eustathius. It is not at all unlikely that the development in the *Asceticon* traced an attenuation of that affinity. Another point of interest concerns what relationship there is, if any, between Basil's ascetic ideals, as represented in his *Asceticon*, and the contemporary ascetic movement known as Messalianism. Apart from a literary affinity in their common predilection for *erotapokriseis*, it is striking that in the final form of the *Great Asceticon* the final prologue is in fact *Homily* 25 of those ascribed to Macarius.

As will be evident from what has been said about the literary form of the *Asceticon*, Basil presents the monastic ideal in a largely episodic fashion. Nevertheless there are a number of distinctive features. First of all, the form of the monastic life envisaged is that of a community: in contrast to many currents in fourth-century and later (especially Byzantine) monasticism, the staggering asceticism of the solitary life holds no attraction for Basil. The essence of Christian asceticism is life together, with the demands on love that this makes. He seems to doubt whether the eremitical ideal can be regarded as Christian at all ('Whose feet will you wash?'). The demands of love are not only made by members of the community, but by those outside the community too: monasteries following Basil's ideals provided hospices for travellers, and hospitals for the sick. Further, though Basil clearly envisages monastic communities as withdrawn from the world, he does not see the ideal of their life as different from that of the ordinary Christian. As with the Macarian Homilies, he provides guidance for the 'Christian' life as such. Another distinctive feature of Basilian monasticism as envisaged by the *Asceticon* is the lack of an single, all-competent leader, an 'abbot' (as in Pachomian or later Benedictine monasticism) to whom all in the community owe obedience: the leaders are usually spoken of in the plural.

Basil wrote two dogmatic works (though several of his letters amount to dogmatic treatises): his *Against Eunomius*, written in 363–5, and *On the Holy Spirit*, written when he was a bishop in about 375. The former was written as a refutation of Eunomius' *Apologia* (or *Defence*), probably delivered at the Council of Constantinople in January 360. Book 1 concentrates on refuting Eunomius' argument that the essence of God consists in unbegottenness, and that consequently the Word cannot be truly divine. Books 2 and 3 are concerned with the divinity of the Son and the Spirit. Books 4 and 5 are not by Basil: they may be by Didymus.[3] *On the Holy Spirit*, dedicated to his friend, Amphilochius, bishop of Iconium, defends the orthodox doctrine that the Holy Spirit is to be worshipped together with the Father and the Son, and is thus co-equal to them. Much of the argument rests on liturgical premises, both in the narrow sense that Basil defends a form of doxology that ranks the Spirit with the Father and the Son, but more deeply in the sense that Basil regards the deity of the Son as revealed in the Church's experience of worship, and to this end proposes a distinction between κήρυγμα and δόγμα, between the faith openly declared and the faith inwardly experienced (and witnessed to in liturgical traditions): it is to δόγμα that the fulness of θεολογία, including acknowledgment of the deity of the Spirit, belongs. Because δόγμα is not to be declared openly, Basil nowhere explicitly states that the Spirit is ὁμοούσιος.

Of Basil's homiletic works there survive two series – on the account of creation in six days (the *Hexaemeron*) and on selected psalms – and twenty or so individual sermons. Despite his early enthusiasm for Origen, in the *Hexaemeron* he dismissed some of Origen's interpretations (without mentioning him by name), and declared his attachment to the literal sense of Scripture. Nevertheless, in his interpretation of the creation story, he displays a wide knowledge of classical and Hellenistic ideas of cosmology, and although he professes to argue against them, in fact he conducts a dialogue with such ideas 'from outside' (ἔξωθεν), to use the Cappadocian term for pagan philosophy, the universe of discourse of which is provided by Plato's *Timaeus*. The question of the relationship of Christianity to Greek culture is directly raised by Basil's *Address to Young Men* on the value of Greek literature. It is probably a late work of Basil's, for there is none of the polemical tone one might expect, had it been written in response to Julian's ban on Christian teaching of Greek literature. Basil sees value in some pagan literature, and clearly envisages no alternative way of learning Greek than using pagan literature.

The collection of Basil's letters includes 368 items, several of them spurious (including, probably, most of the correspondence with Libanios, the great Antiochene rhetor, whose own collected correspondence, by way of comparison, runs to 1,600 items). Many of these letters show us Basil pulling the strings of power, in the accepted classical way, by means of his rhetorical skill. Others give us a glimpse of genuine bonds of friendship – for instance, with Gregory Nazianzen, Eusebius of Samasata (from the letters to whom we learn much of Basil's ill-health), or Amphilochius of Iconium – until those friendships succumbed to Basil's tendency to view friendship, in the classical way, as a means of patronage. Others are essential raw material for the ecclesiastical history of the 370s. There are several letters of consolation, in which Basil clothes a classical theme in Christian garb; others concern the ascetic life, or expound doctrinal matters. A particularly important group of letters provide the canons of St Basil.[4] *Epp.* 361–4, appended to the collection, purport to be a correspondence between Basil and Apollinaris, the heresiarch. If genuine, they portray Apollinaris convincing Basil of the truth of the *homoousion*, and must be among the earliest of Basil's letters to survive. There seems little doubt that the two men corresponded 'as layman to layman' (*Ep.* 224), but whether these are the letters is still disputed.

The *Divine Liturgy of Saint Basil*, used in Orthodox Church of the Byzantine Rite on Sundays in Lent and on Vigils, as well as on the feast of St Basil himself

(1 January) is, at least in its essential elements, genuinely by Basil. The Anaphora, or Eucharistic Prayer, which is much longer than that in the normally used *Divine Liturgy of St John Chrysostom*, begins by calling on God as 'He who is', and continues with a long 'apophatic' invocation of the glory of God, before embarking on a lengthy account of the history of salvation.

Gregory of Nazianzus

Compared with Basil, the ecclesiastical politician and monastic founder, and Gregory of Nyssa, the philosopher and mystic, Gregory of Nazianzus often gets scant attention from modern interpreters, who tend to treat him as ineffectual and unoriginal.[5] Yet he is ranked with Basil among the 'universal teachers' as 'the Theologian', and his sermons probably received more and closer attention than the sermons of any other in the Byzantine period. His works fall into three categories: sermons, letters and poems. In all three categories he demonstrates an unparalleled skill in his use of words: indeed, if poetry be defined as the best words in the best place, there is a strong case for saying that everything that Gregory wrote partakes of poetry. As a result of his natural gifts and his rhetorical training, he was a fine orator, conscious of his way with words. This is revealed in a story Jerome tells of Gregory, a story that portrays not only Gregory's conscious oratorical skill but also his awareness of the limitations of such rhetoric. Jerome encountered Gregory during his brief period in Constantinople, and he tells how once he asked Gregory about the meaning of a particularly obscure expression in St Luke's Gospel (6:1: the expression 'on the "second-first" sabbath', perhaps the first sabbath but one – that is the current best guess). Gregory had been unable to come up with a satisfactory explanation, and had smilingly advised Jerome to come to church and hear him preach about it: there, amidst the wild applause of the congregation, he would understand, or least imagine he understood, its meaning.[6]

The collection of Gregory's letters runs to 249 items in the most recent edition. These letters are much more private than Basil's, with nothing of their importance for Church history, monasticism or canon law. They are invariably elegant, full of classical quotations and allusions. Much is said of the life of 'philosophy', a term Gregory uses for a life of quiet withdrawal and prayerful contemplation: the nuances of this characteristically Christian use of φιλοσοφία are perhaps more surely traced in Gregory's letters than in any other fourth-century source. He frequently talks about his concern for the education of the young, giving advice and recommending teachers:

for him Christianity was a fulfilment of the Greek culture he loved so well. One of his letters gives advice on how to write letters: be brief, write as you speak, be graceful and natural (*Ep.* 51). Three letters stand apart from the rest (and have been, most recently, edited separately): *Epp.* 101, 102, and 202. The first two are addressed to Cledonius, the priest who was looking after the Church of Nazianzus, and the last to Nectarius, Gregory's successor as bishop of Constantinople. They belong to the 380s and their main concern is with Apollinarianism. Although, in their attack on Apollinaris, they reveal many misconceptions about Apollinaris' teaching, the first letter especially exposes the fundamental inadequacy of Apollinarianism, and expresses this with characteristic elegance: 'the unassumed is the unhealed, only that which is united to the Godhead is saved' (*Ep.* 101.32).

A selection of forty-five of Gregory Nazianzen's sermons survive. They were put together shortly after his death, clearly intended to illustrate his rhetorical skill: they became models of Byzantine eloquence, and were frequently commented on.[7] Not all such scholia concerned his eloquence, however: the Origenist influence, patent in many of these sermons, made them popular among the Origenist monks, and caused problems for the orthodox, notably Maximus the Confessor, whose *Ambigua* (especially the earlier set, addressed to John of Cyzikus) are largely devoted to passages in Gregory's works that gave comfort to the Origenists. Many of them were preached during his time of celebrity in Constantinople. Most celebrated are his five Theological Orations (*Or.* 27–31), which expound the orthodox doctrine of the Trinity (and also Christology). Of these the second is devoted to the theme of the ineffability of God, acknowledgment of which is a premise of any true understanding of God. It is worth noting the way in which Gregory uses the doctrine of the angels to underline his theme: if the angels themselves, created though they be, fill us with awe, how unimaginably ineffable must God be; and yet it is with awe that the angels themselves acknowledge God's ineffability, and so it is in worship, rather than simply rational reflection, that God's ineffability, and the possibility of theology itself, is realized. On this basis, the rest of the sermons expound the doctrine of the *homoousion* against the Eunomians, including the explicit attribution of ὁμοούσιος to the Spirit (in contrast to Basil). Other sermons are liturgical (for Christmas/Theophany/Feast of Lights – clearly the same feast, 6 January – Easter and Pentecost). There are encomia of the Maccabees, St Cyprian, St Athanasius, and funeral orations on his father, his brother Caesarius, his sister Gorgonia, his friend Basil. Two bitter sermons attack Julian the Apostate (the first of which, *Or.* 4, is far too long ever to have been delivered). Another long sermon (probably delivered in an earlier shorter form) is his defence of his flight to Annisa, after his ordination (*Or.* 2), which contains a magnificent exposition of the nature of the Christian priesthood (as do the sermons on Athanasius and Basil), which became a model for John Chrysostom's *On the Priesthood* (also a defence of his flight to monastic withdrawal) and Gregory the Great's *Pastoral Rule*. Whatever the subject, Gregory's eloquence carries forward often quite difficult theological arguments, as well as providing memorable phrases encapsulating the truths of the faith, many of which found their way into the liturgical poetry of the Byzantine Church.

The final category of Gregory's works are his poems. Many of these were composed in the retirement in which he lived after his deposition from the see of Constantinople. Taking a variety of classical forms, and demonstrating considerable skill, they are difficult, and may not be to our taste, but they impressed his contemporaries enough for a whole book of the *Palatine Anthology* (book 8) to be devoted to his poems. There are thirty-eight dogmatic poems, several of which are spurious. Eight of these (1–5, 7–9), in hexameters, form a distinct group called the *poemata arcana*. There are forty moral poems (again, several of which are spurious), dealing with various virtues, especially the virtue of virginity. Perhaps most interesting are his historical poems: ninety-nine concern himself (the last is dubious), and eight concern others (the last is probably by Amphilochius of Iconium). The eleventh is a long autobiographical poem; the twelfth ('on himself and the bishops') is revealing of his wit and snobbery. There is a large group of epitaphs and epigrams (most of which found their way into the *Palatine Anthology*), in which form Gregory excelled. There is a tragedy, the *Passion of Christ*, which is generally reckoned to be spurious, though it has recently found defenders.

Gregory of Nyssa

Gregory of Nyssa seems to have been the Cappadocian for the twentieth century. Neglected by tradition, he has been honoured with a fine critical edition, begun in the 1920s and still continuing,[8] and the secondary literature on the younger Cappadocian is far more extensive than that on his elders put together. Part of the reason for this is that Gregory of Nyssa is much more philosophically interesting than the other two: he has a sharp mind and concentrates on large issues. It is also the case that concentration on this Gregory's 'mysticism' has made him much more assimilable in the twentieth century, compared with the institutional concerns of his brother, and the mistrusted rhetoric of his namesake. In his biography, too, he is marked off from the other 'great Cappadocians': they both embraced the celibate life, whereas Gregory in his youth married. Whether, as a bishop, he lived with his wife, as is the general modern view, is much less clear: the *simplest* explanation of the evidence (all preserved by Gregory Nazianzen) is that the Theosebeia, on whose death Nazianzen wrote a letter of consolation to Nyssen, was Gregory of Nyssa's sister.[9] Whatever his domestic arrangements, he was no less a devotee of the ascetic ideal than the other two.

Gregory wrote a great deal that cannot be so easily arranged by literary genre as is the case with the other two. There is a collection of letters, few compared with the other Cappadocians, running to only thirty letters (the first of which is claimed by some for Gregory Nazianzen). The second is of particular interest in recording Gregory's disillusionment with pilgrimage to the Holy Land, and consequent discouragement of the growing practice.

There are a large number of dogmatic works, the most important of which is his *Against Eunomius*. This really consists of four distinct treatises. The first two were written close together in 380 and constitute a defence of Basil against Eunomius' attack on his *Against Eunomius* – Eunomius' *Defence of his defence*. The third, longer treatise (soon divided into ten books) is a later (381–3) refutation of a fresh attack by Eunomius on Basil. The fourth treatise, really independent of the other three which are defences of Basil, was a detailed criticism of Eunomius' *Confession of Faith*, submitted to the Emperor Theodosius in 383. Because of the more speculative character of the second of these treatises, it soon dropped out of the combined work in twelve books, and was replaced by the fourth treatise. When the second treatise was rediscovered with the revival of learning in ninth-century Byzantium, it was simply tagged on to the end, as the second part of book 12 or as 'book 13': an order followed by printed editions until Jaeger's edition in 1921. Central to Gregory's attack on Eunomius, and to the whole of his Christian metaphysics, is his perception that most important ontological distinction is that between the uncreated God and everything else, which is created *ex nihilo*: in comparison with this distinction all other ontological distinctions pale into insignificance, including the fundamental Platonic distinction (which Gregory continues to call 'the supreme division of all beings') between the spiritual and the material. The doctrine of the *homoousion* affirms the uncreatedness of the persons of the Trinity. This distinction is also expressed in terms of the infinity of God's essence, in contrast with the essential finitude of created beings.

There are many other dogmatic works, concerned both with trinitarian doctrine and with Christology (mainly directed against Apollinaris). Of particular importance are his *Great Catechetical Oration* and *On Human Creation*. The *Great Catechetical Oration* is not itself directly a work of catechesis, like the catechetical homilies of Cyril of Jerusalem, but rather a summary for catechists to use, perhaps more like Augustine's *On Catechizing* (*De Catechizandis Rudibus*), or better, his *Enchiridion*. It contains a summary of the Christian faith, which, as well as treating the doctrines of the creed, discusses the creation of human beings in the image of God and the origin of evil in the misuse of human free will, in which that image consists: evil therefore has no substantial reality but is a falling away from the good. It also discusses the sacraments of baptism and the eucharist, in which he attempts to show how through feeding on bread and wine, 'trans-elemented' into the body and blood of Christ, Christians share in immortality. *On Human Creation* was intended as an appendix to his brother's *Hexaemeron*, to treat more fully the creation of human beings. It was an influential treatise, especially for its doctrine of double creation: viz., the teaching that the primary image of God in which humans were created transcends sex, with sexual division belonging to a second stage of creation (a doctrine that Gregory derived, as much else, from Philo).

Another important dogmatic treatise is his *On the Soul and the Resurrection*. This together with his *Life of Macrina* are the sole sources for our knowledge of Macrina, the elder sister of both Basil and Gregory. Basil never mentions her, even though, according to Gregory, it was Macrina who persuaded him to pursue the 'philosophical life' instead of a career as a rhetor. *On the Soul and the Resurrection* takes the form of a dialogue between Gregory and his sister on her deathbed: both situation and literary form invoke Plato's *Phaedo*. The indirectness of the literary form, however, has the effect of enabling Gregory to present his sister publicly as a teacher (he constantly addresses her as 'teacher'), something debarred to her sex in real life. As a teacher, she skilfully meets philosophical objections to the Christian doctrine of the immortality of the soul and the resurrection of the body put to her by her brother, as well as espousing the doctrine of the final restoration of all rational beings. The *Life of Macrina* is more than a work of fraternal *pietas*, influenced as it is by the story and popular cult of St Thekla (Macrina's secret name).

As well as the life of his sister, Gregory wrote various other ascetic works. His *On Virginity*, written probably in 370, provides a theoretical undergirding to Basil's monastic ideal. Drawing on Origen and Methodius, he presents the life of virginity as 'a kind of door and entrance to a more august way of life', and sees the life of the Blessed Virgin as its archetype. *On the Divine Goal and True Asceticism* (usually referred to by its Latin title *De Instituto Christiano*) is an introduction to the ideal of the committed Christian life (as in Basil, there is no suggestion of a double standard), but it is also significant in that the second part of the treatise is based on the *Great Letter*, ascribed to Macarius the Great.

This suggests that with Gregory, as with his brother, there is evidence for links with Messalianism.

Several treatises are concerned with scriptural exegesis. They are mainly homiletic in form: five sermons on the Lord's Prayer, eight sermons on the Beatitudes, eight sermons on Ecclesiastes, fifteen sermons on the Song of Songs. All of them are marked by Gregory's strong sense of connection, ἀκολουθία, i.e., the sense of the connected nature of biblical books and biblical passages, so that there is a strong sense of development, a development that is related to the progress of the Christian life. The beatitudes are not a random group, but a connected sequence, moving from humility, the message of the first beatitude, to the Kingdom of Heaven, the promise of the last. The headings of the psalms (the 'inscriptions', often hardly noticed by modern readers) are similarly interpreted in his treatise (in form, two essays) on the *Inscriptions of the Psalms*. The same pattern is found in his *Life of Moses*, a work, like Philo's work of the same title that clearly forms its inspiration, in two parts, the first an account of his life drawn from Exodus, and the second an allegorical interpretation of this life as a model for the life of the Christian. Both this and the sermons on the Song of Songs contain Gregory's profoundest reflections on the nature of the Christian life as a continual progress towards God. This theology of the Christian life is informed by his dogmatic theology, in particular his doctrine of the ultimate distinction between uncreated and created being. There is nothing in common between the uncreated God and creatures, and consequently no knowledge of the infinite God is possible: God is utterly ineffable. The soul's progress towards God is an entry into deeper and deeper darkness: the soul's longing for God is infinite and never attains satiety. Contemplation is no longer the goal of the spiritual life: rather, a never-ending pursuit into deepening darkness, and a sense of the presence of God which is the result of God's drawing near to the creature, the archetype of which is the incarnation.

Several sermons survive: the three funeral sermons already mentioned, given by Gregory at the height of his fame in Constantinople. There is also an encomium on his brother Basil, and another on St Ephrem the Syrian, which compares him to Basil. There are also hagiographical sermons: two on St Stephen, a long panegyric on St Gregory Thaumaturgus, so important for Basil and Gregory's sense of their place in the Christian tradition (memories of him were preserved by their grandmother, Macrina), a sermon on Theodore the Martyr, and three on the Forty Martyrs of Sebaste. There are also sermons for liturgical feasts and on moral subjects.

Notes

1 Going back at least to H. Weiss, *Die grossen Kappadozier Basilius, Gregor von Nazianz und Gregor von Nyssa als Exegeten* (Braunsberg, 1872), and Karl Holl, *Amphilochius von Iconium in seinem Verhältnis zu den grossen Kappadoziern* (Tübingen, 1904).

2 Jean Gribomont, *Histoire du texte des Ascétiques de saint Basile*, the main results of which so far as the evolution of the *Asceticon* is concerned are summarized by P. Rousseau, *Basil of Caesarea*, Appendix II, 354–9. There is now a critical edition of Rufinus' translation of Basil's Rule by Klaus Zelzer in CSEL 86 (1986).

3 See ch. 24.

4 See ch. 36.

5 For a particularly dismal example of this tendency, see my chapter on the Cappadocians in C. Jones, G. Wainwright and E. Yarnold SJ, eds, *The Study of Spirituality* (London: SPCK, 1986), 161–8.

6 The story is told in Jerome, *Ep*. 52.8, and discussed by J. N. D. Kelly in his *Jerome. His Life, Writings and Controversies*, 70.

7 Geerard, unusually, lists some of the better-known scholia in CPG 3011–31.

8 *Gregorii Nysseni Opera*, ed. W. Jaeger, since 1952 published by E.J. Brill, Leiden.

9 The women lamented in Gregory Nazianzen's consolatory *Ep*. 197 to Gregory Nyssen and in *epitaph* 123, on Theosebeia, the sister of St Basil, are described in remarkably similar terms: both are called Theosebeia, one 'our holy and blessed sister', with whom Nyssen had been living until her death, illustrious 'among brothers of such renown', and having been the 'σύζυγος of a priest' (so the letter); the other sister of St Basil, and therefore of Gregory of Nyssa and Peter of Sebaste, and therefore sister of illustrious brothers, as well as 'σύζυγος of great Gregory' (so the epitaph) – and both lamented by Gregory Nazianzen. It is surely multiplying entities *praeter necessitatem* to have two such Theosebeias!

27

Fourth-century Latin writers: Hilary, Victorinus, Ambrosiaster, Ambrose

DAVID G. HUNTER

The middle to later years of the fourth century witnessed a remarkable proliferation of Christian Latin literature, especially in Italy and Gaul. The earliest Latin poetry and hymns appear at this time, as do the first Latin commentaries on complete books of Scripture. Dogmatic literature abounds in the form of histories and polemical treatises, owing to the controversies surrounding the Council of Nicaea and its creed. The ascetical movement also led to the production of numerous ascetical letters and treatises. Greek philosophical thought, especially Middle Platonism and Neoplatonism, as well as the Platonizing theology of the Greek Fathers, entered the Western literary tradition through the translations and treatises of some of the fourth-century authors under consideration here.[1]

Hilary of Poitiers

One of the great lights of the Gallic Church, Bishop Hilary of Poitiers was born early in the fourth century and became bishop around the year 350. He was exiled by Emperor Constantius II to Phrygia following the Council of Béziers (Baeterrae) in 356 for reasons that remain obscure. The traditional view is that Hilary was exiled for refusing to subscribe to the condemnation of Athanasius and the Nicene faith, but more recently several scholars have suggested that political opposition to Constantius and support of the usurper Silvanus may have led to Hilary's downfall.[2] Whatever the reasons for his exile, while in the East Hilary became more acquainted with the intricacies of the Arian controversy, particularly the perspective of the *homoiousion* party, the large number of Eastern bishops who rejected Arianism but who believed the Nicene formula was susceptible to monarchian interpretations.

During his exile Hilary attended several synods, including the council at Seleucia (359) which saw the triumph of the *homoion* party and the forbidding of all discussion of the divine substance. In 360 Hilary tried unsuccessfully to secure a personal audience with Constantius and to address the council which met at Constantinople in 360. When this council ratified the decisions of Ariminum and Seleucia, Hilary responded with the bitter *In Constantium*, an attack on Emperor Constantius as Antichrist and persecutor of orthodox Christians.

Later that year Hilary returned to Gaul, perhaps encouraged by the growing strength of Constantius' rival Julian.[3] There he began a vigorous campaign to convince the Western clergy that the *homoion* confession was merely a cover for traditional Arian subordinationism. Under Hilary's influence a number of synods were held in Gaul which condemned the creed promulgated at Ariminum.[4] With the assistance of Italian bishops, such as Eusebius of Vercelli, Hilary eventually expanded his activity into Italy, including an unsuccessful attempt in 364 to unseat Auxentius, the bishop of Milan who favoured the *homoion* confession.[5] Hereafter Hilary's activities are unknown. According to Jerome, he returned to Poitiers and died there in 367 (Jerome, *Vir. Ill.* 100 (PL 23, 740); *Chron*. Olympiad 286, year 3, ed. R. Helm, GCS Eusebius, 7, 1956, p. 245).

Among Hilary's earliest writings is a commentary on the Gospel of Matthew, the first Latin commentary on Matthew to have survived in its entirety.[6] Composed some time before his exile in 356, the work offers a continuous reading of the Gospel text and abounds in allegorical and typological interpretations.[7] Hilary's commentary was strongly influenced by Tertullian and Cyprian, and made use of several classical writers, such as Cicero, Quintilian, Pliny and the Roman historians.

Hilary also composed a set of *Tractatus super psalmos* some time after his return from exile in 360. Already in Jerome's day the work was incomplete (*Vir. Ill.* 100), and it is not known whether Hilary originally commented on the whole Psalter. Now extant are the commentaries on Psalms 1, 2, 9, 13, 14, 51–69, 91, and 118–50.[8] Comparison with the remaining fragments of Origen shows that Hilary relied heavily on the great Alexandrian, whose writings he came to know during his exile in the East. For Hilary the entire Psalter prefigured the life, death and resurrection of Christ.

Hilary's third exegetical writing is the *Tractatus mysteriorum*, preserved in a single manuscript first published in 1887 by G. B. Gamurrini.[9] The work discusses a series of Old Testament figures, mainly from Genesis and Exodus: Adam and Eve, Cain and Abel, Lamech, Noah, Abraham, Isaac and Rebecca, Jacob, Moses (book 1); Hosea and Joshua (book 2). Hilary's basic hermeneutical principle is that 'every work contained in the sacred books announces in words, reveals in deeds, and confirms by examples the advent of our Lord Jesus

Christ' (1.1). As a result, details of the biblical stories are taken as prophetic types of Christ and his action in the Church: the creation of Eve from Adam's rib signifies the resurrection of the flesh (1.5); Noah signifies Christ 'who conceals his children in the ark of his doctrine and church' (1.13); Rebecca signifies both marriage and childbirth and thus is a type of the Church: 'she waters the camels, that is, the nations who have submitted to Christ' (1.19). Like the commentary on the Psalms, Hilary's *Tractatus mysteriorum* was composed after his exile and, though not without its originality, betrays the extensive influence of Origen.[10]

Hilary's major theological work was the twelve books now known as *De Trinitate*.[11] Composed largely during his exile, though perhaps not completed until his return to Gaul in 360, the work was influenced by the *homoiousion* theology that Hilary had absorbed while in the East. Hilary also made use of the writings of Novatian and Tertullian, as well as numerous classical authors. Some scholars believe that books 2 and 3 of *De Trinitate* were originally written as an independent work and later fused with the rest by Hilary himself, but there is not universal agreement on this point.[12]

Early in 359 in preparation for the councils of Ariminum and Seleucia, Hilary wrote *De synodis*, an attempt to reconcile the Western supporters of the Nicene *homoousion* formula with the Eastern supporters of the *homoiousion*.[13] Addressed to the bishops of Gaul (1), the first part of the work (1–65) reviews the decisions of Eastern councils held between 341 and 357 and clearly rejects only the creed of 357, the so-called *blasphemia* of Sirmium (*Syn.* 10). The decrees of the other Eastern synods are given a favourable interpretation. In the second part of the work (66–92) Hilary shows that both the *homoousion* and the *homoiousion* formulations are susceptible of orthodox interpretations. In the printed editions *De synodis* is followed by a brief appendix containing Hilary's response to criticism of his work by Lucifer of Cagliari.[14]

Four writings, or sets of writings, comprise Hilary's so-called 'historical' works. These include: (1) *Liber II ad Constantium imperatorem*, a letter to Constantius written in 359, requesting that the emperor allow him to address the council meeting in Constantinople;[15] (2) *Liber in Constantium imperatorem*, a harsh attack on the Emperor Constantius following his ratification of the *homoion* faith at Constantinople in 360;[16] (3) *Contra Arianos vel Auxentium Mediolanensem liber*, an address to fellow Nicene bishops in 364, describing Hilary's unsuccessful effort to charge Auxentius of Milan with heresy;[17] (4) *Fragmenta historica*, also known as the *Collectanea antiariana parisina*, a two-part series of documents relating to the Arian controversy.[18] Appended to the collection in Feder's edition is the so-called *Liber I ad Constantium*, a synodal letter from the Council of Sardica (343), along with a narrative by Hilary describing the proceedings against Athanasius and Eusebius of Vercelli which took place at the Council of Milan (355).[19]

Hilary is also one of the earliest authors of Christian hymns in the Latin language.[20] According to Jerome (*Vir. Ill.* 100) he produced a *liber hymnorum*, but only three hymns have survived, and these are in a fragmentary state. Two are alphabetical hymns, in which each stanza begins with a different letter of the alphabet. Hilary employed a variety of metres and was strongly influenced by the poetic tradition of classical Roman literature.[21] The hymns also reflect Hilary's interest in the Arian controversy and abound in doctrinal themes. For example, Christ appears in Hymn I, *Ante saecula* as: *Lumen fulsit a lumine/ deusque uerus substitit ex deo/uero, non aliud habens/ortus unigena, quam innascibilis pater* (ll. 41–4).[22] Hilary's pioneering work as exegete, theologian and poet strongly influenced later Latin writers.

Marius Victorinus

Our knowledge of the life of Caius Marius Victorinus is virtually limited to several brief notices in Jerome and to Augustine's lengthier discussion in the *Confessions*. According to Jerome, Victorinus was an African by birth who taught rhetoric at Rome under the Emperor Constantius. 'In extreme old age,' Jerome writes, 'yielding himself to faith in Christ, he wrote some very obscure books against Arius in a dialectical style (*more dialectico*), which can be understood only by the learned, as well as commentaries on the apostle' (*Vir. Ill.* 101).[23] Augustine informs us that Victorinus had translated into Latin some 'books of the Platonists' (*quosdam libros platonicorum*), which must have included works of Plotinus and probably of Porphyry as well, but scholars are not agreed on precisely which books are meant.[24] During the reign of the Emperor Julian, Victorinus resigned his professorship when Julian issued his famous edict of 17 June 362, forbidding Christians to teach secular literature.[25] Both Augustine and Jerome mention that Victorinus was honoured during his lifetime with a statue in the forum.[26]

Prior to his conversion to Christianity Victorinus composed a number of works on grammar and rhetoric. The extant writings include an *Ars grammatica*,[27] the *Explanationes in Ciceronis rhetoricam*,[28] and the *Liber de definitionibus* once attributed to Boethius.[29] Victorinus also translated into Latin the *Isagoge* of Porphyry, which formed the basis of Boethius' first commentary on that work.[30] No longer extant are his translations of Aristotle's *Categories*, commentaries on Aristotle's *Categories* and *On Interpretation*, all mentioned by Cassiodorus, and commentaries on the dialogues of Cicero, attested by Jerome.[31]

The writings from Victorinus' Christian period include a series of anti-Arian treatises and hymns, and the first Latin commentary on the Pauline Epistles. Of the latter, the commentaries on Ephesians, Galatians and Philippians survive with minor *lacunae*.[32] In these books Victorinus refers to his previous commentaries on Romans and 1 and 2 Corinthians, which are no longer extant; in the commentary on Ephesians he mentions his intention to discuss the remainder of Paul's letters (*In Eph. 1, prol.*).[33] The commentaries are usually dated to some time after the year 363, that is, immediately following Victorinus' retirement upon the issuance of Julian's edict.[34]

Victorinus' biblical commentaries show no evidence of the use of previous Greek exegetes (e.g., Origen). He appears to have made use of the so-called Marcionite Prologues to the Pauline Epistles that generally circulated in manuscripts of the Old Latin Bible.[35] Victorinus occasionally accentuates the anti-Judaic elements in Paul's thought so strongly that some have seen in him a 'Marcionite' tendency.[36] He maintains, for example, that the God of Jesus Christ 'is far removed from the God of the Jews'.[37] He also notes that in the view of Paul, James the brother of the Lord was not an apostle, but rather was 'in heresy' (*in haeresi*) because he wished to impose Jewish practices on the Christian community.[38] The anti-Arian concerns of his theological writings frequently enter into his Pauline commentaries, as, for example, at Philippians 2:6–11, where he interprets the *forma* of verse 6 as the *imago* and *potentia* of God: as God's image, Christ is the very life (*vivere*), understanding (*intellegere*), and movement (*moveri*) of the Father.[39]

The theological writings of Victorinus closely follow the course of the anti-Nicene reaction that culminated in the rejection of both the *homoousion* and the *homoiousion* formulations by the Council of Sirmium in 357. These years marked the ascendancy of the so-called 'Neo-Arians,' represented by the dialecticians Aetius and Eunomius. According to the chronology established by Pierre Hadot, Victorinus' anti-Arian works were composed in the following order:[40] (1) *Candidi Arriani epistula ad M. Victorinum*, a fictive letter presenting the Neo-Arian view that the Son, by virtue of his character as 'begotten,' is 'unlike' (ἀνόμοιος) the Father; (2) *In Candidi epistula*, Victorinus' response to the first letter of Candidus; (3) *Candidi epistula II*, Candidus' response to Victorinus, consisting primarily of Latin translations of the letter of Arius to

Eusebius of Nicomedia and part of the letter of Eusebius to Paulinus of Tyre. These three documents were probably written in 357/8.

The remainder of the theological writings, composed between 358 and 363, continue the response to Candidus and the letters of Arius; they also attack the *homoiousion* doctrine promulgated by Basil of Ancyra at the Council of Sirmium in 358: (4) *Adversus Arrium IA* (chs 1–47); (5) *Adversus Arrium IB* (chs 48–64); (6) *Adversus Arrium II*, Victorinus' response to the 'Dated Creed' issued in the late summer and autumn of 359 by synods at Ariminum and Seleucia; (7)–(9) (*Adversus Arrium III*; *Adversus Arrium IV*; *De homoousio recipiendo*, less polemical documents, composed after the death of Constantius and under the reign of Julian. The final three items in Victorinus' dogmatic corpus are hymns on the Trinity: *Adesto*, *Miserere Domine* and *Deus Domine*. Their date is unknown, and they may have been composed prior to the theological treatises.

Victorinus' significance as a Christian writer lies in the fact that he, more than anyone else, was 'the one great link between Greek philosophy and the Latin world in the fourth century'.[41] Even before his conversion, Victorinus' work as a translator and commentator indicates that he wished to make the riches of Aristotelian and Neoplatonic philosophy available to the Latin world. While his own daring adaptation of Neoplatonic concepts to Christian trinitarian theology had no discernible impact on the Arian controversy itself, Victorinus exerted some influence on Augustine, whose 'psychological doctrine' of the Trinity shares some similarities with that of his predecessor.[42] Moreover, it is increasingly recognized that Victorinus' biblical commentaries exerted some influence on later Latin interpreters of Paul, such as Ambrosiaster and Augustine.[43]

Ambrosiaster

'Ambrosiaster' ('pseudo-Ambrose') is the name coined by Erasmus to refer to the author of the first complete Latin commentary on the thirteen Pauline Epistles (excluding Hebrews), ascribed in most manuscripts to Ambrose.[44] In 1905 Alexander Souter definitively established that the same author composed the *Quaestiones veteris et novi testamenti*, long attributed to Augustine.[45] Fragments of several other works have been ascribed with some certainty to Ambrosiaster: a commentary on Matthew 24, a discussion of the parable of the three measures of flour into which a woman placed yeast (Matt. 13:33; Luke 13:21), and a treatment of Peter's denial and the arrest of Jesus in Gethsemane. More dubious is the attribution to Ambrosiaster of the *Lex dei sive Mosaicarum et Romanorum legum collatio*, the *De bello iudaico* (a loose translation of Josephus), and the fragments *Contra Arianos* of Ps.-Hilary and *sermo* 246 of Ps.-Augustine.[46]

Although the precise identity of the Ambrosiaster has continued to elude modern scholars, several facts about him can be ascertained. Internal evidence suggests that he was active at Rome during the reign of Pope Damasus (366–84) and almost certainly a member of the Roman clergy. There are strong indications that Ambrosiaster objected to Jerome's efforts to revise the Old Latin versions of the Gospels and that he was critical of Jerome's activity among ascetic women at Rome.[47] Ambrosiaster shows a deep interest in Judaism and often notes that Christian practices derive from Jewish tradition. He was also familiar with Roman legal terminology and customs. Some scholars have suggested that Ambrosiaster may have held public office.[48]

The Pauline commentaries were issued in several editions, probably all from the hand of the same author. Three versions of the commentary on Romans and two versions of the commentaries on the other books are extant. Following the example of Marius Victorinus and the Old Latin Prologues, Ambrosiaster introduces each book with a discussion of the community to which the letter was addressed and Paul's purpose in writing. The *Quaestiones* also exist in multiple editions, each with a different number of questions (127, 150 and 115 (the last is a medieval compilation made from the other two)). It is likely that both the Pauline commentaries and the *Quaestiones* were originally issued anonymously.[49]

Ambrosiaster's *Quaestiones* deal with a variety of topics, not all of them exegetical. There are apologetic tracts against pagans (*Q.* 114), Jews (*Q.* 44), and astral fatalism (*Q.* 115); polemical treatises against Arius (*Q.* 97), Novatian (*Q.* 102), and Photinus (*Q.* 91); even an essay attacking the arrogance of the deacons of Rome (*Q.* 101). But most of the questions concern difficulties in the interpretation of Scripture: e.g., why was Abel's sacrifice accepted by God, but Cain's refused? (*Q.* 5); if God's judgment is just, why were infants destroyed at Sodom along with their parents? (*Q.* 13); why did Abraham receive circumcision as a sign of his faith? (*Q.* 12); are souls passed on in the same way as bodies? (*Q.* 23). Ambrosiaster's *Quaestiones* anticipated many of the theological issues that were to vex Western Christians in the later Origenist and Pelagian controversies.

Ambrosiaster's commentary on Paul also influenced later Latin commentators, among them Augustine and Pelagius. Augustine cited Ambrosiaster under the name of 'Hilary' for his interpretation of Romans 5:12 ('By one man sin entered into the world, and by sin death; and so death passed to all, in whom (*in quo*) all have sinned): 'It is manifest that all have sinned in Adam, as it were in a mass (*quasi in massa*). For he himself was corrupted by sin, and all whom he begot were born under sin.'[50] On the other hand, Ambrosiaster strongly emphasized the freedom of the human will in a manner that foreshadowed Pelagius: 'God gives assistance to our good efforts . . . so that it is ours to will, but God's to complete' (*Ad Phil.* 2:13). Of all the later Latin Fathers, Ambrosiaster is perhaps the most neglected and in need of further study.[51]

Ambrose of Milan

The most prominent and prolific of the later Latin writers under consideration here was Ambrose, bishop of Milan. Born around the year 339 at Trier, the son of the praetorian prefect of Gaul, Ambrose received an education in rhetoric at Rome and began his career as an advocate at the court of the praetorian prefect in Sirmium. Around 372/3 Ambrose received the post of *consularis* of Aemilia and Liguria, whose seat was in Milan. At the death of Auxentius in 374, Ambrose was acclaimed bishop, despite the fact that he was not yet a baptized Christian. Within a week he received baptism, a succession of clerical offices, and episcopal consecration. Ambrose's literary corpus dates entirely from his episcopate which ended with his death in 397.[52]

Ambrose spent his early years as bishop acquiring a Christian education under the tutelage of Simplicianus, the learned presbyter of Milan who had served as mentor to Marius Victorinus and who would later do so to Augustine. He became familiar with the Scriptures, the Greek Fathers, especially Origen and the Cappadocians, and Latin writers such as Tertullian and Cyprian. He also steeped himself in the writings of Philo and Plotinus, from whom he often borrows verbatim.[53] Ambrose's lifelong commitment to study made a deep impression on his contemporaries, most notably Augustine (*Conf.* 6.3.3).

Ambrose's earliest writings date from the years 377–8 and include a pair of treatises on virginity (*De virginibus* and *De virginitate*), a discourse on widows (*De viduis*), and a pair of funeral orations for his brother Satyrus (*De excessu fratris*).[54] In *De virginibus* Ambrose borrowed extensively from a letter to virgins attributed to Athanasius, developing for the first time in the West the ascetical interpretation of the Song of Songs and the image of Mary the mother of Jesus as a model for the consecrated virgin.[55] Promoting the virginal and ascetical lives remained a lifelong preoccupation of Ambrose, as evidenced by his later treatises *De institutione virginis* (*c.* 391) and *Exhortatio virginitatis* (*c.* 393).[56] Ambrose's funeral orations demonstrate his debt to the classical tradition of the *consolatio*, as well as his transformation of the genre by the use of biblical themes.[57]

By far the greater part of Ambrose's literary corpus consists of biblical commentaries, mainly on the Hebrew Scriptures. Most of these originated as homilies which Ambrose subsequently revised and issued for circulation. Among his most popular commentaries are the nine homilies *On the Hexaemeron*, a series preached during the six days of Holy Week.[58] These homilies, which may have been heard by Augustine in 386, explicitly attack the Manichees and rely heavily on a spiritual interpretation of the creation story that Ambrose learned from Philo, Origen and Basil of Caesarea.[59] Ambrose also preached numerous sermons that offered an allegorical treatment of the lives of various figures in Genesis: Cain and Abel, Noah, Abraham, Jacob and Joseph. His sermons *De Nabuthae historia* and *De Tobia* present particularly scathing denunciations of the abuse of wealth and oppression of the poor.[60]

Among Ambrose's most exegetical works are the treatises *De Isaac vel anima* and *De bono mortis*, which were probably originally sermons delivered to the newly baptized in 386 or 387. The former, which has been characterized as 'the first great masterpiece of Western mysticism',[61] focuses on the marriage between Isaac and Rebecca, which Ambrose interprets as an allegory of the spiritual union between God and the soul and, secondarily, between Christ and the Church. In *De Isaac* Ambrose continually employs a spiritual reading of the Song of Songs and borrows extensively from the writings of Plotinus and Porphyry, especially on the theme of the soul's ascent to God.[62] *De bono mortis*, a companion piece to *De Isaac vel anima*, likewise stresses in Platonic and Plotinian fashion the benefit of death as a release from the prison of the body (*Bon*. 2.5).

The Psalms and the life of David provided Ambrose with ample material for several commentaries: *De interpellatione Iob et David* and *De apologia prophetae David*, both of which refer to the vulnerability of human power with apparent allusions to contemporary political events;[63] *Enarrationes in XII psalmos davidicos*, twelve homilies on Psalms 1, 35–40, 45, 47, 48, 61 and 43 (the last incomplete at Ambrose's death);[64] and the *Expositio psalmi CXVIII*, a collection of twenty-two homilies on the twenty-two stanzas of Psalm 118 (119).[65] Ambrose's commentaries on the psalms offer a mixture of moral, typological and messianic interpretations.[66] Ambrose's only commentary on a book of the New Testament is his *Expositio evangelii secundum Lucam*, also originally a set of homilies, which relies extensively on writings by Origen, Eusebius of Caesarea, and Hilary of Poitiers.[67] It was in criticism of Ambrose's commentary on Luke that Jerome made his famous remark that Ambrose was a black crow who adorned himself with coloured feathers taken from other birds.[68]

Homiletic material also served as the basis of several works on the rites of Christian initiation. Ambrose's *De mysteriis* and *De sacramentis* are collections of homilies to the newly baptized concerning the rites of baptism, anointing and eucharist.[69] Also extant is an *Explanatio symboli ad initiandos*, a homily on the creed addressed to those preparing for baptism.[70] Ambrose also composed two books *De paenitentia*, defending the practice of ecclesiastical penance in opposition to the Novatianists, a rigorist sect which still retained vitality in the later fourth century.[71]

One of Ambrose's most famous works is *De officiis* ('On Moral Duties'), which is essentially a treatise on Christian ethics.[72] Based on Cicero's work of the same name, which was itself based on the writings of the Stoic Panaetius with some further influence from Posidonius and Hecaton of Rhodes, Ambrose followed Cicero in organizing the treatise in three books. The first deals with what is 'virtuous' (*honestum*), the second with what is 'expedient' (*utile*), the third with the relationship between the two. While much of the content of Stoic ethics is absorbed in his work (e.g., the four cardinal virtues, the natural law), Ambrose seeks to transform the classical heritage by presenting biblical *exempla* and by introducing specifically Christian virtues, such as *humilitas* and *castitas*. Furthermore, as a recent commentator has noted, Ambrose 'maintains a theocentricity and soteriological-eschatological reference-point which are foreign to Cicero'.[73]

In the area of dogmatic theology Ambrose composed three works of significance. His five books *De fide ad Gratianum* were written between 378 and 380 in response to several requests by the Emperor Gratian.[74] In the work Ambrose argues against a series of Arian propositions (*De fide* 1.34–40) and answers objections to his own views that came from the *homoion* party.[75] Somewhat later (381) Ambrose issued three books *De spiritu sancto*, again addressed to Gratian, in response to the Emperor's earlier request that Ambrose should deal with this new issue that had arisen in the wake of the Arian controversy.[76] His treatise *De incarnationis dominicae sacramento* was composed *c.* 382 in response to a challenge to his teaching regarding the nature of the incarnate Christ.[77] Against the Apollinarian and Arian views that Jesus had no human mind, Ambrose defends the doctrine of two distinct natures in Christ.

Ambrose has recently been characterized as a 'Christian Pliny' because of the ninety-one extant letters which he organized into a collection of ten volumes, nine 'private' and one 'public,' to correspond to the arrangement of his model Pliny.[78] The letters are an important source of documentation regarding their author and the political and religious events of his day, especially the famous struggle with Q. Aurelius Symmachus over the removal of the Altar of Victory from the Roman senate and the various conflicts with Emperor Theodosius I. Finally, Ambrose's achievement as a writer of hymns must be mentioned. Of the numerous hymns ascribed to him only the four attested by Augustine are universally regarded as authentic: *Aeterne rerum conditor, Deus creator omnium, Iam surgit hora tertia* and *Intende qui regis Israel.*[79] The profound impact of Ambrose's hymnody was noted by numerous ancient writers, among them Augustine, Maximus of Turin, and Cassiodorus.[80]

Notes

1 I gratefully acknowledge the assistance of Professor Stephen A. Cooper, Associate Professor of Religious Studies at Franklin and Marshall College, in the preparation of this chapter.

2 The older view can be found in J. Doignon, *Hilaire de Poitiers avant l'exil*, 455–513; and C. F. A. Borchardt, *Hilary of Poitiers' Role in the Arian Struggle*, 24–37. For the newer view: H. C. Brennecke, *Hilarius von Poitiers und die Bischofsopposition gegen Konstantius II: Untersuchungen zur dritten Phase des arianischen Streites*, 210–43; and D. H. Williams, 'A Reassessment of the Early Career and Exile of Hilary of Poitiers', 202–17. But the older view still has its defenders: T. D. Barnes, 'Hilary of Poitiers on His Exile'; and P. C. Burns, review of P. Smulders, *Hilary of Poitiers' Preface to his* Opus Historicum, *JTS* n.s. 47 (1996), 298–301.

3 On the circumstances of Hilary's return, see Y.-M. Duval, 'Vrais et faux problèmes concernant le retour d'exil d'Hilaire de Poitiers et son action en Italie en 360–363'; and D. H. Williams, 'The Anti-Arian Campaigns of Hilary of Poitiers and the "Liber contra Auxentium"'.

4 Sulpicius Severus, *Chronicum* 2.45 (CSEL 1 (1866), 98); Williams, 'Anti-Arian Campaigns,' 14.

5 Described in Hilary's *Contra Auxentium* (PL 10, 609–18).

6 Ed. Jean Doignon, *Hilaire de Poitiers. Sur Matthieu* (SC 254 and 258; 1978–9).

7 An extensive discussion of Hilary's exegetical method can be found in Doignon, *Hilaire de Poitiers avant l'exil*, 227–55.

8 Ed. A. Zingerle, CSEL 22 (1891); cf. A. Wilmart, 'Le dernier tractatus de S. Hilaire sur les psaumes'. The commentary on Ps. 118 has been edited by Marc Milhau in SC 344 and 347 (1988).

9 The most recent critical edition is that of Jean-Paul Brisson, *Hilaire de Poitiers. Traité des Mystères* (SC 19bis; 1967); also by A. Feder, CSEL 65 (1916), 1–38; and in PLS 1 (1958), 246–70.

10 See the commentary in Brisson, SC 19bis, 51–5.

11 Ed. P. Smulders, CCSL 62–62A (1979–80). The original title of Hilary's work is unknown. See P. Smulders, 'Remarks on the Manuscript Tradition of the *De trinitate* of Saint Hilary of Poitiers'.

12 M. Simonetti, 'Note sulla struttura e la cronologia del *De Trinitate* di Ilario di Poities'; also Doignon, *Hilaire de Poitiers avant l'exil*, 82f. Arguing for the original unity of the twelve books is E. P. Meijering, *Hilary of Poitiers on the Trinity*, 1–11.
13 Text in PL 10, 479–546.
14 *Apologetica ad reprehensores libri de synodis responsa* in PL 10, 545–8; also P. Smulders, 'Two Passages of Hilary's *Apologetica responsa* Rediscovered'.
15 Ed. A. Feder, CSEL 65 (1916), 197–205.
16 Ed. A. Rocher, *Hilaire de Poitiers. Contre Constance*, SC 334 (1987).
17 Text in PL 10, 609–18.
18 Ed. A. Feder, CSEL 65 (1916), 43–177.
19 Ibid., 181–7. For a full discussion of the complex history of scholarship on these works, see P. Smulders, *Hilary of Poitiers' Preface to his Opus historicum*, 1–28. All of these documents were probably once part of the work that Jerome refers to as the *liber adversus Valentem et Ursacium, historiam Ariminensis et Seleuciensis synodi continens* (*Vir. Ill.* 100).
20 Ed. A. Feder, CSEL 65, 209–16. Cf. F. J. E. Raby, *A History of Christian Latin Poetry*, 41–3.
21 J. Fontaine, 'L'apport de la tradition poétique romaine à la formation de l'hymnodie latine chrétienne'.
22 CSEL 65, 211.
23 In the prologue to his commentary on Galatians (PL 26, 332), Jerome gives an even less generous estimate of Victorinus' biblical commentaries: *occupatus ille eruditione saecularium litterarum scripturas omnino sanctas ignoraverit et nemo possit, quamvis eloquens, de eo bene disputare quod nesciat.*
24 *Conf.* 8.2.3; cf. 7.9.13. A good discussion can be found in J. J. O'Donnell, *Augustine. Confessions*, II, 413–26; III, 12 –20; cf. also Courcelle, *Les Confessions de saint Augustin dans la tradition littéraire*. Antécédents et Posterité, 31–58. The Porphyrian character of Victorinus' work has been established by P. Hadot, *Porphyre et Victorinus*.
25 *Conf.* 8.5.10. Julian's law is found in *Codex Theodosianus* 13.3.5. The edict itself did not mention Christians specifically, but a subsequent rescript made it plain that Julian's primary aim was to exclude Christians from the schools. See his *Ep.* 61c.423d.
26 *Conf.* 8.2.3; Jerome, *Chron.* a. 2370, specifies the forum of Trajan.
27 Ed. H. Keil, *Grammatici latini* (Leipzig, 1874), VI, 3–184; and with Italian translation by I. Mariotti (Florence: F. Le Monnier, 1967).
28 Ed. C. Halm, *Rhetores latini minores* (Leipzig, 1863; repr. Frankfurt: Minerva GmbH, 1964), 153–304. See Stephen Gersh, 'Marius Victorinus' *Commentarius in Ciceronis Rhetoricam*', Excursus D in his *Middle Platonism and Neoplatonism. The Latin Tradition*, II, 719–27.
29 PL 64, 891–910; also ed. T. Stangl, *Tulliana et Mario-Victoriana* (Munich, 1888), 17–48; repr. in P. Hadot, *Marius Victorinus. Recherches sur sa vie et ses oeuvres*, 331–62.

30 Ed. S. Brant, CSEL 48 (1906), 1–132; reconstructed in Hadot, *Marius Victorinus*, 367–80. For Boethius' use of Victorinus' translation, see H. Chadwick, *Boethius: The Consolations of Music, Logic, Theology, and Philosophy* (Oxford: Clarendon Press, 1981), 115.

31 Cassiodorus, *Inst.* (ed. Mynors, Oxford Classical Texts, 1937), 128–129; Jerome, *Apol. c. Ruf.* 1.16.

32 Ed. F. Gori, CSEL 83/2 (1986).

33 F. Gori, *Praef.* (CSEL 83/2), viii–ix.

34 Hadot, *Marius Victorinus*, 301–3; W. Erdt, *Marius Victorinus Afer, der erste lateinische Paulus Kommentator*, 78–89.

35 K. Th. Schäfer, 'Marius Victorinus und die marcionistischen Prologe zu den Paulusbriefen', *Revue bénédictine* 24 (1970), 7–16; followed by Stephen Cooper, *Metaphysics and Morals in Marius Victorinus' Commentary on the Letter to the Ephesians*, 115–16. The Marcionite character of these Prologues has been seriously challenged by N. Dahl, 'The Origins of the Earliest Prologues to the Pauline Letters', *Semeia* 12 (1978), 233–77.

36 Hadot, *Marius Victorinus*, 292–4; Erdt, *Marius Victorinus Afer*, 198–208, 212–15.

37 *Eph.* 1.17 (CSEL 83/2 (1986), 20–1). In his commentary on this verse, however, Stephen Cooper has argued persuasively that Victorinus' words can be interpreted in a non-Marcionite sense. See his *Metaphysics and Morals*, 146–9.

38 *Ad Galatas* 1.19 (CSEL 83/2, 110).

39 *Ad Phil.* 2.6–8 (CSEL 83/2, 188). Study of Victorinus' biblical commentaries is still in its infancy. In addition to the work of Erdt and Cooper, see now G. Raspanti, *Mario Vittorino esegeta di S. Paolo*.

40 The theological works are edited by Paul Henry and Pierre Hadot, *Marius Victorinus. Traités théologiques sur la Trinité* (SC 68–9; 1960); also in CSEL 83/1 (1971). For the dating, see pp. 28–70; also Hadot, *Marius Victorinus*, 253–82.

41 R. A. Markus, 'Marius Victorinus,' in CHLG, 332.

42 P. Henry, 'The *adversus Arium* of Marius Victorinus: The First Systematic Exposition of the Doctrine of the Trinity'; P. Hadot, 'L'image de la Trinité dans l'âme chez Victorinus et chez saint Augustin'.

43 E. Plumer, 'The Influence of Marius Victorinus on Augustine's Commentary on Galatians'; N. Cipriani, 'Agostino lettore dei commentai paolini di Mario Vittorino', *Augustinianum* 38/2 (1998), 413–28. On the fourth-century 'renaissance' of interest in Paul, see B. Lohse, 'Beobachtungen zum Paulus-Kommentar und zur Wiederentdeckung des Paulus in der lateinischen Theologie des vierten Jahrhunderts'. Still valuable on these questions: A. Souter, *The Earliest Latin Commentaries on the Epistles of St. Paul*.

44 Ed. H. J. Vogels, CSEL 81/1–3 (1966–9).

45 Ed. A. Souter, CSEL 50 (1908). For the demonstration of authorship, see Souter, *A Study of Ambrosiaster*.

46 For a discussion of the authentic and inauthentic works, see C. Martini, *Ambrosiaster. De auctore, operibus, theologia*, 9–73.

47 H. J. Vogels, 'Ambrosiaster und Hieronymus'; D. G. Hunter, '*On the Sin of Adam and Eve*: A Little-known Defense of Marriage and Childbearing by Ambrosiaster'; D. G. Hunter, 'The Paradise of Patriarchy: Ambrosiaster on Woman as (Not) God's Image'.

48 Souter, *A Study of Ambrosiaster*, 172–83; O. Heggelbacher, *Vom römischen zum christlichen Recht. Iuristische Elemente in den Schriften des sog. Ambrosiaster*. The most recent attempt to establish the identity of Ambrosiaster is that of O. Heggelbacher: 'Beziehungen zwischen Ambrosiaster und Maximus von Turin?'

49 C. Martini, 'De ordinatione duarum Collectionum quibus Ambrosiastri "Quaestiones" traduntur'; C. Martini, 'Le recensione delle "Quaestiones Veteris et Novi Testamenti" dell'Ambrosiaster'.

50 Ambrosiaster, *In Epistula ad Romanos* 5.12 (CSEL 81/1 (1966), 165), cited in Augustine, *Contra duas epistulas Pelagii* 4.4.7 (CSEL 60 (1913), 528).

51 For example, there is currently no ET of any significant portion of Ambrosiaster's work. Italian translations of some of the Pauline commentaries have appeared in the *Collana di testi patristici* published by Città Nuova Editrice.

52 The most important source for Ambrose's early life is the *Vita* written by Paulinus of Milan at Augustine's request in 422: *Vita di S. Ambrogio: introduzione, testo critico et note* ed. M. Pellegrino, Verba Seniorum, nuova serie (Rome: Editrice Studium, 1961); for recent accounts, see N. McLynn, *Ambrose of Milan. Church and Court in a Christian Capital*, 1–52; and B. Ramsey, *Ambrose*.

53 Ambrose's debt to Philo and Plotinus has been demonstrated by Pierre Courcelle and others: see P. Courcelle, *Recherches sur les Confessions de saint Augustin*, 93–138, 311–82; H. Savon, *Saint Ambroise devant l'exégèse de Philon le juif*; G. Madec, *Saint Ambroise et la philosophie*. For the Latins, see Y.-M. Duval, 'L'influence des écrivains africains'.

54 *De excessu fratris*, ed. O. Faller, CSEL 73 (1955), 207–325. The most recent edition of Ambrose's writings on virginity and widowhood is that of F. Gori, *Opere morali II/I–II. Verginità e vedovanza* (Opera omnia di sant'Ambrogio 14/I–II; Milan: Biblioteca Ambrosiana; Rome: Città Nuova Editrice, 1989).

55 Y.-M. Duval, 'L'originalité du *De virginibus* dans le mouvement ascétique occidental. Ambroise, Cyprien, Athanase', in *Ambroise de Milan. XVIe Centenaire de son élection épiscopale*, 9–66. On Ambrose's Marian theology in general, see C. W. Neumann, *The Virgin Mary in the Works of Saint Ambrose*.

56 *De institutione virginis*, PL 16, 319–48; *Exhortatio virginitatis*, PL 16, 351–80. All of the works on virginity and widowhood were edited by G. Salvati in Corona Patrum Salesiana, series latina, 6 (Turin, 1955). See also the edition of F. Gori (cited in note 54).

57 Y.-M. Duval, 'Formes profanes et formes bibliques dans les orations funèbres de saint Ambroise'; and H. Savon, 'La première oraison funèbre de saint Ambroise

(*De excessu fratris* I) et les deux sources de la consolation chrétienne'. Ambrose also composed funeral orations for the Emperors Valentinian II and Theodosius; ed. O. Faller, CSEL 73 (1955), 327–401.

58 Ed. C. Schenkl, CSEL 32.1 (1897), 3–261. Also among the early biblical commentaries is *De paradiso*: CSEL 32/1, 265–336.

59 For the possible influence of these homilies on Augustine, see Courcelle, *Recherches*, 93–103.

60 Ed. C. Schenkl, CSEL 32/1 (1897: *De Cain et Abel, De Noe, De Abraham*) and 32/2 (1897: *De Iacob, De Ioseph, De patriarchis, De Nabuthae, De Tobia*). See also M. G. Mara, *Ambrogio. La storia di Naboth. Introduzione, commento, edizione critica, traduzione* (L'Aquila, 1975); and M. Giacchero, *De Tobia. Saggio introduttivo* (Genoa, 1965).

61 B. McGinn, *The Foundations of Mysticism*, 203. Ed. C. Schenkl, CSEL 32/1, 641–700 (*De Isaac*) and 703–53 (*De bono mortis*).

62 Courcelle, *Recherches*, 106–17; also Hadot, 'Platon et Plotin dans trois sermons de saint Ambroise'. For a defence of Ambrose's originality despite his reliance on other sources, see G. Nauroy, 'La structure de *De Isaac vel anima* et la cohérence de l'allegorèse d'Ambroise de Milan'.

63 Ed. C. Schenkl, CSEL 32/2, 211–408; the *Apologia* was also edited by P. Hadot, SC 239 (1977).

64 Ed. M. Petschenig, CSEL 64 (1919), 3–397.

65 Ed. M. Petschenig, CSEL 62 (1913), 3–510.

66 H. J. auf der Maur, *Das Psalmenverständnis des Ambrosius von Mailand*.

67 Ed. M. Adriaen, CCSL 14 (1957); also by G. Tissot, SC 45bis and 52bis (1971, 1976).

68 *Praef. in omelias Origenis super Lucam evangelistam* (SC 87, 94).

69 Ed. B. Botte, SC 25bis (1980), 60–92; also by O. Faller, CSEL 73, 13–116.

70 Ed. R. H. Connolly, *The Explanatio symboli ad initiandos, a work of St. Ambrose* (TS, 10; Cambridge: Cambridge University Press, 1952); also by B. Botte, SC 25bis, 46–58, and O. Faller, CSEL 73 (1955), 1–12.

71 Ed. R. Gryson, SC 179 (1971).

72 Ed. M. Testard, *Saint Ambroise. Les Devoirs*. 2 vols (Paris: Les Belles Lettres, 1984, 1992); also by I. J. Davidson, *Ambrose: De Officiis*. The well-known qualifier '*ministrorum*' is probably not part of the original title: see I. J. Davidson, 'Ambrose's *De officiis* and the Intellectual Climate of the Late Fourth Century'.

73 Davidson, *Ambrose: De Officiis*, 325; cf. Colish, *The Stoic Tradition from Antiquity to the Early Middle Ages*, II, 58–70.

74 Ed. O. Faller, CSEL 78 (1962).

75 On the historical circumstances of *De fide*, see D. H. Williams, *Ambrose of Milan and the end of the Arian-Nicene Conflicts* 141–66.

76 Ed. O. Faller, CSEL 79 (1964), 15–222.

77 Ed. O. Faller, CSEL 79, 223–381.

78 M. Zelzer, '*Plinius Christianus*: Ambrosius als Epistolograph'; and McLynn, *Ambrose of Milan*, xvii. The correspondence can be found in CSEL 82/1–3 (1968–82),

ed. O. Faller, CSEL 82/1 (books 1–6); Faller and M. Zelzer, CSEL 82/2 (books 7–9); Zelzer, CSEL 82/3 (book 10, Epistulae extra collectionem, Gesta).

79 Ed. J. Fontaine et al., *Ambroise de Milan. Hymne* (Paris: Éditions du Cerf, 1992).

80 M.-H. Julien, 'Les sources de la tradition ancienne des hymnes attribuées à Saint Ambroise'; cf. C. P. E. Springer, 'The Concinnity of Ambrose's *Inluminans Altissimus*'.

28

Jerome and Rufinus

MARK VESSEY

Jerome

Jerome obliged all future historians of Christian literature by compiling the first chronological list of Christian writers and their works, beginning with St Peter and ending with himself. His catalogue *De Viris Illustribus* ('On Famous Men') or *De Scriptoribus Ecclesiasticis* ('On Ecclesiastical Writers') was published in 'the fourteenth year of the Emperor Theodosius' (AD 392/3) when he was in his mid-forties and had been living for several years in Bethlehem. His principal generic model was a biobibliography of Roman literature by C. Suetonius Tranquillus (d. AD 160), while for his knowledge of ante-Nicene Christian literature he relied heavily on the *Ecclesiastical History* of Eusebius of Caesarea. Where Suetonius divided his subjects into separate sequences by profession (grammarians, rhetoricians, poets, etc.), Jerome makes one sequence of all who had 'left something on record about the Holy Scriptures (*de scripturis sanctis*)' (*Vir. Ill. prol*). And where Eusebius aimed to recall those 'who in each generation were the ambassadors of the word of God either by speech (*agraphos*) or writing (*dia sungrammaton*)' (*HE* 1.1), he attends mainly to written performance. 'Christian literature', as he conceives and presents it for the first time, is defined in three ways: negatively as a class of writing distinct from the corpus of pagan literature (*litterae gentiles*), positively as an elaboration of the Bible (in the first instance, of the Old Testament), and practically as the life's work of Jerome himself.

In the concluding chapter (135) of the *De Viris Illustribus* Jerome tells us that he was the son of a certain Eusebius and that he was born (probably *c.* 347) at Stridon near the border between the Roman provinces of Dalmatia and Pannonia. He then lists his works to date. Since the underlying structure of the list is chronological, by combining its details with other autobiographical information we can make out the course of a literary career. In so doing, however, we risk overestimating the ease with which this author took his place in literary history. No Latin writer before Petrarch had a finer sense than Jerome of his own life as a work of art. By obvious design, his many letters, prefaces and personal digressions present a strikingly consistent profile of the character, formation and activity of a Christian literatus.

The main stages of Jerome's 'life in letters' are well marked: grammatical and rhetorical education in Rome, where he was also baptized; the beginnings of a secular career, terminated by ascetic conversion; sojourn at Aquileia in the company of fellow ascetics; removal to Antioch in Syria and then, after a trial of his monastic vocation in the 'desert' of Chalcis, to Constantinople (by 381); journey to Rome on business of the Antiochene Church, in which he had been ordained presbyter; residence in Rome, in the entourage of Pope Damasus, until shortly after the latter's death in 384; pilgrimage to Palestine and Egypt; final settlement (386) in a monastery at Bethlehem funded by his patron and companion of many years, the noble Roman widow Paula, where he spent his remaining twenty-five years in a round of study interrupted only by ill-health and the grief occasioned by events such as the Gothic capture of Rome in 410 or Paula's death.

Although few of the facts of this autobiographical narrative can now be independently checked, there is no reason to doubt its general reliability. Matters become more complicated when we begin to correlate biography and bibliography. Much of Jerome's entry in the *De Viris Illustribus* is devoted to works of biblical scholarship published or undertaken after his move to Bethlehem in 386, broadly divisible into the three categories of *translation* (Latin versions of the Old Testament from Greek and Hebrew, extending his earlier work as reviser of the Latin New Testament), *exegesis* (commentaries on St Paul, Ecclesiastes, and the Minor Prophets; tractates on the Psalms; translation of Origen's homilies on Luke; 'Hebrew Questions' on Genesis), and *aids to study* (dictionary of Hebrew names, biblical gazetteer). If we add the commentaries on the Major Prophets and on Matthew begun after 393, a picture emerges of the Christian writer *de scripturis* that exactly answers the implicit prescriptions of the *De Viris Illustribus*. The creation of that role or literary persona is Jerome's masterpiece, as Augustine and Erasmus among others were quick to appreciate and as artists of the Later Middle Ages and Renaissance remind us at every turn. At this distance, it is instructive to realize how little there was of inevitability about it. For a traditionally educated upper-class Roman of the late Empire to make a name (and, within existing structures of patronage, a living) for himself as a *scriptor de scripturis sanctis* required a significant adjustment of cultural assumptions on the part of his readers and a vast labour of improvisation by the writer himself. If the nature of the evidence precludes our reconstructing all the processes behind Jerome's consummate production of his life-and-work, a modern literary history can at least point to his more startling initiatives.

Jerome is the protomartyr of Latin literature. Until he travestied himself as an incorrigible Ciceronian and Christ the Judge as a persecuting magistrate,[1] few would have taken it for granted that a Christian man of letters should suffer for his art. Among the Greeks, a contemporary like Basil of Caesarea could calmly recommend the study of pagan authors to well-born Christian youth. For the Latins, Lactantius, Juvencus and Hilary had already provided models of a confident adaptation of classical norms to the gospel teaching. Even Tertullian, whose polemical opposition of Greek philosophy to biblical revelation Jerome twists in a literary-aesthetic sense,[2] had not made the deceptions of pagan poetry and rhetoric into a stumbling-block for the would-be Christian writer. The illusion of a conflict between classical and Christian literary values in the late fourth-century West may be very largely of Jerome's making. He himself never gave up his favourite Roman authors.[3] Plautus, Cicero, Virgil, Horace and their fellows are always on hand in his work and, on the strength of his reading in the Alexandrian theologians, he can provide an elegant justification for their presence there when called upon to do so.[4] When he chastens his naturally luxurious style – as, for example, in interpreting Scripture – he does so for effect and according to a programme.

It was no part of Jerome's purpose to prescribe a new Christian rhetoric, still less to overturn the classical literary canon. The opposition which he makes between the party of Cicero and that of Christ is contrastive and emulative, calculated to assert the heteronomy of Christian literature – its conformity to a distinct set of rules associated with the Bible –, even as it invites comparisons between the works of Christian writers and the most cherished products of the classical literary system.[5] Classical literary theory taught that writers should seek to outdo their predecessors in particular genres. Jerome generalized the principle, conceiving an entire 'anti-literature' based on Scripture. It is perhaps in this sense that we should construe his otherwise unfathomable comparisons, such as the remark that Hilary of Poitiers in his work *On the Trinity* 'imitated the twelve books of Quintilian both in style and number' (*Ep.* 70.5).

Jerome's biblicism is the other side of his classicism. Like his Constantinian precursors Lactantius and Juvencus or such contemporary classicizing poets as Proba and Paulinus, he was interested in mediating the Bible to a public of cultured Roman readers and conscious that the scriptural text, in its Old Latin versions, was an affront to their sensibilities. However, whereas Juvencus and the centonists seem to have denied the Bible intrinsic 'literary' value by recasting it in classical genres, Jerome contrived to dignify it as the master-text of a separate literature. Now and again he points to 'correspondences' between the genres of the biblical books and those of the classical canon,[6] but this is neither his most original nor his most productive line of thought. The ideal writer *de scripturis* is not an imitator of biblical forms, any more than, strictly speaking, he is an imitator of classical forms. He is an interpreter (*interpres*) of the biblical text itself, one who cleaves to its letter and fastens on its sense. Although previous Latin writers had essayed close and consecutive biblical commentary, Jerome is the first to theorize the art and to make its practice the main burden of the Christian literatus.

The inspiration to do this came chiefly from Origen, whose biblical scholarship Jerome encountered as early as *c.* 380 and whose life's work furnished a fateful model for his own. From Origen he learnt three things which through him would powerfully affect the later Christian culture of the West: a strongly ascetic conception of Bible study as part of a regime of Christian life; a text-centred biblical philology in the exacting tradition of the Hellenistic grammarian-critics; and an ethical hermeneutic which set a premium on spiritual meanings obtained by allegorical exegesis. Convinced by his perusal of Origen's multi-column recension of the Old Testament (the Hexapla) that the 'received' Latin text of the Bible did not – and, even if revised, would still not – convey the plenitude of divine meanings consigned in Scripture, Jerome took it upon himself to provide a kind of hypertextual edition for Latin readers, the components of which (translation, exegesis, study aids) have been listed separately above but demand to be considered together.[7] To think of Jerome principally as 'the author of the Vulgate' is to miss the intricate interdependence of his literary undertakings. The commentaries on the prophets exemplify his approach: lemma by lemma, in strict obedience to the sequence and supposed logic of the original, painstaking collation of the Hebrew and Greek texts (Septuagint and *recentiores*) prepares the way for one or more attempts at translation-and-interpretation.[8] Commentary, as Jerome announces it, is less a genre than a job (*opus commentariorum*),[9] a literary activity subordinate to the Bible as a signifying whole, one which claims neither style nor artistic unity of its own. Any writing that would count as 'Christian literature' in Jerome's book had to be of a piece with the Bible itself.

Jerome's forging of a new 'biblical' literary persona was not his only innovation. Nor would it have succeeded so well without the publicity created by his performances as historian, hagiographer, controversialist and letter-writer. Generic inventiveness is the keynote of Jerome's writings before 386. These include the first Latin universal history (adapting and continuing Eusebius'

Chronicle), the first original Latin *Life* of an ascetic hero (the *Life of Paul the First Hermit*, designed to outdo the Athanasian *Life of Antony* recently translated by his friend Evagrius), a polemical dialogue (the *Altercation between a Luciferian and an Orthodox*, prelude to more vehement and declamatory exchanges with Helvidius, Jovinian, Rufinus and others), and a series of exegetical essays on problems arising from the Hebrew of the Old Testament (to be found among the letters to Damasus and Marcella). The project of revising the Latin New Testament, for which Jerome claimed a commission from Damasus, belongs with these experiments. Some early schemes, such as those for a history of his own times and more extensive translations from Origen, were quietly dropped in favour of the biblical opus.

Yet even after committing himself to his main task, Jerome continued to be an extraordinarily versatile writer. During the 380s he discovered that one literary form, the published 'familiar' letter, was particularly well suited to his purposes as freelance scholar, moralist and occasional dogmatist. His extant correspondence (over 150 items) includes matter of every kind: exhortation, instruction, consolation; satire, complaint, polemic; biography, panegyric – and more. The familiar letter was also his preferred medium for editorializing upon his work-in-progress, and as such a vital means of contact with his newly constituted public. When Jerome addressed letters to well-placed individuals in Africa, Italy, Spain and Gaul, he conscripted them as collaborators in a large-scale literary-religious enterprise. Thus, astonishingly, was he able for a time to make the town of Christ's nativity the centre of the Latin-reading Christian world.

Rufinus

If patristic confirmation were needed of Samuel Johnson's principle that literary judgments are by their nature comparative, the fortunes of Jerome and the companion of his youth, Rufinus, would provide it. When the first Christian *De Viris Illustribus* appeared in 392/3, the latter had still to make his literary début, else he might have received flattering mention in it. The notice given of him by Gennadius of Marseille, continuer of Jerome's catalogue in the second half of the fifth century, is carefully tilted in his favour, as if to redress a balance. 'Rufinus, presbyter of the church at Aquileia,' it begins, 'not least among the doctors of the Church, had an elegant talent for translating Greek into Latin and made a great part of Greek [Christian] literature accessible to Latin readers.'[10] The accompanying list of translations, which is not complete, refers in broad terms to works by Basil of Caesarea (monastic *Rule*, select *Homilies*),

Gregory of Nazianzus (select *Sermons* or *Speeches*), Eusebius of Caesarea (*Ecclesiastical History*, with two-book continuation by Rufinus), Pamphilus (book I of the *Apology for Origen*), Evagrius of Pontus (*Sentences* for monks and virgins), 'Clement of Rome' (pseudepigraphic *Recognitions* and *Letter to James*), 'Sixtus' (*Sentences*, the work of a pagan philosopher, Sextus, misattributed to a martyr-pope), and, reserved for last because of the number and importance of Rufinus' translations of this writer, Origen. 'Not all' of the Latin Origen is Rufinus' work, says Gennadius, but versions with translators' prefaces are his – unless they are by Jerome! As original works of Rufinus he lists a *Commentary on the Apostles' Creed*, an explanation of Jacob's *Benedictions of the Patriarchs* 'in the threefold sense, that is, the historical, moral and mystical', 'many letters exhorting to the fear of God' (not extant), and a two-volume *Apology* in response to a detractor. Gennadius tactfully omits the name of the detractor, whom he certainly knew to be Jerome.

For many years Jerome of Stridon and Rufinus, a native of nearby Concordia in northern Italy, led parallel lives. Schooled together in Rome by the best masters, both became adepts of an oriental-style Christian asceticism in the early 370s, briefly shared the monastic milieux of Aquileia, then pursued their vocations in the East. After eight years in Egypt, visiting the desert monks and studying in Alexandria where he listened to Didymus the Blind and read Origen, Rufinus moved to Jerusalem in 380, there to found a monastery on the Mount of Olives with the financial help of Melania the Elder, an aristocratic widow who befriended and patronized him as Paula did Jerome. As a place of hospitality for pilgrims arriving in the Holy Land from the West and others returning from Egypt, the Latin community on the Mount of Olives quickly became a vital site of Christian cultural exchange. It would have been a natural model for the similar community set up by Jerome and Paula in Bethlehem a few years later. Relations between the two establishments seem to have been cordial until 393 when Jerome, caught in the whirlwind of anti-Origenist propaganda unleashed by Epiphanius of Salamis, decided that his friend and fellow monk was not fierce enough against the works and ideas of a theologian whom they had both long venerated, and denounced him. Their quarrel was patched up in 397, only to break out again even more rancorously when Rufinus, having returned to Italy, claimed Jerome's translations of Origen as a warrant for his own version of that writer's treatise *On First Principles*.

As his friend and rival had eventually found fortune as an exile in the land of the Bible, so Rufinus now aimed to make himself useful as an importer of foreign stuffs into the West. The most precious commodity he could bring home with him, albeit already devalued by Jerome's panicky sale of stock, was the literary heritage of Origen. To explain why he translated the *Apology for Origen*, he tells the story of a Roman friend who dreamt that a ship came to port with answers to certain vexed questions on fate and divine providence; the next day, hearing that Rufinus had arrived from the East, he asked him for Origen's views, which were found conveniently excerpted in the *Apology*.[11] We are told that the translation of *On First Principles*, Origen's classic attempt to mark the limits for a biblical philosophy of creation and human destiny, was motivated by this friend's desire to read more from the same source.

Rufinus may in fact have needed little prompting to pursue an 'edition' of Origen which, even at this awkward juncture, would secure part of his work as a resource for Western theology. Unhappily for him, the editorial principles on which he chose to proceed – that Origen's texts had been interpolated by heretics, and that where he appeared to hold contradictory opinions, the 'orthodox' alternative alone was to be considered his[12] – were too easily ridiculed, and his appeal to Jerome's example in support of his practice too inflammatory, for the latter not to become involved. The ensuing polemics of Rufinus *Against Jerome* and Jerome *Against Rufinus*, in which neither party (certainly not Jerome!) precisely weighed the other's case, witness to the strength of feeling aroused among Latin readers by the contested legacy of Origen.[13] Nowadays they can be read as a disjoint commentary on the hazards of Christian literary activity at a time when episcopal and monastic zeal for orthodoxy, encouraged by the legislation of the militantly Christian emperor, Theodosius I, was threatening to narrow the scope of theological discourse to the hard-won certainties of the Nicene creed. By precipitating controversy over the terms on which Latin Christian writers adapted the texts of their Greek precursors, Rufinus ensured that his enterprise would not be mistaken for a simple extension of Jerome's. Versions from the Greek, adjusted where necessary for intelligibility or doctrinal respectability, were to be the staple of his literary production. In these works, as in those for which he claimed an author's rights,[14] he exhibits a many-sided literary personality. Exponent of the biblical theology of Origen before all else, he is also a skilful moralist in his own fashion and an imaginative narrator of Christian history.

Despite all difficulties, Origen claimed the lion's share of Rufinus' literary labour. In the decade from 400, he translated sets of this teacher's homilies for the whole Heptateuch except Deuteronomy, and others on selected psalms, the Song of Songs and 1 Samuel. Taken with Jerome's commentaries on the prophets, themselves heavily indebted to Alexandrian exegesis, these texts furnished a substantial Latin library on the Old Testament. At the same time, Rufinus' translation of Origen's great commentary on St Paul's Epistle to the

Romans (*c.* 405–6) gave fresh stimulus to discussions of destiny and free will that had been going on in Roman circles since the mid-390s and would shortly come to an issue in Augustine's clash with Pelagius.[15]

These and other literary works were carried out with the support of friends and patrons in Italy, notably in Rome and Aquileia, the two places where Rufinus chiefly resided in the years 397–408, before heading south in flight from Alaric's Goths.[16] Like Jerome, but with a less obvious regard for the processes of literary dissemination and publicity, he regularly gives the appearance of writing to commission or with a local readership in mind. Several of his minor translations, including Origen's homilies on Psalms 36–8 and the collection of moral maxims known as the *Sentences of Sextus*, are commended to women readers as instruction in Christian living. The 'moral' sense is likewise favoured in the threefold exposition of the *Benedictions of the Patriarchs*, written for Paulinus of Nola, as naturally it is too in the translations of Basil's monastic *Rule* (made for the monastery of Pinetum, near Rome) and the Evagrian *Sentences* for monks and virgins. If Jerome in his paraenetic writings at times displays an excessive flair for satire and pathos, the moralist Rufinus – like the dogmatist Rufinus of the *Commentary on the Apostles' Creed* – is invariably lucid, practical and compendious. Had they survived, his 'many' letters would doubtless have confirmed his proficiency as a teacher of ascetic piety.

The emphases and originality of Rufinus' activity as a purveyor of Greek cultural products to Latin Christian readers are well displayed in three narrative works, two of them histories. His translation of Eusebius' *Ecclesiastical History*, undertaken in 401 at the request of Bishop Chromatius of Aquileia as an antidote to the terror caused by the Gothic incursions into Italy, was the first significant addition to the Latin store of Christian historiography since Jerome's pioneering version of the *Chronicle* two decades earlier and would stand almost alone until joined by the *Tripartite History* compiled by Cassiodorus. Rufinus omits much of Eusebius' tenth book and compresses what remains of it into book 9; he also retouches the narrative in several places and adds two books of his own to bring the account down to the death of Theodosius the Great (395). His personal experience and concerns are reflected in the prominence given to events in Alexandria and to the trials and triumphs of Athanasius, whom he revered as confessor of the faith and successor of the martyrs.

Rufinus was as keen to associate the figure of the martyr with the office of Christian writer as Jerome had been, but is content as a rule to leave the association implicit. Stories of Antony and the desert monks in book 11 of the *Ecclesiastical History* provided a natural cue for the translation made soon afterwards of the *History of the Egyptian Monks*, a work which must have sharpened, where it did not cloy, the Western appetite for ascetic miracles whetted by Jerome's hagiography (already followed by Sulpicius Severus) and soon to be exploited to different effect by John Cassian, a fellow enthusiast with Rufinus for the Origenist monasticism of Evagrius of Pontus. As Latinized texts, both Rufinus' histories attest the desire to domesticate an ideal of dedicated, even heroic, Christian spirituality that he himself could claim to have seen realized in foreign lands. That the heroes of the histories were to be regarded as perfectly orthodox, even in cases where doubt was possible (e.g., the Egyptian monks expelled during the recent anti-Origenist purge), goes without saying. A similarly elevated and expansive view of orthodox Mediterranean Christianity commands the translation (*c.* 407) of the *(Pseudo-)Clementine Recognitions*, an elaborate disquisition on cosmology, theodicy and ethics, thinly disguised as sentimental romance. The preface speaks of the laborious transfer of 'goods from overseas', while the story of the future Pope Clement's journey to Caesarea in Palestine and his instruction there by St Peter would have offered at once a reassuring myth of Christian unity in doctrine and a satisfying analogue for the translator's own trade and travel beween Rome and the East.

Notes

1 *Ep.* 22.30 (addressed to the virgin Eustochium at Rome, *c.* 384). The scene is recounted as a vision experienced years earlier, at the outset of the writer's ascetic life.

2 *Ep.* 22.29 ('What has Horace to do with the Psalter, Virgil with the Gospels, Cicero with the Apostle?'), echoing Tertullian, *Praescr.* 7. Where Tertullian asks, 'What has *Athens* to do with Jerusalem?', his successor sets the Bible against three founders of the 'classical' Latin literature of Rome, itself a triumph of Roman Hellenism. As an exceptional Hellenist among westerners of his time, Jerome was conscious – more acutely than Ambrose, in advance of Rufinus – of the possibility of creating a 'classical' Christian literature in Latin by emulation of the Greeks.

3 H. Hagendahl, *Latin Fathers and the Classics: A Study on the Apologists, Jerome and Other Christian Writers*, 91ff.

4 *Ep.* 70 (to the Roman orator Magnus, *c.* 397), a model for many later such defences in the West. The use made by Jerome of the image of the captive woman of Deut. 21:10–13 as a figure for Christian appropriation of pagan learning would become standard, alongside Augustine's preferred image of the spoils of the Egyptians. Both images already served this purpose for Origen.

5 Reinhart Herzog, *Die Bibelepik der lateinischen Spätantike. Formgeschichte einer erbaulichen Gattung*, Bd. 1, 167ff.

6 E.g., *Ep.* 53.8, 17 (the Psalmist as 'our Simonides, Pindar and Alcaeus, our Horace, Catullus and Serenus'); E. R. Curtius, *European Literature and the Latin Middle Ages* (Princeton: Princeton University Press, 1953), 447.

7 H. F. D. Sparkes, 'Jerome as biblical scholar', *Cambridge History of the Bible*, I, ed. P. R. Ackroyd and C. F. Evans (Cambridge: Cambridge University Press, 1970), 510–41.

8 Pierre Jay, *L'exégèse de saint Jérôme d'après son Commentaire sur Isaïe.*

9 *Commentarius in Epistula Pauli ad Galatos* 3, praef. (*PL* 26, 427D). For the formal requirements of Jerome's notion of 'commentary', see Yves-Marie Duval's introduction to the commentary on Jonah (SC 323, 1985).

10 Gennadius, *Vir. Ill.* 17.

11 *Apol. c. Hier.* 1.11.

12 This is the position set forth in the prefaces to the translations of Pamphilus' *Apology* and of *On First Principles*, and in a monograph *On the Adulteration of the Books of Origen* appended by Rufinus to the former work. Jerome's rationale for a selective approach to Origen's oeuvre is first outlined in his *Epp.* 61 and 84.

13 The same context can be assumed for Rufinus' version of the anti-heretical *Dialogue of Adamantius*, falsely ascribed by him to Origen. For particulars, see E. Clark, *The Origenist Controversy: the cultural construction of an early Christian debate*, 121ff. (Jerome) and 159ff. (Rufinus).

14 For the distinction, see the epilogue to his translation of Origen's commentary on Romans (CCSL 20, ed. Simonetti (1961), 276–7), an important statement of his principles and programme as a translator.

15 Further versions of Origen's commentaries on St Paul were projected but never made.

16 For a detailed chronology, see C. P. Hammond, 'The Last Ten Years of Rufinus' Life and the Date of His Move South from Aquileia', *JTS* n.s. 28 (1977), 372–429. Rufinus died in Sicily in 411.

29

Augustine

HENRY CHADWICK

Aurelius Augustinus was born on 13 November 354 at Thagaste (now Souk-Ahras) in the Roman province of Numidia, North Africa, son of a small-time farmer, Patricius, a pagan until near his deathbed, and his Christian wife Mon(n)ica. Gifted in his grasp of Latin literature (Cicero, Sallust, Virgil and Terence he came to know virtually by heart), he studied at nearby Madauros, then at Carthage. Aged seventeen, following the then almost universal custom, he took to his bed and board a Carthaginian girl of low social status, and by her begat a son, Adeodatus, who turned out to be clever but died in adolescence. To his memory Augustine dedicated a dialogue, *De magistro* (the Teacher) on non-verbal communication. Aged eighteen he was profoundly influenced by Cicero's dialogue in defence of the study of philosophy, *Hortensius*, now extant only in fragmentary quotations; Cicero told him that philosophical study (of ethics) was indispensable to finding happiness, which was not achieved by power, honour, wealth or sex. At the time he was already sceptical about his mother's orthodox Christianity, especially offended by the morals of the Israelite patriarchs and the contradictory genealogies of Jesus. But Cicero moved him towards religion; he opted for the sect of theosophists, who followed the third-century gnostic, Mani, the 'Manichees', to whom he remained attached for virtually a decade. Mani reasoned that if God is good and evil is not done away, the supreme power must be less than omnipotent. Augustine thought the argument forceful as an explanation of the problem of evil. However, the pull of philosophical study took him to reading a Latin translation of the *Categories* of Aristotle, and in his twenties, as a self-employed teacher of public speaking at Carthage, he wrote a (lost) book on aesthetic theory, on Beauty and Proportion (*de pulchro et apto*), which may be judged from his own summary of its argument to reflect some knowledge of Neopythagorean musical theories. Mani was not philosophical.

Confidence in Mani was eroded by the total incompatibility of the explanation of eclipses with the best natural science of antiquity. Mani believed that indecisive cosmic battles in the celestial realm (which helped to explain the continuance of evil) aroused horror in the sun and moon which veiled their eyes from the horrible sight. Augustine thought that the ancient astronomers must be right, vindicated by their power to make correct predictions. He gradually moved towards scepticism and suspense of judgment. In the pursuit of truth, risks are improper. A stream of sceptical epistemology long remained an element in Augustine's mind; it is reflected in the discussion of time in *Confessions* 11. Disbelief in human capacity to grasp profound truth, however, is never far distant from a turning to divine revelation and authority. On that path, during his time as city professor of oratory at Milan (384–6), he became converted to Neoplatonism through a Platonic group in the city, some of whom were Christians. Moreover, Ambrose the bishop of Milan was not only a good preacher of much higher intelligence than any he had met in Africa but also a thinker whose sermons reflected reading in Plotinus and Porphyry. The psalm chants also gripped him. Platonizing thinking gave him a very different view of evil as the absence of good rather than a substantial entity.

At Milan influential friends welcomed him at their houses, and he nursed ambitions to become governor of a minor province, since such posts were given to people of high literary culture. But he lacked money. His son's mother, an obstacle to his secular career, was (with mutual pain) sent back to Carthage, vacating a place for a young wife with wealth. The girl was still under age, but in any event in July 386 Augustine became convinced of the emptiness of his ambitions, reinforced by the humiliations of having to ingratiate himself with powerful figures at the emperor's court (Milan being the Western Emperor's residence). Neoplatonic influences would not have helped him to adopt a highly positive view of the physical side of marriage. A fellow African told him of monks in the Western Church both in the suburbs of Milan and at Trier. In the garden of the Milan villa in tearful distress he heard the voice of a young child of indeterminate sex ('a boy or a girl') saying *Tolle lege*, 'take and read'. On a table lay a codex of St Paul's letters. The first words to meet his eye, Romans 13:13f., brought him to decision: he abandoned secular ambition (which ended the proposed marriage), and would resign from his professorship at the end of term a few weeks ahead, and enrol his name for baptism by Ambrose, 24/25 April 387, showing that he was not content to be a fellow-traveller as many intellectuals of the time were.

During the next months between conversion and baptism, in retreat with his mother and pupils at a country villa at Cassiciacum, he wrote philosophical tracts: a refutation of sceptical academics (*Contra academicos*), on the happy life (*De beata vita*) and the order of divine providence (*De ordine*), and Soliloquies

(*Soliloquia*: this last christianizing themes he had read in Porphyry). His mood at the time and after baptism was optimistic about the continuity between the liberal arts and philosophical faith. He wrote a grammar, textbooks of logic and rhetoric, and a work on music – concerning metre rather than pitch, but with a final book integrating music into the Platonizing world-view.

Return to North Africa was delayed by civil war between rival emperors. He used the time, living in Rome, to begin a series of anti-Manichee works: *Freedom of Choice* (*De libero arbitrio*) in three books, partly directed also at sceptics who denied its existence; *On the Morals of the Church and the Manichees*, vindicating the place of the ascetic life within the orthodox community, with some debt to Jerome's *Ep*. 22. Later came a critique of the Manichee doctrine that human beings have two souls, one good, one evil (*De duabus animabus*); the record of a disputation at Hippo on 29 August 392 with Fortunatus, a Manichaean priest who was driven out of tow by the authorities. Full-scale attacks on Manichee myths and criticisms of Scripture appeared about 395 and after: *Against Adimantus*, a disciple of Mani whose books catalogued antitheses between Old and New Testaments; against Mani's 'Fundamental Letter' (with the famous dictum: 'I would not have believed the gospel, if the authority of the catholic Church had not constrained me to do so'); against Faustus of Mileu, in twenty-two books written 398–400 in reply to a book by Faustus attacking Christian orthodoxy, especially the Jewish inheritance from the Old Testament, the morality of the patriarchs, Moses, and Solomon, but also the beliefs that Jesus was born of Mary and was crucified. Faustus thought the gospels interpolated after Jesus' time, and denied Pauline authorship of the Pastoral Epistles. Augustine's disillusioning encounters with Faustus played a part in emancipating him from Manichaeism.

In January 391 Augustine visited the harbour town of Hippo Regius (now Annaba in eastern Algeria) intending to found a monastery. The Greek-speaking bishop of Hippo, Valerius from Southern Italy, needed a Latin-speaking presbyter. He invited his congregation to coerce Augustine into accepting ordination. The radical change of life turned Augustine into a student of Scripture. Paul's Epistle to the Romans had been an influence in his conversion of 386. About 394 he produced an exposition of this letter and of that to the Galatians. Writing against the Manichees he defended the goodness of the created order of 'nature'. Pauline reading led him to the conviction that human nature can reach its end only by the help of divine grace.

Bishop Valerius wanted Augustine to succeed him and asked the senior bishop or primate of Numidia to come to Hippo and consecrate him. For a consecration twelve bishops were normally needed, but in at least one consecration in Numidia (perhaps Augustine's) only two bishops participated. His elevation to be bishop was controversial. People remembered his erotic adolescence, his Manichee years, his secular profession teaching pagan literature and oratory, his claim to have been baptized far away at Milan – without Ambrose making any reference to African bishops informed about his unsatisfactory past. It was contrary to canon law to be consecrated bishop of a see when the previous incumbent was still alive and in office. The most serious charge was that his monastic foundations, new in Africa, were cells for crypto-Manichees. Hence the importance of Augustine's numerous anti-Manichee writings, intended not only to win to orthodoxy the numerous friends he had carried with him to the Manichee conventicle, but also to vindicate his own renunciation of dualist heresy. His consecration was probably in 395.

Between 396 and 400 he wrote his *Confessions*, rapidly to be a best-seller in his lifetime, loved by some, repellent to others, but inevitably a classic of Western literature. Cast in the form of a prose-poem addressed to God but intended to be overheard by critical human ears, the work recounts his troubled youth and secular successes in obtaining teaching positions at Carthage, Rome and Milan. His mother was crucially influential in his gradual discovery that the catholic religion was not what he had once supposed. Monica had followed him to Milan, but died at Ostia on the return journey to Africa. A motive in the *Confessions* is to ask the reader to remember her in prayer.

The *Confessions* is full of anti-Manichee polemic and a further motive is to disavow his association with the sect. At the same time a series of passages in the work vindicate the act of faith against pagan or half-pagan critics who could not understand his decision to give up a successful career with high further prospects. 'Unless we take things on trust, we would achieve nothing in this life.' Therefore to trust in the authority of God mediated through Scripture and through the Church is in no way irrational. He twice declares that he had never doubted God's existence. In *De libero arbitrio*, already mentioned, he devoted much of the second of its three parts to an argument for the existence of God, which is in effect a demonstration that God is wholly incorporeal and outside space and time. The first part of this treatise answers determinists by arguing that if one wants to know whether or not freedom exists, the very wanting decides the issue, and is a condition of knowledge. It is a form of the *Cogito* argument, developed by Descartes: if you doubt, at least you cannot doubt that you are doubting.

The *Confessions* is not simple autobiography. The autobiographic matter, fascinating as it is, does not pretend to present a complete narrative. Augustine was recording those decisions or events that had resulted in his being what he had become as bishop, events in which human foresight and intention played virtually no part. After Monica's death and burial at the end of book 9, book 10 (twice the length of any other part) analyses memory and the subconscious. Book 11 examines eternity and time, the latter being less objective than is ordinarily supposed. The successiveness of things is part of the pain from which eternal salvation is a deliverance. Book 12 offers a synthesis of Platonic and Christian ideas of divine creation. Book 13 discovers in Genesis 1 an allegory of the Church and sacraments and a symbolic mirror of pastoral care. The underlying link between the last four books and the first nine may be discerned in the theme of the soul wandering from God but in tears being led back home to its Maker, a microcosm of the cosmos itself as understood by Plotinus and the Neoplatonists.

Donatism

Since the great persecution of Diocletian, the North African churches were split. The government had demanded the surrender of sacred books and vessels and vestments, with the suspension of all corporate worship. Rigorists judged bishops who surrendered to the authorities guilty of unforgivable pollution. Schism came when a new bishop of Carthage, Caecilian, was consecrated by a bishop rumoured to have retained his see by handing over the Bible to the police. Caecilian won support at Rome and in Gaul, but Roman support was ineffective among the Numidian churches since the bishop of Rome had been among those compromised in the persecution. The rigorists were soon led by Donatus, rival bishop of Carthage. When Augustine came to Hippo almost all Christians in the city were Donatist. In 394–5 he composed an anti-Donatist chant to be recited by the people who would thereby learn the origin of the split. This inaugurated a massive series of polemical tracts, repeatedly insistent that Scripture speaks of a worldwide universal Church, not a Church limited to Africa: *Against the letter of Parmenian* (Donatist bishop of Carthage), *Against the letter of Petilian* (Donatist bishop of Cirta, a convert from the Catholic community and able lawyer), *On baptism* (though baptism is inseparable from the Church, a baptized person can be separated, yet some baptized outside the Church are in intention baptized within; he distinguishes validity from efficacy and both from the worthiness of the minister). In 405–6 he wrote a retort to a Donatist critic of his polemic, Cresconius, an educated teacher of literature, and exploited the fissiparousness of the Donatist community, especially a group adhering to an ultra-rigorist named Maximian who refused to recognize Parmenian's successor, Primianus, in the see of Carthage.

In Numidia Donatists were in a majority, and were supported by bands of peasants wielding clubs, generalled by their rural clergy and intimidating the agrarian population. Donatists called them 'militants' (*agonistici*), Catholics called them *circumcelliones*. Augustine was once saved from a murderous ambush because his guide took the wrong road. The implacable hostility of the Donatists moved Augustine from conciliatory ecumenism to belief in moderate state coercion as the only way of restraining the savagery of circumcellion attacks. One such attack in southern Numidia was so ferocious as to move the emperor to require by edict that Donatists unite with the Catholic Church. In June 411, a conference at Carthage compelled the two episcopates to state their case before an imperial conciliator. Augustine was the spokesman for one, with Petilian for the other. The minutes of the conference in large part survive. Augustine wrote a popular summary of the proceedings (*Breviculus collationis cum Donatistis*), and a plea to the dissidents after the conference (*Contra partem Donati post gesta*). The Donatists were confident they had won the argument and lost only the verdict.

A few intransigent Donatist bishops could not bring themselves to yield. Augustine in 418 tried vainly to reconcile the Donatist ex-bishop Emeritus with a public disputation in church. The last of his anti-Donatist writings is against Gaudentius, Donatist bishop of Thamagadi (Timgad), who had shut himself and his flock in his large church and declared that, if they were molested, they would set the building on fire.

The Pelagian controversy

Pelagius, a British ascetic (and the earliest extant writer from Britain), arrived in Rome about 400 and was valued as a spiritual director by some influential families. He was shocked by the lax attitude of Roman Christians to the high demands of gospel morality, and especially when a bishop condoned an easy-going attitude to sexual faults by quoting Augustine's *Confessions* with his repeated citation of Wisdom of Solomon 8:21: 'no one can be continent except God grants it . . .' Pelagius taught that God has given commandments, and it must be possible for human beings to keep them – of course with divine help through good teaching. He felt it dangerously enervating to read in Augustine that the only thing of our own which we contribute to our salvation is the sin from which we need redemption; or that the condemnation of those not elect is a manifestation of pure justice. Pelagius stated his alternative estimate of human nature in a book, *On Nature*, written at Rome about 406. Some years passed before a copy reached Augustine.

Augustine was only slowly drawn into controversy with Pelagius and those who supported him in Italy. Nevertheless, Pelagius' criticisms reached him and were felt to constitute a negation of everything presupposed in the *Confessions* in which he had stated his case for being a Christian. Pelagius was much respected at Rome. An admirer of Pelagius named Caelestius visited Carthage in 411 and created a storm. Caelestius was accused of teaching that mortality was natural, not a punishment for the sin of Adam's fall, which in any event damaged only himself, not his posterity; that at birth infants are as Adam and Eve were before the Fall; that before the time of Christ there had been sinless saints who got to heaven by keeping the Law. But Caelestius affirmed that it is right to give baptism to infants. Augustine was not present at Caelestius' examination. He would later observe that the unstated issue was whether or not baptism cleansed from original sin.

Caelestius' opinions were derived from a tract written by a Syrian named Rufinus (not Rufinus of Aquileia). This work provoked Augustine to his first anti-Pelagian treatise, *On the deserts of sinners and forgiveness and on the baptism of infants* (*De peccatorum meritis et remissione et de baptismo parvulorum,* written 411–12). The style is a remonstrance with brothers who are mistaken, not an onslaught on heretics. But their errors include denials that Adam's sin entailed corruption and death for his descendants, that infants are in some sense sinful (in the *Confessions* he had portrayed the selfishness and irrational anger of tiny children), and that sexuality, though faultless in marriage, is in itself not 'pure nature'. Augustine concedes that a sinless life is possible by grace and by free choices given by grace, but except for Christ and Mary there has never been a wholly sinless person.

In 412 he wrote *On the Spirit and the Letter*, vigorously disowning the charge that he was eliminating responsible decision in the act of faith by making everything divine grace. Yet grace grants not only the will but also the power to do God's will. In 413–15 he wrote a reply to Pelagius' book *On Nature* entitled *On Nature and Grace*. Pelagius had moved to Jerusalem, and Augustine alerted Jerome at Bethlehem to the dangers. Orosius from Spain travelled to the Holy Land to represent Augustine's position at a synod in Jerusalem, but disastrously conveyed the impression that even with God's help sin is unavoidable. At a synod in Diospolis in December 415, Pelagius was acquitted of heresy, an event alarming to Augustine. After obtaining a copy of the acts of this synod through Cyril of Alexandria, he wrote an attack on Pelagius' integrity in his evidence to his examiners. Pelagius' claim to affirm the need for grace was set aside as mendacious. From this moment onwards the controversy became bitter, and until his death in 430 Augustine never dropped the issue. Pelagius himself ceased to play a part, but the Pelagian cause was taken up by a clever bishop, Julian of Eclanum (near Benevento).

Two questions were thrust into the foreground: could one say that God predestinates the non-elect to hell, in particular unbaptized babies not yet capable of repentance and faith or of freely chosen acts? And could one say that the transmission of original sin from Adam is passed on through heredity, i.e. through the reproductive process, and does this mean that sexual acts carry with them a taint of impurity even in Christian partners? Augustine mitigated the force of the first question by holding that, though God has foreknowledge that many do not respond to the call of faith, nevertheless he allows this freedom.

Julian of Eclanum was not the only critic to be severely critical of Augustine's opinions about both predestination and sexuality. Monks at Hadrumetum thought he abolished moral responsibility, and were appalled by Augustine's frequent dictum: 'In crowning our merits, God rewards only his own gifts.' In Gaul, John Cassian was unimpressed by Augustine's exegesis of 1 Timothy 2:4, 'God wills all to be saved', to mean that a number of representatives of different races or types will be brought to salvation by divine election. To Vincent of Lérins, Augustinianism seemed a dangerous innovation and a departure from the universal consensus of faith. Augustine was defended, however, by Prosper of Aquitaine and by Caesarius of Arles.

Augustine's defence of his understanding of sexuality is in the two books, *On marriage and concupiscence* (418–21). In a work, *On the nature and origin of the soul* in four books (419), he sought to avoid the Manichee implications of attributing original sin to physical heredity (traducianism). He wrote four books *Against two letters of the Pelagians* (419–20), six books *Against Julian* (421–2), and six further books of an uncompleted work *Against Julian* (*Opus imperfectum contra Julianum*, 428–30). The predestination issue was discussed in *On rebuke and grace* (*De correptione et gratia*, 426–7), *On the predestination of the Saints* (429), and *On the gift of perseverance* (428–9). Julian of Eclanum judged that each successive defence revealed an unreconstructed Manichaeism at Augustine's heart.

God the Holy Trinity

Not long after completing the *Confessions*, in which at one point he had outlined an analogy to trinitarian language in being, knowing, and willing, three aspects of one person, Augustine embarked on a large work *De Trinitate*. The first seven books record the teaching of Scripture and the traditional language of Latin theology since Tertullian. From book 8 to the end in book 15 he develops the psychological analogy sketched in the *Confessions*, but with deeper elaboration. If humanity is made in the image of God, one can expect to find vestiges of the divine nature in the human mind. A succession of triads is reviewed in an ascending sequence to that of lover, beloved, and the love between them, and on to memory, self-knowledge, and self-love, finally in book 15 to the intimate link between thought, the expression of thought in words, and the will contained in the utterance.

At the same time Augustine was not claiming that his analogies do more than illustrate the rationality of a unity which is also a triad. His work had the subsidiary motive of answering the pagan mockery of sophisticated critics who laughed at trinitarian terms as meaningless nonsense. To that end he was able to exploit analogous language in Plotinus and Porphyry.

A second motive in the work was to provide a refutation of Arianism, which had long retained adherents in Italy and Illyricum (the Balkans) and remained the form of Christianity followed by the Goths who already constituted the imperial army. Augustine wanted to destroy the notion that the Trinity is a graded hierarchy with three distinct levels of deity. His stress therefore lies throughout on the unity of God, and distinctions in the Trinity are not of being but of relation. An influential Arian thesis subordinated the Holy Spirit to the Father and the Son and exploited the text of John 15:26 (the Spirit proceeds from the Father) to imply inferiority as compared with the begottenness of the Son. Here Neoplatonism, with its graded triad of hypostases – the One, Nous, and the Soul – was of no help to Augustine. He saw that to avert Arianism it would be necessary to affirm that the Son participated in the proceeding of the Spirit from the Father, a doctrine in which he was anticipated by Hilary of Poitiers.

A revision of the Nicene creed of 325 was associated, probably correctly, with the Council of Constantinople of 381, which ended Arian domination of the Greek churches and required assent to the Son's identity of essence with the Father (*homoousios*). That revised creed was designed to justify the full share of the Holy Spirit in the equality of the divine Trinity, as the giver of life and Lord, inspirer of the prophets, 'proceeding from the Father', equal with Father and Son in the baptismal invocation. Augustine betrays no sign of having heard of either the council of 381 or its creed. He was not at the time a baptized Christian anyway, and many of the non-dogmatic decisions of that council were unwelcome at Rome and Milan. He therefore had no reason to think his proposition that the Spirit proceeds from both Father and Son as from one *principium* or first cause could be a source of difficulty or offence. In the middle years of the seventh century it was a shock to the West to discover that the Greek East regarded the Augustinian doctrine as a gross irreverence to a council with ecumenical standing. No Latin bishop had attended the Council of Constantinople in 381.

The City of God

The City of God in twenty-two books had its origin in painful questions about divine providence and protection in 'Christian times' after the sack of Rome in August 410 by Alaric and his Gothic army. The work as a whole is a defence of Christianity against pagan charges that abandonment of the old gods had brought celestial anger, so that the Church was responsible for the political and economic disasters. Augustine first demonstrates from Roman history that the cult of the gods had not brought prosperity, and from the Platonic philosophers that polytheism had not helped anyone to eternal life. A pessimism in the estimate of human history ('what are governments but large-scale banditry?') was reinforced for him by Sallust's history of the Roman republic. The triviality of Roman religion is shown from the vast learning of Varro (of whose writings Augustine is a major witness). The second half of the work from book 11 onwards presents a picture of all history from the standpoint of two 'cities', that is, two societies symbolically represented as Babylon and Jerusalem, which at some moments (not consistently) appear to be the Roman Empire and the Church respectively. The story is divided into six epochs comparable to the ages of man or humanity, culminating in the sixth age, which is that of Christ. The seventh age lies beyond history. But in historical time the two 'cities' are mixed together with a common interest in justice and peace, and there is therefore a positive evaluation of the order and beneficent legal system of the Empire.

Works of exegesis

The Literal Commentary on Genesis in twelve books (404–14) dissatisfied its author, much of the work being in debate with the unnamed Porphyry; that is, the work is concerned with Neoplatonic criticism of the biblical idea of creation as an actual fact rather than a mythical symbol. In this question lay the latent question about the eternity of the world, also acutely discussed in the *City of God* 12. Augustine's central proposition is that the eternal God is outside time, whereas the world is marked by contingency and successiveness; souls come into being, so why is a beginning for the world difficult?

The Harmony of the Evangelists (404) was also directed against pagan criticism, the first book especially answering those who disliked the Church but admired Jesus and his teaching.

Biblical exegesis was presented mainly in the form of sermons, notably those on the Psalms and on the Gospel and First Epistle of John where the passion of the pastor takes precedence over the controversialist. As a presbyter he wrote an exposition of the Sermon on the Mount with some anti-Manichee content. After 404 he wrote a series of brief comments on texts of Matthew and Luke: the *Quaestiones Evangeliorum*.

Shorter treatises

Short works to meet pastoral demands are a substantial list. *On 83 Various Questions* gathered together matters discussed in Augustine's community at Thagaste before he was ordained. Two books answered questions from Simplicianus, Ambrose's successor as bishop of Milan, concerning the exegesis of the Epistle to the Romans and the doctrine that grace precedes good works and even faith, and also concerning the 'spirit', good or evil, in 1 Samuel.

Short treatises include a reply to pagans mocking Christianity's demand for belief in what cannot be seen (*De fide rerum quae non videntur*); a record of alarmed dissent from bishops who were accepting for baptism men who had not first shed concubines (*De fide et operibus*); a summary on faith, hope and charity (*Enchiridion* for Laurentius); an exhortation to understand Christian conflict as a struggle against Satan (*De agone Christiano*); how to teach catechism to uneducated people (*De catechizandis rudibus*); ascetic exhortations (*De sancta virginitate*, on the nun as Christ's bride, and *De opera monachorum*, critical of monks neglecting manual work); a defence of marriage (*De bono conjugali*) and of the legitimacy, though not the public honour, of second or more marriages (*De bono viduitatis*). His rejection of remarriage for the innocent party in a divorce was felt to be rigid, even 'inhuman' (*De adulterinis conjugiis*). Of two treatises on lying, the first (*De mendacio*) discusses arguments for white lies in certain circumstances as well as considerations against them. The second (*Contra mendacium*), written for Consentius of Menorca in 420 and occasioned by the Priscillianist justification of reserve and obfuscation, is absolutist in rejection.

A short work on divination (*De divinatione daemonum*) was occasioned by questions from Christians who observed that in at least some cases soothsayers, astrologers, and fortune-tellers succeed in making correct predictions. The destruction of the great temple of Serapis at Alexandria in 391 had been correctly forecast (in this report Augustine is supported by the pagan historian Eunapius who also knew the story). Christians might not be sorry that the imperial government had forbidden all pagan sacrifices. But some were impressed by accurate forecasts, and were tempted to think that if the Old Testament sacrifices were legitimate for the Hebrews, then pagan sacrifices could be allowed to their polytheistic neighbours. Augustine had to be content to reply that the daimons who inspired divination were evil spirits, and that they were known to make mistakes.

A treatise on care for the dead (*De cura pro mortuis gerenda*) was an answer to Paulinus of Nola who hoped for confirmation of the popular view that to be buried in close proximity to a saint is advantageous to the soul of the departed. Paulinus did not get what he expected. Augustine granted unreservedly that prayer for the faithful departed is the universal custom of the Church, but could provide no compensation for evil lives. 'Fine funerals are to comfort the living, not to help the dead.' (Elsewhere Augustine was sure that the 'saving sacrifice' of the eucharist is powerful intercession for the dead.) But the bodies of believers deserve respect, and to bury them near a saint is a kind of affectionate prayer. It is the prayer which is valuable, not the location of the tomb. One can pray anywhere.

A treatise on Christian teaching (*De doctrina Christiana*), begun early in his time at Hippo and completed near the end of his life, is in four books, the last of which is concerned with the application of Cicero's advice for orators to the needs of a Christian preacher. The first three books concern the interpretation of Scripture, the key principle being love to God and one's neighbour. The work, one of his most interesting and important, enquires into the degree to which secular human culture can help in exegesis: history, natural science, mathematics, logic and philosophy being deemed more of divine than human creation. The third book minimizes the role of allegory, but allows that it is essential for scandalous texts such as the morality of the patriarchs. An issue explicitly raised in the second book is the relation of words to the reality that they signify. Another is the formulation of objective principles of hermeneutic; in that he was helped by the *Book of Rules* of the dissenting Donatist, Tyconius.

The trained Latin orator in Augustine comes to the fore in *De Doctrina Christiana*, as also in the *Confessions*. He was a master of the language, and many sentences contain unmarked verbal reminiscences of Cicero, Virgil, Terence or Sallust. Although he found long sentences of many lines hard to control, terse enigmatic antitheses received masterly formulation. The *Confessions* and *De Trinitate* illustrate his psychological power of introspection and rare ability to articulate feelings. The philosophical tracts of Plotinus taught him that the will is free only when directed towards the good, but that it is fettered by evil.

Letters and sermons

The numerous surviving letters include some substantial treatises, in effect open letters or even manifestos. Virtually all provide a brilliant light for the history of the African churches in Augustine's time (this is especially true of the collection of letters discovered by J. Divjak and published by him in 1981). Of the many thousands of sermons which he preached, about a thousand survive, and these often contain evidence of social history as well as of theology and Christian practice. Polemic against Donatists and, after 419, Pelagians can loom large in the homilies. Manichees seldom receive more than a passing stab, which suggests that the sect was not strong in Hippo or Carthage. The sermons are often very personal statements, and contain autobiographical details. While some of the sermons were carefully edited by Augustine for publication, the majority survive because they were taken down by the private enterprise of shorthand writers, who probably made a modest income by selling copies to less eloquent bishops in the Numidian countryside. It was not Augustine's normal custom to use a written and carefully prepared script. He preached on the lections appointed for the Sunday or saint's commemoration and, if the reader happened to read a lection other than that which he had expected, he still preached on the passage read, not the thoughts which he had prepared. In consequence, his sermons tend to follow the stream of consciousness suggested by the texts read from the Latin Bible.

During his lifetime Jerome produced the revision of the barbarous Old Latin version of Scripture. Augustine knew both texts. He had a painful correspondence with Jerome, then a monk at Bethlehem, about his new version, and also about his interpretation of the quarrel between Peter and Paul (Gal. 2:11ff.) as play-acting, a view that for Augustine undermined apostolic authority.

Retractationes and conclusion

Towards the end of his long life Augustine reviewed his literary output in a work of reappraisals (*Retractationes*). Since the order in which the works are reviewed is more or less chronological, this book is of crucial importance for the dating of his writings. The title cannot be translated 'Retractions', since about 40 per cent consists of argument vindicating what he had written against critics. He regretted the degree to which he had made concessions to the Platonists in his early writings. (As early as the *Confessions* he was writing self-critically about the philosophical dialogues composed on the basis of discussions at Cassiciacum before his baptism, regarding them as too urbane and secular in tone.) The production of this work presupposes awareness of the enormously wide public which his writings had acquired. He had in fact set out to restate the Christian faith for the Latin West and thereby became one of the most influential figures in the history of ideas in Western culture.

Transmission

The manuscript tradition of Augustine's writings is anything but monolithic. For major works such as *Confessions* and the *City of God* the manuscripts are numerous, especially because of lively controversy about predestination and about the eucharist in Carolingian times. For some works manuscripts survive which were written almost during his lifetime, and one manuscript of *De Doctrina Christiana* 1–3, at St Petersburg, was probably written before his death in 430. The oldest manuscript of the *Confessions* in the National Library at Rome (cod. 2099, called Sessorianus) is probably of the sixth century, but has idiosyncratic readings that are not likely to be correct. A seventh-century manuscript in the Vatican Library (3375) contains a valuable anthology of his various writings compiled for a monastery near Naples. The *City of God* is also found in particularly early witnesses, a Verona manuscript XXVIII (26) was written during his lifetime; manuscripts at Lyon and in Paris (from Corbie) are not much later. Manuscripts of *De Trinitate* are not earlier than the ninth century, the National Library at Paris being rich in its holdings. But for minor works the manuscript tradition is much less rich, and for some of the letters and sermons only one or two manuscripts are known to survive.

30

John Chrysostom and the Antiochene School to Theodoret of Cyrrhus

ANDREW LOUTH

Antioch was one of the great cities of the Mediterranean world, ranking alongside Alexandria, Rome, Carthage and, after its foundation in 330, Constantinople. It had a large Jewish population, and was one of the earliest centres of Christianity outside Palestine: it was there that the term 'Christian' was first used (Acts 11:26). It was mentioned, along with Alexandria and Rome, in canon 6 of the Council of Nicaea, as a city whose bishop had some form of primatial (later to be called patriarchal) authority. In addition to its civic and ecclesiastical pre-eminence, Antioch was a centre of learning, especially in rhetoric: according to Libanios, professor of rhetoric in Antioch from 354, Athens and Antioch 'held aloft the torch of rhetoric', Athens for Europe and Antioch for Asia. The traditions of paganism, too, were strong in Antioch, and not simply at a popular level: Libanios was notable in the late fourth century for his adherence to the old religion, and Julian the Apostate's brief campaign to restore paganism was focused in Antioch where he was resident from the end of June 362 until 5 March 363, when he marched east against Persia – and to his death. The vernacular language of the hinterland of Antioch, reaching eastwards through Coele Syria to the river Euphrates and beyond, was Syriac, which by the end of the fourth century had developed its own rich Christian culture, which was not without influence on the Hellenistic culture of the Christians of Antioch.

Even such a brief sketch gives an impression of the complex background of Christian Antioch, which, for rather more than a century from the middle of the fourth, fostered a remarkable group of Christian thinkers and ascetics. They are frequently grouped together as the 'Antiochene School', but this term suggests an institutional identity that is inappropriate, as well as obscuring differences between them and other influences upon them. With the exception of St John Chrysostom, this whole group was condemned, either in person or in their writings, for dividing the person of Christ ('Nestorianism'). This has had two unfortunate consequences for our understanding their thinking: first, many of their writings have not survived, since they were regarded as tainted with heresy, and secondly, it has given rise to a tendency to focus on their Christological teaching (made worse by the fact that many of the surviving fragments address Christological matters). This latter tendency may well distort the balance of their teaching, since it could be argued that Christology was much less central to their teaching than it was to their victorious opponents, which may further explain why they were so easily wrong-footed in the controversy.

Diodore of Tarsus

It is necessary to begin with Diodore of Tarsus, although mention should perhaps be made of a remote ancestor of the 'Antiochene School', Eustathius, bishop of Antioch at the time of the Council of Nicaea, a determined opponent of Arianism, deposed shortly after the council. Only one of his works is extant, *On the Witch of Endor against Origen*, but even that, both in its attack on Origen's allegorical exegesis for depriving Scripture of its historical character, and in the Attic purity of its style (he contrives a complete absence of hiatus), foreshadows characteristics of later Antiochenes, and his criticism of Arius, in one of the fragments preserved, for denying Christ a human soul, points to the central concern of Antiochene Christology.

Diodore was a native of Antioch where he learnt his theology, though he had also studied rhetoric at Athens, as we know from Julian the Apostate. Later he led an ascetic school (ἀσκητήριον) outside Antioch, where among his disciples he counted the young John Chrysostom and Theodore of Mopsuestia (Socrates, *HE* 6.3). As a layman, he, together with Flavian (later bishop of Antioch), had led the pro-Nicene movement in Antioch. By the time John studied with him he had been ordained priest. He was exiled by the Arian Emperor Valens in 372, after whose death in 378 he became bishop of Tarsus in Cilicia. He was present at the Second Œcumenical Council of Constantinople in 381, where he was named one of the inspectors of orthodoxy, and died round about 394. In the next century Cyril of Alexandria attacked him as the source of Nestorianism: he was condemned at a local council in Constantinople in 499 and, by implication, in the condemnation of the 'Three Chapters' at the Fifth Œcumenical Council in 553. In his time, however, he was regarded as a great exegete and teacher of orthodoxy. As the principal opponent in Antioch of Julian's attack on Christianity during his residence there, he attracted the emperor's anger. He was an immensely prolific writer, composing both biblical commentaries and attacks on paganism and Christian heresies, especially varieties of what he regarded as Arianism. All that has survived are fragments in the catenae on the Hexateuch and the Pauline Epistles. Recently a complete commentary on the Psalms has been discovered, which its editor ascribes to Diodore. In his exegesis he avoided allegory, and is said to have written a treatise on the difference between *theoria* (as he termed the deeper meaning of Scripture, based on its historical sense) and allegory.

John Chrysostom

Unlike most of his fellow Antiochenes, though like Nestorius, John Chrysostom ended his life under a cloud: in exile, deposed from his see of Constantinople. But unlike all his fellow Antiochenes, posterity has looked favourably on him: just over thirty years after his death, his relics were brought back to Constantinople, venerated by emperor and patriarch, and placed in the Church of the Holy Apostles. He came to be ranked with St Basil the Great and St Gregory the Theologian as one of the 'universal teachers' of the Church. The learned ninth-century patriarch of Constantinople, Photius, praised him for the 'clarity and purity' of his style, his 'brilliant fluency' which displayed 'a wealth of ideas and a profusion of apt examples', but especially 'because he always, in every sermon, made it his aim to benefit the audience, giving no weight . . . to other considerations, . . . and . . . was quite unconcerned if he gave the impression that certain concepts escaped his attention or that he was not trying to penetrate the deeper meaning of the text'.[1] For such reasons, John Chrysostom's writings were immensely popular with posterity. Very many of his writings survive, and indeed much survives, by attribution to Chrysostom, that is not his, including a long Latin commentary on Matthew that is a precious example of Arian exegesis (of the fourth or fifth century: it is not clear whether the Latin text is the original or a translation from the Greek).

John was born in Antioch around 349. There is much that is disputed about his early years, but he certainly studied rhetoric under Libanios and may have been Diodore's disciple, both in theology and asceticism. He seems to have fled from ordination to the priesthood (such is the obvious interpretation of what he says in his treatise, *On Priesthood*, though this has been disputed) and spent two years in the mountains near Antioch, living an ascetic life under the guidance of a hermit. He returned to Antioch and was made deacon by early 381, and priest in 386. From 386–97 it was his task to preach, principally at the Golden Church, Antioch's cathedral. In 397 he was called to the capital to succeed Nectarius as bishop of Constantinople. His advancement excited the annoyance of Theophilus, bishop of Alexandria, which was experiencing increasing encroachment on its hitherto pre-eminent authority in the East by the growing prestige of Constantinople as imperial capital. Theophilus took advantage of John's apparent support for a group of Egyptian monks, the Tall Brothers, whom he had excommunicated for Origenism, and contrived to have John deposed at the Synod of the Oak, a suburb of Chalcedon, in 403. John was exiled, then restored, but finally, after Pentecost 404, exiled for good. He died at Comana in Pontus on 14 September 407, while on the way from Cucusus in Lesser Armenia, where he had spent three years, to Pityus, a remote spot on the Black Sea.

During his nearly twenty years of active ministry as priest and bishop, John preached several times a week: not surprisingly, the overwhelming bulk of his extant works consists of sermons and commentaries on Scripture. These exist both as systematic exposition of scriptural works in the form of series of homilies, and as individual sermons (or shorter series) on particular texts or passages. Even where the commentary survives in a form other than that of homilies (in the case of both the Psalms and the Epistle to the Galatians, they are described as ἑρμηνείαι, 'interpretations'), there can be little doubt that the commentary represents either material to be used in sermons, or possibly a writing up in the form of a commentary of what had been delivered as a series of sermons. For the Old Testament, there are two series of homilies on Genesis, one of nine sermons dealing with the early chapters, and a series of sixty-seven, which constitute a complete commentary; a series of 'interpretations' of fifty-eight selected psalms; six homilies on Isaiah 6, as well as an extended commentary (Isa. 2:2–Isa. 54, but omitting Isa. 21–30) which exists complete in Armenian, and for Isaiah 2:2–8:10 in the original (as ἑρμηνείαι); and a verse-by-verse commentary (very definitely not homiletic) on Job. For the New Testament, there is a series of ninety homilies on Matthew, of eighty-eight homilies (all very brief) on John, of fifty-five on the Acts of the Apostles, and commentaries (mainly in the form of homilies) on all the Pauline Epistles, including the Pastoral Epistles and Hebrews. We are told that the homilies on Genesis were delivered during Lent, and the homilies on Acts during Paschaltide: this is the earliest evidence for these books being appointed to be read in those seasons. John's exegesis is straightforward, intended to elucidate difficulties in the text, whether difficulties of grammar, syntax, linguistic meaning or historical sequence: he does not use difficulties as an excuse for (or sign of the need for) allegorical exegesis. John's comments, especially on the Greek New Testament, are still of great value, for he, unlike us, spoke the language in which it is written: when he tells us, for example, that the otherwise unknown Greek word ἐπιούσιον in the Lord's Prayer means 'daily' (ἐφήμερον), we should take him seriously. Although he avoids allegory, he is not blind to Scripture's deeper meaning, which he, in common with other Antiochenes, calls θεωρία, contemplation, and sees not as a substitute for the literal meaning, but a further level of meaning. In general this further level of meaning is a matter of a moral lesson (messianic prophecy is, for John, literal, as is the occasionally abstruse dogmatic meaning John finds in prophetic texts). John's moralism is, however, tempered by his sense of awe before God's disclosure of himself in Scripture and the history of salvation. It is not by chance that he returned several times to Isaiah's vision in the Temple, recorded in Isaiah 6.

There are other series of homilies that need to be mentioned. The homilies against the Jews were delivered in 386 and 387 (he broke off the sequence of sermons on Genesis during Lent to deliver some of them); they are evidence of the continuing attraction to the Antiochene Christians of Judaism. The Homilies on the Statues are a series of sermons given in Antioch in 387, during the embassy of his aged bishop Flavian to the Emperor Theodosius to plead for Antioch, threatened with civil annihilation, after the overthrow of imperial statues during riots against the imposition of a special tax. These immensely vivid sermons reveal John's power of oratory, and the way he consoled and warned the people who flocked to hear him. Another remarkable series of sermons are those *On the Unknowability of God*, which in a popular way stated the orthodox case against Eunomianism by evoking the unknowability of God's awesome majesty, drawing on the developing angelology of the Church, and giving a vivid picture of the atmosphere of religious reverence in which the eucharistic liturgy should be celebrated. Also recently discovered are two series of catechetical sermons, one of four and the other of eight homilies, which are important, not just for John's catechesis, but also for the evidence they give of the ceremonies of initiation (baptism, with its accompanying rites, and first communion) in Antioch at the end of the fourth century.

One of John's most interesting works is his treatise *On Priesthood*, written 390/1 and beginning with an account of his early years and a defence of his flight from ordination by Bishop Meletios of Antioch. It is a lively and compelling work, giving insight into both John's nature and his exalted understanding of the priesthood. It draws on Gregory Nazianzen's earlier work *On Priesthood*, also occasioned by his flight (in this case after ordination), but takes the unusual form of a dialogue with his friend Basil, whom he left in the lurch to face Bishop Meletios alone.

Besides all this, there are ascetic works, belonging to various stages of John's life, mainly in the form of encouraging others, or meeting the attacks of those less enamoured of the ascetic life than he. There is also a collection of 242 letters, to which need to be added various other letters, mainly relating to the events that led to his exile. *Epp.* 1–17 constitute a special group of letters to the deaconess Olympias, who was close to John during his time at Constantinople, and deeply shaken by his exile. To this final period in exile belong various other works: a letter from exile, in which he meditates on various biblical examples of suffering, and which forms a kind of introduction to his last work, his treatise *On Providence*, in which in the extreme conditions of his exile he reflects on the nature of providence, and the value of such trials. Both these works were addressed to his friends in Constantinople, and especially to the distressed Olympias. These latter works can be seen as an extended commentary on John's habitual exclamation – and final words: 'Glory to God for everything!'

Theodore of Mopsuestia

Like John, Theodore was born in Antioch and studied there, having Libanios as his teacher of rhetoric, and Diodore as his ascetical and theological master. However, he abandoned this life to become a lawyer and marry. John, in his early letter *To the fallen Theodore*, recalled him to the ascetic life. About 383 Theodore was ordained priest, and in 392 consecrated bishop of Mopsuestia. He died in 428 a revered figure, 'the great exponent of the Scriptures'. Cyril of Alexandria accused him, with Diodore, of being behind Nestorius' heresy. His writings constituted one of the 'Three Chapters', on the basis of which he was condemned at the Fifth Œcumenical Council in 553.

Of his extensive work of commentary – he commented on nearly all the books of the Bible – very little survives, and that mainly in translation, into Latin (for there was little enthusiasm in the West for the condemnation of the 'Three Chapters') and into Syriac (spoken in lands lost to the Byzantine Empire barely two hundred years after his death). The only work to survive in Greek is his commentary on the Twelve Minor Prophets. Substantial fragments survive of his commentary on the Psalms, and these have been supplemented by the recently discovered Latin translation of most of this commentary by Julian of Eclanum.[2] For the rest of the Old Testament there are a few fragments. In the case of the New Testament, his commentary on St John's Gospel survives complete in Syriac, and commentaries on several of the Pauline epistles survive in Latin (Gal., Eph., Phil., Col., 1 and 2 Thess., 1 and 2 Timothy, Titus, Philem.), while fragments of his commentaries on the other Pauline Epistles survive in the catenae. Theodore emerges as firmly rejecting allegorical exegesis (he is known to have rejected the widespread allegorical interpretation of the Song of Songs, a position which even his fellow Antiochene Theodoret repudiated as 'a story not even fitting in the mouth of crazy women'), and a cautious interpreter of messianic prophecy, ascribing many apparently messianic prophecies not to Jesus Christ but to the restoration of the Jewish state or the victories of the Maccabees.

So far as his dogmatic works are concerned, the situation is still worse. He wrote a treatise on the incarnation in at least fifteen books, treatises against Apollinarianism and Eunomianism, and a work on original sin. Of all this only fragments survive, preserved by later writers who cited passages in the course of their refutation of Theodore.

Of considerable importance is his set of catechetical homilies – on the Lord's Prayer, the Creed and the Eucharist – which has survived in Syriac. These sermons reveal similarities with John Chrysostom, both in interpretation and in the structure of the liturgy reflected. Of particular interest is his interpretation of the Real Presence of Christ in the eucharist as being brought about by consecration conceived as the action of the Holy Spirit, and analogous not to the incarnation, but to the resurrection.

Nestorius

Nestorius was born about 381 in Germanicia in Syria Euphratensis. He studied in Antioch, where he may have been one of Theodore's pupils. There he became a monk, and as a priest, like Chrysostom before him, acquired a great reputation for his oratory. His renown was such that in 428 he was made bishop of Constantinople. There he soon attracted censure for his disapproval of the title θεοτόκος ('one who gave birth to God') popularly given to the Blessed Virgin. He required that it be complemented by ἀνθρωποτόκος ('one who gave birth to a man'), or replaced by Χριστοτόκος ('one who gave birth to Christ'). This was reported to Cyril, bishop of Alexandria, who was keen to follow the example of his uncle and predecessor, Theophilus, in humiliating the incumbent of the throne of Constantinople. At a council held in Ephesus in 431, the Third Ecumenical Council, Cyril had Nestorius condemned. This condemnation was confirmed by the emperor, and Nestorius was sent, first to his monastery at Antioch, and then in exile to the Oasis in Upper Egypt, a noisome place, regularly used for exiles, who rarely survived there very long. Nestorius, however, seems to have survived at least until 450.

Of his works, however, very little survives. There are several letters preserved in the records of the Council of Ephesus, and fragments of a few others; about thirty sermons are extant, mostly in fragmentary form. The only complete work we have is the lengthy defence of his theological position, called

The Book of Heraclides,[3] written in exile at the Oasis, which survives in Syriac translation. This must have been completed after 450, as he knows of the death of the Emperor Theodosius II (29 July 450). He knew, too, about the 'Robber Synod' of Ephesus, and regarded himself as vindicated by the Tome of Leo. *The Book of Heraclides* is a rambling work, parts of it in the form of dialogue between Sophronius and Nestorius, and later between Cyril and Nestorius, and parts of it extracts from an otherwise lost work by Nestorius, *On the Faith*.

Theodoret of Cyrrhus

Theodoret was a younger contemporary of Nestorius. Born about 393 in Antioch, he received his considerable education in the monasteries around Antioch and became a monk himself. In 423 he was elected bishop of Cyrrhus. At the Council of Ephesus, he was one of the bishops of the East (the diocese *Oriens*), led by John of Antioch, who were worsted by Cyril. The Formula of Reunion, accepting the ascription of the title θεοτόκος to Mary and balancing it with an affirmation of Christ's double consubstantiality, which formed the basis of the agreement between Cyril and the bishops of the East in 433, has been attributed to Theodoret, though he was loath to endorse reunion with Cyril. In the controversy over Eutyches, Theodoret found himself condemned at the Robber Synod of Ephesus in 449, deposed and exiled. At Chalcedon in 451, he was eventually reinstated as bishop, but only after reluctantly pronouncing anathema on Nestorius. He returned to Cyrrhus until his death, the date of which is disputed: 457 is the traditional date, 466 has held the field for some decades,[4] but 460 is now proposed.[5] His writings against Cyril's twelve anathematisms constituted one of the 'Three Chapters' that were condemned at the Fifth Œcumenical Council in 553.

Several times in his letters (cf. *Epp*. 82, 116, 146), Theodoret mentions the books he has written, from which it is evident, as we should expect, that much has been lost. Nevertheless, a great deal has survived. The most significant category to have survived are his commentaries on Scripture: this is doubtless owing to their qualities of learning and conciseness, for which Photius commended him.[6] There are extant commentaries in the technical exegetical form of 'Questions', or 'Investigations' (ζητήματα) on the Hexateuch and on Kings and Chronicles, and continuous commentaries on Psalms, the Song of Songs (in which he repudiates Theodore's literal interpretation: see above), and all the prophetic books. For the New Testament, there survives a commentary on all fourteen Pauline Epistles.

Many of his dogmatic works have perished, but there are two works, *On the Holy and Lifegiving Trinity* and *On the Incarnation*, that survived through ascription to his opponent Cyril, and two others that were ascribed to Justin Martyr: an *Exposition of the Correct Faith* and *Questions and Answers to the Orthodox*. But his most important dogmatic treatise is his *Eranistes* ('The Collector', or less likely 'The Beggar'). This work, which is interspersed with lengthy *florilegia*, anthologies of patristic citations (which may be the reason for its preservation), takes the form of a dialogue between Eranistes and Orthodox: the three sections of dialogue deal with the questions of the unchangeability of the natures of the union, the unconfused nature of the union, and the question of divine suffering (which Theodoret denies). Theodoret, in his preface, remarks that in his use of the dialogue he has departed from the classical form by placing the names of the participants at the beginning of their sections. Theodoret allows Eranistes to press Orthodox quite hard, especially in the second part: there is genuine dialogue. The *florilegia* provide evidence of Theodoret's considerable theological learning, with 238 texts drawn from eighty-eight works, including pre-Nicene writers such as Ignatius, Irenaeus and Hippolytus, as well as theologians such as Athanasius and the Cappadocian Fathers. This use of *florilegia* heralds a new stage in doctrinal development, in that it creates another explicit authority for Christian theology: that of the 'Fathers'.

Theodoret's learning is also revealed in his two historical works. A *Church History*, a continuation of Eusebius', tells of the rout of the Arians, but finishes in 428 before the Nestorian controversy, although it was completed in 449–50. There is considerable debate about its relationship to the histories of Socrates, Sozomen and Rufinus: it is likely that similarities are due to the use of common material. His *Religious History* (*Historia Philotheos*) is an account of early Syrian monasticism.[7]

A considerable body of letters survives, in three collections: forty-seven letters preserved in a MS belonging to the monastery of Patmos, 147 letters edited by J. Sirmond in the seventeenth century, and thirty-six letters preserved in conciliar records (there is some overlap between these three collections). (The gleeful letter written after the death of Cyril – 'lay a very big heavy stone upon his grave, for fear he should come back again' – is probably not authentic.) They provide precious glimpses of rural Christianity in Northern Syria, as well as insight into episcopal relationships; there are letters of consolation and commendation; throughout there is revealed the generous and sensitive soul of a pastor.

One of Theodoret's most celebrated works is his *Cure for Hellenic Sicknesses*, a work of Christian apologetic. Very high claims have been made for this work:

its most recent editor calls it 'perfectly original and new'.[8] It is not clear that this can be sustained. It is elegant and interesting, but more remarkable for its wealth of classical citations than for the clarity of its argument. This wealth is, alas, largely borrowed; mostly from Eusebius of Caesarea, but also from Clement of Alexandria. His citations often reveal misunderstanding, owing to ignorance of the original context. There are, however, original elements: Theodoret reflects the advance of *Christiana tempora* in his treatment of the traditional apologetic theme of the martyrs, in which he concentrates principally on the power of their relics. The section on divine providence also reveals elements of originality: here there are many citations from Plotinus (mostly from *Enneads* 3.2), which seem to be the fruit of Theodoret's own reading (though he sometimes, pardonably, gets the wrong end of the stick), and his treatment of providence culminates in the incarnation. This is true also of his very different *On Providence*, which is based on the Bible and shorn of classical learning: here, too, the incarnation forms the culmination, and his inspiration, though unstated, seems to be Irenaeus.

Nemesius of Emesa

Theodoret's discussions of providence often recall the similarly inspired, though differently presented, *On Human Nature*, by Nemesius, who was bishop of Emesa at the end of the fourth century.[9] Nemesius belongs to the same thought-world as the Antiochenes, as one might expect from a bishop of Emesa (close to the southern border of Syria Secunda). *On Human Nature* is a distillation of classical learning, drawing on many similar sources as Theodoret, though with much greater control of his material. It attracted the attention of Maximus the Confessor in the seventh century and John Damascene in the eighth, and through them influenced the Middle Ages, both in Byzantium and the West. In many MSS it is ascribed to his contemporary Gregory of Nyssa, owing to confusion with the Cappadocian's rather different *On Human Creation*.

Notes

1 Photius, *Bibliotheca*, codices 172–4 (trans. N. G. Wilson: Photius, *The Bibliotheca* (London: Duckworth, 1994), 157).

2 Ed. by L. De Coninck, CCSL 88A (1977).

3 The ET by G. R. Driver and L. Hodgson, Nestorius, *The Bazaar of Heracleides* (Oxford, 1925) is notoriously inaccurate: those who cannot consult the Syriac should use the older French translation by F. Nau.

4 Following E. Honigmann, 'Theodoret of Cyrrhus and Basil of Seleucia. The time of their death', in *Patristic Studies,* ST 173 (Vatican City, 1953). 174–84.

5 By Y. Azéma, 'La date de la mort de Théodoret de Cyr', *Pallas* 31 (1984), 137–55, 192–3.

6 Photius, *Bibliotheca*, codex 203.

7 See ch. 34.

8 P. Canivet, in the introduction to his edition, Théodoret de Cyr, *Thérapeutique des Maladies Helléniques*, SC 57 (1958), 34.

9 Critical edition by M. Morani (Bibliotheca Scriptorum Graecorum et Romanorum Teubneriana, Leipzig, 1987). ET with commentary by W. Telfer in LCC 4 (1955).

31

Cyril of Alexandria

ANDREW LOUTH

> The patristic understanding of the Incarnation owes more to Cyril of Alexandria than to any other individual theologian. The classic picture of Christ the God-man, as it is delineated in the formulae of the Church from the Council of Chalcedon onwards, and as it has been presented to the heart in liturgies and hymns, is the picture Cyril persuaded Christians was the true, the only credible, Christ.[1]

Despite this, Cyril has suffered such neglect in modern times that, apart from his conciliar letters, he is unrepresented in the standard late-Victorian English translation of the Fathers, the *Library of Nicene and Post-Nicene Fathers*. Part of the reason for this is doubtless his depiction in Charles Kingsley's famous novel, *Hypatia* (1853), as a sinister figure, cruel and unscrupulous. All this, however, provides a poor basis for understanding one whom Christians from at least the seventh century onwards regarded as the 'Seal of the Fathers'.

Cyril was born around 375–80 in Alexandria, where he probably received his education, and he may have spent some time as a monk, though this is disputed. He first appears on the scene of history accompanying his uncle Theophilus at the Synod of the Oak in 403. In 412 he was elected bishop to succeed his uncle: he was not the preferred choice of the civil authorities and the early years of his episcopate were uneasy. The Church historian Socrates tells of outrages – the confiscation of Novatianist churches, troubles with the Augustal Prefect Orestes, mob-violence culminating in the murder of Hypatia the philosopher in 415 and Cyril's (temporary) expulsion of some Jews from Alexandria – which, as Lionel Wickham has put it, should probably be interpreted as the acts 'not of a fanatical priest, hungry for power, heading a howling mob, but of an untried leader attempting, and initially failing, to master popular forces'.[2] But Cyril soon established his control. His episcopate – and his reputation – are dominated by the Nestorian controversy which blew up with the appointment of Nestorius to the see of Constantinople in 428. Nestorius' calling in question the traditional attribution to Mary of the title θεοτόκος ('one who gave birth to God') revealed to Cyril heresy that undermined the reality of the incarnation, and also gave him the opportunity to continue the struggle for pre-eminence between the sees of Alexandria and Constantinople that had inspired his uncle Theophilus against John Chrysostom (the parallel did not escape his contemporaries, as emerges from a letter by Isidore of Pelusium to Cyril himself (*Ep.* 1.310), although by this time John was regarded by Cyril, and everyone else, as one of the 'holy fathers'). Cyril pursued his case against Nestorius by letters – to Nestorius himself, to the imperial court, to the pope – and at a council held at Ephesus in 431, which came to be regarded as the Third Œcumenical Council, where he had Nestorius condemned and deposed. In 433 he achieved reconciliation with John, bishop of Antioch, the leader of the supporters of Nestorius, by assenting to a 'Formula of Reunion', which affirmed Mary's divine motherhood, complementing this with an assertion of Christ's double consubstantiality: with God the Father and 'with us'. All of this was not achieved without the support of the court officials, whose services had to be bought. The huge size of these payments is recorded in a source hostile to Cyril, but, as Wickham comments, 'the bankrupting size is the sincerest testimony to Cyril's wish for a united Church and should, in fairness, bring him credit'.[3] Cyril spent the last decade of his life exposing the roots of Nestorianism in Diodore and Theodore, and replying to attacks from such as Andrew of Samosata and Theodoret of Cyrrhus, as well as composing a defence of Christianity against the Emperor Julian's *Against the Galileans*. He died on 27 June 444.

As a bishop, and maybe before, Cyril was a prolific writer: he has an overloaded style, stuffed with neologisms, which fails, however, to conceal his sharp mind and clear grasp of what for him was the heart of his faith – the union of God and human nature in the single reality of Jesus Christ. The Nestorian controversy forms a watershed. Before the controversy, the catchwords of his attack on Nestorius – θεοτόκος and the formula 'one incarnate nature of God the Word' (μία φύσις τοῦ Θεοῦ λόγου σεσαρκωμένη) – are scarcely to be found, and his concerns are mainly exegetical and pastoral; during the controversy and afterwards, his writings are dominated by a desire to expound Christology with a clarity and polemical edge in order to expose what for him was the muddle and sheer error of Nestorianism.

Though a great deal of Cyril's exegetic work is lost, much remains. On the Pentateuch there are two complementary works: *Adoration and Worship in Spirit and in Truth* and his *Glaphyra* (the Greek word means 'elegant' or 'polished'). The former is a dialogue in which Cyril provides interpretation of various texts from the Pentateuch, presented in a thematic order. The *Glaphyra* discusses much the same texts in a continuous exposition, treating the texts in their biblical order. There also survive commentaries on Isaiah and on the Twelve Minor Prophets. Cyril's exegesis of the Old Testament is dominated by his conviction that its fulfilment is found in Christ, though he does not try to force all passages to yield such a typological meaning. On the New Testament, much the most important work is his commentary on John in twelve books (books 7 and 8 are only preserved in extracts of uncertain authenticity from the catenae), though there is also a commentary in the form of homilies on Luke, and the catenae preserve fragments from his commentaries on Matthew, and Romans, 1 and 2 Corinthians and Hebrews. The Commentary on John is a remarkable work, providing a sustained dogmatic interpretation of the Gospel. It is full of striking reflections on the significance of John's language, and emphasizes the consubstantiality revealed between the Father and the Son, as well as the unity of the incarnate Son. A significant detail is his interpretation of the past tense of the verb 'to be' as used in John 1:1 as indicative of eternal existence: an idea met with in later Byzantine theologians and evidence of their close attention to Cyril on John. This detail he cannot have learnt from the Neoplatonists, but there is evidence, in the Commentary and elsewhere, that Cyril knew of, and borrowed from, the language they used to express their logic of continuity: paradoxical language of distinctness without division and unity without confusion, which Cyril used to express the union of Godhead and manhood in Christ. From the period before the Nestorian controversy there belongs, too, his polemic against the Arians. His *Treasury on the Holy and Consubstantial Trinity* is, for the most part, an anthology of passages from Athanasius, his precedecessor in the see of Alexandria, whose professed disciple he was, and *On the Holy and Consubstantial Trinity* takes the form of seven dialogues, the first six expounding the consubstantiality of the Son and the last that of the Spirit.

The writings from the period of the Nestorian controversy onwards are dominated by his opposition to Nestorianism. They include, however, *Against the Godless Julian*, a massive refutation of the apostate emperor's attack on Christianity. This was composed in twenty books, of which books 1–10 survive in their entirety and the rest in fragments in Greek and Syriac. The mere fact of the work (completed between 433 and 441, since Cyril sent a copy to John of Antioch) indicates the strength of paganism in Egypt (and elsewhere), despite imperial efforts at extirpation from Theodosius I onwards. Like Origen's *Against Celsus*, it is a refutation which quotes Julian passage by passage before responding. Cyril's refutation is, therefore, invaluable for reconstructing Julian's own work which is lost. The learning Cyril employs against Julian is borrowed, largely from Eusebius of Caesarea.

The anti-Nestorian writings take a variety of forms. Many of them are letters: to Nestorius himself, to Acacius, bishop of Melitene, to Eulogius, Cyril's agent in Constantinople, to Succensus, bishop of Diocaesarea in Isauria, and others. Two of the letters to Nestorius are of particular importance. The second (*Ep.* 4) is a concise statement of Cyrilline Christology, presented as an exposition of the Nicene creed. His third letter (*Ep.* 17), written after the Council of Ephesus had been convoked, presents Cyril's position without compromise, and has appended a list of twelve anathematisms (often called Twelve Chapters), with a demand for Nestorius' assent. These begin with an abrupt assertion of the legitimacy of the title θεοτόκος applied to Mary, and continue with a series of propositions rejecting any distinct human agent in Christ, culminating in an affirmation of the deifying power of the eucharistic body of Christ, and the ascription to the incarnate Word of suffering and death. These twelve chapters, upheld at Ephesus but laid to one side at Chalcedon (to be revived in substance at Constantinople II in 553), were the subject of attack from the Antiochene side, to which Cyril responded. Cyril's letter of reconciliation to John of Antioch of 433 (*Ep.* 39) includes the Formula of Reunion, and raises the question as to whether Cyril, after that date, modified his views. As he ceases to insist on the Twelve Chapters, there is little evidence of any change in Cyril's views, other than in the manner of their presentation. Much has been made of the last section of the second letter to Succensus (*Ep.* 46). Here, it is claimed, Cyril recognizes the soul of Christ as a 'theological factor'.[4] That way of putting it reveals a modern theological problematic applied to the ancient theologian. Cyril is making no concession in insisting that human suffering requires a soul, for it to be human suffering as we know it. But that is all he is saying: the human suffering of Christ belongs to the Word incarnate, and no one else. It is worth noting in this connection (it is probably true of Athanasius, too) that Cyril has no room for the idea, found in others such as Origen and Gregory Nazianzen, that Christ's humanity needs a soul to fulfil the role of a 'buffer zone' between the Word and the body: on the contrary, the Word unites itself directly to humanity, even, or especially, to the material body – that is the measure of God's love for humankind.[5] Cyril expounds and defends his Christological position in a host of other treatises: five books *Against the Blasphemies of Nestorius*, his *Scholia on the Incarnation of the Only-begotten*, several works addressed to the emperor and his Augustae, the first of which, a dialogue, circulated separately as *On the Incarnation of the*

Only-begotten, and another dialogue *On the Unity of Christ*. In the second of these dialogues, in particular, Cyril allows his opponent to press his questioning quite hard. Cyril's refutation of the roots of Nestorianism which he found in Diodore of Tarsus and Theodore of Mopsuestia, *Against Diodore and Theodore*, survives only in fragments.

Around a hundred of Cyril's letters survive (including those mentioned above), some preserved only in fragments. Some deal with other than Christological issues: one (to Calosirius, *Ep.* 83) concerns the monastic anthropomorphite controversy (on which Cyril differs from his uncle's eventual position). A few other letters concern matters of canon law, and provide several of the canons of the Fathers. There survive, too, thirty festal letters, announcing the date of Easter and exhorting the priests and people to prepare for it (the exhortation is sometimes doctrinal). About twenty homilies survive on a variety of subjects.

Notes

1 L. R. Wickham, in the introduction to his Cyril of Alexandria, *Selected Letters*, xi. This brief introduction is the best short account of Cyril and his teaching in English (or any other language).

2 Ibid., xvi.

3 Ibid., xxv.

4 See A. Grillmeier, *Christ in Christian Tradition*, I, 474–6.

5 Cf. G. M. de Durand OP in his introduction to: Cyrille d'Alexandrie, *Deux Dialogues Christologiques*, SC 97 (1964), 142.

32

Hagiography

ANDREW LOUTH

Lives of the saints became one of the most popular forms of Christian literature: indeed for some periods of the Middle Ages, both in the East and the West, our literary sources are dominated by the hagiographical. The earliest Christian biography extant is the *Life* of St Cyprian of Carthage (d. 258), by his deacon Pontius, but the most influential without doubt is the *Life* of St Antony, by his contemporary, the pope of Alexandria, Athanasius. Another early Christian biography is the *Life* of Origen, which originally formed part of the *Defence of Origen*, written by Pamphilus and Eusebius of Caesarea in the first decade of the fourth century: it is now lost, but it was almost certainly the source for most of book 6 of Eusebius' *History of the Church*, which is mainly concerned with the life of the great Alexandrian. Both this lost *Life* of Origen and the *Life of St Antony* demonstrate marked similarities with the pagan genre of the *Lives* of the philosophers, which must therefore be counted as a literary source for the genre of the saints' *Lives*.[1] However, the nature of the saint's *Life*, from its beginnings, was more deeply affected by the emerging Christian cult of the saint, of which the *Life* soon came to form a part. The cult of the saint was originally the cult of the martyr, a cult that can be traced back at least to the second century, as the *Martyrdom of St Polycarp* shows. The mortal remains of the martyr – the relics – were buried, if at all possible, and yearly commemorations, involving the celebration of the eucharist, were made at the place of burial. When it became feasible, a small chapel, a *martyrium*, was built, with the altar placed over the relics of the saint. As the cult of the saints developed, it became a common practice for some portion of the relics of one or more saints to be placed beneath every Christian altar, a practice made obligatory by the Seventh Œcumenical Council (canon 7).

The origin of the notion of the saint in the cult of the martyrs had a marked effect on the genre of the saint's *Life*. First, at a literary level, it suggests the already well-developed genre of the *Acts of the Martyrs* as a source for the saint's *Life*, and this is borne out in several ways. The *Acts of the Martyrs* focused on the martyr's death, and saw this death as a struggle (an ἀγών), used metaphors of athletic contest (cf. Heb. 12:1–2) and military combat (cf. Eph. 6:11–20) to depict it, and saw the combat as directed principally against the demons. All this is carried over into the saint's *Life*. Secondly, it explains the close affinity between hagiography and monastic literature, for the ascetic, too, saw himself as a successor to the martyr, and engaged in the same struggle. Further, the very nature of Christian sanctity is affected by this lineage. Although Basil speaks of 'the lives of saintly men, recorded and handed down to us, [as lying] before us like living images of God's government, for our imitation of their good works' (*Ep.* 2: in fact, referring to the holy men of the Scriptures), the Christian saint was not regarded as simply an ethical model from the past: he was seen much more as one who, in his earthly life, demonstrated his closeness to God, not only by his godly life, but by his ready access to God in prayer, and the divine power he was thus able to wield, and who now, as a friend of God in the heavenly court, is able to intercede with God for those for whom he is concerned – in short, a figure of power that can be drawn on by those who cultivate a relationship with him. The saint's *Life*, then, is concerned to depict one whose closeness to God is a source of power, manifest in miracles – not just the miracles worked by the saint during his lifetime, but also the miracles he continues to work through his earthly remains: his relics.

The *Life* of the saint came to conform to a conventional structure (though in our period this is still developing). It began with the birth of the saint, frequently accompanied by some miracle portending his future acclaim; something might be recounted about his childhood years (it would normally be pious invention, in the likely absence of any authentic tradition, and as such, again adorned with the miraculous); often there would be some dramatic conversion experience (more commonly with male than female saints, though inevitably essential in the *Lives* of converted harlots); a period of ascetic training followed, usually involving a spiritual father and often monastic; then the saint is depicted in the fulness of his earthly powers, manifesting his friendship with God and, consequently, his παρρησία, meaning both his ready access to God and his directness with men and women, including those of great rank, together with his miracles, and in appropriate cases evidence of his wisdom (the *Life of St Antony* includes a lengthy sermon: a precedent sometimes followed); much attention was paid to the account of the death of the saint – it was usually disclosed by God to the saint in advance and was his passage into the presence of Christ and the heavenly court; finally, the continued activity of the saint, principally through his relics (though sometimes, also, through dreams), was normally established. In many cases it is clear that the author of the saint's *Life* had little information at his disposal, in which case material was adapted from other saints' *Lives* on the grounds of analogy.

Saints' *Lives* from our period fall into a number of categories: they are not so narrowly focused as later medieval *Lives* (at least in the West), which almost invariably serve to validate some aspect (often the authenticity of wonder-working relics) of what has been called the vast 'thaumaturgy of the dead' that characterized medieval society. The vast majority of saints' *Lives* is monastic: the *Life of St Antony* is an important piece of monastic literature, as well as the archetypal saint's *Life*; there are several versions of the *Life* of St Pachomius: another early monastic saint's *Life* is the *Life of Paul the Hermit* by Jerome. Although, however, there is no reason to doubt that there was an early hermit of that name, there is equally no reason to suppose that Jerome knew much about him: it is a romantic tale of the desert. Many other monastic texts are, in form, collections of saints' *Lives*, notably Palladius' *Lausiac History*, the *History of the Monks of Egypt*, and Theodoret's *Religious History*. Several saints' *Lives* take the form of panegyric sermons or eulogies. Basil gave eulogies on the local Cappadocian saints Julitta and Mamas, as well as on the Forty Martyrs of Sebaste, who were celebrated by many others, including Gregory of Nyssa and Ephrem the Syrian, and became popular saints in Byzantium. Gregory of Nyssa also celebrated his brother, Basil, and Stephen, the first martyr. Gregory of Nazianzus gave eulogies on Athanasius and on Basil, as well as on Cyprian of Carthage, whom he conflates with the legendary Cyprian, the Antiochene magician, thus preparing the way for the Faust legend.[2] John Chrysostom preached several hagiographic sermons, for example on the Antiochene saints, Ignatius, Babylas and Eustathius, as well as on Lazarus, raised from the dead by Jesus, and much celebrated in the East. In the West, Augustine preached many sermons on the martyrs, not least sermons on St Stephen the Protomartyr after the discovery of his relics in 415 and their journey down the Mediterranean. Hilary of Arles' sermon on Honoratus, the founder of the monastic community on Lérins, is a *Vita*. Some of these sermons conform very closely to the form of a *Vita*, though this is no guarantee of historicity, as Gregory's largely fabulous account of Cyprian makes plain (it ends, closely following the form of a saint's *Life*, with the discovery of his relics). Another apparent category of saints' *Lives* is that of *Lives* of bishops. This is very erratic: apart from the eulogistic sermons just mentioned there are no contemporary, or nearly contemporary, *Lives* of such figures as Athanasius, or Cyril, or any of the Cappadocian Fathers (though there is of the 'Cappadocian Mother', Macrina). But in the West there are *Lives* of several bishops, notably Cyprian, Martin, Ambrose and Augustine: the first is linked to the genre of the Acts of the Martyrs, the latter three, however, all present their subjects not simply as bishops, but as monk-bishops, so they are not unrelated to monastic literature. Another, rather different, example of a bishop's *Life* is Palladius' dialogue on the life of John Chrysostom, which is mainly concerned to defend the memory of the victim of the Synod of the Oak. Yet another genre of saints' *Lives* is represented by Prudentius' *Crowns of the Martyrs* (*Peristephanon*), though it is strictly a series of accounts of martyrdom, in verse.

These saints' *Lives*, both by their conventional form and the inclusion of the miraculous, pose problems for modern historians. Traditionally modern historians have approached them, rather in the way Spinoza approached the Bible, by filleting them and removing the indigestible element of the improbable. The classic statement of this approach to the *Lives* of the saints remains the work of the great Bollandist, Hippolyte Delehaye, especially his *Les Légendes hagiographiques*.[3] What survives as historically usable often has little to do with the saints themselves: such material can provide evidence for historical events through which the saint lived, or by which his biographer marked the course of his life; it can also provide evidence for the social history of the period (of the biographer, if not of the saint) – an extreme example might be Kazhdan's account of sexual behaviour in Byzantium, drawn entirely from hagiography.[4] Another way of reading saints' *Lives*, however, is to see them not so much as a rather grubby window through which we can catch glimpses of a few historical events and historical conditions, but rather as a mirror in which we can see reflected the mind and values of the society to which they belong.[5]

Notes

1 For a comparative discussion of the *Lives* of Origen and Plotinus, see Patricia Cox, *Biography in Late Antiquity*.

2 See A.-J. Festugière, *La Révélation d'Hermès Trismégiste*, I, Appendix II, 369–83.

3 Originally published in 1905: ET from the 4th edition, 1955, by D. Attwater, *The Legends of the Saints* (London: Geoffrey Chapman, 1962).

4 A. Kazhdan, 'Byzantine Hagiography and Sex in the Fifth to Twelfth Centuries', in *Dumbarton Oaks Papers* 44 (1990), 131–43.

5 For two recent and complementary discussions of the use of hagiography by historians, see P. Fouracre and R. A. Gerberding, *Late Merovingian France. History and Hagiography 640–720* (Manchester and New York: Manchester University Press, 1996), 26–58, and Rosemary Morris, *Monks and Laymen in Byzantium 843–1118* (Cambridge: Cambridge University Press, 1995), 64–89, and the literature they cite.

33

Ephrem and the Syriac tradition

SEBASTIAN P. BROCK

Virtually every aspect of Syriac Christianity prior to the fourth century remains obscure, and it is only then that one can feel oneself on firmer ground. This is due not only to the presence of more and better historical sources, but also to the fact that three major bodies of writing in Syriac survive from this century: Aphrahat's twenty-three *Demonstrations*, Ephrem's extensive writings in both prose and (above all) poetry, and the anonymous guide to the spiritual life entitled *The Book of Steps*. The first and third of these were produced within the Sasanian Empire, while Ephrem was writing in the easternmost area of the Roman Empire, first in Nisibis, and then in Edessa. Together, these writings provide us with the best evidence we have for the character of Syriac literary culture at a period when it was still comparatively unhellenized.

Aphrahat 'the Persian Sage' was also known at an early date under the name of Jacob, which soon led to confusion with Jacob, bishop of Nisibis, who died in 338. Aphrahat, however, was definitely writing within the Sasanian Empire, and furthermore his works are exactly dated, for *Demonstrations* 1–10 are given the date 337, while 11–22 belong to 344, and 23 to August 345 (1–22 provide an alphabetic acrostic). The title 'Demonstration' happens to correspond exactly to the Greek ἐπίδειξις, but it is unlikely that the Greek genre has had any direct influence on Aphrahat's writing; he himself also describes his short treatises on occasion as 'Letters'. Their subject-matter is very varied. The first half deals with topics concerning general aspects of the Christian life, such as fasting (1), prayer (4), and the ascetic life (6 and 7). *Demonstration* 6, entitled 'On the members of the covenant (*bnay qyama*)' is of especial interest for the light it sheds on the specifically Mesopotamian developments in the consecrated life prior to the advent of Egyptian-style monasticism: these *bnay qyama*, also called *iḥidaye*, lit. 'singles', who were single-minded and celibate followers of Christ the *Iḥida*, or 'Only-Begotten', evidently undertook certain ascetic vows (their *qyama*, or covenant, with Christ), probably made at baptism.[1]

The second half of the *Demonstrations* is largely concerned with relations with Judaism. Although on various occasions a 'Jewish debater' is directly addressed, Aphrahat's concern is not so much dialogue with Jews, but rather argumentation with Judaizing Christians who wished to follow various Jewish practices. *Demonstration* 14, however, stands apart, being an attack on ecclesiastical malpractice in high places; unfortunately the historical setting which gave rise to this outburst remains unclear, despite various attempts to elucidate it. *Demonstration* 21 is an important witness to the beginnings of the persecution of Christianity under Shapur II, while the final *Demonstration*, entitled 'On the Grape Cluster in which there is blessing' (Isa. 65:8) provides a fine example of the way in which typology functioned as a vehicle for Christian teaching.

Certain sections, often quite extensive, of the *Demonstrations* are written in artistic prose, with carefully balanced sentences making abundant use of rhetorical features many of which are also to be found in contemporary Greek *Kunstprosa*. Neither Aphrahat, nor any other early Syriac writer (even Ephrem) who employs this kind of artistic prose writing, can possibly have come under the direct influence of Greek *Kunstprosa*, and it is evident that we have two independent manifestations of the same general phenomenon.

By far the most important figure of early Syriac literature is the theologian-poet Ephrem, most of whose life was spent as a deacon serving the church in Nisibis. When, however, that city was ceded to the Persians in the peace treaty of 363, one of the conditions was that the Christian population should leave, and Ephrem in due course settled in Edessa, where he spent the last ten years of his life (he died in 373). Ephrem's writings are extensive even when the large number of works falsely attributed to him is excluded.[2] His fame as 'the harp of the Spirit' rested primarily on his poetry, for which he employed two different metrical forms, the *memra* and the *madrasha*. The *memra*, in Ephrem's hands, consists of seven-syllable couplets, and is suited to subject-matter of a narrative or didactic content. Only a comparatively small number of *memre* under Ephrem's name, however, are definitely by Ephrem; among these will be the six *memre* on Faith, and the *memre* on the destruction, by an earthquake in 359, of Nicomedia, preserved primarily only in Armenian translation. Probably genuine (though doubt has been expressed) is a famous *memra* on the Repentance of Nineveh, which also survives in Greek translation (where it constitutes one of the rather few items in the extensive corpus of 'Ephrem Graecus' for which a Syriac original exists).[3] Less certain is another well-known narrative *memra*, on the Sinful Woman (Luke 7), where the poet introduces the motif – to prove very influential[4] – of the perfume seller from whom the woman buys the unguent with which she anoints Jesus' feet.

Uncertainty also surrounds the authorship of an epic cycle in twelve books on the patriarch Joseph.

The *madrasha*, conventionally translated 'hymn', is a stanzaic poem which could be written in a variety of different syllabic metres; it had already been employed as the vehicle for theological teaching by Bardaisan and Mani, and at least part of Ephrem's very large output in this medium was specifically intended to counter the influence of these, and other (to him) heretical writers. Ephrem handles the medium with consummate artistry, deftly moving from one striking image to another; he employs a little over forty-five different stanza patterns which could range from the regular and simple (e.g. four lines each of five syllables) to the highly complex. These stanza patterns are identified by their *qale*, or melodies to which they were evidently sung (a single metrical pattern might in fact be known by the names of two or three different *qale*).

Ephrem's *madrashe* come down to us in a small number of fifth- and sixth-century manuscripts (which alone preserve them in an unabbreviated form), and here they are collected together into cycles of various sizes, whose titles do not always give a clear idea of the contents. Thus while the largest cycle (On Faith, 87 *madrashe*) and the small one of fifteen *madrashe* On Paradise are indeed on these topics (the former being largely aimed against later forms of Arianism), the titles of the cycles On the Church and On Virginity (both 52 *madrashe*) give a very inadequate idea of the subjects covered. Even in the case of the volume of *madrashe* on Nisibis (77 *madrashe*, often called the *Carmina Nisibena*), it is only the first half that concerns Nisibis, the second half being devoted largely to the theme of the Descent into Sheol. Among these *madrashe* on the Descent is a small group (52–4) which are in the form of dialogues between Death and Satan, where in alternating stanzas each boasts that he has the greater power over humanity: only to discover in the concluding stanza(s) that the power of them both has been nullified by Christ at his descent into Sheol. Ephrem here adapts to the new context of Christian teaching the ancient Mesopotamian literary genre of the precedence dispute, examples of which are found in both Sumerian and Akkadian.[5] The genre has in fact continued in use – in a variety of different languages – up to the present day in the Middle East; more or less contemporary with Ephrem, the genre is also attested in Jewish Aramaic and in Middle Persian. In Syriac after Ephrem's day it continued to enjoy great popularity, and some fifty or so dialogue poems, mostly anonymous, survive (see further below).

Over 400 *madrashe* by Ephrem survive, a certain number of these in damaged form. From a sixth-century index of the *qale* to his *madrashe* we learn of nine 'volumes' of his *madrashe*, several of the titles of which conform to those of the surviving hymn-cycles; others, however, are unknown, and in the case of some the number of *madrashe* that the index gives is very much larger than that of the cycle(s) we know. It is thus clear that a considerable number of *madrashe* have been lost. Furthermore, in certain of the cycles that do survive there are *madrashe* which must be later than Ephrem's time: this applies in particular to the *madrashe* on Epiphany, and those on the ascetics Julian Saba (the Elder) and Abraham of Qidun.

It is primarily from the *madrashe* that Ephrem's profound theological vision can best be perceived. That he should have chosen poetry, rather than prose, as the vehicle to express this is in itself significant, for to him the best tool of theological language is the paradox, where two poles are held in dynamic tension. Using this, he describes both the divine descent, where God 'puts on', first human language (where he allows himself to be described in the Old Testament) and then the human body, and the possibility opened up by this descent of humanity's ascent to God, using as a ladder the *raze* or 'symbols' (lit. 'mysteries') inherent in both Scripture and Nature, which serve as pointers to the divine reality, or truth, and at the same time indicate the interrelatedness of everything and everyone.[6]

Ephrem's prose works fall into three categories, the *Prose Refutations*, the commentaries, and works written in artistic prose. The *Prose Refutations* is a modern title given to a group of polemical works directed against the teaching of Marcion, Bardaisan and Mani. In these works (and indeed elsewhere) Ephrem shows an awareness of some of the general philosophical issues current among educated Christians writing in Greek,[7] though it is unclear whether he himself was able to read Greek directly: certainly there is no firm evidence that he could.

A number of biblical commentaries have a strong claim either to be by Ephrem himself, or to represent his teaching or that of his immediate followers. These include two Old Testament commentaries, on Genesis and on Exodus (the latter is incomplete), which are of particular interest for the many parallels with Jewish exegetical tradition. The coverage of the two biblical books is very uneven: in the Commentary on Genesis, over a third of the work is devoted to the first four chapters of Genesis, and of the later chapters, only the Blessings of Jacob (Gen. 49) are commented on in any detail. Though a specifically Christian exegesis of certain passages is occasionally found, this is not a regular feature of the commentaries.

Two of the three New Testament commentaries, on Acts, and on the Pauline Epistles, are preserved only in an early Armenian translation, while the third, on the *Diatessaron*, survives complete only in that language, though in recent years quite a large proportion of the Syriac original has come to light. The Commentary on the Diatessaron, or 'Commentary on the Concordant Gospel' as the Armenian title has it (the Syriac is lost), is of particular interest and importance, both as a unique early witness to the text of the Syriac *Diatessaron*, and as an extensive source for knowledge of early Syriac exegesis of the Gospels. The Commentary is in fact curiously uneven in character for, while some passages are in an almost lyrical style verging on artistic prose (notably parts of 21, on the death and resurrection of Jesus), others give the impression of being little more than notes, listing a number of different possible interpretations.

In all the biblical commentaries the normal process is to provide a lemma, consisting of part of a verse, or a whole verse, followed by an exposition. Though the sequence of the biblical text is followed, only a limited number of verses are selected for comment. The exegesis of these commentaries under Ephrem's name is very varied in character, and his approach may be historical or completely ahistorical (the Commentary on Genesis describes these two poles as 'factual' and 'spiritual'). As in the *madrashe* his prime concern is to discern the 'hidden power (or meaning)' behind the words of the biblical text.

Besides the Commentary on the *Diatessaron*, another work entitled 'The Exposition of the Gospel', surviving only in Armenian translation, is also attributed to Ephrem, but in this case the work, though early, is from very different circles.[8]

Two works by Ephrem are written largely in artistic prose: *The Discourse on our Lord*, and the letter addressed to a certain Publius. The former could be described as a doctrinal meditation on various aspects of the life of Christ, while the Letter to Publius, of which only excerpts survive, consists in an extended meditation on the Last Judgment and the nature of Gehenna (which is understood essentially in psychological terms, as an awareness of separation from God).

As is certainly the case with Ephrem's poetry, it is also likely that several of Ephrem's prose works have been lost, and among these will be the work on the Holy Spirit, which Jerome – writing just under twenty years after Ephrem's death – read and admired in translation (*Vir. Ill.* 115).[9]

The name of the third major Syriac author of the fourth century is unknown, but a chance reference indicates that he was probably writing within the Persian Empire. The anonymous *Book of Steps*,[10] written in thirty chapters, could be described as a manual of the Christian life. Running through the work is the distinction between the lesser and the greater commandments of the Gospels: the former are summed up in the Golden Rule of Matthew 7:12 and

Luke 6:31, while the latter involve a complete renunciation of family, marriage and property. The work has a number of features in common with the Greek Macarian Homilies, now known to be of Mesopotamian rather than Egyptian origin, but there is no evidence of any direct literary relationship. The *Book of Steps* has been variously dated, but on the whole somewhere around 400 would seem the most plausible.

The fifth century was to witness a major change in the character of Syriac literature, as it came more and more under the influence of the Greek-speaking world. Furthermore, the Christological controversies produced a three-way split in ecclesiastical allegiance among Syriac speakers: a minority accepted the Council of Chalcedon, while the remainder rejected either that council (thus the West Syriac, or Syrian Orthodox tradition), or the Council of Ephesus (thus the East Syriac tradition of the Church of the East). The effects of these divisions, however, fall largely beyond the bounds of this chapter.

In the early decades of the fifth century, Syriac literature, above all Syriac poetry, still retained a considerable prestige in the Greek-speaking world. It is in fact quite likely that the Syriac poetic form of the *madrasha* served, at least in part, as a model for the development in Greek of the new verse form of the *kontakion*.[11] In any case, one can see from a fragment of Theodore of Mopsuestia that Syriac liturgical poetry must have enjoyed a considerable vogue since both Flavian bishop of Antioch and Diodore bishop of Tarsus had Syriac antiphonal hymns translated into Greek.[12] Syriac hagiography also had an appeal outside a purely Syriac readership, and at least two anonymous *Lives*, of the Man of God (later known as Alexis) and of Abraham of Qidun, were translated in the fifth century into Greek (and thence into Latin, where both proved very influential in the Western Middle Ages).[13] Also translated into Greek were some of the *Acts* of the Persian martyrs who had suffered in the mid-fourth century under Shapur II.[14] A considerable number of martyr *Acts*, of very varying character and historical value, had grown up, probably for the most part in the course of the fifth century, focused on this extensive persecution, whose first victim had been the bishop of Seleucia-Ctesiphon, Simeon bar Sabba'e, martyred in 344 (rather than 341, which has also been claimed).

Although the level of brilliance and profundity achieved by Ephrem's poetry was never again equalled, verse continued to be an important medium for theological writing in the fifth century. Although the names of a few poets, such as Balai and Cyrillona from the beginning of the century, and especially Narsai and Jacob of Serugh from the end, are known, much poetry from this period is anonymous. This applies to writing on biblical topics in two genres in particular, the dramatic dialogue poem, and the narrative poem. Ephrem had been the pioneer in both these verse forms, but the majority of surviving texts employing them are probably the work of anonymous poets of the fifth century. The dialogue poems (a few of which still remain vestigially in liturgical use) provide the author with an opportunity to explore, through an externalized dialogue, the psychological tensions implicit in particular biblical passages (often just a single verse).[15] Thus the dialogue between Joseph and Mary takes as its starting point Matthew 1:18, and Joseph's discovery of his fiancée's pregnancy.[16] The dialogue, formalized into alternating stanzas, combines realism with both insight and, at times, gentle humour. For the most part the surviving dialogue poems are based on biblical sources, though a few introduce persons absent from the relevant biblical text, such as Satan, who is represented as arguing with the Sinful Woman of Luke 7.[17] In a few cases the disputants are personifications; this applies to a dispute between the months,[18] a poem which excellently illustrates the three different components that are to be found, in varying combinations and proportions, in early Syriac literature: the genre is ancient Mesopotamian, the topic has very close parallels in Jewish Aramaic, where there are a number of poems in which the months dispute over who is to have the honour of the Exodus, and the treatment owes something to the Greek tradition of *ekphrasis*.

The number of anonymous narrative poems on biblical topics is not large, but these include some remarkable treatments. Perhaps none is more dramatic than the second of two poems (in seven-syllable couplets) on Abraham and Isaac (Gen. 22):[19] although the biblical narrative makes no mention at all of Sarah, it is she, and not Abraham or Isaac, who emerges as the true heroine, for she has endured, not the single trial that Abraham had experienced, but a double one, the second imposed on her by her husband on his return, when at first he does not disclose that he has brought their son back with him. The author of this extraordinary poem (who conceivably could have been a woman) draws on the distinctive earlier Syriac interpretation of this episode, according to which Sarah was aware of Abraham's intent in taking off their child, but develops this in a way that is without parallel in patristic literature. Another interesting feature of this poem, and others in this genre, lies in various parallels, some quite striking, with rabbinic exegetical homilies. Any direct literary dependency is out of the question, and the presence of these parallels is best explained by seeing both the Syriac poems and the rabbinic homilies as sharing the characteristics of traditional narrative *aggada*, the former expressed in verse, the latter in prose. Interestingly enough, these narrative poems also share some features with Christian Greek writing: as far as the verse form is concerned one can compare the (otherwise very different) versifications of biblical narrative by Eudocia, Apollinaris and others; much closer, as far as content and the treatment of the biblical episodes is concerned, are the homilies of writers like Basil of Seleucia and others.

Towards the end of the fifth century two prolific poets, Narsai (d. *c.* 500) in the East Syriac tradition, and Jacob of Serugh (d. 521) in the West Syriac, adapt the narrative poem into a specifically homiletic context, producing the characteristically Syriac genre of the verse homily. Although biblical topics and passages form the standard subject-matter, these verse homilies can also turn to hagiography (in Jacob's case) and liturgy, the latter exemplified most notably in Narsai's verse commentaries on the baptismal and eucharistic liturgies.[20] It is symptomatic of the growing influence of Greek writing that both these poets show the marked influence of Theodore of Mopsuestia's exegesis. In the case of Narsai this is not a matter for surprise, since he belonged to the strongly dyophysite Antiochene Christological tradition which, as far as the Syriac Church of the East was concerned, was largely based on Theodore's writings. Jacob, however, belonged to the opposite end of the Christological spectrum, and so the influence of Theodore demands explanation. The answer is to be found in Jacob's education at the Persian School in Edessa,[21] where Theodore's biblical commentaries were standard fare; although Jacob (and Philoxenus, another alumnus of that school) rebelled against its Christological teaching, Theodore none the less left his mark on them in matters of biblical exegesis.

As the fifth century advanced the theological and literary agenda of Greek-speaking Christianity grew increasingly influential among Syriac writers, and by the end of the century such was the prestige of Greek that Philoxenus (d. 523), who happens to be one of the finest models of Syriac prose style, considered the Greek Bible as superior in authority to the Syriac. This growing influence of Greek literary culture can be seen in a variety of different ways: thus, for example, the specifically Greek literary form of the philosophical dialogue has been taken over into Syriac for the purpose of discussions on the spiritual life by John of Apamea, a little-known, but important and influential, writer of the first half of the fifth century. Again, Greek rhetorical features such as *ethopoiia* can be found in both prose and verse homilies. Likewise, phraseology from, and exegetical tradition based on, the Greek rather than the Syriac Bible come into currency: thus the 'Ancient of Days' in Ephrem is the Father, in conformity with the Peshitta text of Daniel 7:13, but in fifth-century poetry the Ancient of Days is often identified as the Son, which goes back to an influential reading in the Old Greek text of Daniel.

The ever-increasing prestige of Greek can also be seen in the history of translations made from Greek into Syriac. Over the course of the fourth to the seventh centuries an astonishingly large number of translations, mainly of Greek patristic texts, was made, and in several cases the Syriac translation is now the sole witness to a work, the Greek original having been lost. The pattern of translation technique evidenced by the transition from the Old Syriac to the Peshitta Gospel translation,[22] where an original rather free rendering is brought into closer line with the Greek original, reflects the pattern found in most non-biblical translations as well: here early translations (fourth- and fifth-century) are very much reader-oriented and can sometimes be better described as free re-creations rather than straight translations, while later ones, of the sixth and above all seventh centuries, become more and more oriented to the source text, and increasingly the aim of the translator was to provide as close a mirror reflection of the original as possible.[23] In the sphere of biblical translation the culmination of this process can be seen in the revision of the earlier (lost) Philoxenian revision of the Peshitta New Testament by Thomas of Harkel, made outside Alexandria *c.* 616, and in its companion translation, the *Syrohexapla*, made from Origen's revised text of the Septuagint. In fourth- and fifth-century translations, however, this essentially philological approach is absent. Among the first non-biblical translations into Syriac must have been the *Clementine Recognitions*, Titus of Bostra's work against the Manichaeans, and Eusebius' *Theophaneia* and *Palestinian Martyrs*, for all these are preserved in the earliest dated Syriac literary manuscript, copied in Edessa in November 411. The translators of these particular works, while regularly opting for dynamic as opposed to formal equivalence, nevertheless adhered reasonably closely to the Greek original. This is not, however, the case with some other, probably early fifth-century, translations, such as Athanasius' *Life of Antony* and certain of Basil of Caesarea's works, where the Syriac version ranges between an expanded paraphrase to (at least in parts) a re-creation of the original. Thus, while these translations are often of disappointingly little use as exceptionally early witnesses to the Greek text, nevertheless they offer many insights into the way that Greek literary culture was adapted and received into Syriac Christianity.

As was mentioned in passing earlier, early Syriac literature can be said to have reflected the influence of three different literary cultures, Mesopotamian, Jewish and Greek. The first of these can most clearly be seen in the adaptation of the ancient genre of the precedence dispute, and in some of the poetic imagery employed (a notable example being the phrase 'medicine of life', common in Ephrem and elsewhere); direct links with earlier Aramaic literature, however, seem to be very few, and beside the case of the portions of Ezra and Daniel in biblical Aramaic, the only example is the story of Ahiqar, whose various Syriac forms have their ultimate roots in the Aramaic tale of the Achaemenid period, of which fragments survive from Elephantine in southern Egypt. Elements of Jewish origin are much more prominent, of course. Here it is not just due to the taking over into Syriac of the Hebrew Bible, for many Jewish elements which are not of biblical origin can be found, above all in the fourth-century writers Aphrahat and Ephrem; these may take the form of terminology and phraseology characteristic of Jewish Aramaic literature, especially the Targums, or of Jewish exegetical traditions which have been adapted to Christian use.[24] The Greek element was already the most prominent in the case of Bardaisan and his school, for there we seem to be in the presence of a group (no doubt small) of people who were genuinely bicultural. However, although it is hard to be certain owing to the paucity of Syriac texts from the third century, it would seem likely that the *Acts of Thomas* was a more typical product of that century than the *Book of the Laws of the Countries*. In the *Acts of Thomas*, as in the three major fourth-century writers, while the influence of Greek literary culture is by no means wholly absent, it has not yet begun to become pervasive, as was to prove more and more to be the case as Syriac literature was to develop in the fifth and, above all, in the succeeding two centuries. It is for this reason that a particular interest surrounds Syriac writers of the third and fourth centuries, quite apart from the fact that one of them was certainly the finest poet of early Christianity to write in any language.

Notes

1 Cf. S. Griffith, 'Asceticism in the Church of Syria. The hermeneutics of early Syrian monasticism', in W. L. Wimbush and R. Valantasis, eds, *Asceticism*, 220–48.

2 Cf. S. P. Brock, 'A Brief Guide to the Main Editions and Translations of the Works of St Ephrem'.

3 See S. P. Brock, 'Ephrem's Verse Homily on Jonah and the Repentance of Nineveh', in A. Schoors and P. van Deun, eds, *Polyhistor: Miscellanea in honorem C. Laga*, Orientalia Lovaniensia Analecta 60 (Louvain: Peeters, 1994), 71–86 (repr. in *From Ephrem to Romanos*, ch. V). The best guide to the large corpus of Greek texts under Ephrem's name is M. Geerard, *Clavis Patrum Graecorum*, II and Supplement.

4 See A. C. Mahr, *Relations of Passion Plays to St Ephrem the Syrian*, Ohio State University, Contributions in Languages and Literature 9 (Columbus: The Wartburg Press, 1942).

5 See R. Murray, 'Aramaic and Syriac Dispute Poems and Their Connections', in M. J. Geller, J. C. Greenfield and M. P. Weitzman, eds, *Studia Aramaica* (Journal of Semitic Studies Supplement 4) (Oxford: Oxford University Press, 1995), 157–87.

6 See especially R. Murray, 'The Theory of Symbolism in St Ephrem's Theology', *Parole de l'Orient* 6/7 (1975/6), 1–20.

7 See U. Possekel, *Evidence of Greek Philosophical Concepts in the Writings of Ephrem the Syrian*.

8 ET by G. A. Egan, Saint Ephrem, *An Exposition of the Gospel*, CSCO 292, Scriptores Armeni 6 (1968). On this work see D. Bundy, 'An Anti-Marcionite Commentary on the Lucan Parables (Pseudo-Ephrem A)', *Le Muséon* 103 (1990), 111–23.

9 For the later (misleading) portrait of Ephrem, see J. Amar, 'Byzantine Ascetic Monachism and Greek Bias in the Vita Tradition of Ephrem the Syrian', *Orientalia Christiana Periodica* 58 (1992), 123–56.

10 Ed. with Latin translation by M. Kmosko in *Patrologia Syriaca*, III (Paris: Firmin-Didot, 1926). An ET by R. A. Kitchen is to be published in 2004; two chapters are included in S. P. Brock, *The Syriac Fathers on Prayer and the Spiritual Life*.

11 See S. P. Brock, 'From Ephrem to Romanos', in E. A. Livingstone, ed., *SP* 20 (1989), 139–51 (repr. in *From Ephrem to Romanos*, ch. IV).

12 *PG* 139, 1390C.

13 Cf. M. Schmidt, 'Influence de saint Ephrem sur la littérature latine et allemande du début du moyen-âge', *Parole de l'Orient* 4 (1973), 325–41.

14 Ed. with French translation by H. Delehaye in *PO* 2.4 (1905).

15 A summary survey is given in S. P. Brock, 'Syriac Dispute Poems: the Various Types', in G. J. Reinink and H. L. J. Vanstiphout, eds, *Dispute Poems and Dialogues in the Ancient and Mediaeval Near East*, Orientalia Lovaniensia Analecta 42 (Louvain: Peeters, 1991), 109–19 (repr. in *From Ephrem to Romanos*, ch. VII).

16 ET in S. P. Brock, *Bride of Light. Hymns on Mary from the Syriac Churches*, 118–24.

17 Ed. with ET by S. P. Brock, 'The Sinful Woman and Satan. Two Syriac dialogue poems', *Oriens Christianus* 72 (1988), 21–62, esp. 43–54.

18 Ed. with ET by S. P. Brock, 'A Dispute of the Months and Some Related Syriac Texts', *Journal of Semitic Studies* 30 (1985), 181–211 (repr. in *From Ephrem to Romanos*, ch. VIII).

19 Ed. with ET by S. P. Brock, 'Two Syriac Verse Homilies on the Binding of Isaac', *Le Muséon* 99 (1986), 61–129, esp. 122–9 (repr. in *From Ephrem to Romanos*, ch. VI).

20 ET by R. H. Connolly, *The Liturgical Homilies of Narsai*.

21 Cf. A. Vööbus, *The School of Nisibis*, 7–32, and H. J. W. Drijvers, 'The School of Edessa: Greek learning and local culture', in J. W. Drijvers and A. A. MacDonald, eds, *Centres of Learning. Learning and Location in Pre-Modern Europe and the Near East* (Leiden: Brill, 1995), 49–59.

22 See ch. 15.

23 See S. P. Brock, 'Towards a History of Syriac Translation Technique', in R. Lavenant, ed., *IIIe Symposium Syriacum*, Orientalia Christiana Analecta 221 (Rome: Pontificio Istituto Orientale, 1983), 1–4 (repr. in *Studies in Syriac Christianity*, X).

24 See note 14 to ch. 15.

34
The literature of the monastic movement

ANDREW LOUTH

The very notion of the 'literature of the monastic movement' runs the risk of accepting uncritically the propaganda that this literature constituted. The traditional story of the rise of monasticism as a fourth-century phenomenon, associated *par excellence* with the Egyptian desert, is a Catholic legend, which, unlike many others, was reinforced, rather than questioned, by Protestant scholarship, happy to regard monasticism as a late, and therefore spurious, development. The 'monastic movement' should perhaps be seen rather as a reform movement of an already existing, and flourishing, ascetic tradition: a reform inspired by changes, both within the Church itself, and in the Church's relation to society, brought about by the gradual Christianization of the Roman Empire that began in the fourth century with the conversion of Constantine.[1] The results of this reform movement led to the outlawing (by bishops in councils) of various hitherto acceptable forms of the ascetic life – notably those that involved ascetics of both sexes living together – and the promotion of the ideal of desert or rural monasticism (though urban monasticism continued), as depicted in the 'monastic literature': the net effect was to subordinate ascetic claims to authority to that of the bishop (with only limited success, especially in the East). Although all the forms of reformed monasticism – the eremitical life of solitude, life in community ('coenobitic') and the modified eremitical life of the *laura* or the 'skete' – can be found in Egypt, the reform of monasticism in other parts of the Empire (Syria, for instance, or Asia Minor) is probably an independent response to the changes of the fourth century, rather than evidence of Egyptian influence.

If this revision in our understanding of fourth-century monasticism is allowed, then there is a consequent revision in our notion of monastic literature. 'Traditional' monastic literature – together with its close cousin, hagiography – became the most popular form of literature in the Middle Ages (this is not simply due to a monastic monopoly of learning, for there was no such monopoly in Byzantium). A good example of this, in the form it took in the Middle Ages, can be seen in the Syriac collection called (significantly) the *Paradise of the Fathers*.[2] This consists of Syriac translations (from Greek, ultimately) of Athanasius' *Life of St Antony*, Palladius' *Lausiac History* (called 'The Paradise'), material about Pachomius (which corresponds to the *Paralipomena* of the Greek *Vita*), the *History of the Monks in Egypt* (here ascribed to Jerome), and then a version of the systematic collection of the *Apophthegmata Patrum*. This is the traditional 'literature of the monastic movement', focused on Egypt, telling of both Antony and Pachomius, and culminating in the *Apophthegmata*. Its relationship to the original texts is not, however, simple: the version of the *Life of St Antony* differs significantly from any Greek text we have, and all the other items reveal the presence of complementary material that has attached itself by a process of accretion and miscegenation in the course of being handed down. The same is true of similar collections, which exist in all the Christian languages of the Middle Ages: Latin, Syriac (as we have seen), Armenian, Coptic (both Sahidic and Bohairic), Georgian, Ethiopic, Arabic, Old Slavonic and Sogdian. Like the Syriac version, many of these represent very ancient traditions, interlaced with accretions; some of them include still later monastic literature, such as John Moschus' *Spiritual Meadow* and even Gregory the Great's *Dialogues*. The problems involved in establishing the original version of any of these texts are enormous.

But before we look at this traditional literature, let us look at what else there is. This further literature falls into two categories: the literature of those monastic movements of the fourth century condemned as heretical (or on the fringes of such groups); and literature that is eccentric to the geographical hegemony of Egypt in the traditional literature. Not a lot survives of the 'heretical' literature: that is, literature associated with the 'homoiousian', or Eustathian, ascetics (condemned at the Council of Gangra in 340/1) and with Messalianism (condemned at councils at Antioch and Side in the late fourth century, and frequently thereafter). There is a treatise *On the True Integrity of Virginity* ascribed to Basil of Ancyra (d. after 363),[3] which seems to envisage some of the controls that were being introduced in the fourth century, while belonging to an older tradition, like that found in an anonymous *On Virginity*,[4] usually dated to around the time of the Council of Nicaea (which cannot, therefore, be regarded as homoiousian). These give us glimpses of traditional patterns of asceticism, to be swept away by the reform. For Messalianism we are better informed, since the homilies ascribed to Macarius the Great have some kind of Messalian affinity, even if they are not simply Messalian (and if so manifest a more moderate Orthodox response to this movement). These homilies exist in four collections: collection I consisting of 64 homilies and letters, the first of which is the so-called 'Great Letter'; collection II, the most popular collection, consisting of 50 homilies; collection III, of 43 homilies, 28 of which do not appear in collections I and II; collection IV, of 26 homilies, all of which appear in collection I.[5] Despite their provenance (noted in the Byzantine period, and not simply by modern scholarship), these homilies became enormously popular in Byzantine monasticism: hence their survival. Though called 'homilies' or λόγοι, some of them are clearly letters, and others take the popular monastic form of 'questions and answers' (ἐρωταπόκρισεις). Their teaching lays stress on the paramount importance of prayer for the acquisition of the Holy Spirit, which can alone overcome human ancestral sin and the power of the demons. The influence of such literature can be found in unusual quarters: the community set up by the Cappadocian sister Macrina and her mother Emmelia, which predated Basil's ascetic experiments and which we know about from her brother Gregory's *Life of St Macrina*, has some parallels with 'homoiousian' asceticism, and both Gregory of Nyssa and Basil betray the influence of the Macarian homilies.

The 'geographically non-standard' literature includes such important material as Basil's monastic literature (already discussed in chapter 26), the *Rule* of St Augustine (for it is now generally agreed that Augustine wrote such, even though the importance of the *Rule of St Augustine* in the medieval West has more to do with the authority of the African doctor than any tradition of its use), Sulpicius Severus' literature about St Martin of Tours – a *Life*, three letters and two dialogues – where we should note that Sulpicius' literary models include Suetonius, the literature associated with the influential monastic settlement established by Honoratus on the island of Lérins (scant, unless one includes Cassian), especially Eucherius' *In Praise of the Desert* and *Contempt of the World*, Hilary of Arles' *Sermon on the Life of St Honoratus*, and his own *Life*, probably by a (later) Honoratus. It is interesting to note that Sulpicius Severus' dialogues between the Gallic monk 'Gallus' and Postumianus, who had made the pilgrimage to Egypt, attempt to draw Martin's monasticism under the aegis of the Egyptian desert – and demonstrate the superiority of Martin.

The traditional literature itself falls into several genres. There is the genre of the saint's *Life* (treated on its own in chapter 32); travel literature and reminiscences; what one might call instructional literature – monastic rules, and more discursive 'questions and answers' on issues connected with the monastic life, as well as letters, homilies and 'conferences' (*conlatio* or κατήχησις: something often regarded as the particular duty of the abbot); and finally, the *Sayings of the Holy Fathers*, the *Apophthegmata Patrum*. All these forms overlap: saints' *Lives* contain instruction, and even monastic rules; the travel literature is often a collection of saints' *Lives*; and sayings are to be found everywhere.

The *Life of St Antony*, almost certainly by Athanasius of Alexandria,[6] is the model, not only for all monastic *Lives*, but for the genre of the saint's *Life* itself. Several other *Lives* belong to the core of the traditional literature, notably the various *Lives* of St Pachomius, who founded large coenobitic monasteries in Upper Egypt in the second quarter of the fourth century. For the West this biographical core is supplemented by the *Life of St Martin* (which was as influential as Evagrius' translation of the *Life of St Antony*, if not more so) and Jerome's *Lives* of Hilarion, Malchus and Paul.

The travel literature consists principally of the *Lausiac History*, written by Palladius, friend and biographer of John Chrysostom, and bishop of Helenopolis, though by the time he wrote his history in 419/20 probably bishop of Aspuna, and the anonymous *History of the Monks of Egypt*, originally composed in Greek, translated into Latin by Rufinus, and often ascribed to Jerome. The *Lausiac History*, so-called because its prologue is addressed to Lausus, Theodosius II's chamberlain, tells of Palladius' visit, at the end of the fourth century, to the monks of Egypt, and also Palestine: it consists, largely, of a string of brief saints' *Lives*. The *History of the Monks of Egypt* purports to be the account of a visit by seven travellers to the Egyptian desert in about 394–5. Palladius is generally credited with credulous authenticity; the journey of the seven travellers is usually regarded as a literary fiction. There is considerable overlap between the two works. Both of them promote the primacy of monastic Egypt. Similar to these in that it is a collection of saints' *Lives*, though it is mostly historical reminiscence, not the record of a journey, is Theodoret's *Religious History* or *Ascetic Life*, an account of notable ascetics of Syria from the middle of the fourth century to his own time (it was written in 440). Like the other histories, it is full of miracles and feats of staggering asceticism (one of the longest chapters concerns Symeon the Stylite), but it redresses the balance by the attention it gives to Syria.

Instructional literature obviously includes monastic rules: those of Pachomius, Basil, Augustine, and, for Palestine, what can be discerned of the rules of Chariton and Gerasimus. These were put together for particular communities, but Rufinus' translation of Basil's rules and Jerome's of Pachomius gave them wider currency, and they became the inspiration for further monastic experiments. In the category of letters providing instruction in the monastic life, pre-eminent are probably such letters by Athanasius, Basil the Great, his friend Gregory Nazianzen, John Chrysostom and Theodoret, and in the West, Jerome,[7] as well as Paulinus of Nola and Augustine. But there are also some important letters from the Fathers of the Egyptian desert: seven letters (originally written in Coptic, extant in various versions) by Antony of Egypt himself, and fourteen letters by his successor Ammonas (lost in their original Coptic, preserved in full in Syriac and partially in various other languages). The letters of Antony have attracted a good deal of attention recently on the grounds of their alleged Origenism.[8] There are a good many ascetical homilies from Basil (not to mention those of Messalian provenance ascribed to Macarius, already mentioned), but otherwise comparatively few monastic homilies of our period survive.

The most important monastic literature of an instructional kind is, however, the writings of Evagrius and John Cassian. Evagrius came from Pontus, and was, to begin with, linked with Basil and Gregory Nazianzen (the former ordained him reader and the latter deacon). He is next found in Palestine, in the circle of Melania the Elder. Eventually in 383 he went to Egypt, where he was a disciple of both the Macarii, spending two years in Nitria, before going on the Cellia, where he spent the last fourteen years of his life, dying in 399. Evagrius was at the heart of the Origenist controversy that racked the Egyptian monks in the last decade of the fourth century (he was condemned posthumously by Theophilus of Alexandria in 402) and continued to disturb monasticism in the East for centuries: condemned at the Fifth Œcumenical Council in 553, Origenism was still a live problem in monastic circles in the seventh century, as we can see from the writings of St Maximus the Confessor (d. 662). It is likely that Evagrius caught Origenism from the Cappadocian Fathers, and was further encouraged by the influence of Melania who, according to Palladius, 'turned night into day' reading Origen (*Laus.* 55). Inspired by the Christian Platonism of Origen (and also Clement of Alexandria), Evagrius produced a theoretical analysis of the monastic way of prayer and asceticism of such manifest value that, despite his repeated condemnation for Origenism, his analysis became the basis of all later Eastern Christian spirituality (not just Greek). This analysis drew on the Platonic tripartite analysis of the soul into intellect and two irrational parts: the incensive (or irascible) part and desire. The natural state of the intellect was imageless contemplation of God, in which it regained its original pre-fallen state, and became equivalent to Christ's unfallen soul – ἰσόχριστος. To reach this state, it is necessary to reduce the irrational parts of the soul to a state of calmness, so that they do not disturb the intellect. The way to this is ascetic struggle (the active way, what Evagrius called πρακτική). To help such ascetics Evagrius analysed the dangers faced by the intellect into eight principal λογισμοί (temptations, obsessive trains of thought): gluttony, avarice, fornication, anger, accidie (listlessness), grief, vainglory and pride (the source of the later Western 'seven deadly sins'). The goal of such ascetic struggle was a state of calmness that he called (borrowing a Stoic word, *via* Clement of Alexandria) ἀπάθεια. Once the ascetic had attained ἀπάθεια, he could go on to achieve a state of pure prayer. This teaching Evagrius set out in a variety of treatises and letters, which, because of his condemnation within the Byzantine Empire, are often extant in Syriac translation, or preserved in Greek under a pseudonym, often his younger contemporary, Nilus. Most important, perhaps, are his two trilogies: *Praktikos* or *The Monk*, the *Gnostic*, and his *Gnostic Chapters*; and the more advanced *On Thoughts*, *Reflections* (Σκέμματα), and his *Chapters on Prayer*. The literary form of some of these works is worth noting. The *Praktikos* is a 'century' (ἑκατοντάς), consisting of a hundred (mostly brief) chapters (or paragraphs). The *Gnostic Chapters*, too, consist of six centuries. Evagrius seems to have introduced this genre to Christian monastic literature, where it became immensely popular (later examples include that by Diadochus of Photike, one of the bishops who attended the Council of Chalcedon, who should be mentioned here, as his *Century* essays a thoughtful marriage of Evagrian and Macarian themes). But with Evagrius there is a twist to it: the last ten chapters of the *Praktikos* consist of *apophthegmata*; while the last ten of each of the six centuries of the *Gnostic Chapters* are simply omitted. Perhaps Evagrius wanted to suggest that theory can go only so far: beyond there is practice, or simply silence. The *Chapters on Prayer* consist of 153 chapters, the manifold significance of this number being explained in the introduction.

Cassian was a Latin, a native probably of Scythia (modern Dobrudja), who made his way to the Egyptian desert in the last years of the fourth century, where he became a disciple of Evagrius. He left the desert after Evagrius' death and seems to have gone to Constantinople, probably in connection with the Origenist monks' appeal to John Chrysostom. There he was ordained deacon, but left after the fall of John. He then turns up in Provence, having spent some time in Rome where he became friends with the future Pope Leo. He founded two monasteries at Marseille, one for men and one for women, and advised Castor, bishop of Apt, over a monastic foundation. His monastic writings take the form of two works, his *Institutes*, dedicated to Castor, and his *Conferences* (*Conlationes*); he also wrote, at the request of Leo, then archdeacon of Rome, a refutation of Nestorianism, *On the Incarnation*, to brief the pope for the coming Council of Ephesus (431).

The *Institutes* is in twelve books: the last eight treat of the eight principal vices (Evagrius' eight λογισμοί), the first four of the life of the monk – clothing (book 1), the night office according to Egyptian practice (2), the day office according to Palestinian and Mesopotamian practice (3), and the monastic common life and the virtues it requires (4). There are, however, enormous problems about the integrity of the text as we have it. The *Conferences* are presented as discourses by several of the ascetics of the Egyptian desert: they are set in the context of a tour of monastic sites. They raise various problems. It seems unlikely that, many years later, Cassian can have remembered such lengthy discourses: some of them certainly display the mind of Cassian (notably the thirteenth conference, ascribed to abba Chaeremon, which was taken to be an attack on Augustine's doctrine of grace and predestination). However, the monks to whom Cassian ascribes the teaching of the *Conferences* are not well known, as one would expect if Cassian were seeking to claim for his teaching the authority of the Desert Fathers. A further question concerns the influence of Evagrius. Cassian represents the main structure of Evagrian monastic spirituality, but he avoids anything controversial: so there is no mention of Evagrian ἀπάθεια, which had been attacked by Jerome directly (and implicitly by Augustine)[9] – it becomes the innocuous *puritas cordis*. Except through Cassian, in this modified form, Evagrius' influence on the West was extremely limited: only a very few short works were translated into Latin. Nonetheless, Cassian does seek to assume the mantle of the Desert Fathers, probably to establish himself where there was already a good deal of monastic wisdom on offer: and in this he was successful, as his influence on fifth-century Provençal monasticism and especially Benedict's commendation in his *Rule* (notably the last chapter) bear witness.

But the culmination of the traditional monastic literature is the *Sayings of the Fathers*, the *Apophthegmata Patrum* (called in Greek, τὸ Γεροντικόν, 'the [book] of the old men': γέρων being the usual term for a spiritual father). These are collections of stories about the monks of the Egyptian desert, which contain pithy teaching about prayer and the spiritual life expressed in sayings or proverbs. Sometimes the teaching is in the form of an acted parable. The context of the stories is the search for spiritual wisdom. Such a seeker would approach one of the Fathers, saying, 'Speak to me a word that I may live': the Father's often gnomic replies form the basis of the collections of *Apophthegmata*. With a few notable exceptions such as Basil the Great, Gregory Nazianzen, Epiphanius and Ephrem the Syrian, the monks concerned are those who lived in the Egyptian desert from the mid-fourth to the mid-fifth century. By the middle of the fifth century many of the Fathers had been driven by barbarian raids away from the Egyptian desert to Palestine and beyond.

These collections of sayings exist in a number of different forms, and in many different languages, though the original seems to have been Greek. One form of the sayings collects them according to the different Fathers, arranged in alphabetical order (the 'alphabetical collection'); to this there seems to have been appended a collection of anonymous sayings (the 'anonymous collection'). Yet another form arranges the sayings of the Fathers according to subject: love, humility, fasting, anger, etc. (the 'systematic collection'). The relationship between the alphabetical-anonymous and the systematic collection is much disputed: does one depend on the other, or are they independent? (It seems clear that the answer is not the same for the collections in different languages: the Latin systematic is based on the alphabetical, but this may not be true of the Greek original, or the other versions.) Another disputed issue concerns the source of these sayings: are they drawn from literary sources, or have they been handed down orally? Some sayings (all but one of Evagrius', for instance) certainly come from literary sources: but what of the rest? Another closely related question is whether the sayings have been taken from longer discourses, or whether their gnomic form is original. A strong case has been made that the sayings were handed down as sayings, in the context of monastic spiritual direction.[10] But a final answer awaits a more thorough knowledge of the complex literary tradition than has yet been attained. A further question concerns where, when and by whom such a collection was first made. Palestine, at the end of the fifth century at the earliest, possibly by a monk who had fled the Egyptian desert: these seem plausible answers. The collections as we have them are later than the other literature discussed in this book, and, whether by historical tradition or a retrospective depiction of current monastic ideals, constitute a rhetorical construction in the Egyptian desert of the golden age of monasticism, a veritable Paradise of the Fathers.

Notes

1 For this approach, see especially Elm, *'Virgins of God'. The Making of Asceticism in Late Antiquity*; also, independently of Elm, Richard Price's succinct discussion in the introduction to his translation of Theodoret of Cyrrhus, *A History of the Monks of Syria*, CSS 88 (1985), xxiii–xxvii.

2 I have cited the Syriac collection, as it is easily acccessible in E. A. Wallis Budge's translation: *The Paradise of the Holy Fathers*, popular edn, 2 vols (London: Chatto and Windus, 1907).

3 *CPG* 2827 (*PG* 30, 669–809).

4 D. Amand and M. Ch. Moons, 'Une curieuse homélie grecque inédite sur la virginité adressée aux pères de famille', *RBen* 63 (1953), 18–39, 211–38.

5 See *CPG* 2410–27 (Ps.-Macarius / Symeon) for details of editions, versions, and a few other items.

6 See ch. 24.

7 See ch. 28.

8 See S. Rubenson, *The Letters of St Anthony*.

9 Jerome, *Ep.* 133.3; cf. Augustine's criticism of Stoic *apatheia* in *De Civitate Dei* 9.4. On this see A. M. Casiday, 'Apatheia and Sexuality in the Thought of Augustine and Cassian'.

10 See G. Gould, *The Desert Fathers on Monastic Community*, 17–25.

35

Women and words: texts by and about women

SUSAN ASHBROOK HARVEY

Women's authorship is rarely found in ancient Christianity. The oldest known artistic work of literature by a Christian woman to survive intact is the *Cento Vergilianus de laudibus Christi* by a fourth-century noblewoman commonly identified as Faltonia Betitia Proba (*c.* 320–*c.* 370).[1] Among the very first Christian poems in Latin, Proba's *Cento* is some 694 verses in length, retelling Christianity's sacred history as given in Genesis 1–8 and the New Testament Gospels through one of the most difficult classical literary genres, the cento (from the word for a patchwork cloak; late Gk κέντρων). A cento was a poem consisting solely of lines, half-lines or phrases drawn from earlier, generally epic, works and strung together to present an entirely new subject. Modern scholars have generally scorned the cento, seeing it as a mechanical exercise. But to the ancient eye, the cento in either Greek or Latin was a respected literary form: an artistic challenge of extraordinary difficulty because of its stringent requirements, displaying the highest degree of learning, and paying due reverence to the greatest poetry of the classical era.

Proba constructed her *Cento* entirely from lines of Virgil. Creation is told through the myth of the Golden Age and Christ is cast as an epic hero in the mould of Aeneas – a stern lawgiver, a valiant bringer of peace. Proba displays a dazzling ingenuity in presenting biblical stories through verses containing no biblical names and expressing an altogether different religious view. Jerome (*Ep.* 53.7) castigated her efforts to employ Virgil for Christian purposes, indicating by his very complaint the unusual degree to which Proba had succeeded in appropriating classical tradition for Christian use. Indeed, Proba's *Cento* circulated widely in the eastern and western Roman Empire, for some centuries serving in the West as a school text for teaching children classical Latin literature and Christian stories at one and the same time.

Proba's *Cento* is her only surviving work although we know of at least one other, a poem on the civil war between Constantius II and Magnentius. Neither of Proba's known works fit the rubric of 'women's subjects'; both address patriarchal and politically foundational themes for the Empire of her day, themes that in no way make distinct the location of women's experience. Hence her work illuminates the specific interests to which classical education attended: a civic rather than domestic context, and the perspective of men who could be active players within that sphere, as well as the interlocked relationship between literature as public discourse and its political assumptions.

One other substantial Latin work by a Christian woman has partially survived from the late fourth century, known as the *Itinerarium* ('Journey' or 'Travels') of Egeria, an account of a woman's remarkable pilgrimage from the Western Roman Empire to the Holy Land between 381 and 384.[2] Surviving in a single eleventh-century manuscript, the damaged text has provoked heated debate as to the writer's exact name, dates, and place of origin.[3] The text itself is a narrative apparently written at the end of Egeria's journey from notes she took en route, and addressed to her 'dear ladies': the women of her spiritual community back home. The extant portion is in two parts: first, describing the journey from her approach to Mount Sinai until her stop in Constantinople, and secondly, a detailed account of the liturgical services and observances of the church calendar in Jerusalem.

Interestingly, while Egeria is always attentive to bridging the geographical and cultural distances that separate her spiritual sisters from biblical territory, her focus on her audience lends an exclusivity to her reporting. Despite her vivid accounts of the people who guided, hosted and informed her travels – bishops, abbots and civic dignitaries – no one is named in her text apart from her 'dearest' friend the deaconess and monastic superior Marthana, whom Egeria encountered twice during her travels.

Although virtually contemporary, Egeria's *Itinerarium* is as different from Proba's *Cento* as can be imagined. Written in a strikingly direct colloquial style, the *Itinerarium* appears to represent the vernacular speech of the day. Scholars have tended to view Egeria as literate but unlearned, for the text shows no evidence of training in the Latin classics. However, Egeria's Latin also gives every indication that a high degree of Christian education was becoming possible, without necessarily including classical study. Thus her vocabulary and syntax are steeped in the language of the Old Latin Bible and liturgy, while the liturgical information she provides from Jerusalem required an astute sophistication in matters of ecclesiastical ritual, office and tradition.

Not long after Egeria's pilgrimage, the Empress Eudocia (born Athenaïs; *c.* 400–60), wife of Theodosius II, produced highly accomplished Greek poetry.[4] As empress, Eudocia was part of an extraordinary intellectual flowering in Constantinople fostered by the court of Theodosius II with a sensibility akin to Proba's, one that held classical tradition in deep reverence and sought to engage it for Christian expression.[5]

Eudocia is credited by later writers with having authored six works: hexameter versions of the books of Zechariah and Daniel; a hexameter paraphrase of the Octoteuch; three books in hexameters on the martyrdoms of Cyprian and Justina; a Homeric address to the people of Antioch, delivered *c.* 438; a panegyric on the victory of Theodosius II over the Persians in 422; and a Homeric cento on the Life of Christ. Recently an encomium on the baths of Hammat Gader has also been identified as hers, surviving as a seventeen-line inscription.[6] Apart from this inscription and two stray lines from her other works, we have extant only 800 lines of the *Martyrdom of St. Cyprian*.[7] Eudocia's style has been harshly judged by modern scholars for her uneven command of metrical rules and the apparent lack of originality in her themes and chosen literary forms. If the former charge is strictly speaking true, the latter is more difficult to assess. Like Proba – a calligraphic copy of whose *Cento* was commissioned by Theodosius II, and whose influence on Eudocia thus seems likely – Eudocia wrote Christian literature in the forms and style of classical tradition; like Proba she wrote biblical paraphrases for the didactic purpose of combining classical literature with Christian sacred story; like Proba she wrote primarily on topics of civic import and political persuasion, without specific reference to 'women's experience' (albeit she wrote as empress: hardly a standard vantage point). Her chosen literary mode of expression was one that her culture would value far more than ours. In the sixth century, the noblewoman Anicia Juliana (d. 528) cited Eudocia's model in the elegant epigram she produced for inscription in the Church of Hagios Polyeuktos in Constantinople, a rare and sumptuous joining of literary and visual arts.[8]

These few women are the only known female authors from the fourth to the sixth centuries whose works survive. At the turn of the sixth century, and of entirely different literary quality, two hagiographies authored by women appeared, one each in Latin and Greek. The *Life* of Queen Radegund (d. 587) was written around 600 by her companion the nun Baudonivia.[9] Accounts of Radegund by Venantius Fortunatus and Gregory of Tours emphasize domestic devotional life, (private) individual acts of mercy, and her horrifying self-mortification. By contrast, Baudonivia highlights Radegund's political and civic involvements, as well as her theological and spiritual teachings; the difference is arresting. Around 630, the nun Sergia, superior of the Constantinopolitan convent founded by the late fourth-century holy woman Olympias, wrote a short narrative on the transfer of Olympias' relics and the volatile formation of her cult.[10] These two hagiographies point to a second category of 'women's words' that survive from this period, in the form of teachings ascribed to women saints.

The well-known *Sayings of the Desert Fathers* (*Apophthegmata Patrum*), the collected teachings of Egypt's great fourth- and fifth-century monastic saints, preserve the sayings of three women: Theodora, Sarah and Syncletica.[11] Sayings make use of anecdotes, instructions, insights and admonitions to provide spiritual direction. Because the collections were edited with much reworking from oral tradition, it is difficult to establish authenticity. Many sayings circulated anonymously or under more than one name. The fact that ten sayings are ascribed to Theodora, nine to Sarah, and twenty-seven to Syncletica indicates the surpassing reputations of these women, as well as the poverty of our extant sources. The sayings of Theodora and Syncletica are addressed to religious communities of women, although the sayings of both (and especially Theodora's) are inclusive of the experiences of monks. Sarah seems to have been a solitary, and her sayings affirm grave tension around the issue of gender and spiritual authority.[12]

Syncletica's importance may be measured not only by the large number of sayings attributed to her in the *Apophthegmata*, but also by the anonymous fifth-century hagiography about her.[13] In the *Vita*, eighty of the 113 chapters present Syncletica's teachings to her nuns, in several places closely connected to those attributed to her in the *Apophthegmata*. Heavily influenced by Evagrius Ponticus, her teachings contain lively metaphors drawn from urban and domestic life as well as striking use of imagery related to the suffering of illness.

A similar picture survives for Macrina, the sister of Gregory of Nyssa and Basil of Caesarea. In his *Life of Macrina*, Gregory presents her as a holy woman to be remembered above all as a teacher – of himself, her family and household, her convent, and women throughout the region – styling her as a true philosopher.[14] In his treatise *On the Soul and Resurrection*, Gregory purports to describe the conversation he had with Macrina on her deathbed[15] in a literary form modelled on Plato's *Phaedo*.[16] Scholars are divided as to whether Gregory here honours Macrina by using her as a literary device for his own views – as Plato did with Socrates – or whether he is actually representing her words.[17] In the *Vita* Gregory presents Macrina as one who consciously rejected all classical education, choosing instead devoted study of Scripture and other sacred writings. While Basil, Gregory, and their friend Gregory of Nazianzus epitomized the Christian appropriation of classical education and culture, Gregory depicts Macrina paradoxically as both the antithesis of such education and as the true exemplar of philosophical wisdom: a common topos in hagiographical literature of the time.

Macrina presents the same conundrum as Syncletica, Sarah and Theodora. To what extent can we understand the men who wrote these texts to have reproduced what these women said? Or did literary as well as cultural dictates form a presentation that in fact occluded not only the words of these women but even their effective presence, allowing men to present their own teachings through the fictive voices of women, as Plato did with Diotima in his *Symposium* (a work clearly influencing Gregory's portrait of Macrina)?[18] The problem persists in the array of hagiographical literature from this period that presents holy women as authoritative teachers, especially of women but also of men, with regard to theological, moral and scholarly matters. Melania the Elder, friend of Rufinus; her granddaughter Melania the Younger; the circle of the Roman matron Marcella, well known to Jerome, as well as his beloved companions Paula and her daughter Eustochium; Nonna and Gorgonia, mother and sister of Gregory of Nazianzus; Olympias, deaconess and friend of John Chrysostom: all are portrayed in our ancient sources as exceptionally discerning religious instructors, and some also as distinguished scholars.[19]

Of the teachings of these women, nothing survives to us apart from the descriptions provided by the men who wrote in their praise. Notoriously, even when they were known to be correspondents – Melania with Rufinus; Marcella, Paula, Eustochium and others with Jerome; Olympias with Chrysostom – their letters were not preserved. The one possible exception is Jerome's Letter 46 to Marcella, which some scholars now attribute to Paula and Eustochium, inviting Marcella to join them in the Holy Land.[20] Only a few letters by women survive from this period, almost all of them written by empresses or queens on official matters (for example, to popes).[21] They remind us that women could, in exceptional circumstances, participate in the political discourse of the day, but they do not illuminate us further. Similarly, we know that women were patrons of literature: Gregory of Nazianzus wrote a poem for Olympias' wedding,[22] and Gregory of Nyssa's *Commentary on the Song of Songs* was also dedicated to her.[23] Other works were dedicated to the sisters or women friends of the authors. Does this evidence indicate women's participation in learned literary activity? Or did the education of women encourage their formation as students and scholars, rather than as 'producers' of literature?[24]

The dilemma presented by the hagiographical portraits of holy women applies also when asking whether or not any of the *Vitae* was written by women, a question that has also been raised for some of the Apocryphal Acts.[25] The sixth-century *Life of Febronia*, originally composed in Syriac but popular also in Greek and Latin, claims to have been written by Febronia's companion nun Thomaïs.[26] Its portrayal of convent life is vibrantly positive, both in terms of the spiritual friendships between the nuns and regarding their devotion to learning and philosophical discourse. Because of similar emphases, a woman author has been proposed for the anonymous sixth-century Greek *Life of Matrona of Perge*.[27] Two caveats warn against such assumptions, however. First, hagiographical literature, like its predecessor the Greek novel, by its literary dictates granted a greater visibility to the domestic sphere, including a greater role for female characters. The reasons had to do with ideological shifts in the depiction of proper religious life and with concern about social control during an era of political and religious upheaval, but not with an improved interest in or social status for women.[28] In the case of Febronia, for example, the character of Thomaïs is essential for the story's narrative (parts of which could not have been witnessed by a man); and the depiction of the convent is cast in terms of classical descriptions of the (male) philosophical ideals of friendship and community. Second, men clearly could write with deep admiration about holy women, as did Gregory of Nyssa, Gregory of Nazianzus and Jerome. A positive portrait of a woman does not indicate the gender of the writer.[29] On the other hand, we may take the parallel from apocryphal literature as instructive in the sense that hagiography was both a literary and an oral discourse. It may well be that some of the anonymous hagiographies reflect women's stories as women told them. Certainly, we may be sure that women and men could hear these stories differently in terms of how they addressed women's experience.[30] Beyond this, we cannot say more.

The Christian literature by and about women surviving from late antiquity presents us with substantial evidence that the women authors whose names we know represent the tip of an iceberg. Aristocratic women sometimes obtained the same classical education as men; women of lesser means could still attain a high level of learning, particularly in Bible and other Christian literature, especially in convents where women were clearly expected to cultivate such learning as a part of their religious formation. From both populations, women corresponded with bishops, theologians and spiritual leaders. We know that women wrote, far more than the few extant pieces we have.[31] What survives is the record of words lost. The silence is deafening.

Notes

1 Elizabeth A. Clark and Diane F. Hatch, *The Golden Bough, the Oaken Cross: the Virgilian Cento of Faltonia Betitia Proba* (Chico, CA: Scholars Press, 1981) reproduces the critical edition of Carolus Schenkl in Michael Petschenig, ed., *Poetae Christiani*

Minores, CSEL 16 (Vienna: F. Tempsky, 1888; repr. New York: Johnson, 1972) on pp. 511–640, with ET and excellent commentary. Recently Proba's identity has been questioned, although the view has not met with wide acceptance. See Danuta Shanzer, 'The Anonymous *Carmen contra paganos* and the Date and Identity of the Centonist Proba', *Revue des Études Augustiniennes* 32 (1986), 232–48; Hagith Sivan, 'Anician Women, the Cento of Proba, and Aristocratic Conversion in the Fourth Century', *VigChr* 47 (1993), 140–57.

2 E. Franceschini and R. Weber, *Itinerarium Egeriae*, CCSL 175 (1965), 27–90; Pierre Maraval and Manuel C. Díaz y Díaz, *Journal de voyage (itineraire)*, SC 296 (1982). An exceptionally fine commentary accompanies the ET in John D. Wilkinson, *Egeria's Travels to the Holy Land*, rev. edn (Jerusalem: Ariel; Warminster: Aris and Phillips, 1981). See also George E. Gingras, *Egeria: Diary of a Pilgrimage*, ACW 38 (1970).

3 See the collected bibliography in Marek Starowieyeski, 'Bibliografia Egeriana', *Augustinianum* 19 (1979), 297–318.

4 The ancient *testimonia* as well as extant fragments of her works are collected in Arthur Ludwich, *Eudociae Augustae, Procli Lycii, Claudiani carminum graecorum reliquiae* (Leipzig: Teubner, 1897).

5 See esp. Kenneth G. Holum, *Theodosian Empresses: Women and Imperial Dominian in Late Antiquity* (Berkeley: University of California Press, 1982); Alan Cameron, 'The Empress and the Poet: Paganism and Politics at the Court of Theodosius II', in *Literature and Society in the Early Byzantine World* (London: Variorum Reprints, 1985), III.

6 Judith Green and Yoram Tsafrir, 'Greek Inscriptions from Hammat Gader: A Poem by the Empress Eudocia and Two Building Inscriptions', *Israel Exploration Journal* 32 (1982), 77–96.

7 English translation in M. Thiébaux, *The Writings of Medieval Women: An Anthology*, 49–69.

8 A truly extraordinary achievement in both artistic modes: see Carolyn L. Connor, 'The Epigram in the Church of Hagios Polyeuktos in Constantinople and its Byzantine Response', *Byzantion* 69 (1999), 479–527. The epigram of 76 lines was also preserved in the *Greek Anthology*; see the discussions in Connor, 'Epigram', passim.

9 Translated and discussed in J. M. Petersen, *Handmaids of the Lord: Holy Women in Late Antiquity and the Early Middle Ages*, 365–41, along with the *Vita* by Fortunatus and the account of her funeral by Gregory of Tours. Petersen mistakenly claims to present the first ET of the two hagiographies of Radegund. Both, however, were skilfully translated and discussed in *Sainted Women of the Dark Ages*, ed. and trans. Jo Ann McNamara and John E. Halborg with E. Gordon Whatley (Durham and London: Duke University Press, 1992), at 60–105.

10 Discussed and translated in E. A. Clark, *Jerome, Chrysostom, and Friends: Essays and Translations*, 107–57. The Greek was edited by Hippolyte Delehaye, 'Narratio Sergiae de Translatione Sanctae Olympiadis', *Analecta Bollandiana* 16 (Brussels: Société des Bollandistes, 1897), 44–51.

11 The best source at present is the Greek version in Migne, *PG* 65, cols 71–440, supplemented with J.-C. Guy, *Recherches sur la Tradition Grecques des Apophthegmata Patrum*, Subsidia Hagiographica 36 (Brussels: Société des Bollandistes, 1962). ET in Benedicta Ward, *The Sayings of the Desert Fathers: the Alphabetical Collection*, rev. edn (Kalamazoo, MI: Cistercian Publications, 1984).

12 See Benedicta Ward, 'Apophthegmata Matrum', *SP* 16.2, ed. Elizabeth A. Livingstone, TU 129 (1985), 63–6.

13 *Vita S. Syncleticae*, Migne, *PG* 28, 1487–1558; trans. Elizabeth A. Castelli, 'Pseudo-Athanasius, *The Life and Activity of the Holy and Blessed Teacher Syncletica*', in Vincent Wimbush, ed., *Ascetic Behavior in Greco-Roman Antiquity: A Sourcebook* (Minneapolis: Fortress Press, 1990), 265–311. There is another ET by Elizabeth Bryson Bongie, *The Life of Blessed Syncletica by Pseudo-Athanasius* (Toronto: Peregrina Publishing Co., 1996).

14 *Vita S. Macrinae*, ed. Virginia Woods Callahan in *Gregorii Nysseni Opera*, ed. Werner Jaeger (Leiden: Brill, 1959), VIII.1, 347–414; ET by Virginia Woods Callahan, *Gregory of Nyssa, Ascetical Works*, FC 58 (1967), 161–91. See also Pierre Maraval, *Vie de sainte Macrine*, SC 178 (1971).

15 *Vita S. Macr.*, ed. Callahan, VIII.1, 389–91.

16 Gregory of Nyssa, *De anima et resurrectione dialogus*, *PG* 46, 11–160; trans. Virginia Woods Callahan, *Gregory of Nyssa, Ascetical Works*, 195–272. There is another ET by Catharine P. Roth, *St. Gregory of Nyssa, The Soul and the Resurrection*, PPS (1993).

17 E.g., J. Pelikan, *Christianity and Classical Culture*, *passim*, uses the *Vita S. Macrinae* and the *De anima et resurrectione* to present Macrina as a thinker quite independent of her brother, referring to her throughout his book as 'the Fourth Cappadocian'. See the more subtle treatment in Ruth Albrecht, *Das Leben der heiligen Makrina auf dem Hintergrund der Thekla-Traditionen* (Göttingen: Vandenhoeck and Ruprecht, 1986).

18 See the pivotal works of David M. Halperin, 'Why is Diotima a Woman?' in *One Hundred Years of Homosexuality and Other Essays on Greek Love* (New York: Routledge, 1990) 113–51, 190–211; Averil Cameron, 'Virginity as Metaphor: Women and the Rhetoric of Early Christianity', in Averil Cameron, ed., *History as Text: The Writing of Ancient History* (Chapel Hill: University of North Carolina Press, 1989), 181–205.

19 Palladius, *Lausiac History*, chs 5, 9, 18, 38, 46, 54; Denis Gorce, *Vie de Sainte Mélanie*, SC 90 (1962); ET by Elizabeth A. Clark, *The Life of Melania the Younger* (Lewiston, NY: Edwin Mellen Press, 1984); Jerome, *Ep.* 45, 47, 108, 127; Gregory of Nazianzus, Or. 8 (on Gorgonia) and *Or.* 18 (on his father); 'Vie d'Olympias', ed. Anne-Marie Malingrey, in *Jean Chrysostome: Lettres à Olympias*, 2nd edn, SC 13 bis (1968), 393–449, ET in Clark, *Jerome, Chrysostom, and Friends*, 107–44.

20 The Latin is edited in Isidorus Hilberg, *Sancti Eusebii hieronymi epistolae*, Pt 1, CSEL 54 (Vienna: F. Tempsky; Leipzig: G. Freytag, 1905), 329–44; translation and discussion in P. Dronke, *Women Writers of the Middle Ages: A Critical Study of*

Texts from Perpetua (203) to Marguerite Porete (1310), 17–19, where it is discussed in comparison with Egeria's *Itinerarium*.

21 Editions and translations (where they exist) are listed in A. Kadel, *Matrology: A Bibliography of Writings by Christian Women from the First to the Fifteenth Centuries*, 55–61.

22 'Ad Olympiadem', Migne, *PG* 37, 1542–50.

23 *Gregorii Nysseni Opera*, ed. Jaeger, VI, 3.

24 See the incisive discussion by G. Clark, *Women in Late Antiquity: Pagan and Christian Lifestyles*, 119–38.

25 See especially Ross S. Kraemer, 'Women's Authorship of Jewish and Christian Literature in the Greco-Roman Period', in A.-J. Levine, ed., *'Women Like This': New Perspectives on Jewish Women in the Greco-Roman World*, 221–42.

26 The Syriac is edited in Paul Bedjan, *Acta Martyrum et Sanctorum* 5 (Paris and Leipzig: Otto Harrassowitz, 1895), 573–615; ET and notes in Sebastian P. Brock and Susan Ashbrook Harvey, *Holy Women of the Syrian Orient*, 150–76, 192–3. No known work by a woman survives in Syriac from the ancient Christian period. The *Life of Febronia*, despite its claims, is unlikely to have been authored by a woman. There is the intriguing possibility of one anonymous verse homily (*mimre*) of the sixth century, where the author seems to make one brief self-reference with a feminine singular verb form; see Sebastian P. Brock, 'Two Syriac Verse Homilies on the Binding of Isaac,' *Le Muséon* 99 (1986), 61–129, at 98–9.

27 The Greek is edited by Hippolyte Delehaye, *Acta Sanctorum Novembris* 3 (Brussels: Sociéte des Bollandistes, 1910), 790–813; trans. by Jeffrey Featherstone and Cyril Mango in *Holy Women of Byzantium: Ten Saints' Lives in English Translation*, ed. Alice-Mary Talbot (Washington, DC: Dumbarton Oaks Publications, 1996), 13–64. Female authorship has been suggested by Eva Catafygiotu Topping, 'St. Matrona and Her Friends: Sisterhood in Byzantium', in J. Chrysostomides, ed., *Kathegetria: Essays Presented to Joan Hussey for her 80th Birthday* (Camberley: Porphyrogenitus Press, 1988), 211–24.

28 Cf. the discussion in Susan Ashbrook Harvey, 'Sacred Bonding: Mothers and Daughters in Early Syriac Hagiography', *JECS* 4 (1996), 27–56.

29 Mary R. Lefkowitz, 'Did Ancient Women Write Novels?' in Levine, ed., *'Women Like This'*, 199–219.

30 Harvey, 'Sacred Bonding'; Carolyn Walker Bynum, 'Introduction: The Complexity of Symbols', in Carolyn Walker Bynum, Stevan Harrell and Paula Richman, eds, *Gender and Religion: On the Complexity of Symbols*, (Boston: Beacon Press, 1986), 1–20.

31 I have not treated, for reasons of space, a few secular poems possibly by women and a handful of epitaphs. See Kadel, *Matrology*, 44, 51–2, 54.

36

Conciliar records and canons

ANDREW LOUTH

The first major issue faced by the early Church, that of the terms under which Gentiles could become Christians, was settled, according to the Acts of the Apostles, by a council of the apostles held at Jerusalem. This decided that Gentiles could become Christians, without becoming Jews, subject to renunciation of idolatry and sexual immorality, and certain dietary laws, about which we hear remarkably little in later Church history (see Acts 15:1–21). A very different picture of this dispute is derived from the epistles of St Paul, which make no mention of a council (nor of any dietary regulations), but sees the opening of the Church to the Gentiles as bound up with the authenticity of Paul's apostolic authority (see especially Gal. 2). Here we see two ways of reaching decisions in primitive Christianity – the council and the authority of the individual apostle (the latter of which can be amply illustrated from elsewhere in the New Testament) – both of which ground the authority for any decision in apostolicity.

Both these models of authority can be found in the later history of the Church – indeed, the tension between apostolic authority as conciliar and authority as exercised by an apostolic individual underlies the most fundamental division in later Christendom – but for our period there is little attempt to erase either pole of this tension. By the second century the basic institutional unit of the Church was the Christian congregation of a city and its hinterland (the *chora*) led by a single bishop, who exercised apostolic authority over that community (this is one of the principal themes of the letters of Ignatius of Antioch). Issues that involved the churches of a region were settled by councils (or synods, the Greek word, which Ammianus Marcellinus in the fourth century regarded as Christian terminology: *Res Gestae* 15.7.7; 21.16.18): examples from the second century are Montanism in Phrygia, and the question of the date of Easter (the 'Quartodeciman' controversy), although already there may have been an attempt to settle the latter controversy by the individual *fiat* of the bishop of Rome, Victor. Councils were called in the third century to settle issues of both doctrine and discipline (which were not sharply distinguished in this period). Bishops whose teaching was suspect were tried by synods of their fellow bishops: Bishop Beryllus was tried at his own see of Bostra, Bishop Heraclides at an unknown location, and Paul of Samosata at synods in his see of Antioch. The middle of the century, in the wake of the Decian persecution, saw synods dealing with the problem of mass apostasy occasioned by the persecution, and the related problem of the validity of the sacraments (especially baptism) of schismatical and heretical groups (here again, the bishop of Rome seems to have attempted to settle the issue of the baptism of heretics by his own *fiat*). We know a good deal more about these third-century synods than anything earlier. The record of the trial of Heraclides, in which Origen appears as a theological expert (as he was at the trial of Beryllus), was discovered in 1941 at Tura, south of Cairo, and much has been recovered of the records of Paul of Samosata's trial; records of the trial of Beryllus were known to Eusebius (and probably Socrates).[1] Several synodical letters from the mid-third-century councils survive.

Most of these third-century councils seem to have met for a particular purpose, though it would seem that North Africa already had the custom of regular regional councils (a practice required by the Council of Nicaea in 325: see canon 5). It is not absolutely clear whether anyone other than bishops shared in the decisions made by these councils: presbyters such as Origen and Malchion played an important role in the episcopal trials, but the decision may still have been made by the bishops present. The regional basis of these synods also seems ill-defined: the fact that synods met in provincial capitals may indicate that they were already provincial synods, but that conclusion goes beyond the evidence. Certainly as the fourth century progressed, the institutional structure of the Church came to be modelled on the administrative structure of the Empire, with metropolitan bishops exercising oversight over the city-based churches of the province from the provincial capital (the *metropolis*), and responsible for consecrating bishops and calling provincial synods. In other ways (already in the third century, and maybe earlier) the procedure of synods seems to have echoed Roman practice. Synods reached decisions by following the procedure of the senate. An issue to be decided would be introduced by a *relatio*; the opinions (*sententiae*) of the bishops present would be sought; and a decision (*senatus consultum*) would be reached by voting on these *sententiae* in turn until one of them achieved majority support, which would then be acclaimed by the assembled bishops. The whole discussion seems to have normally been recorded in shorthand, and the publication of the final decision drawn from this shorthand report: in the case of some councils, notably the North African councils and the Council of Serdica (343) this is evident in the form in which the decisions have been preserved. Later on canons were preserved in a more condensed form, simply as the decisions reached.

This decision came to be referred to as a κανών, a rule (the Latins simply transliterated it as *canon*). Other words are also used: ὅρος (definition), τύπος (pattern), and what the canons often referred to as custom, ἔθος, συνήθεια. It is notable that such a decision is rarely called a law: νόμος, *lex*. As Schwartz remarked: 'Nothing contradicts the essence of the ancient church so much as rigid, unchangeable laws; the elastic spirit, adapting itself to reality and yet determined in essentials, is not to be strangled.'[2] Further, canons were not thought to decree anything, rather to recognize already existing custom. So in the fourth century there is often reference to existing canons ('canons of the Fathers', 'canons of the Apostles') of which we have no evidence: these are not necessarily lost, it may simply refer to existing customs that had never been ratified by any council. Later a distinction developed between κανών and ὅρος: the latter came to be exclusively applied to doctrinal definitions, while the former was applied to decisions on matters of discipline, as well as to the anathematisms that frequently accompanied a doctrinal definition. Definitions included creeds (σύμβολα), such as the Nicene creed, though after the fourth century doctrinal decisions were no longer cast in the form of a creed. Another difference emerged between decisions concerning doctrine and those concerning discipline, in that the latter were subject to οἰκονομία, 'economy', which can respect the unique features of an individual case, whereas doctrinal decisions were increasingly regarded as sacrosanct. Disciplinary canons take a variety of forms: many of them are concerned with the administration of the penitential system and lay down the period of exclusion from eucharistic communion required from those guilty of various grave sins (the penance, ἐπιτίμιον, or *poena*); others are procedural (e.g., the rights and duties of the various clerical orders); others still, like doctrinal canons, take the form of anathematisms, outlawing various practices and opinions (all the canons of Gangra take this form).

The production of canons really got under way in the fourth century. To begin with this was partly a recurrence of the situation faced by the mid-third-century councils in the aftermath of the Great Persecution (e.g. the councils of Elvira in Spain, *c.* 306 perhaps, and Arles, 314, and Ancyra, probably 314). But as the century developed conciliar decisions were used to define the Church's own sense of identity, in matters doctrinal, as well as in matters of Christian conduct, mainly moral but also liturgical, and in relation to challenges to an increasingly entrenched episcopal authority (it was bishops who made these decisions!), especially by the growing monastic movement. Some of these councils were initiated by the bishops themselves, some called by the emperor (or by his officials); some came to be regarded as 'œcumenical' ('world-wide': from οἰκουμένη, the region ruled by the 'world-ruler', the emperor), others merely 'local' (τοπική). These two divisions are not the same, though all 'œcumenical' councils were called by the reigning emperor. Œcumenical councils (the term 'œcumenical' may originally have had some link with the Church's bid for tax exemption)[3] came to be regarded as possessing ultimate authority, especially in doctrinal matters (with which they were always concerned): there were four in our period, held at Nicaea (325), Constantinople (381), Ephesus (431), and Chalcedon (451). Local councils could often be no less important, but their canons were mainly disciplinary.

Canons were not only issued by councils. In the fourth century especially, and occasionally later, canons were issued by individual bishops on their own authority. Almost invariably these canons were issued in response to requests for guidance from other bishops, and imitate imperial rescripts. Already in the third century, Dionysius of Alexandria and Gregory Thaumaturgus, bishop of Neocaesarea, had issued canonical letters, the latter's letter largely concerned about compromise with paganism forced on those who had suffered from barbarian invasions. In the fourth century canonical letters were issued by Peter, Athanasius and Timothy of Alexandria, four Cappadocians – Basil of Caesarea, Gregory of Nazianzus, Gregory of Nyssa and Amphilochius of Iconium –, over the turn of the century by Theophilus of Alexandria and in the fifth century by Cyril of Alexandria and Gennadius I of Constantinople. The frequency with which popes of Alexandria issued canonical letters doubtless reflects the immense prestige of the see in this period. The most substantial (and important) of these 'canons of the Fathers' are those issued by Basil the Great. *Epp.* 188, 199 and 217 provide canons 1–85, a paragraph of *Ep.* 236 canon 86, *Epp.* 160, 55, 54, 53 canons 87–90, and *Epp.* 93 and 240 canons 94–5 (canons 91–3, concerning unwritten tradition, are drawn from *On the Holy Spirit*, and canon 96 is a separate *erotapokrisis* on heretics). The canons of Gregory Nazianzen and Amphilochius are both lists of the books of the scriptural canon, in verse.

In a somewhat different category – rather for what they were to become, than for what they were in our period – are the episcopal rescripts issued by the bishop of Rome. Such letters from earlier than the fourth century no longer survive, though we know from Cyprian's replies that Stephen of Rome issued such letters in the third century over the question of rebaptism of heretics. The first 'decretal' letter to survive (so-called because they, too, were modelled on the imperial rescript) is Siricius' letter to Himerius of Tarragona, issued on 11 February 385, though this letter makes it clear, with its reference to the 'general decrees' of his predecessor Liberius, that he regards himself as continuing an already established tradition. The issue of the ultimacy of conciliar *versus* the apostolic authority claimed by the bishop of Rome already emerges in our period with the papal repudiation of the third canon of Constantinople, and its expanded ratification in the twenty-eighth canon of Chalcedon, which granted the see of Constantinople precedence after Rome over all other sees, 'because it is New Rome': a repudiation expressed in terms of such a decision's contravening the sixth canon of Nicaea, but probably expressing a deeper repugnance to the implication that Rome's own authority derived from her status as 'Old Rome', rather than her pre-eminent apostolic foundation.

Canons and conciliar records survive because they were gathered into collections put together to provide a legal basis for the functioning of the Church of the Empire. In late antiquity such a legal basis fulfilled the dual function of providing practical rules and holding up an ideal, the ideal here being that of the 'apostolic' Church. The first collection of canons in the East seems to have originated in Antioch and to have consisted of the canons of the councils of Ancyra and Neocaesarea, enumerated in a single sequence. Later on there were added the canons of the councils of Nicaea, Gangra (340), Antioch (probably 341 but disputed) and Laodicea (uncertain of date, or even existence): this collection existed in Antioch by 381. It is striking that this collection, which remains the core of those canons normative for Byzantine canon law, was put together in an atmosphere hostile to the emerging 'neo-Nicene' orthodoxy: a fact which[4] may warn us against too facile a use of the term 'Arian' in relation to the problems of the mid-fourth century. Collections such as these, later reinforced with the 'canons of the Fathers', were endorsed by œcumenical councils, and formed the canon law of the Church, which by the time of the sixth-century Emperor Justinian had the force of imperial law.

Notes

1 Eusebius, *HE* 6.33; cf. Socrates, *HE* 3.7.

2 E. Schwartz, 'Die Kanonessammlungen der alten Reichskirche', a fundamental study.

3 So H. Chadwick, 'The Origin of the Title "Oecumenical Council"'.

4 Though note that John Chrysostom objected at the Synod of the Oak to being tried by canons drawn up by Arians: Palladius, *Dialogus de vita S. Ioannis Chrysostomi* 9, lines 20 and 79 (ed. A.-M. Malingrey and P. Leclercq, SC 341, 1988).

B.

*

CONTEXT AND INTERPRETATION

37

Social and historical setting

R. A. MARKUS

In the aftermath of the crises of the third century the Roman Empire was transformed in the time of the Emperors Diocletian (284–305) and Constantine (proclaimed emperor 306; in power over Western Empire from 312; sole emperor 324–37). The administrative structure, the society, the imperial office and the court underwent far-reaching changes under their reforms. The secular changes in the Empire could not fail to affect the life of the Christian Church. None, however, cut as deeply into its historical development as the change in its worldly status initiated by the advent of the first Christian emperor. Constantine's victory over his rival in 312, represented as God-given, seemed to usher in a new era. Not – as is often said – because it allowed the Christian Church to grow from a minority cult into a recognized, soon to be a dominant, and eventually legally enforced, religion. It had been well on the way to respectability in the later third century; and its full legal 'establishment' did not come about until the end of the fourth. The significance of the 'Constantinian revolution' lies rather in the fact that it transformed, almost overnight, the conditions of the Church's existence.

The main directions in the Church's development had been established in the first three centuries of its existence. The Church entered the fourth century with a set of beliefs and an organizational structure which gave it a recognizable identity. During the last forty years of the third century it had also spread rapidly and extensively. Its membership was no longer largely confined to the lower social ranks; it was very different from the way its opponents liked to represent it: as a secretive and outlandish sect of underprivileged and uneducated outcasts. In the rare cases where some estimate of the size and composition of the Christian community is possible, its membership seems to have been a cross-section of the Roman urban classes. The Church, though certainly still a minority, was a very much larger minority than it had been in the first half of the third century, and it now embraced the whole range of Roman urban society, from the aristocracy to the urban proletariat. The insecurity of a sect exposed to suspicion and unpopularity, sporadically flaring up into bouts of persecution, was almost a thing of the past when Diocletian launched the last persecution, known since antiquity as the 'Great Persecution'. Far-sighted Christians might have perceived the warning signs: in a time of crisis for the Empire, Diocletian's government sought to rally its subjects around the old traditions which had secured Roman greatness in the past. Christianity was powerful and important enough to be seen as a threat. It was the victim of its own success. Recognizing the ineffectiveness of persecution, the Emperor Galerius called it off on his deathbed in 311.

The Church which emerged from this last persecution was recognizably the Church as it had developed during the second half of the third century. The new conditions accentuated some of the developments already well under way in the third century, and, at the same time, brought new tensions. On the morrow of his victory over his rival Maxentius, Constantine granted freedom to Christians to practise their religion openly and restored to the churches legal rights to property. What began as official toleration quickly grew into imperial favour. Constantine's favours to the Church amounted to far more than the benefactions of a wealthy private patron. An ambitious programme of church building in Rome and the Holy Land sponsored by the emperor began in 313; munificent gifts and endowments to churches flowed from the imperial largesse. Enviable exemptions from onerous public duties and fiscal privileges were granted to Christian clergy, bishops were given the right of arbitrating in legal disputes, and Sunday was made an official day of rest. The enforcement of Christianity by legislation was the work of Constantine's successors. There was a wide gap between a Christian Empire and an emperor who happened to be a Christian: but imperial favour was fast eroding the apparent neutrality of the Roman state as expressed in the so-called Edict of Toleration of 312.

The Constantinian revolution gave a huge new impetus to the Church's spread and to the growth of its public importance. Christianity was becoming a way to prestige; conformity could pay. Christians came gradually to occupy public office and to achieve prominence at the imperial courts. Until the end of the century, however, Roman society remained very mixed. The new social relations of the fourth-century Empire brought greater mobility; a new aristocracy of imperial service came to grow up alongside the old senatorial aristocracy of birth, and provided opportunities for the advancement of new men. Although Christians were to be found increasingly at every level of the official hierarchy, they rubbed shoulders with non-Christians – with people whom the Christians came to call 'pagans'. The rate of Christianization was very uneven. The new religion had made far greater strides in the Eastern provinces than in the West. Towns had been the cradle of Christianity and remained its most natural milieu; the countryside always lagged behind. Among the urban masses, however, it seems to have become the dominant religion by the last quarter of the fourth century. Rioting by Christian mobs against pagans or Jews, sometimes condoned by clergy or incited by monks, was common in cities of the Empire long before the emperors outlawed pagan worship and sought to enforce Christian orthodoxy. By the end of the century which began with the 'Great Persecution', Christianity had become the religion of the majority of townsmen, and there was little opposition among Christians – other than those dissenting from the imperially endorsed orthodoxy – to the official repression of paganism and dissent.

Until the 380s the Christianization of Roman society was not so thorough that it would have seemed irreversible. The reign of the Emperor Julian 'the Apostate' (361–3) shows a very undecided balance of public opinion around 360: although Julian could often count on support for his programme of a pagan revival, he also met resistance to it. Among Christians, too, there was a sense of insecurity: the bad old times might easily return. Julian's immediate successors refrained from direct intervention in the religious conflicts of the fourth century; and it was not until its last decade that the emperors made any real attempt to impose Christianity by compulsion. The legislation of Theodosius I (379–95) and his successors sought to outlaw the public practice of pagan worship, of heretical belief and schism. Not much later, in the 430s, the Christian God took the place of Rome's ancient gods as the Empire's official protector.

The majority of bishops found no difficulty in accepting the new order of things. To the first generation of post-Constantinian Christians the conversion of a Roman emperor to Christianity seemed almost a miracle. They were ready to welcome the new era in terms often extravagant. Messianic language and imagery were applied to the Christian emperor in sermons and historical writings. The established order of Roman society was seen as a divinely sanctioned embodiment of Christian order. Roman imperial ideology and its rituals were reinterpreted in Christian terms. The emperor was God's representative on earth, singled out by divine providence to wield the authority of the *Logos* among his subjects. The reign of Constantine was seen as the fulfilment of the Old Testament's prophecies; in his reign God's purposes were fulfilled. The Empire was a reflection of the Kingdom of God; the Christian Church and the Roman Empire were made for each other, and were now, under the Christian emperor, two facets of a Christian society. The Empire was the natural home of Christianity; beyond it lay pagan darkness and barbarism. Political, cultural and religious exclusiveness merged to give rise to a new sense of *Romania* which was synonymous with civilization and Christianity. Christian preachers and writers from Eusebius of Caesarea on were generally very ready to accept and even to develop such an image of the Christian emperor and his empire. Commonplaces inspired by such an ideology were hardly questioned outside dissenting communities, until Augustine of Hippo radically rejected – and he only late in his career – the underlying ideology.

The emperor was charged with a mission to secure the Church's well-being and unity. His intervention in the Church's affairs was readily accepted; many bishops were prepared to see Constantine as he saw himself: God's agent to guard the unity of His Church. Constantine appeared in this role well before the calling of the Council of Nicaea (325). Almost on the morrow of his assuming control of the Western provinces, he was drawn into the conflicts in the North African Church which had their roots in the years of persecution and were now hardening into the schism between 'Catholics' and 'Donatists', as the opposing communities became known. He found himself driven to intervene in the conflict. The division between orthodoxy and dissent assumed public importance and dissent acquired the character of political opposition. It was in circles opposed to the orthodoxy upheld by the emperor that the emperor's role in the Church's affairs was first questioned. Under Constantine's successors, when the emperors again took sides in the doctrinal controversies following the Council of Nicaea, it was naturally dissenting churchmen who took the lead in protesting against imperial authority in matters of the Church's beliefs. Donatists and the defenders of Nicene orthodoxy against Constantius II, among them Athanasius and others, protested – not often in language as colourful as that of Lucifer, bishop of Caralis – that the Church should not be subject to imperial control. The confrontations between Ambrose of Milan and the Emperor Theodosius I gave a foretaste of a long history of tensions of this kind between bishops and rulers both recognized as orthodox. The extent to which the secular power was entitled to intervene in the life of the worshipping community became one of the perennial problems bequeathed by the Constantinian revolution to later Christian generations; more so in the Western than in the Byzantine world. In the fourth and fifth centuries there was no serious opposition to his calling ecumenical councils and supervising their deliberations. The emperor was readily accepted in this role provided he was seen as orthodox.

Christians had to make a far-reaching adjustment to come to terms with their new position in Roman society. Intellectually and spiritually they were not well prepared for the experience of wealth, privilege, prestige and political power that came their way in the new order of things. A new era had opened with the miracle that turned their persecutor into their patron. The first generation of Christians after Constantine were sharply conscious of a 'generation gap' that had opened up between themselves and their persecuted forefathers. How could they see themselves as the heirs of the Church of the martyrs? A great deal of effort – spiritual, intellectual, liturgical – was invested in the task of reassuring themselves that the newly privileged Church was identical with the persecuted Church. Dissenting churchmen and communities, especially the Donatists in North Africa, found it easier to claim the heritage of the persecuted Church than did their opponents, recognized and favoured by emperors and governors. There was urgent need for some means to allow the Church patronized by emperors to experience itself as continuous with the persecuted Church of the first three centuries.

This need was met in various ways. One was that of the histories of the Church which showed forth its continuity across this 'generation gap'. This was done by a succession of Church historians. A new genre of history-writing, the 'ecclesiastical history', emerged very quickly. A singularly coherent historiographical tradition began with Eusebius of Caesarea, who set out to display just this continuity of his Church with that of the apostles. He therefore laid great stress on continuity in episcopal succession and in the uninterrupted transmission of the pure, unblemished faith. He had many continuators and imitators until the end of the sixth century and provided a model for later historians. These histories, widely read in educated circles, helped literate Christians to see themselves as the heirs of the martyrs.

The other response met the same need in a more widely available form: the cult of the martyrs. Those who died in witnessing to Christ had long been honoured in the Christian community, as had heroes of Jewish resistance to sacrilege among the Jews. The martyr was the human image of perfection. But fourth-century Christians saw the age of the martyrs slip into a past more and more remote from their own experience. The cult of the martyrs brought the heroic past back into the very different present. The calendar of Christian celebrations, hitherto dominated by the festivals commemorating the death and resurrection of Christ, and – eventually added to this – his incarnation, filled up in the fourth century with a large number of feasts commemorating martyrs.

The anniversaries of the martyrs' 'deposition' were at first commemorated near their suburban burial places outside the city walls. In the course of the fourth century the custom of bringing their relics into intra-mural churches spread rapidly, though not without opposition; by the sixth century it was widely practised everywhere. In the relic the martyr's presence and power were venerated. The martyr was made liturgically present in a very immediate, spatially determined, manner in the daily liturgical worship of the urban community. The holiness associated with the martyr's grave was now shared by the church building in which his relic was enshrined. The building itself was more and more often seen as a holy place, a 'gateway to heaven'. The network of urban churches thus created a pattern of holy places within the city.

The cult of the martyrs also facilitated the emergence of a network of 'holy places'. Christians had long been accustomed to the annual excursion to the cemeteries and the martyrs' *memoriae* outside the walls on the martyr's anniversary. Since the time of Constantine, the 'holy places' in Palestine had also become the regular destinations of pilgrimage. The principal sites of Christ's incarnation, crucifixion, resurrection and ascension each received major church buildings. The discovery of Christ's cross by the Empress Helena promoted the practice of pilgrimage, which seems already to have begun quite early in Constantine's reign. Pilgrims came in growing numbers and in increasingly organized groups. Around the focal points marked by the new church buildings in Jerusalem a network of urban ritual developed. The holy places made the biblical past vividly present to the pilgrim, just as the celebration of the martyrs' anniversaries in the presence of their material relics had for a long time made the martyrs present to the devotion of their epigoni. The popularity of pilgrimage gave rise to some first-hand accounts by pilgrims and, eventually, handbooks for their guidance, as well as some polemical literature – most of it focused on the cult of relics, which continued to be opposed until well into the fifth century.

With the Church's new freedom, its further expansion and accelerated growth, questions about its organization became more urgent. Its structure had crystallized around the urban centres of the Empire. To a large extent the Church's organization came to duplicate the administrative geography of the Empire. Bishoprics were located in the cities; the bishop's authority extended over the city's *territorium*; and bishoprics were grouped into metropolitan provinces corresponding, on the whole, to the provinces of the civil administration. This was the normal pattern, and the Council of Nicaea put the stamp of its approval on it, while making some adjustments for exceptions sanctioned by custom. The ancient 'apostolic' sees of Alexandria, Antioch and Rome were accorded a special status; along, eventually, with Jerusalem, they became known as patriarchates. Before long Constantinople was added to their number. Problems about episcopal jurisdiction, however, were not eliminated. They cropped up especially in the case of Constantinople. The city, founded by Constantine as a new and Christian Rome, rapidly grew in status and splendour to rival the 'Old Rome' in the West. The see of Constantinople aspired to a status commensurate with its growing civil importance. The first Council of Constantinople (381) affirmed Constantinople's precedence in rank, second only to the see of Rome. The Eastern imperial court was inclined to endorse the principle that ecclesiastical rank should reflect civil status. The Council of Chalcedon (451) concurred in giving the see of Constantinople equal rights with those of the 'Old Rome', in the teeth of determined opposition from Rome. Similar tensions were later to accompany the rise of the see of Ravenna, which became an imperial residence at the beginning of the fifth century. Rivalry over ecclesiastical status and prestige caused a good deal of friction between the sees of Caesarea in Palestine and Jerusalem, and, later on, in Gaul. Here, too, conflicting claims over metropolitan jurisdiction brought about largely by changes in the civil administrative structure caused much friction in the fifth century.

Councils, both ecumenical and provincial, often concerned themselves with such matters of ecclesiastical jurisdiction. Local and provincial councils were not a new phenomenon of the fourth century; many had been held in the pre-Constantinian period. North Africa had a well-developed tradition of conciliar decisions. The fourth century, however, saw a great development of conciliar activity. Councils began to define the contours of ecclesiastical order, of clerical discipline, privileges, elections and ordination, of episcopal responsibilities and many other subjects. Liturgical development during this period led to more elaborate and also regionally more diversified liturgical traditions.

Christians were as ready to assimilate the culture of Roman society as they were to accept its political framework. The Christian Church had never set up its own educational system; it entered the Constantinian era with no alternative of its own to the existing system of Roman schooling. If Christians wanted to be educated, as many had wanted to be before Constantine and many more still after him, they had to go to the schools frequented by their non-Christian neighbours. Inevitably, in the new conditions, many more Christians were to be found in the middle and higher ranks of society, and education was often a passport to office and advancement. Few Christians had serious misgivings about this. By the middle of the fourth century Christianity had gone a very long way in assimilating the dominant culture of pagan Romans. There was an outcry when the Emperor Julian issued his – in the event short-lived – prohibition of Christians teaching in the schools. His brief attempt to revive a newly defined paganism momentarily helped to polarize the tension between pagan learning and Christian faith. Its effect, however, was largely confined to the Greek-speaking East, and even here it left little mark after Julian's early death. The assimilation by Christians of current secular culture, current practices and celebrations, continued, despite the attempts by bishops to wean their flocks from popular practices – public shows, games, races, banquets – seen more and more as pagan. Aristocratic Christians had no inhibitions about cultivating the classics of Greek or Latin literature, making use of current artistic models and following current fashions, or observing old Roman customs and festivals alongside their own religious celebrations. Cultivated Christians could communicate on easy terms with educated pagans. Religion made very little difference to the style of living at any level of the social scale. Wealthy Christians could adorn their silver with images of pagan gods and enjoy reading their Virgil; others could get drunk at anniversary celebrations in the cemeteries or use charms and consult magicians to cure their ills: just as did their pagan fellows. Bishops and their clergy needed to establish sharp contours within the late antique imaginative landscape to mark off what could be allowed to pass into Christianity as part of a shared culture from what had to be rejected as of demonic origin and tainted by paganism; and their efforts to do so often ran into a heavy weight of attachment to ancient custom or sheer indifference.

The wholesale assimilation of pagan culture provoked acute anxieties in the last decades of the fourth century and at the beginning of the fifth. In the West in the 380s and 390s pagan aristocrats were feeling increasingly isolated and threatened by the growing Christianization of the leading classes in their society. Alienated from an increasingly Christian court they saw their prestige and power being slowly eroded. They saw themselves as the guardians of Rome's ancient traditions, including the traditional literary culture of their class. Their religion, their dedication to the preservation of the Latin classics, their fidelity to ancient models of excellence, blended with their traditional religion. Just as had Julian's 'Hellenism', so their pagan religion became identified with the culture they upheld with determination. Their claim to be the custodians of the traditions of the Republic and the Principate brought them into collision with the Christian court (now in Milan). They looked with apprehension at the Christian bid which was threatening, as it seemed to them, to displace the foundations of traditional Roman society. This confrontation revived ancient tensions within the Christian community: what attitude should Christians take towards the culture of their pagan contemporaries? Classical education and literature were becoming suspect, especially among the most highly educated Christians such as Jerome and Augustine, who felt profoundly ill at ease about a culture they shared with such men. The ancient conflicts between Jerusalem and Athens, a Christian, Scripture-based wisdom and the traditional secular culture, once again opened up a deep division between educated Christians and their pagan contemporaries. Augustine did make a place for secular studies within a Christian curriculum; but it was narrowly conceived: the liberal studies of the schools were to be pursued by Christians only in so far as they were required for a proper understanding of the Bible, and within the framework of a fundamentally Scripture-based wisdom. In their final confrontation, pagan and Christian both found it necessary to define more sharply the boundaries that divided them. This is the reason for the suspicion in which secular culture was again held around AD 400, in the Latin West rather than the Greek East. For complex reasons, Christian and pagan were never as sharply polarized in the East as in the West. Western Christians found themselves more outside the mainstream of upper-class culture and remained less self-confident for rather longer than their fellows in the East. Hence the increased tension and conflict between 'pagan' and Christian in the Latin West in the later fourth century.

This, however, was the last major confrontation between them. By the 430s articulate and educated opposition to Christianity was a thing of the past. Paganism was recollected in tranquillity, its final struggle with the rising tide of Christianity seen through a romantic haze. Subsequent pagan revivals, usually in a time of crisis, were narrowly based and ephemeral. Most of the remaining pagans among the senatorial aristocrats had been converted to Christianity. Their literary tastes, their interests and many of their activities, including the copying of manuscripts and establishing collections of books, were continued by their Christian successors, now more and more often bishops. The heritage of pagan learning, art and literature could be appropriated by Christians with a good conscience. They had a stake in classical antiquity and felt no guilt about it.

A similar accommodation took place in architecture and the pictorial arts. At the time of Constantine's accession Christians had little in the way of building, sculpture or painting. Modest buildings for their communal worship, sometimes adorned with frescos, and some painting and sculpture, much of it funerary in purpose, had long existed. Large-scale public building, sculpture and painting, however, began only in the age of Constantine. The Constantinian basilical buildings combined the conventions of prestige architecture with conventions already established among Christian communities for buildings serving a liturgical purpose; and the new imperially sponsored buildings continued for long to serve as prototypes for large churches for congregational use. A variety of established secular building types – usually centrally planned – were also available as models for other kinds of buildings: memorial buildings to mark a sacred spot (*martyria*), or baptisteries. Around the middle of the fifth century a strongly classicizing trend in architecture was patronized by the popes and the newly Christianized aristocracy in Rome. The astonishing achievement of Christian architecture in the Byzantine East owed less to its classical antecedents, but would scarcely have been possible without them. Existing Late Roman styles and motifs were taken over and adapted by artists and widely utilized in church decoration, funerary sculpture and book-illustration.

With the exception of a decade or so before and after AD 400 there was little resistance among Christians to the rapid assimilation of the current secular culture. Their readiness to adopt the lifestyles and values of their non-Christian contemporaries, their almost heedless haste to assimilate their culture, and the vanishing of any clear line that would mark them out among their fellows, caused anxiety to many dedicated and serious-minded Christians. Many of the debates in Christian circles – not only those concerning the value to be set upon secular culture –, especially in the West, were at bottom related to these anxieties. They had their roots in the uncertainties that surrounded the questions: what is it to be a Christian? what obligations does the name of 'Christian' impose on a person? what is authentic Christianity like, how does it differ from merely outward, fashionable, conformity? Such were the questions that worried Pelagius and the movement named after him. Much of the Latin Christian literature of the decades from about 380 to 430 was related, in one way or another, to perplexities over the meaning of Christian perfection. The conflict over Pelagianism generated new theological problems, concerning grace, freedom and predestination. They continued to be debated, especially in Gaul, long after the deaths of the protagonists, Augustine of Hippo, Jerome, Pelagius, Caelestius and Julian of Eclanum.

Related to these controversies were the problems raised by the growing appeal of the ascetic life. The call to perfection was often interpreted as a call to some form of ascetic renunciation. Virginity, voluntary poverty and self-denial were clearly visible ways of asserting an authentic Christian identity in a world in which this was not easily distinguished from mere outward conformity. Monastic and eremitical life was well established in various parts of the Empire, especially in Egypt and Syria, well before the end of the fourth century, but the new conditions of Christian existence undoubtedly gave greatly increased appeal to asceticism in its varied forms. Renunciation of the pleasures of the body, of riches, of social ties and status could be equated with the martyr's witness to Christ. The life of dedicated virginity was often equated with martyrdom long before the fourth century. The parallel was now taken up with enthusiasm; in a world denied the opportunity to die for Christ renouncing almost any form of self-indulgence could qualify as martyrdom. Monastic communities in varied forms began to multiply in the fourth century. Pachomius and Basil provided models for organized ascetic communities. Late to develop in the West, monastic communities multiplied in the later fourth century, often modelled, or claiming to be modelled, on those of Egypt or Syria. Individual eremitical observance continued to flourish alongside the multiplying communities, as did, in the East, the small monastic settlements of the *laurae*. A very large part of the Christian literature of the late fourth and the fifth centuries concerned itself with the life of dedicated virginity, the ascetic or the monastic life; their outward forms, and even more, their spirituality. The *Lives* of saints, often written by their disciples, usually after their death, achieved wide popularity. Many were modelled on one of the most influential, the *Life of St Antony* attributed to Athanasius. Apocryphal literature also catered for a wide readership and tended to reinforce ascetic world-views.

The explosion of asceticism in the years around 400 itself gave rise to a large body of controversy. Its popularity was not confined to aristocratic families; there was enthusiasm among bishops, some of whom organized their clergy in monastic communities, and even at the imperial court in the time of Theodosius II (408–50). The movement for the adoption of celibacy among the clergy, though by no means unopposed, gained momentum in the Western Church. While the appeal of asceticism in various forms grew, to some dedicated Christians it seemed to bring with it the danger of creating a two-level Church: one for a spiritual elite, another for the ordinary, work-a-day Christian. Anxieties on this score were not confined to Pelagius and his followers, but were voiced by a variety of clergy (especially in Rome) and lay people. These controversies, too, created a fair body of literature, much of it now lost and known only through sources eventually accepted as 'orthodox': a fate common to writings that came to be labelled as 'unorthodox'.

The assumption widely current before the end of the fourth century (see above, pp. 401–2) that the Roman Empire was the proper setting for Christianity and Christianity coextensive with Roman civilization did not encourage a missionary mentality. Outside the imperial frontiers dwelled irredeemable darkness; within the territories of the Empire, 'missionary' preaching was apt to be seen in terms of securing Roman peace and order. Apart from Frumentius, ordained by Athanasius to preach in an area now known as Ethiopia, there is no clear evidence of missionaries being sent by any bishop across imperial frontiers to convert non-Christians until the end of the sixth century. By contrast, from the court down there was general agreement that being a Roman now implied being a Christian, and legal pressures were applied to secure the spread of orthodox Christianity (see above, p. 401). The efficacy of coercive measures has been much debated, and seems likely to have been greatly exaggerated. Subtler pressures towards conformity almost certainly played a far more important part in bringing about a more thorough Christianization in towns and countryside within the Empire. Bishops in many provinces encouraged evangelistic activity by their clergy; monks also often played an important part. The importance of holy men in facilitating the passage from traditional belief and practice to the new faith has only recently received the attention of historians.

Beyond the imperial frontiers Christianity spread by more informal and haphazard means: through the travels of Christians – merchants, soldiers, displaced persons – and through the initiative of rare individuals, such as Patrick's to preach the gospel to the Irish. The most important expansion of Christianity was among the Germanic nations. Some of them, such as particular groups of Goths, had long had contacts with Romans, among them Christians. Christianity took root among the Goths, albeit in a form eventually regarded as unorthodox within the Empire, and was given great impetus through the work of the Gothic Bishop Ulfila. After their establishment within imperial territories the Gothic settlers kept their religion, a moderate 'Arian' homoean Christianity, along with a Gothic version of the Bible and many of their tribal traditions. Other bodies of Germanic settlers also remained Arian in their religion after settlement, seeking to maintain their separate identity within the framework of Roman society. In no case did an Arian Germanic kingdom prove to be lasting. The Visigothic kingdom in Spain was officially converted to orthodox Christianity in 587; the Arian Vandal kingdom was brought to an end by Justinian's reconquest in 533. The Franks and Anglo-Saxons, and later the Lombards, who were largely pagan at the time of their entry, gradually came to conform to the Catholicism of the Romans among whom they settled. The conversion of Germanic rulers and the leading men of the nation generally played a crucial part in their conversion. Subsequent Christianization was the slow work, sometimes of centuries.

The whole period from Constantine to the Council of Chalcedon was a time of doctrinal controversy and articulation. Divergent theological traditions surfaced with the toleration accorded to the Church in 312. Constantine himself had taken the initiative to call together a group of bishops to settle the first ecclesiastical quarrel in which he was called to intervene, the Donatist dispute in North Africa (see above, p. 402). He followed the same pattern in an attempt to settle the trinitarian disputes that had their roots in the rift between the Alexandrian deacon Arius and his bishop. The council he called which met at

Nicaea in 325 became a precedent for imperial initiative in calling councils. Imperial initiative was often seen – especially in the Eastern Church – as a mark of a council being 'ecumenical'. The agreement reached by the bishops at Nicaea under the emperor's patronage failed, however, to settle all the disputes over the question of Christ's divine Sonship. Controversy, imperial interventions, dissenting bishops being sent into exile, continued. Political disturbance and uncertainty exacerbated ecclesiastical confusion. A series of councils attended by only one part or another of the episcopate failed to heal the disagreements; and changeable imperial support compounded the difficulties. At the advent of Julian, in 361, opposition to the Nicene faith seemed to be heading for victory, when the new emperor withdrew from the conflict in the expectation that Christian factionalism would lead to assured mutual destruction. Following the brief moratorium under Julian's reign, serious theological debate, led by the Cappadocian Fathers, prepared the ground for consent. When Theodosius I, a Western general, assumed the imperial office in Constantinople, conditions were right for reconciliation under an emperor who championed Nicene orthodoxy. The doctrinal uncertainty ended with the council he called in Constantinople in 381 and the suppression of Arianism. Though not initiated as an 'ecumenical' council, it was eventually accepted as such at Chalcedon.

Other theological problems, notably over the Holy Spirit, also received attention and caused division during this period. The most significant theological debates after the reaffirmation of the faith of Nicaea at Constantinople concerned questions of Christology – the issue of Christ's humanity and Godhead. Already much discussed during the early Christian centuries, they now came to the fore and dominated theological debate during the whole period until the Council of Chalcedon (and indeed for some two centuries after it – beyond the chronological span covered in this book). Two Councils of Ephesus (431 and 449), one of them subsequently condemned, and Chalcedon (451) concerned themselves with various aspects of these problems. A doctrinal clarification made with the help of a statement by Pope Leo I was accepted by the council, but failed to prevent either subsequent controversy or the rise of separate monophysite and Nestorian communities in the Eastern provinces. How far these – and other – dissident churches articulated separatist sentiments, political or social protest against the imperial establishment, or local and regional cultures, has been the subject of much debate. That some of them, especially monophysitism, came to rally sentiments of political separatism from the Empire is, however, clear.

In the doctrinal self-definition of Christianity Nicaea and Chalcedon were by far the most significant moments. In the Donatist schism (see above, p. 402) the claim of two rival ecclesial communities to being Christ's true Church in Africa was at stake. Although this question was never resolved and the schism never healed, the problem ceased to matter with the eclipse of the Donatist Church during the period of Vandal rule (430–533). Thereafter there is no clear evidence of the schism. It had raised important questions concerning the mode of the Church's being in the world, and the nature of Christian baptism. These matters, like some of those raised by the Origenist controversy and its resonances in monastic circles, and in the Pelagian controversy, were not the subject of conciliar debate and doctrinal articulation.

Controversies, whether doctrinal or disciplinary, are not, however, what is responsible for the huge mass of surviving literature from this period, often, and rightly, seen as the golden age of patristic literature. Polemical writings undoubtedly form a great part of the writings of Jerome, Augustine and John Chrysostom, not to mention the great controversialists active in the trinitarian and Christological debates. But there is a huge corpus of biblical commentary, of letters, of sermons and of straight philosophical or theological exposition as well. The amount of the surviving material – incomparably more than what survives from any other period of the patristic age – has more to do with the intellectual vitality of the period. Christian thought was now on the public stage, open to wide discussion and to questioning. Its defence against Manichaeism, against heresies, against Jews and pagans, called for efforts at self-definition which encouraged much, sometimes highly sophisticated, reflection. At no time before the later fourth century were conditions so favourable to the emergence of Christian intellectual activity. The Christian community now contained a far larger number of educated Christians than at any earlier stage, among them not a few educated at the highest levels. Encounter with non-Christian thought fostered a creative intellectual tension, again on a higher level and on a wider front than ever before, excepting perhaps second- and third-century Alexandria. A range of philosophical disciplines – though usually acquired at second hand – predominantly in the Platonic and Stoic traditions, were brought to bear on the elucidation and elaboration of Christian belief. The vitality this gave to Christian culture has sometimes been contrasted (as by Henri-Irenée Marrou) with the predominant sterility of late antique intellectual culture in this period.

At the beginning of the fourth century the see of Rome already occupied a special if undefined place in the Christian imagination. Among the apostolic sees it was distinguished by the belief that both Peter and Paul had met martyrdom here. The two martyr-apostles were venerated at several shrines, whose nature and mutual relations are still not entirely certain. The bishops of Rome, especially from the late fourth century on, built their claims on this heritage, and elaborated the biblical sayings about Peter into a juridical foundation for papal authority. Faced with the growing importance of Constantinople, the bishops of Rome sought to resist Constantinopolitan claims to a correspondingly higher ecclesiastical status (see above, p. 405). The two sees, however, shared a vast common Christian tradition; not until the Middle Ages could a permanent rift between them be imagined. The separate development of the two sees owed far more to the political conditions in which they found themselves than to squabbles over status or belief, or even to the slowly deepening gulf between Greek and Latin ecclesiastical cultures. Constantinople remained the hub of power in the Byzantine world; its patriarch retained close links with the imperial court. From the end of the fifth century the Western provinces of the Empire fell under Germanic control. At the end of the sixth century the see of Rome still considered itself as part of the Empire and subject to the authority of the emperor. But it was beginning to be detached from the imperial orbit by its situation. Instead of being one of the four great sees in permanent creative tension, Rome was progressively drawn into a Western orbit. In the end this led to its isolation from the ancient apostolic sees, standing alone as the mother-church, the unchallenged teacher and mistress of Germanic Western Europe. The only other great see with a status and an ancient tradition comparable to that of Rome was the see of Carthage. By the end of the seventh century, however, Carthage – along with most of the ancient Near East and Africa – was in Muslim hands. Rome was now alone in the West. This isolation, more than anything else, was to determine its status throughout the European Middle Ages and beyond.

38
Articulating identity

LEWIS AYRES

The purpose of this chapter is to explore some of the ways in which Christian belief and hence some key aspects of Christian identity were articulated and formed from around AD 300 to 451. This subject has far too many facets to be covered in just one chapter. This is especially so in the light of the many different approaches used in contemporary early Christian studies to consider the formation and nature of Christian identity. In this chapter, however, my focus will be fairly narrow: I will primarily consider how the various doctrinal disputes of the fourth and early fifth centuries unfolded and how they led to the development of a particular account of 'orthodox' belief as it is represented in the writings of Christians towards the end of this period. One might conceive of this exercise as exploring how some key aspects of the late antique Christian imagination were shaped through internal and external dispute.

At the turn of the fourth century two of the most important issues facing the Christian community were the place of Christianity in the Roman Empire and the nature of the Church as a unified body (both in terms of organization and teaching). The legitimization of Christianity did not suddenly effect a shift from a pluralistic Church that saw itself as clearly 'apart' from worldly authority and structure to a more monolithic body that was immediately willing to accommodate itself to and desire worldly power, as some older, mostly Protestant, narratives suggested. At the turn of the fourth century Christians already had a long history of *ad hoc* alliances with the Roman authorities, and we know of previous instances where Christians had attempted to involve those authorities in internal disputes. What we see in the fourth century is an increasingly broad interaction between Christian groups and the imperial authorities and an increasing desire by many Roman rulers to control and influence an increasingly important institution in the Roman world. We see this process through virtually all the disputes covered in this chapter. We can begin displaying the character of these interactions by considering two disputes which demonstrate the internal problems caused by emergence from the threat of persecution.

The first dispute is the 'Melitian schism' in Egypt.[1] This dispute is sometimes presented as stemming from the refusal of Melitius, bishop of Lycopolis, and other rigorists to accept the leniency of conditions imposed on those Christians who had lapsed under persecution but now wanted to be readmitted. In fact, the situation appears to be much more complicated than this. During the persecution of 303–13 Melitius seems to have aroused the anger of some fellow bishops who were in prison because he ordained priests and interfered in various dioceses without consulting the official visitors, most notably annoying Peter of Alexandria. At the end of the persecution Melitius seems also to have taken offence at the leniency of Peter's regulations for readmittance and within a few years something of an alternative hierarchy of bishops existed in Egypt. The Council of Nicaea attempted to solve the dispute without success and Melitians became a major source of opposition to Athanasius.

Some scholars have tried to read the two sides in this controversy as revealing two opposed social groups or as ciphers for some sort of underlying political conflict. Such accounts appear increasingly unsustainable and the evidence that does exist seems to present a picture of two communities whose social structure and practice of Christianity were virtually indistinguishable. The conflict is thus extremely complex, and while Melitians seem to have narrated their own origins as an opposition to the leniency of Peter, it seems clear that the role of the bishop of Alexandria and the structure of the Church in Egypt were also at issue. Alexandria had a strong tradition of a powerful and independent priestly office with the bishop acting as an extremely influential *primus inter pares*. From the late third century we seem to see bishops of Alexandria trying to exercise a monarchical episcopacy of the type increasingly common around the Roman world. The struggle to shape such a model in the Egyptian context seems to have been interwoven with apparently distinct disputes there throughout the century. In a wider context a number of scholars have argued that a widely apparent episcopal struggle to control the growing monastic movement within diocesan structures reflects a broader move on the part of bishops to assert a more direct and consistent control over affairs within their diocese. This dispute is also seen in the Egyptian context and may well have helped to prolong the Melitian schism.[2]

Some similar issues are present in the case of Donatism further along the coast of North Africa in the area of modern-day Tunisia and Algeria.[3] Many bishops refused to accept the consecration of Caecilian of Carthage in 311 or

312 on the grounds that his consecrator had been a *traditor* (someone who had 'handed over' the Scriptures to the Roman authorities during persecution). In opposition to him Majorinus was consecrated as rival bishop, and Majorinus' successor was Donatus, after whom the movement was known by its enemies. Both Constantine and, later, his son Constans, intermittently tried coercion to force their submission, but to no avail. Donatists appear to have constituted the majority of the African Church through the late fourth century.

A significant turning point was the Emperor Honorius' equation of Donatists with heretics and his official confiscation of their property in 405. Nevertheless, attempts at reconciliation continued: in 411 a large Donatist and Catholic conference was held in Carthage under the aegis of Marcellinus, an imperial representative. Marcellinus (not surprisingly) declared for the Catholics and in 412 Donatism was banned again by imperial edict. The Catholics also found in Augustine and Aurelius of Carthage energetic partisans who were able to undertake a wide-ranging and sophisticated offensive. Although Donatism went into decline it still existed at Augustine's death in 430. When we try to trace the course of Donatism in the centuries that follow we find our information very scarce. It seems that despite the attempts of some (such as Gregory the Great) to assume the schism still retained its early contours even in the sixth century, the two communities (in Robert Markus' words) 'slowly and imperceptibly coalesced'.[4]

In the last century a number of attempts have been made to treat the dispute as a conflict between the provincial 'nationalism' or 'regionalism' of the Donatists, who were striving to preserve an indigenous form of Christianity, and the imperial authorities' desire to impose a universal form of Christianity under closer imperial control. For some scholars such a view is supplemented by also reading the Donatist controversy as reflecting an incipient class and social conflict. At times such interpretations have been rather reductionist: in recent writing a balance seems to have been achieved in which theological ideas are recognized as being a primary motivating factor in the dispute, but in which it is also recognized that the dispute also occurred in a specific and complex social context.

It seems highly likely that we should think of the Donatists as inheriting a tradition of Christianity that strongly emphasized the purity of the Church over against the world, a theology found clearly in such earlier writers as Tertullian and Cyprian, as well as the importance of staying faithful to those things for which the martyrs had died. For Donatists preserving the purity of the Church was a key issue, and inseparable from preserving the purity of its members. Once the Donatist Church had been in existence for a few decades

Augustine was able to attack them with some force for claiming that the purity of members was of paramount importance and yet for dealing with the moral lives of believers and office holders with (at times) even more leniency than Catholics. In many ways, Augustine offers a fundamentally different account of the Church as 'pure' from that implied by Donatism. For Augustine the Church is pure only because of Christ's presence in it and his union with it, not because of the purity of its members. Indeed, Augustine's developing thoughts on the impossibility of people meriting their own salvation and on the nature of original sin actually help to shape his anti-Donatist ecclesiology and vice versa. Disputes over one theological area thus come to inform and shape dispute in other areas and with other groups.

These two ecclesiological emphases also reflect shifting accounts of the Church within late antique society. Augustine's writing occurs in the context of the Church's greatly increased power and social significance in the Empire resulting over the century since Constantine's legitimization of Christianity. As many writers have noted, Augustine's ecclesiology attempts to combine faithfulness to the traditional vision of the Church as a community drawn out of the world, with a new focus on the Church as a mixed body, the faithful intermingled with those whose Christianity is frequently only inchoate. In this context Augustine's discussions of discipline and penitence are less concerned with securing purity, than with shaping a process of training and education that will encourage distinctive Christian identities and practices. Thus, Augustine's vision of the unity of the Church also reflects both a different theological outlook and the views of a cosmopolitan European-oriented late antique writer.

In the case of the Melitian and Donatist disputes, internal Christian debate was prompted by changing relations with the non-Christian world. Throughout the period covered by this chapter Christians engaged in a polemic against non-Christian traditional polytheistic religion, the religion(s) traditionally sanctioned by the Roman state. Traditionally Christians had written in defence of their faith, arguing for Christianity's antiquity and rationality against non-Christian charges.[5] Through the apologetic of the fourth and fifth centuries, however, we see not simply defence but a new line of attack against the non-Christian world. Eusebius of Caesarea,[6] Augustine and Arnobius present an argument for the failure of Roman traditional religion in the light of the Christian 'triumph' that begins with Constantine. In Augustine the argument is particularly clear. The seemingly ancient and venerable Roman tradition actually embodies a history of moral compromise and half-acknowledged paradox: for instance, he criticizes those classical authors who both think animal sacrifices unnecessary and yet undertake them publicly. For Augustine the Romans could almost sense the failure of their tradition to provide an appropriate training ground in virtue and honesty and yet they continued to sustain its paradox and sinfulness.[7] This shift in polemic seems also to have gone hand in hand with a Christian triumphalism, the Emperors Constantine and Theodosius both attracting particular praise for having advanced the victory of Christianity (Augustine here actually stands almost alone in his eventual rejection of such an attitude).

The character of anti-'pagan' polemic during the fourth and fifth centuries was significantly shaped by the attack on Christianity by Plotinus' disciple Porphyry (*c.* 230–*c.* 305).[8] In his now mostly lost work *Against the Christians*, Porphyry attempted to show up inconsistencies in the New Testament and the general moral turpitude and inconsistency of the Old. Porphyry also attacked allegorical interpretation as only a device to avoid the obvious problems of the text. Porphyry was one of a number of late antique philosophers (Iamblichus being the other major figure) who attempted to shape a vision of non-Christian philosophical and religious life as a unity encompassing an order of practice suitable for all levels of society. In such thinkers we see non-Christians, very probably in response to the rise of Christianity, articulating a new rationale for traditional Roman and Greek religion.[9] This shift began to take on an institutional and aggressively anti-Christian form in the reign of Julian (known to later Christian generations as 'the Apostate').

We should, however, be careful about assuming that we can in this period speak simply either of the 'victory' of Christianity or about the clear separation of 'pagan' and 'Christian'. On the one hand, the rhetoric of Christian triumph is belied by a huge amount of evidence that throughout this period large areas of the countryside remained resolutely non-Christian, and that even many of the major towns and cities allowed traditional temples to exist. The death of public and civic Roman religion was thus a slow one; the death of non-Christian practice and piety was even slower and much more confused. On the other hand, Christian writers throughout the period bear witness to the existence of what they took to be non-Christian practices among their congregations (especially astrology and divination). The definition and then the instilling of a distinctively Christian and anti-'pagan' identity was thus a continuing task for early Christian leaders.[10]

Controversy over fundamental Christian beliefs about Christ and the nature of God is a central feature of developing Christian belief in the period covered in this chapter. One of the most important of these latter controversies concerned 'Manichaeism', a term that labels Manichees by their relation to their founder

Mani. Mani was born in 216 in northern Babylonia and was killed by the Parthian King Bahram I in 274. From the age of twelve he saw himself as a prophetic figure, revealing a cosmic struggle between light and darkness and a way of salvation. After his death his followers continued to grow quickly in number and eventually spread west through the Mediterranean and east into China. For Manichees the cosmos is constituted by a battle between light and dark, good and evil. Although the two principles originally existed in separation from each other, the Father of Greatness or Light was attacked by the Prince of Darkness. To save itself the good principle emanated a series of new divine 'aeons' or 'divine beings' who attempted to release the light that had become interwoven with darkness. The creation of our material world was a further part of a strategy by the Father of Light to save the light entrapped by darkness. The sun and the moon function as collectors of light from the world and transmitters of light back to the Father of Light. Human beings are the creation of the demons of darkness seeking a way to retain the light they have trapped from the work of the Father. Jesus was sent from the realm of light to reveal true saving knowledge to Adam and Eve and the rest of humanity.

Through connection to his true 'light' self, Mani revealed the path to salvation. Central to Manichaean communities were the 'elect' or the 'saints' who were able to aid the release of light from its entrapment. They did so by the digestion of food and the breathing out of light. The elect were to eat only certain foods supposedly high in light content: certain vegetables, grains and fruits – and no meat. In order to separate themselves as far as possible from too much engagement with darkness, the elect were also expected to remain celibate and avoid all killing and lying. One of the key functions of the other Manichees, known as 'hearers', was to assist the elect in their mission. The hearers had to practise their own, less rigorous, asceticism, and were entrusted with the preparation of food for the elect. At death the elect were promised that the light within them would return to the realm of light, while hearers were promised reincarnation among the elect.

The most famous Christian to have had first-hand knowledge of Manichaeism and to have devoted considerable space to refuting its claims was Augustine. However, such detailed knowledge of Manichaeism was very rare. Without detailed knowledge of the group many writers used the label 'Manichee' against other Christians considered to have too strong a view of the body's sinfulness: it is so used, for example, in debates over the good of marriage in fourth-century Italy.[11] It is also used against some of the more subordinationist trends in the trinitarian disputes that we will shortly discuss. Here the term seems to be used not simply because of a supposed parallel between the clearly subordinate status that the Manichaean Jesus (or Jesuses) held with respect to the Father of Light, but because of its sheer rhetorical power. Thus in the use of the label 'Manichaean' we see one facet of the ways in which the move towards a more clearly definable orthodoxy in Christian belief involved also the increasingly clear definition and use of labels for distinct and heretical groups. This move towards a more clearly defined orthodoxy was a key aspect of the fourth century,[12] but it involves *both* the definition of belief *and* the evolution of ways in which one can define as unacceptable those determined to be outside the bounds of the normative.

The most important doctrinal controversy of the fourth century concerned Christians' understanding of God, of the nature of Christ and of the very character of salvation. It is often, but problematically, called the 'Arian' controversy.[13] The story of this controversy used to be narrated in a manner whose basic plot I will summarize in this paragraph. In AD 318 a priest called Arius got into a dispute with the bishop of Alexandria, Alexander. Because Alexander insisted very strongly that the Son of God was always with, was co-eternal with, the Father, Arius accused him of teaching that there were 'two unbegottens': two principles in the universe. It also seemed to Arius that Alexander's account of the Son's generation implied that the Son had emanated from the Father almost as if God were a material substance. For Alexander Arius' own teaching was equally problematic: he appeared to be teaching that the Son was created out of nothing like all other created things. After a number of smaller councils and attempts to deal with the split which ensued in Alexandria, the Emperor Constantine intervened, calling a large council which met at Nicaea, near the imperial capital of Constantinople, in 325. This council condemned Arius and drew up a creed – the Nicene creed – which insisted that Father and Son were ὁμοούσιος, *homoousios*, of one being. This creed is then taken to constitute one of the major defining statements of early Christian belief. In the traditional story, Arius' supporters continued to intrigue on his behalf and against those who had supported Nicaea's creed. Eventually, Arius' supporters were able to influence imperial attitudes towards the Church and promote their 'Arian' theology. Resistance to this policy came largely from Western theologians who traditionally believed strongly in the unity of God and so were shocked by Arius' subordinationism, and from Alexander's successor as bishop of Alexandria, Athanasius. Athanasius was the chief theologian of the Nicene party and he endured many exiles as a result of his uncompromising faithfulness to Nicaea. The three 'Cappadocian' theologians, Basil of Caesarea, Gregory Nazianzen and Gregory of Nyssa, were influenced by Athanasius' efforts and were also key figures in preserving and promoting Nicene orthodoxy, especially after Athanasius' death in 373. Eventually, after the death of the 'Arian' Emperor Valens in 378 and the accession of Theodosius, the Nicene cause triumphed. At the Council of Constantinople in 381 the Nicene creed was reaffirmed with a few changes and orthodoxy was clearly defined.

This standard narrative of the story is inaccurate in a number of important ways. In order for us to understand better how this dispute shaped the character of Christian understanding and identity we need to begin again and tell the story afresh. In retelling the story we cannot begin with Arius; we have to outline a broader account of the different theological traditions current at the beginning of the fourth century. What we will see is a variety of theologies, existing in some tension (almost all drawing on different aspects of Origen's legacy): out of this context came both Arius' own theology and the impetus for the controversy that was to continue for the rest of the century.

Let us begin by outlining four broad theological traditions that can be identified in the period 300–30:

1. A first theological tradition or grouping consists of 'Eusebian' theologies (in either sense: supporters of both Eusebius of Nicomedia and Eusebius of Caesarea).[14] Take Eusebius of Nicomedia: writing in defence of Arius himself, he describes God and his Word as the

> one, the unoriginated, [and] one produced by him truly and not from his substance, not participating at all in the unoriginated nature nor in his substance, but produced as altogether distinct in his nature and in his power . . .[15]

Eusebius thinks of the Father as the source of all in a way that both places him far 'above' all else and regards him as the one true subject of adjectives describing God. Eusebius does not think of the Son as created simply like other things; rather, the Son is the first of all created things, the Lord of everything created and the image of the Father's will and power. He does not in any way share the Father's being but is his perfect likeness. Language of image and likeness here serves to illustrate both the Son's distinction from the Father and his unique status.

Even this last brief paragraph reveals the importance of not falling into the trap of imagining that at the turn of the third century the different theological traditions could be grouped as if they stood on either side of a clear question phrased thus: is the Word of God a creature just like any other or an equal sharer in the one divine nature? Rather, one of the key factors in the development of such a complex dispute stems from the fact that there was not yet an agreed clarity about whether one could speak about degrees of divine beings, degrees by which Christ could be 'close' to God while yet not being the one God.

Eusebius of Caesarea, however, presented the Son in a slightly more complex manner. He emphasized more strongly ways in which the Son is a likeness of the Father that somehow qualify his status as inferior. Eusebius wrote of the Son as 'God from God', being generated in a way beyond our capacity to understand; the Son is also described as a 'ray of light' (*ETh.* 1.8.3). Eusebius also spoke of the Son as coming into being (before all time) through the Father's will. Talk of 'will' here (talk destined to have a long history through the fourth century) emphasized that the Son is clearly distinct in authority. Lastly, but very importantly, in Eusebius' theology the *Logos* or Son comes into being at the Father's will for the particular purpose of being the foundation of the whole creation.

A third 'Eusebian' who deserves mention is Asterius, a key early supporter of Arius. At the core of Asterius' theology was his account of the two powers and wisdoms in God.[16] Asterius spoke first of God's own power and wisdom which is the source of Christ and of all things (it is God's own power and wisdom that Paul describes as being seen in the creation at Rom. 1:20). Christ manifests a different power and wisdom, the first and 'only begotten' of the many powers created by the Father. Asterius insists also that Father, Son and Spirit are three *hypostases*.

Arius himself is also best seen as a particular sort of 'Eusebian', one whose personal theological emphases made him particularly controversial to some non-Eusebians. In his *Thalia* ('The Banquet') Arius not only insists on the Son's subordination in a way either Eusebius would have recognized, but he also seems to rule out many of the ways in which the two Eusebii present the Son as sharing the Father's power and attributes in an incomprehensible way. He writes:

> The one without beginning established the Son as the beginning of all creatures . . . He [the Son] possesses nothing proper to God . . . for he is not equal to God, nor yet is he of the same substance . . . there exists a Trinity in unequal glories, for their *hypostases* are not mixed with each other . . .[17]

Arius' sources and motives are unclear: one suggestion stems from noting the parallel between his thought and contemporary developments in Platonism which insisted ever more strongly on the ways in which the One was transcendent and in which lower realities participated in the activity, but not the essence, of higher realities.[18] For our purposes here it is also important to note that Arius' own theology was of little influence during the rest of the century. While it seems to have been known to some in Alexandria and to a larger group who read Athanasius' summaries of it and compilations from it, outside that milieu it does not seem to have been widely known (for example among the 'Cappadocians').

The Eusebian trajectory thus incorporated a number of conflicting emphases. The emphasis in some Eusebians on continuity of being between Father and Son was so significant that many eventually found themselves alienated by the highly subordinationist theologies that developed during the century and came to form a considerable part of the alliance of theologies that I eventually describe as 'pro-Nicene'. Thus this trajectory is a fascinating combination of theologies that will eventually find themselves on very different sides of these trinitarian controversies.

2. A second theological trajectory we need to note is that apparent in Arius' first major opponent, Alexander of Alexandria, and in Alexander's successor, Athanasius. Both of these theologians spoke very strongly of the eternal correlativity of Father and Son: the Father is eternally Father and hence the Son must eternally be with the Father. Athanasius wrote,

> . . . He is the unchanging image of his own Father. For men, composed of parts and made out of nothing, have their discourse composite and divisible. But God possesses true existence and is not composite, wherefore his Word also has true existence and is not composite, but is the one and only begotten God, who proceeds in his goodness from the Father as from a good fountain . . .
>
> (*CG* 41.1)

Athanasius here thinks of the one God as encompassing both the Father *and* the Father's Word: the language of image and the language of the Son being from the Father as from a fountain are shaped by his overall insistence that these terminologies are commensurate with both together being the one God. Athanasius' argument of course *assumes* the principle that Word and God are both God and that there can be no degrees of deity.[19] It is important to note that Athanasius does not really have any terminology (other than the names themselves) for identifying the individual realities of Father and Son.[20]

We find many of the same themes mirrored in the thought of his predecessor Alexander. Alexander insisted that the Father is called the Father because of the ever-present Son and that the Power and Word of God must always have been with God. He adds that if the brightness of the archetype is not present then we will have to admit that the light itself was not present. At the same time he has a very strong image theology in which the Son is the unchangeable image, alike in all ways to the Father and able to express and reveal the Father. He speaks of the Father and Son as one *hypostasis*, although by this he seems to mean that they share the same nature in some sense. Athanasius and Alexander seem to have been able to claim with some veracity that their theology found traditional precedent in Alexandria, as could their opponents. We can also note links between this theology and some traditions in Antioch and many parts of the Greek-speaking world.

3. A third theological trajectory is apparent in the controversial figure of Marcellus of Ancyra. Marcellus was an important figure in the ecclesiastical politics of the Church around the time of Nicaea (Ancyra was probably the initially proposed site for the Council of Nicaea[21]), but his theology became increasingly controversial. Marcellus' theology appears to be closest to the theologies that we call monarchian, modalist or Sabellian in the third century and to some themes found in the 'Apologists' in the second century. Marcellus spoke of God and God's Word as being parallel to a man and his word.[22] The man and his word are not separate realities and the word has distinct existence only when spoken: the word exists in the man's 'power' and may become distinct in 'activity'.[23] Marcellus seems to have conceived of the eternally inherent and existing (but not distinct) Word as 'spoken' for the work of creation, and as returning to that pre-spoken state when the Son's Kingdom is subjected to the Father (1 Cor. 15:28). Note that saying that the Word exists in a pre-spoken state is distinct from saying that he did not exist: Marcellus himself saw this distinction as enabling his own critique of Sabellianism. Marcellus is also insistent that God is only one *hypostasis*, being and power (ὑπόστασις, οὐσία, δύναμις). Marcellan theologies could make common cause with theologies such as that of Athanasius, as we shall see, but they seemed particularly objectionable to Eusebians of all stripes.

4. All of the trajectories considered so far are Eastern Greek-speaking trajectories. The question of how we should understand Western theology is complicated by a great shortage of evidence. It has become commonplace to say that Western theology showed a consistent preference for God's unity over the diversity of the persons and owed much to Tertullian (*fl.* 200). Tertullian's own Trinitarianism, however, evolved *against* monarchian theologies (theologies which emphasized the unity of God above all and in some cases saw the Son as only a manifestation of the Father). In this context Tertullian began to evolve a terminology for speaking of the unity and yet real distinction between Father, Son and Spirit. The order of generation ensures that the Son may share the Father's being, but that the Father is always the source:

> . . . the tree is not severed from the root, nor the river from the fountain, nor the ray from the sun; nor indeed is the Word separated from God. Following, therefore the form of these analogies, I confess that I call God and his Word – the Father and His Son – two. For the root and the tree are distinctly two things but correlatively joined . . . the Trinity flowing down from the Father through intertwined and connected steps does not at all disturb the monarchy, whilst it at the same time guards the state of the economy. (*Prax.* 8)

Tertullian also insisted that the Son was in some sense always in the Father (*Prax.* 5). Thus while it is correct to point to Tertullian's insistence on the closeness of Father and Son, we need also to note that the desire to highlight the *distinction* between Father and Son – by focusing on the generation of another through the sharing of the Father's being – is a fundamental driving force of his theology.

We can compare Tertullian with two later Latin writers: Novatian (*fl.* *c.* 250) and Lactantius (*c.* 250–*c.* 325). Chapter 31 of Novatian's *On the Trinity* (*c.* 250) offers a brief summary of his theology. The Son is the Word, '[but] not as a sound that strikes the air nor the tone of the voice forced from the lungs, but rather . . . in the substance of a power proceeding from God' (*Trin.* 31). The Father, who has no origin, necessarily precedes the Son, and the Son, who is also God, receives his being only from the Father who is the one God (*Trin.* 4.6). The Son receives his being in a manner that does not compromise the divine unity. Novatian writes: 'Owing his origin to the Father, he could not cause any disunion in the Godhead by making two Gods' (*Trin.* 31). For Lactantius, the Word's role is closely linked with creation, but the speaking of the Word creates a Word that is then necessarily eternal. When Lactantius asks how it is that we speak of two – God the Father and God the Son – but do not speak of different Gods, he writes: '. . . the one is as though an overflowing fount or source, the other as though a stream flowing from that, the one a sun, the other a direct ray from the sun' (*Inst.* 4.29).

Both of these theologians continue the basic dynamics of Tertullian's scheme, but worries about adoptionism (the doctrine that Christ was a man like others given special powers or adopted by God at some point in his ministry) seem to have prompted these third-century Latin writers to emphasize even more clearly that the Son possesses the Father's power. We seem to find the same anti-adoptionist adaptation of previous Latin theology in the early work of Hilary of Poitiers and in some other fragments from the early decades of the fourth century in the West.[24] Hence, while it is inaccurate to talk of Latin theology at the beginning of the fourth century as just being focused on the 'unity' of God, it seems plausible to say that Western theologies tended to emphasize the Son's dependence on the Father and his 'flowing' from the Father's being in ways that were profoundly different from the concerns of contemporary Eusebian theologies in the East.

While I have concentrated on doctrinal distinctions between these four trajectories, we should remember that disputes over these are also disputes between what we might term different imaginative universes.[25] Different accounts of the relationship between Father and Son, and different accounts of the Son's role, implied different conceptions of the cosmos, of the human and Christian condition, of the structure of history. Having laid out something of the complex theological scene in the first decades of the fourth century we can now return to the story of the trinitarian controversies. Against the background of this complex situation, and against the background of widespread existing tensions between these different trajectories, a local dispute between Arius and his bishop set off a controversy of far greater proportions. Although Arius was condemned by local synods in Alexandria, he was able to appeal to supporters (including Eusebius of Nicomedia) in nearby provinces of the Empire and ensure that his cause was not forgotten. These supporters were not necessarily committed to all of Arius' theological positions so much as to opposing common enemies. Finally Constantine summoned a council of bishops which eventually met at Nicaea.

The council drew up a creed ('N') that is of great significance:

> We believe in one God, Father, Almighty, Maker of all things, seen and unseen; and in one Lord Jesus Christ, the Son of God, begotten as only begotten of the Father, that is of the being of the Father (ἐκ τῆς οὐσίας τοῦ Πατρός), God of God, Light of Light, true God of true God, begotten not made, consubstantial (ὁμοούσιος) with the Father, through whom all things came into existence, both things in heaven and things on earth; who for us men and for our salvation came down and was incarnate and became man, suffered and rose again the third day, ascended into the heavens, and is coming to judge the living and the dead.
>
> And in the Holy Spirit.
>
> But those who say 'there was a time when he did not exist', and 'before being begotten he did not exist', and that he came into being from non-existence, or who allege that the Son of God is of another ὑπόστασις or οὐσία, or is alterable or changeable, these the Catholic and Apostolic Church condemns.[26]

What those at the council intended the terminology used in the creed to mean is notoriously unclear, other than the fact that they intended to produce a terminology that would exclude their perceptions of Arius' theology. The very idea of a council producing a creed as part of its judgments was relatively new (we know of only two previous occurrences[27]) and it was thus, and not surprisingly, unclear what status this creed had. As yet it had no place in the liturgy or in catechesis, nor, as we shall see below, was a particular credal wording yet seen as a precise and unalterable statement.

At crucial points the creed deploys what appears to be fairly precise philosophical terminology. The terms *ousia* and *hypostasis* were to be the subject of a great deal of discussion and, importantly, *confusion* during the fourth century.[28] At the beginning of the century, however, the two were frequently treated as interchangeable terms for describing God's being or reality or essence and occasionally even for designating the distinctness of Father, Son and Spirit. It is only during the course of the fourth-century disputes that a clearer division becomes apparent. In N it is thus difficult to understand exactly what is being indicated by the use of *ousia*, *hypostasis* and the phrase 'from the Father's essence' (not to mention *homoousios*, discussed in the next paragraph). It seems to make most sense to attribute to N's signatories a desire to state clearly that the Son was derived from the Father's being or existence. Both Athanasius and Eusebius of Caesarea seem to understand the basic function of N's terminology as asserting that the Son is truly from God: Athanasius sees 'from the Father's essence' as the fundamental phrase which secures the true sense of 'from God' and hence of phrases such as 'light from light'. The seemingly precise terminology was thus actually used without agreement on its sense and in order to shape a position that could secure agreement while excluding Arius.

The intention of the framers of N in deploying the term *homoousios* is equally difficult to interpret. In the early fourth century the term was not, as was once thought, used to indicate identity, to indicate that two *homoousioi* were more truly one than two. Rather, the term seems to mean something like 'of the same kind/class'. The term seems to have been used in a number of contexts with meanings in this wide general range. From its usage in religious thought the term also seems to have acquired the sense that two or more things shared a common substance because of a relationship of origin to the first in a series. In this last sense the term might easily seem to have material connotations, to be most applicable in discussing processes of generation among material beings. As with N's other terminology, much discussion and development were to be necessary before the term had a clearly defined sense.

The development and evolution of what is later thought of as Nicene orthodoxy took many decades after Nicaea itself. In what follows let us divide up this period, the years between 325 and 381, into three sections.

1. Towards a controversy: 325–350

The first thing to note about this initial period is that our sources for the period immediately after Nicaea are sparse. We can, however, make two general observations. On the one hand, it seems at least possible that Constantine and some of his supporters promoted an interpretation of N's phrases 'of the essence of the Father' and *homoousios* against those who were worried that these expressions were too materialistic to be used of God. That these phrases were already seen as requiring this sort of clarification indicates very clearly the perceived problem with N: this text seemed to many to imply or at least permit a materialism about God's being and the Son's generation and a semi-modalist conception of God.

On the other hand, in the years immediately following Nicaea, some of N's strongest supporters seemed to many to be advocating theologies which failed to preserve the distinct existence of the Son and which seemed to offer far too materialistic an account of God. Nicaea offered no clear resources for arguing against these theologians, chief among whom was Marcellus of Ancyra. Marcellus' semi-modalist theology was strongly attacked by those (such as Eusebius of Caesarea) who had been able to sign up to N but who were insistent that they did so believing it was compatible with a strong insistence on the distinction between Father and Son. Eventually, Marcellus was deposed in 336. Thus, in part because Marcellus had been a strong supporter of N, and in part because of its uselessness as a tool against him, the creed disappears from our historical record for around fifteen years.

At the same time, after considerable negotiation, Arius was readmitted to communion. In retrospect it is difficult for many modern readers to understand how this last move could have been made in the face of Nicaea's creed. However, it is precisely at this point that the fourth century demonstrates itself to be so fundamental for later Christian self-definition. The very idea of one universal creed, the terminology of which – itself understood as susceptible to a clearly restricted range of interpretation – could function as a binding statement of faith, evolved *during* this century and should not be read into its early decades. The creed of Nicaea seems to have been understood not simply as an independent part of the council's work but as an integral part and expression of one of its key judgments or decisions, and preserving the spirit of the judgment seems to have been far more important than the particular wording of the creed in which it was expressed. Thus, at later meetings of bishops over the next twenty-five years a variety of other creeds were drawn up, some probably in an attempt to ignore and move beyond N's formulations, some as an attempt to improve on its wording. In all cases credal supplementation and adaptation was an accepted mode of proceeding for all sides in the dispute. It is only during the 350s that we can clearly detect a wide shift in understandings of credal function taking hold.

Alexander of Alexandria's successor, Athanasius, remained an implacable opponent of Arius and refused to accept him back into communion. Eventually Athanasius was deposed in 335 and sent into exile. For the rest of his life Athanasius maintained that he was exiled for theological reasons, while his opponents insisted that his exile had occurred because of maladministration and his violence towards certain opponents. Both were probably partially right. Athanasius and Marcellus were both in exile in Rome in 339. Over the next year Athanasius developed into a fully fledged form earlier lines of polemic against Arius and his supporters, including Eusebius of Nicomedia. Some of this material came from Alexander, some from Marcellus, some from Eustathius and some from earlier texts of Athanasius himself.[29] Athanasius' account can be seen for the first time clearly in his *First Oration Against the Arians* (*c.* 340). Arius is cast as the originator of a heresy, of a group centred around Arius who is likened to Mani as the originator of the Manichaeans. Athanasius' strategy depended on convincing others that the basic motive of those who opposed him was the creation of a sect based on the texts of one (Arius) condemned fifteen years before.

Although Athanasius' Eastern opponents seem to have been unimpressed by what they saw as a diversionary tactic, Athanasius did manage to convince Julius, the bishop of Rome, and some other Western bishops. At this point we might well ask if it makes any sense at all to speak of a 'Nicene' theology in the period 325 to 340. It does, but we must be very careful in definition. It is probably helpful to call some key themes in the theology of Alexander of Alexandria and his supporters, the young Athanasius and Marcellus, 'Nicene', because these were the men who shaped the decisions of Nicaea and found a common interest in their opposition to Arius. But these themes were not embraced by all those who signed up at Nicaea (we know there must have been many who could sign, but did not fully share the creed's emphases), nor do they amount to a clearly uniform theology. Thus, if we speak here of an original 'Nicene' theology, we must recognize that it was as yet ill-defined.

Julius of Rome wrote to his Eastern colleagues complaining that they had unfairly condemned Athanasius and Marcellus, and complaining that they were ignoring the significance of Nicaea by readmitting 'Arians' (*Apol. II* 21ff.).

In response to this challenge by Julius, a group of bishops meeting for the dedication of a new church in Antioch in 341 issued a letter and creed stating their faith. The creed (known as the 'Dedication creed') is long and contains some very significant terminology. Most importantly it describes the Son as the 'exact image of the Godhead and the substance and will and power and glory of the Father'. This phrase appears to be a quotation from Asterius[30] and seems also to echo the sort of theology found in Eusebius of Caesarea.

For Athanasius this creed is to be simply labelled 'Arian', but that is unhelpful. In the later 350s we will see a number of figures claiming it as a source for very different positions, some of them direct precursors of late fourth-century Nicene orthodoxy. It may well be best to see it as one of the finest summaries of 'Eusebian' theology before the various theological strands of this broad tradition began to unravel in the 350s. The exchange between Julius and 'those around Eusebius' helped to turn the initial phase of this controversy into a dispute between those bishops who were most influential in the East and those most influential in the West. This large-scale misunderstanding seems further to have drawn in the imperial authorities, an especially dangerous result as Constantine's different sons ruled different parts of the Empire and resented each other's interference.

An attempt to relieve the tension between East and West was made in 343 when the Western Emperor Constans called a council at Serdica (modern Sofia). This council was a disaster: the two sides never met as one. The 'Western' bishops (including many from Greece and the Balkans but very few from France and Spain) issued a text from Serdica including a long profession of faith insisting that Father, Son and Spirit have one *ousia* or *hypostasis* and exist eternally (Theodoret, *HE* 2.8). The letter does say that 'somehow' the Father must be greater than the Son but offers no terminology for distinguishing the three. Almost any theology which speaks of more than one *hypostasis* is defied. The remainder of the 340s saw a series of attempts at rapprochement between the parties. Athanasius was allowed back to Alexandria, and in the same year we find a party of easterners heading west with a statement of faith and (unsuccessfully) presenting it to a council in Milan. This initial period of the controversy is thus marked by the confused interactions and mutual antipathy between existing theological traditions, the failure of Nicaea to relieve those tensions, and the interweaving of political and theological issues. It was not yet clear that the controversy was basically theological and few thought that the point at issue was the acceptance or rejection of a clearly expressed 'Nicene' theology.

2. The controversy emerges clearly: 350–360

The second of these three periods, 350–360, saw great shifts in the structure of the controversy. During this decade new theological options appeared; the creed of Nicaea and the term *homoousios* began to be significant points of debate; the idea that one creed with a fairly fixed wording should serve as a universal standard of faith emerged – in part through the policies of Constantius and the bishops he supported. These theological shifts need also to be understood in the context of shifts in the Roman Empire. Over the period 351–3 Constantius, originally ruler in the East, achieved control of the whole Empire.[31] Constantius has received a bad press from later history as a ruthless and brutal ruler and as an 'Arian' emperor. In fact the picture is much more complex; a case can be made that, within the fourth-century context, he was a fairly mild ruler.[32] Nevertheless, Constantius did generally promote a subordinationist theology during this decade; this had a great effect on the course of the controversy until his sudden death in 361.

Throughout the 350s a series of councils prolonged earlier Eusebian emphases, but there was an increasingly active antipathy to N's terminology and an increasing willingness to argue for an account of the Son's generation that excludes any ontological continuity between Father and Son. The defence of Nicaea by Athanasius and others may have helped to stimulate this, while continuing antipathy to Marcellus and now to his disciple Photinus also helped to push many in this direction. Two key meetings illustrate the shifts that occurred. The first was the Council of Sirmium in 351, which met while Constantius himself was present in the city (modern Sremska Mitrovica in Serbia). The focus of this council was the examination and condemnation of Photinus, bishop of Sirmium. As the most visible representative of a Marcellan type of theology, Photinus had already been condemned at a number of councils during the latter half of the 340s in the West and East. The creed has attached to it a series of anathemas. Two of these offer a strong condemnation of some different uses of *ousia* language. From these anathemas it seems that the signatories to the creed were particularly worried that linking the Son and Father in terms of *ousia* implies that the Father's being is understood to be 'extended' in the generation of the Son. There are also a number of attacks on the idea that Father and Son are co-eternal or two (equal) Gods.[33] This council in 351 set the trend for a series of subsequent Western councils in which Constantius seems to have attempted to get a clearly subordinationist theology (together with the condemnation of Athanasius) gradually accepted throughout the Empire.

Secondly, there is the meeting of bishops convened, also at Sirmium, in 357. This small meeting (probably not a formal council) produced a summary confession designed to establish a position that was being articulated with growing clarity. This document also demonstrates the increasingly clear views of those who opposed *ousia* language in any form:

> But as for the fact that some, or many, are concerned about substance (*substantia*) which is called *ousia* in Greek, that is, to speak more explicitly, *homoousion* or *homoiousion*, as it is called, there should be no mention of it whatever, nor should anyone preach it.[34]

At this point strong ambivalence regarding Nicaea, or a wish just to ignore its terms, has turned to clear and direct opposition. The clarity of this text in turn provoked a number of responses from bishops who found the direction taken here simply unacceptable. The splits between those who had come to argue for a subordinationist theology envisaging a clear ontological break between Father and Son and those whose theology and imaginative worlds will not allow such a break or at least a break of such clarity is now becoming unavoidable. At Sirmium 357 there emerges a growing confidence among those who can, from around this time, be termed 'homoian'.[35]

Homoian theologians come in distinct varieties but are united in their strong resistance to any theologies that see community of essence between Father and Son. Homoians were willing to talk of the Son being 'like' (ὅμοιος) the Father, or 'like according to the Scriptures', but further description appeared to them blasphemous. Acacius of Caesarea, the successor of Eusebius of Caesarea, was one of the major organizers of this alliance, and for a while had influence with Constantius. This alliance seems to have emerged slowly in the course of Constantius' concerted campaign against Athanasius and initially seems to have focused on the attempt to find a compromise position that would rule out theologies with any Marcellan and Western emphases. These bishops had come to see N and indeed all language about shared *ousia* as problematic. Constantius' support for this theological trajectory and ultimately for a creed to which all bishops should subscribe encouraged its partisans to push a subordinationist agenda with increasing clarity. But, at the same time, the same imperial support for this theology seems to have encouraged a variety of opponents to turn to N as the only possible universally binding standard of faith. Thus, the clarity of the homoian option set the stage for the emergence of the groups amongst whom there would soon develop the solution to the controversies as a whole.

One feature of the decade that provoked many whom I have termed 'Eusebians' into opposition to the emergent homoian theology was the gradual appearance of the theologies of Aetius and Eunomius (whom I shall refer to as 'heterousian' – for such theologies emphasized the difference in essence between Father and Son).[36] Aetius' theology is highly dense in argumentation. In his one surviving work, the *Syntagmation* ('little book'), he refers to those who are willing to countenance either *homoousios* or *homoios kat'ousian* as *chronitoi*, 'temporists', i.e., those who speak about God in temporal terms.[37] For Aetius, if God is truly 'not generated' then no logical sense can be given to an act of generation that results in one who is either *homoousios* or *homoiousios* with God; the 'not generated' cannot logically generate one who shares the quality of being 'not generated'. Thus one strong theme in Aetius' work is detailed reflection on the term 'ingenerate' (ἀγέννητος, *agennetos*). Eunomius was probably twenty-five years younger than Aetius and functioned for some years as a secretary or assistant to him (from about 355).

Initially Aetius and Eunomius are perhaps best viewed as radical homoians, whose radicalism distanced them more and more from other homoians. In his *Apology* (*c.* 361), Eunomius argues that Father and Son must be distinct because the mere fact of the Son being 'begotten' signifies that his essence cannot share the Father's absolute simplicity. There can be no sense given to a theology that alleges a similarity in essence because God's essence is unchangeable and indivisible. Eunomius also speaks of the Son's being given existence by the Father's will, a terminology designed to emphasize the dependence of the Son on the Father and the failure of shared substance language to reflect this basic point. But in this work it is also noticeable that Eunomius gives great weight to 'ingenerate' as a term summing up the character of God's essence, a term present in earlier subordinationist theology but here receiving new force and significance in Aetius' thought.[38]

Elsewhere in the *Apology* we find doctrines shared between Aetius and Eunomius, which, however, appear to have received increasing treatment as Eunomius' position became more radical. Most importantly, Eunomius deploys a particular philosophical understanding of causality to explain the character of divine generation.[39] Eunomius sees something's causal capacity to be distinct from its essence and sees the act of causing something to result in a product that continues in existence only so long as the causal activity exists. Applying this model of causality to divine generation provides a basis on which Eunomius can insist that the Son must be a product which reflects God's activity, not his essence, and that he may be rightly called 'creation' and 'product'.

The radicalism of these two figures seems to have prompted much disquiet, and the fact that they initially received support from leading homoians began, in some eyes, to make it look as if the logical direction of homoian theology was Eunomian.

During this decade we also see Athanasius' theology develop through increasing focus on Nicaea and on the term *homoousios* itself.[40] We see Athanasius turn to a detailed defence of Nicaea for the first time in his long letter entitled *On the Decrees of Nicaea* (usually known simply by the Latin *De Decretis*). This work attempts to refute questions raised by associates of the key homoian bishop Acacius of Caesarea about the non-scriptural terms *homoousios* and 'of the *ousia* of the Father' used at Nicaea. Athanasius begins by arguing (correctly) that Acacius' predecessor Eusebius of Caesarea had signed the creed and was able to interpret its language in a non-modalist, non-materialist sense. The text also directly defends Nicene usage of the language of *ousia* in an argument that possibly draws on Eusebius of Caesarea's own defence of the language (*Dec.* 19–23). Athanasius' main strategy is to present *ousia* language as necessary if the sense of scriptural titles for the Son such as Power, Wisdom and Word and of traditional analogies such as a light and its radiance is to be safeguarded. Athanasius goes on to argue that *homoousios* serves only to safeguard the distinction between Creator and creation and what Athanasius' frequently describes as the Son's status as 'true offspring'.

Having seen these developments in Athanasius' theology, we need now to consider another set of reactions to emerging homoian theology, a reaction from *within* the camp of those who had supported Constantius' policies. Some time in the winter of 358 a small council met at Ancyra. Most immediately the meeting seems to have been prompted by the teaching of Aetius in Antioch. From this gathering an extensive letter survives, probably written by Basil of Ancyra.[41] Basil attaches great weight to the language of Father and Son in his doctrine of God. This pairing indicates something distinct from the language of Creator and creature, but not something that we can directly grasp. When we remove the corporeal connotations of the Father–Son relationship as we know it then we can say 'there remains only the generation of a living being similar in essence'. Thus, confessing the likeness of Father and Son must, if it is to be attentive to the implications of this unique relationship, involve confessing that the two are *like according to essence* (ὅμοιος κατ' οὐσίαν). Basil also argues that, if the Father gives the Son to have life in himself (John 5:26), then the Son must have the same life and thus have 'everything according to essence and absolutely as does the Father'. There is here a certain subordinationism, but also a deep commitment to a unique and incomprehensible sharing of the Son in the very life of God. Thus, at the very time when Constantius seemed to be increasingly interested in imposing the theological perspective of the homoian alliance around Acacius, Basil and his associates were growing in the perception that this very theology failed to do justice to the tradition they saw as central to Eastern theology. In these developments we see beginning a process of gradual convergence of theologians coming from the broad traditions that existed at the beginning of the controversy towards a new broad consensus or tradition that will come to constitute pro-Nicene 'orthodoxy' in the 360 to 380 period.

Returning to our chronological survey, the trajectory of the 350s now reached its culmination. In AD 359 Constantius decided on a further attempt to enforce his theological perspective throughout the Empire by holding a council to which all would be called. Eventually he decided to hold twin councils in East and West. The two councils met in 359: the Eastern council at Seleucia in Cilicia (near Antioch), the Western at Ariminum in Northern Italy (modern Rimini).[42] In Italy, the Western council initially appears to have had a majority in favour of retaining the creed of Nicaea and not introducing any new creed; another smaller party seems to have been in favour of something like the 'dated creed'. This appeal to Nicaea probably reflects growing Western antipathy to the conciliar activity of the 350s, to Constantius and to much of the Eastern conciliar activity of the 340s. In the face of these challenges many Western bishops seem to have turned to Nicaea as the only obvious alternative. Nevertheless, as we shall see, in a few months almost all of those in this majority agreed to a creed worded very differently from N. At that stage they seem to have been mollified by anti-'Arian' public confessions on the part of those whom they most suspected. Thus, a commitment to Nicaea did not yet mean a firm commitment to its wording: the character of that commitment was still evolving.

The Eastern council was divided between those around Acacius, and a larger party who seem to have been in some ways sympathetic to those bishops who had recently sided with Basil of Ancyra. Nothing unified came of this Eastern meeting, and both sides sent delegations to the emperor. At Niké in Thrace (now called Ustodizo), Constantius eventually forced delegations from East and West to sign a creed, closely based on the 'dated creed', except that it missed out 'in all respects' after 'like', and said openly that one should not teach that the Father, Son and Spirit were one *hypostasis* (thus directly contradicting the 'Western' council of Serdica in 343). For about a year after the twin councils Constantius seems to have been strongly influenced by Acacius and many supporters of alternative theologies were deposed and exiled. In 360 a council was convened in Constantinople and presided over by Acacius at which Basil of Ancyra and many of his supporters were deposed. But then Constantius died suddenly in November 361 and many things changed.

3. The emergence of pro-Nicene theology: 360–380

Although much changed with Constantius' death, the pattern of the controversy through the next two decades was in place even before his death. During the later 350s and, now, during the early 360s, we begin to see an increasing number of theologians willing to adopt Nicaea as a standard. At the same time we also see some new emphases in theology and the emergence of theological arguments and principles within which this adoption of Nicaea can be articulated, while the charges of Marcellan modalism can be more strongly warded off. Against this background the 360s and 370s saw a gradual process of rapprochement between groups who had previously been opposed to or deeply suspicious of each other.

With these developments we see the emergence of what we may term 'pro-Nicene' theologies. By 'pro-Nicene' theologies I mean to indicate theologies that:

(a) see the creed of Nicaea as the key standard of belief;
(b) soon come to think that this creed should be supplemented with a confession that the Spirit is equal in glory and power to Father and Son;
(c) offer a supplementary terminology which insists on the unitary power, glory, nature and activity of the three and on the irreducibility of the three distinct persons (and which forms the context for the appropriation and adaptation of traditional considerations of the roles of the divine persons);
(d) share a set of common themes in theological anthropology and Christology that shape a particular approach to the interpretation of Scripture, to the nature of theological speech and to the character of the Christian life.

In watching the emergence of fully fledged pro-Nicene theologies we are seeing the creation of a theological 'culture', not simply the development of a particular set of theological propositions. Pro-Nicene theology offered both a theological world-view, a particular cast to the Christian imagination, and an account of the practices and modes of thinking that would sustain and nurture it.[43]

Brief mention of the imperial succession following Constantius' death is necessary if we are to understand these two decades. On his deathbed Constantius bequeathed the Empire to his cousin Julian, against whose revolt he had been marching when he died. As emperor (361–3) Julian became an active non-Christian. After Julian's own sudden death in war against Persia in 363 (and the further sudden death of his immediate successor Jovian who briefly seemed to many to support the pro-Nicene cause), Constantius' most powerful successors emerged: in the East the Emperor Valens (364–79), in the west the Emperor Valentinian (364–75).[44] While Valens supported a broadly homoian position, Valentinian appears to have had much greater sympathy for the Nicene position, but took a much more light-handed approach to the Church, refusing to support strongly even the party he favoured. However, although Valens has gone down in history as an 'Arian' emperor, he was, like Constantius, largely pragmatic in his support for the homoian cause. During these years the creed of 360 remained the official creed, although only in the East do we really find official support for it.

The realignment of these two decades also involved the transformation of some previously important forces, most importantly the homoiousians. After their political failure in 359, and after the exile of many of their most prominent members in 360, the homoiousian grouping ceased to be an influential force. Many of its key members subscribed to Nicaea as the only obvious alternative to the Niké / Constantinople creed. Others, including some who had made this move to the pro-Nicene side, retained a subordinationist theology of the Spirit and eventually followed a course which led them away from pro-Nicene theology and eventually towards a distinct hierarchy. Some must have decided to accept the homoian line. Despite this realignment among the homoiousians, the attractiveness of their theology, and perhaps their traditional-sounding commitment to a tradition going back to the Dedication creed of 341, continued to draw supporters, and we hear of people proposing their solution to the conflict right to the end of the 370s.

One of the most important attempts at rapprochement in these years occurred under Athanasius' guidance at a council in Alexandria in 362. Coming directly from the council is a text known as the 'Catholic Epistle', which sets out some basic rules for re-establishing communion with bishops who had subscribed to the decision of Ariminum and Seleucia.[45] The council took the pragmatic decision to set fairly minimum conditions centred on subscription to Nicaea, in the realization that many had subscribed to the events of 359–60 with little conviction. Immediately after the council Athanasius and others wrote a letter to the church in Antioch that is usually known more formally as the 'Antiochene Tome'. In this text Athanasius makes a significant move beyond that found in the *De Synodis*. He accepts that not all those who teach three *hypostases* also teach three hierarchically ranked beings, of which only one is 'true' God. Thus, Athanasius admits that *hypostasis* might primarily indicate a logical distinction: indicating only that the persons are truly and eternally distinct, and doing so in the context of a belief that whatever is God is immaterial and simply God. In many ways the pragmatism of the text is evident in its *failure* to produce a theological solution to these differences. Athanasius had found a way in which both sides could recognize each other's views, using Nicaea as a point of reference but without trying to seek unanimity in terminology. This tactic seems to have been copied by design or serendipity throughout much of the Christian world during the next two decades to help shape a common front from among a variety of theological positions and traditions.

Athanasius' letter to the Antiochenes was almost certainly designed to reconcile two parties in Antioch. On the one hand, Athanasius was concerned with the party of Meletius (who spoke of three *hypostases*). Meletius was the bishop of Antioch appointed by homoians, but who soon revealed himself to be far more sympathetic to the homoiousians and eventually to Nicaea. Meletius became one of the key pro-Nicene leaders during the 370s. Athanasius never fully recognized him despite his increasing influence among pro-Nicenes. On the other hand Athanasius was writing to the party of 'Eustathians' (who insisted, in ways parallel to Athanasius, on the terminology of one *hypostasis*). This group traced their ancestry to Eustathius of Antioch, deposed in 327. Athanasius' attempt at reconciliation was not immediately successful, thus demonstrating not simply that the process of rapprochement had now begun but also that this process might, in some cases, take many decades.

At this point we need to observe the emergence of a figure who will play a key role in the next twenty years: Basil of Caesarea (in Cappadocia: modern Kayseri in central Turkey, not Caesarea in Palestine). Basil's early theological allegiances are hard to fathom, but he seems to have been close to homoiousians such as Basil of Ancyra. When we first hear his actual voice, very soon after the events of 359–60, we find Basil in transition: he prefers the key homoiousian phrase ὅμοιος κατ' οὐσίαν with the adverb ἀπαραλλάκτως ('undeviatingly'), but considers this to mean the same as ὁμοούσιος (*Ep.* 9). Early on he seems to have had some problems with *homoousios*, worrying that it seemed to make very difficult appropriate distinctions between Father and Son, but these soon passed.[46]

We see Basil's mature theology beginning to emerge in the course of his *Against Eunomius* (*c.* 364). Basil argues that biblical material such as Colossians 1:15, Hebrews 1:3 and Philippians 2:6 points to a community of essence (τὸ κοινὸν τῆς οὐσίας) between the one who generates and the one generated. Basil then explains that this community of essence is the core of his teaching and writes:

> According to this, divinity (θεότης) is one. That is to say, it is according to the rationale (λόγος) of the substance (οὐσία) that the unity is thought, but, as in number (ἄριθμος), the difference of each rests in the particular properties and in the particular characteristics. (*Eun.* 1.19)

We know that there must be a unity of *ousia* between Father and Son, although what it is remains unknown: we know that there is an essence, but not what it is. At the same time we know the *idioma* or *idiotes* of Father and Son as distinct individuals.

A few sentences later, after explaining that God's image must co-exist before all time, and commenting on Hebrews 1:3, Basil writes,

> And thus, because of this, 'radiance' is said, so that we know what is signified, and 'image of substance', so that *homoousios* is understood. (*Eun.* 1.20)

This text is in some ways unrepresentative, as it is the *only* application of *homoousios* to the relationship of Father and Son in *Against Eunomius*. Nevertheless we see Basil here arguing that the traditional language of the Son's closeness to the Father is best expressed by the terminology of *homoousios*. One further stage in Basil's account appears at *Against Eunomius* 3.3 where he argues that when the Seraphim at Isaiah 6:3 cry 'Holy' three times we see that 'the holiness according to nature (*physis*) is contemplated in the three *hypostases*'. Basil does not yet use *hypostasis* as a standard term for the three persons – sometimes he actually uses *hypostasis* as a synonym for *ousia* or *physis* – but he is beginning to reflect deeply on the need for a vocabulary to distinguish what in God is one from what is three.[47]

The development of a terminology for discussion of divine existence that could allow for the real differentiation of persons within the clearly unitary and indivisible divine existence was fundamental to pro-Nicene theology. Within this new theological context it could gradually become clear in new ways that the relationship of Father and Son was intrinsic to the one divine existence, that the divine 'persons' were in many senses of ontologically equal status, and that this unique mode of existence was the context for all discussion of generation and division. We do not know who first offered a clearly argued version of such a terminology in a pro-Nicene context during these years, although the importance of making these divisions seems to have been recognized by many in quick succession. Basil most certainly is the earliest surviving writer to reflect at length on a terminological distinction central to pro-Nicene theology. In Basil, as in so many writers over the next twenty years, a wide variety of terms are treated as synonymous, as long as the logical distinction is clearly made.

As we have just seen, one feature of Basil's *Against Eunomius* is an increasing willingness to talk about the Spirit's status in parallel terms to that of Father and Son. Basil's language (still in some ways reticent) reflects a widespread pro-Nicene shift. This shift may be seen as the logical conclusion of the pro-Nicene position. Traditional scriptural and liturgical language had long been taken by many to imply that the Spirit's work was inseparable from that of the Son and thus part of the divine activity; but once the activity of Father and Son was treated as unitary, and as theologians asserted with increasing clarity that there was one simple divine nature, then it should not cause surprise that the Spirit was increasingly spoken of as the third *hypostasis* in the divine nature. Nevertheless, however inevitable this shift may seem to us, it was not universally accepted.

We first find clear opposition in a group against whom Athanasius writes *c.* 358–61. One of his Egyptian supporters, Serapion, bishop of Thmuis in the Nile delta, reported a group that was 'Nicene' concerning the divinity of the Son, but seemed to regard the Spirit as a created and superior angel (quoting 1 Tim. 5:21).[48] Against this position Athanasius deploys arguments he had earlier used in the case of the Son. Just as the Son's coming forth from the Father is only logically comprehensible as an immaterial generation within the Godhead, not as the generation of an intermediate being who shares partially in divinity, so the Spirit proceeds from the Father, fully within the Godhead. At the same time, just as the Son shares the Father's being with us and so must be true God, so the Spirit draws us to the Son and brings us gifts from heaven. The Spirit must also be God.

In Cappadocia, possibly beginning in 368, and clearly evident in the early 370s, we find a number of references to those who deny the divinity of the Spirit. During the late 370s and 380s a specific group is frequently mentioned called Macedonians (after Macedonius the bishop of Constantinople) or *Pneumatomachoi* ('Spirit fighters'). Many of those being described in this way during the 370s were former homoiousians. Many or most of these figures seem to have believed in the divinity of the Son in ways that satisfied pro-Nicene commentators, but they seem to have been worried that pro-Nicene insistence on according an equal position to the Spirit reflected either a non-scriptural modalism or a confession of three equal Gods. In the second case these thinkers seem to have grasped how one might speak of the Son sharing the Father's nature, but they were unhappy with the next step of speaking clearly and simply of one divine nature encompassing three still distinct beings. Against them Basil explains that pro-Nicenes are not in the business of adding further divine beings to a list of divine beings, but of providing an account of irreducible simplicity and unity within which all talk of God must occur (*SpS* 16). Basil's opponents had, in many ways, missed the context within which emerging pro-Nicene theology made this assertion. One of the most fundamental moves of pro-Nicene theology was to articulate this context *without* making the persons reducible to a prior essence.

It is time now to turn again to events in the Western half of the Empire, which have not been mentioned since describing the Council of Ariminium in 359. During the second half of the 350s some westerners had already begun to see Nicaea as the obvious alternative standard of faith to the emerging homoian theology, and as a rallying point against the decisions forced on westerners as Constantius' power increased westwards. This response was particularly strong after 357, one of the key figures being Hilary of Poitiers. Hilary was a bishop who had been sent into exile in 356 by order of Constantius, for his opposition to Constantius' main ecclesiastical supporter and agent in Gaul.[49] Hilary is clear that until the mid-350s he had never heard the creed of Nicaea used publicly at a council, although he soon came to grant it great significance. In exile, Hilary went to the region of Phrygia in Asia Minor where he made the acquaintance of a number of key figures, including Basil of Ancyra. In 359, after attending the council at Seleucia, he was allowed back to Gaul and played a major role in opposing Constantius' homoian settlement. Hilary's theology provides a fascinating example of how someone with what we might term a traditional Latin interest in language that emphasizes the shared being between God and his Word gradually offers a more distinctly pro-Nicene account that overcomes the ambiguities of earlier Nicene theology. We find Hilary treating the ineffable generation of one who is truly God from God as the core of the Christian account of God, but we also see him increasingly offering a sophisticated and clearly pro-Nicene account of the Father and Son as distinct from each other, but sharing one nature and power – specifically the power that is creative activity. Hilary was active at a number of councils, trying to rally people behind Nicaea as the only alternative standard comparable to the Ariminum creed. One feature of these pro-Nicene campaigns in the West during the 360s and 370s was the importance of conducting them cautiously, without creating the impression with the imperial authorities that there would be large-scale public disorder. In particular, while it was possible for small synods to meet and articulate a common adherence to Nicaea, we have no evidence during this period that pro-Nicenes had the means to depose (rather than just censure or excommunicate) homoian bishops. Rarely did pro-Nicenes attempt to incite the direct removal of their opponents.

For much of these two decades the West was under the control of Valentinian I (366–75). Valentinian has gone down in history as a 'Nicene' emperor; in fact his public policy was one of pragmatic non-interference in ecclesiastical affairs (whatever his private sympathies). This public policy allowed the pro-Nicene campaigns gradually to have a serious effect even while certain avenues for change remained closed. Valentinian's young successor Gratian was a far more open supporter of the pro-Nicene cause, especially after the accession of Theodosius in the East.

One other Western figure from the 370s and 380s demands brief mention: Ambrose, bishop of Milan 374–97. Ambrose was a provincial governor and an unbaptized layman when he was chosen as successor to the important homoïan bishop of Milan, Auxentius, in 374.[50] His appointment probably reflects the imperial authorities' intention of ensuring that Milan would henceforth have as bishop a less controversial figure than Auxentius. For the first few years of his episcopate, despite apparently having pro-Nicene leanings, he appears to have taken little action against homoïans. However, by 378 there appears to have been considerable pressure on Ambrose from homoïans in Milan, aided by an influx of refugees from Illyricum following the Gothic invasion. Ambrose gradually evolved a sophisticated theological response to these opponents, incorporating much contemporary Greek pro-Nicene theology.[51]

Ambrose became increasingly influential over Gratian, and under this influence, as well as the influence of Theodosius' policies in the East, Gratian began to pursue a much more directly pro-Nicene line. In many ways the highpoint of this new policy was the small council held at Aquileia (at the very top of the Adriatic) in 381. At this council a number of the key remaining homoïans were deposed at Ambrose's instigation. This council does not, as it has sometimes been presented, mark the end of the homoians in the West, but it does mark an important juncture. After this homoeans seem to have begun the process of becoming a clearly distinct group, although their theology continued to develop.

We are now in a position to narrate the institutional victory of the emergent pro-Nicene theology. Events in the Eastern half of the Empire during the years 378–82, both secular and ecclesiastical, take their cue from the disastrous battle of Adrianople in 378. At this battle against the Goths, the Emperor Valens was among those killed. A general called Theodosius was eventually summoned from retirement in Spain by the remaining Emperor Gratian and commissioned as co-emperor to take charge of the problem. In 379 Meletius called a council in Antioch after returning from the last of a series of exiles under Valens (365–6, 371–8). The uncertainty following the battle of Adrianople and the change in imperial administration provided an opportunity to change the status quo that was not missed by pro-Nicenes. Meletius' council (which probably met with at least the tacit approval of the new emperor) indicated that many in both East and West favoured the pro-Nicene cause. Within months Theodosius declared for the pro-Nicenes. In 380 Theodosius issued an edict which insisted on the profession of 'Nicene' faith, defined as that taught by Damasus, bishop of Rome, and Peter, Athanasius' successor in Alexandria. Then, in 381, Theodosius summoned a council to meet in Constantinople.[52]

It is important to realize that our knowledge of this famous council is surprisingly patchy. The council seems not to have been large – around 150 bishops attended – and to have been drawn from areas under Meletius' influence. We have no surviving copy of the theological definition that followed the council's creed, and most surprisingly there is no certain account of the creed until the Council of Chalcedon. However, there are enough hints to make it fairly certain that this council did actually issue the creed later associated with it.[53] That creed probably read as follows:

> We believe in one God, the Father Almighty, maker of heaven and earth and of all things visible and invisible; and in one Lord Jesus Christ, the Son of God, the Only-begotten, begotten by his Father before all ages, Light from light, true God from true God, begotten not made, consubstantial with the Father, through whom all things came into existence, who for us men and for our salvation came down from the heavens and became incarnate by the Holy Spirit and the Virgin Mary and became a man, and was crucified for us under Pontius Pilate and suffered and was buried and rose again on the third day in accordance with the Scriptures and ascended into the heavens and is seated at the right hand of the Father and will come again with glory to judge the living and the dead, and there will be no end to his kingdom; and in the Holy Spirit, the Lord and Life-giver, who proceeds from the Father, who is worshipped and glorified together with the Father and the Son, who spoke by the prophets; and in one holy catholic and apostolic Church; we confess one baptism for the forgiveness of sins; we wait for the resurrection of the dead and the life of the coming age.[54]

The creed of this council makes a number of adjustments to the Nicene creed, subtly changing the wording of the central accounts of the Son's generation and extending the clause on the Spirit to insist on the Spirit's being worshipped with Father and Son. This last change is somewhat ambiguously worded and the creed does not say directly that the Spirit is God or that the Spirit is *homoousios*. This may well reflect something of a compromise at the council, and very possibly the personal influence of Gregory of Nyssa, although from Theodosius' subsequent decree the basic intention of those setting the theological pace was very clear.

Theodosius issued a decree in 382 known as *Episcopiis tradi* that is of considerable significance because of the manner in which it attempts to define orthodoxy. The beginning of the text says,

> [W]e order that all the churches now be handed over to bishops who confess the Father, Son and Spirit to be of one majesty and power and glory and splendour, making no discordance by profane division, but with a declaration of the order of the persons of the Trinity and in the unity of the divinity . . .

The significance of this decree lies in its attempt to define pro-Nicene orthodoxy without trying to impose one particular terminology. Rather, the text attempts to define the logic of the relationship between persons and essence. This strategy reflects the reality that different pro-Nicene theologies had become able to recognize a variety of terminologies as compatible because they could identify the logical overlap in the deep structures of their theologies. It is also noteworthy that the text does not define orthodoxy by reference to the term *homoousios* or the terms of Nicaea, but by a trinitarian formula: this was now clearly the focus of Christian doctrine, the articulating principle behind other doctrinal themes.

Two other key figures in the development of pro-Nicene theology were Gregory Nazianzen, a long-term friend and close associate of Basil's, and Gregory of Nyssa, Basil's younger brother. Their theology represents a less cautious approach (at least with respect to the Spirit) than their contemporary Basil. Basil's work during the 360s seems to have prepared the way for them, but it is their writing through into the 380s that stands as the full flowering of pro-Nicene thought. After Basil's death Gregory of Nyssa in particular seems to have taken up his role as chief pro-Nicene opponent of Eunomius.

When we consider pro-Nicene theologies in general, instead of attempting to define pro-Nicene orthodoxy by reference simply to particular propositions, we should perhaps speak of the development of a pro-Nicene theological 'culture'. In this way we will better understand how these theological developments came to have such a fundamental role in shaping Christian identity. The use of 'culture' here is one that stems from discussions in cultural anthropology, and a brief definition might perhaps be 'a system of learned patterns of behaviour (including thought, speech and human action), ideas and products that together shape conceptions of the order of existence'. Two other observations are needed to complement this definition. First, 'cultures', in this sense, do not necessarily have clearly defined boundaries. Boundaries between different cultures may be fluid; while one can define their core attributes and point to those who exhibit them well, it may be very difficult to identify clear boundaries. Secondly, one may belong to a variety of cultures simultaneously and be in a continual process of negotiating the boundaries between them.[55]

To define pro-Nicene culture thoroughly we would need to look at a variety of intellectual, social, political and ritual practices and attitudes to see the concrete forms of these patterns of behaviour. Here, where there is space only for a summary account, I shall focus on some of the key ideas that shaped pro-Nicene theologies. We might begin to indicate the structure of this culture by identifying three broad sets of themes found between different pro-Nicene theologies. Together these themes – although still developing – were central to shaping the mainstream Christian imagination and identity at the end of the fourth century.

First, and seemingly most specifically concerned with trinitarian theology, pro-Nicenes insisted that God was one simple power, glory, majesty and nature. The unity of God is also reflected in the central pro-Nicene tenet that the persons of the Trinity are inseparable in their activity. It is important to understand that this insistence provides the basic context within which pro-Nicenes situate *all* talk about the persons and their irreducibility. However, arguing that the divine unity and simplicity are right at the heart of pro-Nicene theology is not intended to constitute a suggestion that pro-Nicenes somehow thought of the divine unity as more important than the differences between the persons. This is so *only insofar as* they thought that the indivisibility and simplicity of the divine being was the context within which we should speak about division or hierarchical ordering within God. Within this context pro-Nicenes insisted on the irreducibility of the divine persons. Although it is still commonplace to speak as if the terminology of *ousia* and *hypostasis* was the central terminology of pro-Nicene theology, it is actually the case that a variety of logically compatible terminologies were used, and not simply within different pro-Nicene traditions, but even within the same writer.[56]

The second major set of themes in pro-Nicene theology follows directly on from the first and focuses on an overlapping set of principles concerning human speech about God, its nature and possibility. For all pro-Nicenes whose work survives at any length, discussions of trinitarian theology are interwoven with questions of anthropology, psychology and epistemology. On the one hand, pro-Nicenes insist that the divine nature exceeds our intellectual grasp. If one asks in what precise sense God is incomprehensible, pro-Nicenes rarely provide clear answers, insisting that we cannot know in what ways the divine exceeds our grasp precisely because God is the Creator of all and the Lord of all who is truly distinct from the created order. Some, such as Augustine, articulate clearly the principle that no formal analogies are possible; others, such as Gregory of Nyssa, use the language of 'analogy' more openly but simultaneously insist on the impossibility of fully understanding the God to whom we apply the analogies. On the other hand, pro-Nicenes link their accounts of divine incomprehensibility very clearly to their accounts of how human beings in need of redemption fail even to comprehend what they should, and how the search for knowledge of God must be accompanied by practices that purify soul and mind. Thus, developed psychologies and anthropologies become key parts of good trinitarian theology. In a more extended investigation it might also be possible to show how pro-Nicenes link these presumptions to accounts of bodily ascetic practice. This collection of themes must also be seen as including pro-Nicene accounts of Scripture. For pro-Nicenes Scripture is the focal resource in our attempts to speak of God and our attempts to learn how to go on speaking meaningfully. Figural reading practices enable Scripture to function as a resource for the purification of the soul and the constant advance of the human understanding within the context of pro-Nicene anthropologies and psychologies.[57]

The third and last major set of pro-Nicene themes is Christological, and again follows closely on from the last. On the one hand, pro-Nicene theologies do not so much abandon but rather transform traditional accounts of the Son's intermediary role. The role of the incarnate *Logos* in drawing us together before the Father, through the incorporation of our existence within that of the *Logos*, becomes perhaps more prominent. The work of Son and Spirit can thus now shape new accounts of the ways in which Christians conceive of themselves as being encompassed within the life of the three divine persons.

This account has referred to pro-Nicenes in the plural. It is important to realize that there were different groups of pro-Nicene theologians who could certainly recognize each other's theologies as mutually compatible. Much scholarly work remains to be done on identifying the different groups and their characteristic emphases. Contrary to some common presentations, it is more and more clear that an East *versus* West distinction is not a primary dividing mark between different pro-Nicene theologies. These overlapping theologies were also themselves in a state of flux; over the course of the emergence of pro-Nicene orthodoxy and through the decades that followed, various terminologies and emphases came to spread more and more widely, and distinct traditions changed and evolved.

Having discussed at some length the course of the trinitarian controversies of the fourth century we need now to outline the course of the Christological controversies that occupied much energy over the seventy years from 380 to 450. However, it is important to note that the previous sentence is problematic in its assumptions. In many textbook presentations the 'Christological' disputes are treated as a separate and subsequent theological controversy occurring once the trinitarian controversies of the fourth century were over. This account is problematic, first, because it does not take account of the fact that the divergent Christologies with which we are concerned emerged in the context of the trinitarian debates. Secondly, the assumption that one can easily separate these disputes leads one to neglect ways in which the trinitarian controversy shaped the fundamental assumptions of all the protagonists in the later disputes between 380 and 450.

The first stage in the Christological debates was controversy around the figure of Apollinaris of Laodicea in the 370s and 380s.[58] Apollinaris (*c.* 315–92) was the son of a priest and rhetor also called Apollinaris, and like his father was highly trained in classical literature and literary style. He was a friend and ally of Athanasius, sided with the Eustathian Bishop Paulinus in Antioch against Meletius, and wrote strongly in defence of pro-Nicene theology in the mid 360s. Even at this stage he seems to have possessed a distinctive Christology, which eventually became the subject of strong censure and criticism. However serious Apollinaris' theological errors seemed, his decision to ordain his own supporter Vitalis bishop in Antioch against Meletius in 378 and then to allow other supporters to establish an alternative hierarchy in some other bishoprics greatly increased the anger of many in the East towards him.

Traditionally Apollinaris' theology has been described through reference to his supposed insistence that Christ did not have a human soul, the *Logos* 'ensouling' the human person of Christ. Paradoxically, Apollinaris' doctrine, if this it was, found much support in third- and fourth-century writing, even among some of those who had been strong supporters of Nicaea. For a number of earlier Nicene writers a concern to show that the truly divine *Logos* was directly at work in Christ led them to show little interest in whether Christ possessed a human soul, and in some cases to deny it directly. However, rather than assuming that Apollinaris imagined Christ simply without a human soul, it seems much more likely that Apollinaris held to a trichotomous understanding of the human being. That is, he seems to have envisaged the soul as divided into two levels, there being an animating soul controlling the functions of the body, and a rational soul which 'contained' the will and self-governing rational power of human existence: in this scheme the *Logos* replaced the higher level or division of the soul. For Apollinaris this was the only way of preserving the true presence of the *Logos* in the incarnate Christ; the idea that the human Christ possessed both a rational soul and the presence of the *Logos* implied to him that the full depth of union between man and *Logos* was being avoided.

Apollinaris' account of the soul of Christ needs also to be set in the context of one other key theme in his theology. Apollinaris makes significant use of Paul's terminology of the 'heavenly man' for Christ and seems in some sense to speak of Christ's flesh as having existed before the incarnation. Apollinaris perhaps conceived of the Word as existing before the ages in a form that prefigured the flesh of Christ, a spiritual form of Christ's glorified body that was already in some sense the mediating union between God and creation that would appear through a human birth. Brian Daley has recently argued that this theme of Apollinaris' theology seemed to imply to Gregory of Nyssa that Apollinaris misunderstood the true narrative of the incarnation.[59] For Nyssa, Daley argues, Apollinaris fails to give sufficient weight to the *Logos'* status both as one in the divine nature (by envisaging the *Logos* as somehow eternally enfleshed) and as freely descending to become incarnate in Christ. Once we have seen Apollinaris' views on the soul and on the Word's eternal enfleshment it becomes easier to understand one of the most important of his ideas, and one that prefigures and even influences Christological debate over the next seventy years. Apollinaris speaks famously of 'the one enfleshed nature of God the *Logos'* (μία φύσις τοῦ Θεοῦ Λόγου σεσαρκωμένη). While Apollinaris does at times speak of or imply two different aspects to Christ, his two natures, his main focus is on ensuring that we understand Christ to be a unity, constituted by the saving presence of the *Logos*.

Dispute over Apollinaris continued for some decades. For the purposes of understanding the Christological controversies of the fifth century it is important to understand that the dispute with Apollinaris established a polemical terminology: those throughout the next few decades who wished to insist that the incarnate Christ was one unified reality, constituted by the presence of the *Logos*, could always be accused of Apollinarianism. Questions concerning Christ's soul also now received new focus: to offer a theology in which Christ's soul seemed dispensable could now be accused of being 'Apollinarian'. Thus, dispute over Apollinaris' theology was in many ways the opening salvo in a Christological battle that was to run for many centuries, the initial skirmish of which might be said to end at the Council of Chalcedon in 451.

One of the targets (and opponents) of Apollinaris was the Christology associated with Diodore of Tarsus. Diodore was bishop of Tarsus only from 378, but he had already had a long career in the pro-Nicene cause, having become a supporter of Meletius of Antioch in the 360s. His work has tended to be seen as one of the early examples of what is frequently called the 'Antiochene' school, exhibiting a Christology and a style of reading scriptural texts that stand as one of two key theological traditions of the early fifth century. While it does seem fair to talk of an Antiochene tradition in the fifth century, it is not the case that 'Antioch' and 'Alexandria' represent two traditions equally long-standing and all-encompassing in Christian thought.[60] The Antiochene tradition in terms of Christology is limited in scope, largely from Diodore to Nestorius. The Alexandrian tradition of Cyril (discussed below) is in many ways a particular version of a style of Christology found in many places in the fourth- and fifth-century Christian world. Treating them as two equal traditions can easily give one a distorted sense of their relative size.

Despite the state of Diodore's remaining corpus, the basic lines of his position are clear: he insisted that in Christ there is a clear separation between the *Logos*, 'the Son of God', and 'the one born of Mary' or 'the son of David'. Diodore insisted on distinguishing the two subjects of talk about Christ for a sound pro-Nicene reason: the divine, impassible and omniscient *Logos* could not in any way be subject to change or suffering. At every stage his animus against Apollinaris stemmed from his worry that Apollinaris envisaged Christ as a mixture and thus compromised the truly divine status of the *Logos*. We can say, then, that pro-Nicene theology shaped the early stages of this dispute in two ways: first, one side insisted that our descriptions of Christ must constantly bear in mind the immutability and impassibility of the divine *Logos*; secondly, both sides insisted that salvation comes through the presence of the *Logos* in Christ, but for Apollinaris, as earlier for Athanasius and later for Cyril of Alexandria, this conception implies that the *Logos* must somehow have become truly one with Christ's humanity, transforming it into the unitary locus of salvation.

Diodore died around 390, but his theology and teaching lived on, especially in the Theodore who became bishop of Mopsuestia in 392.[61] Theodore's main Christological concern, like Diodore's, was with preserving the *Logos* as immutable and hence with not confusing the two different subjects of talk about the incarnate Christ. Theodore clearly argues that Christ had a human soul: 'the man assumed' must be a fully human being. When he spoke of the incarnation, Theodore sometimes used phrases that easily seemed problematic to those outside his particular tradition: he spoke of the *Logos* becoming flesh only κατὰ τὸ δοκεῖν, a Greek phrase we might gloss as 'seemingly' or 'metaphorically'. However, we misinterpret Theodore unless we notice that he does also have a sophisticated account of the union that is the incarnate

Christ. God is present in all things and everywhere, but by a specific act of love or grace he chooses to be specially present, or present for particular purposes. In the Son, the *Logos* is present 'as in a Son' so that there is one person (πρόσωπον) to which all the actions of the Saviour can be referred. This union enabled the participation of Christ's human nature in the divine life and was eternal. The union that occurs in the incarnate Christ is then the model for our own adoption as sons of God.

Although it is difficult to narrate the course of events with certainty, it seems that the work of Diodore and Theodore was well known, and had created a context in which differing pro-Nicene Christologies were in an increasingly tense relationship. It is against this background that the next stage of the controversy erupted. In 428 Nestorius, a disciple of Theodore, became bishop of Constantinople.[62] Nestorius' theology offered another version of the 'Antiochene' tradition as we have seen it in Diodore and Theodore, but his personality appears also to have been a factor in the events that followed. Within a year of his consecration controversy with Cyril, the bishop of Alexandria, erupted. It is important to note that both of the protagonists in this controversy were well-known and established figures. Two events were key in the public emergence of this controversy. First, Nestorius preached in Constantinople arguing that Mary should not be addressed by the title Θεοτόκος ('one who gave birth to God'). Secondly, Cyril wrote to Nestorius (in 429) claiming that the Nicene creed implies the necessity of the title *Theotokos*. Nestorius' reply to Cyril avoided the issues, and Cyril wrote again: his *Second Letter to Nestorius* became a document that was eventually identified by the Council of Chalcedon as a standard of orthodoxy.[63]

Nestorius' theology in many ways followed clearly on from Theodore's. Nestorius insisted that Christ may be spoken of as both one and two realities, but at different levels. The incarnate Christ is indivisible as Christ, as the person (πρόσωπον) of Christ – and πρόσωπον for Nestorius seems to have specifically indicated the person as a concrete manifestation. However, Christ is also two in the sense that the two natures of divinity and humanity are distinct. Christ is made up of two sorts of realities, which cannot lose or change their essential features. Although Nestorius tries hard to insist that the one *prosopon* of the incarnate Christ means that we can attribute saying and actions of Christ, not simply to his human or his divine nature, but to the incarnate *prosopon* as a unity, at other times his language is looser, and he even speaks of two *prosopa* in Christ.

For Nestorius Cyril's language was dangerous because it seemed to envisage a change in the nature of the *Logos*, the two natures for him being always the unchangeable grounds from which Christ is constituted. After he had lost his battle with Cyril, Nestorius composed a long text called *The Book of Heraclides of Damascus* (known at times as the *Bazaar of Heraclides*), in which he seems to have moved much more closely towards admitting that in the union of incarnation the two natures interpenetrate in some sense. Many modern scholars have argued that Nestorius was not a 'Nestorian', that he is not at all fairly represented by his opponents and by the caricature condemned under his name.

Cyril's own theology found its early bearings in reinterpreting Athanasius' anti-'Arian' themes.[64] In his early works on the Trinity and in his commentary on John Cyril defends strongly the status of the *Logos* as divine, and he emphasizes the Word's *kenosis*, self-emptying, in the incarnation. Cyril does not (again unsurprisingly) imagine that the Word voluntarily ceases to possess those qualities intrinsic to being divine; rather, in a mysterious and ineffable way the *Logos* chose to unite himself to a human nature and to take the flesh and soul *as his own*. At times this leads to descriptions (not unlike some Athanasian themes) in which the human actions and sufferings of Christ seem to be the *Logos'* performance of human suffering rather than actual suffering. One helpful way of explaining the core of Cyril's thought is, Richard Norris suggests, to think about the narrative Cyril wishes to tell. Cyril's fundamental Christological narrative takes its form from Philippians 2. The *Logos* remains in the form of God and yet descends, not assuming a person who might potentially have existed independently, but becoming one subject with a human nature so that a human life and death (and resurrection) would be his eternally. The concern in this narrative is not to offer a metaphysical analysis of the constitution of Christ's person, but to describe how the *Logos*, as the one subject of the story, assumes flesh for our salvation.

At times Cyril faced accusations of Apollinarianism, the earlier controversy having shaped what one might term the polemical imagination of the early fifth century. His strong talk of the union between the two natures gave rise to charges that he believed the flesh to have come down from heaven. Cyril denies these charges directly in his letter to John of Antioch, but there is a fascinating twist to his denial of Apollinarianism. As the controversy progressed, Cyril's account of Christ came to focus more and more clearly on language that emphasized the unity of the person of Christ, and one of the tools that enabled this shift was the discovery of phraseology and texts that were Apollinaris', but which had survived under the name of Athanasius and Didymus the Blind. In particular Apollinaris' terminology of 'the one enfleshed nature of the *Logos*' seems to have helped Cyril develop his increasing insistence on there being one nature in Christ.

We left the story of the controversy with Cyril and Nestorius starting a war by correspondence in 429. Cyril's tactics were masterly: at the same time as his correspondence campaign he also won over Celestine the bishop of Rome. Cyril was able to persuade Celestine to hold a synod (August 430) at which Nestorius was to be condemned if he did not recant. However, these moves were forestalled by the imperial summoning of a council to meet in the following year. The Council of Ephesus was, to say the least, problematic. Cyril orchestrated the proceedings: Nestorius was condemned; Mary proclaimed Theotokos; John of Antioch and the bishops of the dioceses of the East, amongst whom Nestorius might have expected support, arrived in Ephesus late, after Cyril had already concluded the council with those already present.

There were those, John of Antioch and Theodoret of Cyrrhus among them, who found unacceptable the council's simple proclamation that Cyril was right. Something of a rapprochement came in 433 when a document known as the Formula of Reunion and composed in Antioch was signed by both Cyril and John of Antioch. Nestorius remained deposed, Cyril conceded that in matters of exegesis one might attribute sayings to either of the two natures or to the one person of Christ, and the Antiochenes confessed Mary as Theotokos. The text also speaks of an 'unconfused union' of two natures, the divine '*homoousios* with the Father' (as Nicaea had affirmed), and the human, which includes a rational soul, '*homoousios* with us', in the 'One Christ, one Son, one Lord'. This agreement seems to have angered some of Cyril's supporters, but he held to it until he died in 444.

Although the treatment of individual writers in this volume stops with the death of Cyril, it is important to continue the narrative briefly through to 451. In the late 440s the controversy erupted again, and two issues were central, the case of Eutyches in Constantinople and the theology of Theodoret of Cyrrhus. Theodoret emerged as a fundamental defender of Nestorius and is clearly dependent on the themes found in Diodore and Theodore, but, like Nestorius, he was trying to deal with the ambiguities inherited from them.[65] After much reluctance Theodoret eventually accepted the Formula of Reunion but he refused to condemn Nestorius. Eutyches, an aged and much respected archimandrite in Constantinople, was condemned for his insistence that in the incarnation one must speak of only one nature, and indeed a nature not 'consubstantial with us'.

In 449 a synod was held in Ephesus under the control of Dioscorus, Cyril's successor. Eutyches was declared orthodox and Flavian was deposed, as was Theodoret of Cyrrhus. Dioscorus used imperial troops to harass those who opposed him. Among those whose views were not heard was Leo, the bishop of Rome. Leo was deeply offended and termed the meeting the 'robber council'. In 451, under a new emperor, the Council of Chalcedon met.[66] Three aspects of its work need to be noted here. First, and at imperial insistence, Dioscorus and some of his key supporters were deposed. Secondly, the council defined a series of works as embodying Christological orthodoxy. The creeds of Nicaea and Constantinople were reaffirmed, but the council also accepted as standards of orthodoxy Leo's Letter to Flavian (ignored in 449; known as Leo's 'Tome' from the Latin *tomus* for letter), Cyril's *Second Letter to Nestorius*, and Cyril's letter to John of Antioch which contained the Formula of Reunion. Thirdly, the council drew up a famous definition of Christological faith. This definition affirms that the 'mystery of the dispensation' should not be split 'into a duality of sons'; at the same time it rejects any 'mixture or confusion' of the two natures, and rejects any language of one nature after the union. The central part of the definition is closely related to the Formula of Reunion. It insists that 'one and the same Son, Our Lord Jesus Christ' is to be acknowledged 'in two natures' (a modification of the theology avowed by Cyril and Dioscorus insisted on by the papal legates), adding the adverbs unconfusedly, unalterably, undividedly and inseparably. Finally, the text insists that the natures come together 'in one person or *hypostasis*'. The four adverbs have been the subject of much debate ever since. Our narrative ends with Chalcedon, but the dispute did not. From the many debates over Chalcedon splits occurred in the Church in the East, which continue today.

The bulk of this chapter has been concerned with debates over trinitarian and Christological issues, and these were indeed fundamental in shaping Christian belief and imagination during these years. But interwoven with these disputes was a series of other controversies centred on the nature of humanity and the origins and powers of the soul. In discussing the origins of the trinitarian controversies we have already encountered third-century controversy over Origen's work: towards the end of the fourth century controversy over Origen again became prominent. As Elizabeth Clark makes clear in her recent study of this controversy, we need almost to speak of controversies in the plural here, different participants having different views about what was actually at stake, and a number of highly personal disputes becoming foci of the debate.[67] One of the earliest stages in the dispute began with Epiphanius of Salamis' strong denunciation of Origen in the 370s. For Epiphanius, Origen's teaching on the fall of souls into the body and the possibility that the devil would be saved were unacceptable. Epiphanius also treated Origen as the ultimate source of 'Arianism' because of his subordinationism.

Epiphanius' attacks seem to have reflected debate about Origen's works that was already prominent, especially in ascetic circles in Egypt. The debate over Origen in Egypt would soon take centre stage in the debate, but here subtly different issues seem to have been at stake. The strong spiritualizing tendencies in Origen's exegesis of scriptural material concerning the nature of the Word seemed to some Egyptian ascetics to run against the scriptural tendency to speak of God in anthropomorphic terms. Some also thought that asserting God's incorporeality and incomprehensibility failed to acknowledge the implications of the doctrine that human beings are created in God's image. Lastly, some also seem to have understood the Son as possessing a visible form or glory, possibly in connection with exegesis of Daniel 7 and Ezekiel 1:[68] a theme that has a long pre-Nicene pedigree in Christian thought and which may well be connected with the account of Christ's glorified body found in Apollinarian circles.

Eventually, in the 380s, Epiphanius convinced Jerome in Palestine that these charges were just (particularly interesting as Jerome had long been virtually a copier of Origen in his biblical commentaries). In 395 Epiphanius visited Jerusalem and effectively charged John of Jerusalem with Origenism. He was able to enlist Jerome on his side against both John and Jerome's erstwhile friend Rufinus. Theophilus, bishop of Alexandria, had been dismissive of Epiphanius' views in the mid-390s. However, his position soon changed. In his Easter Letter of 399 Theophilus argued strongly in favour of God's incorporeality and the invisibility of the *Logos*, but then he abruptly changed course and took the side of Jerome and Epiphanius. He also expelled from Egypt some of the leading Origenist monks to whom he had formerly been close. When these were to some extent sheltered, pending further investigation, by John the bishop of Constantinople (who became known as Chrysostom), Theophilus engineered the removal of John from his bishopric in 403. At this point Theophilus appears to have again changed his mind and returned to a qualified support for and study of Origen, claiming that one simply had to choose what in Origen one studied.

These debates also were heard and followed in the Western half of the Empire, Rufinus acting as a principal conduit for transferring ideas and translations to the West. Of particular importance here were debates over the origin of the soul and to what extent one could hold to any version of an Origenist cosmic scheme in which souls are created separate from bodies and are then give a chance to work towards salvation through being born in material bodies. Some issues concerning free will and the origin of the soul appear in a transmuted form in debate over 'Pelagianism'.

As remarked above, in the West some aspects of the Origenist controversy came to affect disputes over what became known as 'Pelagianism', a dispute particularly associated with the figure of Augustine of Hippo.[69] However, this dispute, which had such an impact on defining Western Christian identity for future centuries, involved many other thinkers than Augustine and Pelagius. Pelagius himself had had a long career before the controversy and we should beware lest the name 'Pelagianism' make us forget that a host of related thinkers were involved. The precise origins of the dispute are, as with so many such disputes, unclear. At the turn of the fourth century there seems to have been a growing debate in Rome over the nature of sin, death and human nature. One issue in debate was the question of whether infants were baptized not because of their own sin but because of the results of Adam's sin. Also in debate at this time were a variety of questions about the value of the body and the relative virtues of chastity and marriage. These latter questions are particularly associated with debate over Jovinian, who died *c.* 406.[70]

Pelagius, who was the leader of a group of ascetics in Rome, had already been involved in controversy with Jerome in 394. Pelagius' writing was primarily practical, exhorting his disciples and readers to strive for moral perfection and sinlessness. For Pelagius, baptism removes the punishment due to our sins and restores our original abilities to know and do the good. The grace of baptism, one might say, provides a new law for us to follow. Thus it is not surprising that Pelagius places much emphasis on obedience to law and on the baptized possessing the ability to obey what has been commanded. This theology seems to have found a willing audience among some social groups in late fourth-century Rome. In particular, there seems to have been a willing lay aristocratic audience, for whom Pelagius' exhortations accorded with their own ascetic desires, while his emphasis on the human ability to act well encouraged them to continue their traditional function as benefactors (some other 'Pelagian' supporters, especially in Sicily, took a much stronger line against all human clinging to riches).[71]

Although we are not certain, one or other of Pelagius' associates or Pelagius himself may well have begun to react to Augustine around 400, in response to his growing emphasis on grace and human inability to act by itself towards the good, which is apparent both in the second book of Augustine's *Ad Simplicianum* and in the *Confessions*. However, the controversy with Augustine came clearly into the open only in 412. Pelagius and Caelestius arrived in North Africa in 411 following increasing barbarian incursion into Italy and the sack of Rome the year before. Pelagius himself travelled on to Palestine but Caelestius stayed and was immediately criticized for teaching that Adam would have died naturally and that babies are born into the same state as Adam. He was condemned at a council in Carthage in 412 and left for Ephesus. Pelagius himself had mixed fortunes in the East, finding both much more sympathy for his views and some strong opponents. Indeed, the term 'Pelagian' and the assumption that Pelagius was the author of a uniform heretical grouping appeared in Palestine in 415, first being used by Jerome.

Augustine was not present at the council in Carthage that condemned Caelestius in 412 but, being informed of the proceedings, he wrote his *On Merit and the Forgiveness of Sins* in response to Caelestius. A little later, in 415, Augustine also wrote his *On Nature and Grace* in response to Pelagius' own *On Nature*. Pelagius and Caelestius were both exonerated by a synod in Palestine, which stimulated Augustine and the African bishops to launch a strong campaign for the reversal of this decision. After a complex series of events the Africans managed to persuade the Western imperial authorities to condemn Pelagius as a heretic in 418. Zosimus, bishop of Rome, who had previously been opposed to this move, acquiesced and even excommunicated the few bishops in Italy who refused to agree with his official condemnation, including Julian, bishop of Eclanum, who now came to assume a key role in the dispute.

At this point we can see that this conflict also reflects emerging issues and regional conflicts in church authority and structure. On the one hand the African bishops were keen to enlist Rome's support, and yet at the same time they were happy to press their case in the face of Roman lack of interest, to the extent of simultaneously trying to court the emperor. We should not speak simply of the Africans acknowledging Rome as their superior; they seem to have treated Rome as an appropriate appellate court but were simultaneously keen to assert their traditional independence.[72] At the same time Roman bishops were keen to expand their power and exert authority where possible, whether in defence of Pelagius *or* Augustine. Eastern bishops were traditionally very wary of Rome's seeking to assert a right to interfere in the actual jurisdiction of the East. So once Pelagius had been condemned in the West his case had been caught up in a continuing struggle over power in the Church and the structure of authority.

From 418 until Augustine's death in 430 Julian and Augustine waged a fierce literary battle. Augustine's own position continued to develop, with an increasingly clear account of the human race's family unity in Adam, of the almost inevitably sinful character of fallen sexual desire, and of the irresistible draw of divine grace within the human will. During this debate Julian presents Augustine's teaching as having a Manichaean tendency, denigrating the natural human condition, marriage and the purpose of human desire. Julian found himself both repeatedly condemned after 418 and caught up in the results of other controversies. He seems to have spent a good deal of the 420s in the East with Theodore of Mopsuestia, and appealed to Nestorius for reinstatement in 428. These connections probably did him no good and he was again condemned at Ephesus in 431. He died around 454. Late in Augustine's life aspects of the same controversy also appear in North Africa with some monks from Hadrumetum writing to Augustine asking if their ascetic struggle is in vain. And again after Augustine's death, the same issues reappear in southern Gaul, with some trying to claim that grace becomes operative only after the will has made its free choice. The frequency with which these ideas recur shows the extent to which they got to the heart of some key questions about Christian identity in the late fourth century.[73]

One last movement that illustrates debates about the nature of human activity within the Church needs to be discussed here. However, 'Messalianism' as a movement or set of ideas is notoriously difficult to define and as a discrete group of people very difficult to identify.[74] Messalianism seems to have originated in Syriac-speaking areas of the Eastern Christian world. Unfortunately, little literature survives that we can definitely associate with this movement or set of movements. During the 380s and through the early fifth century a number of writers speak of a group with a distinctive set of doctrines focused on the place of prayer in the Christian life, the presence of demons and the Spirit in the human soul, and the necessity or otherwise of participation in the sacraments. Although the course of events remains in dispute, Messalians are first mentioned in the mid- and late-370s by Epiphanius, who was particularly concerned with their 'idleness', holding that they taught that the work which constituted a normal part of a monastic lifestyle is only a distraction from prayer.

At some point towards the end of the fourth century Flavian the bishop of Antioch held a synod to condemn a Messalian leader called Adelphius, and we know also of a related synod at Side in Pamphylia (on the southern coast of modern Turkey). Messalians were specifically condemned by the Council of Ephesus, but it is noteworthy that Cyril of Alexandria himself suggests that they should only be required to abjure the name 'Messalian' in order to be reconciled to the Church. This perhaps reflects a contemporary sense that they were a very diffuse movement with little interest in separating themselves from the rest of the Church, and that some of the themes they held dear were common (in some form) among ascetics.

When we try to understand what those termed 'Messalians' actually taught we have some clues and can make some reasonable conjectures. It is likely that those concerned placed great emphasis on fervent prayer and on the importance of giving this activity complete priority within one's ascetic life, and hence had less interest in shaping ascetic lives around monastic work. 'Messalians' also appear to have possessed a complex demonology and doctrine of evil in which each person was indwelt by a demon who was an active power within the soul. Only the practice of prayer and the indwelling of the Spirit could drive out this demon. The Spirit's presence seems to have been described in very strong terms, often using the language of mixture and of being joined to the Spirit. Those accused of 'Messalianism' seem to have sat lightly to the need for normal ecclesiastical ritual practice. Thus, it is probably also the case that accusations of disobedience to ecclesiastical authorities and lack of interest in the established life of the Church reflect the response of bishops to a group whose asceticism originated in a context very different from the increasingly clearly defined episcopal hierarchies of the imperial Church.

Throughout the period covered here developments and controversies over Christian beliefs served to shape accounts of God, salvation, Church and cosmos that provided fundamental building blocks for the Christian imagination, or, better, imaginations. This period was a pivotal one in shaping such imaginations, but the themes the emergence or refinement of which we have explored here continued to develop and arguments about their consequences continued to rage in the centuries that followed.

Notes

1 For the best recent discussion of the complex beginnings of this dispute see R. Williams, *Arius. Heresy and Tradition*, 32ff.

2 Brakke, *Athanasius*, esp. 83ff.

3 On Donatism see W. H. C. Frend, *The Donatist Church*; B. Kriegbaum, *Kirche der Traditoren oder kirche der Martyrer?: die vorgeschichte des Donatismus*; R. A. Markus, *Saeculum: History and Society in the Theology of St Augustine*; R. A. Markus, 'Christianity and Dissent in Roman Africa: changing perspectives in recent work'.

4 R. A. Markus, 'Donatus, Donatism', 285.

5 On this traditional polemic see U. Simon, *Verus Israel. A study of the relations between Christians and Jews in the Roman Empire (AD 135–425)*; S. Benko, 'Pagan Criticism of Christianity During the First Two Centuries AD'; Daniélou, *Gospel Message*; Edwards, *Apologetics in the Roman Empire*.

6 On Eusebius especially see A. Kofsky, *Eusebius of Caesarea against Paganism.*

7 On Augustine's polemic see Markus, *Saeculum*, J.-C. Guy, *Unité et structure logique de la ≪Cité de Dieu≫ de Saint Augustin* and the bibliography; D. F. Donnelly, *Augustine's 'De civitate Dei': An Annotated Bibliography of Modern Criticism, 1960–1990*. On Arnobius see M. B. Simmons, *Arnobius of Sicca: Religious Conflict and Competition in the Age of Diocletian.*

8 On late antique Roman religion in this phase see G. Fowden, *The Egyptian Hermes*, and his summary treatment in *CAH*, XIII, 538–60. On Porphyry and his attack on Christianity see R. R. L. Wilken, *The Christians as Romans Saw Them*; *CHLG*, 272ff; A. Smith, *Porphyry's Place in the Neoplatonic Tradition*. Much useful introductory material on the character of late antique non-Christian religion (and especially Platonism) is to be found in A. H. Armstrong, ed., *Classical Mediterranean Spirituality: Egyptian, Greek, Roman.*

9 See P. Athanassiadi and M. Frede, *Pagan Monotheism in Late Antiquity.*

10 Salzman, *On Roman Time.*

11 See ch. 27.

12 On the difficulty and possibility of speaking of 'orthodoxy' before this period see R. Williams, 'Does It Make Sense To Speak of Pre-Nicene Orthodoxy?'. On the ways in which a set of related religious groups might simply not opt for one normative definition see the discussion of 'gnosticism' in B. A. Pearson, *Gnosticism, Judaism and Egyptian Christianity.*

13 See L. Ayres, *Nicaea and Its Legacy: An Approach to Fourth-Century Trinitarian Theology*; M. R. Barnes, 'The Fourth Century as Trinitarian Canon', in L. Ayres and G. Jones, eds, *Christian Origins. Theology, Rhetoric and Community*; J. T. Lienhard, 'The "Arian" Controversy: Some Categories Reconsidered' for treatments which strongly question the use of 'Arianism' as a useful category for historical description. For other key treatments of this controversy see M. Simonetti, *La Crisi ariana nel IV secolo* and R. P. C. Hanson, *The Search for the Christian Doctrine of God. The Arian Controversy 318–381*.

14 Thus following the usage of J. T. Lienhard, *Contra Marcellum: Marcellus of Ancyra and Fourth-Century Theology.*

15 Eusebius in Theodoret, *HE* 1.6.1.

16 For Asterius' theology see Hanson, *Search*, 32–8; Lienhard, *Contra Marcellum*, 89–98; Vinzent, *Asterius von Kappadokien: Die Theologische Fragmente. Einleitung, Kritischer Text, Ubersetzung und Kommentar.*

17 Arius ap. Athanasius, *Syn.* 15.

18 See Williams, *Arius* and 'Does It Make Sense To Speak of Pre-Nicene Orthodoxy?'.

19 See K. Anatolios, *Athanasius. The Coherence of His Thought.*

20 Thus, for instance, Athanasius only ever uses *hypostasis* in his *Contra Arianos* in connection with exegesis of Heb. 1:3; it does not function as an independent piece of theological terminology.

21 See A. H. B. Logan, 'Marcellus of Ancyra and the Councils of 325: Antioch, Ancyra, and Nicaea'; A. H. B. Logan 'Marcellus of Ancyra, Defender of the Faith against Heretics – and Pagans'.

22 Marcellus, frg. 52 and 61. The fragments are available with German translation in the recent edition of Vinzent: *Asterius von Kappadokien*.

23 Marcellus appears to make strong use of the terminology, but it is not found exclusively in Marcellus' work, cf. Eusebius of Caesarea's *Letter to the People of His Diocese*, 10.

24 See Williams, *Arius*.

25 R. P. Vaggione, *Eunomius of Cyzicus and the Nicene Revolution* attempts to explore the conflict in this way, arguing that the widespread nature of the controversy and the seemingly frequent involvement of non-elite Christians is explained by this clash of world-views. Vaggione, however, presents the conflict as between two imaginative universes, Nicene and non-Nicene: it is not at all clear that such a division can be made this easily given the complexity of the different trajectories and parties.

26 This translation is Hanson's: *Search*, 163.

27 Both in Antioch, the first in 268 in the case of Paul of Samosata, the second in early 325.

28 For a discussion of and bibliographical notes on this complex question see Stead, *Philosophy in Late Antiquity*, chs 14–15; Hanson, *Search*, ch. 7.

29 On the creation of 'Arianism' see Ayres, *Nicaea and Its Legacy*, ch. 5.

30 Asterius, ap. Eusebius, *Marc*. I.4.

31 For a brief summary see *CAH*, XIII, ch. 1.

32 On the character of Constantius' reign see R. Klein, *Constantius II. und die christliche kirche* and Barnes, *Athanasius and Constantius*.

33 For the text of the creed and anathemas see Athanasius, *Syn*. 27; Socrates, *HE* 2.30.

34 The text is preserved at Hilary, *Syn*. 11. On this text see Hanson, *Search*, 343–5, whose translation I follow.

35 Hanson, *Search*, 557–97, offers an account of homoean theology. See also R. Gryson, ed., *Scolies ariennes sur le Concile d'Aquilée*, 173–200; Brennecke, *Studien zur Geschichte der Homöer. Der Osten bis zum Ende der homöischen Reichskirche*. Williams, *Ambrose of Milan*, 243ff. offers a very useful list of surviving Latin homoìan credal texts.

36 On heterousian theology see M. R. Barnes, *The Power of God: Dunamis in Gregory of Nyssa's Trinitarian Theology*, ch. 5; J. Daniélou, 'Eunome l'arien et l'exégèse néo-platonicienne du ≪Cratyle≫'; T. A. Kopecek, *A History of Neo-Arianism*; R. Mortley, *From Word to Silence*, II, ch. 8; Vaggione, *Eunomius of Cyzicus*.

37 L. R. Wickham, 'The *Syntagmation* of Aetius the Anomean', *JTS* 19 (1968), 540–1.

38 It has been suggested that one stimulus for this focus was Athanasius' own discussion of the term in his *Contra Arianos* in the 340s.

39 On this question see Barnes, 'The Fourth Century as Trinitarian Canon'.

40 For the sake of clarity it may be helpful to summarize Athanasius' movements and exiles here. Athanasius had first been in exile (mostly in what is now the city of Trier in Germany) between 335 and the end of 337, and was also in exile between 339 and 346. He had probably been allowed back to Alexandria in 346, but once Constantius was in sole charge of the Empire Athanasius' fortunes turned again, and he may well have been formally deposed both at a small council in Antioch in 349 and at the Sirmium council in 351. However, it was not until 356 that Constantius sent troops to Alexandria to have him actually removed. From the beginning of 356 to the end of 361 Athanasius could not openly occupy his see, though he spent most of these years in hiding in Egypt.

41 The text is preserved in Epiphanius' *Panarion*, 73.2.1ff.

42 For an account of these complex events see Hanson, *Search*, 371–86.

43 On the meaning of 'pro-Nicene' and the history of parallel terminologies see Ayres, *Nicaea and Its Legacy*, ch. 8.

44 For a useful introduction to Valens and Valentinian, focusing on political and military issues, see *CAH*, XIII, 80–101.

45 A critical edition and German translation of this text are provided in M. Tetz, 'Ein enzyklisches Schreiben der Synode von Alexandrien (362)'.

46 See Basil, *Epp*. 361–4.

47 See B. Sesboüé, *Saint Basile et La Trinité. Un acte théologique au IV*[e] *siècle*, 130–7, for Basil's developing use of this term.

48 For a brief summary of recent scholarship on these letters see M. A. G. Haykin, *The Spirit of God. The Exegesis of 1 & 2 Corinthians in the Pneumatomachian Controversy of the Fourth Century*, 59–61.

49 On Hilary's role see Williams, *Ambrose of Milan*, ch. 2; Brennecke, *Hilarius von Poitiers*.

50 See Williams, *Ambrose of Milan*, chs 4ff.; N. McLynn, *Ambrose of Milan. Church and Court in a Christian Capital*.

51 On Ambrose's development see Barnes, *The Power of God*, 167ff.; Williams, *Ambrose of Milan*.

52 *CTheod*. 16.1.2, 16.1.3. Hanson, *Search*, 791ff. provides a very useful account. See also the seminal text, A. M. Ritter, *Das Konzil von Constantinopel und sein Symbol. Studien zur Geschichte und Theologie des 2. Ökumenishcen Konzils*.

53 On this particular question see the account in J. N. D. Kelly, *Early Christian Creeds* (1972[3]), ch. 10, which takes account of Ritter's research.

54 Hanson's translation: *Search*, 816.

55 For a good discussion of this terminology see K. Tanner, *Theories of Culture: a New Agenda for Theology*, chs 2 and 3.

56 See esp. J. T. Lienhard, '*Ousia* and *Hypostasis*: The Cappadocian Settlement and the Theology of "One *Hypostasis*" '. It is, however, the case that over the decades that followed the 380s the terminology of *ousia* and *hypostasis* became increasingly prominent.

57 On the term 'figural reading' see Dawson, *Allegorical Readers*, D. Dawson, *Christian Figural Reading and the Shaping of Christian Identity*; Ayres, *Nicaea and Its Legacy*, ch. 1.

58 For more detailed introduction to Apollinaris and the other figures discussed in this section of this chapter see F. M. Young, *From Nicaea to Chalcedon*. On Apollinaris see also the fundamental study of E. Muhlenberg, *Apollinarius von Laodicea*. See also the very helpful J. O'Keefe, 'Impassible Suffering? Divine Passion and Fifth-Century Christology'.

59 B. E. Daley, 'Nature and the "Mode of Union": Late Patristic Models for the Personal Unity of Christ'.

60 Fourth-century disputes in Antioch demonstrate the existence of a variety of Antiochene traditions, while the Alexandrian context gave rise to both Arius and Athanasius.

61 See R. A. Greer, *Theodore of Mopsuestia. Exegete and Theologian*; R. A. Norris, *Manhood and Christ. A Study in the Theology of Theodore of Mopsuestia*.

62 On Nestorius' understanding of the incarnate Christ see M. V. Anastos, 'Nestorius was Orthodox'; Greer, 'The Image of God and the Prosopic Union in Nestorius' *Bazaar of Heraclides*'; R. C. Chesnut, 'The Two *Prosopa* in Nestorius' *Bazaar of Heraclides*'.

63 Many of the relevant texts can be found in translation in *DEC*.

64 For Cyril's theology see M.-O. Boulnois, *La paradoxe trinitaire chez Cyrille d'Alexandrie*; J. Liébaert, *La doctrine christologique de saint Cyrille d'Alexandrie avant la querelle nestorienne*; J. McGuckin, *St Cyril of Alexandria: The Christological Controversy*; R. V. Sellers, *Two Ancient Christologies*. An excellent brief account and further bibliography are to be found in N. Russell, *Cyril of Alexandria* (with a very useful collection of translations).

65 For a longer introduction and bibliography see Young, *From Nicaea to Chalcedon*, 265ff.

66 On Chalcedon itself R. V. Sellers, *The Council of Chalcedon* is still useful. See also A. Grillmeier SJ and H. Bacht SJ, eds, *Das Konzil von Chalkedon*.

67 Clark, *The Origenist Controversy*.

68 Ibid., ch. 2 gives a useful summary of these themes, without mentioning this last.

69 For studies of the Pelagian controversy as a whole see B. R. Rees, *Pelagius: a Reluctant Heretic*; G. Greshake, *Gnade als konkrete Freiheit. Eine Untersuchung zur Gnadenlehre des Pelagius*; F. G. Nuvolone and A. Solignac, 'Pelage et Pelagianisme'.

70 Here see D. Hunter, 'Resistance to the Virginal Ideal in Late Fourth-Century Rome: The Case of Jovinian'; and ch. 27.

71 See P. Brown, 'The Patrons of Pelagius: The Roman Aristocracy between East and West'; B. R. Rees, *The Letters of Pelagius and His Followers*, 147–298, for the texts known as the 'Caspari Corpus' relating to Sicily.

72 Most recently on this theme see J. E. Merdinger, *Rome and the African Church in the Time of Augustine.*

73 There is still much debate about whether Augustine's theology of free will and grace is directly mirrored in late fourth-century and early fifth-century Greek contexts. For a taste of this debate see L. R. Wickham, 'Pelagianism in the East'; E. Muhlenberg, *Das Unendlichkeit Gottes bei Gregor von Nyssa.*

74 On Messalianism see C. Stewart OSB, *'Working the Earth of the Heart': The Messalian Controversy in History, Texts and Language to AD 341*; R. Staats, *Gregor von Nyssa und die Messalianer*; A. Louth, 'Messalianism and Pelagianism', *SP* 17 (1982), 127–35; J. Gribomont, 'Le dossier des origines du messalianisme'; K. Fitschen, *Messalianismus und Antimessalianismus. Ein Beispiel ostkirchliche Ketzergeschichte.*

39
Christian teaching

FRANCES YOUNG

It has been argued (chapter 9) that the early Church was school-like, and that the importance of *dogma* or *doctrina* (both words which simply mean 'teaching') has its roots in that characteristic. Ancient religion was not 'dogmatic', but philosophy was. It has also been evident (chapters 9 and 19) that Christian teachers played a significant role, often like Justin Martyr without having any official institutional position, or alongside the hierarchy and with shifting relationships with it, as in the case of Origen. Whether or not the bishop of Alexandria appointed Origen head of a Catechetical School, the account of his educational activities in Caesarea suggests the formation of a school of Christian higher education, alongside regular homiletic activity as a priest within the Church for the whole spectrum of believers. Control of such semi-independent teachers was far from achieved prior to the fourth century.

The post-Nicene period can be seen as a time of tightening up, of a determined effort to achieve uniformity, and so establish the doctrines which form Christianity's dogmatic core, thus shifting the nuance of those ancient words for 'teaching'. The tendencies that produced this had long been around: councils of bishops already had the custom of meeting to exclude teaching they found at variance with the Christian tradition, and so teaching authority was already in the process of being transferred from scholars to the episcopate, particularly acting collectively. A strong assertion of the unity of truth had long accompanied the apologetic attack on the many different options (*haereses*) offered by philosophers, and this would drive the thrust towards uniformity. Initiation had long involved formulaic affirmations of faith in response to questions, while the developing norms of catechesis encouraged the development of credal declarations to be committed to memory. The political desire to unite the Empire through the worship of the One God proclaimed by the Christians reinforced these tendencies, and facilitated œcumenical councils charged with making authoritative doctrinal decisions in the face of conflict and disagreement.

The changed political situation also led to the influx of huge numbers of new converts. Whereas Origen could celebrate the achievement of Christianity in terms of its power to make all kinds of people good, not just educated philosophers, the post-Constantinian Church was faced with a split between the ignorant masses, whose behaviour was hard to change and who often remained catechumens most of their lives, and the committed extremists in the fast-growing monastic movement for whom baptism was the sign of their rejection of the world. In what sense could the school-like character of Christianity survive under these conditions?

One fact that is often overlooked is the change that conversion to Christianity made to the physical context as well as the practice of worship. The temples of the ancient world were invariably the palaces where the gods resided, entered only by priests and acolytes who attended the particular deity as slaves and servants would a king. Crowds of worshippers might gather in the sacred courts outside; communities, or individual worshippers, might make offerings at an altar outside, or through the mediation of a priest. Entering a temple was not customary, often taboo. Freed to create their own public buildings, and with the patronage to do so, Christians did not build temples but 'basilicas'. Basilicas were great halls for public gathering, places where all kinds of business, political, economic, social, and indeed educational, were transacted, places that people entered, places where people participated, or listened and learned, where speeches were delivered. As Christians gained predominance, they broke the old taboos, entered the temples, claimed them for Christ, and turned them into basilicas: that entering was somewhat like democrats storming the residence of a hated or defunct regime. This radical shift implies a very different understanding of the nature of the relationship between divine and human: people, not places, were the locus of the indwelling divine, the Holy Spirit, and the congregation constituted the Body of Christ, which was the Temple of the Spirit. It is also clear evidence of the fact that the school-like features of the synagogue and the early church remain significant. People gathered to learn.

There was, of course, a massive need to re-educate with the stories of the Bible a populace whose minds were filled with myths of the gods, and the emergence of mural and mosaic as more than mere decoration of the new church buildings might be seen as the development of innovative teaching methods alongside the continued regular exposition of Scripture in worship. The formalized development of catechesis was given greater impetus, as was the transmission of a creed to the initiates, for whom initiation was a teaching and learning process. Orthodoxy, or right belief, was as important as lifestyle;

both had to be taught. But increasingly the Church would be obliged to fulfil the functions of traditional religion, assimilating to familiar rituals and mysteries, accepting popular assumptions about prayer and offerings, or initiation and patronage, sacralizing old sacred sites and transforming local deities and heroes into Christian saints, while, conversely, shifting 'religion' into a matter of dogma and belief. A new discourse was being formed which would shape a Christianized society, and shift the emphasis from acts of piety to acceptance of a faith structure.

In other words, the fourth century sees a great cultural shift which both retains something of the school-like character of early Christianity and yet leaves no room for the semi-independent Christian philosopher or exegete. It has been suggested[1] that the misfortune of Arius was that his Origen-like activities were out of joint with the times. Be that as it may, it was certainly in this century that Origen's influence was repudiated and some of his speculations, interpreted as *dogmata*, were condemned. Orthodoxy was increasingly defined (see chapter 38). The sections of this chapter will trace the impact of this with respect to Christian teaching, while arguing that space remained for intellectual enquiry in the area of spirituality, and that exegesis continued to reflect the norms of *paideia* inherited from the educational culture of antiquity.

Catechesis and the role of creeds

The fourth century is the period from which we receive bodies of teaching material delivered to catechumens during the period of Lent in preparation for baptism on Easter night, the candidates then dying with Christ as they entered the water to rise with him on Easter Sunday morning. If we include alongside these catechetical lectures a number of works to aid catechists, we have material from East and West, from Cyril of Jerusalem, Theodore of Mopsuestia, Gregory of Nyssa, John Chrysostom, Ambrose and Augustine.

Clearly the practice of using Lent for instruction did not emerge or spread overnight – it had probably been developing over at least the previous century; and while, on the one hand, this evidence demonstrates a widespread common practice, on the other, it shows considerable local variation in style and content, and indeed in the form of the creed taught to the initiates. At the Nicene Council Eusebius[2] spoke of reciting the creed he had received from his bishop, and of its being approved with the addition of the new formula, the *homoousion*. In the post-Nicene period it would appear that local creeds became 'Nicene' in this way. The reaffirmation of the Nicene creed at Constantinople appears to be the adoption of such an adapted creed[3] – for textually it is not a development of the creed agreed some fifty-five years earlier.

This being the case, it is evident that creeds did not have their origins in authoritative conciliar statements. The form of the creed was adopted and adapted by councils, and the story of the fourth century is of one council after another drawing up statements of belief in credal form. By the time of Chalcedon there was a general consensus that further creed-making was unsatisfactory, and the creeds of 325 and 381 were simply reaffirmed with an expository definition appended to indicate how their words were to be understood in relation to the person of Christ. The conciliar 'take-over' of creeds meant they were turned into 'articles of belief', and became potentially restrictive. By contrast, Cyril of Jerusalem in his *Catechetical Lectures* presents creeds as a simple summary of the Scriptures[4] for the convenience of those who cannot devote themselves to further study, and as a key to the gates of the heavenly mystery. They provided elementary education for those at the beginning of the Christian way.

The story of the creeds is a clear example, therefore, of the tendencies noted in introducing this chapter. They began in a school-like context, but became one element in the development of dogmatism and institutional uniformity. Not that that is really surprising. The credal format seems to have two precursors. On the one hand the three questions asked of candidates within the liturgy of baptism, already evidenced in the third century, seem to have provided the threefold framework: a declaration of belief about the one God, about Jesus Christ, the Son of God, and about the Holy Spirit of God. On the other hand, the verbal form of the phrases that spell out each of these three clauses clearly draws upon the looser summaries of faith known as the 'rule of faith' or 'canon of truth', found in the writings of Irenaeus, Tertullian, Origen and others, where more often than not they are appealed to against the contrary teachings of heretics.

The social context for that situation lay in the rivalry between philosophical schools. Each offered statements of their teachings, to be mocked and criticized, especially by Christians, for their divisions (*haereses*) and lack of consensus about the truth. The Christian claim to know the truth revealed through the *Logos* of God had always generated a thrust towards excluding those who did not subscribe to the same core teachings about morals and theology. But that observation reinforces the point that dogmatism derives from the Church's character as a philosophical school. In the writings of an Epiphanius[5] any vestiges of philosophical enquiry have evaporated – indeed, are entirely misunderstood. There is one truth, enshrined in the creeds and formulae approved by the Church, and clung to by the 'well-anchored man'. Any departure from that is divisive and therefore heretical. The story of the world is a story of division, of *haereses*, but soon the number of heresies predicted in Scripture will be filled up, God's purpose fulfilled and a monolithic faith established to unite the world.

The character of the catechetical lectures that are extant demonstrates that the old anti-heretical thrust of the rule of faith remains crucial in the exposition of the creeds. Invariably the rival accounts of gnostics and Manichees, adoptionists and Sabellians, are sketched and condemned, so that the true understanding can be grasped. But the development of catechesis in this period also illustrates the other tendency sketched earlier. If the process of teaching and learning the truth provides the obvious framework for this activity, increasingly the analogy with initiation into the mysteries turns this educational activity into a religious and ritual practice.

The analogy between the mysteries and Christianity had of course been drawn long before, casually by Justin, more systematically by Clement of Alexandria. But the idea of secrecy or reserve, of an elite who are in the know because they have passed through an initiation rite, becomes much more obvious in the language of liturgy and doctrine in the fourth century. For Basil of Caesarea the truth about the divinity of the Holy Spirit lies in the esoteric traditions imparted to those who are fully initiated (cf. *SSp*.), while Cyril of Jerusalem (or a successor) delivered *Mystagogical Catecheses* explaining the sacraments only after baptism had occurred. Thus a convergence of religious rite and school-like dogma is creating a new understanding of what religion is. Belief is as important, if not more important, than practice; practice involves correct belief.

The rich deposit of material that has survived to give us access to the process of catechesis in the fourth century is also important for the light it sheds on what was thought to be significant in the re-education of the people. If, as many have assumed, the lectures of Cyril of Jerusalem give us insight into 'popular' Christianity, then a surprising level of intellectual understanding was demanded of even illiterate people. That Cyril treats the creed as a convenient summary for those who have not the leisure or ability to read Scripture suggests that such a conclusion is not necessarily unrealistic. The Church still claimed to be a comprehensive, not an elitist, school.

Indeed, in this century, people like Basil of Caesarea and Gregory of Nazianzus[6] would have to defend the benefits of secular, or rather pagan, education so that Christian leaders could function as effectively as other educated people in the society of the day. This would, of course, increasingly undermine any residual claim on the part of the Church to be an educational institution. Education in grammar and rhetoric would continue to be based on the traditional literature, now regarded as 'pagan' in an increasingly Christianized society, treated as useful but not true. Yet the Church remained the locus of teaching based on the Scriptures. To this characteristic and fundamentally school-like activity of scriptural exegesis we must now turn.

Scripture and its reading

As we have seen, education in the ancient world was almost entirely based upon the reading of literature, and the place of Scripture-reading in the Jewish synagogue, subsequently adopted by the Christian Church, made both communities analogous to a school. This tradition remains central in the fourth century. All adherents, baptized or not, participated in the first part of the liturgy when not only were prayers said, but Scripture was read and expounded. Only then did the catechumens depart while the initiates shared in the eucharist. So people entered a public hall, a basilica not a temple, to listen to speeches interpreting written texts which enshrined the word of God. To that extent there can be no doubt that the Church was perceived to be a religious school. But what happens to the interpretation of Scripture in the fourth century, under the pressures of the new situation and the needs of mass education?

It is important to recognize that there was no sudden break in the traditions of exegesis. Eusebius inherited Origen's biblical scholarship, and acknowledges spiritual meanings beyond the historical, using allegorical techniques to move from one plane to another. Since the discovery of some works of Didymus the Blind in a munitions dump in the Second World War, there has been a lively scholarly debate about the extent to which we can trace in his exegesis a more consistently worked out hermeneutic and methodology than Origen achieved.[7] Whatever conclusion is reached one thing is clear: allegory was alive and well in the Alexandrian tradition. Nor was it confined to those we know were influenced by Origen. At least prior to the Origenist controversy, Jerome plundered the works of Didymus in his Latin commentaries, so transmitting the tradition to the medieval West. The notion that Christ and the Church can be traced in the Old Testament Scriptures through signs to be recognized through allegorical techniques is not only presupposed in the work of Augustine,[8] but remains almost universal.

Almost, but not quite: for it is in the fourth century that we find a self-conscious reaction against allegory[9] in some quarters, which becomes associated with the movement against Origenism. This reaction is characterized usually as an espousal of the literal or historical meaning of the text, and that view has tended to be reinforced by the extreme case of Theodore of Mopsuestia who challenged many of the by then traditional readings which understood Old Testament prophecies and psalms in oracular and Christological terms. To claim as Theodore did that the prophets were addressing the circumstances of their own time seems at first sight to anticipate the historico-critical methods of modern scholars. But there are some real difficulties with this analysis. For one thing, the so-called Antiochene School which is associated with this anti-allegorical reaction certainly found moral and doctrinal meanings in Scripture, and were far from having the concerns about historicity that have dominated modern interpretation. The challenge to allegory must be set in the cultural and intellectual climate of the fourth century.

One suggestion has been that doctrinal debate drove church leaders to rest their case on texts interpreted according to the letter rather than with the imaginative freedom of allegory.[10] The motivation came from the need to pin down meaning, to arrive at an authoritative interpretation. Literalism was adopted so as to determine orthodoxy. Plausible though this might seem, it is not borne out by the texts.[11] In his debate with Arius, Athanasius has to appeal to the 'mind' of Scripture against the surface meaning of a number of problematic texts which were taken literally by his opponent.[12] The metaphorical nature of language was recognized, and so both sides in the Christological debates continued to assume that Old Testament texts long understood as prophetic did refer to Christ through symbols. There was debate about words and their meanings, but this was not straightforwardly a difference between literal and allegorical reading: did 'the Word became flesh' mean that the eternal *Logos* suffered change, or was it that the *Logos* 'assumed' human nature? As here, one text (Phil. 2:7) might be used to interpret another (John 1:14); for since Scripture was referring to things beyond human language, its meaning had to be discerned by enquiry, not simply read off in a simplistic way.[13] God could not literally have a Son by physical generation since God has no physical organs; yet there must be some divine and true meaning to the word 'Son' applied to the *Logos* since Scripture is the word of God.[14]

To understand fourth-century debates about the interpretation of Scripture it is necessary to look at both methodology and objectives. Methodologically both sides in the disputes were indebted to the way texts were used and interpreted in the educational traditions of the Greco-Roman world.[15] In the rhetorical schools, the canon of classical literature provided the basis on which students learned about language and style, about the need to determine the appropriate linguistic dress in which to clothe the subject-matter, and the necessity of determining what the underlying argument or thrust of the text was so as to ape classical exemplars in their own composition. To effect this, exegesis concentrated first on matters of vocabulary and syntax, on figures of speech and other stylistic devices (τὸ μεθοδικόν), then on explanatory notes dealing with the subject-matter or with allusions to myths and events, or references to geographical, astronomical, musical or other matters (τὸ ἱστορικόν); while composition focused on εὕρησις or *inventio*, the determination of the subject-matter, as the vital stage prior to determining style. These processes were fundamental to both Alexandrian and Antiochene exegesis.

So what made the difference? Origen and his followers were influenced by tendencies among philosophical schools. They exploited the figure of speech called ἀλληγορία, identifying its presence systematically across literary texts, especially those of a mythological character, so as to discern a deeper meaning behind the stories. Their objective was to find philosophical truths hidden in texts whose surface-meaning they could not accept as straightforwardly true. The instructive thing is to notice how Origen utilizes standard literary-critical techniques to expose the difficulties in Scripture, the *aporiai*, the metaphoricity of language, in order to show that some other meaning must be hinted at by the Holy Spirit, who is taken to be the author of the text. The Holy Spirit's intention is the subject-matter of the Bible, dressed up in the linguistic expression of the diverse books and parables of Scripture. Those who reacted against this did so both on methodological grounds and out of concern for the overarching thrust of what the Bible and its narratives are about, which they took to be enshrined in the rule of faith, or the Creed.

Those reacting against Origen insisted that the figure of speech ἀλληγορία should only be found where there was some indication present in the text that this figure of speech was intended. It was one among many figures of speech which had to be identified if one was to do justice to the particular discourse of Scripture.[16] On the one hand, they were as alert to metaphor as ever the Origenists were, and recognized that references to God's eyes or hands were ways of speaking of divine oversight or power. On the other hand they accepted hyperbole as a clue to meanings beyond the immediate reference of the text, such as implied prophecy. The two sides had more in common than is often supposed: it is not in the end so surprising that Theodoret could offer a spiritual interpretation of the Song of Songs not all that far removed from that of Origen. They too believed that the Bible pointed beyond itself. They looked for insight (θεωρία) through contemplation of the text.

The crucial difference lay in their commitment to the shape (σχῆμα, *schema*) of the text, the narrative logic (ἀκολουθία, *akolouthia*), a feature attributable to the methodology of the rhetorical schools with their insistence on attention to the subject-matter or flow of the argument. Origen's allegory became piecemeal because it was verbal in its focus: words became symbols or tokens, and texts were decoded. His critics rejected this procedure, saying he should pay attention to 'deeds', that is, facts or events (πράγματα), rather than words (ὀνόματα). Eustathius in his treatise *On the Witch of Endor and against Origen* shows how Origen misreads the text in terms of resurrection because he fails to take seriously the implication in the story that Saul is deceived about the appearance of Samuel by one whose very description (ἐγγαστρίμυθος) implies that she generates myths in her womb: Samuel simply did not emerge from the underworld, as Origen infers. Paradoxically Origen is too literal! And it is scandalous that he takes this story literally and then allegorizes the narratives of Creation and Paradise, Gospel stories and many other things.

And it is here that we light upon the radical difference in objective which underlies the methodological debate. Time and again the Antiochenes reproach Origen for not taking the key biblical narratives seriously. Diodore was just as anxious about a talking serpent as Origen was, but he took it that the serpent embodied the devil, that this was an account of the origin of human sin, that God's creation of the material world, the reality of Christ's humanity, the resurrection of the flesh and restoration of creation to the perfection God intended were essential to the truth of the Christian faith and no mere parable of spiritual realities. The Antiochenes cared for the overarching narrative logic of the Bible summarized in the creed, and protested at the tendency of allegory to evacuate this.[17]

Difference there was, then, but this must not be allowed to obscure the essentially identical roots of scriptural exegesis in the educational norms of antiquity. Nor should we overlook the fact that much exegesis was practised without being affected by this controversy. The exegesis of many major figures has been characterized as eclectic, precisely because it shares features with both Alexandrian and Antiochene approaches. But this is probably to misrepresent the situation. Alexandrian and Antiochene are simply labels for two sides of an explicit debate, whereas in practice people simply interpreted the Bible in homily, commentary and treatise according to the norms picked up at school and through the ongoing traditions of ecclesiastical practice. From this period a rich treasury of exegetical material survives which testifies to the centrality of the Bible in liturgy and teaching, and so to the continued 'school-like' character of early Christianity.

These conclusions are confirmed by a brief turn to the West, where there was no parallel controversy over allegory. Augustine's *De Doctrina Christiana* is essentially a treatise on scriptural interpretation.[18] Augustine practised as a rhetorician for years before his conversion, and Latin rhetoric was an adaptation of Greek traditions and practices, exemplified in Cicero, set out in Quintilian's handbook, *Institutio oratoria*. In the *De Doctrina* Augustine provides the Christian equivalent. His first book focuses on discerning the subject-matter of Scripture, subsequent books on the linguistic 'signs', the vocabulary and style, in which that subject-matter is conveyed, and the final book on communication of the message, the rhetoric the Christian teacher needs so as to provide instruction in what Scripture is about. The fact that Augustine broke off somewhere in the middle of book 3, and completed the work some years later, does not seem to have modified the overall conception with which he started. His demonstration of Scripture's own rhetoric allows him to claim that this literature has both wisdom and eloquence, and that the Bible can play the same role in Christian education as the classics had in pagan society.

Books 2–3 come nearest to providing what we would suppose a treatise on interpretation to contain. Here Augustine discusses language, the need to discern the intended meaning behind the expression, or what the signs signify, while acknowledging the obscurities, the need for humility of mind before the text. He is not simply aware of the complexities of translation, approving some knowledge of Hebrew and Greek in the interpreter, but like any other rhetorically trained practitioner, he is acutely aware of metaphor and figures of speech, of linguistic tropes such as 'allegory', 'enigma' and 'parable', of the need for inference, for grammatical analysis, for knowledge of many subjects, so as to provide an exegesis of the text. But book 1 has provided a discussion of the intent or subject-matter, defining it as love of God, expounding it in terms of the rule of faith, Trinity and incarnation, and this becomes the criterion whereby judgments are made concerning the obscurities of scriptural language.

This position is in principle very close to that of the Antiochenes, though much of Augustine's exegetical practice is allegorical to the extent that his reading of the Old Testament is profoundly Christological. To describe the majority of exegetes in this period as 'eclectic' is to misconceive the situation, setting up the controversy over allegory as the yardstick. Rather, encouraged by Augustine's attempt to form the Christian teacher, we should conceive of scriptural exegesis as continuing to be rooted in the 'school-like' character of the Church, and as deeply indebted to the methods and procedures current in the educational norms of antiquity. Yet the distilling of norms of truth, summarized in creeds, formulated into dogmas, began to restrict the possibilities of meaning by providing criteria, limits on what the text could mean. Scripture and creed are inseparable, and the role of both in the life of the Church testifies to the most significant factor in modifying the ancient conception of what religion was about. The Church remained in large part a teaching institution, and its buildings were not temples but places of learning.

Christian *paideia*

Discussion of exegesis has revealed something of the extent to which the teaching and learning activity of the Church was indebted to Greek *paideia*. But whereas previously there was implicit a rejection of the education based on classical literature, the substituting of Scripture for the classics, a challenge to the philosophers – indeed, an alternative Christian *paideia*, dramatically encapsulated in Tertullian's well-known outburst, 'What has Athens to do with Jerusalem?' –, with the gradual Christianization of the Roman Empire, the relationship was perceived in more ambiguous terms.[19] Leading churchmen were increasingly drawn from the educated elite and realized the potential weakness of a Church with leaders who could not compete with their peers on the same terms. The attempt by the apostate Emperor Julian to take at face value the old-style Christian rhetoric of rejection and exclude Christians from the schools, sharpened up the issues.

Two different reactions reflect essentially the same position. The Apollinarii, father and son, set about writing epics and lyrics, tragedies and comedies, using the style of the classics and the content of the Bible.[20] Somehow Christian schools had to be able to pursue a curriculum of the same quality as pagan schools, and the disadvantage of the Bible had always been its barbarian style. The other reaction emerged in the aftermath, when it was safe, namely that of the Cappadocians. Gregory of Nazianzus wrote *Orations against Julian*, in which he made a distinction between, on the one hand, Greek language and culture which no one could claim exclusively to possess, and on the other, Greek religion. He laid claim to λόγος (language, reasoning), refusing to allow that Julian had any right to deprive people of the advantages of education in Attic eloquence. Less directly provoked by Julian's challenge, yet testifying to the importance of the issue, is the address of Basil of Caesarea *To the Young on how they might benefit from Greek Literature*: they should follow the usual curriculum so as to get a good training of the mind, but learn to distinguish between what is morally useful and what is harmful. Interestingly, Basil's advice reflects the long-standing response offered in the face of Plato's challenge to the morality of the gods and the use of poetry in education, a response clearly evidenced in Plutarch.[21]

What is most evident in all this is the need to grapple with the relationship between the Church and its cultural context. The notion that the Church was an alternative society, with an alternative culture and an alternative literature, was becoming less sustainable. There were groups which sought to regain the older ethos of protest, notably those involved in the monastic movement and the withdrawal from civilization into the desert: in many respects the monk succeeded the martyr. Illiteracy was celebrated in some quarters in the Egyptian desert, not just because the commitment of the simple was honoured, but as part of the protest against the world and its values. Yet the educated elite also espoused the ideology of the desert. Consciously or unconsciously they linked ascetic withdrawal with the traditions of philosophic contemplation. The cultural ambiguities cannot be resolved by a stark contrast between the desert and the increasingly encultured city churches, compromised by riches and endowments, led by power-hungry bishops. If some of the characters of this period, such as Theodoret, spent their childhood being raised and educated by monks, and others, like Chrysostom, turned from pagan to Christian masters in the course of their youth, the influence of Greek *paideia* marks them all, both implicitly and explicitly.

Of course this would be the more so, one might think, in the case of those who converted later in life. A figure like Augustine not only had the benefit of an elite education, but himself practised as an educator for years. The intention of his move from North Africa to Italy was precisely to advance his career as a rhetorician, different though the outcome was to be. The works of the mature Augustine, however, show that reaction against his past enabled a self-conscious critique as well as an intelligent appropriation of skills acquired in his previous career. By contrast Synesius of Cyrene, a member of the local elite with a Neoplatonic cast of mind, found himself elected bishop and embraced by the Church while unable, it seems, to identify any profound change in his fundamental philosophical position. Interestingly enough the Cappadocians, who were brought up in Christian families but sent, in the case of Basil and Gregory Nazianzen as far as Athens, to gain the best available education, exemplify most dramatically the conscious and unconscious tensions, but also evidence the continuing development of a Christian *paideia* which enabled intellectuals to engage with the faith and progress beyond the memorization of credal affirmations.

The tensions are evidenced not least in the lives the three Cappadocians lived: Basil of Caesarea returned from Athens to take up a career as rhetorician in his local city. He seems to have enjoyed success. Probably under family influence, he soon gave up his career, to be baptized and follow a life of withdrawal, only to re-emerge as bishop's assistant, then bishop, in the capital city of Cappadocia. His younger brother, Gregory of Nyssa, claims that he owed his education to his brother; certainly he did not have the same opportunities and seems to have begun life destined for office in the Church. But some evidence points to the fact that he rebelled against this and briefly became a rhetor. Certainly his writings show no less sophistication, not to mention philosophical ability. But it is Basil's student friend, Gregory of Nazianzus, whose career reveals the ambiguities most dramatically,[22] as his heart pulls him to ascetic withdrawal, demands are made on his talents by those who would have him serve the Church, and his love of λόγοι becomes his greatest asset and his deepest temptation. If he defends rhetoric for Christians against Julian, his personal poems reveal him keeping silence during a fast, for that is the most telling self-denial. Thus is apparent in the lives of all three the tension between public success and philosophic asceticism, and their public success even within the Church hung upon their prowess in the arts which constituted Greek *paideia*.

The extant writings of the Cappadocians bear the marks of their education, implicitly and explicitly, but also testify to their ambivalence. Basil's *Homilies on the Hexaemeron* may scorn philosophers and scientists who seek solutions to unanswerable questions with human reason and come up with contradictions, suggesting that Christians should avoid 'busy-bodying' curiosity about the universe, the shape of the earth, the number of the heavens – Scripture alone is enough; but what he offers is an exegesis of Genesis' creation-narrative which provides a Christian cosmogony, drawing on the astronomical knowledge of the time, offering the doctrine of creation out of nothing as a solution to the questions of the philosophers. His methods are those of his opponents. What Basil achieves is a synthesis of biblical teaching and philosophical enquiry, so providing material for a Christian *paideia*. It is not so surprising that the Basil who renounced pagan culture at the time of his baptism could defend its usefulness in educating the young. His mature work displays a marriage of cultures, while rehearsing traditional Christian polemic against philosophy.

No less is this true of the two Gregories, who explicitly model Christian works on pagan precedents in panegyric and poem, epistle and dialogue, while renouncing rhetoric and philosophy for their own sake and accusing heretics of exploiting these tools for their own ends. The public achievement of Gregory of Nazianzus in creating an anti-Arian community in Arian Constantinople depended upon exercising arts and talents forged in the schools of Greek *paideia* just as much as did his private self-conscious literary efforts in retirement. His *Orations*, when set in that context, are as important for their contribution to the emerging Christianized Hellenism as for their setting of doctrinal norms. The writings of Gregory of Nyssa generate a Neoplatonist Christianity in the process of providing instruction for monks, catechists and priests.

Indeed, Gregory of Nyssa, under the unacknowledged influence of Neoplatonism but with some characteristically Christian features, develops an intellectual spirituality. The *Life of Moses* is a classic example, but exegesis of the *Song of Songs* and many other works provide material for reconstructing the mystical journey envisaged by Gregory.[23] That this is a journey of the intellect rather than a mysticism of absorption and loss of consciousness is important.[24] It is expressed in metaphorical terms, using the language of Scripture to provide images of entering clouds as mountains are ascended, of suffering vertigo, of luminous darkness. Yet fundamentally it is about knowledge of God, about the moral and intellectual progress required, and about the recognition that the infinite God is in principle beyond the comprehension or containment of any created intellect, so that the journey into understanding is never-ending. The mutability of the creature means either fall and loss, or the possibility of constant 'becoming', growth and the attainment of deeper and deeper riches. It has been suggested[25] that this dynamic sense of eternal progress in perfection was Gregory's way of dealing with some of the problems inherent in Origen's notion of a static perfection.

Indeed, the crucial background to the Christian *paideia* produced by the Cappadocians is the Origenist tradition. That the young ascetic Basil and his friend Gregory produced the *Philocalia* is explicit evidence for what later lies implicit in their writings, doubtless because of the Origenist controversy which took place in this period. The profound contrast between the works of Epiphanius and those considered here demonstrates the perennial conflict between any Christian intellectualism and teaching which is dogmatic in the negative sense that that word has latterly acquired simply because of the tendency within the Church to intolerant assertion of the truth. Yet these opposing trends equally bear witness to the continuing 'school-like' character of Christianity. Teaching and education in morals, lifestyle and the faith were fundamental. This very observation demands that we attend to the question if and how orthodoxy was integrated with the kind of sophisticated intellectual spirituality just sketched.

Spirituality and orthodoxy

Integrated they certainly were. Indeed, the argument with Eunomius was possibly another crucial factor in the development of Gregory's ideas. Eunomius, it will be recalled, was the heretic contemporary with the Cappadocians who represented Arianism in an extreme form. Both Basil and, after Basil's death, his brother Gregory expended much ink refuting his views. Basil initiated the argument that God's Being could not be defined in terms of ἀγεννησία; Gregory developed the argument against the knowability of God.

Essential to Eunomius' position was the notion that God was completely comprehensible because God is simple unity. God being One, the divine nature is not separable or divided into more, nor is God 'becoming sometimes one, sometimes another, nor changing from being what he is or split from one οὐσία into a threefold ὑπόστασις: for he is always and absolutely one, remaining uniformly and unchangeably God' (*Ref.* 33). Gregory agrees, of course, that God is incomposite, homogeneous, unchangeable and indivisible. What he will not agree to is the privileging of ἀγεννησία as a comprehensive definition of God's Being in a way that excludes Son and Spirit from the incomposite, indivisible divine nature. For Eunomius ἀγεννησία guaranteed God's unity and simplicity. For Gregory any exclusive definition reduced the transcendent God to a conception of a creaturely mind.

God's infinity, God's boundlessness, for Gregory meant that no human language or conception could define or delimit God, and Eunomius' claim was a proud boast: 'the infinity of God exceeds all the significance and comprehension that names can furnish' (*Eun.* 1.620–33). Nevertheless, God accommodated the divine self to the limitations of human perception, providing in Scripture a language which could be used, but only by multiplying many names and critically evaluating them. The gulf between the Creator and created, finite and Infinite, was such that every name was misleading at the same time as being appropriate. 'Son of God' would not do taken literally as if God had genital organs; yet God did not deceive, so the language pointed to some genuine reality.

It is significant that Gregory's argument presents a contrast between Eunomius and the figure of Abraham (*Eun.* 2.84ff.). Abraham's setting out is characterized as 'leaving his lowly and earthly mind', so as to 'raise his conception as far as possible above the common bounds of nature', and 'walking by faith not sight', to be 'lifted so high by the sublimity of his knowledge that he came to be regarded as the acme of human perfection, knowing as much of God as it was possible for finite human capacity at full stretch to attain'. It is at this point that Gregory's intellectual spirituality becomes a fundamental element in doctrinal argument. The so-called definition of the doctrine of the Trinity emerged from resistance to definition before the mystery of God. Abraham could use various human conceptions, such as God's power or goodness, as stepping-stones, yet all fell short of what he sought. Only 'when he had outstripped every supposition with respect to the divine nature, every single conception of God suggested by any designation', could he discern an 'unmisleading sign of the knowledge of God, namely the conviction that God is greater and more sublime than any known signification'.

That Gregory saw no tension between – rather indeed the mutual interdependence of – the conceptions that shaped his so-called mystical exegesis and the essential teachings of orthodoxy is further demonstrated by his use of similar arguments in the *Great Catechesis*. Here he was providing guidance for catechists, so we can presume his audience, at least at one remove, was a more popular one. That the liturgy shared by the Christian populace also expressed a coherence between spirituality and orthodoxy is clear from the preaching of John Chrysostom. His sermons *On the Incomprehensibility of God* were directed against Eunomius, but take a less philosophical and more biblical stance, encouraging humility before the transcendent object of worship. That the theologian cannot proceed without such humility is a key point made by Gregory of Nazianzus in his *Five Theological Orations*. Theology requires a certain moral character and spiritual attitude. It is the appropriate *aporia* of the worshipper before the mystery of God which undergirds the doctrine of the Trinity. Orthodoxy is not simply an arid intellectual conclusion reached through argument. It both fosters and is fostered by worship. The Fathers also assume a coherence between right belief and righteousness.

The works of the Syrian Ephrem provide confirmation of this.[26] Expressed in the form of poetry and the language of praise, the tenets of orthodoxy become the inspiration of worship and spirituality. The heart of gratitude responds to the extraordinary grace of an unknowable God who is incarnated in human language so that human minds can get a glimmering of what they cannot encompass. Paradox and symbolism are linguistic tools that enable theology, as well as characterizing poetry. They bridge the chasm between creatures and their Creator. God is both hidden and revealed; investigation is blasphemous prying, yet faith enables understanding. The metaphors and images without the proper critical balance of apophaticism become blasphemous and idolatrous; yet God clothed the divine self in these inadequate terms for the benefit of humankind, reaching down to the level of human childishness.

The types and images that express Ephrem's theology are drawn from the Bible, but melded together in remarkably fresh visions. At the same time they are constantly informed by the sense of an overarching narrative of human fall and redemption which is at the same time the story of 'everyman'. The divine descent enables the re-ascent of the sinner, and the pattern of divine grace and human salvation is replayed time and again: through Adam and Christ, Eve and Mary, with Noah and David, Passover and Exodus, anticipating Christ, baptism, eucharist. But Ephrem goes beyond the traditional types, linking the womb of Mary with womb of Jordan river, finding in Christ's incarnate body the restoration of the robe of glory lost at the Fall. Ephrem's spirituality is imaginative, symbolic and poetic. Yet it is deeply formed by Scripture and by the orthodox doctrine of the Trinity. The parallels between his thought and that of the Cappadocians, especially Gregory of Nyssa, are striking: Ephrem's grasp of the chasm between Creator and created bridged nevertheless by the gracious condescension of the divine mirrors the distinction found in both Cappadocian Gregories between the energies or activities of God recognizable in the created order and the unknowable essence of God on which only silence is appropriate. That both Ephrem and Gregory, in their different ways, reflect upon scriptural 'names', 'types' and symbols in their articulation of God's accommodation to human language is of particular interest. So far from being rigid dogma (using the word in the pejorative sense it has acquired), the teaching of orthodox doctrine undergirds a spirituality of intellectual journeying, moral maturing and θέωσις ('deification'). Orientals found similar reasons to those of the Greek tradition for resisting Arianism, and those reasons went far deeper than intellectual argument.

A somewhat parallel account can also be given with respect to the Latin-speaking Church of the West, taking Augustine as an example. It is not that the same issues figure in parallel ways, but rather that trinitarian orthodoxy turns out again to undergird a spirituality of restoration, and the really important thing about it is not its character as dogma but its expression of the core relationship of love, within the Godhead, in the divine outreach of grace, in the experience of worship and praise, in the image of God realized again in human being.

The early books of the *De Trinitate* follow the path of arguments blazed in the heat of the controversy in the East, arguments about scriptural exegesis, about the meaning of terms that were becoming technical, arguments which have a primarily intellectual edge. Gradually, however, we move into a different key. Augustine recognizes that now 'we see by means of a mirror', through an enigma; whereas when the promised vision 'face to face' comes it will be possible to see the Trinity. Yet that will evoke humility rather than pride in achievement, not so much knowing as being known. The work, which was many years in the making, ends with a prayer. Augustine has desired to see with his understanding what he has believed, he has sought God's face with an eager heart, and now he acknowledges in direct address to God that his ignorance and knowledge are in the divine hands; for God responds to his knocking, God opens, God shuts. 'Let me remember you, understand you, love you,' he prays; 'increase in me all these until you restore me to your perfect pattern.' The final words attribute what is rightly said in this massive theological work to God not himself, and ask pardon for what has missed the mark. The *De Trinitate* is as much a work of spirituality as the *Confessions*.

The characteristic element in Augustine's thought reinforces this. For his contribution to the doctrine of the Trinity lies in his use of psychological analogies, carefully crafted, judiciously safeguarded from potentially idolatrous use. Justified on the grounds that a human being is made in God's image, they are treated as signs, as pointers to what is a mystery beyond comparison within the created order. If God is the object of our longing and love, that very relationship can inform our understanding as long as we do not dare to think we can possess God. The lover, the beloved and the love that exists between them form a trinity, as also the knower, the known and knowledge. Thus we experience a kind of inner relationship in self-knowledge and self-love, but this is imperfect unless we participate in God. Our discursive reasoning is a poor representation of God's knowledge, and yet our spiritual threefoldness, also expressed in terms of the unity of memory, understanding and will, provides a clue to the mystery of God.

As in the case of the easterners, the coherence of orthodoxy and spirituality rests ultimately on the way in which the story of fall and redemption informs both. It is possible in the case of both Augustine and Gregory of Nyssa to argue about the extent to which this paradigm is shaped by Neoplatonic thought; yet the biblical and credal foundations are universally evident. Dogma turns out invariably to be an attempt at formulating a conceptual basis adequate to the overarching narrative Christianity discerned in Scripture: from creation, through fall and redemption, to the eschaton. In the case of Augustine, his own life becomes an expression of this narrative as he tells it in the *Confessions*. Few would dispute that work's claim to be an expression of his spirituality, of the restless heart seeking its rest in God. Yet it is clearly informed by a particular reading of Scripture, especially the epistles of Paul, and by acceptance of the teachings of orthodoxy.

When immersed in the controversial literature of the fourth century, or confronted by the writings of an anti-heretical warrior such as Epiphanius, it is all too easy to stereotype the Christian discourse of this period as increasingly dogmatic and exclusive. The element of enquiry and of search was, however, inherent in the spiritual journey, and in the end orthodoxy, with its emphasis upon humility before the infinite divine mystery which confronts and cannot be encompassed by the creaturely intellect, provided a context in which overweening intellectual pride could be challenged while engagement in a boundless quest for truth was encouraged. The Christian way remained an education, a *paideia*, a training and discipline, moral, intellectual and spiritual.

Conclusion

There can be little doubt that in the fourth and subsequent centuries the Church adopted more and more of the characteristics of a traditional religion, answering to the needs of the wider populace by 'baptizing' local shrines, encouraging the veneration of saints and martyrs who often replaced local gods, receiving gifts and endowments not unlike the offerings and sacrifices traditionally made in the religious practices of antiquity, turning the eucharist into a kind of *mysterion* for those initiated by baptism, and so on. Its school-like legacy, however, meant that dogma or teaching had a much higher profile than religion normally demanded, and correct belief, or orthodoxy, was increasingly imposed. Like a philosophy, Christianity claimed to impart wisdom and teach the truth.

This claim was, of course, focused in Christology. That Christ was the Wisdom and *Logos* of God was maintained through the controversies. The incarnate Christ spoke divine truth as the one who came from the Father's bosom. As the wisdom of prophecy, Gospel and apostle witnessed to the coming of the one who revealed, redeemed and restored the divine image in humanity, the Scriptures remained central to the life of the Church. The regular practice of expounding authoritative texts could not help but maintain something of the school-like character of the Church, even as its character shifted in other ways. Authority was invested in bishops not least because they had the teaching office, and spoke the word of God.

Education always has to wrestle with the tension between the didactic delivery of what is known and the process of search and discovery aided by teachers who act as 'midwives'. Christianity demonstrates in this period just such a tension. On the one hand the Church had received an authoritative revelation of the truth and had to preserve the tradition handed down unadulterated by speculation; novelty was increasingly condemned, yet often necessary, if unacknowledged, to meet novel challenges. On the other hand, Christian teaching characterized human life and history as a journey, as progress under the guidance of the Spirit, even justifying some doctrinal developments in these terms as well as spiritual insights. It could be that such a tension necessarily lies at the very heart of Christian theology. Be that as it may, the Christian tradition is clearly rooted in educational practice, and in this period retained something of its legacy as a teaching institution.

Notes

1 Williams, *Arius*.
2 Eusebius' letter to the people of his diocese after the Nicene Council: appended to Athanasius' *De Decretis*; also found in Socrates, *HE* 1.8 and Theodoret, *HE* 1.11.
3 Kelly, *Early Christian Creeds*.
4 Cyril of Jerusalem, *Cat.* 5.12.
5 See F. M. Young, 'Did Epiphanius Know What He Meant by heresy?'; and F. M. Young, '*Paideia* and the Myth of Static Dogma'.
6 Basil, *Ad Adolescentes de legendis libris gentilium*; Gregory Nazianzen, *Or.* 4–5 (against Julian).
7 W. A. Bienert, *'Allegoria' und 'Anagoge' bei Didymus dem Blinden*; J. H. Tigcheler, *Didyme l'Aveugle et l'exégèse allégorique, son commentaire sur Zacharie*.
8 E.g. Augustine, *Enarrationes in Psalmos*.
9 Discussed in F. M. Young, 'The Fourth-century Reaction against Allegory'.
10 M. Simonetti, *Biblical Interpretation in the Early Church: An Historical Introduction to Patristic Exegesis*, appendix.
11 See F. M. Young, 'Exegetical Method and Scriptural Proof: the Bible in Doctrinal Debate'.
12 Athanasius, *De Decretis*; see Young, *Biblical Exegesis*.
13 E.g. Theodoret's arguments in his *Eranistes*.
14 Gregory of Nyssa, *Eun.* 1.620–33 and elsewhere.
15 See F. M. Young, 'The Rhetorical Schools and Their Influence on Patristic Exegesis'.
16 Hadrianus, *Isagoge ad sacras scripturas*, *PG* 98, 1273–1312; CPG 6527.
17 With reference to the discussion in the previous paragraphs, see further, Young, 'Rhetorical Schools'; 'Fourth-century Reaction'; and *Biblical Exegesis*.
18 The following discussion owes much to Young, *Biblical Exegesis*, ch. 12.
19 See ibid., ch. 3.
20 Sozomen, *HE* 5.18.
21 See above ch. 9, p. 92.

22 See R. Ruether, *Gregory of Nazianzus. Rhetor and Philosopher*, and also J. A. McGuckin, *St Gregory of Nazianzus. An Intellectual Biography.*

23 H. Musurillo, ed., *From Glory to Glory: Texts from Gregory of Nyssa's Mystical Writings.*

24 Against Danielou and others, Mühlenberg (*Die Unendlichkeit Gottes*) and R. E. Heine (*Perfection in the Virtuous Life: a study in the relationship between edification and polemical theology in Gregory of Nyssa's De Vita Moysis*) have argued the case for the doctrinal and controversial grounding of Gregory's thought.

25 By Heine in his *Perfection in the Virtuous Life.*

26 See Sebastian Brock, *The Luminous Eye. The Spiritual World Vision of St Ephrem.*

40

Retrospect: interpretation and appropriation

FRANCES YOUNG

In the eighteenth century, John Wesley took up the study of ancient Christian literature in Oxford. The last half of the seventeenth century had seen a revival of patristic[1] interest and the production of new editions made the texts available. It is said that 'in the thought and piety of the early Church [Wesley] discovered what he thereafter regarded as the normative pattern of catholic Christianity'.[2] According to his *Journal*, Wesley daily checked his reading of Scripture against the early authors as he crossed the Atlantic to America. In his *Address to the Clergy* of 1796, he said:

> Can any who spend several years in those seats of learning [the universities] be excused if they do not add to that of the languages and sciences, the knowledge of the fathers – the most authentic commentators on Scripture, as being both nearest the fountain and eminently endued with that Spirit by whom 'all scripture was given'? . . . I speak chiefly of those who wrote before the Council of Nicaea. But who would not likewise desire to have some acquaintance with those that followed them – with St. Chrysostom, Basil, Jerome, Austin, and, above all, the man of a broken heart, Ephraim Syrus?[3]

Wesley provides a clear example of how the Fathers have been valued, particularly as providing a hermeneutic of Scripture. The Reformation did not immediately occasion a devaluation of the Fathers, despite the watchword *sola scriptura*. Eastern theology has always affirmed that all theology is in the Fathers,[4] thus implying that theology is simply exegetical of the patristic material; and Western theology, though somewhat less explicit, has in practice accepted that the doctrinal orthodoxy defined in the patristic texts provides the criteria by which essays in systematic theology are to be judged. Appropriation was unproblematic prior to the rise of the historico-critical method. Wesley published translations of texts he knew as the Spiritual Homilies of St Macarius of Egypt for his largely uneducated, working-class preachers, and 'Macarius' sounds just like Wesley as the perfectionism of the old ascetic movement is democratized and promulgated as the true gospel of transformation. There was no hermeneutical gap.

Between Wesley and ourselves readers have lost their innocence. In the nineteenth century, despite an awareness of the fact that 'the past is a foreign country',[5] it was still possible to believe that if one learned the language and customs of that time, one could think the thoughts of a great author after him: indeed, interpretation came to be regarded as the discernment of the author's intention, the rediscovery of the original meaning, which was to be ascertained by research into the life and background of the author, and by dialogue with his work so as to resolve problems and contradictions. By taking authors and their situation seriously it was possible to re-establish what they really meant, to assess the greatness of each contribution, to challenge received traditions about what really happened, to discover the truth in an objective way.

Such a project has remained dominant in studies of the early Church, and has enabled historians and theologians to make common cause as they shared the same methods. But not infrequently their different prior agendas produced contradictory conclusions. So the historical method turned out not to bring agreement about objective truth after all. Furthermore, theologians working with historical methodologies began to worry about the strange world of patristic discourse, such as its outdated substance language, and to enquire whether patristic formulae did not have to be abandoned in the interests of communication in the modern world. By focusing on what it meant then without minding what it might mean now, theologians had forfeited their right to claim that the study of the Fathers could contribute directly to the current theological enterprise. There was now developing a glaring hermeneutical gap.

Anxiety about this gap first hit biblical studies, but it should exercise all theologians who study the first few centuries of Christian existence. For the doctrinal conclusions of the fourth and fifth centuries have remained the identity-markers of mainstream Christianity, and this was the period through which earlier traditions, whether scriptural or patristic, were transmitted. For a long time the notion of development permitted theologians to escape the questions. Students followed reconstructed accounts of the development of doctrine, and took it for granted that the development was right, even providential, and having once got to the truth that was fine: the search for the Christian doctrine of God[6] and Christ, Trinity and incarnation, was complete. But if the creed of Nicaea and the definition at Chalcedon are rooted historically in problems that arose back then in the context of ancient discourse and rationality, how can the churches go on interpreting Scripture as if these culture-bound criteria were not open to question? Why should liturgical language and theological exposition simply assume that the conclusions reached then are truth for all time? Clearly the gap must be faced, and if, in the interests of continuity of identity, the old formulae are to be retained, along with respect for the Fathers and the literature surveyed in this volume, then ways of appropriation need to be considered.

The imperative for this is reinforced by recent developments in critical theory and hermeneutics.[7] Biblical studies have already wrestled for some time with the questions arising from these. Some of the issues have been foreshadowed in chapters 10 and 20. Clearly the brief discussion here can only lift the curtain on possibilities, but we can begin by noting that there are some interesting ways in which new approaches to interpretation enable a greater appreciation of many features of ancient rhetoric in general and early Christian literature in particular.

1. One way in which new perspectives have challenged historico-critical presuppositions is the suggestion that meaning does not lie behind a text, in its background or precedents, in its sources and prior history; rather, meaning is in front of the text, in the effect the text may have in the future.[8] Now all texts from the ancient world were affected by rhetoric, all discourse was intended to persuade. To that extent we are likely to read the intention of early Christian texts better if we ask about their implied effect, their future.

As noted in chapter 10, texts were close to speech and were meant to carry conviction. Belief, or acceptance of the truth of the discourse, was the outcome of interplay between a speaker who was authoritative because of his *ethos* (character), an argument which was convincing because of its *logos*, and an audience moved to respond (*pathos*). Each of these will reward attention.

The author's biography or *persona* mattered only insofar as it endorsed a character worthy of respect and lent authority. In critical theory this is mirrored by the response of Foucault to the supposed death of the author: true, the author in the flesh is largely irrelevant to the meaning of his/her work (Barthes),[9] true, the author has no control over the text once it has left his/her desk (Ricoeur), but the author-function can still be important. Certain early Christian works became authoritative because they were attributed to figures of authority such as Justin or Athanasius. The right kind of author's *ethos* was essential.

But so was the response (*pathos*) of the audience or reader. The significance of this has become more and more apparent as reader response theory has come into vogue: different readings are generated by different readers, even by the same reader on different occasions. A pluralism of readings seems inevitable. Yet a text has certain readers implied within it; the ancient art of persuasion took the nature of the audience very seriously and directed its attention to appropriate techniques for effecting the intended response. All the more important then is the identification of the implied audience for the interpretation of texts from the ancient world.

But prior to the development of reader response theory attention had swung from the old interest in the original author's intention to the text in itself, to the attempt to interpret the work as it disclosed itself to the interpreter, in other words, to the nature of the discourse and its effect. This interest on the part of the interpreter corresponds with that of the ancient rhetorician who recognized the overriding importance of *heuresis* or *inventio*, that is, determining the subject-matter and then arriving at a suitable style for dealing with the topics to be covered. The power of discourse has been rediscovered.

But there is one key difference between ancient and modern discussions: there seems to have been far greater confidence in the past that language corresponded with the world it described. Postmodern scepticism has deconstructed the notion of such simple reference, while recognizing the extent to which the discourse we use about the world also contributes to its creation. Yet the philosopher's critique of rhetoric even in antiquity was precisely that it could make lies plausible and falsehood seem like truth. The slipperiness of language has always been evident. Hence the need for analysis, for the identification of figures of speech, for the laboured explanations in patristic texts that much of what the Bible says about God cannot be literally true. Much of our apparently sophisticated postmodern discussion is anticipated in Augustine, the Cappadocians, even Ephrem the Syrian. The metaphoricity of language is a perception we can now share with them.

It is this more than anything else which can enable us to enter their world and share their imagination. If we begin by suspending disbelief so as to journey with Moses, as Gregory of Nyssa did, or construct a self providentially saved from guilt, as Augustine did, the literature may generate possibilities into which we, and not just the original implied audience, are invited. This empathy will be enhanced by Christian faith, for there is continuity at some level between modern believers and Christians of the past; the hermeneutical gap is not absolute but bridgeable. Beyond the purging fires of criticism may lie a new naivety, where appropriation becomes as innocent as that of John Wesley. For the meaning of the text lies in its future, a future and potential which may be released by taking seriously both the historical and rhetorical ambience of the text.

2. The method of 'deconstruction' associated with the name of Derrida has, like reader response theories, challenged the idea that a text has a single meaning.[10] Gaps or *aporias* in the text are not problems to be solved so as to make the whole work consistent: rather, they are the generative moments, the points which both deconstruct the meaning of the text and provide opportunities for alternative readings.

This may at first sight seem the diametric opposite of allegorical readings; for such reading is often treated as if it subverts a text by bringing to it an alien construction. Yet careful attention to the hermeneutical theories that lay behind the allegorical approach shows that it was precisely in the gaps, *aporias* and inconsistencies that clues were found to the fact that the Holy Spirit did not intend the text to be read at face value. Furthermore, it was the uncertainties introduced by the metaphoricity of the language that pointed to a deeper meaning than the literal one.

If truth lies between the lines, if signs and symbols are all we have, then there is much to learn from attempts to analyse these, such as those found in the Cappadocians, Ephrem and Augustine. A standard rhetorical distinction was that between the subject-matter and the diction. Like Origen, Augustine distinguished between the realities signified in Scripture and the signs by which that signification took place. The medium of language is both transparent and opaque; interpretation is vital. The standard analyses of figures of speech, logic and grammar were borrowed to enable exegesis. Gregory of Nyssa insisted that a literal interpretation of 'Son of God' was false if it implied physical begetting; yet God condescended to use human language and expressed the truth as nearly as possible in this inadequate medium. Ephrem spoke of a divine incarnation in language as God stooped to communicate with us; for him it was like someone using a mirror in an attempt to teach a parrot to speak!

For Ephrem, Scripture was a well, never exhausted:

> Anyone who encounters Scripture should not suppose that the single one of its riches that he has found is the only one to exist; rather he should realize that he himself is only capable of discovering that one out of the many riches which exist in it . . . A thirsty person rejoices because he has drunk: he is not grieved because he proved incapable of drinking the fountain dry.[11]

Postmodernism has liberated us to share the same sense that a plurality of meanings is good. We can abandon the superiority complex of modernity which aimed to find THE meaning and rejected past readings in its favour. Instead the postmodern interpreter deconstructs the self of the reader and offers respect for other readings, so mirroring something of that challenging humility with respect to human intellect upon which the Fathers insisted. We cannot encompass God; for, as Ephrem and the Cappadocians never tire of asking, how could the infinite be contained in a finite mind? It is precisely for that reason that God clothes the divine self in symbols and metaphors, adopting our language in order to communicate with us. A plurality of meanings, a relativism with respect to human cultures and languages which anticipates the postmodern perspective, is allied with a confidence that all is contingent in relation to the divine Being which transcends all thought, all expression, all conception. The Fathers might help us to challenge some of the assumptions of our culture both intellectually and morally.

Furthermore, deconstruction of the normative interpretations of the texts and formulae which have shaped Christian identity has a significant role to play in ensuring that the ancient attack on idolatry is reflexive upon the current tendency to literalize images and concepts. After modernity we need a spirituality of repentance, encouraged by the fact that even the doctrine of the Trinity was finalized as a protest against the Eunomian claim to be able to define God. The Fathers, for all their theological talk and writing, ultimately stand before the Mystery in silence. They understood the inadequacy of all language and the creative importance of deconstruction. But that never undermined their confidence in God as the basis and source of all truth, no matter how relativistic and inadequate our reception of it. Ultimately God was the author in whom one could have confidence, the text was revelation of truth through divine condescension, and its readers responded with conviction because the Holy Spirit was shed abroad in their hearts. Postmodernism is both anticipated and challenged.

3. Perhaps the most fruitful direction for a hermeneutic of patristic texts lies in the rediscovery of typology. It can be argued that typology was invented by modern scholars anxious to distinguish between allegory and a method of interpretation they saw as more attentive to history. But another approach is fostered by more recent literary interest in intertextuality.[12] Even within the Bible it is possible to trace the modelling of one story upon another,[13] producing patterns and prophecies through narrative *mimesis*. It is characteristic of early Christian interpretation to identify such narrative prophecies, to develop them in liturgy and preaching, and to create models of Christian lifestyle or destiny out of the characters of Scripture. They provide an interpretative key to Scripture and a way of reading oneself into the text. In other words, typology provides a way of appropriation.

Christian discourse was fundamentally intertextual. The writings of the New Testament constantly quote, mirror or allude to the Jewish Scriptures, and this is true of all the subsequent literature we have surveyed. Collages of biblical texts would be created for purposes of *paraenesis* or prayer. Later the Bible would replace the classics in providing the 'myths' and maxims, virtues and values to which allusion would be made in constructing Christian encomia according to the norms of classical rhetoric. Homilies would equate the implied audience of the scriptural text and the audience gathered before the preacher. Typology was a great facilitator of this natural appropriation, as was the sense of an overarching narrative from creation to eschaton into which was fitted the lives of individuals and the history of the Church, with the key to it all found in the story of the incarnation in Christ.

It is with the rediscovery of perspectives of this kind that literary critics such as Northrop Frye[14] have challenged the historico-critical approach to the Bible. It is surely time that the intertextuality of the Fathers played a larger role in informing current approaches to hermeneutics; and it is not for nothing that earlier discussions in chapters 10 and 20 turned to typology as a model for the appropriation of patristic material itself. In particular the current climate is ready to respond to a focus on narrative as being more than mere story and a significant vehicle of identity, meaning and truth, just as the Fathers did. And the melding of significant narratives in works like the poems of Ephrem shows a kind of typological imagination which surely has potential for creative appropriation.

We have briefly surveyed some ways in which postmodern critical theory enables a new appreciation of a body of literature whose features have often seemed alien to the modern world. But inevitably there are ways in which postmodernism is postmodern and reaches into realms not dreamed of by the Fathers. One aspect of this is found in the social location of meaning. In some ways this radicalizes the historico-critical perception of distance and change. The texts we have chosen to study came from a society quite differently structured from our own in which all kinds of assumptions were made which we no longer share. The obvious example, already describable as classic, is found in the patriarchal presuppositions embedded in these texts, for feminists dangerously so embedded precisely because these authoritative texts have created authoritarian Christian societies which have resisted change. The extent to which Christian institutions took over and developed those of the Roman Empire has been noted in this volume. This may be even more challenging to ecclesiastical norms, if taken seriously, than the controversial evidence for the early existence and subsequent suppression of women priests; for why should the Church perpetuate offices and structures belonging to such an utterly different society? Furthermore, in a democratic society their association of monotheism with monarchy is deeply disturbing, and the hierarchical nature of their whole outlook and theology may for us undermine the validity of everything found in these texts.

It is here that Gadamer's hermeneutical analysis becomes important: we cannot avoid dialogue between the 'two horizons' of text and reader.[15] We cannot go back on the perception of historical difference. The 'otherness' of the world of early Christianity justifies our making common cause with historians of late antiquity and Byzantinists. For we need to set the texts in their social world if we are to understand them, and progress can be made only by facing up to their difference. Taking the world of the texts seriously involves first a hermeneutic of suspicion, for all the reasons sketched above. The hermeneutic of suspicion also validates the rehabilitation of heretics, those on the losing side of history who almost certainly had more good in their characters and ideas than the vitriolic and contentious defenders of orthodoxy allowed for. Indeed, their damning rhetoric is for us one of the most distasteful features of these texts, even as it reflects the norms of the society in which they were written. The recognition of otherness and difference is a prerequisite for dialogue. We cannot simply take over these texts as pre-modern readers did.

The recognition of difference is also essential to an 'ethical' reading of this literature. For it is only when we respect and articulate the otherness of these texts that we can offer hospitality to them, allowing ourselves to be challenged or engaged. This is when real dialogue is possible, because we are prepared to enter their world with a degree of empathy and then return to our different world with changed perspectives and an awareness of different horizons.

But who is this 'we'? There are of course many different individuals and groups who read this literature for different reasons and with different outcomes; for there is no 'innocent' reading of these texts, and there are different 'informed' readings. Some of us inhabit a variety of different interpretative communities, reading the texts as scholars, as women, as believers, oscillating in our reading stance between different perspectives, sharing interests with different groups. But one significant 'we' must be those of us who belong to Christian communities which have both continuity and discontinuity with the past community which produced this literature.

It is significant that this literature is a community deposit, preserved to build up the community that treasured it. It is important that it is seen as a total deposit; for the reception of Scripture demonstrates that much which seems utterly alien in one generation may chime with another. Ongoing dialogue with this deposit is essential to the enterprise of Christian theology. Simple historical reconstruction followed by dogmatic reassertion of the formulae resulting from the process is simply not adequate. The *logos* that matters is the whole discourse of this literature, whether persuasive to us or not, not just the doctrinal outcomes in creeds interpreted as formulae binding for the preservation of Christian identity.

We need the focus on all the texts and the world from which they issued. It enables common cause with other scholars and readers; but more than that it enables an appropriation which results from immersion in the world of the texts so that we can identify continuities and possibilities beyond difference, and so begin to accept Gregory of Nazianzus as theologian, John Chrysostom as exegete and instructor, Gregory of Nyssa as spiritual guide, and so on. It is the empathetic imagination that will release dimensions of spirituality and theology which can prove enriching. It is the critical imagination that can analyse the discourse of polemics and debate so as to identify issues which should still inform the faith's struggle for understanding.

Notes

1 The term 'patristic' is used in much of the following discussion because it raises issues concerning the reception of this literature as the product of the 'Fathers' of the Church. This conception is doubtless patriarchal and hierarchical; but that is the significant reality about the preservation and influence of these texts with which we have to deal.

2 Albert Outler, Introduction to *John Wesley*, a volume of A Library of Protestant Thought, (New York: Oxford University Press, 1964), 9.

3 Quoted in a footnote, ibid.

4 Though Eastern Orthodox theology does not confine the period of the Fathers to the remote past (editors).

5 L. P. Hartley, *The Go-Between*, prologue.

6 The title of the book by R. P. C. Hanson, *The Search for the Christian Doctrine of God*, exemplifies the point.

7 The background to the issues raised in this chapter may be pursued by turning to the author's article, 'From Suspicion and Sociology'. Detailed footnotes concerning the wider issues are not provided here.

8 Paul Ricoeur has had a great influence upon theological hermeneutics, and two of his classic points are referred to in this and following paragraphs. Of his many writings, reference may be made to *Hermeneutics and the Human Sciences* (Cambridge: Cambridge University Press, 1981); and *Time and Narrative* (3 vols, Chicago: University of Chicago Press, 1984, 1985, 1988).

9 Cf. the classic article by Roland Barthes, 'The Death of the Author'; reprinted in *Image Music Text*, ed. and trans. S. Heath (London: Fontana Press, 1977), 142–8.

10 The work of Derrida has become prolific, as has the discussion about reader response theory; some formative texts are gathered in David Lodge, ed., *Modern Criticism and Theory. A Reader* (London and New York: Longman, 1988).

11 *Commentary on the Diatesseron* 1.18–19; quoted from Brock, *The Luminous Eye*, 36.

12 For fuller discussion of the material in the following paragraphs, see Young, *Biblical Exegesis*.

13 Michael Fishbane, *Biblical Interpretation in Ancient Israel* (Oxford: Clarendon, 1985).

14 Northrop Frye, *The Great Code. The Bible and Literature* (New York and London: Harcourt Brace Jovanovich, 1981).

15 The classic contribution of Gadamer is discussed by Anthony Thiselton, *The Two Horizons* (Exeter: Paternoster, 1980).

Bibliographies

The bibliographies are arranged as follows: first there are general bibliographies that apply to the whole work; then follow bibliographies arranged according to the three parts of the book, these begin with a general bibliography for the whole part, followed by more detailed bibliographies arranged by chapters of the sections A of each part (there are no specific bibliographies for the chapters of sections B, as these chapters are, of their nature, general).

Lexica, dictionaries and encyclopedias

L'Année philologique: bibliographie critique et analytique de l'antiquité gréco-latine (Paris: Les Belles Lettres, 1928–).

Biblia patristica: index des citations et allusions bibliques dans la littérature patristique, J. Allenbach et al., eds (Paris: Centre Nationale de la Recherche Scientifique, 1975–).

Bibliotheca sanctorum, 12 vols (Rome: Istituto Giovanni XXIII nella Pontificia Università lateranense, 1961–1970); *Indici* (Rome: Città Nuova, 1991); *Prima appendice* (Rome: Città Nuova, 1992); *Seconda appendice* (Rome: Città Nuova, 2000).

Bibliotheca sanctorum orientalium: Enciclopedia dei santi: le chiese orientali, J. N. Cañellas and S. Virgulin, eds, 2 vols (Rome: Città Nuova, 1998–9).

Biographisch-bibliographisches Kirchenlexikon, F. W. Bautz and T. Bautz, eds (Hamm: Bautz, 1970–).

The Blackwell Dictionary of Eastern Christianity, K. Parry and J. Hinnells, eds (Oxford: Blackwell, 2000).

Clavis Apocryphorum Veteris Testamenti, J.-C. Haelewyck, ed. (Turnhout: Brepols, 1998).

Clavis Patrum Graecorum, M. Geerard, ed., 5 vols (Turnhout: Brepols, 1974–87); *Supplementum*. M. Geerard and J. Noret, eds (Turnhout: Brepols, 1998). Cited by item number.

Clavis Patrum Latinorum, E. Dekkers, ed. (Turnhout: Brepols, 1995^3). Cited by item number.

A Compendious Syriac Lexicon, J. Payne Smith, ed. (Oxford: Clarendon Press, 1903).

A Coptic Dictionary, W. E. Crum, ed. (Oxford: Clarendon Press, 1939).

The Coptic Encyclopedia, A. Z. Atiya, ed., 8 vols (New York: Macmillan, 1991).

Dictionary of Christian Biography, M. J. Walsh, ed. (London: Continuum and Collegeville, MN: Liturgical Press, 2001).

Dictionary of Christian Biography, Literature, Sects and Doctrines, W. Smith and H. Wace, eds, 4 vols (London: J. Murray, 1877–87).

Dictionnaire d'archéologie chrétienne et de liturgie, F. Cabrol, ed., 15 vols (Paris: Letouzy et Ané, 1907–53).

Dictionnaire d'histoire et de géographie ecclésiastiques, A. Baudrillart et al., eds (Paris: Letouzey, 1912–).

Dictionnaire de spiritualité, ascétique et mystique, histoire et doctrine, M. Viller et al., eds, 16 vols (Paris: Beauchesne, 1932–95).

Dictionnaire de théologie catholique, A. Vacant et al., eds, 15 vols (Paris: Letouzey et Ané, 1908–50).

Dictionnaire latin-français des auteurs chrétiens, A. Blaise and H. Chirat, eds (Turnhout: Brepols, 1954).

Dizionario enciclopedico dell'Oriente cristiano, E. G. Farrugia, ed. (Rome: Pontificio Istituto Orientale, 2000).

Dizionario patristico e di antichità cristiane, A. di Berardino, ed., 3 vols (Marietti: Casale Montferrato, 1983). ET: *Encyclopedia of the Early Church*, W. H. C. Frend, ed., 2 vols (Cambridge: James Clarke, 1992).

Dizionario sintetico di patristica, C. Vidal Manzanares, ed. (Città del Vaticano: Libreria Editrice Vaticana, 1995).

Encyclopedia of Early Christianity, Everett Ferguson, ed., New York: Garland Publishing, 1990, 1998^2).

A Glossary of Later Latin to 600 A.D., A. Souter, ed. (Oxford: Oxford University Press, 1949).

A Greek-English Lexicon, H. G. Liddell and R. Scott, eds (Oxford: Clarendon Press, 1996^9).

Greek Lexicon of the Roman and Byzantine Periods (from B.C. 146 to A.D. 1100), E. A. Sophocles, ed. (Cambridge, MA: Harvard University Press, 1914).

Latin Dictionary, C. T. Lewis and C. Short, eds (Oxford: Oxford University Press, 1963).

Lexikon für Theologie und Kirche, M. Buchberger et al., eds (Freiburg im Breisgau: Herder, $1993–^3$).

The Oxford Dictionary of the Christian Church, F. L. Cross and E. A. Livingstone, eds (Oxford: Oxford University Press, 1998^3).

Oxford Latin Dictionary, P. G. W. Glare, ed. (Oxford: Oxford University Press, 1982).

A Patristic Greek lexicon, G. W. H. Lampe, ed. (Oxford: Clarendon Press, 1968).

Reallexikon für Antike und Christentum: Sachwörterbuch zur Auseinandersetzung des Christentums mit der antiken Welt, T. Klauser et al., eds (Stuttgart: Hiersemann, 1950–).

Theologische Realenzyklopädie, H. R. Balz et al., eds (Berlin and New York: Walter de Gruyter, 1977–).

Thesaurus Linguae Graecae CD-ROM, version E, M. C. Pantelia, ed. (Irvine, CA: University of California, 1999).

Thesaurus Linguae Latinae (Leipzig: Teubner, 1900–).

Thesaurus Syriacus, R. Payne Smith et al., eds (Oxford: Clarendon Press, 1879–1901).

Series

Texts

Acta Conciliorum Oecumenicorum, Series I, ed. E. Schwartz and J. Straub (Strasbourg, 1914; Berlin, 1922–84); Series II, ed. sub auspiciis Academiae Scientiarum Bavaricae (Berlin, 1984–).

Biblioteca de Autores Cristianos (Madrid: [various imprints], 1945–).
Biblioteca Patristica (Bologna: [various imprints], 1981–).
Corpus Christianorum. Series Apocryphorum (Turnhout: Brepols, 1983–).
Corpus Christianorum. Series Graeca (Turnhout: Brepols, 1977–).
Corpus Christianorum. Series Latina (Turnhout: Brepols, 1953–).
Corpus Scriptorum Christianorum Orientalium (Louvain: [various imprints], 1903–).
Corpus Scriptorum Ecclesiasticorum Latinorum (Vienna: [various imprints], 1866–).
Decrees of the Ecumenical Councils, N. P. Tanner, ed., 2 vols (London: Sheed and Ward and Washington, DC: Georgetown University Press, 1990).
Gnostische Schriften in Koptischer Sprache aus dem Codex Brucianus, C. Schmidt, ed., *TU* 8.1–2 (Leipzig, 1892).
Die Griechischen Christlichen Schriftsteller der ersten drei Jahrhunderte (Leipzig: J. C. Hinrich'sche Buchhandlung, 1897–1941; Berlin and Leipzig: Akademie Verlag, 1953; Berlin: Akademie Verlag, 1954–).
Monumenta Germaniae Historica (Hanover: Hahnsche Buchhandlung, 1890–).
Patristische Texte und Studien (Berlin: Walter de Gruyter, 1964–).
Patrologiae Cursus Completus . . . Series Graeca, J.-P. Migne, ed., 162 vols (Paris: Garnier, 1857–66).
Patrologiae Cursus Completus . . . Series Latina, J.-P. Migne, ed., 221 vols (Paris: Garnier, 1844–64). *Supplementum*, A. Hamman, ed., 5 vols (Paris, 1958–70).
Patrologia Orientalis (Paris: Firmin-Didot, 1903–66; Turnhout: Brepols, 1968–).
Scrittori Greci e Latini (Milan: A. Mondadori, 1974–).
Sources Chrétiennes (Paris: Les Éditions du Cerf, 1941–).
Texte und Untersuchungen (Leipzig: J.C. Hinrich'sche Buchhandlung, 1882–1943; Berlin: Akademie Verlag, 1951–).

N. B.: The standard reference works for critical editions are *CPG*, for the Greek, and *CPL*, for the Latin, to which works the reader is referred for further particulars (see also the articles in *ODCC*). Only in exceptional cases will the detailed bibliographies for each chapter include references to particular critical editions.

Translations

Ancient Christian Writers, ed. J. Quasten and others (Westminster, MD. Newman Press and London: Longman, Green and Co., 1946–67; Westminster, MD: Newman Press, 1970–).
The Ante-Nicene Fathers. Translations of the Writings of the Fathers down to A.D. 325, Alexander Roberts and James Donaldson, eds, 9 vols (Edinburgh: T & T Clark, 1882).
Cistercian Studies Series (Kalamazoo: Cistercian Publications, 1969–).
Classics of Western Spirituality (Mahwah, NJ: Paulist Press, 1946–).
Early Church Fathers, Carol Harrison, ed. (London and New York: Routledge, 1996–).
Fathers of the Church (New York: Fathers of the Church, Inc., 1949–1960; Washington, DC: Catholic University of America Press, 1962–).
Library of Christian Classics, 26 vols (London: SCM and Philadelphia: Westminster Press, 1953–1966.
Oxford Early Christian Texts, Henry Chadwick, ed. (Oxford: Clarendon Press, 1970–).

Popular Patristics Series (Crestwood, NY: St Vladimir's Seminary Press, 1977–).

A Select Library of the Nicene and Post-Nicene Fathers of the Christian Church, Philip Schaff et al., eds, 14 vols, (Buffalo: Christian Literature Co., 1886–90).

Translated Texts for Historians, ed. G. Clark et al. (Liverpool: Liverpool University Press, 1985–).

General bibliography

B. Altaner, *Patrology* (New York: Herder and Herder, 1961²).

A. H. Armstrong, ed., *Cambridge History of Later Greek and Early Medieval Philosophy* (Cambridge: Cambridge University Press, 1967).

Classical Mediterranean Spirituality: Egyptian, Greek, Roman, World Spirituality 15 (London: Routledge and Kegan Paul, 1986).

P. Athanassiadi and Michael Frede, eds, *Pagan Monotheism in Late Antiquity* (Oxford: Clarendon Press, 1999).

W. Bauer, *Orthodoxy and Heresy in Earliest Christianity*, ET of *Rechglaubigkeit und Ketzerei im altesten Christentum* (Tübingen: Mohr, 1964²) by R. Kraft et al. (Philadelphia: Fortress Press, 1971/London: SCM, 1972).

A. Baumstark, *Geschichte der syrischen Literatur* (Bonn: A. Marcus und E. Webers Verlag, 1922; repr. Berlin: Walter de Gruyter, 1968).

J. Behr, *The Way to Nicaea*, The Formation of Christian Theology, I (Crestwood, NY: St Vladimir's Seminary Press, 2001).

A. Di Berardino and B. Studer, *History of Theology*, I, ET by Matthew O'Connell (Collegeville, MN: Liturgical Press 1996).

Bible de tous les temps, I: *Le monde grec ancien et la Bible*, ed. C. Mondesert, II: *Le monde latin antique et la Bible*, ed. J. Fontaine and Ch. Pietri, III: *Saint Augustin et le Bible*, ed. A.-M. de la Bonnardière (Paris: Beauchesne, 1984–6).

P. Brown, *The World of Late Antiquity* (London: Thames and Hudson, 1971).

The Making of Late Antiquity (Cambridge, MA and London: Harvard University Press, 1978).

The Body and Society (London: Faber, 1989).

Philip Burton, *The Old Latin Gospels* (Oxford: Clarendon Press, 2000).

The Cambridge History of the Bible, I, ed. P. Ackroyd and C. F. Evans; II, ed. G. W. H. Lampe (Cambridge: Cambridge University Press, 1969–70).

Averil Cameron, *Christianity and the Rhetoric of Empire. The Development of Christian Discourse*, Sather Classical Lectures (Berkeley: University of California Press, 1991).

H. von Campenhausen, *The Fathers of the Greek Church*, ET of *Griechische Kirchenväter* (Stuttgart: Kohlhammer, 1955/London: Adam and Charles Black, 1963).

The Fathers of the Latin Church, ET of *Lateinische Kirchenväter* (Stuttgart: Kohlhammer, 1960/London: Adam and Charles Black, 1964).

F. Cayré, *Manual of Patrology and History of Theology* (Paris: Desclée, 1940).

H. Chadwick, *History and Thought of the Early Church* (London: Variorum Reprints, 1982).

The Early Church, rev. edn (London and New York: Penguin Books, 1993).

The Church in Ancient Society. From Galilee to Gregory the Great (Oxford: Clarendon Press, 2001).

M. L. Colish, *The Stoic Tradition from Antiquity to the Early Middle Ages*, II, *Stoicism in Christian Latin Thought through the Sixth Century* (Leiden: Brill, 1985).
M. B. Cunningham and P. Allen, eds, *Preacher and Audience. Studies in Early Christian and Byzantine Homiletics*, A New History of the Sermon, I (Leiden: Brill, 1998).
J. Daniélou, *A History of Early Christian Doctrine before the Council of Nicaea*, 3 vols (I *The Theology of Jewish Christianity*, II *Gospel Message and Hellenistic Culture*, III *The Origins of Latin Christianity*, London: Darton, Longman and Todd, 1964–77). ET of *Histoires des doctrines chrétiennes avant Nicée*, 3 vols (Bruges: Desclée, 1958–78).
D. Dawson, *Christian Figural Reading and the Shaping of Christian Identity* (Berkeley: University of California Press, 2002).
L. Duchesne, *The Early History of the Church*, 3 vols (London: John Murray, 1909–24; ET of *Histoire ancienne de l'Église*, 1906–10).
M. J. Edwards, ed., *Apologetics in the Roman Empire: Pagans, Jews and Christians* (Oxford: Clarendon Press, 1999).
P. F. Esler, ed., *The Early Christian World* (London and New York: Routledge, 2000).
A.-J. Festugière, *La Révélation d'Hermès Trismégiste*, 4 vols (Paris: J. Gabalda et Compagnie, 1950–4).
G. Fowden, *The Egyptian Hermes* (Cambridge: Cambridge University Press, 1986).
R. Lane Fox, *Pagans and Christians* (New York: Alfred A. Knopf, Inc., 1986).
W. H. C. Frend, Martyrdom and Persecution in the Early Church (Oxford: Blackwell, 1965).
The Rise of Christianity (Philadelphia: Fortress Press, 1984).
C. W. Griggs, *Early Egyptian Christianity: From its Origins to 451 CE* (Leiden: Brill, 1991).
A. Grillmeier SJ, *Christ in Christian Tradition*, I, ET of *Jesus der Christus im Glauben der Kirche* by J. Bowden (London: Mowbrays and Atlanta, GA/Louisville, KY: John Knox Press, 1975[2]).
C. Haas, *Alexandria in Late Antiquity. Topography and Social Conflict* (Baltimore and London: The John Hopkins University Press, 1997).
A. von Harnack, *Lehrbuch der Dogmengeschichte*, 3 vols, 4th edn (Tübingen, 1909); ET (from 3rd edn), *History of Dogma*, 7 vols (London and Edinburgh: Norgate and Williams, 1894–9).
Ian Hazlett, ed., *Early Christianity, Origins and Evolution to AD 600* (London: SPCK, 1991).
W. Jaeger, *Early Christianity and Greek Paideia* (Oxford: Oxford University Press, 1962).
J. A. Jungmann, *The Early Liturgy* (London: Dorton, Longman and Todd, 1959, 1980[2]).
J. N. D. Kelly, *Early Christian Doctrines* (London: Adam and Charles Black, 1960[2]).
Early Christian Creeds (London: Longman, 1972[3]).
R. Lamberton, *Homer the Theologian: Neoplatonist Allegorical Reading and the Growth of the Epic Tradition*. TCH 9 (Berkeley and Los Angeles: University of California Press, 1986).
H. Lietzmann, *A History of the Early Church*, 4 vols (Cleveland and New York: Meridian Books, 1961; revised, though still imperfect, ET of *Geschichte der alten Kirche*, Berlin, 1932–44).
A. Louth, *Origins of the Christian Mystical Tradition* (Oxford: Clarendon Press, 1981).
B. McGinn, *The Foundations of Mysticism. Origins to the Fifth Century* (New York: Crossroad, 1991).
R. MacMullen, *Paganism in the Roman Empire* (New Haven: Yale University Press, 1981).
H.-I. Marrou, *A History of Education in Antiquity*, ET of *L'Education dans l'Antiquité* (Paris: Editions du Seuil, 1948[3]) by G. Lamb (London: Sheed and Ward, 1956).

W. A. Meeks and R. L. Wilken, *Jews and Christians in Antioch in the First Four Centuries of the Common Era* (Missoula, MT: Scholars Press, 1978).

F. van der Meer and C. Mohrmann, eds, *Atlas of the Early Christian World* (London: Nelson, 1958).

F. Millar, *The Roman Near East, 31 BC–AD 337* (Cambridge, MA: Harvard University Press, 1993).

R. Mortley, *From Word to Silence*, 2 vols (Bonn: Peter Hanstein, 1986).

L.-S. le Nain de Tillemont, *Mémoires pour servir à l'histoire ecclésiastique des six premiers siècles*, 16 vols (Paris: Charles Robustel, 1693–1712).

I. Ortiz de Urbina, *Patrologia Syriaca* (Rome: PIOS, 1965^2).

J. Pelikan, *The Christian Tradition: A History of the Development of Doctrine*, 5 vols (Chicago: University of Chicago Press, 1971–83).

J. Quasten with A. di Berardino, *Patrology*, 4 vols (Westminster, MD: Newman Press, 1986).

B. Ramsey, *Beginning to Read the Fathers* (London: SCM, 1993).

M.-J. Rondeau, *Les commentaires patristiques du Psautier*, vol. I *OCA* 219 (Rome: PIOS, 1982).

P. Rousseau, *The Early Christian Centuries* (London, etc.: Longman, 2002).

A. Rousselle, *Porneia: On Desire and the Body in Antiquity*, ET of *Porneia: de la maîtrise du corps à la privation sensorielle* (Paris: Presses Universitaires de France, 1983) by F. Pheasant (Oxford: Blackwell, 1988).

M. Simon, *Verus Israel. A study of the relations between Christians and Jews in the Roman Empire (AD 135–425)* (Oxford: Oxford University Press for the Littmann Library, 1986).

M. Simonetti, *Biblical Interpretation in the Early Church: An Historical Introduction to Patristic Exegesis*. ET of *Profilo storico dell'esegesi patristica* (Rome: Augustinianum, 1981) by J. Hughes, A. Bergquist, M. Bockmuehl, and W. Horbury (Edinburgh: T & T Clark, 1994).

M. Sordi, *The Christians and the Roman Empire*, trans. A. Bedini (Norman and London: University of Oklahoma, 1986).

G. C. Stead, *Divine Substance* (Oxford: Clarendon Press, 1977).

Philosophy in Late Antiquity (Cambridge: Cambridge University Press, 1994).

J. Stevenson, *A New Eusebius* (London: SPCK, 1963; revised edn, 1987).

Creeds, Councils and Controversies (London: SPCK, 1966; revised edn 1987).

B. Studer, *Trinity and Incarnation. The Faith of the Early Church* (Edinburgh: T & T Clark, 1993); ET of *Gott und unsere Erlösung im Glauben des Alten Kirche*, Düsseldorf, 1985).

K. Tanner, *Theories of Culture: a New Agenda for Theology* (Minneapolis: Fortress Press, 1997).

H. E. W. Turner, *The Pattern of Christian Truth* (London: Mowbray, 1954).

M. P. Weitzman, *From Judaism to Christianity: Studies in the Hebrew and Syriac Bibles*, Journal of Semitic Studies Supplement 8 (Oxford: Oxford University Press, 1999).

M. White, *Building God's House in the Roman World. Architectural Adaptation among Pagans, Jews and Christians* (London: Nelson, 1990).

R. R. L. Wilken, *The Christians as Romans Saw Them* (New Haven and London: Yale University Press, 1984).

W. L. Wimbush and R. Valantasis, eds, *Asceticism* (New York: Oxford University Press, 1995).

F. W. Young, *Biblical Exegesis and the Formation of Christian Culture* (Cambridge: Cambridge University Press, 1997).

Part I. The Beginnings: the New Testament to Irenaeus

General

S. Bacchiocchi, *From Sabbath to Sunday* (Rome: Gregorian, 1977).

S. Benko, 'Pagan Criticism of Christianity During the First Two Centuries AD', *ANRW* 23/2 (1980), 1055–118.

S. Benko and J. J. O'Rourke, eds, *The Catacombs and the Colosseum: The Roman Empire as the Setting of Primitive Christianity* (Valley Forge, PA: Judson Press, 1971).

A. Brent, *Hippolytus and the Roman Church in the Third Century: Communities in Tension before the Emergence of a Monarch-Bishop* (Leiden: Brill, 1995).

R. E. Brown and J. P. Meier, *Antioch and Rome: New Testament Cradles of Catholic Christianity* (New York: Paulist Press, 1983).

J. T. Burtchaell, *From Synagogue to Church. Public services and offices in the earliest Christian communities* (Cambridge: Cambridge University Press, 1992).

H. von Campenhausen, *Ecclesiastical Authority and Spiritual Power in the Church of the First Three Centuries*, ET of *Kirchliches Amt und geistliche Vollmacht in den ersten drei Jahrhunderten* (Tübingen: Mohr, 1953) by J. A. Baker (London: A. & C. Black, 1969).

The Formation of the Christian Bible. ET of *Die Entstehung der christlichen Bibel* (Tübingen: Mohr, 1968) by J. A. Baker (Philadelphia: Fortress, 1972).

J. Carcopino, *Daily Life in Ancient Rome* (New Haven: Yale University Press, 1940).

James Carleton Paget, 'Anti-Judaism and Early Christian Identity', *ZAC* 1 (1997), 195–225.

H. Chadwick, *Early Christian Thought and the Classical Tradition* (Oxford: Clarendon Press, 1966).

A. Deissmann, *Light from the Ancient East*, ET of *Licht vom Osten* (Tübingen: Mohr, 1909^2) by L. Strachan (London: Hodder and Stoughton, 1910).

L. R. Donelson, *Pseudepigraphy and Ethical Argument in the Pastoral Epistles*, HUT 22 (Tübingen: Mohr, 1986).

A. J. Droge, *Homer or Moses? Early Christian Interpretations of the History of Culture*, HUT 26 (Tübingen: Mohr, 1989).

J. D. G. Dunn, *Christology in the Making* (London: SCM, 1980, 1989).

A. Faivre, *The Emergence of the Laity in the Early Church* (New York: Paulist Press, 1990).

M. Fishbane, *Biblical Interpretation in Ancient Israel* (Oxford: Clarendon Press, 1985).

H. Y. Gamble, *Books and Readers in the Early Church: A History of Early Christian Texts* (New Haven and London: Yale University Press, 1995).

R. M. Grant, *Heresy and Criticism* (Louisville: Westminster/John Knox Press, 1993).

Kim Haines-Eitzen, *Guardians of Letters. Literacy, Power and the Transmitters of Early Christian Literature* (New York: Oxford University Press, 2000).

A. Harnack, *The Expansion of Christianity in the First Three Centuries*, ET of *Mission und Ausbreitung des Christentums in den ersten drei Jahrhunderten* (Leipzig: Hinrichs, 1902) by J. Moffatt (London: Williams and Norgate, 1904).

J. S. Jeffers, *Conflict at Rome: Social Order and Hierarchy in Early Christianity* (Minneapolis: Fortress Press, 1991).

P. Lampe, *Die stadtrömischen Christen in den ersten beiden Jahrhunderten* (Tübingen: Mohr, 1989[2]); ET: *From Paul to Valentinus: Christians at Rome in the First Two Centuries*, trans. M. Steinhammer, ed. M. D. Johnson (Minneapolis: Fortress Press, 2003).

R. MacMullen, *Roman Social Relations, 50BC to AD 284* (New Haven: Yale University Press, 1974).

Paganism in the Roman Empire (New Haven: Yale University Press, 1981).

Christianizing the Roman Empire, AD 100–400 (New Haven: Yale University Press, 1984).

L. H. Martin, *Hellenistic Religions* (Oxford: Oxford University Press, 1987).

G. May, *Creatio ex nihilo. The Doctrine of 'Creation out of Nothing' in Early Christian Thought*, ET of *Schopfung aus dem Nichts* (Berlin: de Gruyter, 1978) by A. S. Worrall (Edinburgh: T & T Clark, 1994).

W. A. Meeks, *The First Urban Christians: The Social World of the Apostle Paul* (New Haven: Yale University Press, 1983).

The Origins of Christian Morality: The First Two Centuries (New Haven: Yale University Press, 1993).

W. A. Meeks and R. L. Wilken, *Jews and Christians in Antioch in the First Four Centuries of the Common Era*, Sources for Biblical Study 13 (Missoula, MT: Scholars Press, 1978).

T. Morgan, *Literate Education in the Hellenistic and Roman Worlds* (Cambridge: Cambridge University Press, 1998).

C. H. Roberts, 'Books in the Greco-Roman World and in the New Testament', in *The Cambridge History of the Bible* (Cambridge: Cambridge University Press, 1963–70), I, 48–66.

Manuscript, Society and Belief in Early Christian Egypt (London: Oxford University Press, 1979).

W. Rordorf, *Sunday* (London: SCM, 1968).

A. F. Segal, *Paul the Convert* (New Haven: Yale University Press, 1990).

J.-A. Shelton, *As the Romans Did: A Source Book in Roman Social History* (New York and Oxford: Oxford University Press, 1988).

R. Stark, *The Rise of Christianity: A Sociologist Reconsiders History* (Princeton: Princeton University Press, 1996).

A. Strobel, *Ursprung und Geschichte des frühchristlichen Osterkalenders* (Berlin: Akademie Verlag, 1977).

G. Theissen, *Social Reality and the Early Christians: Theology, Ethics and the World of the New Testament*, ET of *Studien zur Soziologie des Urchristentums* (Tübingen: Mohr-Siebeck, 1989) by M. Kohl (Edinburgh: T & T Clark and Minneapolis: Fortress Press, 1992).

C. Trevett, *Montanism: Gender, Authority and the New Prophecy* (Cambridge: Cambridge University Press, 1996).

D. Verner, *The Household of God. The Social World of the Pastoral Epistles* (Chico, CA: Scholars Press, 1983).

Rowan Williams, ed., *The Making of Orthodoxy* (Cambridge: Cambridge University Press, 1989).

S. G. Wilson, *Related Strangers: Jews and Christians 70–170CE* (Minneapolis: Fortress Press, 1995).

F. Young, '"*Creatio ex nihilo*": a Context for the Emergence of the Christian Doctrine of Creation', *Scottish Journal of Theology* 44 (1991), 139–51.

The Pastoral Letters (Cambridge: Cambridge University Press, 1994).
'From Suspicion and Sociology to Spirituality: on Method. Hermeneutics and Appropriation with Respect to Patristic Material', *SP* 29 (1997), 421–35.

Chapter 2. The apostolic and sub-apostolic writings: The New Testament and the Apostolic Fathers

Critical editions by O. Gebhardt, A Harnack and T. Zahn (3 vols, Leipzig, 1875–7); by J. B. Lightfoot (5 vols in 4, 1885–90, Clement, Ignatius and Polycarp only); by F. X. Funk (2 vols, Tübingen, 1878–81; 3rd edn of vol. I by K. Bihlmeyer and W. Schneemelcher, 1970).
L. W. Barnard, *Studies in the Apostolic Fathers and Their Background* (Oxford: Blackwell, 1966).
A. Brent, 'The Relations between Ignatius and the *Didascalia*', *SecCent* 8.3 (1991), 129–56.
V. Corwin, *St Ignatius and Christianity in Antioch* (New Haven: Yale University Press, 1960).
C. Jefford et al., *Reading the Apostolic Fathers: An Introduction* (Peabody, MA: Hendrickson, 1996).
A. P. O'Hagan, *Material Re-Creation in the Apostolic Fathers*, TU 100 (1968).
C. Richardson, *The Christianity of Ignatius of Antioch* (New York: Columbia University Press, 1935).
C. Trevett, *A Study of Ignatius of Antioch in Syria and Asia* (Lewiston, NY: Mellen, 1992).
S. Tugwell OP, *The Apostolic Fathers* (London: Geoffrey Chapman, 1989).

Chapter 3. Gnostic literature

U. Bianchi, ed., *Le origini dello Gnosticismo* (Leiden: Brill, 1967).
G. Filoramo, *L'attesa della fine. Storia della gnosi* (Rome: Laterza, 1983); ET by Anthony Alcock, *A History of Gnosticism* (Oxford: Blackwells, 1990).
H. Jonas, *The Gnostic Religion* (London: Routledge, 1992).
B. Layton, *The Rediscovery of Gnosticism*, 2 vols (Leiden: Brill, 1980–1).
The Gnostic Scriptures (Garden City, NY: Doubleday & Co., 1987).
A. Logan, *Gnostic Truth and Christian Heresy: A Study in the History of Gnosticism* (Edinburgh: T & T Clark, 1996).
E. Pagels, *The Gnostic Gospels* (New York: Random House, 1979).
B. A. Pearson, *Gnosticism, Judaism and Egyptian Christianity* (Minneapolis: Fortress Press, 1990).
J. M. Robinson, ed., *The Nag Hammadi Library in English* (San Francisco: Harper & Row, 3rd revised edn, 1988).
M. A. Williams, *Rethinking 'Gnosticism'* (Princeton: Princeton University Press, 1996).
F. Wisse, 'The Nag Hammadi Library and the Heresiologists', *VigChr* 25 (1971), 205–23.

Chapter 4. (a) Apocryphal writings

V. Burrus, *Chastity as Autonomy: Women in the Stories of the Apocryphal Acts* (Lewiston: E. Mellen, 1987).
J. H. Charlesworth, ed., *The Old Testament Pseudepigrapha*, 2 vols (Garden City, NY: Doubleday, 1983–5).

J. H. Charlesworth and C. A. Evans, eds, *The Pseudepigrapha and Early Biblical Interpretation* (Sheffield: JSOT Press, 1993).

J. H. Charlesworth and Walter P. Weaver, eds, *The Old and New Testaments: their relationship and the 'intertestamental' literature* (Valley Forge, PA: Trinity Press International, 1993).

O. Eissfeldt, *The Old Testament: an introduction*, ET of *Einleitung in das Alte Testament* (Tübingen: Mohr, 1964[3]) by P. Ackroyd (Oxford: Blackwell, 1965).

J. K. Elliott, *The Apocryphal New Testament* (Oxford: Clarendon Press, 1993).

A. Resch, *Agrapha; aussercanonische Schriftfragmente; gesammelt und untersucht und in zweiter völlig neu bearbeiteter durch alttestamentliche Agrapha vermehrter Auflage*, TU 30.3–4 (Leipzig: J. C. Hinrichs, 1906).

W. Schneemelcher, ed., *New Testament Apocrypha*, ET of *Neutestamentliche Apokryphen* (Tübingen: Mohr, 1989[5]) by R. McL. Wilson, 2 vols (Louisville, KY: Westminster/John Knox Press, 1991–2).

L. Di Tommaso, *A Bibliography of Pseudepigrapha Research, 1850–1999* (Sheffield: Sheffield Academic Press, 2001).

(b) Acts of the martyrs

T. D. Barnes, 'Legislation against the Christians', *Journal of Roman Studies* 58 (1968), 32–50.

G. W. Bowersock, *Martyrdom and Rome* (Cambridge: Cambridge University Press, 1995).

H. von Campenhausen, *Die Idee des Martyriums in der alten Kirche* (Göttingen: Vanderhoeck & Ruprecht, 1964[2]).

H. Delehaye, *Les Passions des Martyrs et les genres littéraires* (Brussels: Société des Bollandistes, 1921).

G. Lazzati, *Gli sviluppi della litteratura sui martiri nei primi Quattro secoli* (Turin: Società Editrice Internazionale, 1956).

H. Musurillo, *Acts of the Christian Martyrs*, OECT (1972).

G. E. M. de Ste. Croix, 'Aspects of the "Great" Persecution', *HTR* 47 (1954), 75–113.

'Why Were the Early Christians Persecuted?', *Past and Present* 26 (1963), 6–38.

Chapter 5. The Apologists

Critical editions of Apologists by J. C. T. Otto, *Corpus Apologetarum* (9 vols, Jena, 1847–72); E. Goodspeed, *Die ältesten Apologeten* (Göttingen: Vanderhoeck & Ruprecht, 1914); in OECT with ET (Theophilus of Antioch, ed. R. M. Grant, 1970; Athenagoras, ed. W. R. Schoedel, 1972; Tatian, ed. M. Whittaker, 1982); and by M. Marcovitch (Justin: PTS 38 (1994); Athenagoras: PTS 31 (1990); Tatian: PTS 43 (1995).

Critical editions of Melito and *Peri Pascha* by O. Perler (SC 123, 1966) and S. G. Hall (OECT, 1979).

L. W. Barnard, *Justin Martyr: His Life and Thought* (Cambridge: Cambridge University Press, 1967).

Athenagoras: A Study in Second Century Christian Apologetic (Paris: Beauchesne, 1972).

A. Casamassa, *Gli apologisti greci* (Rome: Lateranum, 1944).

H. Chadwick, 'Justin Martyr's Defence of Christianity', *Bulletin of the John Rylands Library* 47 (1965), 275–97 (= item VII in *History and Thought of the Early Church*).

L. Cohick, *The Peri Pascha attributed to Melito of Sardis: setting, purpose, and sources*, Brown Judaic Studies (Providence, RI: Brown, 2000).

M. Edwards et al., *Apologetics in the Roman Empire: Pagans, Jews and Christians* (Oxford: Oxford University Press, 1999).

M. Elze, *Tatian und seine Theologie* (Göttingen: Vandenhoeck & Ruprecht, 1960).

R. Grant, *Greek Apologists of the Second Century* (Philadelphia: Westminster and London: SCM, 1988).

P. Keresztes, 'The Literary Genre of Justin's First Apology', *VigChr* 19 (1965), 99–110.

K. W. Noakes, *Studies in Melito of Sardis: some attempts to set Melito in his second century Asia Minor context*, Oxford Faculty of Theology, DPhil thesis, 1971.

E. F. Osborn, *Justin Martyr*, Beiträge zur historischen Theologie 47 (Tübingen: Mohr, 1973).
The Emergence of Christian Theology (Cambridge: Cambridge University Press, 1993).

M. Pellegrino, *Gli apologisti greci del II secolo* (Rome: Anonima Veritas editrice, 1947).

W. Petersen, *Tatian's Diatessaron*, Supplements to *VigChr* 25 (Leiden: Brill, 1994).

J. Pinell, OSB, *Il mistero della pasqua in Melitone di Sardi* (Rome: Pontificio Istituto Liturgico, 1970).

A. Puech, *Les apologistes grecs du IIe siècle de notre ère* (Paris: Hachette, 1912).

O. Skarsaune, *The Proof from Prophecy. A Study in Justin Martyr's Proof-Text Tradition: Text-Type, Provenance, Theological Profile* (Leiden: Brill, 1987).

A. Stewart-Sykes, *On Pascha: with the fragments of Melito and other material related to the Quartodecimans*, PPS (Crestwood, NY: St Vladimir's Seminary Press, 2001).

Chapter 6. Irenaeus of Lyon

Critical editions of Adversus Haeresis by W. W. Harvey (Cambridge, 1857) and A. Rousseau, L. Doutreleau et al. (SC 100, 152–3, 210–11, 263–4, 293–4, 1965–82).

English translations of *Proof of the Apostolic Preaching* by J. P. Smith (ACW 16, 1952) and John Behr (PPS 1997).

Y. de Andia, *'Homo Vivens'. Incorruptibilité et divinisation de l'homme selon Irénée de Lyon* (Paris: Études augustiniennes, 1986).

J. Behr, *Asceticism and Anthropology in Irenaeus and Clement*, OECS (Oxford: Oxford University Press, 2000).

A. Benoit, *Saint Irénée. Introduction à l'étude de sa théologie* (Paris: Presses universitaires de France, 1960).

G. Bentivegna, *Economia di salvezza e creazione nel pensiero di S. Ireneo* (Rome: Herder, 1973).

Y.-M. Blanchard, *Aux sources du canon: le témoinage d'Irénee* (Paris: Les Éditions du Cerf, 1993).

R. Grant, *Irenaeus of Lyons*, ECF (London: Routledge, 1997).

S. Lundström, *Die Überlieferung der lateinischen Irenaeusübersetzung* (Uppsala and Stockholm: Almqvist & Wiksell International, 1985).

D. Minns, *Irenaeus* (London: Geoffrey Chapman and Washington, DC: Georgetown University Press, 1994).

Part II. The Third Century

General

G. Bardy, *Paul de Samosate*, Spicilegium sacrum Lovaniense études et documents, 4 (Louvain: Spicilegium sacrum bureaux, 1923).

Alexander Beck, *Römisches Recht bei Tertullian und Cyprian* (Halle: Max Niemeyer Verlag, 1930).

Peter Brown, *Power and Persuasion in Late Antiquity* (Madison, WI: University of Wisconsin Press, 1992).

H. Chadwick, 'Philo and the Beginning of Christian Thought', in A. H. Armstrong, ed., *The Cambridge History of Later Greek and Early Medieval Philosophy* (Cambridge: Cambridge University Press, 1967).

Kate Cooper, *The Virgin and the Bride* (Cambridge, MA: Harvard University Press, 1996).

P. Cox, *Biography in Late Antiquity*, TCH 5 (Berkeley: University of California Press, 1983).

Suzanne Dixon, *The Roman Mother* (Norman: University of Oklahoma Press, 1988).

Ute E. Eisen, *Arztsträgerinnen im frühen Christentum* (Göttingen: Vandenhoeck & Ruprecht, 1996).

I. Hadot, 'Les introductions aux commentaires exégétiques chez les auteurs néoplatoniciens et les auteurs chrétiens', in M. Tardieu, ed., *Les règles de l'interprétation* (Paris: Cerf, 1987), 99–122.

H. Hagemann, *Die Römische Kirche* (Freiburg: Herder, 1864).

Judith Hallett, *Fathers and Daughters in Roman Society* (Princeton: Princeton University Press, 1984).

E. Havelock, *Preface to Plato* (Cambridge, MA: Belknap Press, 1963).

R. E. Heine, *The Montanist Oracles and Testimonia*, Patristic Monograph Series 14 (Macon, GA: The Philadelphia Patristic Foundation Ltd, 1989).

'The Christology of Callistus', *JTS* n.s. 49 (1998), 56–91.

Elisabeth Herrmann, *Ecclesia in Re Publica* (Frankfurt: Peter D. Lang, 1980).

Theodore Klauser, 'Bischöfe als staatliche Prokuratoren im dritten Jahrhundert?' *Jahrbuch fur Antike und Christentum*, Jahrgang 14 (1971), 140–9.

R. Lamberton, *Homer the Theologian: Neoplatonist Allegorical Reading and the Growth of the Epic Tradition*, TCH 9 (Berkeley: University of California Press, 1986).

F. Loofs, *Paulus von Samosata*, TU 44.5 (1924).

J. R. Lyman, *Christology and Cosmology*, Oxford Theological Monographs (Oxford: Clarendon Press, 1993).

A. McGowan, *Ascetic Eucharists. Food and Drink in Early Christian Ritual Meals*, OECS (Oxford: Clarendon Press, 1999).

F. Millar, 'Paul of Samosata, Zenobia and Aurelian: The Church, Local Culture and Political Allegiance in Third-Century Syria', *Journal of Roman Studies* 61 (1971), 1–17.

P. Nautin, *Lettres et écrivains chrétiens des IIe et IIIe siècles* (Paris, 1961).

F. W. Norris, 'Paul of Samosata: Procurator Ducenarius', *JTS* n.s. 34 (1984), 50–70.

Giorgio Otranto, 'Note sul sacerdozio femminile nell'antichità in margine a una testimonianze di Gelasio', *Vetera Christianorum* 19 (1982), 341–60.

Judith Perkins, *The Suffering Self* (New York: Routledge, 1995).

T. E. Pollard, *Johannine Christology and the Early Church* (Cambridge: Cambridge University Press, 1970).

Amy Richlin, 'Carrying Water in a Sieve: Class and Body in Roman Women's Religion', Karen King, in ed., *Women and Goddesses* (Minneapolis: Fortress Press, 1997), 330–74.

H. de Riedmatten, *Les actes du procès de Paul de Samosate*, Paradosis 6 (Fribourg: Éditions St-Paul, 1952).

J. B. Rives, *Religion and Authority in Ancient Carthage* (Oxford: Clarendon Press, 1995).
Mary Ann Rossi, 'Priesthood, Precedent and Prejudice', *Journal of Feminist Studies in Religion* 7 (Spring 1991), 73–94.
R. L. Sample, 'The Messiah as Prophet: The Christology of Paul of Samosata', Northwestern University, dissertation, 1977.
A. Smith, *Porphyry's Place in the Neoplatonic Tradition* (The Hague: M. Nijhoff, 1974).
Karen Jo Torjesen, *When Women Were Priests* (San Francisco: HarperSanFrancisco, 1995).
R. Walzer, *Galen on Jews and Christians* (Oxford: Clarendon Press, 1949).
P. Widdicombe, *The Fatherhood of God from Origen to Athanasius*, Oxford Theological Monographs (Oxford: Clarendon Press, 1994).
R. Williams, 'Does It Make Sense To Speak of Pre-Nicene Orthodoxy?', R. Williams, ed., *The Making of Orthodoxy* (Cambridge: Cambridge University Press, 1989).

Chapter 11. The Alexandrians

Critical editions of Clement and Origen in GCS.
Y. Baer, 'Israel, the Christian Church, and the Roman Empire', *Scripta Hierosolymitana* 7 (1961), 79–149.
G. Bardy, 'Aux origines de l'école d'Alexandrie', *RechSR* 27 (1937), 65–90.
R. M. Berchman, *From Philo to Origen*, Brown Judaic Studies 69 (Chico: Scholars Press, 1984).
J. Bernard, *Die apologetische Methode bei Klemens von Alexandria* (Leipzig: St. Benno-Verlag, 1968).
H. Bietenhard, *Caesarea, Origenes und die Juden* (Stuttgart: W. Kohlhammer, 1974).
C. Bigg, *The Christian Platonists of Alexandria* (Oxford: Clarendon Press, 1913[2]).
R. P. Casey, *The Excerpta ex Theodoto of Clement of Alexandria*. Studies and Documents 1 (London: Christophers, 1934).
H. Chadwick, 'Rufinus and the Tura Papyrus of Origen's Commentary on Romans', *JTS* n.s. 10 (1959), 10–42.
Early Christian Thought and the Classical Tradition (Oxford: Clarendon Press, 1966).
H. Chadwick, trans. Origen, *Contra Celsum* (Cambridge: Cambridge University Press, 1965).
E. A. Clark, *Clement's Use of Aristotle* (New York: Mellen, 1977).
A. H. Criddle, 'On the Mar Saba Letter Attributed to Clement of Alexandria', *Journal of Early Christian Studies* 3 (1995), 215–20.
H. Crouzel, *Origène et la «connaissance mystique»* (Bruges: Desclée de Brouwer, 1961).
Origène et la philosophie (Paris: Aubier, 1962).
'Origène s'est-il en Cappadoce pendant la persécution de Maximin le Thrace?', *BLE* 64 (1963), 195–203.
Bibliographie critique d'Origène. Instrumenta Patristica 8 (Steenbrugis: Abbatia s. Petri, 1971).
Bibliographie critique d'Origène. Supplement 1. Instrumenta Patristica 8 A. (Steenbrugis: Abbatia s. Petri, 1982).
Origen, ET of *Origène* (Paris: Lethielleux, 1985) by A. S. Worrall (Edinburgh: T & T Clark, 1989).
H. Crouzel and M. Simonetti, eds, Origène, *Traité des Principes*, SC 252 (1978), SC 253 (1978), SC 268 (1980), SC 269 (1980), and SC 312 (1984).

J. Daniélou, *Origen*, ET of *Origène* (Paris: La Table Ronde, 1948), by W. Mitchell (New York: Sheed and Ward, 1955).

D. Dawson, *Allegorical Readers and Cultural Revision in Ancient Alexandria* (Berkeley: University of California Press, 1992).

'Allegorical Reading and the Embodiment of the Soul in Origen', in L. Ayres and G. Jones, eds, *Christian Origins: Theology, Rhetoric and Community* (London and New York: Routledge, 1998).

G. Dorival, 'Remarques sur la forme du Peri Archôn', *Origeniana*, I, 33–45.

E. de Faye, *Clément d'Alexandrie* (Paris: Leroux, 1898).

Origène: sa vie, son oeuvre, sa pensée, 3 vols (Paris: Leroux, 1923, 1927, 1928).

J. Ferguson, *Clement of Alexandria* (New York: Twayne Publishers, 1974).

J. Ferguson, 'The Achievement of Clement of Alexandria', *Religious Studies* 12 (1976), 59–80.

trans., *Clement of Alexandria. Stromateis Books One to Three*, FC 85 (1991).

R. Girod, 'La traduction latine anonyme du commentaire sur Matthieu', *Origeniana*, I, 125–38.

Origène, Commentaire sur l'Évangile selon Matthieu, I, SC 162 (1970).

P. Gorday, *Principles of Patristic Exegesis*, Studies in the Bible and Early Christianity 4 (New York: Mellen, 1983).

R. Grant, 'Eusebius and His Lives of Origen', in *Forma Futuri: Studi in Onore del Cardinale Michele Pellegrino* (Turin, 1975), 647–9.

R. Greer, *Origen: An Exhortation to Martyrdom; Prayer; First Principles, book IV; Prologue to the Commentary on The Song of Songs; Homily XXVII on Numbers*, CWS (1979).

C. W. Griggs, *Early Egyptian Christianity*, Coptic Studies 2 (Leiden: Brill, 1990).

O. Guéraud and P. Nautin, *Origène, Sur la Pâque* (Paris, 1979).

T. Halton, 'Clement's Lyre: A Broken String, a New Song', *SecCent* 3 (1983), 177–99.

C. P. Hammond (Bammel), 'Notes on the Manuscripts and Editions of Origen's Commentary on the Epistle to the Romans in the Latin Translation by Rufinus', *JTS* n.s. 16 (1965), 338–57.

'Die fehlenden Bände des Römerbriefkommentars des Origenes', *Origeniana*, IV, 16–20.

Der Römerbriefkommentar des Origenes. Kritische Ausgabe der Übersetzung Rufins, Buch 1–3, 16 (Freiburg: Herder, Aus der Geschichte der lateinischen Bibel 1990), *Buch 4–6*, 33 (1997), *Buch 7–10*, 34 (1998).

R. P. C. Hanson, *Origen's Doctrine of Tradition* (London: SPCK, 1954).

M. Harl, *Origène et la fonction révélatrice du Verbe Incarné* (Paris: Seuil, 1958).

'Structure et cohérence du Peri Archôn', *Origeniana*, I, 11–32.

M. Harl and N. de Lange, eds, *Origène: Philocalie, 1–20 et la lettre à Africanus*, SC 302 (1983).

R. E. Heine, *Origen: Homilies on Genesis and Exodus*, FC 71 (1982).

Origen: Commentary on the Gospel according to John, Books 1–10, FC 80 (1989),

Origen: Commentary on the Gospel according to John, Books 13–32, FC 89 (1993).

'Stoic Logic as Handmaid to Exegesis and Theology in Origen's Commentary on the Gospel of John', *JTS* n.s. 44 (1993), 90–117.

'Three Allusions to Book 20 of Origen's *Commentary on John* in Gregory Thaumaturgus's *Panegyric to Origen*', *SP* 26 (1993), 261–6.

'The Introduction to Origen's Commentary on John Compared with the Introductions to the Ancient Philosophical Commentaries on Aristotle', *Origeniana*, VI, 3–12.

The Commentaries of Origen and Jerome on St Paul's Epistle to the Ephesians, OECS (Oxford: Oxford University Press, 2002).

A. van den Hoek, *Clement of Alexandria and His Use of Philo in the Stromateis*, Supplements *VigChr* 3 (Leiden: Brill, 1988).

'How Alexandrian was Clement of Alexandria? Reflections on Clement and his Alexandrian Background', *HeyJ* 31 (1990), 179–94.

M. Hornschuh, 'Das Leben des Origenes und die Entstehung der alexandrinischen Schule,' *ZKG* 71 (1960), 1–25, 193–214.

A. Jakab, *Ecclesia Alexandrina. Evolution sociale et institutionnelle du christianisme alexandrin (IIe et IIIe siècles)*, Christianismes anciens, I (Berne etc.: Peter Lang, 2001).

É. Junod, 'Wodurch unterscheiden sich die Homilien des Origenes von seinen Kommentaren?', in E. Mühlenberg and J. van Oort, eds, *Predigt in der alten Kirche* (Kampen: Kok Pharos, 1994), 62–81.

C. Kannengiesser, 'Divine Trinity and the Structure of *Peri Archon*', in C. Kannengiesser and W. L. Petersen, eds, *Origen of Alexandria: His World and His Legacy* (Notre Dame: University of Notre Dame Press, 1988), 231–49.

R. Kimelman, 'Rabbi Yohanan and Origen on the Song of Songs: A Third-Century Jewish-Christian Disputation', *HTR* 73 (1980), 567–95.

H. Koch, *Pronoia und Paideusis* (Berlin: Walter de Gruyter, 1932).

N. R. M. de Lange, *Origen and the Jews* (Cambridge: Cambridge University Press 1976).

L. I. Levine, *Caesarea Under Roman Rule* (Leiden: Brill 1975).

B. Leyerle, 'Clement of Alexandria on the Importance of Table Etiquette', *JECS* 3 (1995), 123–41.

S. R. Lilla, *Clement of Alexandria: A Study in Christian Platonism and Gnosticism*, Oxford Theological Monographs (London: Oxford University Press, 1971).

J. C. McLelland, *God the Anonymous: A Study in Alexandrian Philosophical Theology* (Cambridge, MA: Philadelphia Patristic Foundation, 1976).

H. O. Maier, 'Clement of Alexandria and the Care of the Self', *Journal of the American Academy of Religions* 62 (1994), 719–45.

A. Méhat, *Étude sur les 'Stromates' de Clément d'Alexandrie*, Patristica Sorbonensia 7 (Paris: Éditions du Seuil, 1966).

P. Nautin, *Origène: Homélies sur Jérémie*, I, SC 232 (1976).

Origène: sa vie et son oeuvre (Paris: Beauchesne, 1977).

P. Nautin and M.-T. Nautin, *Origène: Homélies sur Samuel*, SC 328 (1986).

B. Neuschäfer, *Origenes als Philologe*, SBAW 18.1–2 (Basel: Reinhardt, 1987).

A. Orbe, 'Origenes y los Monarquianos', *Greg.* 72 (1991), 39–72.

Origeniana: Premier colloque international des études origéniennes (Bari, 1975) = *Origeniana*, I.

Origeniana Quarta, ed. L. Lies (Innsbruck, 1987) = *Origeniana*, IV.

Origeniana Sexta. Origène et la Bible. Origen and the Bible. Actes du Colloquium Origenianum Sextum, Chantilly, 30 août–3 septembre 1993, ed. G. Dorival and A. Le Boulluec (Leuven: Uitgeverij Peeters, 1995) = *Origeniana*, VI.

E. F. Osborn, *The Philosophy of Clement of Alexandria* (Cambridge: Cambridge University Press, 1957).

'Clement of Alexandria: A Review of Research, 1958–1982', *SecCent* 3 (1983), 219–44.

J. E. L. Oulton and H. Chadwick, eds, *Alexandrian Christianity*, LCC 2 (1954).

A. Outler, 'Origen and the *Regulae Fidei*', *SecCent* 4 (1984), 133–41.

V. Peri, *Omelie origeniane sui Salmi*, ST 289 (Vatican, 1980).
J. M. Rist, 'Beyond Stoic and Platonist: A Sample of Origen's Treatment of Philosophy (Contra Celsum: 4.62–70)', in H. Blume and F. Mann, eds, *Platonismus und Christentum: Festschrift für Heinrich Dörrie*, Jahrbuch für Antike und Christentum. Ergänzungsband 10 (Münster Westfallen: Aschendorff, 1983), 228–38.
L. Roberts, 'The Literary Form of the *Stromateis*', *SecCent* 1 (1981), 211–22.
J. Scherer, *Entretien d'Origène avec Héraclide et les évêques, ses collègues sur le Père, le Fils, et l'âme* (Cairo: Publications de la Société, Fouad Ier de Papyrologie, Textes et Documents IX, 1949).
Le commentaire d'Origène sur Rom. III.5–V.7 d'après les extraits du papyrus No 88748 du Musée du Caire et les fragments de la Philocalie et du Vaticanus Gr. 762 (Cairo: Institut français d'archéologie orientale, Bibliothèque d'Étude, 27, 1957).
Entretien d'Origène avec Héraclide, SC 67 (1960).
M. Smith, *Clement of Alexandria and a Secret Gospel of Mark* (Cambridge, MA: Harvard University Press, 1973).
The Secret Gospel (New York: Harper and Row, 1973).
'Clement of Alexandria and Secret Mark: The Score at the End of the First Decade', *HTR* 75 (1982), 449–61.
R. W. Smith, *The Art of Rhetoric in Alexandria* (The Hague: Martinus Nijhoff, 1974).
B. Steidl, 'Neue Untersuchungen zu Origenes' Peri Archon', *ZNW* 40 (1941).
J. W. Trigg, 'A Decade of Origen Studies', *Religious Studies Review* 7 (1981), 21–7.
Origen (Atlanta: John Knox, 1983).
E. E. Urbach, 'The Homiletical Interpretations of the Sages and the Expositions of Origen on Canticles, and the Jewish-Christian Disputation', *Scripta Hierosolymitana* 22 (1971), 247–75.
W. Völker, *Das Vollkommenheitsideal des Origenes* (Tübingen: Mohr, 1930).
H. J. Vogt, *Der Kommentar zum Evangelium nach Mattäus*, vol. I, BGL 18 (Stuttgart: Anton Hiersemann, 1983).
R. Williams, 'Angels Unawares: Heavenly Liturgy and Earthly Theology in Alexandria', *SP* 30 (1997), 350–63.

Chapter 12. The beginnings of Latin Christian literature

Critical edition of Tertullian in CCSL.
K. M. Abbott, 'Commodian and His Verse', in *Classical Studies Presented to Ben Edwin Perry*, Illinois Studies in Language and Literature 58 (Urbana: University of Illinois Press, 1969), 272–83.
T. D. Barnes, 'Tertullian's Scorpiace', *JTS* n.s. 20 (1969), 105–32.
Tertullian. A Historical and Literary Study (Oxford: Clarendon Press, 1971, 1985[2]).
G. L. Bray, *Holiness and the Will of God: Perspectives on the Theology of Tertullian* (London: Marshall, Morgan & Scott, 1979).
S. T. Carroll, 'An Early Church Sermon Against Gambling', *SecCent* 8 (1991), 83–95.
'Chronica Tertullianea', an annual annotated bibliography appearing in *Revue des Études Augustiniennes* since 1976 (from 1986 entitled 'Chronica Tertullianea et Cyprianea').
L. Countryman, 'Tertullian and the *Regula Fidei*', *SecCent* 2 (1982), 208–27.

C. B. Daly, *Tertullian the Puritan and His Influence* (Dublin, Blackrock: Four Courts Press, 1993).
J. Daniélou, 'La littérature latine avant Tertullien', *REL* 48 (1970), 357–75.
E. Evans, *Tertullian's Treatise Against Praxeas* (London: SPCK, 1948).
E. Ferguson, 'Canon Muratori: Date and Provenance,' *SP* 18 (1982), 677–83.
J.-C. Fredouille, *Tertullien et la conversion de la culture antique* (Paris: Études augustiniennes, 1972).
J.-C. Fredouille, ed., Tertullien, *Contre les Valentiniens*, I, SC 280 (1980).
G. M. Hahneman, *The Muratorian Fragment and the Development of the Canon* (Oxford: Clarendon Press, 1992).
C. Micaelli and C. Munier, eds, Tertullien, *La Pudicité*, SC 394 (1993).
J. Moingt, *Théologie trinitaire de Tertullien*, Théologie 68–70, 75 (Paris: Aubier, 1966–9).
T. P. O'Malley, *Tertullian and the Bible* (Nijmegen-Utrecht: Dekker & Van de Vegt, 1967).
A. P. Orbán, 'Die Frage der ersten Zeugnisse des Christenlateins', *VigChr* 30 (1976), 214–38.
E. Osborn, *Tertullian: First Theologian of the West* (Cambridge: Cambridge University Press, 1997).
G. Quispel, 'African Christianity before Minucius Felix and Tertullian', in J. den Boeft and A. H. M. Kessels, eds, *Actus* (Utrecht Instituut voor Klassieke Talen, 1982), 307–8.
D. Rankin, *Tertullian and the Church* (Cambridge: Cambridge University Press, 1995).
R. D. Sider, *Ancient Rhetoric and the Art of Tertullian* (Oxford: Oxford University Press, 1971).
'On Symmetrical Composition in Tertullian', *JTS* n.s. 24 (1973), 408–23.
'Approaches to Tertullian: A Study of Recent Scholarship', *SecCent* 2 (1982), 228–60.
H. Steiner, *Das Verhältnis Tertullians zur antiken Paideia* EOS-Verlag, (St. Ottilien: 1989).
A. C. Sundberg, Jr, 'Canon Muratori: A Fourth-Century List', *HTR* 66 (1973), 1–41.
J. C. Waszink, 'Observations on Tertullian's Treatise against Hermogenes', *VigChr* 9 (1955), 127–47.
'Tertullian's Principles and Methods of Exegesis', in W. R. Schoedel and R. L. Wilken, eds, *Early Christian Literature and the Classical Intellectual Tradition*, ThH 54 (Paris: Beauchesne, 1979), 17–31.

Chapter 13. Hippolytus, Ps.-Hippolytus and the early canons

H. Achelis, *Die Canones Hippolyti*, TU 6.4 (1891).
B. Botte, *La tradition apostolique de saint Hippolyte*, Liturgiewissenschaftliche Quellen und Forschungen 39 (Münster: Aschendorffsche Verlagsbuchhandlung, 1963).
H. Brakmann, 'Alexandreia und die Kanones des Hippolyt', *JAC* 22 (1979), 139–49.
P. Bradshaw, ed., and G. Bebawi, trans., *The Canons of Hippolytus*, AGLS 2 (Bramcote: Grove, 1987).
A. Brent, *Hippolytus and the Roman Church in the Third Century*, Supplements *VigChr* 31 (Leiden: Brill, 1995).
R. Butterworth, *Hippolytus of Rome: Contra Noetum*, Heythrop Monographs 2 (London: Heythrop College, 1977).
R. H. Connolly, *The So-called Egyptian Church Order and Derived Documents*, TS 8.4 (Cambridge, 1916).
R.-G. Coquin, *Les canons d'Hippolyte*, *PO* 31.2 (Paris: Firmin-Didot, 1966).

G. J. Cuming, *Hippolytus: A Text for Students*, AGLS 8 (Bramcote: Grove, 1991²).
G. Dix, *The Treatise on the Apostolic Tradition of St Hippolytus of Rome* I (London: SPCK, 1937); corrected edn: G. Dix and H. Chadwick (London: SPCK, 1968²).
J. Frickel, *Das Dunkel um Hippolyt von Rom* (Graz: Eigenverlag des Instituts für Ökumenische Theologie und Patrologie an der Universität Graz, 1988).
G. Garitte, *Traités d'Hippolyte sur David et Goliath, sur le Cantique des cantiques et sur l'Antéchrist*, CSCO 264, Scriptores Iberici 16 (1965), i–ii.
M. Lefèvre, Hippolyte, *Commentaire sur Daniel*, SC 14 (1947).
W. J. Malley, 'Four Unedited Fragments of the *De Universo* of the Pseudo-Josephus Found in the *Chronicon* of George Hamartolus (Coislin 305)', *JTS* n.s. 16 (1965), 13–25.
J. Mansfield, *Heresiography in Context: Hippolytus' Elenchos as a source for Greek philosophy*, Philosophia Antiqua 56 (Leiden: Brill, 1992).
M. Marcovich, *Hippolytus Refutatio Omnium Haeresium*, PTS 25 (1986).
S. N. Mouraviev, 'Hippolyte, Héraclite et Noët (Commentaire d'Hippolyte, Refut. omn. haer. IX 8–10)', *ANRW* II. 36. 6 (1992), 4375–402.
I. Mueller, 'Heterodoxy and Doxography in Hippolytus' "Refutation of All Heresies", *ANRW* II. 36. 6 (1992), 4310–74.
P. Nautin, *Hippolyte et Josipe* (Paris: Éditions du Cerf, 1947).
Hippolyte, Contre les hérésies: fragment, étude, et édition critique (Paris: Éditions du Cerf, 1949).
Le dossier d'Hippolyte et de Méliton dansles florilèges dogmatiques et chez les historiens modernes (Paris: Éditions du Cerf, 1953).
'Hippolytus', *EEC*, I, 383–5.
E. Norelli, *Ippolito. L'Anticristo*, Bibliotheca Patristica 10 (Florence: Nardini, 1987).
Nuove Ricerche su Ippolito, SEA 30 (Rome: Augustinianum, 1989).
C. Osborne, *Rethinking Early Greek Philosophy* (London: Duckworth, 1987).
E. Prinzivalli, 'Hippolytus, Statue of'. *EEC*, I, 385.
Ricerche su Ippolito, SEA 13 (Rome: Augustinianum, 1977).
M. Richard, 'Hippolyte de Rome', in *Opera Minora*, I (Turnhout / Leuven: Brepols / University of Leuven Press, 1976), 10, cols 531–71.
G. Schöllgen and W. Geerlings, *Didache, Zwölf-Apostel-Lehre; Traditio Apostolica, Apostolische Überlieferung* (Freiburg: Herder, 1991).
E. Schwartz, *Über die pseudoapostolische Kirchenordnung*, SWGS 6, (Strasbourg, 1910).
G. Vallée, *A Study in Anti-Gnostic Polemics* (Waterloo, Ontario, 1981).

Chapter 14. Cyprian and Novatian

Critical editions of Cyprian and Novatian in CCSL.
A. d'Alès, *Novatien: Étude sur la théologie Romaine au milieu du IIIe siècle* (Paris: Beauchesne, 1924).
M. Bévenot, *Cyprian: De Lapsis and De Ecclesiae Catholicae Unitate*, OECT (1971).
C. A. Bobertz, 'Cyprian of Carthage as Patron: A Social Historical Study of the Role of Bishop in the Ancient Christian Community of North Africa'. Yale University, dissertation, 1988.
'The Historical Context of Cyprian's *De Unitate*', *JTS* n.s. 41 (1990), 107–11.

G. W. Clarke, trans., *The Letters of St. Cyprian of Carthage*, ACW 43, 44, 46, 47, (New York: Newman, 1984–9).

R. J. DeSimone, *The Treatise of Novatian the Roman Presbyter on the Trinity*, *SEA* 4 (Rome: Augustinianum, 1970).

R. J. DeSimone, trans., *Novatian*, FC 67 (1974).

C. V. Groves, 'Cyprian of Carthage. His Understanding of Religious Leadership in the Controversy with the Lapsed'. University of Chicago Divinity School, dissertation, 1985.

H. Gülzow, *Cyprian und Novatian: Die Briefwechsel zwischen den Gemeinden in Rom und Karthago zur Zeit der Verfolgung des Kaisers Decius*, Beiträge zur historischen Theologie 48 (Tübingen: Mohr, 1975).

P. Monceaux, *Histoire littéraire de l'Afrique chrétienne*: II, *Saint Cyprien et son temps* (Paris: Leroux, 1902).

H. Montgomery, 'The Bishop Who Fled: Responsibility and Honour in Saint Cyprian', *SP* 21 (1989), 264–7.

M. M. Sage, *Cyprian*, Patristic Monograph Series 1 (Cambridge, MA: Philadelphia Patristic Foundation, 1975).

C. E. Straw, 'Cyprian and Mt 5:45: The Evolution of Christian Patronage', *SP* 18/3 (1990), 329–39.

M. Szarmach, '"Ad Donatum" des heiligen Cyprian als rhetorischer Protreptik', *Eos* 77 (1989), 289–97.

H. J. Vogt, *Coetus Sanctorum: der Kirchenbegriff des Novatian und die Geschichte seiner Sonderkirche*, Theophaneia 20 (Bonn: Hanstein, 1967).

'Cyprian – Hindernis für die Ökumene?', *Theologische Quartalschrift* 164 (1984), 1–15.

Chapters 15 and 33. The Syriac tradition

M. Albert, *Christianismes orientaux. Introduction a l'étude des langues et des littératures* (Paris: Éditions du Cerf, 1993), ch. 6.

S. Beggiani, *Early Syriac Theology* (Lanham, MD: University Press of America, 1983).

P. Bettiolo, 'Letteratura siriaca', in A. Quacquarelli, ed., *Complementi interdisciplinari di Patrologia* (Rome: Città Nuova, 1989), 503–603.

T. Bou Mansour, *La pensée symbolique de s. Ephrem le Syrien* (Kaslik: Université Saint Esprit, 1988).

La théologie de Jacques de Saroug, I–II (Kaslik: Université Saint Esprit, 1993, 2000).

S. P. Brock, *The Harp of the Spirit. Eighteen Poems of Saint Ephrem*, Studies Supplementary to Sobornost 4 (London: Fellowship of St Alban and St Sergius, 1983[2]).

The Syriac Fathers on Prayer and the Spiritual Life, Cistercian Studies Series 101 (Kalamazoo: Cistercian Publications, 1987).

Syriac Perspectives on Late Antiquity (London: Variorum, 1984).

'A Brief Guide to the Main Editions and Translations of the Works of St Ephrem', *The Harp: A Review of Syriac and Oriental Studies* 3 (1990), 7–29.

St Ephrem the Syrian. Hymns on Paradise, PPS (1990).

Studies in Syriac Christianity (Aldershot: Variorum, 1992).

The Luminous Eye. The Spiritual World Vision of St Ephrem, revised edn (Kalamazoo: Cistercian Publications, 1992).

Bride of Light. Hymns on Mary from the Syriac Churches (Kottayam: St Ephrem Ecumenical Research Institute, 1994).

From Ephrem to Romanos. Interactions between Syriac and Greek in Late Antiquity (Aldershot: Variorum, 1999).

P. Bruns, *Das Christusbild Aphrahats des Persischen Weisen*, Hereditas 4 (Bonn: Borengässer, 1990).

F. C. Burkitt, *Early Eastern Christianity* (London: John Murray, 1904).

J. H. Charlesworth, *The Odes of Solomon* (Oxford: Clarendon Press, 1973).

R. H. Connolly, *The Liturgical Homilies of Narsai*, TS 8, 1 (Cambridge: Cambridge University Press, 1909).

W. Cureton, *Ancient Syriac Documents* (London: Williams and Norgate, 1864; repr. Amsterdam: Oriental Press, 1967).

Spicilegium Syriacum (London: Rivingtons, 1855).

H. J. W. Drijvers, *The Book of the Laws of Countries* (Assen: Van Gorcum, 1965).

Bardaisan of Edessa (Assen: Van Gorcum, 1966).

East of Antioch. Studies in Early Syriac Christianity (London: Variorum, 1984).

History and Religion in Late Antique Syria (Aldershot: Variorum, 1994).

Mary Hansbury, *Jacob of Serug. On the Mother of God*, PPS (Crestwood, NY: St Vladimir's Seminary Press, 1998).

I. Hausherr, *Jean le Solitaire (Pseudo-Jean de Lycopolis). Dialogue sur l'âme et les passions des hommes*, OCA 120 (Rome: PIOS, 1939).

G. Howard, *The Teaching of Addai* (Chico: Scholars Press, 1981).

A. F. J. Klijn, *The Acts of Thomas*, Supplements to *Novum Testamentum* 5 (Leiden: Brill, 1962).

T. Kollamparampil, *Jacob of Serugh: Select Festal Homilies* (Rome: Centre for Indian and Inter-Religious Studies and Bangalore: Dharmaram, 1997).

Salvation in Christ According to Jacob of Serugh (Bangalore: Dharmaram, 2001).

T. Kronholm, *Motifs from Genesis 1–11 in the Genuine Hymns of Ephrem*, Coniectanea Biblica, OT Series 11 (Lund: C.W.K. Gleerup, 1978).

M. Lattke, *Die Oden Salomos in ihrer Bedeutung fur Neues Testament und Gnosis*, Orbis Biblicus et Orientalis 25/1–4 (Freiburg: Universitätsverlag and Göttingen: Vandenhoeck & Ruprecht, 1979–1998).

Oden Salomos. Text, Ubersetzung, Kommentar, Novum Testamentum et Orbis Antiquus 41/1– (Freiburg: Universitätsverlag and Göttingen: Vandenhoeck & Ruprecht, 1999–).

R. Lavenant, *Jean d'Apamée. Dialogues et Traités*, SC 311 (1984).

C. McCarthy, *Saint Ephrem's Commentary on Tatian's Diatessaron*, Journal of Semitic Studies Supplement 2 (Oxford: Oxford University Press, 1993).

K. E. McVey, *Ephrem the Syrian. Hymns*, CWS (1989).

E. G. Mathews and J. Amar, *St Ephrem the Syrian. Prose Works: Commentary on Genesis, Letter to Publius, Homily on our Lord*, FC 91 (1995).

B. M. Metzger, *Early Versions of the New Testament* (Oxford: Clarendon Press, 1977).

C. W. Mitchell, *S. Ephraim's Prose Refutations*, I–II (London: Williams and Norgate, 1912, 1921).

R. Murray, *Symbols of Church and Kingdom. A Study in Early Syriac Tradition* (Cambridge: Cambridge University Press, 1975).

G. Phillips, *The Doctrine of Addai the Apostle* (London: Trubner, 1876).
M.-J. Pierre, *Aphraate le sage persan. Les Exposés, I–II*, SC 349, 359 (1988, 1989).
U. Possekel, *Evidence of Greek Philosophical Concepts in the Writings of Ephrem the Syrian*, CSCO 580, Subsidia 102 (1999).
K. Valavanolickal, *The Use of the Gospel Parables in the Writings of Aphrahat and Ephrem* (Frankfurt a/M: Lang, 1996).
Aphrahat, Demonstrations, I (Changanassery: Higher Institute for Religious Studies, 1999).
A. Vööbus, *A History of Asceticism in the Christian Orient*, I–III, CSCO 184, 197, 500, Subsidia 14, 17, 81 (1958, 1960, 1988).
The School of Nisibis, CSCO 266, Subsidia 26 (1965).
Note: Bibliography on Syriac literature can conveniently be found in C. Moss, *Catalogue of Syriac Printed Books and Related Literature in the British Museum* (London: British Museum, 1962); and, for subsequent years, in S. P. Brock, *Syriac Studies. A Classified Bibliography (1960–1990)* (Kaslik: Université Saint Esprit, 1996); and 'Syriac Studies: a classified bibliography (1991–1995)', *Parole de l'Orient* 23 (1998), 242–350.

Part III. Foundation of a new culture: from Diocletian to Cyril

General

L. Ayres, *Nicaea and Its Legacy: An Approach to Fourth-Century Trinitarian Theology* (Oxford: Clarendon Press, 2004).
L. Ayres and G. Jones, eds, *Christian Origins. Theology, Rhetoric and Community* (London: Routledge, 1998).
R. S. Bagnall, *Egypt in Late Antiquity* (Princeton: Princeton University Press, 1993).
M. R. Barnes and D. H. Williams, eds, *Arianism after Arius. Essays on the Development of the Fourth-Century Trinitarian Controversies* (Edinburgh: T & T Clark, 1993).
T. D. Barnes, *New Empire of Diocletian and Constantine* (Cambridge, MA: Harvard University Press, 1982).
G. W. Bowersock, *Julian the Apostate* (London: Duckworth, 1978).
Hellenism in Late Antiquity (Cambridge: Cambridge University Press, 1990).
H. C. Brennecke, *Studien zur Geschichte der Homöer. Der Osten bis zum Ende der homöischen Reichskirche* (Tübingen: Mohr, 1988).
P. Brown, 'The Patrons of Pelagius: The Roman Aristocracy between East and West', *JTS* n.s. 21 (1970), 56–72 (reprinted in *Religion and Society*).
Religion and Society in the Age of Saint Augustine (London: Faber, 1972).
Society and the Holy in Late Antiquity (London: Faber, 1982).
Power and Persuasion in Late Antiquity. Towards a Christian Empire (Madison, WI: University of Wisconsin Press, 1992).
Authority and the Sacred (Cambridge: Cambridge University Press, 1995).
The Rise of Western Christendom. Triumph and Diversity, AD 200–1000, The Making of Europe (Oxford: Blackwell, 1996).
Virginia Burrus, *The Making of a Heretic: Gender Authority and the Priscillianist Controversy* (Berkeley: University of California Press, 1995).

Begotten, Not Made: Conceiving Manhood in Late Antiquity (Stanford: Stanford University Press, 2000).

Averil Cameron and P. Garnsey, eds, *The Cambridge Ancient History*, XIII: *The Late Empire, A.D. 337–425* (Cambridge: Cambridge University Press, 1998).

A. M. Casiday, 'Apatheia and Sexuality in the Thought of Augustine and Cassian', *St Vladimir's Theological Quarterly* 45 (2001), 359–94.

E. Caspar, *Geschichte des Papsttums*, II (Tübingen: Mohr, 1933).

C. N. Cochrane, *Christianity and Classical Culture* (Oxford: Clarendon Press, 1957).

C. Conybeare, *Paulinus Noster. Self and Symbols in the Letters of Paulinus of Nola*, OECT (2000).

B. E. Daley, 'Nature and the "Mode of Union": Late Patristic Models for the Personal Unity of Christ', in Gerald O'Collins et al., eds, *The Incarnation: An Interdisciplinary Symposium on the Incarnation of the Son of God* (Oxford: Clarendon Press, 2002), 164–96.

J. Daniélou, 'Eunome l'arien et l'exégèse néo-platonicienne du «Cratyle»', *Revue des etudes grecques* 69 (1956), 412–32.

J. Drinkwater and H. Elton, eds, *Fifth-Century Gaul: a Crisis of Identity?* (Cambridge: Cambridge University Press, 1992).

M. Edwards, ed. and trans., *Neoplatonic Saints. The Lives of Plotinus and Proclus by their Students*, TTH 35 (2000).

K. Fitschen, *Messalianismus und Antimessalianismus. Ein Beispiel ostkirchliche Ketzergeschichte* (Göttingen: Vandenhoeck & Ruprecht, 1998).

W. H. C. Frend, *The Donatist Church* (Oxford: Clarendon Press, 1952).

J. Geffcken, *Der Ausgang des griechisch-römischen Heidentums* (Heidelberg: C. Winter, 1929).

G. Greshake, *Gnade als konkrete Freiheit. Eine Untersuchung zur Gnadenlehre des Pelagius* (Mainz: Matthias-Grunwald-Verlag, 1972).

J. Gribomont, 'Le dossier des origines du messalianisme', in J. Fontaine and Ch. Kannengiesser, eds, *Epectasis. Mélanges patristiques offerts au Cardinal Jean Daniélou*, (Paris: Beauchesne, 1972), 611–25.

A. Grillmeier SJ and H. Bacht SJ, eds, *Das Konzil von Chalkedon*, 3 vols (Würzburg: Echter-Verlag, 1951–4).

R. Gryson, ed., *Scolies ariennes sur le Concile d'Aquilée*, SC 267 (1980).

R. P. C. Hanson, *The Search for the Christian Doctrine of God. The Arian Controversy 318–381* (Edinburgh: T & T Clark, 1988).

M. A. G. Haykin, *The Spirit of God. The Exegesis of 1 & 2 Corinthians in the Pneumatomachian Controversy of the Fourth Century* (Leiden: Brill, 1994).

R. Herzog, *Die Bibelepik der lateinischen Spätantike. Formgeschichte einer erbaulichen Gattung*, Bd. 1 (Munich: Wilhelm Fink Verlag, 1975).

M. Humphries, *Communities of the Blessed. Social Environment and Change in Northern Italy, AD 200–400*, OECS (Oxford: Clarendon Press, 1999).

D. Hunter, 'Resistance to the Virginal Ideal in Late Fourth-Century Rome: The Case of Jovinian', *Theological Studies* 48 (1987), 45–64.

A. H. M. Jones, *The Later Roman Empire, 284–602*, 3 vols + maps (Oxford: Blackwell, 1964).

R. Klein, *Constantius II. und die christliche Kirche* (Darmstadt: Wissenschaftliche Buchgesellschaft, 1977).

T. A. Kopecek, *A History of Neo-Arianism*, Patristic Monographs Series 8 (Philadelphia: Philadelphia Patristic Foundation, 1979).

B. Kriegbaum, *Kirche der Traditoren oder kirche der Martyrer?: die vorgeschichte des Donatismus* (Innsbruck: Tyrolia, 1986).

C. Leyser, *Authority and Asceticism from Augustine to Gregory the Great* (Oxford: Oxford University Press, 2000).

J. T. Lienhard, 'The "Arian" Controversy: Some Categories Reconsidered', *Theological Studies* 48 (1987), 415–37.

Contra Marcellum: Marcellus of Ancyra and Fourth-Century Theology (Washington, DC: Catholic University of America, 1999).

'*Ousia* and *Hypostasis*: The Cappadocian Settlement and the Theology of "One *Hypostasis*" ', in S. Davis, D. Kendall SJ and G. O'Collins SJ, eds, *The Trinity* (Oxford: Oxford University Press, 1999), 99–121.

A. H. B. Logan, 'Marcellus of Ancyra and the Councils of 325: Antioch, Ancyra, and Nicaea', *JTS* n.s. 43 (1992), 428–46.

'Marcellus of Ancyra, Defender of the Faith against Heretics – and Pagans', *SP* 37 (2001), 550–64.

R. MacMullen, *Christianity and Paganism in the Fourth to Eighth Centuries* (New Haven and London: Yale University Press, 1997).

R. A. Markus, 'Christianity and Dissent in Roman Africa: changing perspectives in recent work', *SCH* 9 (1972), 21–36.

Christianity in the Roman world (London: Thames and Hudson, 1974).

From Augustine to Gregory the Great (London: Variorum Reprints, 1983).

The End of Ancient Christianity (Cambridge: Cambridge University Press, 1990).

'Donatus, Donatism', in A. Fitzgerald, ed., *Augustine through the Ages: An Encyclopedia* (Grand Rapids, MI: Eerdmans, 1999) 284–7.

H.-I. Marrou, *Saint Augustin et la fin de la culture antique* (Paris: E de Boccard, 1938; with *Retractatio*, 1946).

J. E. Merdinger, *Rome and the African Church in the Time of Augustine* (New Haven and London: Yale University Press, 1997).

A. Momigliano, ed., *The Conflict between Paganism and Christianity in the Fourth Century* (Oxford: Clarendon Press, 1963).

E. Mühlenberg, *Apollinarius von Laodicea* (Göttingen: Vandenhoek & Ruprecht, 1969).

F. G. Nuvolone and A. Solignac, 'Pelage et Pelagianisme', *DSp* XII. 2 (1987), 2889–924.

J. O'Keefe, 'Impassible Suffering? Divine Passion and Fifth-Century Christology', *Theological Studies* 58 (1997), 39–60.

E. Rébillard and C. Sotinel, eds, *L'Évêque dans la cité du IVe au Ve siècle*, (Rome: École française de Rome, 1998).

B. R. Rees, *Pelagius: a Reluctant Heretic* (Woodbridge: The Boydell Press, 1988).

The Letters of Pelagius and His Followers (Woodbridge: The Boydell Press, 1991).

A. M. Ritter, *Das Konzil von Konstantinopel und sein Symbol. Studien zur Geschichte und Theologie des 2. Ökumenischen Konzils* (Göttingen: Vandenhoek & Ruprecht, 1965).

P. Rousseau, *Ascetics, Authority and the Church* (Oxford: Oxford University Press, 1978).

Michele Renee Salzman, *On Roman Time. The Codex-Calender of 354 and the Rhythms of Urban Life in Late Antiquity*, TCH 17 (Berkeley / Los Angeles / Oxford: University of California Press, 1990).

R. V. Sellers, *Two Ancient Christologies* (London and New York: SPCK, 1940).

The Council of Chalcedon (London: SPCK, 1953).
H. J. Sieben SJ, *Das Konzilsidee der alten Kirche*, Konziliengeschichte, Reihe B: Untersuchungen (Paderborn and Zurich: Ferdinand Schöningh, 1979).
M. Simonetti, *Studi sull' Arianesimo*, Verba Seniorum n.s. 5 (Rome: Editrice Studium, 1965).
La Crisi ariana nel IV secolo, Studia Ephemeridis «Augustinianum» 11 (Rome: Institutum Patristicum «Augustinianum», 1975).
C. Stewart OSB, *'Working the Earth of the Heart': The Messalian Controversy in History, Texts and Language to AD 431* (Oxford: Clarendon Press, 1991).
M. Tetz, 'Ein enzyklisches Schreiben der Synode von Alexandrien (362)', *ZNW* 79 (1988), 262–81.
F. R. Trombley, *Hellenic Religion and Christianization c.370–529*, 2 vols (Leiden: Brill, 1993, 1995).
R. P. Vaggione, *Eunomius of Cyzicus and the Nicene Revolution*, OECS (Oxford: Clarendon Press, 2000).
M. Vinzent, *Asterius von Kappadokien: Die Theologische Fragmente. Einleitung, Kritischer Text, Ubersetzung und Kommentar* (Leiden: Brill, 1993).
L. R. Wickham, 'The *Syntagmation* of Aetius the Anomean', *JTS* n.s.19 (1968), 532–69.
'Pelagianism in the East', in Rowan Williams, ed., *The Making of Orthodoxy* (Cambridge: Cambridge University Press, 1989), 200–13.
R. Williams, *Arius. Heresy and Tradition* (London: DLT, 1987; 2nd edn, revised with appendix, London: SCM, 2001).
F. M. Young, 'The God of the Greeks and the Nature of Religious Language', in W. R. Schoedel and R. Wilken, eds, *Early Christian Literature and the Greek Intellectual Tradition: Festschrift for R. M. Grant*, Théologie Historique 53 (Paris: Beauchesne, 1980).
From Nicaea to Chalcedon (London: SCM, 1983).
'The Rhetorical Schools and Their Influence on Patristic Exegesis', in R. Williams, ed., *The Making of Orthodoxy. Essays in honour of Henry Chadwick* (Cambridge: Cambridge University Press, 1989), 182–99.
'Exegetical Method and Scriptural Proof: the Bible in Doctrinal Debate', *SP* 24 (1989), 291–304.
'*Paideia* and the Myth of Static Dogma', in S. Coakley and D. Pailin, eds, *The Making and Remaking of Christian Doctrine: Essays in Honour of Maurice Wiles* (Oxford: Clarendon Press, 1993), 265–83.
'The Fourth-century Reaction against Allegory', *SP* 30 (1997), 120–5.

Chapter 22. Arnobius and Lactantius

Critical editions of Arnobius in CSEL, and of Lactantius in CSEL and SC.
T. D. Barnes, 'Lactantius and Constantine', *Journal of Roman Studies* 63 (1973), 29–46.
F. J. Bryce, 'Lactantius' *De Ave Phoenice* and the Religious Policy of Constantine the Great', *SP* 19 (1989), 13–19.
The Library of Lactantius, Harvard Dissertations in Classics (New York: Garland Press, 1990).
V. Buchheit, 'Goldene Zeit und Paradies auf Erden (Laktanz, *Inst.* 5, 5–8)', *Würzburger Jahrbucher für Altertumswissenschaft* n.f. 4 (1978), 161–85, 5 (1979), 219–35.
P. Courcelle, 'Les sages de Porphyre et les "viri novi" d'Arnobe', *REL* 31 (1953), 257–71.

V. Fáberga, 'Die chiliastiche Lehre des Laktanz: methodische und theologische Voraussetzungen und religionsgeschichtlicher Hintergrund', *JAC* 17 (1974), 126–46.

A.-J. Festugière, 'La Doctrine des "viri novi" sur l'Origine et le Sort des âmes' in *Hermétisme et mystique païenne* (Paris: Aubier-Montaigne, 1967), 261–312.

J. Fontaine and M. Perrin, eds, *Lactance et son temps: recherches actuelles*, Théologie historique 48 (Paris: Beauchesne, 1978).

E. Heck, *Die dualistischen Zusätze und die Kaiseranreden bei Lactantius. Untersuchungen zur Textgeschichte der Divinae Institutiones und der Schrift De Opificio Dei*, Abhandlungen der Heidelberger Akademie der Wissenschaften, Phil.-hist. Klasse 1972/2.

'Die dualistischen Zusätze und die Kaiseranreden bei Lactantius', *SP* 13/ TU 116 (1975), 185–8.

V. Loi, *Lattanzio nella storia della linguaggio e del pensiero teologico preniceno* (Zurich: Pas-Verlag, 1970).

G. E. McCracken, *Arnobius of Sicca: The Case Against the Pagans*, ACW 7, 8 (1949).

P. McGuckin, 'The Non-Cyprianic Scripture Texts in Lactantius' *Divinae Institutiones*', *VigChr* 36 (1982), 145–63.

P. Monat, *Lactance et la Bible: une propédeutique latine à la lecture de la Bible dans l'Occident constantinien*, 2 vols (Paris: Études augustiniennes, 1982).

O. Nicholson, 'The Source of the Dates in Lactantius's Divine Institutes', *JTS* n.s. 36 (1985), 291–310.

'Flight in Persecution as Imitation of Christ: Lactantius, *Divine Institutes* IV, 18, 1–2', *JTS* n.s. 30 (1989), 48–65.

R. M. Ogilvie, *The Library of Lactantius* (Oxford: Clarendon Press, 1978).

M. Perrin, *L'homme antique et chrétien: l'anthropologie de Lactance*, Théologie historique 59 (Paris: Beauchesne, 1981).

R. Pichon, *Lactance: étude sur le mouvement philosophique et religieux sous le règne de Constantin* (Paris: Hachette, 1901).

P. A. Roots, 'The *De Opificio Dei*: the Workmanship of God and Lactantius', *Classical Quarterly* 37 (1982), 466–86.

M. B. Simmonds, *Arnobius of Sicca: Religious Conflict and Competition in the Age of Diocletian*, OECS (Oxford: Oxford University Press, 1995).

J. Spiegl, 'Zum Kirchenbegriff des Laktanz', *Römische Quartalschrift* 65 (1970), 15–28.

J. Stevenson, 'The Life and Literary Activity of Lactantius', *SP* 1/TU 63 (1957), 661–71.

A. Wlosok, *Laktanz und die philosophische Gnosis: Untersuchungen zu Geschichte und Terminologie der gnostischen Erlosungsvorstellung* (Heidelberg: C. Winter, 1960).

Chapter 23. Eusebius and the birth of church history

Critical editions of the Greek Church historians in GCS.

H. Attridge and G. Hata, eds, *Eusebius, Christianity, and Judaism* (Leiden: Brill, 1992).

T. D. Barnes, 'The Composition of Eusebius' *Onomasticon*', *JTS* n.s. 26 (1975), 412–15.

Constantine and Eusebius (Cambridge, MA: Harvard University Press, 1981).

G. Chesnut, *The First Christian Histories: Eusebius, Socrates, Sozomen, Theodoret, and Evagrius* (Paris: Beauchesne, 1977).

B. Croke, *Christian Chronicles and Byzantine History, 5th–6th Centuries* (Aldershot: Variorum, 1992).

R. Grant, *Eusebius as Church Historian* (Oxford: Clarendon Press, 1980).
M. J. Hollerich, *Eusebius of Caesarea's* Commentary on Isaiah, OECS (Oxford: Clarendon Press, 1999).
A. Kofsky, *Eusebius of Caesarea against Paganism* (Leiden: Brill, 2000).
H. J. Lawlor, *Eusebiana* (Oxford: Clarendon Press, 1912).
H. J. Lawlor and J. E. L. Oulton, *Eusebius of Caesarea: The Ecclesiastical History and Martyrs of Palestine*, 2 vols (London: SPCK, 1928).
H. Leppin, *Von Constantin dem Grossen zu Theodosius II : das christliche Kaisertum bei den Kirchenhistorikern Socrates, Sozomenus und Theodoret* (Göttingen: Vandenhoeck & Ruprecht, 1996).
E. des Places, *Eusèbe de Césarée commentateur. Platonisme et écriture sainte*, Théologie Historique 63 (Paris: Beauchesne, 1982).
T. Urbainczyk, *Socrates of Constantinople: historian of church and state* (Ann Arbor, MI: University of Michigan Press, 1997).
D. S. Wallace-Hadrill, *Eusebius of Caesarea* (London: Mowbray, 1960).
G. A. Williamson, revised with introduction and notes by A. Louth: Eusebius, *The History of the Church* (Harmondsworth: Penguin, 1989²).

Chapter 24. The fourth-century Alexandrians: Athanasius and Didymus

Critical edition of Athanasius for the Berlin Academy, begun by H. G. Opitz, still in progress, Berlin, 1934ff. Critical edition of *De Trinitate* by J. Hönscheid and I. Seiler (Beiträge zur klassischen Philologie, 44, 52, etc., Meisenheim am Glam, 1975ff.), and of the commentaries on Zechariah and Genesis in SC. For further details see *CPG* and *ODCC*.
K. Anatolios, *Athanasius. The Coherence of His Thought* (London: Routledge, 1998).
D. Arnold, *The Early Episcopal Career of Athanasius of Alexandria* (Notre Dame: University of Notre Dame Press, 1991).
G. Bardy, *Didyme l'Aveugle* (Paris: Beauchesne, 1910).
T. D. Barnes, *Athanasius and Constantius* (Cambridge, MA: Harvard University Press, 1993).
W. A. Bienert, *'Allegoria' und 'Anagoge' bei Didymus dem Blinden*, PTS 13 (1972).
D. Brakke, *Athanasius and the Politics of Asceticism* (Oxford: Clarendon Press, 1995).
A. Camplani, *Le Lettere festali di Atanasio di Alessandria: Studio storico-critico* (Rome: C.I.M., 1989).
W. Dietsche, *Didymus von Alexandrien als Verfasser der Schrift über die Seraphenvision* (Freiburg i. B.: Blümer, 1946).
Charles Kannengiesser, *Athanase d'Alexandrie, Évêque et Écrivain. Une lecture des traités* Contre les Ariens, Théologie Historique 70 (Paris: Beauchesne, 1983).
Charles Kannengiesser, ed., *Politique et Théologie chez Athanase d'Alexandrie*, Théologie Historique 27 (Paris: Beauchesne, 1974).
J. Leipoldt, *Didymus der Blinde von Alexandria*, TU 29.3 (1905).
A. Martin, *Athanase d'Alexandrie et l'église d'Égypte au IVᵉ siècle (328–373)* (Rome: École française de Rome, 1996).
A. Pettersen, *Athanasius and the Human Body* (Bristol: The Bristol Press, 1990).
Athanasius (London: Geoffrey Chapman, 1995).
E. Prinzivalli, *Didimo il Cieco e l'interpretazione dei Salmi* (Rome: L'Aquila, 1988).

J. Roldanus, *Le Christ et l'homme dans la théologie d'Athanase d'Alexandrie* (Leiden: Brill, 1968).

M. D. Sánchez, *El 'Comentario al Eclesiastés' de Dídimo Alejandrino* (Rome: Augustinianum, 1990).

J. H. Tigcheler, *Didyme l'Aveugle et l'exégèse allégorique, son commentaire sur Zacharie* (Nijmegen: Dekker & van de Vegt, 1977).

Chapter 25. Palestine: Cyril of Jerusalem and Epiphanius

Critical edition of Epiphanius in GCS.

A. Bonato, *La dottrina trinitaria di Cirillo di Gerusalemme*, *SEA* 18 (Rome: Augustinianum, 1983).

A. J. Doval, *Cyril of Jerusalem, Mystagogue: the authorship of the Mystagogic catecheses* (Washington, DC: Catholic University of America Press, 2001).

L. A. Eldridge, *The Gospel Text of Epiphanius* (Salt Lake City, UT: University of Utah, 1969).

R. Lipsius, *Zur Quellenkritik des Epiphanios* (Vienna: Braumüller, 1865).

B. Niederberger, *Die Logoslehre des hl. Cyrill von Jerusalem: Eine Dogmengeschichtliche Studie*, Forschungen zur christlichen Literatur- und Dogmengeschichte 14.4 (Paderborn: Schönigh, 1923).

A. Pourkier, *L'hérésiologie chez Epiphane de Salamine* (Paris: Beauchesne, 1992).

H. M. Riley, *Christian Initiation: a comparative study of the interpretation of the baptismal liturgy in the mystagogical writings of Cyril of Jerusalem, John Chrysostom, Theodore of Mopsuestia, and Ambrose of Milan* (Washington, DC: Catholic University of America Press, 1974).

B. Schultze, 'Filioque bei Epiphanius von Cypern', *Ostkirchliche Studien* 36 (1987), 281–300.

E. Yarnold, *Cyril of Jerusalem*, ECF (2000).

F. W. Young, 'Did Epiphanius Know What He Meant by Heresy?' *SP* 18 (1982), 199–205.

Chapter 26. The Cappadocians

Critical editions of some works of Basil in SC, of many of Gregory Nazianzen's homilies in SC, with a comprehensive critical edition just begun in CCSG, and of Gregory of Nyssa's works begun by W. Jaeger, still continuing (*Gregorii Nysseni Opera*, Leiden: Brill, 1958ff.).

D. L. Balás, *Μετουσία Θεοῦ. Man's Participation in God's Perfections according to Saint Gregory of Nyssa*, Studia Anselmiana 55 (Rome: Herder, 1966).

H. U. von Balthasar, *Présence et pensée. Essai sur la philosophie religieuse de Grégoire de Nysse* (Paris: Beauchesne, 1952).

M. R. Barnes, *The Power of God: Dunamis in Gregory of Nyssa's Trinitarian Theology* (Washington DC: Catholic University of America Press, 2000).

M. Canevet, *Grégoire de Nysse et l'herméneutique biblique. Étude des rapports entre le langage et la connaissance de Dieu* (Paris: Études Augustiniennes, 1983).

J. Daniélou, *Platonisme et théologie mystique. Doctrine spirituelle de Saint Grégoire de Nysse* (Paris: Aubier-Éditions Montaigne, 1944).

K. Demoen, *Pagan and Biblical Exempla in Gregory Nazianzen: A Study in Rhetoric and Hermeneutics* (Turnhout: Brepols, 1996).

P. J. Fedwick, ed., *Basil of Caesarea: Christian, Humanist, Ascetic*, 2 vols (Toronto: Pontifical Institute of Mediaeval Studies, 1981).

B. Gain, *L'Église de Cappadoce au IVe siècle d'après la correspondance de Basile de Césarée (330–379)* (Rome: PIOS, 1985).

J. Gaïth, *La conception de la liberté chez Grégoire de Nysse* (Paris: Vrin, 1953).

Jean Gribomont, *Histoire du texte des Ascétiques de saint Basile*, *BMus* 32 (Louvain: Publications universitaires, 1953).

R. E. Heine, *Perfection in the Virtuous Life: a study in the relationship between edification and polemical theology in Gregory of Nyssa's* De Vita Moysis, Patristic Monograph Series 2 (Philadelphia: Philadelphia Patristic Foundation, 1975).

Gregory of Nyssa's Treatise on the Inscriptions of the Psalms, OECS (Oxford: Clarendon Press, 1995).

C. Junck, ed. and trans., Gregor von Nazianz, *De Vita Sua* (Heidelberg: Carl Winters Universitäts Verlag, 1974).

J. A. McGuckin, *St Gregory of Nazianzus: An Intellectual Biography* (Crestwood, NY: St Vladimir's Seminary Press, 2001).

A. Meredith, *The Cappadocians* (London: Geoffrey Chapman and Crestwood, NY: St Vladimir's Seminary Press, 1995).

Gregory of Nyssa, ECF (1999).

C. Moreschini and D. A. Sykes, *St Gregory of Nazianzus: Poemata Arcana* (Oxford: Clarendon Press, 1997).

E. Mühlenberg, *Die Unendlichkeit Gottes bei Gregor von Nyssa* (Göttingen: Vandenhoeck & Ruprecht, 1966).

H. Musurillo, ed., *From Glory to Glory: Texts from Gregory of Nyssa's Mystical Writings* (New York: Charles Schribner's Sons, 1961).

F. W. Norris, with translations by L. Wickham and F. Williams, *Faith Gives Fullness to Reasoning. The Five Theological Orations of Gregory of Nazianzus* (Leiden: Brill, 1990).

B. Otis, 'Cappadocian Thought as a Coherent System', *Dumbarton Oaks Papers* 12 (1958), 95–124.

J. Pelikan, *Christianity and Classical Culture* (New Haven: Yale University Press, 1993).

P. Rousseau, *Basil of Caesarea*, TCH 20 (Berkeley: University of California Press, 1995).

R. Ruether, *Gregory of Nazianzus. Rhetor and Philosopher* (Oxford: Clarendon Press, 1969).

B. Sesboüé, *Saint Basile et La Trinité. Un acte théologique au IVe siècle* (Paris: Desclée, 1998).

T. Špidlík, C. Moreschini and G. Menestrina, eds, *Gregorio Nazianzeno teologo e scrittore* (Bologna: Edizioni Dehoniane Bologna, 1992).

R. Staats, *Gregor von Nyssa und die Messalianer*, PTS 8 (1968).

Walther Völker, *Gregor von Nyssa als Mystiker* (Wiesbaden: Franz Steiner Verlag, 1955).

C. White, ed. and trans., Gregory of Nazianzus, *Autobiographical Poems*, Cambridge Medieval Classics 6 (Cambridge: Cambridge University Press, 1996).

Chapter 27. Fourth-Century Latin writers: Hilary, Victorinus, Ambrose, Ambrosiaster

Critical editions in CSEL and CCSL, also in SC.

T. D. Barnes, 'Hilary of Poitiers on His Exile', *VigChr* 46 (1992), 129–40.

C. F. A. Borchardt, *Hilary of Poitiers' Role in the Arian Struggle* (The Hague: Martinus Nijhoff, 1966).

H. C. Brennecke, *Hilarius von Poitiers und die Bischofsopposition gegen Konstantius II: Untersuchungen zur dritten Phase des arianischen Streites* (337–361) (Berlin: Walter de Gruyter, 1984).

H. Chadwick, *Boethius: The Consolations of Music, Logic, Theology, and Philosophy* (Oxford: Clarendon Press, 1981).

S. Cooper, *Metaphysics and Morals in Marius Victorinus' Commentary on the Letter to the Ephesians* (New York: Peter Lang, 1995).

P. Courcelle, *Les Confessions de saint Augustin dans la tradition littéraire. Antécédents et postérité* (Paris: Études Augustiniennes, 1963).

Recherches sur les Confessions de saint Augustin, nouvelle édition augmentée et illustrée (Paris: Boccard, 1968).

Late Latin Writers and their Greek Sources, ET of *Les lettres grecques en Occident de Macrobe à Cassiodore* (Paris: Boccard, 1948[2]) by Harry E. Wedeck (Cambridge, MA: Harvard University Press, 1969).

I. J. Davidson, 'Ambrose's *De officiis* and the Intellectual Climate of the Late Fourth Century', *VigChr* 49 (1995), 315–16.

Ambrose: De Officiis, 2 vols, OECS (Oxford: Clarendon Press, 2002).

J. Doignon, *Hilaire de Poitiers avant l'exil* (Paris: Études Augustiniennes, 1971).

Y.-M. Duval, 'Vrais et faux problèmes concernant le retour d'exil d'Hilaire de Poitiers et son action en Italie en 360–363', *Athenaeum* n.s. 48 (1970), 251–75.

'L'influence des écrivains africains du IIIe chrétiens de l'Italie du nord dans la seconde moitié du IVe siècle', *Antichità Altoadriatiche* 5 (1974), 191–225.

Ambroise de Milan. XVIe Centenaire de son élection épiscopale (Paris: Études Augustiniennes, 1974).

'Formes profanes et formes bibliques dans les orations funèbres de saint Ambroise (*De excessu fratris* I) et les deux sources de la consolation chrétienne', *REL* 58 (1980), 370–402.

M. Edwards, ed. and trans., *Optatus: Against the Donatists*, *TTH* 27 (1997).

W. Erdt, *Marius Victorinus Afer, der erste lateinische Paulus Kommentator* (Frankfurt am Main: Peter Lang, 1980).

J. Fontaine, 'L'apport de la tradition poétique romaine à la formation de l'hymnodie latine chrétienne', *REL* 52 (1974), 318–55.

S. Gersh, *Middle Platonism and Neoplatonism. The Latin Tradition*, 2 vols (Notre Dame: University of Notre Dame Press, 1986).

P. Hadot, 'Platon et Plotin dans trois sermons de saint Ambroise', *REL* 34 (1956), 202–20.

'L'Image de la Trinité dans l'âme chez Victorinus et chez saint Augustin', *SP* 6/TU 81 (1962), 409–42.

Porphyre et Victorinus (Paris: Études Augustiniennes, 1968).

Marius Victorinus. Recherches sur sa vie et ses oeuvres (Paris: Études Augustiniennes, 1971).

O. Heggelbacher, *Vom römischen zum christlichen Recht. Iuristische Elemente in den Schriften des sog. Ambrosiaster* (Freiburg: Universitätsverlag, 1959).

'Beziehungen zwischen Ambrosiaster und Maximus von Turin?', *Freiburger Zeitschrift für Philosophie und Theologie* 41 (1994), 5–44.

P. Henry, 'The *adversus Arium* of Marius Victorinus: The First Systematic Exposition of the Doctrine of the Trinity', *JTS* n.s. 1 (1950), 42–55.

D. G. Hunter, '*On the Sin of Adam and Eve*: A Little-known Defense of Marriage and Child-bearing by Ambrosiaster', *HTR* 82 (1989), 283–99.

'The Paradise of Patriarchy: Ambrosiaster on Woman as (Not) God's Image', *JTS* n.s. 43 (1992), 447–69.

M.-H. Julien, 'Les Sources de la tradition ancienne des hymnes attribuées à Saint Ambroise', *Revue d'histoire des textes* 19 (1989), 57–189.

B. Lohse, 'Beobachtungen zum Paulus-Kommentar und zur Wiederentdeckung des Paulus in der lateinischen Theologie des vierten Jahrhunderts', in A. M. Ritter, ed., *Kerygma und Logos. Festschrift für Carl Andresen zum 70 Geburtstag* (Göttingen: Vandenhoeck & Ruprecht, 1979), 351–66.

N. McLynn, *Ambrose of Milan. Church and Court in a Christian Capital*, TCH 22 (Berkeley: University of California Press, 1994).

G. Madec, *Saint Ambroise et la philosophie* (Paris: Études augustiniennes, 1974).

C. Martini, *Ambrosiaster. De auctore, operibus, theologia* (Rome: Pontificium Athenaeum Antonianum, 1944).

'De ordinatione duarum Collectionum quibus Ambrosiastri "Quaestiones" traduntur', *Antonianum* 21 (1947), 23–48.

'Le recensione delle "Quaestiones Veteris et Novi Testamenti" dell'Ambrosiaster', *Ricerche di storia religiosa* 1 (1954), 40–62.

H. J. auf der Maur, *Das Psalmenverständnis des Ambrosius von Mailand* (Leiden: Brill, 1977).

E. P. Meijering, *Hilary of Poitiers on the Trinity. De Trinitate I, 1–19, 2, 3*, Philosophia Patrum 6 (Leiden: Brill, 1982).

G. Nauroy, 'La structure de *De Isaac vel anima* et la cohérence de l'allégorèse d'Ambroise de Milan', *REL* 63 (1985), 210–36.

C. W. Neumann, *The Virgin Mary in the Works of Saint Ambrose* (Fribourg: The University Press, 1962).

E. Plumer, 'The Influence of Marius Victorinus on Augustine's Commentary on Galatians', *SP* 33 (1970), 221–8.

F. J. E. Raby, *A History of Christian Latin Poetry* (Oxford: Clarendon Press, 1953[2]).

B. Ramsey, *Ambrose*, ECF (1997).

G. Raspanti, *Mario Vittorino esegeta di S. Paolo* (Palermo: L'epos società editrice, 1996).

H. Savon, *Saint Ambroise devant l'exégèse de Philon le juif* (Paris: Études augustiniennes, 1977).

'La première oraison funèbre de saint Ambroise (*De excessu fratris* I) et les deux sources de la consolation chrétienne', *Revue des études latines* 58 (1980), 370–402.

M. Simonetti, 'Note sulla struttura e la cronologia del *De Trinitate* di Ilario di Poitiers', *Studi Urbinati* 39 (1965), 274–300.

P. Smulders, 'Remarks on the Manuscript Tradition of the *De trinitate* of Saint Hilary of Poitiers', *SP* 3/TU 78 (1961), 129–38.

'Two Passages of Hilary's *Apologetica responsa* Rediscovered', *Bijdragen* 39 (1978), 234–43.

Hilary of Poitiers' Preface to his Opus historicum (Leiden: Brill, 1995).

A. Souter, *A Study of Ambrosiaster*, Texts and Studies 7 (Cambridge: Cambridge University Press, 1905).

The Earliest Latin Commentaries on the Epistles of St. Paul (Oxford: Clarendon Press, 1927).

C. P. E. Springer, 'The Concinnity of Ambrose's *Inluminans Altissimus*', in *Panchaia. Festschrift für Klaus Thraede*, Jahrbuch für Antike und Christentum, Ergänzungsband 22 (Münster: Aschendorff, 1995), 235–6.
H. J. Vogels, 'Ambrosiaster und Hieronymus', *RBen* 66 (1956), 14–19.
C. White, *Early Christian Latin Poets*, ECF (2000).
L. Wickham, *Hilary of Poitiers. Conflicts of Conscience and Law in the Fourth-century Church*, *TTH* 25 (1997).
D. H. Williams, 'A Reassessment of the Early Career and Exile of Hilary of Poitiers', *Journal of Ecclesiastical History* 42 (1991), 202–17.
'The Anti-Arian Campaigns of Hilary of Poiters and the "Liber contra Auxentium"', *Church History* 61 (1992), 7–22.
Ambrose of Milan and the End of the Arian-Nicene Conflicts, OECS (Oxford: Clarendon Press, 1995).
A. Wilmart, 'Le Dernier tractatus de S. Hilaire sur les psaumes', *RBen* 43 (1931), 277–83.
M. Zelzer, '*Plinius Christianus*: Ambrosius als Epistolograph', *SP* 23 (1989), 203–8.

Chapter 28. Jerome and Rufinus

No critical edition of Rufinus; critical edition of Jerome in CCSL (in progress).

J. Brochet, *Saint Jérome et ses ennemis: étude sur la querelle de Saint Jérome avec Rufin d'Aquilée et sur l'ensemble de son oeuvre polémique* (Paris: Fontemoing, 1906).
D. Brown, *Vir Trilinguis: a study in the biblical exegesis of Saint Jerome* (Kampen, The Netherlands: Kok Pharos, 1992).
E. Clark, *The Origenist Controversy: the cultural construction of an early Christian debate* (Princeton: Princeton University Press, 1992).
G. Fedalto, *Rufino di Concordia (345 c.–410/411): tra Oriente e Occidente* (Rome: Città Nuova, 1990).
Harald Hagendahl, *Latin Fathers and the Classics: A Study on the Apologists, Jerome and Other Christian Writers* (Göteborg: Almqvist & Wiksell, 1958).
C. P. Hammond Bammel, *Origeniana et Rufiniana* (Freiburg: Herder, 1996).
Pierre Jay, *L'exégèse de saint Jérôme d'après son Commentaire sur Isaïe* (Paris: Études Augustiniennes, 1985).
B. Jeanjean, *Saint Jérôme et l'hérésie* (Paris: Institut d'Études Augustiniennes, 1999).
J. N. D. Kelly, *Jerome. His Life, Writings and Controversies* (London: Duckworth, 1975).
P. Lardet, *L'Apologie de Jérôme contre Rufin: un commentaire*, Supp. *VigChr* 15 (Leiden: Brill, 1993).
F. X. Murray, *Rufinus of Aquileia (345–411): his life and works* (Washington, DC: Catholic University of America Press, 1945).
S. Rebenich, *Hieronymus und sein Kreis: prosopographische und sozialgeschichtliche Untersuchungen* (Stuttgart: Steiner, 1992).
Rufino di Concordia e il suo tempo, 2 vols (Udine: Arti grafiche friulane, 1987).
Storia ed esegesi in Rufino di Concordia (Udine: Arti grafiche friulane, 1992).
M. Wagner, *Rufinus, the Translator: a study of his theory and his practice as illustrated in his version of the Apologetica of St. Gregory Nazianzen* (Washington, DC: Catholic University of America Press, 1945).

Chapter 29. Augustine

Critical edition in CCSL, and with French translation and notes in *Bibliothèque Augustinienne* (Paris: Desclée de Brouwer, later volumes Études Augustiniennes), both still in progress.

Augustinus Magister: Congrès International Augustinienne, Paris 21–4 septembre 1954, 3 vols (Paris: Études augustiniennes, 1954–5).

G. Bonner, *St. Augustine of Hippo: Life and Controversies* (Norwich: Canterbury Press, 2002³).

P. Brown, *Augustine of Hippo: A Biography* (London: Faber, 2000; new edn with an epilogue).

J. Burnaby, *Amor Dei: A Study of the Religion of St Augustine* (Norwich: Canterbury Press, 1991; reissue with corrections of the London 1938 edition).

H. Chadwick, *Augustine* (Oxford: Oxford University Press, 1986).

P. Courcelle, *Les Confessions de saint Augustin dans la tradition littéraire. Antécédents et Póstérité* (Paris: Études Augustiniennes, 1963).

R. Dodaro and G. Lawless, eds, *Augustine and His Critics: essays in honour of Gerald Bonner* (London: Routledge, 2000).

D. F. Donnelly, *Augustine's 'De civitate Dei': An Annotated Bibliography of Modern Criticism, 1960–1990* (New York: Peter Lang, 1991).

J.-C. Guy, *Unité et structure logique de la «Cité de Dieu» de Saint Augustin* (Paris: Études Augustiennes, 1961).

C. Harrison, *Beauty and Revelation in the Thought of Saint Augustine* (Oxford: Clarendon Press, 1992).

Augustine: Christian Truth and Fractured Humanity (Oxford: Oxford University Press, 2000).

A. Fitzgerald, ed., *Augustine through the Ages: An Encyclopedia* (Grand Rapids, MI: Eerdmans, 1999).

S. Lancel, *St Augustine*, ET by Antonia Nevill (London: SCM Press, 2002, originally published Paris: Arthème Fayard, 1999).

G. Madec, *Le Dieu d'Augustin* (Paris: Cerf, 1998).

Petites études augustiniennes (Paris: Institut des études augustiniennes, 1994).

R. Markus, *Saeculum: History and Society in the Theology of St Augustine* (Cambridge: Cambridge University Press, 1970).

C. Mayer, ed., *Augustinus-Lexikon* (Basel: Schwabe, 1986–).

ed., *Homo spiritalis: Festgabe für Luc Verheijen zu seinem 70. Geburtstag* (Würzburg: Augustinus-Verlag, 1987).

G. O'Daly, *Augustine's Philosophy of Mind* (London: Routledge, 1987).

J. J. O'Donnell, *Augustine. Confessions*, 3 vols (Oxford: Clarendon Press, 1992).

O. O'Donovan, *The Problem of Self-Love in St Augustine* (New Haven and London: Yale University Press, 1980).

E. Plumer, *Augustine's Commentary on Galatians*, OECS (Oxford: Oxford University Press, 2002).

J. Rist, *Augustine: Ancient Thought Baptized* (Cambridge: Cambridge University Press, 1994).

Eugene TeSelle, *Augustine the Theologian* (London, 1970).

L. Verheijen, *Nouvelle approche de la Règle de saint Augustin* (Bégrolles-en-Mauges: Abbaye de Bellefontaine, 1988).

Chapter 30. John Chrysostom and the Antiochene School to Theodoret of Cyrrhus

Critical edition of many of Chrysostom's homilies in SC.
P. Allen and W. Mayer, *John Chrysostom*, ECF (2000).
M. V. Anastos, 'Nestorios was Orthodox', *Dumbarton Oaks Papers* 16 (1962), 117–39.
G. W. Ashby, *Theodoret of Cyrrhus as Exegete of the Old Testament* (Grahamstown: Rhodes University Press, 1972).
C. Baur, *John Chrysostom and His Time*, 2 vols, ET of *Der heilige Johannes Chrysostomus und seine Zeit* (Munich: Hueber, 1929–1930) by M. Gonzaga (Vaduz: Büchervertriebsanstalt, 1988²).
R. C. Chesnut, 'The Two *Prosopa* in Nestorius' *Bazaar of Heraclides*', *JTS* n.s. 29 (1978), 85–102.
R. Devreesse, *Essai sur Théodore de Mopsueste* (Città del Vaticano: Biblioteca apostolica vaticana, 1949).
G. H. Ettlinger, ed., Theodoret of Cyrus, *Eranistes* (Oxford: Clarendon Press, 1975).
A.-J. Festugière, *Antioche païenne et chrétienne* (Paris: Boccard, 1959).
R. A. Greer, *Theodore of Mopsuestia. Exegete and Theologian* (London: The Faith Press, 1961).
'The Image of God and the Prosopic Union in Nestorius' *Bazaar of Heraclides*', in R. A. Norris, ed., *Lux in Lumine. Essays to honor W. N. Pittenger* (New York: Seabury Press, 1966), 46–61.
The Captain of Our Salvation (Tübingen: Mohr, 1973).
J.-N. Guinot, *L'Éxégèse de Théodoret de Cyr* (Paris: Beauchesne, 1995).
J. N. D. Kelly, *Golden Mouth: the Story of John Chrysostom – Ascetic, Preacher, Bishop* (London: Duckworth, 1996).
H. de Lubac, *L'écriture dans la tradition* (Paris: Aubier-Montaigne, 1966).
M. Mitchell, *The Heavenly Trumpet: John Chrysostom and the art of Pauline interpretation* (Tübingen: Mohr-Siebeck, 2000).
F. Nau, trans., Nestorius, *Le Livre d'Héraclide de Damas* (Paris: Letouzey et Ané, 1910; reprinted Farnborough: Gregg International Publishers, 1969).
R. A. Norris, *Manhood and Christ. A Study in the Theology of Theodore of Mopsuestia* (Oxford: Clarendon Press, 1963).
M. Simonetti, 'Note sull'esegesi veterotestamentaria di Teodoro di Mopsuestia', *Vetera Christianorum* 1 (1977), 69–102.
R. Taft, SJ, *A History of the Liturgy of St John Chrysostom* (Rome: PIOS, 1975ff.).
R. Tonneau OP and R. Devreesse, *Les Homélies catéchetiques de Théodore de Mopsueste*, ST 145 (Città del Vaticano: Biblioteca Apostolica Vaticana, 1949).

Chapter 31. Cyril of Alexandria

Critical edition of much of Cyril by P. E. Pusey (Oxford: Clarendon Press, 1868–77); select letters in OECT, several works in SC.
M.-O. Boulnois, *Le paradoxe trinitaire chez Cyrille d'Alexandrie*. Collection d'Études Augustiennes, Série Antiquité 143 (Paris: Études Augustiniennes, 1994).
M. Diepen, *Aux origins de l'anthropologie de Saint Cyrille d'Alexandrie* (Bruges: Desclée de Brouwer, 1957).

A. Kerrigan, *St. Cyril of Alexandria, Interpreter of the Old Testament* (Rome: Pontificio Istituto Biblico, 1952).

J. Liébaert, *La Doctrine christologique de saint Cyrille d'Alexandrie avant la querelle nestorienne* (Lille: Facultés catholiques, 1951).

J. McGuckin, *St Cyril of Alexandria: The Christological Controversy* (Leiden: Brill, 1994).

S. A. McKinion, *Words, Imagery and the Mystery of Christ: A Reconstruction of Cyril of Alexandria's Christology*, Supp. *VigChr* 55 (Leiden: Brill, 2000).

G. Münch-Labacher, *Naturhaftes und geschichtliches Denken bei Cyrill von Alexandrien: die verschiedenen Betrachtungsweisen der Heilsverwirklichung in seinem Johannes-Kommentar*, Hereditas 10 (Bonn: Borengässer, 1996).

N. Russell, *Cyril of Alexandria*, ECF (2000).

L. Scipioni, *Nestorio e il concilio di Efeso* (Milan: Vita e pensiero, 1974).

E. Weigl, *Die Heilslehre des hl. Cyrill von Alexandrien* (Mainz: Kirchheim, 1905).

L. R. Wickham, ed. and trans., Cyril of Alexandria, *Selected Letters*, OECT (1983).

Chapter 32. Hagiography

P. Brown, *The Cult of the Saints* (London: SCM, 1981).

P. Cox, *Biography in Late Antiquity* (Berkeley / Los Angeles / London: University of California Press, 1983).

A. G. Elliott, *Roads to Paradise. Reading the Lives of the Early Saints* (Hanover, NH and London: Brown University Press, 1987).

S. J. Davis, *The Cult of St Thecla, A Tradition of Women's Piety in Late Antiquity*, OECS (Oxford: Clarendon Press, 2001).

H. Delehaye, *Les Légendes hagiographiques* (Brussels: Société des Bollandistes, 1905); ET from the 1955[4] edn, by D. Attwater, *The Legends of the Saints* (London, 1962).

T. J. Heffernan, *Sacred Biography. Saints and Their Biographers in the Middle Ages* (New York: Oxford University Press, 1988).

J. Howard-Johnston and P. A. Hayward, *The Cult of Saints in Late Antiquity and the Early Middle Ages* (Oxford: Oxford University Press, 1999).

Chapter 33. Ephrem and the Syriac tradition

See the bibliography for chapter 15.

Chapter 34. The literature of the monastic movement

W. Bossuet, *Apophthegmata. Studien zur Geschichte des ältesten Mönchtums* (Tübingen: Mohr, 1923).

G. Bunge, *Evagrios Pontikos: Briefe aus der Wüste*, Sophia 24 (Trier: Paulinus-Verlag, 1986).

D. Burton-Christie, *The Word in the Desert* (New York: Oxford University Press, 1993).

C. Butler, *The Lausiac History of Palladius*, *TS* 6.1–2 (Cambridge: Cambridge University Press, 1898, 1904).

O. Chadwick, *John Cassian* (Cambridge: Cambridge University Press, 1950[1]; 1964[2]).

D. J. Chitty, *The Desert a City* (Oxford: Blackwell, 1966).

R. Draguet, 'L' "Histoire Lausiaque", une œuvre écrite dans l'esprit d'Évagre', *Revue d'Histoire Ecclésiastique* 41 (1946), 321–46; 42 (1945), 5–49.

J. Driscoll, *The 'Ad monachos' of Evagrius Ponticus: Its Structure and a Select Commentary, SA* 104 (Rome: S. Anselmo, 1991).
Susanna Elm, *'Virgins of God'. The Making of Asceticism in Late Antiquity* (Oxford: Clarendon Press, 1994).
H. G. Evelyn White, *The monasteries of the Wâdi 'n Natrûn . . .*, 3 vols (New York: Metropolitan Museum of Art, 1926–33).
C. Fraggiana di Sarzana, *'Apophthegmata Patrum'*, *SP* 29 (1997), 455–67.
G. Gould, *The Desert Fathers on Monastic Community*, OECS (Oxford: Clarendon Press, 1993).
A. Guillaumont, *Aux origines du monachisme chrétien: pour une phénomenologie du monachisme* (Bégrolles-en-Mauges: Abbaye de Bellefontaine, 1979).
Études sur la spiritualité de l'Orient chrétien (Bégrolles-en-Mauges: Abbaye de Bellefontaine, 1996).
J.-C. Guy, 'Les Apophthegmata Patrum', in *Théologie de la vie monastique* (Paris: Aubier, 1961), 73–83.
Recherches sur la tradition grecque des Apophthegmata Patrum, Subsidia Hagiographica 36 (Brussels: Société des Bollandistes, 1984²).
K. Heussi, *Der Ursprung des Mönchtums* (Tübingen: Mohr, 1936).
S. Marsili, *Giovanni Cassiano ed Evagrio Pontico, SA* 5 (Rome: Editrice Anselmiana, 1936).
P. Miquel, *Lexique du desert*, Spiritualité Orientale 44 (Bégrolles-en-Mauge: Abbaye de Bellefontaine, 1986).
P. Rousseau, *Ascetics, Authority, and the Church in the Age of Jerome and Cassian* (Oxford: Oxford University Press, 1978).
S. Rubenson, *The Letters of St Anthony: Monasticism and the Making of a Saint* (Minneapolis: Fortress Press, 1995; revised version of thesis originally published by Lund University Press in 1990).
M. Sheridan, 'Il mondo spirituale e intellectuale del primo monachesimo egiziano', in A. Camplani, ed., *L'Egitto cristiano: Aspetti e problemi in età tardo-antica* (Rome: Augustinianum, 1997), 177–216.
C. Stewart, *Cassian the Monk* (New York: Oxford University Press, 1998).
A. de Vogüé, *De Saint Pachôme à Jean Cassien: etudes littéraires et doctrinales sur le monachisme égyptien à ses débuts, SA* 120 (Rome: S. Anselmo, 1996).

Chapter 35. Women and words: Texts by and about women

Sebastian P. Brock and Susan Ashbrook Harvey, *Holy Women of the Syrian Orient* (Berkeley: University of California Press, 1987, updated edn 1998).
E. A. Clark, *Jerome, Chrysostom, and Friends: Essays and Translations*, Studies in Women and Religion 2 (Lewiston, NY: Edwin Mellen Press, 1979).
G. Clark, *Women in Late Antiquity: Pagan and Christian Lifestyles* (New York: Oxford University Press, 1993).
P. Dronke, *Women Writers of the Middle Ages: A Critical Study of Texts from Perpetua (203) to Marguerite Porete (1310)* (Cambridge: Cambridge University Press, 1984).
A. Kadel, *Matrology: A Bibliography of Writings by Christian Women from the First to the Fifteenth Centuries* (New York: Continuum, 1995).
A.-J. Levine, ed., *'Women Like This': New Perspectives on Jewish Women in the Greco-Roman World* (Atlanta: Scholars Press, 1991).

J. M. Petersen, *Handmaids of the Lord: Holy Women in Late Antiquity and the Early Middle Ages* (Kalamazoo, MI: Cistercian Publications, 1996).

M. Thiébaux, *The Writings of Medieval Women: An Anthology* (New York: Garland Publishing, 1994²).

Chapter 36. Conciliar records and canons

Records and canons are collected in:

P.-P. Joannou, ed., *Discipline générale antique (IVᵉ–IXᵉ siècles)*, 3 vols in 2: I. 1: Les canons des conciles œcuméniques; I. 2: Les canons des Synodes Particuliers; II: Les canons des Pères Grecs, *Fonti* fasc. IX, (Grottaferrata, Rome: Tipografia Italo-Orientale «S. Nilo», 1962–3).

C. H. Turner, ed., *Ecclesiae Occidentalis Monumenta Iuris Antiquissima* (Oxford: Clarendon Press, 1899–1930).

N. P. Tanner, SJ, *Decrees of the Ecumenical Councils*, 2 vols (London: Sheed and Ward and Washington, DC: Georgetown University Press, 1990).

W. Bright, *The Canons of the First Four General Councils . . . with notes* (Oxford: Clarendon Press, 1892²).

H. Chadwick, 'The Origin of the Title "Oecumenical Council" ', *JTS* n.s. 23 (1972), 132–5.

J. Erickson, *The Challenge of Our Past* (Crestwood, NY: St Vladimir's Seminary Press, 1991).

C. Gallaher, *Church Law and Church Order in Rome and Byzantium. A Comparative Study*, Birmingham Byzantine and Ottoman Studies 8 (Aldershot and Burlington, Vermont: Ashgate Variorum, 2002).

H. Hess, *The Early Development of Canon Law and the Council of Sardica* (Oxford: Oxford University Press, 2002).

G. Le Bras and J. Gaudemet, *Histoire du droit et des institutions de l'Église en Occident* (Paris: Sirey, 1955ff.).

P. L'Huillier, *The Church of the Ancient Councils* (Crestwood, NY: St Vladimir's Seminary Press, 1996).

N. Milasch, *Das Kirchenrecht der morgenländischen Kirche*, German translation from the Serbian by Alexander von Pessic (Mostar: Pacher & Kisic, 1905²).

E. Schwartz, 'Die Kanonessammlungen der alten Reichskirche', in *Gesammelte Schriften*, (Berlin, 1960; originally published in *Zeitschrift der Savigny-Stifung für Rechtsgeschichte* 42, K. 11 (1921), 208–53).

Index